GW00992123

Yamaha
YZF750R, YZF750SP and
YZF1000R Thunderace
Service and Repair Manual

by Matthew Coombs

Models covered

(3720 - 288)

YZF750R. 1993 to 1997 (UK), 1994 to 1998 (US)
YZF750SP. 1993 to 1997 (UK only)
YZF1000R Thunderace. 1996 to 2000 (UK), 1997 only (US)

ABCDE
FGHIJ
KLMNO
P

© Haynes Publishing 2000

A book in the **Haynes Service and Repair Manual Series**

All rights reserved. No part of this book may be reproduced or transmitted in any form or by any means, electronic or mechanical, including photocopying, recording or by any information storage or retrieval system, without permission in writing from the copyright holder.

ISBN 1 85960 720 9

British Library Cataloguing in Publication Data
A catalogue record for this book is available from the British Library.

Library of Congress Catalog Card Number **99-76572**

Printed in the USA

Haynes Publishing
Sparkford, Yeovil, Somerset BA22 7JJ, England

Haynes North America, Inc
861 Lawrence Drive, Newbury Park, California 91320, USA

Editions Haynes
4, Rue de l'Abreuvoir
92415 COURBEVOIE CEDEX, France

Haynes Publishing Nordiska AB
Box 1504, 751 45 UPPSALA, Sweden

Contents

Contents

REPAIRS AND OVERHAUL

Engine, transmission and associated systems

Chassis and bodywork components

Electrical system

Wiring diagrams

REFERENCE

Index

Yamaha
Musical instruments to motorcycles

**The FS1E -
first bike of many sixteen year olds in the UK**

The Yamaha Motor Company

The Yamaha name can be traced back to 1889, when Torakusu Yamaha founded the Yamaha Organ Manufacturing Company. Such was the success of the company, that in 1897 it became Nippon Gakki Limited and manufactured a wide range of reed organs and pianos.

During World War II, Nippon Gakki's manufacturing base was utilised by the Japanese authorities to produce propellers and fuel tanks for their aviation industry. The end of the war brought about a huge public demand for low cost transport and many firms decided to utilise their obsolete aircraft tooling for the production of motorcycles. Nippon Gakki's first motorcycle went on sale in February 1955 and was named the 125 YA-1 Red Dragonfly. This machine was a copy of the German DKW RT125 motorcycle, featuring a single cylinder two-stroke engine with a four-speed gearbox. Due to the outstanding success of this model the motorcycle operation was separated from Nippon Gakki in July 1955 and the Yamaha Motor Company was formed.

The YA-1 also received acclaim by winning two of Japan's biggest road races, the Mount Fuji Climbing race and the Asama Volcano race. The high level of public demand for the YA-1 led to the development of a whole series of two-stroke singles and twins.

Having made a large impact on their home market, Yamahas were exported to the USA in 1958 and to the UK in 1962. In the UK the signing of an Anglo-Japanese trade agreement during 1962 enabled the sale of Japanese lightweight motorcycles and scooters in Britain. At that time, competition between the many motorcycle producers in Japan had reduced numbers significantly and by the end of the sixties, only the big-four which are familiar with today remained.

Yamaha Europe was founded in 1968 and based in Holland. Although originally set up to market marine products, the Dutch base is now the official European Headquarters and distribution centre. Yamaha motorcycles are built at factories in Holland, Denmark, Norway, Italy, France, Spain and Portugal. Yamahas are imported into the UK by Yamaha Motor UK Ltd, formerly Mitsui Machinery Sales (UK) Ltd. Mitsui and Co. were originally a trading house, handling the shipping, distribution and marketing of Japanese products into western countries. Ultimately Mitsui Machinery Sales was formed to handle Yamaha motorcycles and outboard motors.

Based on the technology derived from its motorcycle operation, Yamaha have produced many other products, such as automobile and lightweight aircraft engines, marine engines and boats, generators, pumps, ATVs, snowmobiles, golf cars, industrial robots, lawnmowers, swimming pools and archery equipment.

Two-strokes first

Part of Yamaha's success was a whole string of innovations in the two-stroke world. Autolube engine lubrication, torque induction, multi-ported engines, reed valves and power valves kept their two-strokes at the forefront of technology. Many advances were achieved with the use of racing as a development laboratory. They went to the USA in the late 1950s with an air-cooled 250cc twin but didn't hit the GPs until the early 1960s when Fumio Ito scored a hat-trick of sixth places in the Isle of Man TT, the Dutch TT and the Belgian GP. This experiment gave rise to the idea of the over-the-counter racer, an idea that became reality in the TD1, the first in an unmatched series of two-stroke racers that were the standard issue for privateers at national and international level for years and helped Yamaha develop their road engines. While privateers raced the twins, Yamaha built the outrageously complicated vee-four 250 for Phil Read and followed it with a vee-four 125 that Bill Ivy lapped the Isle of Man on at over 100mph! When the FIM regulations were changed to limit the smaller GP classes to two cylinders, these exotic bikes died but set the scene for an unparalleled dynasty of mass-produced racers based on the same technology as the road bikes.

In the 1960s and 70s the two-stroke engined YAS3 125, YDS1 to YDS7 250 and YR5 350 formed the core of Yamaha's range. By the mid-70s they had been superseded by the RD (Race-Developed) 125, 250, and 350

range of two-stroke twins, featuring improved 7-port engines with reed valve induction. Braking was improved by the use of an hydraulic brake on the front wheel of DX models, instead of the drum arrangement used previously, and cast alloy wheels were available as an option on later RD models. The RD350 was replaced by the RD400 in 1976.

Running parallel with the RD twins was a range of single-cylinder two-strokes. Used in a variety of chassis types, the engine was used in the popular 50 cc FS1-E moped, the V50 to 90 step-thrus, RS100 and 125, YB100 and the DT trail range.

The TD racers got water-cooling in 1973 to become the TZs, the most successful and numerous over-the-counter racers ever built. That same year, Jarno Saarinen became the first rider to win a 500cc GP on a four-cylinder two-stroke on the new in-line four which was effectively a pair of TZs side-by-side. TZs won everywhere – including the Daytona 200 and 500 races when overbored to 351cc. A 700cc TZ also appeared, one year later taken out to 750cc. Steve Baker won the first Formula 750 world title – one of the precursors of Superbike – on one in 1977. The

following year Kenny Roberts won Yamaha's first world 500 title and would be succeeded by Wayne Rainey and Eddie Lawson before Mick Doohan and the NSR500 took over.

The air-cooled single and twin cylinder RD road bikes were eventually replaced by the LC series in 1980, featuring liquid-cooled engines, radical new styling, spiral pattern cast wheels and cantilever rear suspension (Yamaha's Monoshock). Of all the LC models, the RD350LC, or RD350R as it was later known, has made the most impact in the market. Later models had YPVS (Yamaha Power Valve System) engines, another first for Yamaha – this was essentially a valve located in the exhaust ports which was electronically operated to alter port timing to achieve maximum power output. The RD500LC was the largest two-stroke made by Yamaha and differed from the other LCs by the use of its vee-four cylinder engine.

With the exception of the RD350R, now manufactured in Brazil, the LC range has been discontinued. Two-stroke engined models have given way to environmental pressure, and thus with a few exceptions, such as the TZR125 and TZR250, are used only in scooters and small capacity bikes.

The distinctive paintwork and trim of the RD models

The Four-strokes

Yamaha concentrated solely on two-stroke models until 1970 when the XS1 was produced, their first four-stroke motorcycle. It was perhaps Yamaha's success with two-strokes that postponed an earlier move into the four-stroke motorcycle market, although their work with Toyota during the 1960s had given them a sound base in four-stroke technology.

The XS1 had a 650 cc twin-cylinder SOHC engine and was later to become known as the XS650, appearing also in the popular SE custom form. Yamaha introduced a three cylinder 750 cc engine in 1976, fitted in a sport-tourer frame and called the XS750, TX750 in the USA . The XS750 established itself well in the sport tourer class and remained in production with very few changes until uprated to 850 cc in 1980.

Other four-strokes followed in 1976, with the introduction of the XS250/360/400 series twins. The XS range was strengthened in 1978 by the four-cylinder XS1100.

The 1980s saw a new family of four-strokes, the XJ550, 650, 750 and 900 Fours. Improvements over the XS range amounted to a slimmer DOHC engine unit due to the relocation of the alternator behind the cylinders, electronic ignition and uprated braking and suspension systems. Models were available mainly in standard trim, although custom-styled Maxims were produced especially for the US market. The

The XS650 led the way for Yamaha's four-stroke range

Yamaha's XS750 was produced from 1976 to 1982 and then uprated to 850 cc

XJ650T was the first model from Yamaha to have a turbo-charged engine. Although these early XJ models have now been discontinued, their roots live on in the XJ600S and XJ900S Diversion (Seca II) models.

The FZR prefix encompasses the pure sports Yamaha models. With the exception of the 16-valve FZR400 and FZR600 models, the FZ/FZR750 and FZR1000 used 20-valve engines, two exhaust valves and three inlet valves per cylinder. This concept was called Genesis and gave improved gas flow to the combustion chambers. Other features of the new engine were the use of down-draught carburetors and the engine's inclined angle in the frame, plus the change to liquid-cooling. Lightweight Deltabox design aluminium frames and uprated suspension improved the bikes's handling. The Genesis engine lives on in the YZF750 and 1000 models.

The Genesis concept was the basis of Yamaha's foray into four-stroke racing, first with a bike known simply as 'The Genesis', an FZ750 motor in a TT Formula 1 bike with which the factory attempted to steal the Honda RVF750's thunder at important events like the Suzuka 8 Hours and the Bol d'Or although they never fielded it for a whole World Championship season. That had to wait for the advent of the World Superbike Championship, although there was no full works team until 1995, instead it was left to individual importers to support teams. It was the Australian Dealer Team Yamaha which scored the factory's first World Superbike win in the series debut year of 1988. The rider? Mick Doohan. Slightly, embarrassingly, it was the steel framed FZ750

A new family of four-strokes was released in 1980 with the introduction of the XJ range

rather than the FZR homologation special that won races. The OW01 was a race winner, mainly in the hands of Fabrizio Pirovano, the factory's most successful Superbike racer with ten victories, but national success in the UK, Japan, and in the Daytona 200 has not been translated into World Championships for any of Yamaha's 750s.

The vee-twin engine has been the mainstay of the XV Virago range. Since 1981 XVs have been produced in 535, 700, 750, 920, 1000 and 1100 engine sizes, all using the same basic air-cooled sohc vee-twin engine. Other uses of vee engines have been in the XZ550 of the early 1980s, the XVZ12 Venture and the mighty VMX-12 V-Max.

The XV535 Virago vee-twin

The YZF750R

Yamaha has always been a sporting-orientated company whose motto could be 'Racing Improves the Breed', so it's no surprise that the latest generation of lightweight sportsters are at the cutting edge of performance on and off the track. The R6 won more races than any other machine in the inaugural year of the World Supersports Championship, the R7 won a race in its debut year in World Superbike in the hands of the mercurial Noriyuki Haga, and the mighty 1000cc R1 ended Honda's domination of the

Isle of Man F1 TT when David Jefferies won three races in a week in 1999.

In Grand Prix racing, the factory took several years to get over the shock of Wayne Rainey's crippling accident. and first 500cc win since the American's enforced retirement didn't come until 1998 when Simon Crafar won at Donington Park. For 1999, Yamaha refocussed their ambitions and signed Italian superstar Max Biaggi plus Spanish trier Carlos Checa for the works team, while dashing young Frenchman Regis Laconi and tough

little Aussie Gary McCoy rode for the WCM satellite team. Both teams got a win in the '99 season and with a new TZ250 being developed for 2000 it looks as if Yamaha's spirit of competition will go on unabated into the new Millenium.

In the shade

The 750 and 1000 cc YZF Yamahas share more than just a common design, they share the same reputation. Or rather lack of it. Neither is in any way a bad bike, quite the reverse, but both followed and preceded Yamahas of greater reputations.

The YZF750R first appeared in 1993 and if it had a problem it was that it was the last of the in-line fours of its generation. Suzuki's GSX-R750 and Kawasaki's ZXR750 had already been around for a couple of years and while the Yamaha was just as good a bike it was a bit late in arriving for the party. Developed from the old OW01, the YZF was a typical refinement of the older bike but atypically it was a long-lived model.

There was also a YZF750SP version for Superbike racing with close-ratio box, single seat, multi-adjustable suspension and flat-slide carbs, nevertheless Yamaha teams still had to start with something much closer to a road bike than an £18,000 homologation special like the Honda RC45. That didn't stop the bike winning domestic Championships in Germany, Japan and the UK or first Eddie Lawson and then Scott Russell dominating the Daytona 200. The YZF750 also won Yamaha's first Bol d'Or since 1978 when Christian Sarron finally won in 1994 after trying for years. Not a bad record, but somehow the racing success didn't translate into showroom traffic.

Clever buyers did note, however, that the sporty YZF made a brilliant secondhand buy and a very effective trackday tool. And why shouldn't it? It was lighter, with a better power-to-weight ratio than its immediate competitors and when in 1995 it came with Ohlins suspension as standard it was sharper than ever. The only other significant change happened the same year, a big curved radiator that looked like it came straight out of the race kit.

Those clever enough to buy an underpriced YZF ended up basking happily in the reflected glory of the Superbike team when Noriyuki Haga burst on the scene and in 1997 won the only World Championship road race for the Yamaha factory that year. As the factory was about to end the season without a victory for the first time since they started racing, you could say Yamaha have a lot to be grateful to the YZF750 for.

The YZF750 came between the OW01 and R-7, but the YZF1000R Thunderace had two much bigger problems: the EXUP and the R-1. Both of those were the benchmark sportsbikes of their time but the YZF1000R was not as focused. It was big, comfortable, easy to ride, and very fast but without the cutting edge

The YZF750SP

handling of its siblings. In fact when put up against the opposition's top-of-the-range race-replica sportsters it looked more and more like a sports tourer. Or it would have done if the pillion seat had been more accommodating. The Thunderace looked big alongside the opposition but that was mainly due to the capacious bodywork that cosseted the rider.

Underneath the fibreglass was a totally reworked FZR1000 motor with all-new internals, new carbs and new gearbox. Cooling was by a big curved radiator as fitted to the later 750 and the chassis bears a very close resemblance to the smaller YZF's frame, not surprising as the 1000 arrived in '96, the year after the 750 got its only major update. In fact the two bikes' chassis are so similar that the 1000 is only 5 mm longer in the wheelbase than the 750. You wouldn't guess that by looking at them, such is the impression of bulk that the Thunderace imparts.

The motor's engine characteristics reinforce that impression. There is, not surprisingly, a lot of power on tap. Unlike the 13,000 rpm 750, the bigger bike has a flat torque curve and linear power delivery. Peak torque arrives at 8500 rpm, nearly 1500 revs before peak power. You can stick it in top and leave the gear pedal alone. Try that on most sportsters and you'll disappear down a hole in the power curve the first time you try and pull out of a slow corner.

With hindsight, it's possible to see that both YZF models were very good bikes indeed, it's just that when they were new no-one was quite sure how they fitted into the great scheme of things. Fortunately, time has put both bikes in perspective and revealed them as stonking bargains. Yamaha's five-valve motor has always combined useability with longevity, and the YZFs are no exceptions. Buy a well cared for example and you're onto a winner.

Acknowledgements

Our thanks are due to Fowlers of Bristol and John Welsh Motorcycles of Weston-super-Mare who supplied the machines featured in the illustrations throughout this manual. We would also like to thank Mitsui Machinery Sales (UK) Ltd for permission to reproduce certain illustrations used in this manual and for supplying some of the cover photographs, also NGK Spark Plugs (UK) Ltd for supplying the colour spark plug condition photos and the Avon Rubber Company for supplying information on tyre fitting.

Thanks are also due to Kel Edge who supplied the colour transparency of the YZF750 on the rear cover.

About this manual

The aim of this manual is to help you get the best value from your motorcycle. It can do so in several ways. It can help you decide what work must be done, even if you choose to have it done by a dealer; it provides information and procedures for routine maintenance and servicing; and it offers diagnostic and repair procedures to follow when trouble occurs.

We hope you use the manual to tackle the work yourself. For many simpler jobs, doing it yourself may be quicker than arranging an appointment to get the motorcycle into a dealer and making the trips to leave it and pick it up. More importantly, a lot of money can be saved by avoiding the expense the shop must pass on to you to cover its labour and overhead costs. An added benefit is the sense of satisfaction and accomplishment that you feel after doing the job yourself.

References to the "left" or "right" side of the motorcycle assume you are sitting on the seat, facing forward.

We take great pride in the accuracy of information given in this manual, but motorcycle manufacturers make alterations and design changes during the production run of a particular motorcycle of which they do not inform us. No liability can be accepted by the authors or publishers for loss, damage or injury caused by any errors in, or omissions from, the information given.

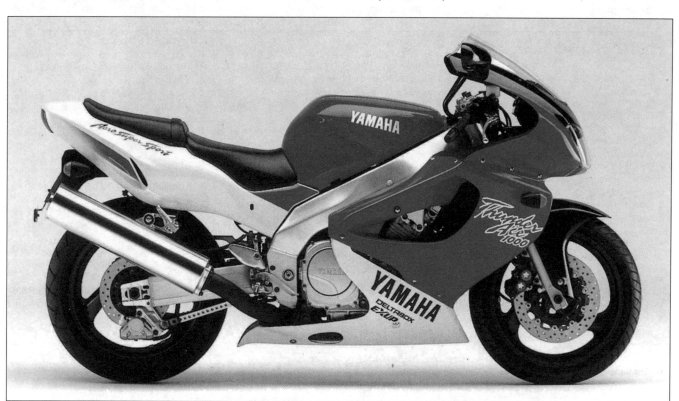

The YZF1000R Thunderace

Professional mechanics are trained in safe working procedures. However enthusiastic you may be about getting on with the job at hand, take the time to ensure that your safety is not put at risk. A moment's lack of attention can result in an accident, as can failure to observe simple precautions.

There will always be new ways of having accidents, and the following is not a comprehensive list of all dangers; it is intended rather to make you aware of the risks and to encourage a safe approach to all work you carry out on your bike.

Asbestos

● Certain friction, insulating, sealing and other products - such as brake pads, clutch linings, gaskets, etc. - contain asbestos. Extreme care must be taken to avoid inhalation of dust from such products since it is hazardous to health. If in doubt, assume that they do contain asbestos.

Fire

● Remember at all times that petrol is highly flammable. Never smoke or have any kind of naked flame around, when working on the vehicle. But the risk does not end there - a spark caused by an electrical short-circuit, by two metal surfaces contacting each other, by careless use of tools, or even by static electricity built up in your body under certain conditions, can ignite petrol vapour, which in a confined space is highly explosive. Never use petrol as a cleaning solvent. Use an approved safety solvent.

● Always disconnect the battery earth terminal before working on any part of the fuel or electrical system, and never risk spilling fuel on to a hot engine or exhaust.
● It is recommended that a fire extinguisher of a type suitable for fuel and electrical fires is kept handy in the garage or workplace at all times. Never try to extinguish a fuel or electrical fire with water.

Fumes

● Certain fumes are highly toxic and can quickly cause unconsciousness and even death if inhaled to any extent. Petrol vapour comes into this category, as do the vapours from certain solvents such as trichloro-ethylene. Any draining or pouring of such volatile fluids should be done in a well ventilated area.
● When using cleaning fluids and solvents, read the instructions carefully. Never use materials from unmarked containers - they may give off poisonous vapours.
● Never run the engine of a motor vehicle in an enclosed space such as a garage. Exhaust fumes contain carbon monoxide which is extremely poisonous; if you need to run the engine, always do so in the open air or at least have the rear of the vehicle outside the workplace.

The battery

● Never cause a spark, or allow a naked light near the vehicle's battery. It will normally be giving off a certain amount of hydrogen gas, which is highly explosive.

● Always disconnect the battery ground (earth) terminal before working on the fuel or electrical systems (except where noted).
● If possible, loosen the filler plugs or cover when charging the battery from an external source. Do not charge at an excessive rate or the battery may burst.
● Take care when topping up, cleaning or carrying the battery. The acid electrolyte, evenwhen diluted, is very corrosive and should not be allowed to contact the eyes or skin. Always wear rubber gloves and goggles or a face shield. If you ever need to prepare electrolyte yourself, always add the acid slowly to the water; never add the water to the acid.

Electricity

● When using an electric power tool, inspection light etc., always ensure that the appliance is correctly connected to its plug and that, where necessary, it is properly grounded (earthed). Do not use such appliances in damp conditions and, again, beware of creating a spark or applying excessive heat in the vicinity of fuel or fuel vapour. Also ensure that the appliances meet national safety standards.
● A severe electric shock can result from touching certain parts of the electrical system, such as the spark plug wires (HT leads), when the engine is running or being cranked, particularly if components are damp or the insulation is defective. Where an electronic ignition system is used, the secondary (HT) voltage is much higher and could prove fatal.

Remember...

✗ **Don't** start the engine without first ascertaining that the transmission is in neutral.
✗ **Don't** suddenly remove the pressure cap from a hot cooling system - cover it with a cloth and release the pressure gradually first, or you may get scalded by escaping coolant.
✗ **Don't** attempt to drain oil until you are sure it has cooled sufficiently to avoid scalding you.
✗ **Don't** grasp any part of the engine or exhaust system without first ascertaining that it is cool enough not to burn you.
✗ **Don't** allow brake fluid or antifreeze to contact the machine's paintwork or plastic components.
✗ **Don't** siphon toxic liquids such as fuel, hydraulic fluid or antifreeze by mouth, or allow them to remain on your skin.
✗ **Don't** inhale dust - it may be injurious to health (see Asbestos heading).
✗ **Don't** allow any spilled oil or grease to remain on the floor - wipe it up right away, before someone slips on it.
✗ **Don't** use ill-fitting spanners or other tools which may slip and cause injury.
✗ **Don't** lift a heavy component which may

be beyond your capability - get assistance.
✗ **Don't** rush to finish a job or take unverified short cuts.
✗ **Don't** allow children or animals in or around an unattended vehicle.
✗ **Don't** inflate a tyre above the recommended pressure. Apart from overstressing the carcass, in extreme cases the tyre may blow off forcibly.
✔ **Do** ensure that the machine is supported securely at all times. This is especially important when the machine is blocked up to aid wheel or fork removal.
✔ **Do** take care when attempting to loosen a stubborn nut or bolt. It is generally better to pull on a spanner, rather than push, so that if you slip, you fall away from the machine rather than onto it.
✔ **Do** wear eye protection when using power tools such as drill, sander, bench grinder etc.
✔ **Do** use a barrier cream on your hands prior to undertaking dirty jobs - it will protect your skin from infection as well as making the dirt easier to remove afterwards; but make sure your hands aren't left slippery. Note that long-term contact with used engine oil can be a health hazard.
✔ **Do** keep loose clothing (cuffs, ties etc. and long hair) well out of the way of moving

mechanical parts.
✔ **Do** remove rings, wristwatch etc., before working on the vehicle - especially the electrical system.
✔ **Do** keep your work area tidy - it is only too easy to fall over articles left lying around.
✔ **Do** exercise caution when compressing springs for removal or installation. Ensure that the tension is applied and released in a controlled manner, using suitable tools which preclude the possibility of the spring escaping violently.
✔ **Do** ensure that any lifting tackle used has a safe working load rating adequate for the job.
✔ **Do** get someone to check periodically that all is well, when working alone on the vehicle.
✔ **Do** carry out work in a logical sequence and check that everything is correctly assembled and tightened afterwards.
✔ **Do** remember that your vehicle's safety affects that of yourself and others. If in doubt on any point, get professional advice.
● If in spite of following these precautions, you are unfortunate enough to injure yourself, seek medical attention as soon as possible.

Frame and engine numbers

The frame serial number is stamped into the right-hand side of the steering head. The engine number is stamped into the top of the crankcase on the right-hand side of the engine. The model code label is on the top of the left-hand sub-frame spar under the seat. These numbers should be recorded and kept in a safe place so they can be furnished to law enforcement officials in the event of a theft. There is also a carburettor identification number on the intake side of each carburettor body.

The frame serial number, engine serial number, carburettor identification number and model code should be recorded and kept in a handy place (such as with your driver's licence) so that they are always available when purchasing or ordering parts for your machine.

The procedures in this manual identify the bikes by year and model (eg 1998 YZF1000R). The model codes for all years and models covered are tabled below. Where available, the initial frame and engine numbers are also given.

Buying spare parts

Once you have found all the identification numbers, record them for reference when buying parts. Since the manufacturers change specifications, parts and vendors (companies that manufacture various components on the machine), providing the ID numbers is the only way to be reasonably sure that you are buying the correct parts.

Whenever possible, take the worn part to the dealer so direct comparison with the new component can be made. Along the trail from the manufacturer to the parts shelf, there are numerous places that the part can end up with the wrong number or be listed incorrectly.

The two places to purchase new parts for your motorcycle – the accessory store and the franchised dealer – differ in the type of parts they carry. While dealers can obtain virtually every part for your motorcycle, the accessory dealer is usually limited to normal high wear items such as shock absorbers, tune-up parts, various engine gaskets, cables, chains, brake parts, etc. Rarely will an accessory outlet have major suspension components, cylinders, transmission gears, or cases.

Used parts can be obtained for roughly half

750 models (UK)	Year	Code	Frame No.	Engine No.
YZF750R	1993	4HD1	000101-on	000101-on
YZF750R	1994	4HD3	015101-on	015101-on
YZF750R	1995	4HD5	028101-on	028101-on
YZF750R	1996/7	4HD7	Not available	Not available
YZF750SP	1993	4HS1	000101	000101
YZF750SP	1994	4HS3	002101	002101
YZF750SP	1995	4HS5	005101	005101
YZF750SP	1996/7	4HS7	Not available	Not available
750 models (US)	**Year**	**Code**	**Frame No.**	**Engine No.**
YZF750R(F) – 49-state	1994	4LE1	001101	001101
YZF750R(FC) – California	1994	4LE2	000101	000101
YZF750R(H) – 49-state	1996	4LE3	003101	003101
YZF750R(HC) – California	1996	4LE4	004101	004101
YZF750R(J) – 49-state	1997	4LES	Not available	Not available
YZF750R(JC) – California	1997	4LE6	Not available	Not available
YZF750R(K) – 49-state	1998	4LE7	Not available	Not available
YZF750R(KC) – California	1998	4LE8	Not available	Not available
1000 models (UK)	**Year**	**Code**		
YZF1000R Thunderace	1996	4SV1		
YZF1000R Thunderace	1997	4SV3		
YZF1000R Thunderace	1998/9	4SV4		
YZF1000R Thunderace	2000	4SV5		
1000 models (US)	**Year**	**Code**		
YZF1000R(K) – 49-state	1997	4XV4		
YZF1000R(KC) – California	1997	4XV6		

the price of new ones, but you can't always be sure of what you're getting. Once again, take your worn part to the breaker's yard for direct comparison.

Whether buying new, used or rebuilt parts, the best course is to deal directly with someone who specialises in parts for your particular make.

Model code label (arrowed) is on the left-hand side of the sub-frame

The engine number is stamped into the top of the crankcase on the right-hand side of the engine

The frame number is stamped into the right-hand side of the steering head

Note: *The daily (pre-ride) checks outlined in the owner's manual covers those items which should be inspected on a daily basis.*

1 Engine/transmission oil level check

Before you start

✔ Support the motorcycle in an upright position, using an auxiliary stand if required. Make sure it is on level ground.

✔ Start the engine and let it idle for several minutes to allow it to reach normal operating temperature.

Caution: Do not run the engine in an enclosed space such as a garage or workshop.

✔ Leave the motorcycle undisturbed for a few minutes to allow the oil level to stabilise.

The correct oil

● Modern, high-revving engines place great demands on their oil. It is very important that the correct oil for your bike is used.

● Always top up with a good quality oil of the specified type and viscosity and do not overfill the engine.

Caution: Do not use chemical additives or oils with a grade of CD or higher, or use oils labelled "ENERGY CONSERVING II". Such additives or oils could cause clutch slip.

Oil type	API grade SE, SF or SG
Oil viscosity*	
UK models	SAE 10W30 or 10W40
US models	SAE 10W30 or 20W40

Refer to the viscosity table to select the oil best suited to your conditions.

Bike care

● If you have to add oil frequently, you should check whether you have any oil leaks. If there is no sign of oil leakage from the joints and gaskets the engine could be burning oil (see *Fault Finding*).

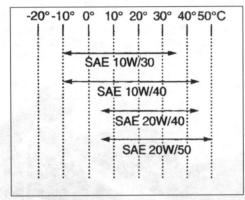

Oil viscosity table; select the oil best suited to the conditions

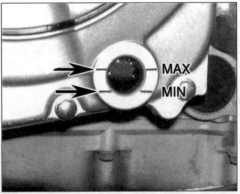

1 Wipe the oil level inspection window, located on the right-hand side of the engine, so that it is clean. With the motorcycle vertical, the oil level should lie between the maximum and minimum levels on the window (arrowed).

2 If the level is below the minimum line, remove the right-hand fairing side-panel (see Chapter 8). Remove the filler cap from the top of the clutch cover.

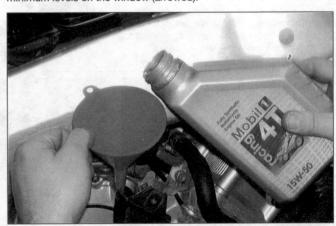

3 Top the engine up with the recommended grade and type of oil, to bring the level up to the maximum level on the window.

2 Coolant level check

Warning: DO NOT remove the cooling system pressure cap to add coolant. Topping up is done via the coolant reservoir tank filler. DO NOT leave open containers of coolant about, as it is poisonous.

Before you start

✔ Make sure you have a supply of coolant available – a mixture of 50% distilled water and 50% corrosion inhibited ethylene glycol anti-freeze is needed. **Note:** *Yamaha specify that soft tap water can be used, but NOT hard water. If in doubt, boil the water first or use only distilled water.*

✔ Always check the coolant level when the engine is cold.
✔ Support the motorcycle in an upright position, using an auxiliary stand if required. Make sure it is on level ground.

Bike care

● Use only the specified coolant mixture. It is important that anti-freeze is used in the system all year round, and not just in the winter. Do not top the system up using only water, as the system will become too diluted.
● Do not overfill the reservoir. If the coolant is significantly above the "FULL" level line at any time, the surplus should be siphoned or drained off to prevent the possibility of it being expelled out of the overflow hose.
● If the coolant level falls steadily, check the system for leaks (see Chapter 1). If no leaks are found and the level continues to fall, it is recommended that the machine is taken to a Yamaha dealer for a pressure test.

1 Remove the seat to access the coolant reservoir (see Chapter 8). The coolant FULL and LOW level lines are marked on the reservoir – if they are difficult to see, remove the reservoir cap and look inside.

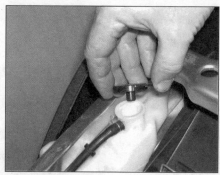

2 If the coolant level does not lie between the FULL and LOW level lines, remove the reservoir filler cap.

3 Top the coolant level up with the recommended coolant mixture. Fit the cap securely, then install the seat (see Chapter 8).

3 Brake fluid level checks

Warning: Brake hydraulic fluid can harm your eyes and damage painted surfaces, so use extreme caution when handling and pouring it and cover surrounding surfaces with rag. Do not use fluid that has been standing open for some time, as it absorbs moisture from the air which can cause a dangerous loss of braking effectiveness.

Before you start

✔ Support the motorcycle in an upright position, using an auxiliary stand if required. Turn the handlebars until the top of the front master cylinder is as level as possible. The rear master cylinder reservoir is located behind the right-hand side cover.
✔ Make sure you have the correct hydraulic fluid. DOT 4 is recommended.
✔ Wrap a rag around the reservoir being worked on to ensure that any spillage does not come into contact with painted surfaces.

Bike care

● The fluid in the front and rear brake master cylinder reservoirs will drop slightly as the brake pads wear down.
● If any fluid reservoir requires repeated topping-up this is an indication of a hydraulic leak somewhere in the system, which should be investigated immediately.

● Check for signs of fluid leakage from the hydraulic hoses and components – if found, rectify immediately.
● Check the operation of both brakes before taking the machine on the road; if there is evidence of air in the system (spongy feel to lever or pedal), it must be bled as described in Chapter 7.

FRONT BRAKE FLUID LEVEL

(CONTINUED OVERLEAF)

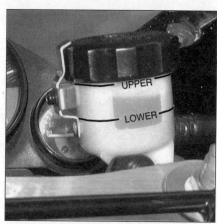

1 The front brake fluid level is visible through the reservoir body – it must be between the UPPER and LOWER level lines.

FRONT BRAKE FLUID LEVEL (CONTINUED)

2 If the level is below the LOWER level line, remove the reservoir cap clamp screw, then unscrew the cap and remove the diaphragm plate and the diaphragm.

3 Top up with new clean DOT 4 hydraulic fluid, until the level is above the LOWER level line. Take care to avoid spills (see **Warning** on previous page).

4 Ensure that the diaphragm is correctly seated before installing the plate and cap. Secure the cap with its clamp.

REAR BRAKE FLUID LEVEL

5 On YZF750R and SP models, the rear brake fluid level is visible through the reservoir body – it must be above LOWER level line. If the level is below the LOWER level line, remove the reservoir cap clamp screw (arrowed) and remove the clamp. Support the reservoir upright, then unscrew the cap and remove the diaphragm plate and the diaphragm.

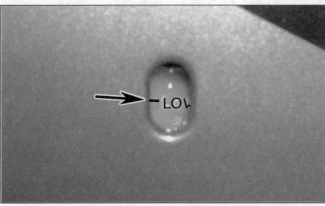

6 On YZF1000R models, the rear brake fluid level is visible through the cutout in the right-hand side cover – it must be above LOWER level line (arrowed). If the level is below the LOWER level line, remove the right-hand side cover (see Chapter 8) . . .

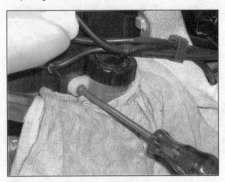

7 . . . slacken the reservoir mounting screw and displace the reservoir to provide clearance, then unscrew the cap and remove the diaphragm plate and the diaphragm.

8 Top up with new clean DOT 4 hydraulic fluid, until the level is above the lower mark. Take care to avoid spills (see **Warning** on the previous page).

9 Ensure that the diaphragm is correctly seated before installing the plate and cap. Tighten the cap securely. On YZF750R and SP models, fit the cap clamp. On YZF1000R models, tighten the mounting screw. Install the side cover(s) or seat cowling (see Chapter 8).

4 Clutch fluid level check

 Warning: *Brake and clutch hydraulic fluid can harm your eyes and damage painted surfaces, so use extreme caution when handling and pouring it and cover surrounding surfaces with rag. Do not use fluid that has been standing open for some time, as it absorbs moisture from the air which can cause a loss of clutch effectiveness.*

Before you start:
✔ Support the motorcycle in an upright position, using an auxiliary stand if required. Turn the handlebars until the top of the master cylinder is as level as possible.
✔ Make sure you have the correct hydraulic fluid. DOT 4 is recommended.
✔ Wrap a rag around the reservoir to ensure that any spillage does not come into contact with painted surfaces.

Bike care:
● If the fluid reservoir requires repeated topping-up this is an indication of an hydraulic leak somewhere in the system, which should be investigated immediately.

● Check for signs of fluid leakage from the hydraulic hose and components – if found, rectify immediately.
● Check the operation of the clutch; if there is evidence of air in the system (spongy feel to the lever), bleed the clutch as described in Chapter 2.

1 On YZF750R and SP models, the clutch fluid level is visible through the reservoir body – it must be above the LOWER level line. If the level is below the LOWER level line, remove the reservoir cap clamp screw (arrowed), then unscrew the cap and remove the diaphragm plate and the diaphragm.

2 On YZF1000R models, the fluid level is visible through the window in the reservoir body – it must be above the LOWER level line . . .

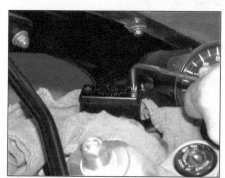

3 . . . If the level is below the LOWER level line, remove the two reservoir cover screws and remove the cover, the diaphragm plate and the diaphragm.

4 Top up with new clean DOT 4 hydraulic fluid, until the level is above the LOWER level line. Take care to avoid spills (see **Warning** above).

5 Ensure that the diaphragm is correctly seated before installing the plate and cover or cap. On YZF750R and SP models, secure the cap with its clamp.

5 Tyre checks

The correct pressures
● The tyres must be checked when **cold**, not immediately after riding. Note that low tyre pressures may cause the tyre to slip on the rim or come off. High tyre pressures will cause abnormal tread wear and unsafe handling.
● Use an accurate pressure gauge.
● Proper air pressure will increase tyre life and provide maximum stability and ride comfort.

Tyre care
● Check the tyres carefully for cuts, tears, embedded nails or other sharp objects and excessive wear. Operation of the motorcycle with excessively worn tyres is extremely hazardous, as traction and handling are directly affected.

● Check the condition of the tyre valve and ensure the dust cap is in place.

● Pick out any stones or nails which may have become embedded in the tyre tread. If left, they will eventually penetrate through the casing and cause a puncture.
● If tyre damage is apparent, or unexplained loss of pressure is experienced, seek the advice of a tyre fitting specialist without delay.

Tyre tread depth
● At the time of writing, UK law requires that tread depth must be at least 1 mm over 3/4 of the tread breadth all the way around the tyre, with no bald patches. Many riders, however, consider 2 mm tread depth minimum to be a safer limit. Yamaha recommend a minimum of 1.6 mm.
● Many tyres now incorporate wear indicators in the tread. Identify the triangular pointer or "TWI" mark on the tyre sidewall to locate the indicator bar and replace the tyre if the tread has worn down to the bar.

Loading/speed	Front	Rear
Rider only	33 psi (2.25 Bar)	36 psi (2.50 Bar)
Rider and passenger, or high speed riding	36 psi (2.50 Bar)	42 psi (2.90 Bar)

1 Check the tyre pressures when the tyres are **cold** and keep them properly inflated.

2 Measure tread depth at the centre of the tyre using a tread depth gauge.

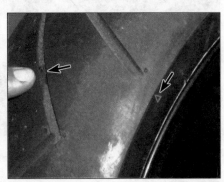

3 Tyre tread wear indicator bar and its location marking (usually either an arrow, a triangle or the letters TWI) on the sidewall (arrowed).

6 Suspension, steering and final drive checks

Suspension and Steering
● Check that the front and rear suspension operates smoothly without binding.

● Check that the suspension is adjusted as required.

● Check that the steering moves smoothly from lock-to-lock.

Final drive
● Check that the drive chain slack isn't excessive, and adjust if necessary (see Chapter 1).
● If the chain looks dry, lubricate it (see Chapter 1).

7 Legal and safety checks

Lighting and signalling
● Take a minute to check that the headlight, taillight, brake light, instrument lights and turn signals all work correctly.
● Check that the horn sounds when the switch is operated.
● A working speedometer graduated in mph is a statutory requirement in the UK.

Safety
● Check that the throttle grip rotates smoothly, and snaps shut when released, in all steering positions. Also check for the correct amount of freeplay (see Chapter 1).
● Check that the engine shuts off when the kill switch is operated.
● Check that sidestand return spring holds the stand securely up when retracted.

Fuel
● This may seem obvious, but check that you have enough fuel to complete your journey. If you notice signs of fuel leakage – rectify the cause immediately.
● Ensure you use the correct grade fuel – see Chapter 4 Specifications.

Chapter 1
Routine maintenance and Servicing

Contents

Degrees of difficulty

| Easy, suitable for novice with little experience | 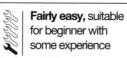 | Fairly easy, suitable for beginner with some experience | | Fairly difficult, suitable for competent DIY mechanic | | Difficult, suitable for experienced DIY mechanic | 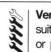 | Very difficult, suitable for expert DIY or professional | |

Engine

Spark plugs
  YZF750R and SP models
    Type . . . . NGK CR9E or Nippondenso U27ESR-N
    Electrode gap . . . . 0.7 to 0.8 mm
  YZF1000R
    Type . . . . NGK DR8EA or Nippondenso X24ESR-U
    Electrode gap . . . . 0.6 to 0.7 mm

Engine idle speed
  YZF750R and SP models . . . . 1150 to 1250 rpm
  YZF1000R models . . . . 1050 to 1150 rpm

Carburettor synchronisation – intake vacuum
  YZF750R and SP models . . . . 200 mmHg
  YZF1000R models . . . . 250 mmHg

Carburettor synchronisation – max. difference between carburettors
  YZF750R and SP models . . . . 10 mmHg
  YZF1000R models . . . . 10 mmHg

Valve clearances (COLD engine)
  Intake valves . . . . 0.11 to 0.20 mm
  Exhaust valves . . . . 0.21 to 0.30 mm

Cylinder compression
  YZF750R and SP models
    Standard . . . . 192 psi (13.25 Bar)
    Maximum . . . . 196 psi (13.52 Bar)
    Minimum . . . . 179 psi (12.35 Bar)
    Max. difference between cylinders . . . . 14.5 psi (1.0 Bar)
  YZF1000R models
    Standard . . . . 202 psi (13.94 Bar)
    Maximum . . . . 213 psi (14.69 Bar)
    Minimum . . . . 190 psi (13.11 Bar)
    Max. difference between cylinders . . . . 14.5 psi (1.0 Bar)
Engine oil pressure (YZF1000R models) . . . . 50 to 64 psi (3.45 to 4.42 Bar) @ 4000 rpm

Cycle parts

Drive chain slack . . . . 20 to 35 mm

Chain stretch limit (see text)
  YZF750R and SP models . . . . 150 mm
  YZF1000R models . . . . 149.1 mm

Rear brake pedal height (see text)
  YZF750R and SP models . . . . 57 mm
  YZF1000R models . . . . 50 mm

Throttle cable freeplay . . . . 3 to 7 mm

EXUP cable freeplay . . . . 1.5 mm

Tyre pressures (cold) . . . . see *Daily (pre-ride) checks*

Recommended lubricants and fluids

Engine/transmission oil type . . . .   see *Daily (pre-ride) checks*
Engine/transmission oil capacity
  YZF750R and SP models*
    Oil change . . . .   3.0 litres
    Oil and filter change . . . .   3.2 litres
    Following engine overhaul – dry engine, new filter . . . .   4.0 litres
Note that the capacity of 2.7 litres (2700 cc) indicated on the crankcase on some R models is incorrect and should be ignored
  YZF1000R models
    Oil change . . . .   3.0 litres
    Oil and filter change . . . .   3.2 litres
    Following engine overhaul – dry engine, new filter . . . .   3.5 litres
Coolant type . . . .   50% distilled water, 50% corrosion inhibited ethylene glycol anti-freeze. **Note:** *Yamaha specify that soft tap water can be used, but NOT hard water. If in doubt, boil the water first or use only distilled water.*

Coolant capacity
  1993 and 1994 YZF750R and SP models . . . .   2.4 litres
  1995-on YZF750R and SP models . . . .   2.6 litres
  YZF1000R models . . . .   2.7 litres
Brake/clutch fluid . . . .   DOT 4
Drive chain . . . .   SAE 30 to 50 W engine oil or chain lubricant suitable for O-ring chains
Steering head bearings . . . .   Lithium-based multi-purpose grease
Swingarm pivot and bearings . . . .   Molybdenum disulphide grease
Suspension linkage bearings . . . .   Molybdenum disulphide grease
Bearing seal lips . . . .   Lithium-based multi-purpose grease
Gearchange lever/clutch lever/front brake lever/
  rear brake pedal/sidestand pivots . . . .   Lithium-based multi-purpose grease
Cables . . . .   10W30 motor oil
Throttle grip . . . .   Multi-purpose grease or dry film lubricant

Torque wrench settings

Rear axle nut
  1993 and 1994 YZF750R and SP models . . . .   203 Nm
  1995-on YZF750R and SP models . . . .   150 Nm
  YZF1000R models . . . .   150 Nm
Rear brake torque arm nuts . . . .   30 Nm
Spark plugs
  YZF750R and SP models . . . .   12.5 Nm
  YZF1000R models . . . .   18 Nm
EXUP pulley cover bolts . . . .   10 Nm
Oil drain plug . . . .   43 Nm
Oil filter . . . .   17 Nm
Steering head bearing adjuster nut
  Initial setting . . . .   48 Nm
  Final setting . . . .   16 Nm
Steering stem nut . . . .   110 Nm
Fork clamp bolts (top yoke)
  YZF750R and SP models . . . .   25 Nm
  YZF1000R models . . . .   26 Nm
Handlebar positioning bolts . . . .   13 Nm
Handlebar clamp bolts
  YZF750R and SP models . . . .   13 Nm
  YZF1000R models . . . .   17 Nm
Cooling system drain plug(s) . . . .   10 Nm
Crankshaft end-cover screws . . . .   7 Nm
Oil gallery bolt (YZF750R and SP) . . . .   10 Nm
Main oil gallery plug (YZF1000R) . . . .   12 Nm

1

Note: *The daily (pre-ride) checks outlined in the owner's manual covers those items which should be inspected on a daily basis. Always perform the pre-ride inspection at every* *maintenance interval (in addition to the procedures listed). The intervals listed below are the intervals recommended by the manufacturer for each particular operation* *during the model years covered in this manual. Your owner's manual may have different intervals for your model.*

Daily (pre-ride)
- [ ] See *Daily (pre-ride) checks* at the beginning of this manual.

After the initial 600 miles (1000 km)
Note: *This check is usually performed by a Yamaha dealer after the first 600 miles (1000 km) from new. Thereafter, maintenance is carried out according to the following intervals of the schedule.*

Every 300 miles (600 km) – YZF750R and SP
- [ ] Check, adjust, clean and lubricate the drive chain (Section 1)

Every 600 miles (1000 km) – YZF1000R
- [ ] Check, adjust, clean and lubricate the drive chain (Section 1)

Every 4000 miles (6000 km) or 6 months (whichever comes sooner)
- [ ] Check the spark plug gaps (Section 2)
- [ ] Check and adjust the idle speed (Section 3)
- [ ] Check/adjust the carburettor synchronisation (Section 4)
- [ ] Clean and check the air filter element (Section 5)
- [ ] Check the fuel system and EXUP system (Section 6)
- [ ] Change the engine/transmission oil (Section 7)
- [ ] Check the brake pads (Section 8)
- [ ] Check the brake system and brake light switch operation (Section 9)
- [ ] Check the clutch (Section 10)
- [ ] Check the battery (Section 11)
- [ ] Check the condition of the wheels and tyres (Section 12)
- [ ] Check the wheel bearings (Section 13)
- [ ] Check the sidestand (Section 14)
- [ ] Check the tightness of all nuts, bolts and fasteners (Section 15)
- [ ] Check the cooling system (Section 16)
- [ ] Check and adjust the throttle and choke cables (Section 17)
- [ ] Lubricate the clutch/gearchange/brake lever/brake pedal/sidestand pivots and the throttle/choke cables (Section 18)
- [ ] Check the suspension (Section 19)
- [ ] Check and adjust the steering head bearings (Section 20)

Every 8000 miles (12,000 km) or 12 months (whichever comes sooner)
Carry out all the items under the 4000 mile (6000 km) check, plus the following
- [ ] Change the engine/transmission oil and filter (Section 21)
- [ ] Renew the spark plugs (Section 2)

Every 16,000 miles (24,000 km) or two years (whichever comes sooner)
Carry out all the items under the 8000 mile (12,000 km) check, plus the following
- [ ] Change the coolant (Section 22)
- [ ] Re-grease the swingarm and suspension linkage bearings (Section 23).
- [ ] Re-grease the steering head bearings (Section 24).
- [ ] Change the brake and clutch fluid (Section 25)
- [ ] Renew the brake and clutch master cylinder and caliper/slave cylinder seals (Section 26)

Every 28,000 miles (42,000 km) or 42 months (whichever comes sooner)
Carry out all the items under the 4000 mile (6000 km) check, plus the following
- [ ] Check and adjust the valve clearances (Section 27)

Every 60,000 miles (100,000 km)
- [ ] Renew the alternator brushes (Section 28)

Every four years
- [ ] Renew the brake and clutch hoses (Section 29)

Non-scheduled maintenance
- [ ] Check and adjust the headlight aim (Section 30)
- [ ] Check the cylinder compression (Section 31)
- [ ] Check the engine oil pressure (Section 32)
- [ ] Renew the fuel hoses (Section 33)
- [ ] Change the front fork oil (Section 34)

Component locations on right-hand side – YZF750R and SP models

1 Coolant reservoir
2 Rear brake fluid reservoir
3 Battery
4 Air filter
5 Front brake fluid reservoir
6 Cooling system pressure cap
7 Coolant drain plug in cylinder block
8 Idle speed adjuster (YZF750SP)
9 Engine/transmission oil inspection window
10 Engine/transmission oil filler cap

Component locations on left-hand side – YZF750R and SP models

1 Clutch fluid reservoir
2 Steering head bearings
3 Idle speed adjuster (YZF750R)
4 Alternator
5 EXUP pulley cover
6 Coolant drain plug in water pump
7 Engine/transmission oil drain plug
8 Coolant drain plug in cylinder block
9 Engine/transmission oil filter

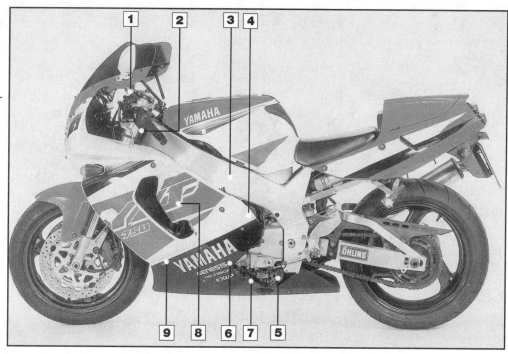

1

Component locations on right-hand side – YZF1000R model

1 Coolant reservoir
2 Rear brake fluid reservoir
3 In-line fuel filter
4 Air filter
5 Front brake fluid reservoir
6 Cooling system pressure cap
7 Idle speed adjuster
8 Coolant drain plug in cylinder block
9 Engine/transmission oil level inspection window
10 Engine/transmission oil filler cap

Component locations on left-hand side – YZF1000R model

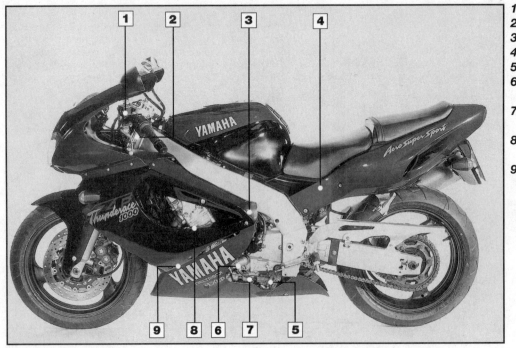

1 Clutch fluid reservoir
2 Steering head bearings
3 Alternator
4 Battery
5 EXUP pulley cover
6 Coolant drain plug in water pump
7 Engine/transmission oil drain plug
8 Coolant drain plug in cylinder block
9 Engine/transmission oil filter

Introduction

1 This Chapter is designed to help the home mechanic maintain his/her motorcycle for safety, economy, long life and peak performance.

2 Deciding where to start or plug into the routine maintenance schedule depends on several factors. If the warranty period on your motorcycle has just expired, and if it has been maintained according to the warranty standards, you may want to pick up routine maintenance as it coincides with the next mileage or calendar interval. If you have owned the machine for some time but have never performed any maintenance on it, then you may want to start at the beginning and include all frequent procedures to ensure that nothing important is overlooked. If you have just had a major engine overhaul, then you should start the engine maintenance routines from the beginning. If you have a used machine and have no knowledge of its history or maintenance record, you should combine all the checks into one large initial service and then settle into the maintenance schedule prescribed.

3 Before beginning any maintenance or repair, the machine should be cleaned thoroughly, especially around the oil filter, spark plugs, valve cover, side panels, carburettors, etc. Cleaning will help ensure that dirt does not contaminate the engine and will allow you to detect wear and damage that could otherwise easily go unnoticed.

4 Certain maintenance information is sometimes printed on decals attached to the motorcycle. If any information on the decals differs from that included here, use the information on the decal.

Every 300 miles (500 km) – YZF750R and SP

Every 600 miles (1000 km) – YZF1000R

1   Drive chain and sprockets – check, adjustment and lubrication

Check

1 A neglected drive chain won't last long and can quickly damage the sprockets. Routine chain adjustment and lubrication isn't difficult and will ensure maximum chain and sprocket life.

2 To check the chain, place the bike on its

sidestand and shift the transmission into neutral.

3 Push up on the bottom run of the chain and measure the slack midway between the two sprockets, then compare your measurement to that listed in this Chapter's Specifications **(see illustration)**. As the chain stretches with wear, adjustment will periodically be necessary (see below). Since the chain will rarely wear evenly, roll the bike forwards so that another section of chain can be checked; do this several times to check the entire length of chain.

4 If the chain has reached the end of its adjustment it has probably stretched beyond its service limit. This can be checked by measuring a section of the chain **(see illustration)** with the chain held taught, and comparing the measurement to the limit in the Specifications. Ideally this should be done with the chain removed, although it is possible to take the measurement on the bike if the chainguard is removed and the measurement is taken on the chain's top run, midway between the sprockets. Take three measurements in different places on the chain. If the chain has stretched beyond the limit, replace it with a new one (see Chapter 6).

5 In some cases where lubrication has been neglected, corrosion and galling may cause the links to bind and kink, which effectively shortens the chain's length. Such links should be thoroughly cleaned and worked free. If the chain is tight between the sprockets, rusty or kinked, it's time to replace it with a new one. If you find a tight area, mark it with felt pen or paint, and repeat the measurement after the bike has been ridden. If the chain's still tight in the same area, it may be damaged or worn. Because a tight or kinked chain can damage the transmission output shaft bearing, it's a good idea to replace it with a new one (see Chapter 6).

6 Check the entire length of the chain for damaged rollers, loose links and pins, and missing O-rings and replace with a new one it if damage is found. **Note:** *Never install a new chain on old sprockets, and never use the old chain if you install new sprockets – renew the chain and sprockets as a set.*

7 Remove the front sprocket cover (see Chapter 6). Check the teeth on the engine sprocket and the rear wheel sprocket for wear **(see illustration)**.

8 Inspect the drive chain slider on the swingarm for excessive wear and renew it if worn (see Chapter 6).

1

1.3 Push up on the chain and measure the slack 20 to 35 mm

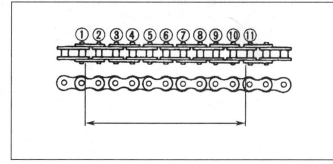

1.4 Check the amount of stretch by measuring as shown

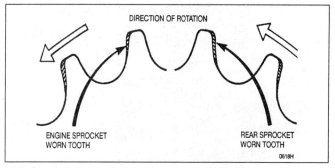

DIRECTION OF ROTATION

ENGINE SPROCKET WORN TOOTH

REAR SPROCKET WORN TOOTH

0618H

1.7 Check the sprockets in the areas indicated to see if they are worn excessively

1.10a Slacken the rear axle nut (arrowed)

1.10b Remove the split pin (arrowed) and slacken the nut on each end of the torque arm

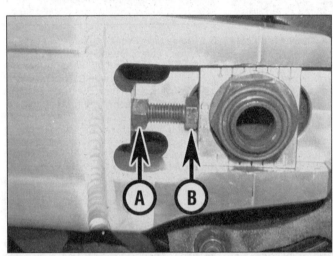

1.11a Slacken the locknut (A) and turn the adjuster (B) as required

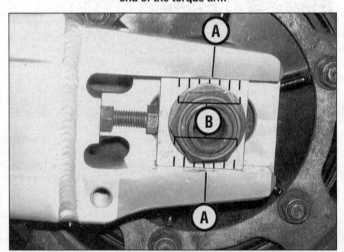

1.11b Check the relative position of the static marks (A) and the adjustment marks (B) on each side

Adjustment

9 Rotate the rear wheel until the chain is positioned with the tightest point at the centre of its bottom run, then place the machine on its sidestand.

10 Where fitted, remove the split pin from the axle nut. Slacken the axle nut **(see illustration)**. Also remove the split pin from

1.13 Tighten the axle nut to the specified torque

the bolt on each end of the brake torque and slacken the nuts – this will allow easier movement of the wheel as the adjustment is made **(see illustration)**.

11 Slacken the adjuster locknut on each side of the swingarm, then turn the adjusters evenly until the amount of freeplay specified at the beginning of the Chapter is obtained at the centre of the bottom run of the chain **(see illustration)**. Following chain adjustment, check that each chain adjustment marker is in the same position in relation to the marks on the swingarm **(see illustration)**. It is important each adjuster aligns with the same notch; if not, the rear wheel will be out of alignment with the front. Also check that there is no clearance between the adjuster and the adjustment marker – push or kick the wheel forwards to eliminate any freeplay.

> **HAYNES HINT** *Refer to Chapter 7 for information on checking wheel alignment.*

12 If there is a discrepancy in the chain adjuster positions, adjust one of them so that its position is exactly the same as the other. Check the chain freeplay as described above and readjust if necessary.

13 Tighten the axle nut to the torque setting specified at the beginning of the Chapter, then tighten the adjuster locknuts securely **(see illustration)**. Also tighten the brake torque arm nuts to the specified torque and fit the split pins to lock them.

Lubrication

14 If required, wash the chain in paraffin (kerosene), then wipe it off and allow it to dry, using compressed air if available. If the chain is excessively dirty it should be removed from the machine and allowed to soak in the paraffin (see Chapter 6).

Caution: Don't use petrol (gasoline), solvent or other cleaning fluids which might damage the internal sealing properties of the chain. Don't use high-pressure water. The entire process shouldn't take longer

than ten minutes – if it does, the O-rings in the chain rollers could be damaged.

15 For routine lubrication, the best time to lubricate the chain is after the motorcycle has been ridden. When the chain is warm, the lubricant will penetrate the joints between the side plates better than when cold. **Note:** *Yamaha specifies SAE 30 to 50 W engine oil; do not use chain lube, which may contain solvents that could damage the O-rings, unless it is specified for O-ring chains.* Apply the lubricant to the area where the side plates overlap – not the middle of the rollers **(see illustration).**

 HAYNES HiNT *Apply the lubricant to the top of the lower chain run, so centrifugal force will work it into the chain when the bike is moving. After applying the lubricant, let it soak in a few minutes before wiping off any excess.*

1.15 Apply the lubricant to the overlap between the sideplates

Every 4000 miles (6000 km) or 6 months

2 Spark plugs – gap check and adjustment

1 Make sure your spark plug socket is the correct size before attempting to remove the plugs – a suitable one is supplied in the motorcycle's tool kit which is stored under the seat. Remove the fairing side panels (see Chapter 8).

2 Using compressed air if available, clean the area around the base of the spark plugs to prevent any dirt falling into the engine when the plugs are removed.

3 Check that the cylinder location is marked on each plug lead, then pull the spark plug cap off each spark plug **(see illustration)**. Using either the plug removing tool supplied in the bike's toolkit or a deep socket type wrench, unscrew the plugs from the cylinder head **(see illustration)**. Lay each plug out in relation to its cylinder; if any plug shows up a problem it will then be easy to identify the troublesome cylinder.

4 Inspect the electrodes for wear. Both the centre and side electrodes should have square edges and the side electrodes should be of uniform thickness. Look for excessive deposits and evidence of a cracked or chipped insulator around the centre electrode. Compare your spark plugs to the colour spark plug reading chart at the end of this manual. Check the threads, the washer and the ceramic insulator body for cracks and other damage.

5 If the electrodes are not excessively worn, and if the deposits can be easily removed with a wire brush, the plugs can be re-gapped and re-used (if no cracks or chips are visible in the insulator). If in doubt concerning the condition of the plugs, replace them with new ones, as the expense is minimal. Note that the spark plugs should be renewed at every second service interval, ie every 8000 miles.

6 Cleaning spark plugs by sandblasting is permitted, provided you clean the plugs with a high flash-point solvent afterwards.

7 Before installing the plugs, make sure they are the correct type and heat range and check the gap between the electrodes **(see illustrations)**. Compare the gap to that specified and adjust as necessary. If the gap must be adjusted, bend the side electrodes only and be very careful not to chip or crack the insulator nose **(see illustration)**. Make sure the washer is in place on the plug before installing it.

1

2.3a Remove the spark plug cap . . .

2.3b . . . then unscrew the spark plug

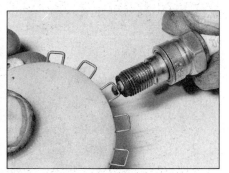

2.7a Using a wire type gauge to measure the spark plug electrode gap

2.7b Using a feeler gauge to measure the spark plug electrode gap

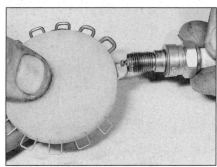

2.7c Adjust the electrode gap by bending the side electrode only

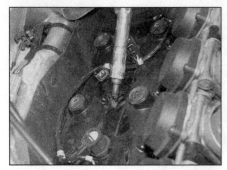

2.8 Thread the plug as far as possible turning the tool by hand

8 Since the cylinder head is made of aluminium, which is soft and easily damaged, thread the plugs into the heads turning the tool by hand **(see illustration)**. Once the plugs are finger-tight, the job can be finished with a spanner on the tool supplied or a socket drive **(see illustration 2.3b)**. If a torque wrench can be applied, tighten the spark plugs to the specified torque setting. Otherwise tighten them by 1/4 to 1/2 turn after they have been fully hand tightened and have seated. Do not over-tighten them.

 HAYNES HiNT *As the plugs are quite recessed, you can slip a short length of hose over the end of the plug to use as a tool to thread it into place. The hose will grip the plug well enough to turn it, but will start to slip if the plug begins to cross-thread in the hole – this will prevent damaged threads.*

9 Reconnect the spark plug caps, making sure they are securely connected to the correct cylinder **(see illustration 2.3a)**. Install the fairing side panels (see Chapter 8).

 HAYNES HiNT *Stripped plug threads in the cylinder head can be repaired with a Heli-Coil thread insert – see 'Tools and Workshop Tips' in the Reference section.*

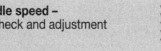
3 Idle speed –
check and adjustment

1 The idle speed should be checked and adjusted before and after the carburettors are synchronised (balanced) and when it is obviously too high or too low. Before adjusting the idle speed, make sure the valve clearances and spark plug gaps are correct, and the air filter is clean. Also, turn the handlebars back-and-forth and see if the idle speed changes as this is done. If it does, the throttle cables may not be adjusted or routed correctly, or may be worn out. This is a dangerous condition that can cause loss of control of the bike. Be sure to correct this problem before proceeding.

2 The engine should be at normal operating temperature, which is usually reached after 10 to 15 minutes of stop-and-go riding. Make sure the transmission is in neutral, and place the motorcycle on its stand.

3 On YZF750R models, the idle speed adjuster is located on the left-hand side of the motorcycle and is accessed using a screwdriver inserted through the hole in the frame beam – remove the blanking cap from the hole **(see illustrations)**. On YZF750SP and YZF1000R models, the idle speed adjuster is located on the right-hand side of the engine above the clutch cover **(see illustration)**. With the engine idling, adjust the idle speed by turning the adjuster screw until the idle speed listed in this Chapter's Specifications is obtained. Turn the screw clockwise to increase idle speed, and anti-clockwise to decrease it.

4 Snap the throttle open and shut a few times, then recheck the idle speed. If necessary, repeat the adjustment procedure.

5 If a smooth, steady idle can't be achieved, the fuel/air mixture may be incorrect (check the pilot screw settings – see Chapter 4) or the carburettors may need synchronising (see Section 4). Also check the intake manifold rubbers for cracks which will cause an air leak, resulting in a weak mixture.

4 Carburettors –
synchronisation

⚠ *Warning: Petrol (gasoline) is extremely flammable, so take extra precautions when you work on any part of the fuel system. Don't smoke or allow open flames or bare light bulbs near the work area, and don't work in a garage where a natural gas-type appliance is present. If you spill any fuel on your skin, rinse it off immediately with soap and water. When you perform any kind of work on the fuel system, wear safety glasses and have a fire extinguisher suitable for a Class B type fire (flammable liquids) on hand.*

⚠ *Warning: Take great care not to burn your hand on the hot engine unit when accessing the gauge take-off points on the intake manifolds. Do not allow exhaust gases to build up in the work area; either perform the check outside or use an exhaust gas extraction system.*

1 Carburettor synchronisation is simply the process of adjusting the carburettors so they pass the same amount of fuel/air mixture to each cylinder. This is done by measuring the vacuum produced in each cylinder. Carburettors that are out of synchronisation will result in decreased fuel mileage, increased engine temperature, less than ideal throttle response and higher vibration levels. Before synchronising the carburettors, make sure the valve clearances and idle speed are properly set.

2 To properly synchronise the carburettors you will need a set of vacuum gauges or a manometer. These instruments measure engine vacuum, and can be obtained from motorcycle dealers or mail order parts suppliers. The equipment used should be suitable for a four cylinder engine and come complete with the necessary adapters and hoses to fit the take off points. **Note:** *Because of the nature of the synchronisation procedure and the need for special instruments, most owners leave the task to a Yamaha dealer.*

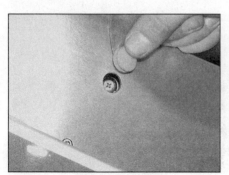

3.3a On YZF750R models, remove the blanking cap . . .

3.3b . . . and insert a screwdriver through the hole

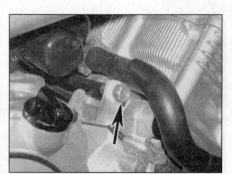

3.3c Idle speed adjuster screw (arrowed) – YZF1000R and 750 SP models

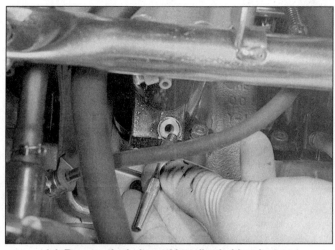

4.4 Remove the bolts and install suitable adapters

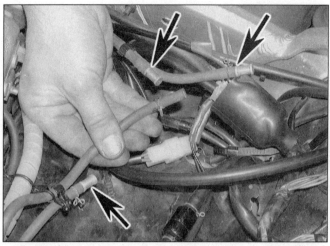

4.5 Pull the blanking plugs out of the hoses for cylinders 2, 3 and 4 (arrowed)

3 Start the engine and let it run until it reaches normal operating temperature, then shut it off.
4 On 1993 and 1994 YZF750R and all SP models, remove the carburettors (see Chapter 4). Unscrew the blanking bolts from the take-off points on the intake manifolds of Nos. 2, 3 and 4 cylinders and attach the gauge or manometer hoses to them using suitable

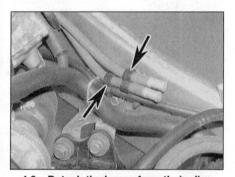

4.6a Detach the hoses from their clips (arrowed) . . .

adapters **(see illustration)**. Disconnect the fuel tap vacuum hose from the take-off point on No. 1 cylinder intake manifold and connect the gauge/manometer hose. Make sure the No. 1 gauge is attached to the hose from the No. 1 (left-hand) carburettor manifold, and so on. Install the carburettors.
5 On 1995-on YZF750R models, remove the fuel tank (see Chapter 4). Detach the three vacuum hoses for Nos. 2, 3 and 4 carburettor manifolds from their clips (there are two hoses on the right-hand side and one on the left), then pull the blanking plug out of the end of each hose in turn **(see illustration)**. The vacuum hose from the No. 1 carburettor manifold has already been detached from the fuel tap. Attach the gauge or manometer hoses to the vacuum hoses using a suitable union. Make sure the No. 1 gauge is attached to the hose from the No. 1 (left-hand) carburettor, and so on.
6 On YZF1000R models, remove the fuel tank

(see Chapter 4). Detach the vacuum hoses from their clips (there are two hoses on each side), then pull the blanking plug out of the end of each hose in turn and attach the gauge or manometer hoses to them using a suitable union **(see illustrations)**. On California models, only three of the hoses will have blanking plugs, while the other one will be attached to a union on one of the EVAP system components. Make sure the No. 1 gauge is attached to the hose from the No. 1 (left-hand) carburettor, and so on.
7 Arrange a temporary fuel supply using an auxiliary tank and some hosing.
8 Start the engine and let it idle. If the gauges are fitted with damping adjustment, set this so that the needle flutter is just eliminated but so that they can still respond to small changes in pressure.
9 The vacuum readings for all cylinders should be the same **(see illustration)**. If the vacuum readings differ, proceed as follows.

1

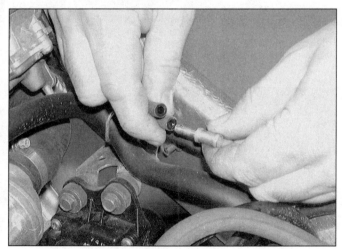

4.6b . . . . then remove the blanking plugs . . .

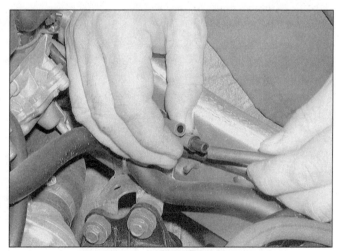

4.6c . . . and connect the gauge hoses using suitable unions

4.9 Carburettor synchronisation set-up

4.10a The screws are located in the throttle linkage between the carburettors – YZF1000R models

10 On YZF750R and YZF1000R models, the carburettors are balanced by turning the synchronising screws situated in-between each carburettor, in the throttle linkage **(see illustrations)**. **Note:** *Do not press on the screws whilst adjusting them, otherwise a false reading will be obtained.* First synchronise No. 1 carburettor to No. 2 using the left-hand synchronising screw until the readings are the same. Then synchronise No. 3 carburettor to No. 4 using the right-hand screw. Finally synchronise Nos. 1 and 2 carburettors to Nos. 3 and 4 using the centre screw, on YZF1000R models accessing it as shown using a long screwdriver **(see illustration)**. When all the carburettors are synchronised, open and close the throttle quickly to settle the linkage, and recheck the gauge readings, readjusting if necessary.

11 On YZF750SP models, the carburettors are balanced by turning the synchronising screw situated in the slide assembly in the top of each carburettor. **Note:** *Do not press on the screws whilst adjusting them, otherwise a false reading will be obtained.* Unscrew the bolts securing the top covers on Nos. 1, 3 and 4 carburettors and remove the covers – No. 2 is the reference and should not be adjusted. First synchronise No. 1 carburettor to No. 2 by slackening the locknut in the top of No. 1 carburettor and turning the synchronising screw until the readings are the same. Then synchronise No. 3 carburettor to No. 2 using the screw in No. 3 carburettor. Finally synchronise No. 4 carburettor to No. 2. When all the carburettors are synchronised, open and close the throttle quickly to settle the linkage, and recheck the gauge readings, readjusting if necessary.

12 When the adjustment is complete, recheck the vacuum readings, then adjust the idle speed (see Section 3) until the speed listed in this Chapter's Specifications is obtained. Remove the gauges and refit the blanking plugs or bolts as required by your model (see Steps 4, 5 and 6). On California models, do not forget to attach the vacuum hose to the EVAP system. Detach the temporary fuel supply and install the fuel tank (see Chapter 4).

5 Air filter – cleaning and renewal

1 Remove the fuel tank (see Chapter 4).
2 On YZF750R and SP models, remove the screws securing the air filter cover to the filter housing, then remove the cover and withdraw the filter element from the housing **(see illustrations)**.

4.10b Carburettor synchronisation screws (arrowed) – YZF750R models

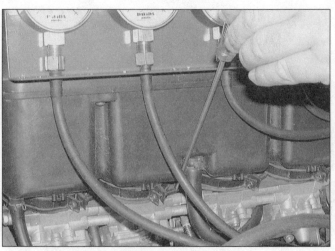

4.10c On YZF1000R models, access the centre screw as shown

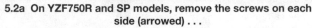

5.2a On YZF750R and SP models, remove the screws on each side (arrowed) . . .

5.2b . . . then lift off the cover . . .

3 On YZF1000R models, remove the screw(s) securing the air filter cover to the filter housing, then remove the cover and withdraw the filter element from the housing (see illustrations).

4 Tap the element on a hard surface to dislodge any large particles of dirt, then if compressed air is available, use it to clean the element, directing the air in the opposite direction of normal airflow.

Caution: If the machine is continually ridden in dusty conditions, the filter should be cleaned more frequently.

5 Check the element for signs of damage. If the element is torn or cannot be cleaned, or is obviously beyond further use, replace it with a new one.

6 Install the filter element, making sure it is properly seated – on YZF750R and SP models the element fits with the mesh side facing back **(see illustration 5.2c)**. On YZF1000R models make sure the ↑FWD mark is at the top and pointing forward (see illustration). Fit the air filter cover, making sure the rubber seal is in place **(see illustration 5.2b or 5.3b)**. Install the fuel tank (see Chapter 4).

7 Check that the collector in the air filter housing drain hose has not become blocked, and drain it if necessary – the hose comes out of the rear left side of the housing.

8 Check the crankcase breather hose between the engine and the air filter housing for loose connections, cracks and deterioration and replace it with a new one if necessary.

6	Fuel system and EXUP system – check

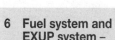

⚠️ *Warning: Petrol (gasoline) is extremely flammable, so take extra precautions when you work on any part of the fuel system. Don't smoke or allow open flames or bare light bulbs near the work area, and don't work in a garage where a natural gas-type appliance is present. If you spill any fuel on your skin, rinse it off immediately with soap and water. When you perform any kind of work on the fuel system, wear safety glasses and have a fire extinguisher suitable for a Class B type fire (flammable liquids) on hand.*

Fuel system – check

1 Remove the fuel tank (see Chapter 4) and check the tank, the fuel tap and the fuel hoses, and on YZF1000R models the filter and the fuel pump, for signs of leakage, deterioration or damage; in particular check that there is no leakage from the fuel hoses.

5.2c . . . and withdraw the element

5.3a On YZF1000R models, undo the screw . . .

5.3b . . . then lift off the cover . . .

5.3c . . . and withdraw the element

5.6 On YZF1000R models make sure the ↑FWD mark is at the top and pointing forward

1

6.7a In-line fuel filter (arrowed) – YZF1000R models

6.7b Detach the fuel hose . . .

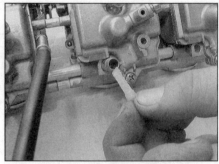

6.7c . . . and carefully draw out the strainer

Renew any hoses which are cracked or have deteriorated. On YZF750R and SP models, the filter and pump are mounted inside the fuel tank – check around the mounting plate gasket in the bottom of the tank for leaks.

2 If the fuel tap is leaking, tighten the assembly screws and mounting bolts (see Chapter 4). If leakage persists remove the tap and disassemble it, noting how the components fit. Inspect all components and replace any that are worn or damaged with new ones, if available. Otherwise fit a new tap.

3 If the carburettor gaskets are leaking, the carburettors should be disassembled and rebuilt using new gaskets and seals (see Chapter 4).

4 On California models, check the EVAP system hoses for loose connections, cracks and deterioration and replace them with new ones if necessary.

Fuel strainer/filter cleaning and renewal

5 Cleaning of the fuel strainer is advised after a high mileage has been covered. It is also necessary if fuel starvation is suspected. If the strainer is dirty, check the condition of the inside of your tank – if there is evidence of rust, remove, drain and clean the tank (see Chapter 4). The in-line filter fitted to YZF1000R models should be inspected periodically; if it is dirty renew it – this type of filter cannot be cleaned. Note that Yamaha recommend that the in-line filter should be renewed every 19,000 miles (30,000 km) on US models.

6 On YZF750R and SP models, the fuel strainer is mounted in the tank and is integral with the fuel pump. Remove the fuel tank and the fuel pump (see Chapter 4). Clean the filter to remove all traces of dirt and fuel sediment. Check the filter for holes. If any are found, a new pump assembly should be fitted – the filter is not available separately. Install the fuel pump (see Chapter 4). Start the engine and check that there are no leaks.

7 On YZF1000R models, a fuel strainer is mounted in the tank and is integral with the fuel tap. Remove the fuel tank and the fuel tap (see Chapter 4). Clean the gauze strainer to remove all traces of dirt and fuel sediment. Check the gauze for holes. If any are found, a new tap should be fitted – the strainer is not available

separately. An in-line fuel filter is fitted in the hose from the fuel tap to the fuel pump (see illustration). Remove the fuel tank for access (see Chapter 4). If the filter is dirty or clogged, or otherwise needs renewal, have a rag handy to soak up any residual fuel, then release the clamps and disconnect the hoses from the filter. Release the filter from its holder and discard it. Install the new filter so that its arrow points in the direction of fuel flow (ie towards the pump). Fit the hoses to the unions on the filter and secure them with the clamps. There is also a small strainer fitted inside the fuel hose union on the carburettors – release the clamp and detach the hose, then carefully draw out the strainer and clean it in new fuel (see illustrations). Refit the strainer and attach the hose. Install the fuel tank (see Chapter 4). Start the engine and check that there are no leaks.

EXUP system – check

8 When the ignition is first switched 'ON', or while the engine is running, the EXUP system on 1995-on YZF750R and SP models and all YZF1000R models performs its own self-diagnosis. If a fault occurs, the tachometer will be seen to display zero rpm for 3 seconds, then 9000 rpm (YZF750R and SP models) or 7000 rpm (YZF1000R models) for 2.5 seconds, then the actual engine speed for 3 seconds, whereupon it will repeat the cycle until the engine is switched off.

9 Remove the lower fairing (see Chapter 8) and the fuel tank (see Chapter 4).

10 Unscrew the bolts securing the EXUP pulley cover on the exhaust and remove the cover (see illustration).

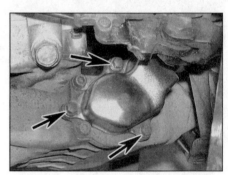

6.10 Unscrew the bolts (arrowed) and remove the cover

11 Start the engine and increase the revs to 2000 rpm. The servo should turn. As it turns, simultaneously check that the pulley on the exhaust is turning the valve. If the servo turns but the pulley doesn't, remove the cables and check them, and lubricate or replace them with new ones as necessary (see Chapter 4). If the pulley operates, but the movement of the valve is sticky or not complete, first check the cables, and if they are good, disassemble the valve for cleaning and inspection (see Chapter 4). If the servo does not operate, refer to Chapter 4 for further tests.

12 Measure the amount of freeplay in each EXUP cable as shown and check that it is as specified at the beginning of the Chapter (see illustration). If not, slacken the lockring on the adjuster in each cable and turn the adjusters in to create freeplay in the cable (see illustration). Now turn the cable pulley on the valve until the notch in the pulley aligns with

6.12a Check the freeplay in the cables. If it is incorrect, adjust it as described, inserting the pin into the hole (arrowed) so it locks the pulley

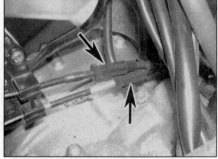

6.12b EXUP cable freeplay adjusters (arrowed)

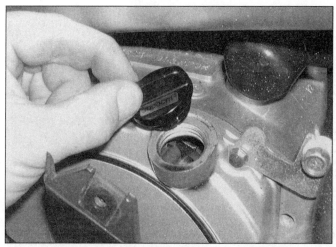

7.3 Remove the oil filler cap from the clutch cover

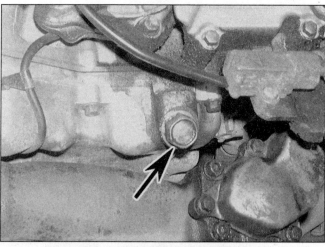

7.4a Unscrew the crankcase oil drain plug . . .

the hole in the housing, then insert a 4 mm pin into the hole **(see illustration 6.12a)**. Turn each cable adjuster out until it becomes tight, then turn it in by 1/4 turn on YZF750R and SP models, and 1/2 turn on YZF1000R models, then tighten the lockrings. Remove the pin from the hole and check that the freeplay is as specified and equal for each cable.

13 Install the cover and tighten the bolts to the torque setting specified at the beginning of the Chapter **(see illustration 6.10).**

7 Engine/transmission – oil change

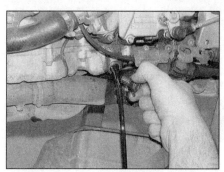

7.4b . . . and allow the oil to drain

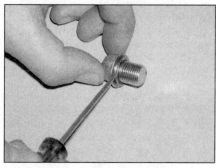

7.4c To remove the old sealing washer, cut it off

> ⚠️ **Warning:** *Be careful when draining the oil, as the exhaust pipes, the engine, and the oil itself can cause severe burns.*

1 Consistent routine oil and filter changes are the single most important maintenance procedure you can perform on a motorcycle. The oil not only lubricates the internal parts of the engine, transmission and clutch, but it also acts as a coolant, a cleaner, a sealant, and a protectant. Because of these demands, the oil takes a terrific amount of abuse and should be changed often with new oil of the recommended grade and type. Saving a little money on the difference in cost between a good oil and a cheap oil won't pay off if the engine is damaged. The oil filter should be changed with every second oil change.

2 Before changing the oil, warm up the engine so the oil will drain easily. Remove the lower fairing and the right-hand fairing side panel (see Chapter 8).

3 Put the motorcycle on its sidestand, and position a clean drain tray below the engine. Unscrew the oil filler cap from the clutch cover to vent it and to act as a reminder that there is no oil in the engine **(see illustration)**.

4 Unscrew the oil drain plug from the left-hand side of the crankcase and allow the oil to flow into the drain tray **(see illustrations)**.

Check the condition of the sealing washer on the drain plug and discard it if it is damaged or worn – it will probably be necessary to cut the old one off using pliers **(see illustration)**.

5 When the oil has completely drained, fit the plug into the crankcase, using a new sealing washer if required, and tighten it to the torque setting specified at the beginning of the Chapter **(see illustrations)**. Avoid overtightening, as damage to the crankcase will result.

6 Refill the engine to the proper level using the recommended type and amount of oil (see *Daily (pre-ride) checks*). With the motorcycle vertical, the oil level should lie between the maximum and minimum level lines on the inspection window (see *Daily (pre-ride) checks*).

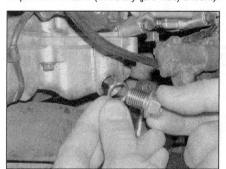

7.5a Install the drain plug, using a new sealing washer if necessary . . .

Install the filler cap. Start the engine and let it run for two or three minutes. Stop the engine, wait a few minutes, then check the oil level. If necessary, add more oil to bring the level up to the maximum level line on the window. Check around the drain plug that there are no leaks.

> **HAYNES HINT** *Saving a little money on good and cheap oils won't pay off if the engine is damaged as a result.*

7 Every so often, and especially as Yamaha do not fit an oil pressure switch and warning light (the system fitted uses an oil level

7.5b . . . and tighten it to the specified torque

1

sensor), it is advisable to perform an oil pressure check (see Section 32).

8 The old oil drained from the engine cannot be re-used and should be disposed of properly. Check with your local refuse disposal company, disposal facility or environmental agency to see whether they will accept the used oil for recycling. Don't pour used oil into drains or onto the ground.

HAYNES HiNT *Check the old oil carefully – if it is very metallic coloured, then the engine is experiencing wear from break-in (new engine) or from insufficient lubrication. If there are flakes or chips of metal in the oil, then something is drastically wrong internally and the engine will have to be disassembled for inspection and repair. If there are pieces of fibre-like material in the oil, the clutch is experiencing excessive wear and should be checked.*

9 Install the right-hand fairing side panel and the lower fairing (see Chapter 8).

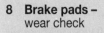

Note: It is antisocial and illegal to dump oil down the drain. To find the location of your nearest oil recycling bank in the UK, call this number free. In the USA, note that any oil supplier must accept used oil for recycling.

OIL CARE FOLLOW THE CODE

OIL BANK LINE
0800 66 33 66

8 Brake pads – wear check

1 Each brake pad has wear indicators that can be viewed without removing the pads from the caliper.

2 The turned in corners of the brake pad backing material form the wear indicators – when they are almost contacting the disc itself the pads must be renewed. The indicators are visible by looking at the bottom corner of the pads **(see illustrations)**. **Note:** *Some after-*

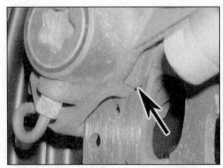

8.2a Brake pad wear indicator (arrowed) – YZF1000R shown

market pads may use different indicators (such as a groove cut into the friction material); the pad is worn when the groove is no longer visible.

Caution: Do not allow the pads to wear to the extent that the indicators contact the disc itself as the disc will be damaged.

3 If the pads are worn to the indicators, new ones must be installed. If the pads are dirty or if you are in doubt as to the amount of friction material remaining, remove them for inspection (see Chapter 7). If required, measure the amount of friction material remaining – the minimum is 0.5 mm.

4 Refer to Chapter 7 for details of pad renewal.

9 Brake system – check

1 A routine general check of the brake system will ensure that any problems are discovered and remedied before the rider's safety is jeopardised.

2 Check the brake lever and pedal for looseness, improper or rough action, excessive play, bends, and other damage. Replace any damaged parts with new ones (see Chapter 7). Clean and lubricate the lever and pedal pivots if their action is stiff or rough (see Section 18).

3 Make sure all brake fasteners are tight. Check the brake pads for wear (see Section 8) and make sure the fluid level in the reservoirs is correct (see *Daily (pre-ride) checks*). Look

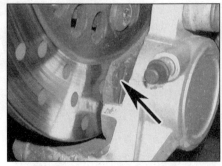

8.2b Rear brake pad wear indicator (arrowed)

for leaks at the hose connections and check for cracks in the hoses themselves **(see illustration)**. If the lever or pedal is spongy bleed the brakes (see Chapter 7). The brake fluid should be changed every two years (see Section 25) and the hoses renewed if they deteriorate, or every four years irrespective of their condition (see Section 29). The master cylinder and caliper seals should be renewed every two years, or if leakage from them is evident (see Section 26).

4 Make sure the brake light operates when the front brake lever is pulled in. The front brake light switch, mounted on the underside of the master cylinder, is not adjustable. If it fails to operate properly, check it (see Chapter 9).

5 Make sure the brake light is activated just before the rear brake takes effect. If adjustment is necessary, hold the switch and turn the adjuster nut on the switch body until the brake light is activated when required **(see illustration)**. If the brake light comes on too late, turn the nut clockwise. If the brake light comes on too soon or is permanently on, turn the nut anti-clockwise. If the switch doesn't operate the brake light, check it (see Chapter 9).

6 The front brake lever has a span adjuster which alters the distance of the lever from the handlebar. Each setting is identified by a number on the adjuster which aligns with the arrow on the lever bracket. Pull the lever away from the handlebar and turn the adjuster ring until the setting which best suits the rider is obtained **(see illustration)**. There are four settings – setting 1 gives the largest span, and

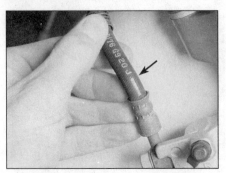

9.3 Flex the brake hose and check for cracks, bulges and leaking fluid

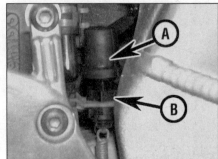

9.5 Hold the brake light switch (A) and turn the adjuster nut (B)

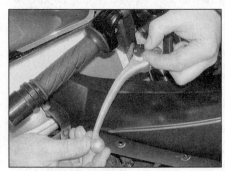

9.6 Adjusting the front brake lever span

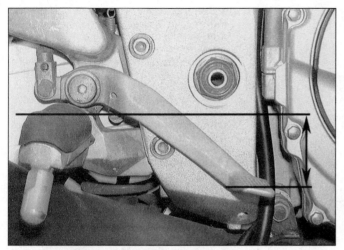

9.7a Measure the distance between the top of the footrest and the top of the brake pedal as shown

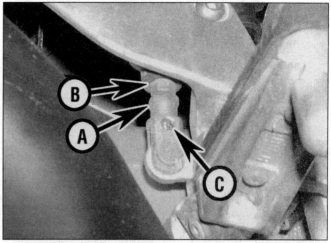

9.7b Slacken the locknut (A) and turn the pushrod using the hex (B) making sure the rod end is still visible in the hole (C)

setting 4 the smallest. When making adjustment ensure that the pin set in the level bracket is engaged in its detent hollow on the adjuster.

7 Check the position of the brake pedal. Yamaha recommend the distance between the tip of the brake pedal and the top of the rider's footrest should be as specified at the beginning of the Chapter (see illustration). If the pedal height is incorrect, or if the rider's preference is different, slacken the clevis locknut on the master cylinder pushrod, then turn the pushrod using a spanner on the hex at the top of the rod until the pedal is at the correct or desired height (see illustration). After adjustment check that the pushrod end is still visible in the hole in the clevis. On completion tighten the locknut securely. Adjust the rear brake light switch after adjusting the pedal height (see Step 5).

10 Clutch – check

1 All models are fitted with an hydraulic clutch, for which there is no method of adjustment.
2 Check the fluid level in the reservoir (see Daily (pre-ride) checks).
3 Inspect the hose and its connections for signs of fluid leakage, cracking, deterioration and wear. The clutch fluid should be changed every two years (see Section 25), and the hoses replaced with new ones either if they deteriorate, or every four years irrespective of their condition (see Section 29). The master and slave cylinder seals should be changed every two years, or if leakage from them is evident (see Section 26).
4 Check the operation of the clutch. If there is evidence of air in the system (spongy feel to the lever), bleed the clutch (see Chapter 2).
5 The clutch lever has a span adjuster which

alters the distance of the lever from the handlebar. Each setting is identified by a number on the adjuster which aligns with the arrow on the lever bracket. Pull the lever away from the handlebar and turn the adjuster ring until the setting which best suits the rider is obtained (see illustration). There are four settings – setting 1 gives the largest span, and setting 4 the smallest. When making adjustment ensure that the pin set in the level bracket is engaged in its detent hollow on the adjuster.

11 Battery – check

1 All models are fitted with a sealed (maintenance-free) battery which requires no maintenance. Note: Do not attempt to remove the battery caps to check the electrolyte level or battery specific gravity. Removal will damage the caps, resulting in electrolyte leakage and battery damage.
2 All that should be done is to check that the terminals are clean and tight and that the casing is not damaged or leaking. See Chapter 9 for further details.

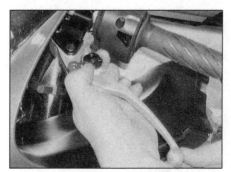

10.5 Adjusting the front clutch lever span

Caution: Be extremely careful when handling or working around the battery. The electrolyte is very caustic and an explosive gas (hydrogen) is given off when the battery is charging.
3 If the machine is not in regular use, disconnect the battery and give it a refresher charge every month to six weeks (see Chapter 9).

12 Wheels and tyres – general check

Tyres

1 Check the tyre condition and tread depth thoroughly – see Daily (pre-ride) checks.

Wheels

2 Cast wheels are virtually maintenance free, but they should be kept clean and checked periodically for cracks and other damage. Also check the wheel runout and alignment (see Chapter 7). Never attempt to repair damaged cast wheels; they must be replaced with new ones. Check the valve rubber for signs of damage or deterioration and have it replaced with a new one if necessary. Also, make sure the valve cap is in place and tight.

13 Wheel bearings – check

1 Wheel bearings will wear over a period of time and result in handling problems.
2 Support the motorcycle upright using an auxiliary stand. Check for any play in the bearings by pushing and pulling the wheel against the hub (see illustration). Also rotate the wheel and check that it rotates smoothly.

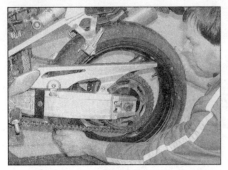

13.2 Checking for play in the wheel bearings

3 If any play is detected in the hub, or if the wheel does not rotate smoothly (and this is not due to brake or transmission drag), the wheel bearings must be removed and inspected for wear or damage (see Chapter 7).

14 Sidestand – check

1 The stand return springs must be capable of retracting the stand fully and holding the stand retracted when the motorcycle is in use. If a spring is sagged or broken it must be replaced with a new one.
2 Lubricate the stand pivot regularly (see Section 18).
3 The sidestand switch prevents the motorcycle being started if the stand is extended. Check its operation by shifting the transmission into neutral, retracting the stand and starting the engine. Pull in the clutch lever and select a gear. Extend the sidestand. The engine should stop as the sidestand is extended. If the sidestand switch does not operate as described, check its circuit (see Chapter 9). The clutch switch is also part of the same circuit – to check it, retract the sidestand, then select a gear. With the clutch lever pulled in, start the engine – if the engine starts, the switch is good. Otherwise, check the circuit (see Chapter 9).

15 Nuts and bolts – tightness check

1 Since vibration of the machine tends to loosen fasteners, all nuts, bolts, screws, etc. should be periodically checked for proper tightness.
2 Pay particular attention to the following:
Spark plugs
Engine oil drain plug
Gearchange lever, brake and clutch lever, and brake pedal bolts
Footrest and stand bolts
Engine mounting bolts
Shock absorber and suspension linkage bolts and swingarm pivot bolts
Handlebar clamp bolts
Front axle bolt and axle clamp bolts
Front fork clamp bolts (top and bottom yoke)
Rear axle nut
Brake caliper mounting bolts
Brake hose banjo bolts and caliper bleed valves
Brake disc bolts
Exhaust system bolts/nuts
3 If a torque wrench is available, use it along with the torque specifications at the beginning of this and other Chapters.

16 Cooling system – check

⚠️ *Warning: The engine must be cool before beginning this procedure.*

1 Check the coolant level (see *Daily (pre-ride) checks*).
2 The entire cooling system should be checked for evidence of leakage. Remove the fairing side panels (see Chapter 8) and the fuel tank (see Chapter 4). Examine each rubber coolant hose along its entire length. Look for cracks, abrasions and other damage. Squeeze each hose at various points. They should feel firm, yet pliable, and return to their original shape when released. If they are dried out or hard, replace them with new ones.

3 Check for evidence of leaks at each cooling system joint. If necessary, tighten the hose clips carefully to prevent future leaks.
4 Check the radiator for leaks and other damage. Leaks in the radiator leave tell-tale scale deposits or coolant stains on the outside of the core below the leak. If leaks are noted, remove the radiator (see Chapter 3) and have it repaired by a professional.
Caution: Do not use a liquid leak stopping compound to try to repair leaks.
5 Check the radiator fins for mud, dirt and insects, which may impede the flow of air through the radiator. If the fins are dirty, remove the radiator (see Chapter 3) and clean it using water or low pressure compressed air directed through the fins from the backside. If the fins are bent or distorted, straighten them carefully with a screwdriver. If the air flow is restricted by bent or damaged fins over more than 30% of the radiator's surface area, install a new radiator.
6 On YZF1000R models remove the fairing if required (see Chapter 8), though access is reasonable by removing the rear screw on the fairing trim panel and carefully lifting the end of the panel up **(see illustration)**. Remove the pressure cap from the filler neck (YZF1000R models) or radiator (YZF750R and SP models) by turning it anti-clockwise until it reaches a stop **(see illustrations)**. If you hear a hissing sound (indicating there is still pressure in the system), wait until it stops. Now press down on the cap and continue turning the cap until it can be removed. Check the condition of the coolant in the system. If it is rust-coloured or if accumulations of scale are visible, drain, flush and refill the system with new coolant (See Section 22). Check the cap seal for cracks and other damage. If in doubt about the pressure cap's condition, have it tested by a Yamaha dealer or replace it with a new one. Install the cap by turning it clockwise until it reaches the first stop then push down on the cap and continue turning until it can turn further.
7 Check the antifreeze content of the coolant with an antifreeze hydrometer. Sometimes coolant looks like it's in good condition, but might be too weak to offer adequate protection. If the hydrometer indicates a weak mixture, drain, flush and refill the system (see Section 22).

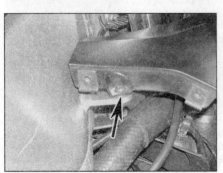

16.6a On YZF1000R models, remove the screw and carefully lift the trim panel . . .

16.6b . . . and remove the pressure cap as described

16.6c Pressure cap (arrowed) – YZF750R and SP models

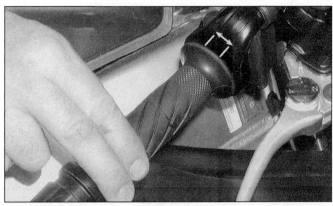

17.3 Measure the amount of freeplay in the throttle as shown

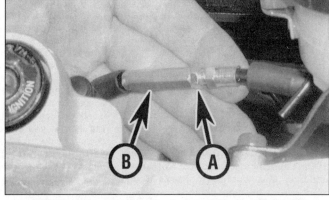

17.4 Throttle cable adjuster locknut (A) and adjuster (B)

8 Start the engine and let it reach normal operating temperature, then check for leaks again. As the coolant temperature increases beyond normal, the fan should come on automatically and the temperature should begin to drop. If it doesn't, refer to Chapter 3 and check the fan switch, fan motor and fan circuit carefully.

9 If the coolant level is consistently low, and no evidence of leaks can be found, have the entire system pressure checked by a Yamaha dealer.

17 Throttle and choke cables – check

Throttle cables

1 Make sure the throttle grip rotates easily from fully closed to fully open with the front wheel turned at various angles. The grip should return automatically from fully open to fully closed when released.

2 If the throttle sticks, this is probably due to a cable fault. Remove the cables (see Chapter 4) and lubricate them (see Section 18). Install the cables, making sure they are correctly routed. If this fails to improve the operation of the throttle, new cables must be installed. Note that in very rare cases the fault could lie in the carburettors rather than the cables, necessitating the removal of the carburettors and inspection of the throttle linkage (see Chapter 4).

3 With the throttle operating smoothly, check for a small amount of freeplay in the cables, measured in terms of the amount of twistgrip rotation before the throttle opens, and compare the amount to that listed in this Chapter's Specifications **(see illustration)**. If it's incorrect, adjust the cables to correct it.

4 Freeplay adjustments can be made at the throttle end of the cable. Pull back the rubber cover on the adjuster, then loosen the locknut **(see illustration)**. Turn the adjuster until the specified amount of freeplay is obtained (see this Chapter's Specifications), then retighten the locknut. Turn the adjuster in to increase freeplay and out to reduce it. Refit the rubber boot on completion.

5 If the adjuster has reached its limit of adjustment, reset it so that the freeplay is at a maximum, then adjust the cable at the carburettor end as follows. Remove the air filter housing (see Chapter 4) and the rubber cover. Slacken the accelerator (opening) cable top nut and slide the cable down in the bracket until the bottom nut is clear of the lug, then thread the bottom nut up or down as required – thread it down to reduce freeplay, and thread it up to increase it **(see illustrations)**. Draw the cable up into the bracket so the bottom nut becomes captive against the lug, then tighten the top nut down onto the bracket. Further adjustments can now be made at the throttle end. If the cable cannot be adjusted as specified, renew the cable (see Chapter 4).

Warning: Turn the handlebars all the way through their travel with the engine idling. Idle speed should not change. If it does, the cable may be routed incorrectly. Correct this condition before riding the bike.

6 Check that the throttle twistgrip operates smoothly and snaps shut quickly when released.

Choke cable

7 If the choke does not operate smoothly this is probably due to a cable fault. Remove the cable (see Chapter 4) and lubricate it (see Section 18). Install the cable, routing it so it takes the smoothest route possible.

8 If this fails to improve the operation of the choke, a new cable must be installed. Note that in very rare cases the fault could lie in the carburettors rather than the cable, necessitating the removal of the carburettors and inspection of the choke plungers (see Chapter 4).

9 Make sure there is a small amount of freeplay in the cable before the plungers move. If there isn't, check that the cable is seating correctly at the carburettor end – remove the air filter housing for access (see Chapter 4). You can create some freeplay in the cable by slackening the outer cable clamp screw on the carburettor and sliding the cable further into the clamp **(see illustration)**. Otherwise, renew the cable.

1

17.5a Slacken the accelerator cable top nut and slide the cable down in the bracket until the bottom nut is clear of the lug . . .

17.5b . . . then thread the bottom nut up or down as required

17.9 Slacken the clamp screw (arrowed) and slide the cable into the clamp a little

18.3a Lubricating a cable with a pressure lubricator. Make sure the tool seals around the inner cable

18 Stand, lever pivots and cables – lubrication

1 Since the controls, cables and various other components of a motorcycle are exposed to the elements, they should be lubricated periodically to ensure safe and trouble-free operation.

2 The footrests, clutch and brake levers, brake pedal, gearshift lever linkage and sidestand pivots should be lubricated frequently. In order for the lubricant to be applied where it will do the most good, the component should be disassembled. However, if chain and cable lubricant is being used, it can be applied to the pivot joint gaps and will usually work its way into the areas where friction occurs. If motor oil or light grease is being used, apply it sparingly

19.3a Lever off the dust seal . . .

19.3b . . . and check underneath it for signs of oil leakage

as it may attract dirt (which could cause the controls to bind or wear at an accelerated rate). **Note:** *One of the best lubricants for the control lever pivots is a dry-film lubricant (available from many sources by different names).*

3 To lubricate the throttle and choke cables, disconnect the relevant cable at its upper end, then lubricate the cable with a pressure adapter, or if one is not available, using the set-up shown **(see illustrations)**. See Chapter 4 for the throttle and choke cable removal procedures, and Chapter 2 for the clutch cable.

4 To lubricate the speedometer cable, remove it (see Chapter 9), then withdraw the inner cable from the outer cable and lubricate the inner cable with motor oil or cable lubricant. Do not lubricate the upper few inches of the cable as the lubricant may travel up into the instrument head.

19 Suspension – check

1 The suspension components must be maintained in top operating condition to ensure rider safety. Loose, worn or damaged suspension parts decrease the motorcycle's stability and control.

Front suspension

2 While standing alongside the motorcycle, apply the front brake and push on the handlebars to compress the forks several times. See if they move up-and-down smoothly without binding. If binding is felt, the forks should be disassembled and inspected (see Chapter 6).

3 Inspect the area around the dust seal for signs of oil leakage, then carefully lever off the dust seal using a flat-bladed screwdriver and inspect the area around the fork seal **(see illustrations)**. If leakage is evident, new seals must be fitted (see Chapter 6). Check the fork tubes for scratches, corrosion and pitting as these will cause premature seal failure. If the damage is excessive new tubes should be installed (see Chapter 6).

4 Check the tightness of all suspension nuts and bolts to be sure none have worked loose, referring to the torque settings specified at the beginning of Chapter 6.

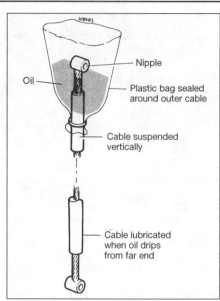

18.3b Lubricating a cable with a makeshift funnel and motor oil

Oil — Nipple
Oil — Plastic bag sealed around outer cable
Cable suspended vertically
Cable lubricated when oil drips from far end

Rear suspension

5 Inspect the rear shock for fluid leakage and tightness of its mountings. If leakage is found, a new shock should be installed (see Chapter 6).

6 With the aid of an assistant to support the bike, compress the rear suspension several times. It should move up and down freely without binding. If any binding is felt, the worn or faulty component must be identified and renewed. The problem could be due to either the shock absorber, the suspension linkage components or the swingarm components.

7 Support the motorcycle using an auxiliary stand so that the rear wheel is off the ground. Grab the swingarm and rock it from side to side – there should be no discernible movement at the rear (Yamaha specify a maximum of 1 mm) **(see illustration)**. If there's a little movement or a slight clicking can be heard, inspect the tightness of all the rear suspension mounting bolts and nuts, referring to the torque settings specified at the beginning of Chapter 6, and re-check for movement. Next, grasp the top of the rear wheel and pull it upwards – there should be

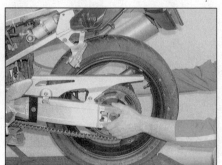

19.7a Checking for play in the swingarm bearings

19.7b Checking for play in the suspension linkage bearings

20.4 Checking for play in the steering head bearings

20.6a Unscrew the brake reservoir bolt (arrowed) . . .

20.6b . . . and on 750's the clutch reservoir bolt (arrowed) and displace them

no discernible freeplay before the shock absorber begins to compress **(see illustration)**. Any freeplay felt in either check indicates worn bearings in the suspension linkage or swingarm, or worn shock absorber mountings. The worn components must be renewed (see Chapter 6).

8 To make an accurate assessment of the swingarm bearings, remove the rear wheel (see Chapter 7) and the bolt securing the suspension linkage rods to the swingarm (see Chapter 6). Grasp the rear of the swingarm with one hand and place your other hand at the junction of the swingarm and the frame. Try to move the rear of the swingarm from side-to-side. Any wear (play) in the bearings should be felt as movement between the swingarm and the frame at the front. If there is any play the swingarm will be felt to move forward and backward at the front (not from side-to-side). Alternatively, measure the amount of freeplay at the swingarm end – Yamaha specify a maximum of 1 mm. Next, move the swingarm up and down through its full travel. It should move freely, without any binding or rough spots. If any play in the swingarm is noted or if the swingarm does not move freely, the bearings must be removed for inspection or renewal (see Chapter 6).

20 Steering head bearings – freeplay check and adjustment

1 This motorcycle is equipped with caged ball steering head bearings which can become dented, rough or loose during normal use of the machine. In extreme cases, worn or loose bearings can cause steering wobble – a condition that is potentially dangerous.

Check

2 Support the motorcycle in an upright position using an auxiliary stand. Raise the front wheel off the ground either by having an assistant push down on the rear, or by placing a support under the engine, in which case remove the lower fairing first (see Chapter 8).

3 Point the front wheel straight-ahead and slowly move the handlebars from side-to-side. Any dents or roughness in the bearing races will be felt and the bars will not move smoothly and freely.

4 Next, grasp the fork sliders and try to pull and push them forward and backward **(see illustration)**. Any looseness in the steering head bearings will be felt as front-to-rear movement of the forks. If play is felt in the bearings, adjust the steering head as follows.

HAYNES HiNT *Freeplay in the fork due to worn fork bushes can be misinterpreted as steering head bearing play – do not confuse the two.*

Adjustment

5 Remove the fuel tank (see Chapter 4). Remove the fairing (see Chapter 8). **Note:** *Although it is not strictly necessary to remove the fairing, doing so will prevent the possibility of damage should a tool slip. Alternatively, remove the rear view mirrors, then unscrew the two bolts securing the fairing stay and remove the stay.*

6 Unscrew the bolt securing the front brake master cylinder, and on YZF750R and SP models also the clutch master cylinder, to the top yoke and displace it/them **(see illustrations)**. Keep the master cylinder(s) upright to prevent fluid leakage.

7 Remove the blanking caps from the handlebar positioning bolts using a small flat-bladed screwdriver **(see illustration)**. Unscrew the handlebar positioning bolts, then slacken the handlebar clamp bolts and the fork clamp bolts in the top yoke **(see illustration)**.

1

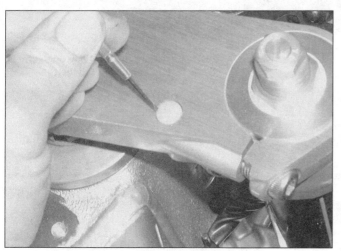

20.7a Remove the blanking caps . . .

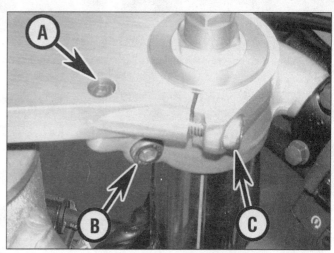

20.7b . . . then unscrew the handlebar positioning bolt (A), the handlebar clamp bolt (B) and the fork clamp bolt (C) on each side

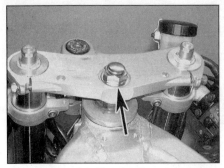

20.8 Unscrew the steering stem nut (arrowed)

20.9 Ease the top yoke up off the steering stem and forks

20.10a Remove the tabbed lockwasher . . .

8 Unscrew the steering stem nut and remove it along with its washer, where fitted **(see illustration)**.

9 Gently ease the top yoke upwards off the fork tubes and position it clear, using a rag to protect the tank or other components **(see illustration)**.

10 Remove the tabbed lockwasher, noting how it fits, then unscrew and remove the locknut using either a C-spanner, a peg spanner or a drift located in one of the notches **(see illustrations)**. Remove the rubber washer **(see illustration)**.

11 To adjust the bearings as specified by Yamaha, a special service tool (Pt. No. 90890-01403) and a torque wrench are required. If the tool is available, first slacken the adjuster nut, then tighten it to the initial torque setting specified at the beginning of the Chapter, making sure the torque wrench handle is at right-angles (90°) to the line between the

adjuster nut and the wrench socket in the special tool **(see illustration)**. Now slacken the nut so that it is loose, then tighten it to the final torque setting specified. Check that the steering is still able to move freely from side to side, but that all freeplay is eliminated.

12 If the Yamaha tool is not available, using either a C-spanner, a peg spanner or a drift located in one of the notches, slacken the adjuster nut slightly until pressure is just released, then tighten it until all freeplay is removed, then tighten it a little more **(see illustration)**. This pre-loads the bearings. Now slacken the nut, then tighten it again, setting it so that all freeplay is just removed yet the steering is able to move freely from side to side. To do this tighten the nut only a little at a time, and after each tightening repeat the checks outlined above (Steps 2 to 4) until the bearings are correctly set. The object is to set the adjuster nut so that the bearings are under

a very light loading, just enough to remove any freeplay.

Caution: Take great care not to apply excessive pressure because this will cause premature failure of the bearings.

13 With the bearings correctly adjusted, install the washer and the locknut **(see illustrations 20.10c and b)**. Tighten the locknut finger-tight, then tighten it further until its notches align with those in the adjuster nut. If necessary, counter-hold the adjuster nut and tighten the locknut using a C-spanner or drift until the notches align, but make sure the adjuster nut does not turn as well. Install the tabbed lockwasher so that the tabs fit into the notches in both the locknut and adjuster nut **(see illustration 20.10a)**.

14 Fit the top yoke onto the steering stem **(see illustration 20.9)**, then install the washer (where fitted) and steering stem nut and tighten it to the torque setting specified at the

20.10b . . . then unscrew the locknut . . .

20.10c . . . and remove the rubber washer

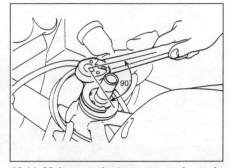

20.11 Make sure the torque wrench arm is at right angles (90°) to the tool

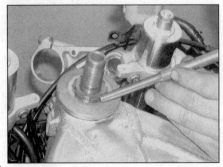

20.12 If the tool is not available, adjust the bearings as described

20.14a Fit the washer . . .

20.14b . . . and the steering stem nut . . .

20.14c . . . and tighten it to the specified torque

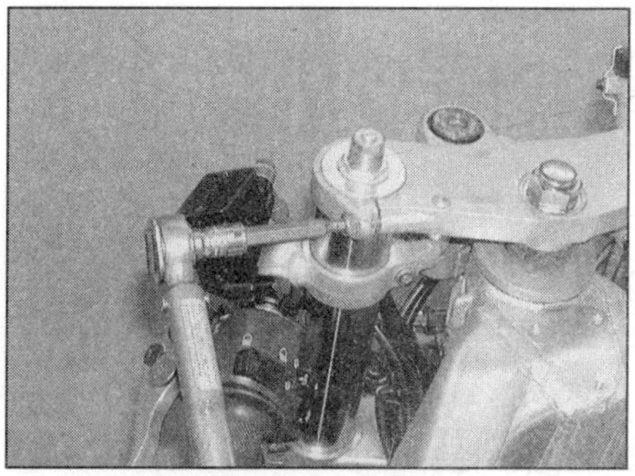

20.14d Now tighten the fork clamp bolts to the specified torque

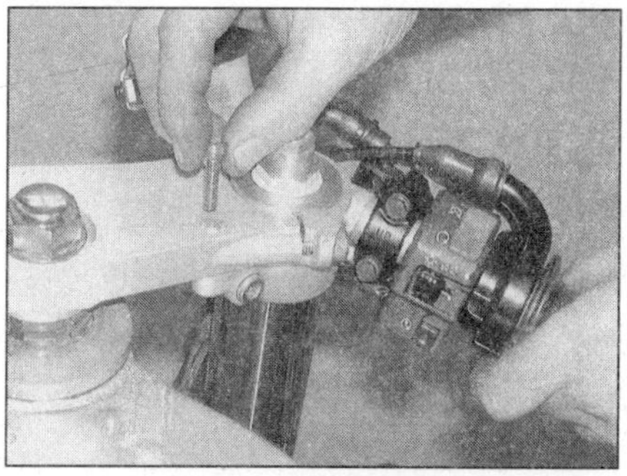

20.15a Align the handlebar, then install the bolt . . .

beginning of the Chapter **(see illustrations)**. Now tighten both the fork clamp bolts to the specified torque setting **(see illustration)**.

15 Install the handlebar positioning bolts and tighten them to the specified torque setting, then tighten the handlebar clamp bolts to the specified torque **(see illustrations)**. Fit the blanking caps into the positioning bolts **(see illustration 20.7a)**.

16 Install the front brake master cylinder, and on YZF750R and SP models the clutch master cylinder, onto the top yoke and tighten the bolt(s) securely **(see illustrations 20.6a and b)**.

17 Re-check the bearing adjustment as described above and re-adjust if necessary.

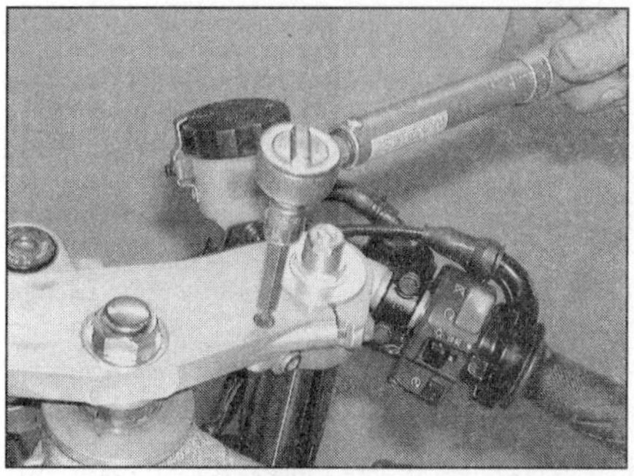

20.15b . . . and tighten it to the specified torque . . .

20.15c . . . then tighten the clamp bolts to the specified torque

Every 8000 miles (12,000 km) or 12 months

Carry out all the items under the 4000 mile (6000 km) check, plus the following:

21 Engine/transmission – oil and filter change

Warning: Be careful when draining the oil, as the exhaust pipes, the engine, and the oil itself can cause severe burns.

1 Drain the engine oil as described in Section 7, Steps 1 to 5.

2 Now place the drain tray below the oil filter, which is at the front of the engine. Unscrew the oil filter using a filter removing strap, chain or wrench and tip any residue oil into the drain tray **(see illustrations)**. Wipe any oil off the exhaust pipes to prevent too much smoke when you start it.

3 Smear clean engine oil onto the rubber seal on the new filter, then manoeuvre it into position and screw it onto the engine until the seal just seats **(see illustrations)**. If the correct tools are available, tighten the filter to the torque setting specified at the beginning

21.2a Unscrew the filter . . .

21.2b . . . and drain it into the tray

21.3a Smear some clean oil onto the seal . . .

of the Chapter (see illustration). Otherwise, tighten the filter as tight as possible by hand, or by the number of turns specified on the filter or its packaging. Note: *Do not use a strap or chain filter removing tool to tighten the filter as you will damage it.*

HAYNES HINT *Saving a little money on the difference between good and cheap oils won't pay off if the engine is damaged as a result.*

4 Refill the engine to the proper level as described in Section 7, Steps 6 to 8.

21.3b . . . then thread the filter onto the cooler . . .

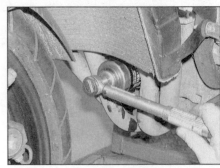
21.3c . . . and tighten it as described

Every 16,000 miles (24,000 km) or two years

Carry out all the items under the 4000 mile (6000 km) and 8000 mile (12,000 km) checks:

22 Cooling system –
draining, flushing and refilling

 Warning: Allow the engine to cool completely before performing this maintenance operation. Also, don't allow antifreeze to come into contact with your skin or the painted surfaces of the motorcycle. Rinse off spills immediately with plenty of water. Antifreeze is highly toxic if ingested. Never leave antifreeze lying around in an open container or in puddles on the floor; *children and pets are attracted by its sweet smell and may drink it. Check with local authorities (councils) about disposing of antifreeze. Many communities have collection centres which will see that antifreeze is disposed of safely. Antifreeze is also combustible, so don't store it near open flames.*

Draining

1 Remove the lower fairing and the fairing side panels, the seat(s) and the right-hand side cover (YZF1000R), side covers (YZF750R) or seat cowling (YZF750SP) (see Chapter 8). On YZF1000R models remove the fairing if required (see Chapter 8), though access is reasonable by removing the rear screw on the fairing trim panel and carefully lifting the end of the panel up (see illustration 16.6a). Remove the pressure cap from the filler neck (YZF1000R models) or radiator (YZF750R and SP models) by turning it anti-clockwise until it reaches a stop (see illustrations 16.6b and c). If you hear a hissing sound (indicating there is still pressure in the system), wait until it stops. Now press down on the cap and continue turning the cap until it can be removed. Also remove the filler cap from the coolant reservoir.

2 Position a suitable container beneath the water pump. Remove the coolant drain plug from the water pump and allow the coolant to completely drain from the system (see illustrations). Retain the old sealing washer for use during flushing.

3 Now position the container beneath one end of the cylinder block, then remove the drain plug from the front (YZF750R and SP models), or side (YZF1000R models) of one end of the block, and allow the coolant to completely drain from the engine (see illustrations). Repeat on the other end of the block. Retain the old sealing washers for use during flushing.

4 Position the container beneath the coolant reservoir. Remove the reservoir cap, then release the clamp and detach the hose from the bottom of the reservoir and allow the remaining coolant to completely drain (see illustration). Fit the hose back onto the reservoir and secure it with the clamp. Fit the cap.

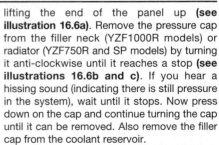

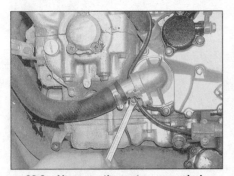
22.2a Unscrew the water pump drain plug . . .

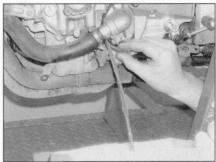
22.2b . . . and allow the coolant to drain

22.3a Unscrew the cylinder drain plug on each side . . .

22.3b . . . and allow the coolant to drain

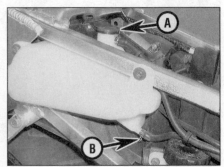
22.4 Remove the cap (A) and detach the hose (B)

Flushing

5 Flush the system with clean tap water by inserting a garden hose in the radiator or filler neck. Allow the water to run through the system until it is clear and flows cleanly out of the drain hole(s). If the radiator is extremely corroded, remove it (see Chapter 3) and have it cleaned professionally.

6 Clean the drain holes then install the drain plugs using the old sealing washers.

7 Fill the cooling system with clean water mixed with a flushing compound. Make sure the flushing compound is compatible with aluminium components, and follow the manufacturer's instructions carefully. Install the pressure cap.

8 Start the engine and allow it to reach normal operating temperature. Let it run for about ten minutes.

9 Stop the engine. Let it cool for a while, then cover the pressure cap with a heavy rag and turn it anti-clockwise to the first stop, releasing any pressure that may be present in the system. Once the hissing stops, push down on the cap and remove it completely.

10 Drain the system once again.

11 Fill the system with clean water and repeat the procedure in Steps 8 to 10.

Refilling

12 Fit new sealing washers onto the drain plugs and tighten them to the torque setting specified at the beginning of the Chapter.

13 Fill the system via the radiator or filler neck with the proper coolant mixture (see this Chapter's Specifications). **Note:** *Pour the coolant in slowly to minimise the amount of air entering the system.* When the system appears full, pull the bike off its stand and shake it slightly to dissipate the coolant, then place the bike back on the stand and top the system up.

14 When the system is full (all the way up to the top of the radiator or filler neck), install the pressure cap. Now fill the coolant reservoir to the UPPER level mark (see *Daily (pre-ride) checks*).

15 Start the engine and allow it to idle for 2 to 3 minutes. Flick the throttle twistgrip part open 3 or 4 times, so that the engine speed rises to approximately 4000 – 5000 rpm, then stop the engine. Any air trapped in the system should have bled back to the radiator filler neck via the small-bore air bleed hoses.

16 Let the engine cool then remove the pressure cap as described in Step 1. Check that the coolant level is still up to the top of the radiator or filler neck. If it's low, add the specified mixture until it reaches the top. Refit the pressure cap.

17 Check the coolant level in the reservoir and top up if necessary.

18 Check the system for leaks.

19 Do not dispose of the old coolant by pouring it down the drain. Instead pour it into a heavy plastic container, cap it tightly and take it into an authorised disposal site or service station – see **Warning** at the beginning of this Section.

20 Install the body panels and seat as required by your model (see Chapter 8).

23 Swingarm and suspension linkage bearings – re-greasing

1 Over a period of time the grease will harden and dirt will penetrate the bearings.

2 The rear suspension components are not equipped with grease nipples. Remove the swingarm and the suspension linkage as described in Chapter 6 for greasing of the bearings.

24 Steering head bearings – re-greasing

1 Over a period of time the grease will harden or may be washed out of the bearings by incorrect use of jet washes.

2 Disassemble the steering head for re-greasing of the bearings. Refer to Chapter 6 for details.

25 Brakes and clutch – fluid change

1 The brake and clutch fluid should be replaced every two years or whenever a master cylinder or caliper/release cylinder overhaul is carried out. Refer to the brake bleeding section in Chapter 7 or the clutch bleeding section in Chapter 2, noting that all old fluid must be pumped from the fluid reservoir and hydraulic line before filling with new fluid.

 HAYNES HiNT *Old brake fluid is invariably much darker in colour than new fluid, making it easy to see when all old fluid has been expelled from the system.*

26 Brake and clutch master cylinder and caliper/release cylinder seals – renewal

1 The seals will deteriorate over a period of time and lose their effectiveness, leading to sticky operation or fluid loss, or allowing the ingress of air and dirt. Refer to Chapter 7 (brakes) or Chapter 2 (clutch) and dismantle the components for seal renewal every two years.

1

Every 28,000 miles (42,000 km) or 42 months

Carry out all the items under the 4000 mile (6000 km) check, plus the following

27 Valve clearances – check and adjustment

1 The engine must be completely cool for this maintenance procedure, so let the machine sit overnight before beginning.

2 Remove the valve cover (see Chapter 2). Each cylinder is referred to by a number. They are numbered 1 to 4 from left to right.

3 Make a chart or sketch of all valve positions so that a note of each clearance can be made against the relevant valve.

4 Remove the left-hand crankshaft end-cover, secured by three screws, and the timing inspection plug **(see illustration)**. The O-rings can be reused if they are in good condition, otherwise discard them. In order to turn the engine a suitable bolt and collar must be threaded into the end of the crankshaft. Obtain the required parts as shown in the diagram, then fit the collar onto the bolt and thread the bolt into the crankshaft and tighten it – select a gear and apply the rear brake to prevent the engine turning **(see illustration 10.2b in Chapter 2)**. A flange nut

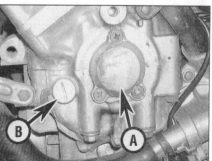

27.4a Remove the end-cover (A) and the inspection plug (B)

27.4b Thread the bolt in then tighten the nut against the crankshaft

27.4c Turn the bolt anti-clockwise as shown

27.5a Turn the engine until the 'T' mark aligns with the pointer

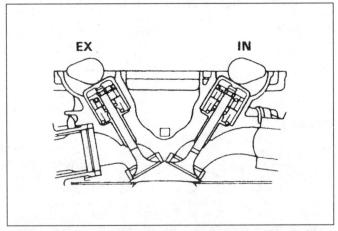

27.5b The camshaft lobes for No. 1 cylinder should be facing away from each other as shown

with the same thread as the bolt can be used instead of a collar – tighten the nut against the end of the crankshaft to lock the bolt **(see illustration)**. The engine can now be turned using the bolt hex, turning it in an anti-clockwise direction only **(see illustration)**. Alternatively, place the motorcycle on an auxiliary stand so that the rear wheel is off the ground, select a high gear and rotate the rear wheel by hand in its normal direction of rotation. If available, Yamaha's special tool assembly, consisting of a timing rotor, a bolt

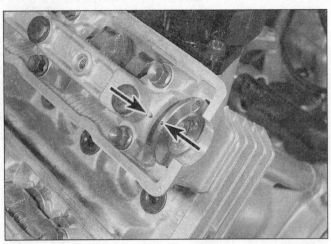

27.5c Align the punchmark on each camshaft with the mark on the holder (arrowed)

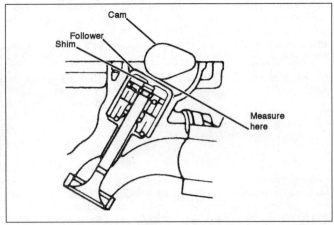

27.6a Make sure the cam lobes are not depressing the valves and are facing away from each other, then insert the feeler gauge between the cam and the follower

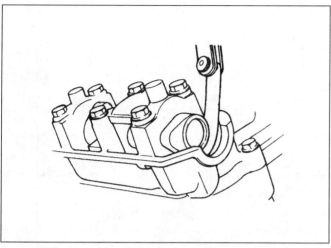

27.6b Measuring the clearance using a feeler gauge

27.7 Turn the engine until the cutout aligns with the static timing mark in the inspection window

and a dowel pin (Pt. Nos. 4U8-81673-10 or 33M-81673-10, 91317-08030 and 93604-08071) can also be used – fit the pin into the hole in the end of the crankshaft, then locate the rotor over the pin and tighten the bolt (see illustration 10.2e in Chapter 2). Use the flats on the rotor, not the bolt, to turn the engine.

5 Turn the engine until the 'T' mark aligns with the pointer in the inspection window (see illustration), and the camshaft lobes for the No. 1 (left-hand) cylinder face away from each other, and the dot on each camshaft aligns with the dot on the camshaft holder (see illustrations). If the cam lobes are facing towards each other and the dots do not align, rotate the engine anti-clockwise 360° (one full turn) so that the 'T' mark again aligns with the pointer in the inspection window. The camshaft lobes will now be facing away from each other and the dots will be aligned, meaning the No. 1 cylinder is at TDC (top dead centre) on the compression stroke.

6 With No. 1 cylinder at TDC on the compression stroke, check the clearances on the No. 1 cylinder intake and exhaust valves (see illustration). Insert a feeler gauge of the same thickness as the correct valve clearance (see Specifications) between the camshaft lobe and follower of each valve and check that it is a firm sliding fit – you should feel a

slight drag when the you pull the gauge out (see illustration). If not, use the feeler gauges to obtain the exact clearance. Record the measured clearance on the chart.

7 Now turn the engine anti-clockwise 180° (half a turn) so that the cutout aligns with the pointer in the inspection window as shown and the camshaft lobes for the No. 2 cylinder are facing away from each other (see illustration). The No. 2 cylinder is now at TDC on the compression stroke. Measure the clearances of the No. 2 cylinder valves using the method described in Step 6.

8 Now turn the engine anti-clockwise 180° (half a turn) so that the 'T' mark on the rotor again aligns with the pointer in the inspection window and the camshaft lobes for the No. 4 cylinder are facing away from each other. The No. 4 cylinder is now at TDC on the compression stroke. Measure the clearances of the No. 4 cylinder valves using the method described in Step 6.

9 Now turn the engine anti-clockwise 180° (half a turn) so that the cutout aligns with the pointer in the inspection window as shown and the camshaft lobes for the No. 3 cylinder are facing away from each other. The No. 3 cylinder is now at TDC on the compression stroke. Measure the clearances of the No. 3 cylinder valves using the method described in Step 6.

10 When all clearances have been measured and charted, identify whether the clearance on any valve falls outside that specified. If it does, the shim between the cam follower and the valve must be replaced with one of a thickness which will restore the correct clearance.

11 Shim replacement requires removal of the camshafts (see Chapter 2). There is no need to remove both camshafts if shims from only one side of the engine need replacing. Place rags over the spark plug holes and the cam chain tunnel to prevent a shim from dropping into the engine on removal.

12 With the camshaft removed, remove the cam follower of the valve in question, then retrieve the shim from the inside of the follower (see illustrations). If it is not in the follower, pick it out of the top of the valve using either a magnet, a small screwdriver with a dab of grease on it (the shim will stick to the grease), or a screwdriver and a pair of pliers (see illustration 27.15a). Do not allow the shim to fall into the engine.

13 A size mark should be stamped on the upper face of the shim – a shim marked 175 is 1.75 mm thick. If the mark is not visible the shim thickness will have to be measured. It is recommended that the shim is measured anyway to check that it has not worn (see illustration).

1

27.12a Lift out the follower . . .

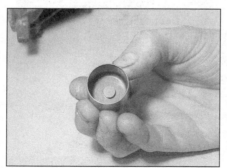

27.12b . . . and remove the shim from inside the follower

27.13 Measure the shim using a micrometer

INSTALLED PAD NUMBER

MEASURED CLEARANCE	120	125	130	135	140	145	150	155	160	165	170	175	180	185	190	195	200	205	210	215	220	225	230	235	240
0.00 ~ 0.02				120	125	130	135	140	145	150	155	160	165	170	175	180	185	190	195	200	205	210	215	220	225
0.03 ~ 0.07			120	125	130	135	140	145	150	155	160	165	170	175	180	185	190	195	200	205	210	215	220	225	230
0.08 ~ 0.10		120	125	130	135	140	145	150	155	160	165	170	175	180	185	190	195	200	205	210	215	220	225	230	235
0.11 ~ 0.20	RECOMMENDED CLEARANCE																								
0.21 ~ 0.22	125	130	135	140	145	150	155	160	165	170	175	180	185	190	195	200	205	210	215	220	225	230	235	240	
0.23 ~ 0.27	130	135	140	145	150	155	160	165	170	175	180	185	190	195	200	205	210	215	220	225	230	235	240		
0.28 ~ 0.32	135	140	145	150	155	160	165	170	175	180	185	190	195	200	205	210	215	220	225	230	235	240			
0.33 ~ 0.37	140	145	150	155	160	165	170	175	180	185	190	195	200	205	210	215	220	225	230	235	240				
0.38 ~ 0.42	145	150	155	160	165	170	175	180	185	190	195	200	205	210	215	220	225	230	235	240					
0.43 ~ 0.47	150	155	160	165	170	175	180	185	190	195	200	205	210	215	220	225	230	235	240						
0.48 ~ 0.52	155	160	165	170	175	180	185	190	195	200	205	210	215	220	225	230	235	240							
0.53 ~ 0.57	160	165	170	175	180	185	190	195	200	205	210	215	220	225	230	235	240								
0.58 ~ 0.62	165	170	175	180	185	190	195	200	205	210	215	220	225	230	235	240									
.063 ~ 0.67	170	175	180	185	190	195	200	205	210	215	220	225	230	235	240										
0.68 ~ 0.72	175	180	185	190	195	200	205	210	215	220	225	230	235	240											
0.73 ~ 0.77	180	185	190	195	200	205	210	215	220	225	230	235	240												
0.78 ~ 0.82	185	190	195	200	205	210	215	220	225	230	235	240													
0.83 ~ 0.87	190	195	200	205	210	215	220	225	230	235	240														
0.88 ~ 0.92	195	200	205	210	215	220	225	230	235	240															
0.93 ~ 0.97	200	205	210	215	220	225	230	235	240																
0.98 ~ 1.02	205	210	215	220	225	230	235	240																	
1.03 ~ 1.07	210	215	220	225	230	235	240																		
1.08 ~ 1.12	215	220	225	230	235	240																			
1.13 ~ 1.17	220	225	230	235	240																				
1.18 ~ 1.22	225	230	235	240																					
1.23 ~ 1.27	230	235	240																						
1.28 ~ 1.32	235	240																							
1.33 ~ 1.37	240																								

27.14a Shim selection chart – intake camshaft

INSTALLED PAD NUMBER

MEASURED CLEARANCE	120	125	130	135	140	145	150	155	160	165	170	175	180	185	190	195	200	205	210	215	220	225	230	235	240
0.00 ~ 0.02						120	125	130	135	140	145	150	155	160	165	170	175	180	185	190	195	200	205	210	215
0.03 ~ 0.07					120	125	130	135	140	145	150	155	160	165	170	175	180	185	190	195	200	205	210	215	220
0.08 ~ 0.12				120	125	130	135	140	145	150	155	160	165	170	175	180	185	190	195	200	205	210	215	220	225
0.13 ~ 0.17			120	125	130	135	140	145	150	155	160	165	170	175	180	185	190	195	200	205	210	215	220	225	230
0.18 ~ 0.20		120	125	130	135	140	145	150	155	160	165	170	175	180	185	190	195	200	205	210	215	220	225	230	235
0.21 ~ 0.30	RECOMMENDED CLEARANCE																								
0.31 ~ 0.32	125	130	135	140	145	150	155	160	165	170	175	180	185	190	195	200	205	210	215	220	225	230	235	240	
0.33 ~ 0.37	130	135	140	145	150	155	160	165	170	175	180	185	190	195	200	205	210	215	220	225	230	235	240		
0.38 ~ 0.42	135	140	145	150	155	160	165	170	175	180	185	190	195	200	205	210	215	220	225	230	235	240			
0.43 ~ 0.47	140	145	150	155	160	165	170	175	180	185	190	195	200	205	210	215	220	225	230	235	240				
0.48 ~ 0.52	145	150	155	160	165	170	175	180	185	190	195	200	205	210	215	220	225	230	235	240					
0.53 ~ 0.57	150	155	160	165	170	175	180	185	190	195	200	205	210	215	220	225	230	235	240						
0.58 ~ 0.62	155	160	165	170	175	180	185	190	195	200	205	210	215	220	225	230	235	240							
0.63 ~ 0.67	160	165	170	175	180	185	190	195	200	205	210	215	220	225	230	235	240								
0.68 ~ 0.72	165	170	175	180	185	190	195	200	205	210	215	220	225	230	235	240									
0.73 ~ 0.77	170	175	180	185	190	195	200	205	210	215	220	225	230	235	240										
0.78 ~ 0.82	175	180	185	190	195	200	205	210	215	220	225	230	235	240											
0.83 ~ 0.87	180	185	190	195	200	205	210	215	220	225	230	235	240												
0.88 ~ 0.92	185	190	195	200	205	210	215	220	225	230	235	240													
0.93 ~ 0.97	190	195	200	205	210	215	220	225	230	235	240														
0.98 ~ 1.02	195	200	205	210	215	220	225	230	235	240															
1.03 ~ 1.07	200	205	210	215	220	225	230	235	240																
1.08 ~ 1.12	205	210	215	220	225	230	235	240																	
1.13 ~ 1.17	210	215	220	225	230	235	240																		
1.18 ~ 1.22	215	220	225	230	235	240																			
1.23 ~ 1.27	220	225	230	235	240																				
1.28 ~ 1.32	225	230	235	240																					
1.33 ~ 1.37	230	235	240																						
1.38 ~ 1.42	235	240																							
1.43 ~ 1.47	240																								

27.14b Shim selection chart – exhaust camshaft

27.15a Fit the shim into the recess in the top of the valve . . .

27.15b . . . then install the follower

27.17 Install the end-cover and plug using new O-rings

14 Using the appropriate shim selection chart, find where the measured valve clearance and existing shim thickness values intersect and read off the shim size required **(see illustrations)**. **Note:** *If the existing shim is marked with a number not ending in 0 or 5, round it up or down as appropriate to the nearest number ending in 0 or 5 so that the chart can be used.* Shims are available in 0.05 mm increments from 1.20 mm to 2.40 mm. **Note:** *If the required replacement shim is greater than 2.40 mm (the largest available), the valve is probably not seating*

correctly due to a build-up of carbon deposits and should be checked and cleaned or resurfaced as required (see Chapter 2).
15 Obtain the replacement shim, then lubricate it with molybdenum disulphide grease and fit it into its recess in the top of the valve, with the size marking on each shim facing down **(see illustration)**. Check that the shim is correctly seated, then lubricate the follower with molybdenum disulphide oil (a 50/50 mixture of molybdenum disulphide grease and engine oil) and install it onto the valve **(see illustration)**. Repeat the process

for any other valves until the clearances are correct, then install the camshafts (see Chapter 2).
16 Rotate the crankshaft several turns to seat the new shim(s), then check the clearances again.
17 Install all disturbed components in a reverse of the removal sequence. Install the timing inspection plug and the crankshaft end-cover using new O-rings and tighten the end-cover screws to the torque setting specified at the beginning of the Chapter **(see illustration)**.

Every 60,000 miles (100,000 km)

28 Alternator brushes –
renewal

1 The brushes will wear down with use and should be replaced with new ones. Refer to Chapter 9 for details.

Every four years

29 Brake and clutch hoses –
renewal

1 The hoses will deteriorate with age and should be replaced with new ones every two years regardless of their apparent condition.
2 Refer to Chapter 7 (brakes) or Chapter 2 (clutch) and disconnect the hoses from the

master cylinders and calipers/slave cylinder. Always replace the banjo union sealing washers with new ones.

1

Non-scheduled maintenance

30 Headlight aim –
check and adjustment

Note: *An improperly adjusted headlight may cause problems for oncoming traffic or provide poor, unsafe illumination of the road ahead. Before adjusting the headlight aim, be sure to consult with local traffic laws and regulations – for UK models refer to MOT Test Checks in the Reference section.*
1 The headlight beam can be adjusted both horizontally and vertically. Before making any adjustment, check that the tyre pressures are

correct and the suspension is adjusted as required. Make any adjustments to the headlight aim with the machine on level ground, with the fuel tank half full and with an assistant sitting on the seat. If the bike is usually ridden with a passenger on the back, have a second assistant to do this.
2 On YZF750R and SP models, vertical adjustment is made by turning the adjuster screw on the top inner corner of the headlight unit **(see illustration)**. Turn it clockwise to raise the beam, and anti-clockwise to lower it. Horizontal adjustment is made by turning the adjuster screw on the bottom outer corner of the headlight unit. For the right-hand light unit,

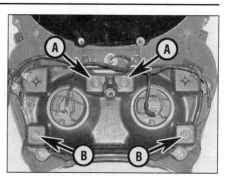

30.2 Vertical adjusters (A), horizontal adjusters (B) – YZF750R and SP models

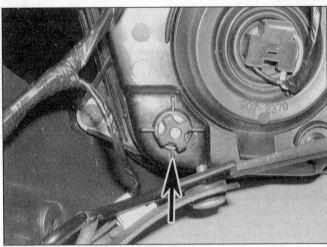

30.3a Vertical adjuster (arrowed) – YZF1000R models

30.3b Horizontal adjuster (arrowed) – YZF1000R models

turn it clockwise to move the beam to the right, and anti-clockwise to move it to the left. For the left-hand light unit, turn it clockwise to move the beam to the right, and anti-clockwise to move it to the left.

3 On YZF1000R models, vertical adjustment is made by turning the adjuster knob on the bottom outer corner of each headlight unit (see illustration). Turn it anti-clockwise to raise the beam, and clockwise to lower it. Horizontal adjustment is made by turning the adjuster screw on the bottom inner corner of each headlight unit, using a screwdriver inserted from below the headlight (see illustration). For the left-hand beam, turn it clockwise to move the beam to the right, and anti-clockwise to move it to the left. For the right-hand beam, turn it clockwise to move the beam to the left, and anti-clockwise to move it to the right. Remove the fairing side panels for best access to the adjusters (see Chapter 8).

31 Cylinder compression – check

1 Among other things, poor engine performance may be caused by leaking valves, incorrect valve clearances, a leaking head gasket, or worn pistons, rings and/or cylinder walls. A cylinder compression check will help pinpoint these conditions and can also indicate the presence of excessive carbon deposits in the cylinder heads.

2 The only tools required are a compression gauge and a spark plug wrench. A compression gauge with a threaded end for the spark plug hole is preferable to the type which requires hand pressure to maintain a tight seal. Depending on the outcome of the initial test, a squirt-type oil can may also be needed.

3 Make sure the valve clearances are

correctly set (see Section 27) and that the cylinder head nuts are tightened to the correct torque setting (see Chapter 2).

4 Refer to *Fault Finding Equipment* in the Reference section for details of the compression test. Refer to the specifications at the beginning of this Chapter for compression figures.

32 Engine oil pressure – check

1 None of the models covered in this manual are fitted with an oil pressure switch and warning light, only an oil level sensor and light (see Chapter 9 for further information). If a lubrication problem is suspected, first check the oil level (see *Daily (pre-ride) checks*).

2 If the oil level is correct, an oil pressure check must be carried out. The check provides useful information about the condition of the engine's lubrication system.

YZF750R and SP models

3 To check the oil pressure on YZF750R and SP models, remove the right-hand fairing side panel (see Chapter 8). Slacken the oil gallery bolt in the right-hand side of the cylinder head

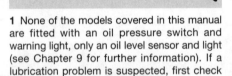

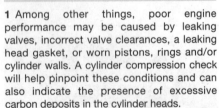

32.3 Oil gallery plug (arrowed) – YZF750R and SP models

– there is no need to remove it (see illustration). Start the engine and allow it to idle.

4 After a short while oil should begin to seep out from the oil gallery plug. If no oil has appeared after one minute, stop the engine immediately. If the oil does not appear after a further minute, either the pressure regulator is stuck open, the oil pump is faulty, the oil strainer or filter is blocked, or there is other engine damage.

5 Begin diagnosis by checking the oil filter, strainer and regulator, then the oil pump (see Chapter 2). If no problems are found with those items, it may well be that the bearing oil clearances are excessive and the engine needs to be overhauled.

6 If the oil appears very quickly and spurts out, the pressure may be too high, meaning either an oil passage is clogged, the regulator is stuck closed or the wrong grade of oil is being used.

7 Tighten the oil gallery bolt to the torque setting specified at the beginning of the Chapter.

YZF1000R models

8 To check the oil pressure on YZF1000R models, remove the lower fairing (see Chapter 8). A suitable gauge and adapter piece (which screws into the crankcase) will be needed. Yamaha provide a kit (Pt. Nos. 90890-03153 and 90890-03139) for this purpose.

9 Warm the engine up to normal operating temperature then stop it.

10 Place a suitable container below the main oil gallery plug, which is below the crankshaft end-cover on the right-hand side of the engine, to catch any oil (see illustration).

11 Unscrew the plug and swiftly screw the adapter into the crankcase threads. Connect the gauge to the adapter. If oil is lost, replenish it to the correct level before proceeding (see *Daily (pre-ride) checks*).

12 Start the engine and increase the engine speed to 4000 rpm whilst watching the gauge reading. The oil pressure should be similar to that given in the Specifications at the start of this Chapter.

13 Stop the engine and unscrew the gauge and adapter from the crankcase. Install the main oil gallery plug using a new sealing washer, and tighten it to the torque setting specified at the beginning of the Chapter.

14 Check the oil level (see *Daily (pre-ride) checks*). If the pressure is significantly lower than the standard, either the pressure regulator is stuck open, the oil pump is faulty, the oil strainer or filter is blocked, or there is other engine damage.

15 Begin diagnosis by checking the oil filter, strainer and regulator, then the oil pump (see Chapter 2). If no problems are found with those items, it may well be that the bearing oil clearances are excessive and the engine needs to be overhauled. If the pressure is too high, either an oil passage is clogged, the regulator is stuck closed or the wrong grade of oil is being used.

All models

16 Refer to Chapter 2 and rectify any problems before running the engine again.

17 If the oil pressure and oil level are both good, then the oil level sensor or its warning light may be faulty. Check them and the circuit and replace with a new one if necessary (see Chapter 9).

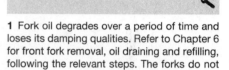

33 Fuel hoses – renewal

⚠️ *Warning: Petrol (gasoline) is extremely flammable, so take extra precautions when you work on any part of the fuel system. Don't smoke or allow open flames or bare light bulbs near the work area, and don't work in a garage where a natural gas-type appliance is present. If you spill any fuel on your skin, rinse it off immediately with soap and water. When you perform any kind of work on the fuel system, wear safety glasses and have a fire extinguisher suitable for a Class B type fire (flammable liquids) on hand.*

1 The fuel delivery hoses should be renewed after a few years regardless of their condition.

2 Remove the fuel tank (see Chapter 4). Disconnect the fuel hoses from the fuel tap, filter, fuel pump and from the carburettors as required by your model, noting the routing of each hose and where it connects (see Chapter 4 if required). It is advisable to make a sketch of the various hoses before removing

32.10 Main oil gallery plug (arrowed) – YZF1000R models

them to ensure they are correctly installed.

3 Secure each new hose to its unions using new clamps. Run the engine and check for leaks before taking the machine out on the road.

34 Front forks – oil change

1 Fork oil degrades over a period of time and loses its damping qualities. Refer to Chapter 6 for front fork removal, oil draining and refilling, following the relevant steps. The forks do not need to be completely disassembled.

Chapter 2
Engine, clutch and transmission

Contents

Degrees of difficulty

Easy, suitable for novice with little experience	Fairly easy, suitable for beginner with some experience	Fairly difficult, suitable for competent DIY mechanic	Difficult, suitable for experienced DIY mechanic	Very difficult, suitable for expert DIY or professional

Specifications – YZF750R and SP

General

Type	Four-stroke in-line four
Capacity	749 cc
Bore	72.0 mm
Stroke	46.0 mm
Compression ratio	11.5 to 1
Cylinder numbering	1 to 4 from left to right
Cooling system	Liquid cooled
Clutch	Wet multi-plate
Transmission	Six-speed constant mesh
Final drive	Chain

Camshafts

Intake lobe height

  Standard . . . . 32.60 to 32.70 mm

  Service limit (min) . . . . 32.50 mm

Exhaust lobe height

  Standard . . . . 33.00 to 33.10 mm

  Service limit (min) . . . . 32.90 mm

Journal diameter . . . . 24.437 to 24.450 mm

Holder diameter

  Cylinders 1 and 4 . . . . 24.470 to 24.491 mm

  Cylinders 2 and 3 . . . . 24.500 to 24.521 mm

Journal oil clearance

  Cylinders 1 and 4 . . . . 0.020 to 0.054 mm

  Cylinders 2 and 3 . . . . 0.050 to 0.084 mm

Runout (max) . . . . 0.03 mm

Cylinder head

Warpage (max) . . . . 0.03 mm

Valves, guides and springs

Valve clearances . . . . see Chapter 1

Intake valve

  Stem diameter

    Standard . . . . 4.475 to 4.490 mm

    Service limit (min) . . . . 4.445 mm

  Guide bore diameter

    Standard . . . . 4.500 to 4.512 mm

    Service limit (max) . . . . 4.550 mm

  Stem-to-guide clearance

    Standard . . . . 0.010 to 0.037 mm

    Service limit (max) . . . . 0.08 mm

  Head diameter . . . . 22.9 to 23.1 mm

  Face width . . . . 1.49 to 2.48 mm

  Seat width . . . . 0.9 to 1.1 mm

  Margin thickness . . . . 0.6 to 0.8 mm

  Valve lift . . . . 7.55 to 7.75 mm

Exhaust valve

  Stem diameter

    Standard . . . . 4.460 to 4.475 mm

    Service limit (min) . . . . 4.430 mm

  Guide bore diameter

    Standard . . . . 4.500 to 4.512 mm

    Service limit (max) . . . . 4.550 mm

  Stem-to-guide clearance

    Standard . . . . 0.025 to 0.052 mm

    Service limit (max) . . . . 0.10 mm

  Head diameter . . . . 24.4 to 24.6 mm

  Face width . . . . 1.76 to 2.76 mm

  Seat width . . . . 0.9 to 1.1 mm

  Margin thickness . . . . 0.85 to 1.15 mm

  Valve lift . . . . 7.95 to 8.15 mm

Valve stem runout (max) . . . . 0.01 mm

Valve springs free length

  Intake . . . . 40.38 mm

  Exhaust . . . . 44.40 mm

Valve spring bend (max)

  Intake . . . . 1.7 mm

  Exhaust . . . . 1.9 mm

Cylinder block

Bore . . . . 71.98 to 72.02 mm

Warpage (max) . . . . 0.03 mm

Ovality (out-of-round) (max) . . . . 0.05 mm

Taper (max) . . . . 0.05 mm

Cylinder compression . . . . see Chapter 1

Pistons

Piston diameter (measured 3.5 mm up from skirt, at 90° to piston pin axis)	71.90 to 71.94 mm
Piston-to-bore clearance	
Standard	0.07 to 0.09 mm
Service limit (max)	0.11 mm
Piston pin diameter	18.991 to 19.000 mm
Piston pin bore diameter in piston	19.004 to 19.015 mm
Piston pin-to-piston pin bore clearance	
Standard	0.004 to 0.024 mm
Service limit	0.070 mm

Piston rings

Top ring	
Ring width	2.8 mm
Ring thickness	0.8 mm
Ring end gap (installed)	0.2 to 0.4 mm
Piston ring-to-groove clearance	0.03 to 0.07 mm
2nd ring	
Ring width	2.8 mm
Ring thickness	0.8 mm
Ring end gap (installed)	0.2 to 0.4 mm
Piston ring-to-groove clearance	0.02 to 0.06 mm
Oil ring	
Ring width	2.5 mm
Ring thickness	1.5 mm
Side-rail end gap (installed)	0.2 to 0.7 mm

Clutch

Friction plates	
Quantity	9
Thickness	
Standard	2.9 to 3.1 mm
Service limit (min)	2.8 mm
Plain plates	
Quantity	8
Thickness	1.9 to 2.1 mm
Warpage (max)	0.1 mm
Clutch springs	
Quantity	6
Spring free length	
Standard	55 mm
Service limit (min)	54 mm
Pushrod runout (max)	0.5 mm

Lubrication system

Oil pressure	see Chapter 1
Relief valve opening pressure	69.69 to 81.07 psi (4.81 to 5.60 Bar)
Oil pump	
Inner rotor tip-to-outer rotor clearance	0.09 to 0.15 mm
Outer rotor-to-body clearance	0.03 to 0.08 mm

Connecting rods

Big-end side clearance	0.160 to 0.262 mm
Big-end oil clearance	0.032 to 0.056 mm

Crankshaft and bearings

Main bearing oil clearance	0.040 to 0.064 mm
Runout (max)	0.03 mm

Transmission

YZF750R

Gear ratios (no. of teeth)

Primary reduction	1.896 to 1 (91/48T)
Final reduction	2.688 to 1 (43/16T)
1st gear	2.571 to 1 (36/14T)
2nd gear	1.941 to 1 (33/17T)
3rd gear	1.556 to 1 (28/18T)

2

Transmission (continued)

YZF750R (continued)
4th gear	1.368 to 1 (26/19T)
5th gear	1.217 to 1 (28/23T)
6th gear	1.083 to 1 (26/24T)
Shaft runout (max)	0.08 mm

YZF750SP
Gear ratios (no. of teeth)
Primary reduction	1.896 to 1 (91/48T)
Final reduction	2.438 to 1 (39/16T)
1st gear	2.462 to 1 (32/13T)
2nd gear	1.941 to 1 (33/17T)
3rd gear	1.632 to 1 (31/19T)
4th gear	1.435 to 1 (33/23T)
5th gear	1.300 to 1 (26/20T)
6th gear	1.190 to 1 (25/21T)
Shaft runout (max)	0.08 mm

Selector drum and forks
Selector fork shaft runout (max)	0.1 mm

Specifications – YZF1000R

General
Type	Four-stroke in-line four
Capacity	1002 cc
Bore	75.5 mm
Stroke	56.0 mm
Compression ratio	11.5 to 1
Cylinder numbering	1 to 4 from left to right
Cooling system	Liquid cooled
Clutch	Wet multi-plate
Transmission	Five-speed constant mesh
Final drive	Chain

Camshafts
Intake lobe height
Standard	32.50 to 32.60 mm
Service limit (min)	32.40 mm

Exhaust lobe height
Standard	32.95 to 33.05 mm
Service limit (min)	32.85 mm
Journal diameter	24.437 to 24.450 mm

Holder diameter
Cylinders 1 and 4	24.470 to 24.491 mm
Cylinders 2 and 3	24.500 to 24.521 mm

Journal oil clearance
Cylinders 1 and 4	0.020 to 0.054 mm
Cylinders 2 and 3	0.050 to 0.084 mm
Runout (max)	0.03 mm

Cylinder head
Warpage (max)	0.10 mm

Valves, guides and springs
Valve clearances	see Chapter 1

Intake valve
Stem diameter
Standard	4.475 to 4.490 mm
Service limit (min)	4.445 mm

Guide bore diameter
Standard	4.500 to 4.512 mm
Service limit (max)	4.550 mm

Stem-to-guide clearance
Standard	0.010 to 0.037 mm
Service limit (max)	0.08 mm

Head diameter	23.4 to 23.6 mm
Face width	1.63 to 2.90 mm
Seat width	0.9 to 1.1 mm
Margin thickness	0.45 to 0.95 mm
Valve lift	7.45 to 7.65 mm

Exhaust valve
  Stem diameter

Standard	4.460 to 4.475 mm
Service limit (min)	4.430 mm

  Guide bore diameter

Standard	4.500 to 4.512 mm
Service limit (max)	4.550 mm

  Stem-to-guide clearance

Standard	0.025 to 0.052 mm
Service limit (max)	0.10 mm
Head diameter	24.9 to 25.1 mm
Face width	1.63 to 2.90 mm
Seat width	0.9 to 1.1 mm
Margin thickness	0.75 to 1.25 mm
Valve lift	7.75 to 7.95 mm
Valve stem runout (max)	0.01 mm

Valve springs free length

Intake	40.73 mm
Exhaust	44.01 mm
Valve spring bend (max)	1.7 mm

Cylinder block

Bore	75.500 to 75.505 mm
Warpage (max)	0.03 mm
Ovality (out-of-round) (max)	0.05 mm
Taper (max)	0.05 mm
Cylinder compression	see Chapter 1

Pistons

Piston diameter (measured 3.0 mm up from skirt, at 90° to piston pin axis)	75.425 to 75.440 mm

Piston-to-bore clearance

Standard	0.06 to 0.08 mm
Service limit (max)	0.1 mm
Piston pin diameter	18.991 to 19.000 mm
Piston pin bore diameter in piston	19.004 to 19.015 mm

Piston pin-to-piston pin bore clearance

Standard	0.004 to 0.024 mm
Service limit	0.070 mm

Piston rings

Top ring

Ring width	2.8 mm
Ring thickness	0.8 mm
Ring end gap (installed)	0.3 to 0.5 mm
Piston ring-to-groove clearance	0.03 to 0.07 mm

2nd ring

Ring width	2.8 mm
Ring thickness	0.8 mm
Ring end gap (installed)	0.3 to 0.5 mm
Piston ring-to-groove clearance	0.02 to 0.06 mm

Oil ring

Ring width	2.5 mm
Ring thickness	1.5 mm
Side-rail end gap (installed)	0.2 to 0.8 mm

Clutch

Friction plates

Quantity	9

  Thickness

Standard	2.9 to 3.1 mm
Service limit (min)	2.8 mm

2

Clutch (continued)

Plain plates
  Quantity 8
  Thickness . . . . 1.9 to 2.1 mm
  Warpage (max) . . . . 0.1 mm
Clutch springs
  Quantity 6
  Spring free length
    Standard . . . . 50 mm
    Service limit (min) . . . . 48 mm
Pushrod runout (max) . . . . 0.5 mm

Lubrication system

Oil pressure . . . . see Chapter 1
Relief valve opening pressure . . . . 52.63 to 65.43 psi (3.63 to 4.51 Bar)
Oil pump
  Inner rotor tip-to-outer rotor clearance . . . . 0.09 to 0.15 mm
  Outer rotor-to-body clearance . . . . 0.03 to 0.08 mm

Connecting rods

Big-end side clearance . . . . 0.160 to 0.262 mm
Big-end oil clearance . . . . 0.032 to 0.056 mm

Crankshaft and bearings

Main bearing oil clearance . . . . 0.020 to 0.044 mm
Runout (max) . . . . 0.03 mm

Transmission

Gear ratios (no. of teeth)
  Primary reduction . . . . 1.659 to 1 (68/41T)
  Final reduction . . . . 2.706 to 1 (46/17T)
  1st gear . . . . 2.571 to 1 (36/14T)
  2nd gear . . . . 1.778 to 1 (32/18T)
  3rd gear . . . . 1.381 to 1 (29/21T)
  4th gear . . . . 1.174 to 1 (27/23T)
  5th gear . . . . 1.037 to 1 (28/27T)
Shaft runout (max) . . . . 0.08 mm

Selector drum and forks

Selector fork shaft runout (max) . . . . 0.1 mm

Torque wrench settings – all models

Engine mounting bolts
  YZF750R and SP models
    Lower rear mounting bolt nut . . . . 55 Nm
    Upper rear mounting bolt nut . . . . 55 Nm
    Upper rear mounting bolt pinchbolts . . . . 15 Nm
    Front mounting bolts . . . . 40 Nm
    Right-hand front mounting bolt pinchbolts . . . . 22 Nm
  YZF1000R models
    Lower rear mounting bolt nut . . . . 50 Nm
    Upper rear mounting bolt nut . . . . 50 Nm
    Upper rear mounting bolt pinchbolts . . . . 22 Nm
    Front mounting bolts . . . . 40 Nm
    Right-hand front mounting bolt pinchbolts . . . . 22 Nm
Oil cooler bolt . . . . 63 Nm
Valve cover bolts . . . . 10 Nm
Cam chain tensioner mounting bolts . . . . 10 Nm
Cam chain tensioner cap bolt . . . . 20 Nm
Crankshaft end-cover screws . . . . 7 Nm
Cam chain top guide bolts . . . . 10 Nm
Camshaft case oil pipe bolts . . . . 10 Nm
Camshaft case bolts . . . . 10 Nm
Camshaft holder bolts
  YZF750R and SP models
    Rear outer bolts on exhaust holders (see text) . . . . 8 Nm
    All other bolts . . . . 10 Nm
  YZF1000R models . . . . 10 Nm

Camshaft sprocket bolts	24 Nm
Cylinder head nuts	41 Nm
Oil hose banjo bolts (YZF750R)	21 Nm
Oil pipe banjo bolts (YZF1000R)	20 Nm
Oil pipe clamp bolt (YZF1000R)	10 Nm
Coolant outlet union to cylinder head bolts	10 Nm
Coolant inlet union to cylinder block bolts	10 Nm
Clutch nut	70 Nm
Clutch spring bolts	8 Nm
Clutch cover bolts	
YZF750R and SP models	10 Nm
YZF1000R models	12 Nm
Clutch master cylinder clamp bolts	
YZF750R and SP models	10 Nm
YZF1000R models	13 Nm
Clutch hose banjo bolts	
YZF750R and SP models	26 Nm
YZF1000R models	30 Nm
Clutch release cylinder mounting bolts	10 Nm
Clutch release cylinder bleed valve	6 Nm
Stopper arm and retainer plate bolts	10 Nm
Oil pump assembly screw	7 Nm
Oil pump mounting bolts	10 Nm
Oil pipe bolts	10 Nm
Oil strainer bolts	10 Nm
Oil baffle plate bolts	10 Nm
Oil spray pipe bolts	10 Nm
Oil sump bolts	
YZF750R and SP models	10 Nm
YZF1000R models	12 Nm
Crankcase 9 mm bolts	32 Nm
Crankcase 8 mm bolts	24 Nm
Crankcase 6 mm bolts	12 Nm
Bearing retainer plate screws	10 Nm
Oil nozzle plate bolt	10 Nm
Cam chain tensioner blade bolts	10 Nm
Connecting rod cap nuts	
Initial setting (see Text)	20 Nm
Final setting	36 Nm
Selector drum retainer bolt	10 Nm
Starter clutch bolts	25 Nm
Hy-Vo chain guide bolts	10 Nm
Alternator drive shaft bearing retainer bolts	10 Nm

1 General information

The engine/transmission unit is a liquid-cooled in-line four cylinder with five valves per cylinder. The valves are operated by double overhead camshafts which are chain driven off the crankshaft. The engine/transmission assembly is constructed from aluminium alloy. The crankcase is divided horizontally.

The crankcase incorporates a wet sump, pressure-fed lubrication system which uses a gear-driven, dual-rotor oil pump, an oil filter and by-pass valve assembly, a relief valve and an oil level switch. The pump is driven by a gear on the back of the clutch housing. The oil is cooled by a cooler which is fed off the engine cooling system.

A Hy-Vo chain running off the crankshaft drives a shaft which has the alternator on its left-hand end and the starter clutch on its right-hand end.

Power from the crankshaft is routed to the transmission via the clutch. The clutch is of the wet, multi-plate type and is gear-driven off the crankshaft. The transmission is a six-speed (750 models) or five-speed (1000 models) constant-mesh unit. Final drive to the rear wheel is by chain and sprockets.

2 Operations possible with the engine in the frame

The components and assemblies listed below can be removed without having to remove the engine/transmission assembly from the frame. If however, a number of areas require attention at the same time, removal of the engine is recommended.

Valve cover
Camshafts
Cylinder head
Cylinder block, pistons and piston rings
Clutch
Oil pump
Gearchange mechanism
Alternator
Pick-up coil assembly
Oil filter and cooler
Oil sump, oil strainer and oil pressure relief valve
Starter motor
Water pump

3 Operations requiring engine removal

It is necessary to remove the engine/transmission assembly from the frame to gain access to the following components.

Transmission shafts
Selector drum and forks
Starter clutch
Connecting rods and bearings
Crankshaft and bearings

2

4 Major engine repair – general information

1 It is not always easy to determine when or if an engine should be completely overhauled, as a number of factors must be considered.

2 High mileage is not necessarily an indication that an overhaul is needed, while low mileage, on the other hand, does not preclude the need for an overhaul. Frequency of servicing is probably the single most important consideration. An engine that has regular and frequent oil and filter changes, as well as other required maintenance, will most likely give many miles of reliable service. Conversely, a neglected engine, or one which has not been run in properly, may require an overhaul very early in its life.

3 Exhaust smoke and excessive oil consumption are both indications that piston rings and/or valve guides are in need of attention, although make sure that the fault is not due to oil leakage.

4 If the engine is making obvious knocking or rumbling noises, the connecting rods and/or main bearings are probably at fault.

5 Loss of power, rough running, excessive valve train noise and high fuel consumption rates may also point to the need for an overhaul, especially if they are all present at the same time. If a complete tune-up does not remedy the situation, major mechanical work is the only solution.

6 An engine overhaul generally involves restoring the internal parts to the specifications of a new engine. The piston rings and main and connecting rod bearings are usually replaced with new ones and the cylinder walls honed or, if necessary, rebored, during a major overhaul. Generally the valve seats are re-ground, since they are usually in less than perfect condition at this point. The end result should be a like new engine that will give as many trouble-free miles as the original.

7 Before beginning the engine overhaul, read through the related procedures to familiarise yourself with the scope and requirements of the job. Overhauling an engine is not all that difficult, but it is time consuming. Plan on the

5.6 Disconnect the negative wire wiring connector

motorcycle being tied up for a minimum of two weeks. Check on the availability of parts and make sure that any necessary special tools, equipment and supplies are obtained in advance.

8 Most work can be done with typical workshop hand tools, although a number of precision measuring tools are required for inspecting parts to determine if they must be renewed. Often a dealer will handle the inspection of parts and offer advice concerning reconditioning and replacement. As a general rule, time is the primary cost of an overhaul so it does not pay to install worn or substandard parts.

9 As a final note, to ensure maximum life and minimum trouble from a rebuilt engine, everything must be assembled with care in a spotlessly clean environment.

5 Engine – removal and installation

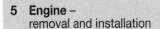

Caution: The engine is very heavy. Engine removal and installation should be carried out with the aid of at least one assistant. Personal injury or damage could occur if the engine falls or is dropped. An hydraulic or mechanical floor jack should be used to support and lower or raise the engine if possible.

Removal

1 Support the motorcycle securely in an upright position using an auxiliary stand. Work

can be made easier by raising the machine to a suitable working height on an hydraulic ramp or a suitable platform. Make sure the motorcycle is secure and will not topple over (see Section 1 of Tools and Workshop Tips in the Reference section). When disconnecting any wiring, cables and hoses, it is advisable to mark or tag them as a reminder to where they connect.

2 If the engine is dirty, particularly around its mountings, wash it thoroughly before starting any major dismantling work. This will make work much easier and rule out the possibility of caked-on lumps of dirt falling into some vital component.

3 Remove the seat, side covers or seat cowling, lower faring, fairing side panels and fairing (see Chapter 8). Note: The fairing can stay on the bike, though it is wise to remove it as it could get in the way and could be damaged – if its not there, it can't do either!

4 Remove the fuel tank (see Chapter 4).

5 Drain the engine oil and the coolant (see Chapter 1).

6 Disconnect the negative (–ve) lead from the battery, then disconnect the positive (+ve) lead (see Chapter 9). Also disconnect the wiring connector joining the negative wire to the negative lead (see illustration). Feed the lead through to the engine, noting its routing, and coil it on the crankcase so that it does not impede engine removal.

7 Remove the carburettors (see Chapter 4). Plug the intake manifolds with clean rag. On 1995-on YZF750R models and YZF1000R models, either detach the vacuum take-off hoses from the intake manifolds and position them clear, or release the hoses from their clips on each side and coil them around the manifolds (see illustration). On YZF1000R models, free the relay assembly from its mount, then unscrew the single bolt securing the fuel pump and filter holders and remove them with their hoses (see illustrations).

8 Make a note or sketch of all the cooling system hoses between the radiator and the engine. Detach the overflow hose to the reservoir from its union just below the pressure cap on the radiator filler neck. Remove the radiator (see Chapter 3), but detach the hoses from their unions on the engine components rather than from the

5.7a Release the vacuum hoses (arrowed) on each side from any clips or ties

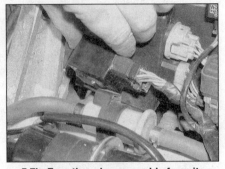

5.7b Free the relay assembly from its mount . . .

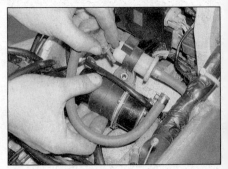

5.7c . . . then unscrew the bolt and remove the pump/filter assembly

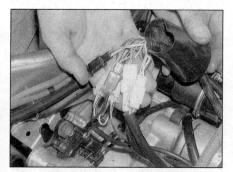

5.10 Disconnect the relevant wiring connectors as described

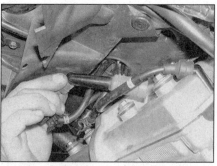

5.14 Pull the caps off the spark plugs

5.15 Unscrew the nut (arrowed) and detach the starter motor lead from the relay

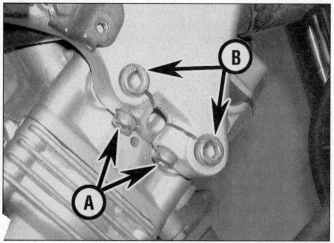

5.19a Slacken the pinchbolts (A), then remove the right-hand front mounting bolts (B) . . .

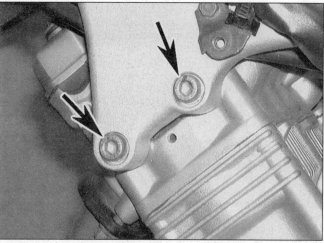

5.19b . . . and the left-hand front mounting bolts (arrowed)

radiator itself, then remove the radiator along with the hoses, noting their routing, and releasing them from any ties.
9 Remove the exhaust system (see Chapter 4).
10 Trace the alternator wiring from the alternator and disconnect it at the connector (see illustration). Release the wiring from any clips or ties, noting its routing, and coil it so that it does not impede engine removal.
11 Trace the ignition pick-up coil wiring from the coil on the right-hand side of the engine and disconnect it at the connector (see illustration 5.10). Release the wiring from any clips or ties, noting its routing, and coil it so that it does not impede engine removal.
12 Trace the neutral switch and oil level sensor wiring from the left-hand side of the engine and disconnect it at the connector (see illustration 5.10). Release the wiring from any clips or ties, noting its routing, and coil it so that it does not impede engine removal.
13 Trace the sidestand switch wiring from the stand and disconnect it at the connector (see illustration 5.10). Release the wiring from any clips or ties, noting its routing, and feed it down to the switch.

14 Disconnect the spark plug caps from the spark plugs and secure them clear of the engine (see illustration).
15 Pull back the rubber cover on the starter motor terminal, then unscrew the nut and detach the lead (see illustration). Secure it clear of the engine.
16 Remove the front sprocket (see Chapter 6).
17 If required, detach the crankcase breather hose from the crankcase and remove it.
18 At this point, position an hydraulic or mechanical jack under the engine with a block of wood between the jack head and crankcase. Make sure the jack is centrally positioned so the engine will not topple in any direction when the last mounting bolt is removed. Take the weight of the engine on the jack. It is also advisable to place a block of wood between the rear wheel and the ground, or under the swingarm, in case the bike tilts back onto the rear wheel when the engine is removed. Check around the engine and frame to make sure that all wiring, cables and hoses that need to be disconnected have been disconnected, and that any remaining connected to the engine are not retained by any clips, guides or brackets connected to the

frame. Check that any protruding mounting brackets will not get in the way and remove them if necessary.
19 Slacken the pinchbolts on the mounting lugs for the right-hand front mounting bolts (see illustration). Unscrew and remove the right-hand and left-hand front mounting bolts, noting the washers with the left-hand ones (see illustration). Unscrew the nut securing the exhaust system mounting bracket to the right-hand end of the lower rear engine mounting bolt and remove the bracket and the washer (see illustration). Now unscrew the

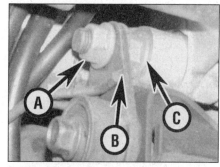

5.19c Unscrew the nut (A) and remove the bracket (B), then unscrew the nut (C)

2

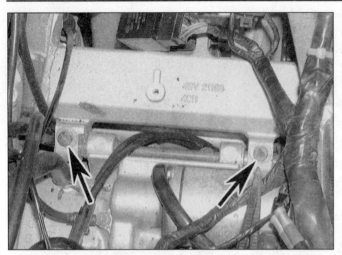

5.19d Slacken the pinchbolts (arrowed) then unscrew the mounting bolt nut

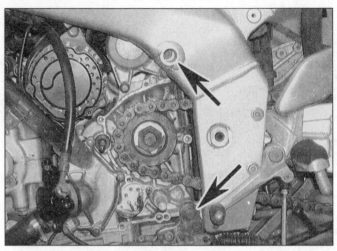

5.19e Withdraw the upper and lower rear mounting bolts (arrowed)

nut on the mounting bolt but do not yet withdraw the bolt. Slacken the pinchbolts on the mounting lugs for the upper rear mounting bolt, then unscrew the nut on the mounting bolt, but do not yet withdraw the bolt **(see illustration)**. Make sure the engine is properly supported on the jack, and have an assistant support it as well, then withdraw the upper and lower rear mounting bolts, noting the washer with the lower bolt on 1993 YZF750R and SP models **(see illustration)**. Carefully lower the engine a little, then bring it forward slightly so that the gearchange shaft is clear of the sidestand switch, then lower it more and manoeuvre it out from the right-hand side. Either remove the collars from the right-hand front mounting bolt lugs and the upper rear mounting bolt left-hand lug for safekeeping, noting which way round they fit, or tighten the pinchbolts so that they are held securely and cannot fall out.

Installation

20 Installation is the reverse of removal, noting the following points:

a) Make sure no wires, cables or hoses become trapped between the engine and the frame when installing the engine.

b) Many of the engine mounting bolts are of different size and length. Make sure the correct bolt is installed in its correct location, with its washer if fitted. Install all of the bolts and nuts finger-tight only until they are all located, then tighten them in the order below to their torque settings as specified at the beginning of the Chapter.

c) Before the engine is mounted, either install the collars for the right-hand front mounting bolt lugs and the upper rear mounting bolt left-hand lug, making sure the shouldered ends face the inside, or slacken the pinchbolts to release them if they were not removed. With the aid of an

assistant place the engine unit on top of the jack and block of wood and carefully raise the engine into position in the frame, making sure the mounting bolt holes align. Also make sure no wires, cables or hoses become trapped between the engine and the frame. Locate all the mounting bolts, not forgetting the washers with the lower rear mounting bolt (1993 YZF750R and SP models only) and left-hand front mounting bolts, and tighten them finger-tight. Now tighten the lower rear mounting bolt nut, then the upper rear mounting bolt nut, then the upper rear mounting bolt lug pinchbolts, then the front mounting bolts, and finally the left-hand front mounting bolt lug pinchbolts, tightening them all to their specified torque settings **(see illustrations 5.19e, d, c, b and a)**. Slide the washer and exhaust system mounting bracket onto the right-hand end of the lower rear engine mounting bolt, but leave the nut loose so that the bracket can be aligned with the exhaust system when it is installed, and then tighten the nut to the specified torque.

d) Use new gaskets on the exhaust pipe connections.

e) Make sure all wires, cables and hoses are correctly routed and connected, and secured by any clips or ties.

f) Refill the engine with oil and coolant (see Chapter 1).

g) Adjust the throttle and clutch cable freeplay and engine idle speed (see Chapter 1).

h) Adjust the drive chain slack (see Chapter 1).

i) Start the engine and check for any oil or coolant leaks before installing the body panels.

6 Engine disassembly and reassembly – general information

Disassembly

1 Before disassembling the engine, the external surfaces of the unit should be thoroughly cleaned and degreased. This will prevent contamination of the engine internals, and will also make working a lot easier and cleaner. A high flash-point solvent, such as paraffin (kerosene) can be used, or better still, a proprietary engine degreaser such as Gunk. Use old paintbrushes and toothbrushes to work the solvent into the various recesses of the engine casings. Take care to exclude solvent or water from the electrical components and intake and exhaust ports.

 Warning: The use of petrol (gasoline) as a cleaning agent should be avoided because of the risk of fire.

2 When clean and dry, arrange the unit on the workbench, leaving suitable clear area for working. Gather a selection of small containers and plastic bags so that parts can be grouped together in an easily identifiable manner. Some paper and a pen should be on hand so that notes can be made and labels attached where necessary. A supply of clean rag is also required.

3 Before commencing work, read through the appropriate section so that some idea of the necessary procedure can be gained. When removing components it should be noted that great force is seldom required, unless specified. In many cases, a component's reluctance to be removed is indicative of an incorrect approach or removal method – if in any doubt, re-check with the text.

4 An engine support stand can be made from short lengths of 2 x 4 inch wood bolted together into a rectangle to help support the

6.4 An engine support made from pieces of 2 x 4 inch wood

engine if required **(see illustration)**, though the engine will sit nicely on the flat bottom of the sump, and there are two pegs at the front to keep it stable. The perimeter of the mount should be just big enough to accommodate the sump within it so that the engine rests on its crankcase.

5 When disassembling the engine, keep 'mated' parts together (including gears, cylinders, pistons, connecting rods, valves, etc. that have been in contact with each other during engine operation). These 'mated' parts must be reused or renewed as an assembly.

6 A complete engine/transmission disassembly should be done in the following general order with reference to the appropriate Sections.

Remove the valve cover
Remove the camshafts
Remove the cylinder head
Remove the cylinder block
Remove the pistons
Remove the clutch
Remove the pick-up coil assembly (see Chapter 5)
Remove the alternator (see Chapter 9)
Remove the starter motor (see Chapter 9)
Remove the gearchange mechanism
Remove the oil pump
Remove the oil sump
Separate the crankcase halves

Remove the crankshaft
Remove the transmission shafts
Remove the selector drum and forks
Remove the starter clutch and idle/reduction gears

Reassembly

7 Reassembly is accomplished by reversing the general disassembly sequence.

7 Oil cooler – removal and installation

Note: *The oil cooler can be removed with the engine in the frame. If the engine has been removed, ignore the steps which do not apply.*

Removal

1 Drain the engine oil and remove the oil filter (see Chapter 1). Drain the cooling system (see Chapter 1), or have some means of blocking or clamping the hoses to avoid excessive loss of coolant.
2 The cooler is located on the front of the engine below the radiator, and has the oil filter mounted on it. Slacken the clamp securing each hose to the cooler and detach the hoses.
3 Unscrew the cooler bolt using a socket and remove the cooler, noting how the tab on the cooler locates on the crankcase **(see illustration)**. Discard the O-ring as a new one must be used.
4 Check the cooler body for cracks and dents and any evidence of coolant leakage and replace it with a new one if necessary. Also check the hoses for splits, cracks, hardening and deterioration and fit new ones if required.

Installation

5 Installation is the reverse of removal, noting the following:
a) Clean the mating surfaces of the crankcase and the cooler with a rag and some thinners.
b) Use a new O-ring and smear it with clean

7.3 Unscrew the oil cooler bolt (arrowed)

engine oil. Make sure it seats in its groove **(see illustration)**.
c) Locate the tab on the cooler between the lugs on the crankcase **(see illustration)**.
d) Tighten the cooler bolt to the torque setting specified at the beginning of the Chapter.
e) Make sure the coolant hoses are pressed fully onto their unions and are secured by the clamps.
f) Fit a new oil filter and fill the engine with oil (see Chapter 1).
g) Refill the cooling system if it was drained, or check the level in both the radiator and the reservoir and top up if necessary (see Chapter 1).

8 Valve cover – removal and installation

Note: *The valve cover can be removed with the engine in the frame. If the engine has been removed, ignore the steps which do not apply.*

Removal

1 Remove the seat and the fairing side panels (see Chapter 8), the fuel tank and the air filter housing (see Chapter 4), and the radiator (see Chapter 3).

2

7.5a Use a new O-ring when installing the cooler

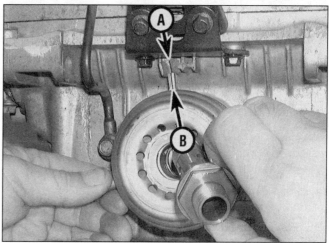

7.5b Locate the tab (B) between the lugs (A)

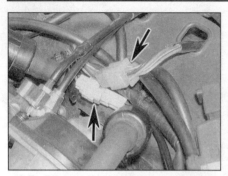

8.2a Disconnect the wiring connectors (arrowed)

8.2b Unscrew the bolts (arrowed) on each side and remove the plate

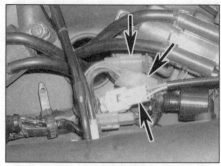

8.3a Disconnect the wiring connectors (arrowed)

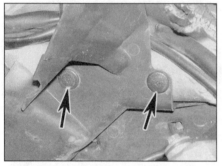

8.3b Remove the trim clips (arrowed) on each side . . .

8.3c . . . and remove the plate

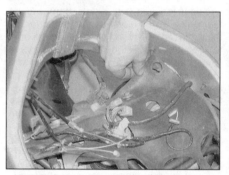

8.3d Lift the rubber baffle off the valve cover

2 On YZF750R and SP models, remove the ignition coils (see Chapter 5). Disconnect the right-hand handlebar switch and throttle position sensor wiring connectors **(see illustration)**. Detach the throttle cables from the carburettors (see Chapter 4). Unscrew the four bolts securing the coil mounting plate and remove it noting how it fits **(see illustration)**. Lift the rubber baffle off the valve cover, noting how it fits **(see illustration 8.3d)**.

3 On YZF1000R models, remove the ignition coils (see Chapter 5). Release the cable ties and free the wiring loom, then disconnect the

right-hand handlebar switch and throttle position sensor wiring connectors **(see illustration)**. Release the four trim clips securing the coil mounting plate to the underside of the frame beams and remove the plate, noting how it fits **(see illustrations)**. Lift the rubber baffle off the valve cover, noting how it fits **(see illustration)**.

4 Unscrew the bolts securing the valve cover and remove it **(see illustrations)**. If the cover is stuck, do not try to lever it off with a screwdriver. Tap it gently around the sides with a rubber hammer or block of wood to dislodge it.

Installation

5 Examine the valve cover gasket for signs of damage or deterioration and fit a new one if necessary. Similarly check the rubber grommets on the cover bolts for cracks, hardening and deterioration **(see illustration)**.
6 Clean the mating surfaces of the cylinder head and the valve cover with lacquer thinner, acetone or brake system cleaner.
7 Fit the gasket into the valve cover, making sure it locates correctly into the groove and the small tab in the middle section faces the front **(see illustration)**. Use a few dabs of

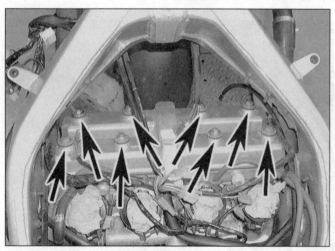

8.4a Unscrew the cover bolts (arrowed) . . .

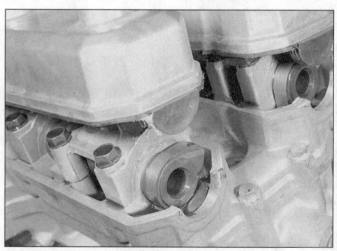

8.4b . . . and lift the cover off the engine

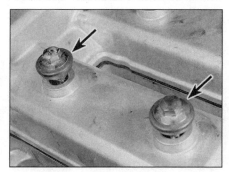

8.5 Check the rubber grommets (arrowed) and use new ones if necessary

8.7 The tab on the gasket must be at the front of the cover

8.8 Apply the sealant to the cutouts in the head

grease to keep the gasket in place while the cover is fitted.

8 Apply a suitable sealant to the cut-outs in the cylinder head where the gasket half-circles fit **(see illustration)**. Position the valve cover on the cylinder head, making sure the gasket stays in place **(see illustration 8.4b)**. Install the cover bolts and tighten them to the torque setting specified at the beginning of the Chapter.

9 Install the remaining components in the reverse order of removal.

9 Cam chain tensioner and guides – removal, inspection and installation

Note: *The cam chain tensioner and guides can be removed with the engine in the frame.*
Caution: *Once you start to remove the tensioner bolts, you must remove the tensioner all the way and reset it before tightening the bolts. The tensioner extends itself and locks in place, so if you loosen the bolts partway and then retighten them, the tensioner or cam chain will be damaged.*

Cam chain tensioner

Removal

1 On YZF1000R models, pull the carburettor heater system hose holder off the tensioner body **(see illustration)**.
2 Unscrew the tensioner cap bolt and withdraw the springs from the tensioner body **(see illustrations)**.

9.1 Pull the hose holder off the tensioner body

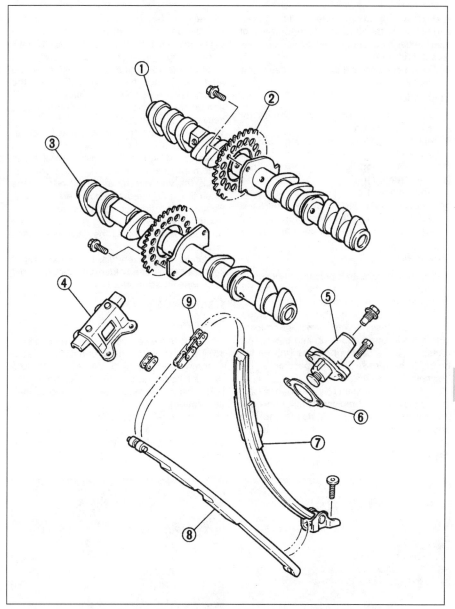

9.2a Camshafts, cam chain and tensioner components

1 Intake camshaft
2 Sprocket
3 Exhaust camshaft
4 Top cam chain guide
5 Cam chain tensioner
6 Gasket
7 Tensioner blade
8 Front cam chain guide
9 Cam chain

2

9.2b Unscrew the cap bolt . . .

9.2c . . . and remove it together with the springs (one spring fits inside the other)

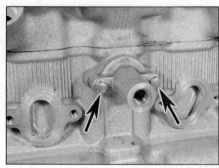

9.3 Unscrew the tensioner bolts (arrowed) and remove the tensioner

3 Unscrew the two tensioner mounting bolts and withdraw the tensioner from the back of the cylinder block, noting which way up it fits (see illustration).

4 Discard the tensioner body gasket as a new one must be used.

Inspection

5 Examine the tensioner components for signs of wear or damage.

6 Release the ratchet mechanism from the tensioner plunger and check that the plunger moves freely in and out of the tensioner body (see illustration).

7 If the tensioner or any of its components are worn or damaged, or if the plunger is seized in the body, the tensioner must be renewed. Individual internal components are not available.

Installation

8 Release the ratchet mechanism and press the tensioner plunger all the way into the tensioner body (see illustration 9.6).

9 Fit a new gasket onto the tensioner body, then fit the tensioner into the engine, making sure the 'UP' mark faces up and the ratchet release lever is on the bottom. Tighten the bolts to the torque setting specified at the beginning of the Chapter.

10 Check the condition of the sealing washer on the cap bolt and replace it with a new one if it is worn or damaged. Install the springs and cap bolt and tighten the bolt to the specified torque setting (see illustration 9.2b).

11 Refer to Section 10, Step 2 and remove the left-hand crankshaft end-cover, then turn the crankshaft anti-clockwise through two full turns using the method described (see illustrations 10.2a and b). This will allow the tensioner to set itself properly. Install the cover, using a new O-ring if necessary, and tighten the screws to the specified torque setting.

12 It is advisable to remove the valve cover (see Section 8) and check that the cam chain is tensioned and all the timing marks are in alignment (see Section 10). If the chain is slack, the tensioner plunger did not release when the spring and cap bolt were installed. Remove the tensioner again and re-check it. Again check the timing marks (see Section 10), then install the valve cover (see Section 8).

13 On YZF1000R models, fit the carburettor heater system hose holder onto the tensioner body (see illustration 9.1).

Cam chain guides

Removal

14 Remove the valve cover (see Section 8).

15 To remove the cam chain top guide, unscrew the four bolts securing it to the cylinder head, noting that these bolts also partly secure the inner camshaft holders (see illustration).

16 To remove the cam chain front guide, lift it out of the front of the cam chain tunnel, noting which way round it fits and how it locates (see illustration).

Inspection

17 Check the sliding surfaces of the guides for excessive wear, deep grooves, cracking and other obvious damage, and renew them if necessary.

Installation

18 Install the front guide blade into the front of the cam chain tunnel (see illustration 9.16), making sure it locates correctly onto its seat and its lugs locate in their cut-outs.

19 Install the top guide onto the cylinder head and tighten the mounting bolts to the torque setting specified at the beginning of the Chapter (see illustration 9.15).

20 Install the valve cover (see Section 8).

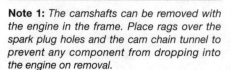

10 Camshafts and followers – removal, inspection and installation

Note 1: *The camshafts can be removed with the engine in the frame. Place rags over the spark plug holes and the cam chain tunnel to prevent any component from dropping into the engine on removal.*

Note 2: *Do not separate the camshaft case from the cylinder head unless a new case is being installed. Refer to Step 10 for details on separation.*

Removal

1 Remove the valve cover (see Section 8).

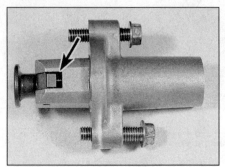

9.6 Release the ratchet mechanism to free the plunger

9.15 Unscrew the bolts (arrowed) and remove the cam chain top guide

9.16 Lift the front guide out of the engine noting how the lugs locate in the cutouts

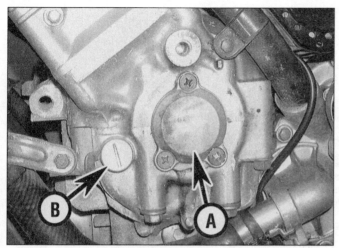

10.2a Remove the crankshaft end-cover (A) and the timing inspection plug (B)

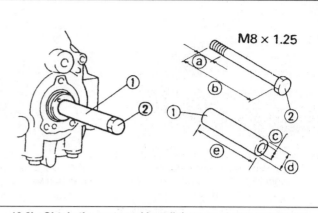

10.2b Obtain the parts and install them as shown to turn the engine

| 1 | Collar | a | 15 mm | c | 8 mm | e | 60 mm |
| 2 | Bolt | b | 75 mm | d | 12 mm | | |

2 Remove the left-hand crankshaft end-cover, secured by three screws, and the timing inspection plug **(see illustration)**. The O-rings can be reused if they are in good condition, otherwise discard them. In order to turn the engine a suitable bolt and collar must be threaded into the end of the crankshaft. Obtain the required parts as shown in the diagram, then fit the collar onto the bolt and thread the bolt into the crankshaft and tighten it – select a gear and apply the rear brake to prevent the engine turning **(see illustration)**. A flange nut with the same thread as the bolt can be used instead of a collar – tighten the nut against the end of the crankshaft to lock the bolt **(see illustration)**. The engine can now be turned using the bolt hex, turning it in an anti-clockwise direction only **(see illustration)**. Alternatively, place the motorcycle on an auxiliary stand so that the rear wheel is off the ground, select a high gear and rotate the rear wheel by hand in its normal direction of rotation. If available, Yamaha's

10.2c Thread the bolt in then tighten the nut against the crankshaft

10.2d Turn the bolt anti-clockwise as shown

special tool assembly, consisting of a timing rotor, a bolt and a dowel pin (Pt. Nos. 4U8-81673-10 or 33M-81673-10, 91317-08030 and 93604-08071) can also be used – fit the pin into the hole in the end of the crankshaft, then locate the rotor over the pin and tighten the bolt **(see illustration)**. Use the flats on the rotor, not the bolt, to turn the engine.

3 Turn the engine until the 'T' mark aligns with the pointer in the inspection window **(see illustration)**, and the camshaft lobes for the No. 1 (left-hand) cylinder face away from each other, and the dot on each camshaft aligns with the dot on the camshaft holder **(see illustrations)**. If the cam lobes are facing towards each other and the dots do not align,

2

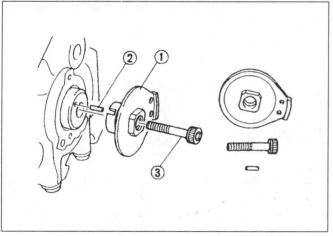

10.2e Yamaha's special tool can also be used as shown

| 1 | Timing rotor | 2 | Dowel pin | 3 | Bolt |

10.3a Turn the engine until the 'T' mark aligns with the pointer

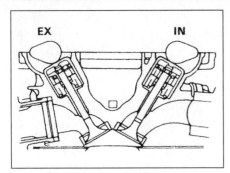

10.3b The camshaft lobes for no. 1 cylinder should be facing away from each other as shown

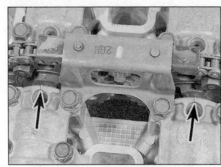

10.3c Align the punchmark on each camshaft with the mark on the holder (arrowed)

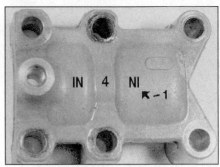

10.7 Note the identification marks which denote the location of each holder

rotate the engine anti-clockwise 360° (one full turn) so that the 'T' mark again aligns with the pointer in the inspection window. The camshaft lobes will now be facing away from each other and the dots will be aligned, meaning the No. 1 cylinder is at TDC (top dead centre) on the compression stroke.

4 Before disturbing the camshafts, make a note of the timing markings described above and how they align. If you are in any doubt as to the alignment of the markings, or if they are not visible, make your own alignment marks between all components, and also between a tooth on each sprocket and its corresponding link on the chain, before disturbing them. These markings ensure that the valve timing can be correctly set up on assembly without difficulty. As it is easy to be a tooth out on installation, marking between a tooth on each sprocket and its link in the chain is especially useful.

5 Remove the cam chain tensioner (see Section 9).

6 Remove the cam chain top and front guides (see Section 9).

7 Before removing the camshaft holders, make a note of which fits where. All the holders are marked with letters and a number to denote their location – 'IN' denotes that the holder is for the intake camshaft at the back, 'EX' denotes it is for the exhaust camshaft at the front. The number denotes the cylinder above which it fits, ie 1 to 4 from left to right. If the marks are not visible, make your own before disturbing them – it is essential they

are returned to their original locations on installation **(see illustration)**.

8 Unscrew the camshaft holder bolts for the camshaft being worked on, slackening them evenly and a little at a time in a criss-cross pattern, starting from the outside and working towards the centre. Slacken the bolts above any lobes that are pressing onto a valve last in the sequence so that the pressure from the open valves cannot cause the camshaft to bend **(see illustration)**. Note that one bolt on each inner holder secures the cam chain top guide and has already been removed.

Caution: A camshaft could break if the holder bolts are not slackened as described and the pressure from a depressed valve causes the shaft to bend. Also, if the holder does not come squarely away from the head, the holder is likely to break. If this happens the camshaft case must be renewed ; the holders are matched to the case and cannot be replaced separately.

Remove the bolts, then lift off the camshaft holders, noting how they fit. Retrieve the dowels from either the holder or the camshaft case if they are loose **(see illustration 10.26a)**. Remove the camshafts, rotating them towards the centre of the engine as you do so. Keep all mated parts together. While the camshafts are out, don't allow the cam chain to go slack and do not rotate the crankshaft – the chain may drop down and bind between the crankshaft and case, which could damage these components. Wire the

chain to another component or secure it using a rod of some sort to prevent it from dropping.

9 If the followers and shims are being removed from the camshaft case, obtain a container which is divided into twenty compartments, and label each compartment with the location of its corresponding valve in the cylinder head and whether it belongs with an intake or an exhaust valve. If a container is not available, use labelled plastic bags (egg cartons also work very well!). Remove the cam follower of the valve in question, then retrieve the shim from the inside of the follower **(see illustrations)**. If it is not in the follower, pick it out of the top of the valve using either a magnet, a small screwdriver with a dab of grease on it (the shim will stick to the grease), or a screwdriver and a pair of pliers **(see illustration 10.21a)**. Do not allow the shim to fall into the engine.

Inspection

10 Inspect the bearing surfaces of the camshaft case and holders and the corresponding journals on the camshaft **(see illustrations)**. Look for score marks, deep scratches and evidence of spalling (a pitted appearance). If damage is noted or wear is excessive, the components must be replaced with new ones. To separate the camshaft case from the cylinder head, unscrew the eleven bolts holding them together and lift off the case **(see illustration)**. If it is stuck, tap around the joint faces of the case with a soft-faced mallet. Do not attempt to free it by inserting a screwdriver between the case and the head –

10.8 Unscrew the camshaft holder bolts as described

10.9a Lift out the follower . . .

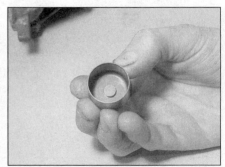

10.9b . . . and remove the shim from inside the follower

you'll damage the sealing surfaces. Remove the old gasket and discard it as a new one must be used. Note the two dowels and remove them from the case (if they are not there, they will be in the head). Remove the oil pipes from the underside of the case and discard the O-rings, then fit the pipes onto the new case using new O-rings and tighten the bolts to the torque setting specified at the beginning of the Chapter. Fit the dowels into the head if removed, then lay the new gasket over the dowels, making sure the 'UP' mark faces up. Fit the case onto the head, then apply molybdenum disulphide oil (a 50/50 mixture of molybdenum disulphide grease and engine oil) to the bolt threads and tighten them evenly and a little at a time in a criss-cross sequence starting from the centre and working outwards to the specified torque setting.

11 Check the camshaft lobes for heat discoloration (blue appearance), score marks, chipped areas, flat spots and spalling **(see illustration)**. Measure the height of each lobe with a micrometer **(see illustration)** and compare the results to the minimum lobe height listed in this Chapter's Specifications. If damage is noted or wear is excessive, the camshaft must be replaced with a new one. Also, be sure to check the condition of the followers.

12 Check the amount of camshaft runout by supporting each end of the camshaft on V-blocks, and measuring any runout using a dial gauge. If the runout exceeds the specified limit the camshaft must be replaced with a new one.

 HAYNES HiNT *Refer to Tools and Workshop Tips (Section 3) in the Reference section for details of how to read a micrometer and dial gauge.*

13 Next, check the camshaft journal oil clearances. Check each camshaft in turn rather than at the same time – the exhaust camshaft is identifiable by its two lobes per cylinder, and the intake camshaft by its three lobes per cylinder **(see illustration 10.24a)**. Clean the camshaft, the bearing surfaces in the cylinder head and camshaft holders with a clean lint-free cloth, then lay the camshaft in place in the case.

14 Cut some strips of Plastigauge and lay one piece on each journal, parallel with the camshaft centreline **(see illustration)**. Make sure the camshaft holder dowels are installed **(see illustration 10.26a)**. Lay the holders in their correct place in the case (see Step 7). Lubricate the threads of the holder bolts with

10.10a Inspect the bearing surfaces in the camshaft case and holder . . .

engine oil then install them and tighten them evenly and a little at a time in a criss-cross pattern, working from the centre of the camshaft outwards, (ie starting with the bolts that are above valves that will be opened when the camshaft is tightened down), to the torque setting specified at the beginning of the Chapter **(see illustration 10.26b)**. Note that on YZF750R and SP models, the rear outer bolt on each exhaust holder is tightened to a lower torque than the rest. Whilst tightening the bolts, make sure the holders are being pulled squarely down and are not binding on the dowels. While doing this, don't let the camshaft rotate.

2

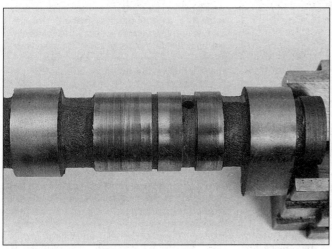

10.10b . . . and the journal surfaces of the camshaft for scratches or wear

10.10c Camshaft case bolts (arrowed)

10.11a Check the lobes of the camshaft for wear – here's an example of damage requiring camshaft repair or renewal

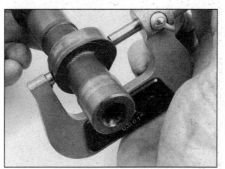

10.11b Measure the height of the camshaft lobes with a micrometer

10.14 Lay a strip of Plastigauge across each bearing journal, parallel with the camshaft centreline

10.16a Compare the width of the crushed Plastigauge to the scale printed on the Plastigauge container

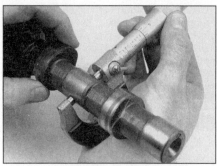

10.16b Measure the cam bearing journals with a micrometer

to maintain proper tension, or if it is stiff or the links are binding or kinking, replace it with a new one. Refer to Section 25 for replacement.

18 Check the sprockets for wear, cracks and other damage. If the sprockets are worn, the cam chain is also worn, and so is the sprocket on the crankshaft. If severe wear is apparent, the entire engine should be disassembled for inspection.

19 Inspect the cam chain guides and tensioner blade (see Sections 9 and 25).

20 Inspect the outer surfaces of the cam followers for evidence of scoring or other damage. If a follower is in poor condition, it is probable that the bore in which it works is also damaged. Check for clearance between the followers and their bores. Whilst no specifications are given, if slack is excessive, renew the followers. If the bores are seriously out-of-round or tapered, the camshaft case and the followers must be replaced.

Installation

21 If removed, lubricate each shim and its follower with molybdenum disulphide oil (a 50/50 mixture of molybdenum disulphide grease and engine oil) and fit each shim into its recess in the top of the valve, with the size marking on each shim facing up **(see illustration)**. Make sure each shim is correctly seated in the top of the valve assembly, then install each follower, making sure it fits squarely in its bore **(see illustration)**. **Note:** *It is most important that the shims and followers are returned to their original valves otherwise the valve clearances will be inaccurate.*

22 Make sure the bearing surfaces on the camshafts and in the cylinder head are clean, then apply molybdenum disulphide oil (a 50/50 mixture of molybdenum disulphide grease and engine oil) to each of them. Also apply it to the camshaft lobes.

23 Check that the 'T' mark on the rotor still aligns with the pointer in the inspection window (see Step 3) **(see illustration 10.3a)**.

24 Fit the exhaust camshaft, identifiable by its two lobes per cylinder **(see illustration)**, through the cam chain and onto the front of the head, making sure the No. 1 (left-hand) cylinder lobes are facing forwards and the punchmark on the camshaft is facing up **(see illustration)**. Fit the cam chain around the exhaust sprocket, aligning the marks between sprocket tooth and link if made. When fitting the chain, pull up on the front run to remove all slack from it.

25 Now fit the intake camshaft, identifiable by its three lobes per cylinder **(see illustration 10.24a)**, through the cam chain and onto the back of the case, making sure the No. 1 cylinder lobes are facing back and the punchmark on the camshaft end is facing up **(see illustration 10.24b)**. Fit the cam chain around the intake sprocket, aligning the marks between sprocket tooth and link if made. When fitting the chain, pull it tight to make sure there is no slack between the two camshaft sprockets.

10.21a Fit the shim into the recess in the top of the valve . . .

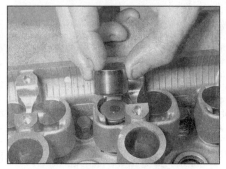

10.21b . . . then install the follower

15 Now unscrew the bolts evenly and a little at a time in a criss-cross pattern, starting from the outside and working towards the centre, and carefully lift off the camshaft holders.

16 To determine the oil clearance, compare the crushed Plastigauge (at its widest point) on each journal to the scale printed on the Plastigauge container **(see illustration)**. Compare the results to this Chapter's Specifications. If the oil clearance is greater than specified, measure the diameter of the camshaft journal with a micrometer **(see illustration)**. If the journal diameter is less than the specified limit, replace the camshaft with a new one and recheck the clearance. If the clearance is still too great, or if the camshaft journal is within its limit, replace the camshaft case and holders with new ones (see Step 10 for separation of the case from the cylinder head).

> **HAYNES HINT** *Before renewing the camshafts, camshaft case or holders because of damage, check with local machine shops specialising in motorcycle engine work. In the case of the camshafts, it may be possible for cam lobes to be welded, reground and hardened, at a cost far lower than that of a new camshaft. If the bearing surfaces in the case or holders are damaged, it may be possible for them to be bored out to accept bearing inserts. Due to the cost of new components it is recommended that all options be explored!*

17 Except in cases of oil starvation, the cam chain wears very little. If the chain has stretched excessively, which makes it difficult

10.24a The camshafts are identifiable by lobes per cylinder – the exhaust has two and the intake three

10.24b Lay the camshaft in the case with the punchmark (arrowed) facing up

10.26a Make sure all the dowels (arrowed) are installed

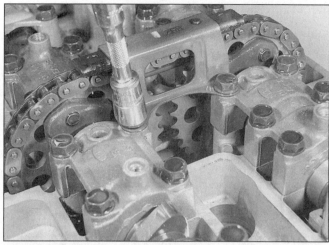

10.26b Tighten the holder bolts as described to the specified torque

26 Fit the camshaft holder dowels into the cylinder head **(see illustration)**. Make sure the bearing surfaces in the holders are clean, then apply molybdenum disulphide oil (a 50/50 mixture of molybdenum disulphide grease and engine oil) to them. Lay the holders in their correct place in the case (see Step 7), then position the cam chain top guide **(see illustration 9.15)**. Lubricate the threads of the holder bolts with engine oil then install them and tighten them evenly and a little at a time in a criss-cross pattern, working from the centre of the camshaft outwards, (ie starting with the bolts that are above valves that will be opened when the camshaft is tightened down), to the torque setting specified at the beginning of the Chapter **(see illustration)**. Note that on YZF750R and SP models, the rear outer bolt on each exhaust holder is tightened to a lower torque than the rest. Whilst tightening the bolts, make sure the holders are being pulled squarely down and are not binding on the dowels.

Caution: The camshaft is likely to break if it is tightened down onto the closed valves before the open valves. The holders are likely to break if they are not tightened down evenly and squarely.

27 Using a piece of wooden dowel, press on the back of the cam chain tensioner blade via the tensioner bore in the cylinder block to ensure that any slack in the cam chain between the crankshaft and the intake camshaft, and between the two camshafts, is taken up and transferred to the rear run of the chain (where it will later be taken up by the tensioner). At this point check that all the timing marks are still in **exact** alignment as described in Steps 3 and 4. Note that it is easy to be slightly out (one tooth on the sprocket) without the marks appearing drastically out of alignment. If the marks are out, verify which sprocket is misaligned, then unscrew its bolts and slide it off the camshaft, then disengage it from the chain. Move the

camshaft round as required, then fit the sprocket back into the chain and onto the camshaft, and check the marks again. With everything correctly aligned, tighten the sprocket bolts to the torque setting specified at the beginning of the Chapter.

Caution: If the marks are not aligned exactly as described, the valve timing will be incorrect and the valves may strike the pistons, causing extensive damage to the engine.

28 Install the cam chain front guide (see Section 9).

29 Install the cam chain tensioner (see Section 9). Turn the engine anti-clockwise through two full turns and check again that all the timing marks still align (see Steps 3 and 4).

30 Check the valve clearances and adjust them if necessary (see Chapter 1).

31 If used, remove the collar or nut and bolt or timing plate assembly from the left-hand end of the crankshaft – select a gear and use the rear brake to prevent the engine turning while slackening the bolt. Install the left-hand crankshaft end-cover and the timing inspection plug using new O-rings if necessary **(see illustration)**. Tighten the end-cover screws to the specified torque setting.

32 Install the valve cover (see Section 8).

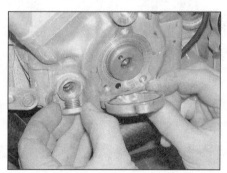

10.31 Install the end-cover and inspection plug using new O-rings if required

11 Cylinder head –
removal and installation

Caution: The engine must be completely cool before beginning this procedure or the cylinder head may become warped.

Note 1: The cylinder head can be removed with the engine in the frame. If the engine has been removed, ignore the steps which don't apply.

Note 2: As it is possible to split the cam chain, it is not necessary to remove the camshafts when removing the cylinder head – refer to Section 25 for details on how to split and join the chain, taking note of all the information given, and do not split the chain until the camshafts are correctly positioned as described in Section 10, Steps 3 and 4. The camshafts and holders have access holes in them for the cylinder head nuts. Remove the rubber bungs in each camshaft holder to access the holes. Refer to Section 10 and position the camshafts as described in Steps 3 and 4 – the holes will then be correctly positioned. If the engine has been correctly built, this will automatically position the split-link between the camshaft sprockets, so there is no need to turn the camshafts after the chain is removed, which should not be done. If the chain is not positioned with the split-link visible when the camshafts are correctly positioned, the engine will have to be turned until the link is visible. This will mean the camshafts are not correctly positioned, which means they will have to be be turned after the chain has been removed to align the holes – this could cause a valve to contact a piston, causing serious damage, and so the camshafts should therefore be removed prior to removing the cylinder head (see Section 10). Unscrew the cylinder head nuts using a suitable hex key in a socket extension.

2

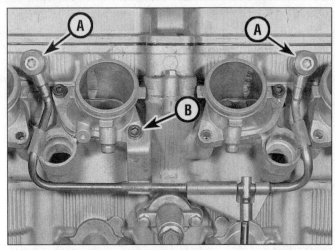

11.6a Unscrew the banjo bolts (A) and the clamp bolt (B) from the cylinder head . . .

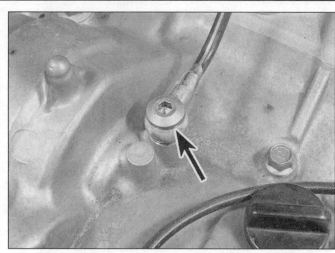

11.6b . . . and the banjo bolt (arrowed) from the crankcase

With the camshafts in situ, it is not possible to fully remove the cylinder head nuts and washers, so great care must be taken on installation not to cock the washers or cross-thread the nuts. Before splitting the cam chain, make a reference mark between a link on the chain and a tooth on the sprocket on each side of the split link so that it can be installed in exactly the same position, making the timing easier to set up. If the cylinder head is being removed purely to access the pistons or cylinder block, then removal of the camshafts is not necessary, as long as you are certain that they are in good condition and do not need checking. If however the engine is being taken down because of general wear and age, it is of course necessary to remove the camshafts and to check them carefully along with all other components. In the event of any damage in an engine, tiny particles of metal could enter the lubrication system and affect every bearing surface and component, so if, for instance, on checking the pistons you find a broken ring, and you have not removed

the camshafts, you should do so.

Note 3: *Do not separate the camshaft case from the cylinder head unless a new head is being installed. Refer to Section 10, Step 10 for details of separation.*

Removal

1 Remove the exhaust system (see Chapter 4). Plug the exhaust ports with clean rag.

2 Remove the carburettors (see Chapter 4). Plug the intake manifolds with clean rag.

3 Remove the valve cover (see Section 8) and the camshafts and followers (see Section 10) (see Note 2 above).

4 On all except 1993 and 1994 YZF750R and all SP models, either detach the vacuum take-off hoses from the intake manifolds, or release the hoses from their clips and coil them around the manifolds so they do not get in the way **(see illustration 5.7a)**.

5 Drain the cooling system (see Chapter 1). Remove the thermostat housing (see Chapter 3).

6 On YZF750R and SP models, unscrew the banjo bolts securing the oil hoses to the cylinder head and detach the hoses. On YZF1000R models, unscrew the oil pipe banjo bolts and bracket bolt and remove the pipe **(see illustrations)**. Discard the banjo bolt sealing washers as new ones must be used.

7 Slacken the pinchbolts on the mounting lugs for the right-hand front engine mounting bolts, then unscrew and remove the right-hand and left-hand front engine mounting bolts, noting the washers with the left-hand ones **(see illustrations 5.19a and b)**.

8 The cylinder head is secured by twelve nuts **(see illustration)**. Slacken the nuts evenly and a little at a time in a **reverse** of the numerical tightening sequence shown until they are all slack, then remove the nuts and their washers, using either a magnet, a screwdriver, or a piece of wire hooked over at the end to lift them out where necessary **(see illustrations)**.

9 Pull the cylinder head up off the block **(see illustration)**. If it is stuck, tap around the

11.8a Cylinder head nut TIGHTENING sequence – slacken the nuts in reverse order

11.8b Remove the end nuts using a socket . . .

11.8c . . . and the centre nuts using an Allen bit

11.9a Carefully lift the head up off the block . . .

11.9b . . . then remove the gasket

joint faces of the cylinder head with a soft-faced mallet to free the head. Do not attempt to free the head by inserting a screwdriver between the head and cylinder block – you'll damage the sealing surfaces. Remove the old cylinder head gasket and discard it as a new one must be used **(see illustration)**.

10 If they are loose, remove the dowels from the cylinder block **(see illustration 11.14a)**. If they appear to be missing they are probably stuck in the underside of the cylinder head. Remove the collars from the right-hand front engine mounting lugs for safekeeping if required, or tighten the pinchbolts to keep them in place.

11 Check the cylinder head gasket and the mating surfaces on the cylinder head and block for signs of leakage, which could indicate warpage. Refer to Section 13 and check the flatness of the cylinder head.

Installation

12 Clean all traces of old gasket material from the cylinder head and block. If a scraper is used, take care not to scratch or gouge the soft aluminium. Be careful not to let any of the gasket material fall into the crankcase, the cylinder bores or the oil passages. Lubricate the cylinder bores with new engine oil.

HAYNES HiNT *Refer to Tools and Workshop Tips (Section 7) for details of gasket removal methods.*

13 If removed, install the collars for the left-hand front mounting bolts, making sure their shouldered ends face the inside.

14 Ensure both cylinder head and block mating surfaces are clean. If removed, fit the dowels into the cylinder block, then lay the new head gasket in place on the block, making sure it locates correctly over the dowels, the 'UP' mark faces up, and all the holes are correctly aligned **(see illustrations)**. Never re-use the old gasket.

15 Carefully fit the cylinder head onto the block, making sure it locates correctly onto the dowels **(see illustration 11.9a)**.

16 Lubricate the threads of the cylinder head nuts with clean engine oil. Install the nuts with their washers and tighten them finger-tight. Now tighten the nuts in the correct numerical sequence **(see illustrations 11.8a, b and c)** and in two stages, to the torque setting specified at the beginning of the Chapter.

17 Install the right-hand and left-hand engine front mounting bolts, not forgetting the washers with the left-hand ones, and tighten them to the specified torque setting **(see illustrations 5.19b**

and a). Now tighten the pinchbolts on the mounting lugs for the left-hand front mounting bolts to the specified torque.

18 On YZF750R and SP models, fit the oil hoses onto the cylinder head, using new sealing washers on each side of the unions, and tighten the banjo bolts to the specified torque setting. On YZF1000R models, install the oil pipe, using new sealing washers on each side of the unions, and tighten the banjo bolts and the clamp bolt to the specified torque settings **(see illustrations 11.6a and b)**.

19 If removed, install the coolant outlet union onto the back of the cylinder head, using new O-rings smeared with grease, and tighten the bolts to the specified torque setting. Attach the hose to the union and tighten the clamp securely. Fit the thermostat housing onto the union (see Chapter 3).

20 On all except 1993 and 1994 YZF750R and all SP models, either attach the vacuum take-off hoses to the intake manifolds or secure the hoses in their clips, according to your removal procedure **(see illustration 5.7a)**.

21 Install the remaining components in a reverse of their removal sequence, referring to the relevant Sections or Chapters (see Steps 1, 2 and 3). Fill the cooling system (see Chapter 1).

2

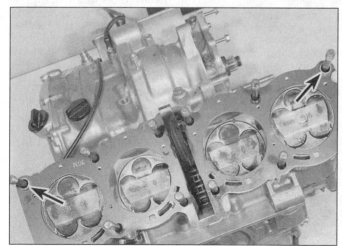

11.14a Lay the new gasket over the dowels (arrowed) and onto the head . . .

11.14b . . . . making sure the 'UP' cutout (arrowed) reads the right way

12.1 Check all around the edge of each valve for solvent leakage

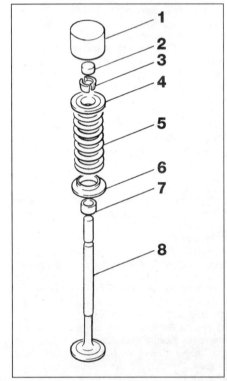

13.3 Valve components

1	Follower	5	Valve spring
2	Shim	6	Spring seat
3	Collets	7	Valve stem oil
4	Spring		seal
	retainer	8	Valve

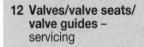

12 Valves/valve seats/ valve guides – servicing

1 Because of the complex nature of this job and the special tools and equipment required, most owners leave servicing of the valves, valve seats and valve guides to a professional. However, you can make an initial assessment of whether the valves are seating, and therefore sealing, correctly by pouring a small amount of solvent into each of the valve ports. If the solvent leaks past any valve into the combustion chamber area the valve is not seating and sealing correctly **(see illustration)**.

2 You can also remove the valves from the cylinder head, clean the components, check them for wear to assess the extent of the work needed, and, unless a valve service is required, grind in the valves (see Section 13). The head can then be reassembled.

3 The dealer service department will remove the valves and springs, renew the valves and guides, recut the valve seats, check and renew the valve springs, spring retainers and collets (as necessary), replace the valve seals with new ones and reassemble the valve components.

4 After the valve service has been performed, the head will be in like-new condition. When the head is returned, be sure to clean it again very thoroughly before installation on the engine to remove any metal particles or abrasive grit that may still be present from the valve service operations. Use compressed air, if available, to blow out all the holes and passages.

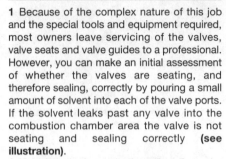

13 Cylinder head and valves – disassembly, inspection and reassembly

1 As mentioned in the previous section, valve overhaul should be left to a Yamaha dealer. However, disassembly, cleaning and inspection of the valves and related components can be done (if the necessary special tools are available) by the home

mechanic. This way no expense is incurred if the inspection reveals that overhaul is not required at this time.

2 To disassemble the valve components without the risk of damaging them, a valve spring compressor is absolutely essential. Make sure it is suitable for motorcycle work.

Disassembly

3 Before proceeding, arrange to label and store the valves along with their related components in such a way that they can be returned to their original locations without getting mixed up **(see illustration)**. A good way to do this is to use the same container as the shims are stored in (see Section 10), or to obtain a separate container which is divided into twenty compartments, and to label each compartment with the identity of the valve which will be stored in it (ie number of cylinder, intake or exhaust side, inner, centre or outer valve). Alternatively, labelled plastic bags will do just as well.

4 Clean all traces of old gasket material from the cylinder head. If a scraper is used, take care not to scratch or gouge the soft aluminium.

 HAYNES HiNT *Refer to Tools and Workshop Tips (Section 7) for details of gasket removal methods.*

5 Compress the valve spring on the first valve with a spring compressor, making sure it is correctly located onto each end of the valve assembly **(see illustrations)**. On the underside of the head make sure the plate on the compressor only contacts the valve and not the soft aluminium of the head – if the plate is too big for the valve, use a spacer between them **(see illustration)**. Do not compress the springs any more than is absolutely necessary. Remove the collets, using either needle-nose pliers, tweezers, a magnet or a screwdriver with a dab of grease on it **(see illustration)**. Carefully release the valve spring compressor and remove the spring retainer, noting which way up it fits, the spring, the spring seat, and the valve from the head **(see illustration 13.3)**. If the valve binds in the guide (won't pull through), push it back

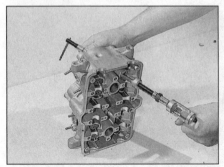

13.5a Compressing the valve springs using a valve spring compressor

13.5b Make sure the compressor is a good fit both on the top . . .

13.5c . . . and the bottom of the valve assembly

13.5d Use a spacer between the plate and the valve if the plate is too big

13.5e Remove the collets with needle-nose pliers, tweezers, a magnet or a screwdriver with a dab of grease on it

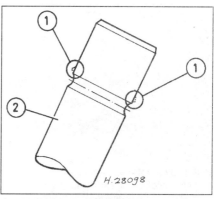

13.5f If the valve stem (2) won't pull through the guide, deburr the area above the collet groove (1)

into the head and deburr the area around the collet groove with a very fine file or whetstone **(see illustration)**.

6 Repeat the procedure for the remaining valves. Remember to keep the parts for each valve together and in order so they can be reinstalled in the same location.

7 Once the valves have been removed and labelled, pull the valve stem seals off the top of the valve guides with pliers and discard them (the old seals should never be reused).

8 Next, clean the cylinder head with solvent and dry it thoroughly. Compressed air will speed the drying process and ensure that all holes and recessed areas are clean.

9 Clean all of the valve springs, collets, retainers and spring seats with solvent and dry them thoroughly. Do the parts from one valve at a time so that no mixing of parts between valves occurs.

10 Scrape off any deposits that may have formed on the valve, then use a motorised wire brush to remove deposits from the valve heads and stems. Again, make sure the valves do not get mixed up.

Inspection

11 Inspect the head very carefully for cracks and other damage. If cracks are found, a new head will be required. Check the cam bearing surfaces for wear and evidence of seizure. Check the camshafts for wear as well (see Section 10).

12 Using a precision straight-edge and a feeler gauge set to the warpage limit listed in the specifications at the beginning of the Chapter, check the head gasket mating surface for warpage. Refer to *Tools and Workshop Tips* (Section 3) in the Reference section for details of how to use the straight-edge.

13 Examine the valve seats in the combustion chamber. If they are pitted, cracked or burned, the head will require work beyond the scope of the home mechanic. Measure the valve seat width and compare it to this Chapter's Specifications **(see illustration)**. If it exceeds the service limit, or if it varies around its circumference, valve overhaul is required. If

available, use Prussian blue to determine the extent of valve seat wear. Uniformly coat the seat with the Prussian blue, then install the valve and rotate it back and forth using a lapping tool. Remove the valve and check whether the ring of blue on the valve is uniform and continuous around the valve, and of the correct width as specified.

14 Measure the valve stem diameter **(see illustration)**. Clean the valve guides to remove any carbon build-up, then measure the inside diameters of the guides (at both ends and the centre of the guide) with a small hole gauge and micrometer **(see illustrations)**. The guides are measured at the

ends and at the centre to determine if they are worn in a bell-mouth pattern (more wear at the ends). Subtract the stem diameter from the valve guide diameter to obtain the valve stem-to-guide clearance. If the stem-to-guide clearance is greater than listed in this Chapter's Specifications, renew whichever components are worn beyond their specification limits. If the valve guide is within specifications, but is worn unevenly, it should be renewed.

15 Carefully inspect each valve face, stem and collet groove area for cracks, pits and burned spots **(see illustration)**. Measure the valve margin thickness and compare it to the

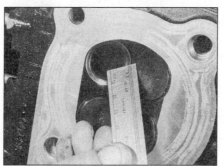

13.13 Measure the valve seat width with a ruler (or for greater precision use a vernier caliper)

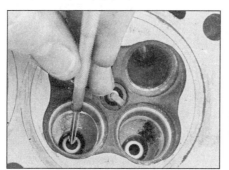

13.14b Insert a small hole gauge into the valve guide and expand it so there's a slight drag when it's pulled out

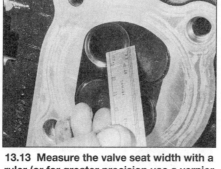

13.14a Measure the valve stem diameter with a micrometer

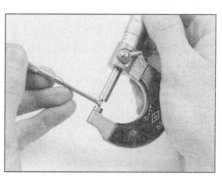

13.14c Measure the small hole gauge with a micrometer

2

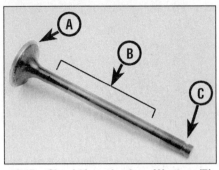

13.15a Check the valve face (A), stem (B) and collet groove (C) for signs of wear and damage

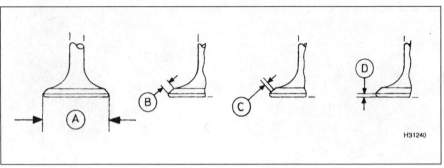

13.15b Valve head measurement points

A Head diameter   B Face width   C Seat width   D Margin thickness

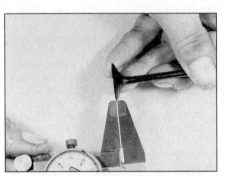

13.15c Measure the valve margin thickness as shown

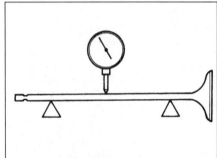

13.16 Check the valve stem for runout using V-blocks and a dial gauge

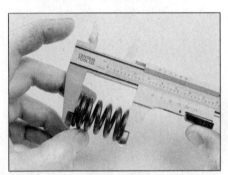

13.17a Measure the free length of the valve springs

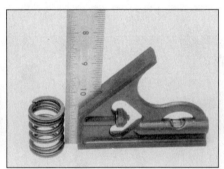

13.17b Check the valve springs for squareness

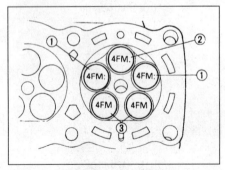

13.19a Valve locations – YZF750R and SP models

1 Outer intake valves
2 Centre intake valve
3 Exhaust valves

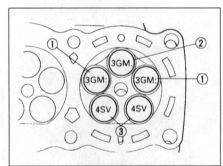

13.19a Valve locations – YZF1000R models

1 Outer intake valves
2 Centre intake valve
3 Exhaust valves

specifications (see illustrations). If it is thinner than specified, replace the valve with a new one. The margin is the portion of the valve head which is below the valve seat.

16 Rotate the valve and check for any obvious indication that it is bent. Using V-blocks and a dial gauge if available, measure the valve stem runout and compare the results to the specifications (see illustration). If the measurement exceeds the service limit specified, the valve must be replaced with a new one. Check the end of the stem for pitting and excessive wear. The presence of any of the above conditions indicates the need for valve servicing. The stem end can be ground down, provided that the amount of stem above the collet groove after grinding is sufficient.

17 Check the end of each valve spring for wear and pitting. Measure the spring free length and compare it to that listed in the specifications (see illustration). If any spring is shorter than specified it has sagged and must be replaced with a new one. Also place the spring upright on a flat surface and check it for bend by placing a ruler against it (see illustration). If the bend in any spring is excessive, it must be replaced with a new one.

18 Check the spring retainers and collets for obvious wear and cracks. Any questionable parts should not be reused, as extensive damage will occur in the event of failure during engine operation.

19 If the inspection indicates that no overhaul work is required, the valve components can be reinstalled in the head. If any new valves are being installed, they can be identified as follows: on YZF750R and SP models, the exhaust valves are marked '4FM', the outer intake valves are marked '4FM:', and the centre intake valve is marked '4FM.' (see illustration). On YZF1000R models, the exhaust valves are marked '4SV', the outer intake valves are marked '3GM:', and the centre intake valve is marked '3GM.' (see illustration).

Reassembly

20 Unless a valve service has been performed, before installing the valves in the head they should be ground in (lapped) to ensure a positive seal between the valves and

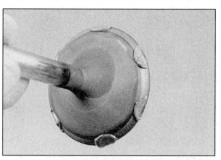

13.21 Apply the lapping compound very sparingly, in small dabs, to the valve face only

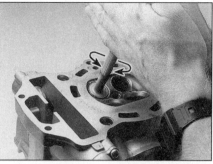

13.22a Rotate the valve grinding tool back and forth between the palms of your hands

13.22b The valve face and seat should show a uniform unbroken ring . . .

seats. This procedure requires coarse and fine valve grinding compound and a valve grinding tool. If a grinding tool is not available, a piece of rubber or plastic hose can be slipped over the valve stem (after the valve has been installed in the guide) and used to turn the valve.

21 Apply a small amount of coarse grinding compound to the valve face and some molybdenum disulphide oil (a 50/50 mixture of molybdenum disulphide grease and engine oil) to the valve stem, then slip the valve into the guide **(see illustration)**. **Note:** *Make sure each valve is installed in its correct guide and be careful not to get any grinding compound on the valve stem.*

22 Attach the grinding tool (or hose) to the valve and rotate the tool between the palms of your hands. Use a back-and-forth motion (as though rubbing your hands together) rather than a circular motion (ie so that the valve rotates alternately clockwise and anti-

clockwise rather than in one direction only) **(see illustration)**. Lift the valve off the seat and turn it at regular intervals to distribute the grinding compound properly. Continue the grinding procedure until the valve face and seat contact area is of uniform width and unbroken around the entire circumference of the valve face and seat **(see illustrations)**.

23 Carefully remove the valve from the guide and wipe off all traces of grinding compound. Use solvent to clean the valve and wipe the seat area thoroughly with a solvent soaked cloth.

24 Repeat the procedure with fine valve grinding compound, then repeat the entire procedure for the remaining valves.

25 Working on one valve at a time, lay the spring seat in place in the cylinder head, with its shouldered side up so that the spring fits into it, then fit a new valve stem seal on the guide **(see illustration)**. Use an appropriate

size deep socket to push the seal over the end of the valve guide until it is felt to clip into place. Don't twist or cock the seal, or it will not seal properly against the valve stem. Also, don't remove it again or it will be damaged.

26 Coat the valve stem with molybdenum disulphide oil (a 50/50 mixture of molybdenum disulphide grease and engine oil), then install it into its guide, rotating it slowly to avoid damaging the seal **(see illustration)**. Check that the valve moves up and down freely in the guide. Next, install the spring, with its closer-wound coils facing down into the cylinder head, followed by the spring retainer, with its shouldered side facing down so that it fits into the top of the spring **(see illustrations)**.

27 Apply a small amount of grease to the collets to help hold them in place as the pressure is released from the spring **(see illustration)**. Compress the spring with the

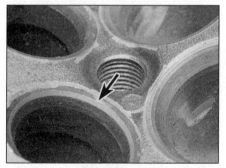

13.22c . . . and the seat (arrowed) should be the specified width all the way round

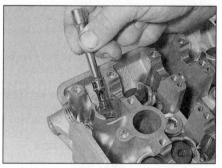

13.25 Press the valve stem seal into position using a suitable deep socket

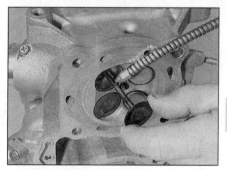

13.26a Lubricate the stem and slide the valve into its correct location

13.26b Fit the valve spring with its closer wound coils facing down. . .

13.26c . . . then fit the spring retainer

13.27a A small dab of grease will help to keep the collets in place on the valve while the spring is released

2

13.27b Compress the springs and install the collets, making sure they locate in the groove

14.2 Unscrew the bolt (arrowed) and remove the pipe

14.3 Lift the block up off the studs

valve spring compressor and install the collets **(see illustration)**. When compressing the spring, do so only as far as is necessary to slip the collets into place. Make certain that the collets are securely locked in the retaining groove.

28 Support the cylinder head on blocks so the valves can't contact the workbench top, then very gently tap the valve stem with a soft-faced hammer. This will help seat the collets in the groove.

 Check for proper sealing of the valves by pouring a small amount of solvent into each of the valve ports. If the solvent leaks past any valve into the combustion chamber area the valve grinding operation on that valve should be repeated.

29 Repeat the procedure for the remaining valves. Remember to keep the parts for each valve together and separate from the other valves so they can be reinstalled in the same location.

14 Cylinder block –
removal, inspection and installation

Note: *The cylinder block can be removed with the engine in the frame.*

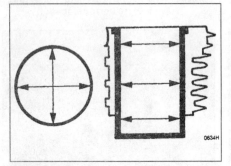

14.8 Measure the cylinder bore in the directions shown with a telescoping gauge, then measure the gauge with a micrometer

Removal

1 Remove the cylinder head (see Section 11).
2 Unscrew the bolt securing the coolant pipe from the water pump to the inlet union on the back of the block and remove the pipe **(see illustration)**. Discard the O-rings as new ones must be used. Slacken the clamp screw securing the oil cooler hose to the right-hand end of the inlet union and detach the hose. If required, unscrew the bolts securing the union to the back of the block and remove the union, noting the carburettor breather hose clamp where fitted. Discard the O-rings as new ones must be used.
3 Hold the cam chain up and lift the cylinder block up, then pass the cam chain down through the tunnel **(see illustration)**. Do not let the chain fall into the crankcase – secure it with a piece of wire or metal bar to prevent it from doing so. If the block is stuck, tap around the joint faces of the block with a soft-faced mallet to free it from the crankcase. Don't attempt to free the block by inserting a screwdriver between it and the crankcase – you'll damage the sealing surfaces. When the block is removed, stuff clean rags around the pistons to prevent anything falling into the crankcase.
4 Remove the gasket and clean all traces of old gasket material from the cylinder block and crankcase mating surfaces. If a scraper is used, take care not to scratch or gouge the soft aluminium. Be careful not to let any of the gasket material fall into the crankcase or the oil passages.
5 Remove the dowels from the mating surface of the crankcase or the underside of the block if they are loose **(see illustration 14.16a)**. Be careful not to drop them into the engine.

Inspection

Caution: Do not attempt to separate the liners from the cylinder block.
6 Check the cylinder walls carefully for scratches and score marks.
7 Using a precision straight-edge and a feeler gauge set to the warpage limit listed in the specifications at the beginning of the Chapter, check the block gasket mating surface for warpage. Refer to *Tools and Workshop Tips* (Section 3) in the Reference section for details of how to use the straight-edge. If warpage is

excessive the block must be replaced with a new one.
8 Using telescoping gauges and a micrometer (see Section 3 of *Tools and Workshop Tips*), check the dimensions of each cylinder to assess the amount of wear, taper and ovality. Measure near the top (but below the level of the top piston ring at TDC), centre and bottom (but above the level of the oil ring at BDC) of the bore, both parallel to and across the crankshaft axis **(see illustration)**. Compare the results to the specifications at the beginning of the Chapter.
9 If the precision measuring tools are not available, take the block to a Yamaha dealer or specialist motorcycle repair shop for assessment and advice.
10 If the cylinders are worn beyond the service limit, or badly scratched, scuffed or scored, the cylinder block must be rebored. Yamaha supply one oversize piston (+0.5 mm).
11 If the block and cylinders are in good condition and the piston-to-bore clearance is within specifications (see Section 15), the cylinders should be honed (de-glazed). To perform this operation you will need the proper size flexible hone with fine stones (see Specialist Tools in *Tools and Workshop Tips* in the Reference section), or a bottle-brush type hone, plenty of light oil or honing oil, some clean rags and an electric drill motor.
12 Hold the block sideways (so that the bores are horizontal rather than vertical) in a vice with soft jaws or cushioned with wooden blocks. Mount the hone in the drill motor, compress the stones and insert the hone into the cylinder. Thoroughly lubricate the cylinder, then turn on the drill and move the hone up and down in the cylinder at a pace which produces a fine cross-hatch pattern on the cylinder wall with the lines intersecting at an angle of approximately 60 degrees. Be sure to use plenty of lubricant and do not take off any more material than is necessary to produce the desired effect. Do not withdraw the hone from the cylinder while it is still turning. Switch off the drill and continue to move it up and down in the cylinder until it has stopped turning, then compress the stones and withdraw the hone. Wipe the oil from the cylinder and repeat the procedure on the other cylinder. Remember, do not take too much material from the cylinder wall.

14.16a Make sure there is a dowel (arrowed) at each front corner, then fit the gasket . . .

14.16b . . . making sure the 'UP' mark (arrowed) reads correctly

14.19 Carefully feed the rings in using a screwdriver and/or fingernails

13 Wash the cylinders thoroughly with warm soapy water to remove all traces of the abrasive grit produced during the honing operation. Be sure to run a brush through the bolt holes and flush them with running water. After rinsing, dry the cylinders thoroughly and apply a thin coat of light, rust-preventative oil to all machined surfaces.

14 If you do not have the equipment or desire to perform the honing operation, take the block to a Yamaha dealer or specialist motorcycle repair shop.

Installation

15 Check the condition of the O-rings fitted around the base of each cylinder and replace them with new ones if necessary. Check that the mating surfaces of the cylinder block and crankcase are free from oil or pieces of old gasket.

16 If removed, fit the dowels into the crankcase (see illustration). Remove the rags from around the pistons. Lay the new base gasket in place on the crankcase, making sure the 'UP' mark faces up, it locates correctly over the dowels and all the holes are correctly aligned (see illustration). Never re-use the old gasket.

17 If required, install piston ring clamps onto the pistons to ease their entry into the bores as the block is lowered. This is not essential as each cylinder has a good lead-in enabling the piston rings to be hand-fed into the bore. If possible, have an assistant to support the block while this is done.

> **HAYNES HiNT**
>
> *Rotate the crankshaft until the inner pistons (2 and 3) are uppermost and feed them into the block first. Access to the lower pistons (1 and 4) is easier since they are on the outside.*

18 Lubricate the cylinder bores, pistons and piston rings, and the connecting rod big- and small-ends, with clean engine oil, then install the block down over the studs until the uppermost piston crowns fit into the bores. At this stage feed the cam chain up through the block and secure it in place with a piece of wire to prevent it from falling back down.

19 Gently push down on the cylinder block, making sure the pistons enter the bores squarely and do not get cocked sideways. If piston ring clamps are not being used, carefully compress and feed each ring into the bore as the block is lowered (see illustration). If necessary, use a soft mallet to gently tap the block down, but do not use force if the block appears to be stuck as the pistons and/or rings will be damaged. If clamps are used, remove them once the pistons are in the bore.

20 When the pistons are correctly installed in the cylinders, press the block down onto the base gasket, making sure it locates correctly onto the dowels.

21 If removed, install the coolant inlet union using new O-rings and tighten the bolts to the torque setting specified at the beginning of the Chapter, not forgetting the carburettor breather hose clamp where fitted. Attach the oil cooler hose and secure it with the clamp.

Fit a new O-ring onto each end of the coolant pipe, then press the pipe into the water pump and inlet union simultaneously until the O-rings are felt to locate. Install the pipe bolt and tighten it securely (see illustration 14.2).

22 Install the cylinder head (see Section 11).

15 Pistons – removal, inspection and installation

Note: *The pistons can be removed with the engine in the frame.*

Removal

1 Remove the cylinder block (see Section 14).

2 Before removing the piston from the connecting rod, and if not already done, stuff a clean rag into the hole around the rod to prevent the circlips or anything else from falling into the crankcase. Use a sharp scriber or felt marker pen to write the cylinder identity on the crown of each piston (or on the inside of the skirt if the piston is dirty and going to be cleaned) as it must be installed in its original cylinder. Each piston should also have an arrow on its crown which should point to the exhaust (front) side of the bore (see illustration). If this is not visible, mark the piston accordingly so that it can be installed the correct way round.

3 Carefully prise out the circlip on one side of the piston using needle-nose pliers or a small flat-bladed screwdriver inserted into the notch (see illustration). Push the piston pin out from the other side to free the piston from the connecting rod (see illustration). Remove the

2

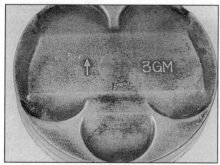

15.2 Note the arrow on the piston which must point forwards

15.3a Prise out the circlip . . .

15.3b . . . then push out the pin and remove the piston

15.5 Removing the piston rings using a ring removal and installation tool

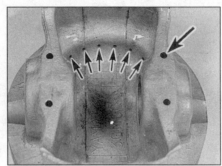

15.8 Make sure the oil return holes (arrowed) are clear

15.11 Measure the piston ring-to-groove clearance with a feeler gauge

other circlip and discard them as new ones must be used. When the piston has been removed, install its pin back into its bore so that related parts do not get mixed up. Rotate the crankshaft so that the best access is obtained for each piston.

HAYNES HiNT *To prevent the circlip from pinging away, pass a rod or screwdriver, whose diameter is greater than the gap between the circlip ends, through the piston pin. This will trap the circlip if it springs out.*

HAYNES HiNT *If a piston pin is a tight fit in the piston bosses, soak a rag in boiling water then wring it out and wrap it around the piston – this will expand the alloy piston sufficiently to release its grip on the pin. If the piston pin is particularly stubborn, extract it using a drawbolt tool, but be careful to protect the piston's working surfaces.*

Inspection

4 Before the inspection process can be carried out, the pistons must be cleaned and the old piston rings removed.

5 Using your thumbs or a piston ring removal and installation tool, carefully remove the rings from the pistons **(see illustration)**. Do not nick or gouge the pistons in the process.

Carefully note which way up each ring fits and in which groove as they must be installed in their original positions if being re-used. The upper surface of each ring should have a manufacturer's mark or letter at one end.

6 Scrape all traces of carbon from the tops of the pistons. A hand-held wire brush or a piece of fine emery cloth can be used once most of the deposits have been scraped away. Do not, under any circumstances, use a wire brush mounted in a drill motor to remove deposits from the pistons; the piston material is soft and will be eroded away by the wire brush.

7 Use a piston ring groove cleaning tool to remove any carbon deposits from the ring grooves. If a tool is not available, a piece broken off an old ring will do the job. Be very careful to remove only the carbon deposits. Do not remove any metal and do not nick or gouge the sides of the ring grooves.

8 Once the deposits have been removed, clean the pistons with solvent and dry them thoroughly. If the identification previously marked on the piston is cleaned off, be sure to re-mark it with the correct identity. Make sure the oil return holes below the oil ring groove are clear **(see illustration)**.

9 Carefully inspect each piston for cracks around the skirt, at the pin bosses and at the ring lands. Normal piston wear appears as even, vertical wear on the thrust surfaces of the piston and slight looseness of the top ring in its groove. If the skirt is scored or scuffed, the engine may have been suffering from overheating and/or abnormal combustion,

resulting in excessively high operating temperatures. The oil pump should be checked thoroughly. Also check that the circlip grooves are not damaged.

10 A hole in the piston crown, an extreme to be sure, is an indication that abnormal combustion (pre-ignition) was occurring. Burned areas at the edge of the piston crown are usually evidence of spark knock (detonation). If any of the above problems exist, the causes must be corrected or the damage will occur again.

11 Measure the piston ring-to-groove clearance by laying each piston ring in its groove and slipping a feeler gauge in beside it **(see illustration)**. Make sure you have the correct ring for the groove (see Step 5). Check the clearance at three or four locations around the groove. If the clearance is greater than specified, renew both the piston and rings as a set. If new rings are being used, measure the clearance using the new rings. If the clearance is greater than that specified, the piston is worn and must be renewed.

12 Check the piston-to-bore clearance by measuring the bore (see Section 14) and the piston diameter. Make sure each piston is matched to its correct cylinder. Measure the piston 3.5 mm (YZF750R and SP) or 3.0 mm (YZF1000R) up from the bottom of the skirt and at 90° to the piston pin axis **(see illustration)**. Subtract the piston diameter from the bore diameter to obtain the clearance. If it is greater than the specified figure, the piston must be renewed (assuming the bore itself is within limits, otherwise the cylinder block must be rebored).

13 Apply clean engine oil to the piston pin, insert it into the piston and check for any freeplay between the two **(see illustration)**. Measure the pin external diameter, and the pin bore in the piston **(see illustrations)**. Calculate the difference to obtain the piston pin-to-piston pin bore clearance. Compare the result to the specifications at the beginning of the Chapter. If the clearance is greater than specified, renew the components that are worn beyond their specified limits. Repeat the checks between the pin and the connecting rod small end (see Section 27).

14 Remove the two small-end oil jets – they are a push-fit **(see illustration)**. Discard their

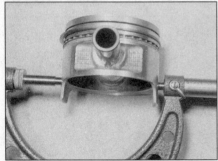

15.12 Measure the piston diameter with a micrometer at the specified distance from the bottom of the skirt

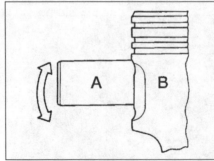

15.13a Slip the pin (A) into the piston (B) and try to rock it back and forth. If it's loose, renew the piston and pin

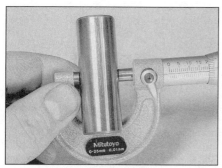

15.13b Measure the external diameter of the pin . . .

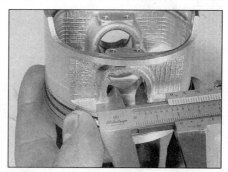

15.13c . . . and the internal diameter of the bore in the piston

15.14 Pull the two oil jets out of the crankcase (arrowed)

O-rings as new ones must be used. Clean the jets in solvent and blow them through, using compressed air if available, to ensure they are not blocked. Fit a new O-ring onto each jet and press them back into the crankcase.

Installation

15 Inspect and install the piston rings (see Section 16).
16 Lubricate the piston pin, the piston pin bore and the connecting rod small-end bore with clean engine oil.
17 Install a new circlip in the inner side of the piston (do not re-use old circlips). Line up the piston on its correct connecting rod, making sure the arrow on the piston crown points forwards (see illustration 15.2), and insert the piston pin from the other side (see illustration 15.3b). Secure the pin with the other new circlip (see illustration). When installing the circlips, compress them only just enough to fit them in the piston, and make sure they are properly seated in their grooves with the open end away from the removal notch.
18 Install the cylinder block (see Section 14).

16 Piston rings –
inspection and installation

1 It is good practice to renew the piston rings when an engine is being overhauled. Before installing the new piston rings, the ring end gaps must be checked with the rings installed in the cylinder.

2 Lay out the pistons and the new ring sets so the rings will be matched with the same piston and cylinder during the end gap measurement procedure and engine assembly.
3 To measure the ring end gap, insert the top ring into the top of the first cylinder and square it up with the cylinder walls by pushing it in with the top of the piston. The ring should be about 20 mm below the top edge of the cylinder. Slip a feeler gauge between the ends of the ring and compare the measurement to the specifications at the beginning of the Chapter (see illustration).
4 If the gap is larger or smaller than specified, double check to make sure that you have the correct rings before proceeding.
5 If the gap is too small, it must be enlarged or the ring ends may come in contact with each other during engine operation, which can cause serious damage. The end gap can be increased by filing the ring ends very carefully with a fine file. When performing this operation, file only from the outside in (see illustration).
6 Excess end gap is not critical unless it exceeds the service limit. Again, double-check to make sure you have the correct rings for your engine and check that the bore is not worn.
7 Repeat the procedure for each ring that will be installed in the cylinders. When checking the oil ring, only the side-rails can be checked as the ends of the expander ring should contact each other. Remember to keep the rings, pistons and cylinders matched up.

15.17 Do not over-compress the circlips and make sure they seat in the groove (arrowed)

8 Once the ring end gaps have been checked/corrected, the rings can be installed on the pistons.
9 The oil control ring (lowest on the piston) is installed first. It is composed of three separate components, namely the expander and the upper and lower side rails. Slip the expander into the groove, then install the upper side rail (see illustration). Do not use a piston ring installation tool on the oil ring side rails as they may be damaged. Instead, place one end of the side rail into the groove between the expander and the ring land (see illustration). Hold it firmly in place and slide a finger around the piston while pushing the rail into the groove. Next, install the lower side rail in the same manner. Make sure the ends of the expander do not overlap.
10 After the three oil ring components have been installed, check to make sure that both

2

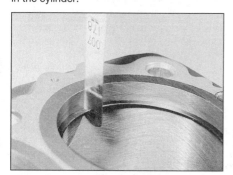

16.3 Measuring piston ring end gap

16.5 Ring end gap can be enlarged by clamping a file in a vice and filing the ring ends

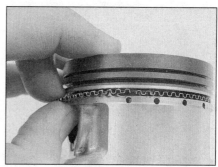

16.9a Install the oil ring expander in its groove . . .

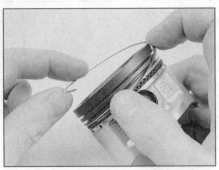

16.9b ... and fit the side rails each side of it. The oil ring must be installed by hand

the upper and lower side rails can be turned smoothly in the ring groove.

11 The upper surface of each compression ring should have a mark or letter at one end which must face up when the ring is installed on the piston.

12 Fit the second ring into the middle groove in the piston. Do not expand the ring any more than is necessary to slide it into place. To avoid breaking the ring, use a piston ring installation tool **(see illustration 15.5)**, or pieces of old feeler gauge blades **(see illustration)**.

13 Finally, install the top ring in the same manner into the top groove in the piston.

14 Once the rings are correctly installed, check they move freely without snagging and stagger their end gaps as shown **(see illustration)**.

17 Clutch –
removal, inspection and installation

Note: *The clutch can be removed with the engine in the frame. If the engine has been removed, ignore the steps which don't apply.*

Removal

1 Remove the lower fairing and the right-hand fairing side panel (see Chapter 8). Drain the engine oil (see Chapter 1).

2 On YZF1000R models, release the idle speed adjuster from its holder.

3 Working evenly in a criss-cross pattern, unscrew the clutch cover bolts, on YZF1000R

17.3 Unscrew the bolts (arrowed) and remove the cover

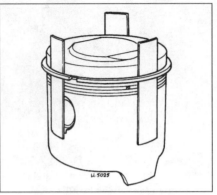

16.12 Old pieces of feeler gauge blade can be used to guide the ring over the piston

models noting the position of the idle speed adjuster bracket **(see illustration)**. Lift the cover away from the engine, being prepared to catch any residual oil which may be released as the cover is removed.

4 Remove the gasket and discard it. Note the

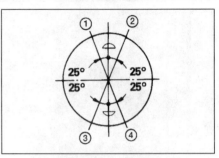

16.14 Stagger the ring end gaps as shown

1   *Top ring*
2   *Lower oil ring side rail*
3   *Upper oil ring side rail*
4   *Second ring*

positions of the two locating dowels fitted to the crankcase and remove them for safe-keeping if they are loose.

5 Working in a criss-cross pattern, gradually slacken the clutch spring bolts until spring pressure is released **(see illustrations)**.

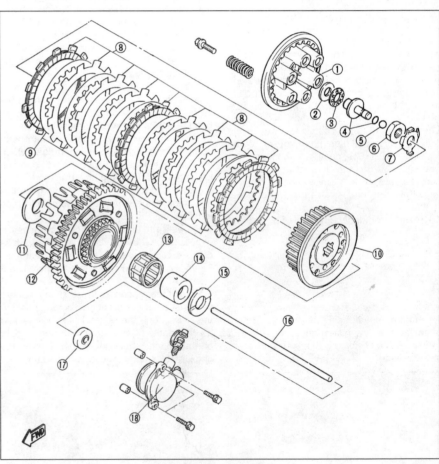

17.5a Clutch components

1	Pressure plate	7	Lockwasher	13 Needle bearing
2	Thrust washer	8	Friction plates	14 Sleeve
3	Bearing	9	Plain plates	15 Inner thrust plate
4	Pushrod end-piece	10	Clutch centre	16 Pushrod
5	Ball bearing	11	Outer thrust plate	17 Oil seal
6	Clutch nut	12	Clutch housing	18 Release cylinder

17.5b Unscrew the clutch pressure plate bolts as described

17.5c The pushrod can be withdrawn from the left

17.6 Draw off the clutch plates as a pack

17.7a Bend back the lockwasher tabs . . .

17.7b . . . then unscrew the clutch nut as described . . .

17.7c . . . and remove the lockwasher

Counter-hold the clutch housing to prevent it turning. Remove the bolts and springs, then remove the clutch pressure plate. Remove the pushrod end-piece from either the pressure plate or the shaft, noting the thrust washer and bearing **(see illustrations 17.27c and b)**. Discard the O-ring on the end-piece as a new one must be used. If required also remove the ball bearing and pushrod from inside the shaft – you may need a magnet or magnetised

screwdriver to draw them out **(see illustration 17.27a)**. Otherwise, remove the front sprocket cover (see Chapter 6), then push the rod into the engine from the left-hand side until the ball bearing comes out of the right-hand end of the shaft, then withdraw the pushrod from the left-hand side **(see illustration)**.
6 Grasp the complete set of clutch plates and remove them as a pack **(see illustration)**.

Unless the plates are being replaced with new ones, keep them in their original order. On YZF1000R models, note the notch in the outer friction plate – it is supposed to be there.
7 Bend back the tabs on the clutch nut lockwasher **(see illustration)**. To remove the clutch nut the transmission input shaft must be locked. This can be done in several ways. If the engine is in the frame, engage 1st gear and have an assistant hold the rear brake on hard with the rear tyre in firm contact with the ground. Alternatively, the Yamaha service tool (Pt. No. 90890-04086), or a similar commercially available or home-made tool **(see Tool tip)**, can be used to stop the clutch centre from turning whilst the nut is slackened. Unscrew the nut and remove the lockwasher from the input shaft, noting how it fits **(see illustrations)**. Discard the lockwasher, as a new one must be used on installation.
8 Remove the clutch centre and the outer thrust plate from the shaft **(see illustrations)**.

2

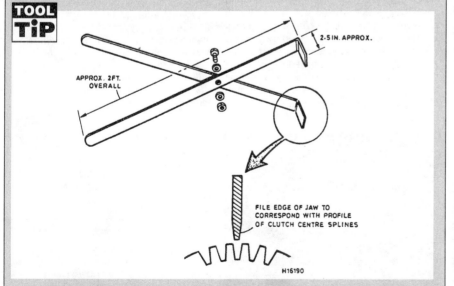

TOOL TiP

2.5 IN. APPROX.

APPROX. 2FT. OVERALL

FILE EDGE OF JAW TO CORRESPOND WITH PROFILE OF CLUTCH CENTRE SPLINES

H16190

A clutch centre holding tool can easily be made using two strips of steel with the ends bent over, and bolted together in the middle

17.8a Slide the clutch centre (arrowed) off the shaft . . .

17.8b . . . and remove the outer thrust plate

17.9 Remove the inner sleeve and bearing as described . . .

17.10 . . . then remove the clutch housing . . .

9 Support the clutch housing and withdraw the large sleeve from its centre. To get a grip on the sleeve, grasp the housing and wiggle it out and in – it should draw the sleeve out far enough to grip it. If difficulty is experienced in getting a grip on the sleeve, install a suitable bolt into one or both of the threaded holes and pull the sleeve from the housing **(see illustration)**.

10 Withdraw the caged needle roller bearing from the housing if it didn't come away with the sleeve, and then remove the housing from the engine, noting how it engages with the primary drive gear and the oil pump driven gear **(see illustration)**.

11 Remove the inner thrust plate from the shaft **(see illustration)**.

Inspection

12 After an extended period of service the clutch friction plates will wear and promote

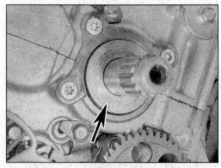

17.11 . . . and the inner thrust plate (arrowed)

clutch slip. Measure the thickness of each friction plate using a vernier caliper **(see illustration)**. If any plate has worn to or beyond the service limit given in the Specifications at the beginning of the Chapter, the friction plates must be renewed as a set. Also, if any of the plates smell burnt or are glazed, they must be renewed as a set.

13 The plain plates should not show any signs of excess heating (bluing). Check for warpage using a flat surface and feeler gauges **(see illustration)**. If any plate exceeds the maximum permissible amount of warpage, or shows signs of bluing, all plain plates must be renewed as a set.

14 Measure the free length of each clutch spring using a vernier caliper **(see illustration)**. If any spring is below the service limit specified, renew all the springs as a set.

15 Inspect the clutch assembly for burrs and indentations on the edges of the protruding tangs of the friction plates and/or slots in the edge of the housing with which they engage. Similarly check for wear between the inner tongues of the plain plates and the slots in the clutch centre. Wear of this nature will cause clutch drag and slow disengagement during gear changes as the plates will snag when the pressure plate is lifted. With care a small amount of wear can be corrected by dressing with a fine file, but if this is excessive the worn components should be renewed.

16 Inspect the sleeve and caged needle roller bearing in conjunction with the clutch housing's internal bearing surface. If there are

any signs of wear, pitting or other damage the affected parts must be renewed.

17 Check the pressure plate and its bearing for signs of wear or damage and roughness. Check the pushrod end piece and ball bearing for signs of roughness, wear or damage. Replace any parts as necessary with new ones.

18 The clutch release mechanism, housed in the front sprocket cover, should be also be checked (see Section 18).

19 Check that the pushrod is straight by rolling it on a flat surface – if it is bent by more than the runout limit specified, replace it with a new one. Check the pushrod oil seal for signs of leakage and replace it with a new one if necessary. To replace it, first remove the front sprocket cover (if not already done – see Chapter 6). Lever out the old seal using a screwdriver. Apply grease to the lips of the new seal, then drive it squarely into place. Install the front sprocket cover (see Chapter 6).

Installation

20 Remove all traces of old gasket from the crankcase and clutch cover surfaces.

21 Slide the inner thrust plate onto the shaft **(see illustration 17.11)**.

22 Lubricate the needle roller bearing and sleeve with clean engine oil. Install the clutch housing, without its needle roller bearing and sleeve, and support it in position, making sure it is engaged correctly with the primary drive gear on the crankshaft **(see illustration 17.10)**.

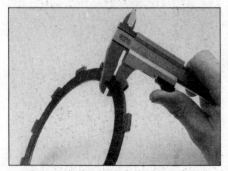

17.12 Measuring clutch friction plate thickness

17.13 Check the plain plates for warpage

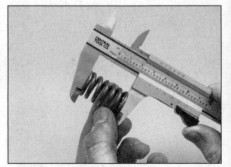

17.14 Measure the free length of the springs as shown

17.23a Fit the sleeve . . .

17.23b . . . and the needle bearing into the middle of the housing

17.25a Install the lockwasher, fitting the smaller bent tabs into the slots in the centre (arrowed)

17.25b Fit the nut and tighten it to the specified torque, then bend up the washer tabs

17.26a Fit a friction plate first then a plain plate and so on

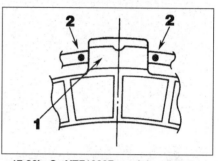

17.26b On YZF1000R models, align the notched tab (1) with the marked tangs (2) as shown

23 Install the sleeve, with its bolt holes facing out, and the needle bearing into the middle of the clutch housing (see illustrations).

24 Lubricate the outer thrust plate with clean engine oil and fit it onto the shaft (see illustration 17.8b).

25 Install the clutch centre onto the shaft splines (see illustration 17.8a), then install the new lockwasher, engaging its tabs with the slots (see illustration). Install the clutch nut and, using the method employed on removal to lock the input shaft (see Step 7), tighten the nut to the torque setting specified at the beginning of the Chapter (see illustration 17.7b). Note: Check that the clutch centre rotates freely after tightening. Bend up the tabs of the lockwasher to secure the nut (see illustration).

26 Coat each clutch plate with engine oil prior to installation. Build up the plates as follows: first fit a friction plate, then a plain plate, then alternate friction and plain plates until all are installed, making sure the outer-most friction plate is the one with a notch in one of its tabs, aligning that tab between the marked tangs on the clutch housing (see illustrations).

27 Fit a new O-ring onto the pushrod end-piece. Lubricate the thrust bearing and washer, the pushrod end-piece, O-ring, ball bearing and pushrod with a lightweight lithium soap based grease. Slide the pushrod into the shaft so that its rounded end faces the left-hand side – if the sprocket cover has been removed it can be inserted from the left-hand side (see illustration 17.5c). Fit the ball bearing and the end-piece (see illustrations).

Slide the bearing and thrust washer onto the end-piece (see illustration).

28 Install the pressure plate onto the clutch, aligning the dot on the plate with the one on the clutch centre (see illustration). Install the

springs and the bolts and tighten them evenly in a criss-cross sequence to the specified torque setting (see illustration 17.5b). Counter-hold the clutch housing to prevent it turning when tightening the spring bolts.

17.27a Insert the ball bearing . . .

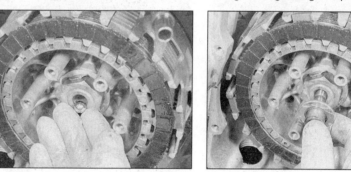

17.27b . . . and the end-piece . . .

17.27c . . . then fit the bearing and thrust washer

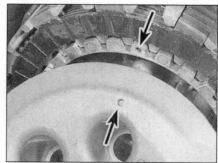

17.28 Install the pressure plate, aligning the dots (arrowed)

2

17.29 Fit the cover using a new gasket, locating it onto the dowels

29 Insert the dowels in the crankcase, then install the clutch cover using a new gasket and tighten its bolts evenly in a criss-cross sequence to the specified torque setting **(see illustration)**.
30 Refill the engine with oil (see Chapter 1).
31 Install the lower fairing and the fairing side panel (see Chapter 8).

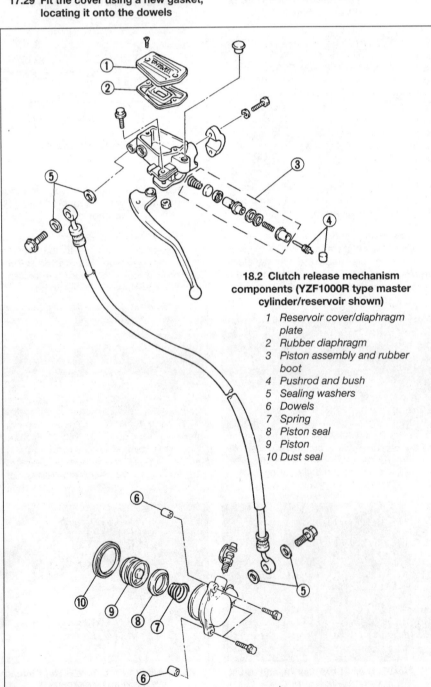

18.2 Clutch release mechanism components (YZF1000R type master cylinder/reservoir shown)

1 Reservoir cover/diaphragm plate
2 Rubber diaphragm
3 Piston assembly and rubber boot
4 Pushrod and bush
5 Sealing washers
6 Dowels
7 Spring
8 Piston seal
9 Piston
10 Dust seal

18 Clutch release mechanism – removal, overhaul and installation

Master cylinder

1 If the master cylinder is leaking fluid, or if the clutch does not work properly when the lever is applied, and bleeding the system does not help (see Section 19), and the hydraulic hoses are all in good condition, then master cylinder overhaul is recommended.
2 Before disassembling the master cylinder, read through the entire procedure and make sure that you have the correct rebuild kit **(see illustration)**. Also, you will need some new DOT 4 hydraulic brake and clutch fluid, some clean rags and internal circlip pliers. **Note:** *To prevent damage to the paint from spilled brake fluid, always cover the fuel tank and fairing when working on the master cylinder.*
Caution: Disassembly, overhaul and reassembly of the master cylinder must be done in a spotlessly clean work area to avoid contamination and possible failure of the hydraulic system components.

Removal

3 On YZF750R and SP models, remove the reservoir cap clamp and partially unscrew the cap **(see illustration)**. On YZF1000R models, loosen, but do not remove, the screws holding the reservoir cover in place **(see illustration)**.

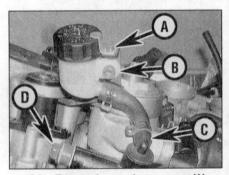

18.3a Reservoir cap clamp screw (A), mounting bolt (B), and hose union (C), and clutch hose banjo bolt (D) – YZF750R and SP models

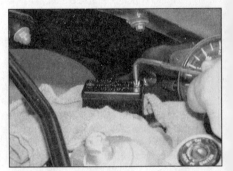

18.3b Slacken the reservoir cover screws

18.4 Disconnect the clutch switch wiring connector (arrowed) – YZF1000R model shown

18.5 Clutch hose banjo bolt (arrowed) – YZF1000R models

18.7 Master cylinder clamp bolts (arrowed)

4 Disconnect the clutch switch wiring connector **(see illustration)**. Remove the clutch lever (see Chapter 6). Take care not to lose the pushrod bush from its socket in the lever.

5 Unscrew the clutch hose banjo bolt and separate the hose from the master cylinder, noting the alignment **(see illustration)**. Discard the sealing washers as they must be replaced with new ones. Wrap the end of the hose in a clean rag and suspend it in an upright position or bend down carefully and place the open end in a clean container. The objective is to prevent excessive loss of brake fluid, fluid spills and system contamination.

6 On YZF750R and SP models, unscrew the bolt securing the reservoir to the bracket, then release the clamp securing the reservoir hose to the union on the master cylinder **(see illustration 18.3a)**. Remove the reservoir cap and lift off the diaphragm plate and the rubber

18.10 Draw the pushrod and the rubber boot out of the cylinder

diaphragm. Drain the brake fluid from the reservoir into a suitable container, then detach the reservoir hose from its union on the master cylinder. Wipe any remaining fluid out of the reservoir with a clean rag.

7 Unscrew the master cylinder clamp bolts, noting how the 'UP' mark faces up and the top mating surfaces of the clamp align with the punchmark on the handlebar, then lift the master cylinder away from the handlebar **(see illustration)**.

8 On YZF1000R models, remove the reservoir cover retaining screws and lift off the cover, the diaphragm plate and the rubber diaphragm. Drain the brake fluid from the reservoir into a suitable container. Wipe any remaining fluid out of the reservoir with a clean rag.

9 If required, remove the clutch switch (see Chapter 9).

Caution: Do not tip the master cylinder upside down or fluid will run out.

Overhaul

10 Draw the pushrod out of the master cylinder, noting how it locates in the rubber boot – the boot may come away with the pushrod **(see illustration)**.

11 If it didn't come with the pushrod, remove the rubber boot from the end of the piston in the cylinder.

12 Using circlip pliers, remove the circlip, then slide out the piston assembly and the spring, noting how they fit **(see illustrations)**. Lay the parts out in the proper order and the right way round to prevent confusion during reassembly.

13 On YZF750R and SP models, remove the

fluid reservoir hose union rubber cap, then remove the circlip and detach the union from the master cylinder. Discard the O-ring as a new one must be used. Inspect the reservoir hose for cracks or splits and renew if necessary.

14 Clean all parts with clean brake fluid. If compressed air is available, use it to dry the parts thoroughly (make sure it's filtered and unlubricated).

Caution: Do not, under any circumstances, use a petroleum-based solvent to clean brake parts.

15 Check the master cylinder bore for corrosion, scratches, nicks and score marks. If damage or wear is evident, the master cylinder must be replaced with a new one. If the master cylinder is in poor condition, then the release cylinder should be checked as well. Check that the fluid inlet and outlet ports in the master cylinder are clear.

16 The dust boot, circlip, piston assembly and spring are included in the rebuild kit. Use all of the new parts, regardless of the apparent condition of the old ones. If the seal and cup are not already on the piston, fit them according to the layout of the old piston assembly. Also fit the washer onto the outer end of the piston.

17 Fit the spring into the master cylinder so that its narrow end faces out.

18 Lubricate the piston assembly with clean brake fluid. Fit the assembly into the master cylinder, making sure it is the correct way round **(see illustration 18.12b)**. Make sure the lips on the cup do not turn inside out when they are slipped into the bore. Depress the piston and install the new circlip, making sure that it locates in the groove **(see illustration)**.

2

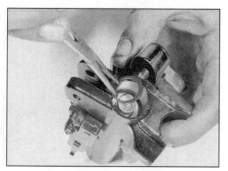

18.12a Remove the circlip . . .

18.12b . . . and draw out the piston assembly and spring

18.18 Make sure the circlip locates correctly into its groove

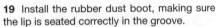

18.29 Make sure the diaphragm is correctly seated before installing the plate and cover or cap

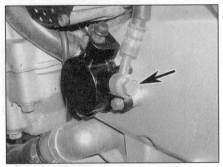

18.32 Clutch hose banjo bolt (arrowed)

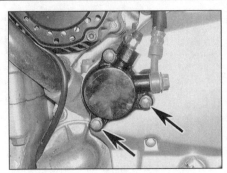

18.33a Unscrew the bolts (arrowed) . . .

19 Install the rubber dust boot, making sure the lip is seated correctly in the groove.

20 Fit the pushrod into the end of the master cylinder, making sure the rubber boot locates in the groove **(see illustration 18.10)**. If removed, fit the pushrod bush into the socket in the clutch lever, then install the lever, making sure the pushrod end locates into the hole in the bush (see Chapter 6, Section 5).

21 On YZF750R and SP models, fit a new O-ring onto the reservoir hose union, then press the union into the master cylinder and secure it with the circlip. Fit the rubber cap over the circlip.

22 Inspect the reservoir cover rubber diaphragm and renew if damaged or deteriorated.

Installation

23 If removed, install the clutch switch (see Chapter 9).

24 Attach the master cylinder to the handlebar and fit the clamp with its 'UP' mark facing up, aligning the top mating surfaces of the clamp with the punchmark on the handlebar **(see illustration 18.7)**. Tighten the upper bolt first, then the lower bolt to the torque setting specified at the beginning of the Chapter.

25 Connect the clutch hose to the master cylinder, using new sealing washers on each side of the union, and aligning the hose as noted on removal **(see illustration 18.5 or 18.3a)**. Tighten the banjo bolt to the torque setting specified at the beginning of this Chapter.

26 On YZF750R and SP models, mount the reservoir and tighten the bolt securely **(see illustration 18.3a)**. Connect the reservoir hose to the union and secure it with the clamp.

27 Connect the clutch switch wiring **(see illustration 18.4)**.

28 Fill the fluid reservoir with new DOT 4 clutch fluid as described in *Daily (pre-ride) checks*. Refer to Section 19 of this Chapter and bleed the air from the system.

29 Fit the rubber diaphragm, making sure it is correctly seated, the diaphragm plate and the cover or cap onto the master cylinder reservoir **(see illustration)**. On YZF750R and SP models, fit the cap clamp **(see illustration 18.3a)**.

30 Check the operation of the front brake before riding the motorcycle.

Release cylinder

Removal

31 If required for improved access, remove the lower fairing (see Chapter 8).

32 If the release cylinder is just being displaced and not completely removed or overhauled, do not disconnect the clutch hose. Otherwise, unscrew the clutch hose banjo bolt and separate the hose from the release cylinder, noting its alignment **(see illustration)**. Plug the hose end or wrap a plastic bag around it to minimise fluid loss and prevent dirt entering the system. Discard the sealing washers as new ones must be used on installation. **Note:** *If you're planning to overhaul the release cylinder and don't have a source of compressed air to blow out the piston, just loosen the banjo bolt at this stage and retighten it lightly. The hydraulic system can then be used to force the piston out of the body once the cylinder has been*

unbolted. Disconnect the hose once the piston has been sufficiently displaced.

33 Unscrew the three bolts securing the release cylinder to the sprocket cover and remove the cylinder **(see illustrations)**. Retrieve the two dowels if they are loose. If required, withdraw the pushrod. Do not operate the clutch lever with the release cylinder removed.

> **HAYNES HINT** *If the release cylinder is not being disassembled, the piston can be prevented from creeping out of the release cylinder by restraining it with a couple of cable ties passed through the mounting bolt holes.*

Overhaul

34 Remove the dust seal from the cylinder, noting how it fits **(see illustration)**.

35 Have a supply of clean rags on hand, then pump the clutch lever to expel the piston under hydraulic pressure. If the hose has already been detached, use a jet of compressed air directed into the fluid inlet to expel the piston.

> ⚠️ *Warning: Use only low air pressure, otherwise the piston may be forcibly expelled causing injury. Wrap the cylinder in a rag before applying the air.*

36 Remove the spring from the piston **(see illustration 18.41)**.

37 Using a plastic or wooden tool, remove the piston seal from the piston groove **(see**

18.33b . . . and withdraw the release cylinder

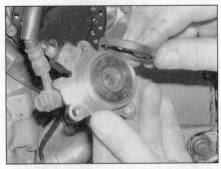

18.34 Remove the dust seal, noting how it fits

18.37 Remove the seal from the piston using a non-metallic tool

illustration). Discard both seals as new ones must be used.

38 Clean the piston and release cylinder bore with clean hydraulic fluid.

Caution: Do not, under any circumstances, use a petroleum-based solvent to clean hydraulic parts.

39 Inspect the piston and release cylinder bore for signs of corrosion, nicks and burrs and loss of plating. If surface defects are found, the piston and cylinder should be replaced with new ones. If the release cylinder is in poor condition the master cylinder should also be overhauled (see above).

40 Refer to Section 17, Step 19, and check the clutch pushrod and its oil seal.

41 Lubricate the new piston seal with clean hydraulic fluid and fit it into the groove in the piston. Fit the narrow end of the spring over the lug on the inner end of the piston **(see illustration)**. Lubricate the piston and seal with clean hydraulic fluid and insert the assembly into the cylinder. Use your thumbs to press it fully into the cylinder.

Installation

42 If removed, lubricate the pushrod with a lightweight lithium soap based grease. Slide the pushrod into the engine so that its rounded end faces the left-hand side **(see illustration 17.5c)**.

43 Fit the dowels into the sprocket cover if removed, then install the release cylinder and tighten the bolts to the torque setting specified at the beginning of the Chapter **(see illustrations 18.33b and a)**.

44 If the hydraulic hose was disconnected, use a new sealing washer on each side of the banjo union. Position the union as noted on removal and tighten the banjo bolt to the specified torque setting **(see illustration 18.32)**.

45 Remove the master cylinder reservoir cap or cover and remove the diaphragm plate and diaphragm (see above). Fill the reservoir with new hydraulic fluid (see *Daily (pre-ride) checks*) and bleed the system as described in section 19. Check for fluid leaks.

19 Clutch – bleeding

1 Bleeding the clutch is simply the process of removing all the air bubbles from the master cylinder, the hydraulic hose and the release cylinder. Bleeding is necessary whenever a clutch system hydraulic connection is loosened, when a component or hose is renewed, or when the master cylinder or release cylinder is overhauled. Leaks in the system may also allow air to enter, but leaking clutch fluid will reveal their presence and warn you of the need for repair.

2 To bleed the clutch, you will need some new DOT 4 brake and clutch fluid, a length of clear vinyl or plastic tubing, a small container

18.41 Fit the narrow end of the spring over the lug on the piston

partially filled with clean fluid, a supply of clean rags and a spanner to fit the bleed valve.

3 Cover the fuel tank and other painted components to prevent damage in the event that fluid is spilled.

4 Position the bike so that the master cylinder is level. Remove the master cylinder reservoir cap or cover, then remove the diaphragm plate and diaphragm (see Section 18). Slowly pump the clutch lever a few times until no air bubbles can be seen floating up from the bottom of the reservoir. Doing this bleeds air from the master cylinder end of the hose.

Caution: Do not pump the lever too quickly as fluid could spurt out of the reservoir and onto a painted component.

5 Pull the dust cap off the bleed valve on the release cylinder and attach one end of the clear tubing to the valve **(see illustration)**. Submerge the other end in the fluid in the container. Check the fluid level in the reservoir. Do not allow it to drop below the lower mark during the bleeding process.

6 Pump the clutch lever slowly three or four times and hold it in against the handlebar whilst opening the bleed valve. When the valve is opened, fluid will flow out of the release cylinder into the clear tubing.

7 Tighten the bleed valve, then release the lever gradually. Repeat the process until no air bubbles are visible in the fluid leaving the release cylinder, and the clutch action feels smooth and progressive. On completion, tighten the bleed valve to the torque setting specified at the beginning of the Chapter.

8 Ensure that the reservoir is topped up above the lower level mark, install the diaphragm,

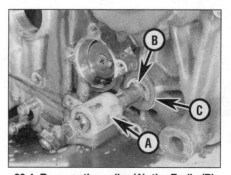
20.4 Remove the collar (A), the E-clip (B) and the washer (C)

19.5 Clutch release system bleed valve (arrowed)

diaphragm plate and cap or cover. Wipe up any spilled fluid and check that there are no leaks from the system when activated. Refit the dust cap over the bleed valve.

20 Gearchange mechanism – removal, inspection and installation

Note: The gearchange mechanism can be removed with the engine in the frame. If the engine has been removed, ignore the steps which don't apply.

Removal

1 Make sure the transmission is in neutral. Remove the lower fairing and the fairing side panels (see Chapter 8).

2 Remove the front sprocket cover (see Chapter 6). There is no need to detach the clutch release cylinder from the cover (see Section 18).

3 Remove the clutch (see Section 17), and if the stopper arm and selector drum are being removed, also remove the oil pump (see Section 21).

4 Slide the collar off the left-hand end of the gearchange shaft, then remove the E-clip and the washer **(see illustration)**.

5 Note how the gearchange shaft centralising spring ends fit on each side of the locating pin in the casing, and how the pawls on the selector arm locate onto the pins on the end of the selector drum **(see illustration 20.11)**. Grasp the end of the shaft and withdraw the shaft/arm assembly **(see illustration)**.

2

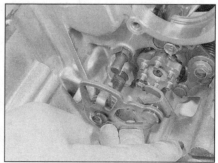
20.5 Withdraw the shaft from the engine

20.6 Unscrew the stopper arm bolt and the retainer plate bolt (arrowed) and remove the arm, plate and spring

20.10a Fit the return spring as shown . . .

20.10b . . . then install the retainer plate . . .

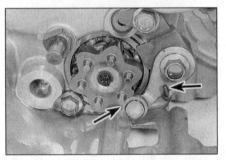

20.10c . . . and the stopper arm, locating the roller and spring end as shown (arrowed)

20.11 The installed assembly should be as shown

6 If required, note how the stopper arm spring ends locate and how the roller on the arm locates in the neutral detent on the selector drum, then unscrew the stopper arm bolt and the retainer plate bolt and remove the arm, the plate and the spring, noting how they locate **(see illustration)**.

Inspection

7 Check the selector arm for cracks, distortion and wear of its pawls, and check for any corresponding wear on the selector pins on the selector drum. Also check the stopper arm roller and the detents in the selector drum for any wear or damage, and make sure the roller turns freely. Replace any components that are worn or damaged with new ones.
8 Inspect the shaft centralising spring and the stopper arm return spring for fatigue, wear or damage. If any faults are found, renew the components. Also check that the centralising

spring locating pin in the crankcase is securely tightened. If it is loose, remove it and apply a non-permanent thread locking compound to its threads, then tighten it securely.
9 Check the gearchange shaft for straightness and damage to the splines. If the shaft is bent you can attempt to straighten it, but if the splines are damaged the shaft must be renewed. Also check the condition of the shaft oil seal in the left-hand side of the crankcase. If it is damaged, deteriorated or shows signs of leakage it must be replaced with a new one. Lever out the old seal and drive the new one squarely into place, with its lip facing inward, using a seal driver or suitable socket.

Installation

10 If removed, apply a suitable non-permanent thread locking compound to the stopper arm and retainer plate bolts. Locate

the stopper arm spring, then install the plate and the stopper arm, locating the arm onto the neutral detent on the selector drum and making sure the spring ends are positioned correctly **(see illustrations)**. Tighten the bolts to the torque setting specified at the beginning of the Chapter.
11 Apply some grease to the lips of the gearchange shaft oil seal in the left-hand side of the crankcase. Slide the shaft into place and push it all the way through the case until the splined end comes out the other side **(see illustration 20.5)**. Locate the selector arm pawls onto the pins on the selector drum and the centralising spring ends onto each side of the locating pin **(see illustration)**.
12 Slide the washer onto the left-hand end of the shaft, then fit the E-clip, making sure it locates in its groove **(see illustration 20.4)**. Slide the collar onto the shaft.
13 Install the oil pump if removed (see Section 21), and the clutch (see Section 17).
14 Install the front sprocket cover (see Chapter 6), and if removed the clutch release cylinder (see Section 18).

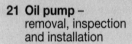

21 Oil pump –
removal, inspection and installation

Note: *The oil pump can be removed with the engine in the frame. If the engine has been removed, ignore the steps which don't apply.*

Removal

1 Drain the engine oil (see Chapter 1).
2 Remove the clutch (see Section 17).
3 Turn the oil pump driven gear to align the holes in the gear with the pump mounting bolts **(see illustration)**.
4 Unscrew the bolts and withdraw the pump from the engine, being prepared to catch any residual oil **(see illustration)**. Discard the gasket, as a new one must be used. Remove the dowel from either the pump housing or the crankcase if it is loose **(see illustration)**.

Inspection

5 If required, the pump can be disassembled for cleaning and inspection. Remove the single assembly screw, then draw the pump body, the outer rotor, and the inner rotor off

21.3 Oil pump bolts (arrowed) – align the holes in the gear with the bolts as shown

21.4a Withdraw the pump . . .

the drive shaft (see illustrations). Note which way round the rotors fit and how the drive pin in the shaft locates in the slots in the inner rotor. Remove the drive pin, then slide the washer and pump cover off the shaft (see illustration). Remove the locating pins from the cover for safekeeping if they are loose.

6 Clean all the components in solvent.

7 Inspect the pump body and rotors for scoring and wear (see illustration). If any damage, scoring or uneven or excessive wear is evident, replace the pump with a new one (individual components are not available).

8 Fit the outer rotor into the pump body, then fit the inner rotor into the outer rotor. Measure the clearance between the outer rotor and the pump body with a feeler gauge and compare it to the maximum clearance listed in the specifications at the beginning of the Chapter (see illustration). If the clearance measured is greater than the maximum listed, replace the pump with a new one.

9 Measure the clearance between the inner rotor tip and the outer rotor with a feeler gauge and compare it to the maximum clearance listed in the specifications at the beginning of the Chapter (see illustration 21.8). If the clearance measured is greater than the maximum listed, replace the pump with a new one.

10 Check the pump driven gear for wear or damage, and replace it with a new one if

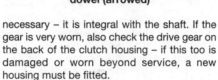

21.4b ... and remove the gasket and dowel (arrowed)

necessary – it is integral with the shaft. If the gear is very worn, also check the drive gear on the back of the clutch housing – if this too is damaged or worn beyond service, a new housing must be fitted.

11 If the pump is good, make sure all the components are clean, then lubricate them with new engine oil. Fit the locating pins into the cover if removed (see illustration 21.5c). Slide the pump cover followed by the washer onto the shaft, then fit the drive pin through the hole in the shaft (see illustrations 21.5c). Slide the inner rotor onto the shaft, with the slots in the rotor facing down so that they locate over the drive pin (see illustration 21.5b). Fit the outer rotor onto the

21.5a Remove the screw ...

inner rotor, then fit the pump body over the outer rotor (see illustration 21.5b). Install the assembly screw and tighten it to the torque setting specified at the beginning of the Chapter (see illustration 21.5a).

12 Rotate the pump shaft by hand and check that the rotors turn smoothly and freely. If not, replace the pump with a new one. Before installing the pump, prime it by filling it with clean engine oil.

Installation

13 If removed, fit the dowel into the pump body, then fit a new gasket onto the pump, making sure it locates over the dowel (see illustration). Align the tab on the end of the

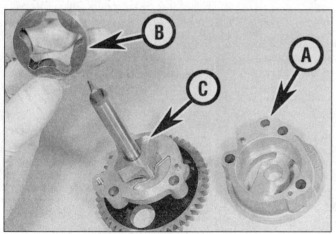

21.5b ... and draw the body (A), outer rotor (B) and inner rotor (C) off the shaft

21.5c Remove the drive pin (A), washer (B) and locating pins (C), then draw the cover off the shaft

21.7 Look for scoring and wear, such as on this outer rotor

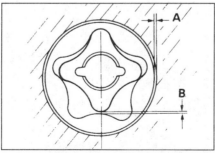

21.8 Measure outer rotor to body clearance (A) and inner rotor tip to outer rotor clearance (B)

21.13a Align the tab on the shaft (arrowed) with the slot in the water pump shaft

2

pump drive shaft so that it will locate into the slot in the water pump drive shaft, then install the pump, aligning the arrow on the pump body with that on the crankcase and making sure the dowel locates correctly **(see illustration)**. Wiggle the gear if necessary to locate the shaft end in the water pump. Turn the pump gear to align the holes in the gear with the pump mounting bolt holes **(see illustration 21.3)**. Apply a suitable non-permanent thread locking compound to the mounting bolts and tighten them to the torque setting specified at the beginning of the Chapter.

14 Install the clutch (see Section 17).

15 Fill the engine with the specified quantity and type of new engine oil (see Chapter 1).

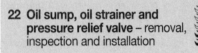

22 Oil sump, oil strainer and pressure relief valve – removal, inspection and installation

Note: *The oil sump, strainer and pressure relief valve can be removed with the engine in the frame. If the engine has been removed, ignore the steps which don't apply.*

Removal

1 Remove the exhaust system (see Chapter 4).

2 Drain the engine oil (see Chapter 1). Either remove the oil level sensor if required (see Chapter 9), or trace the wire from the switch and disconnect it at the single bullet connector – you may have to remove the front sprocket cover to access it (see Chapter 6).

21.13b Install the pump, aligning the arrows (arrowed), making sure the shaft end locates correctly in the water pump

3 Unscrew the sump bolts, slackening them evenly in a criss-cross sequence to prevent distortion, and remove the sump **(see illustration)**. Note the positions of the wiring clamp and fairing side panel brackets. Discard the gasket, as a new one must be used. Note the positions of the dowels and remove them if they are loose.

4 Unscrew the oil strainer bolts and remove the strainer.

5 Pull the pressure relief valve out of the crankcase **(see illustration)**. Discard the O-ring, as a new one must be used. If required, unscrew the bolts securing the oil pipes and pull out the pipes. Discard their O-rings.

Inspection

6 Remove all traces of gasket from the sump and crankcase mating surfaces, and clean the inside of the sump with solvent. Remove the baffle plate if required **(see illustration)**.

7 Clean the oil strainer and pipes in solvent and remove any debris caught in the strainer mesh. Inspect the strainer for any signs of wear or damage and replace it with a new one if necessary. Check that the oil pipes are clear by blowing them through with compressed air.

8 Push the relief valve plunger into the valve body and check that it moves smoothly and freely against the spring pressure. If not, remove the circlip, noting that it is under spring pressure, and remove the spring seat, spring and plunger **(see illustrations)**. Clean all the components in solvent and check them for scoring, wear or damage. If any is found, replace the relief valve with a new one – individual components are not available. Otherwise, coat the inside of the valve body and the plunger with clean engine oil, then insert the plunger, spring and spring seat and secure them with the circlip. Check the action of the valve plunger again – if it is still suspect, replace the valve with a new one.

Installation

9 Fit a new O-ring onto the relief valve and smear it with grease, then push the valve into its socket in the crankcase **(see illustration 22.5)**. Fit new O-rings onto the oil pipes and fit them into their sockets. Apply a suitable non-permanent thread locking compound to the pipe bolt threads and tighten them to the torque setting specified at the beginning of the Chapter.

10 Install the oil strainer housing, making sure the arrow points to the front of the engine. Apply a suitable non-permanent thread locking

22.3 Unscrew the sump bolts, noting the positions of the brackets and clamp

22.5 Pull the pressure relief valve out of its socket

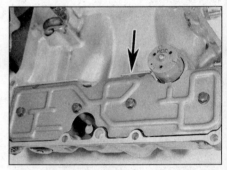

22.6 Remove the baffle plate (arrowed) if required

22.8a Remove the circlip and the spring seat . . .

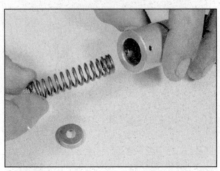

22.8b . . . then draw out the spring . . .

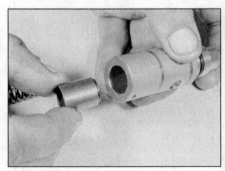

22.8c . . . and the plunger

compound to the bolts and tighten them to the specified torque setting.

11 If removed, install the baffle plate in the sump, then apply a suitable non-permanent thread locking compound to the bolt threads and tighten them to the specified torque setting **(see illustration 22.6)**. If removed, fit the sump dowels into the crankcase. Lay a new gasket onto the sump (if the engine is in the frame) or onto the crankcase (if the engine has been removed and is positioned upside down on the work surface). Make sure the holes in the gasket align correctly with the bolt holes.

12 Position the sump onto the crankcase **(see illustration)**, then install the bolts, not forgetting the oil level sensor wiring clamp and fairing side panel brackets **(see illustration 22.3)**, and tighten them evenly and a little at a time in a criss-cross pattern to the specified torque setting.

13 Either install the oil level sensor if removed (see Chapter 9), or connect the wire at the connector. Install the sprocket cover if removed (see Chapter 6).

14 Fill the engine with the correct type and quantity of oil (see Chapter 1).

15 Install the exhaust system (see Chapter 4). Start the engine and check for leaks around the sump.

23 Crankcase halves – separation and reassembly

Note: *To separate the crankcase halves, the engine must be removed from the frame.*

Separation

1 To access the cam chain and tensioner blade, connecting rods, crankshaft, bearings, transmission shafts, alternator drive shaft and starter clutch, the crankcase must be split into two parts.

2 To enable the crankcases to be separated, the engine must be removed from the frame (see Section 5). Before the crankcases can be separated the following components must be removed:
  a) *Valve cover (Section 8).*
  b) *Cam chain tensioner and guides (Section 9).*
  c) *Cylinder head (Section 11).*
  d) *Cylinder block (Section 14).*
  e) *Oil sump (Section 22).*
  f) *Clutch (Section 17).*

3 If the crankcases are being separated to remove the crankshaft, remove the pistons (see Section 15).

4 If the crankcases are being separated as part of a complete engine overhaul, remove the following components:
  a) *Oil cooler (Section 7).*
  b) *Pistons (Section 15).*
  c) *Gearchange mechanism (Section 20).*
  d) *Oil pump (Section 21).*
  e) *Water pump (Chapter 3).*
  f) *Starter motor (Chapter 9).*

22.12 Fit the sump, making sure it locates correctly onto the dowels

  g) *Alternator (Chapter 9).*
  h) *Oil strainer, pressure relief valve and oil pipes (Section 22).*
  i) *Neutral and oil level switches (Chapter 9).*
  j) *Pick-up coil (Chapter 5).*

5 Remove the screws securing the right-hand crankshaft end-cover and remove the cover **(see illustration)**. Discard the O-ring, as a new one must be used.

6 Remove the Torx screws securing the bearing retainer plate to the right-hand side of the engine and remove the plate **(see illustration)**.

7 Unscrew the upper crankcase bolts evenly and a little at a time in a reverse of the numerical sequence shown and as marked on the crankcase (the number of each bolt is cast into the crankcase – access bolt 25 from the underside of the engine), until they are finger-tight, then remove them **(see illustration)**. Note any washers, leads and wiring guides fitted with the bolts. **Note:** *As each bolt is removed, store it in its relative position, with its washer, lead or guide where applicable, in a cardboard template of the crankcase halves. This will ensure all bolts are installed in the correct location on reassembly.*

8 Turn the engine upside down so that it rests on the cylinder head studs.

9 Unscrew the lower crankcase bolts evenly and a little at a time in a reverse of the numerical sequence shown and as marked on the crankcase (the number of each bolt is cast into the crankcase), until they are finger-tight, then remove them **(see illustration 23.7)**. Note the washers fitted with some of the

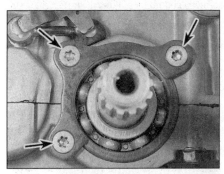

23.6 ... and the bearing retainer plate – you will need a Torx bit for the screws (arrowed)

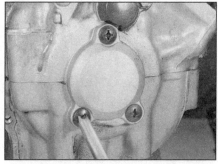

23.5 Remove the right-hand crankshaft end-cover ...

bolts, and the radiator brackets (according to model). **Note:** *As each bolt is removed, store it in its relative position, with its washer and cable guide or bracket where applicable, in a cardboard template of the crankcase halves. This will ensure all bolts are installed in the correct location on reassembly.*

10 Carefully lift the lower crankcase half off the upper half, using a soft-faced hammer to

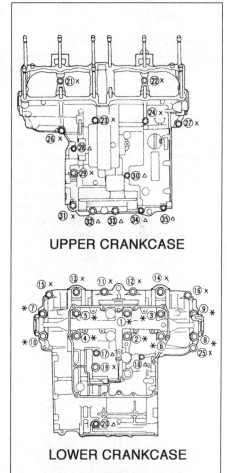

UPPER CRANKCASE

LOWER CRANKCASE

23.7 Crankcase bolt size identification and tightening sequence

✳ = 9 mm bolt Δ = 6 mm bolt
x = 8 mm bolt

23.10 Carefully lift the lower half off the upper half

23.11a Remove the large dowel (arrowed) . . .

23.11b . . . the small dowel (arrowed) . . .

23.11c . . . and its O-ring (arrowed)

tap around the joint to initially separate the halves if necessary **(see illustration)**. **Note:** *If the halves do not separate easily, make sure all fasteners have been removed. Do not try and separate the halves by levering against the crankcase mating surfaces as they are easily scored and will leak oil. Tap around the joint faces with a soft-faced mallet.*

11 Remove the large locating dowel from the back of the crankcase and the small dowel and its O-ring from the middle of the right-hand side of the case (they could be in either crankcase half) **(see illustrations)**.

12 Refer to Sections 24 to 32 for the removal and installation of the components housed within the crankcases.

Reassembly

13 Remove all traces of sealant from the crankcase mating surfaces.

14 Ensure that all components and their bearings are in place in the upper and lower crankcase halves. If the transmission shafts have not been removed, check the condition of the oil seal on the left-hand end of the output shaft and the clutch pushrod oil seal on the left-hand end of the input shaft and replace them with new ones if they are damaged or deteriorated. Check that the selector drum is in the neutral position (see Section 31).

15 Generously lubricate the crankshaft, transmission shafts and selector drum and forks (if installed), particularly around the bearings, with clean engine oil, then use a rag soaked in high flash-point solvent to wipe

over the mating surfaces of both crankcase halves to remove all traces of oil.

16 If removed, fit the large locating dowel into its hole in the back of the crankcase, and the small dowel into the middle of the right-hand side, using a new O-ring **(see illustrations 23.11a, b and c)**.

17 Apply a small amount of suitable sealant (such as Yamaha Bond 1215) to the outer mating surface of one crankcase half.

Caution: Do not apply an excessive amount of sealant as it will ooze out when the case halves are assembled and may obstruct oil passages. Do not apply the sealant on or too close (within 2 to 3 mm) to any of the bearing inserts or surfaces.

18 Check again that all components are in position, particularly that the bearing shells are still correctly located in the lower crankcase half. Carefully fit the lower crankcase half onto the upper crankcase half, making sure the selector forks locate correctly into their grooves in the transmission shaft gears, the cam chain tensioner blade locates in the tunnel, and the dowels locate correctly **(see illustration 23.10)**.

19 Check that the lower crankcase half is correctly seated. **Note:** *The crankcase halves should fit together without being forced. If the casings are not correctly seated, remove the lower crankcase half and investigate the problem. Do not attempt to pull them together using the crankcase bolts as the casing will crack and be ruined.* Make sure the output shaft and clutch pushrod oil seals are correctly seated **(see illustration)**.

20 Clean the threads of the 9 mm lower crankcase bolts (Nos. 1 to 10) and apply molybdenum disulphide oil (a 50/50 mixture of molybdenum disulphide grease and new engine oil) to their threads. Insert them, with the washers on bolts 7 to 10 **(see illustration)**, in their original locations **(see illustration 23.7)**. Clean the threads of the 8 and 6 mm lower crankcase bolts and apply new engine oil to their threads. Insert them (with the radiator brackets where fitted) in their original locations **(see illustration 23.7)**. Secure all bolts finger-tight at first, then tighten them evenly and a little at a time in the correct numerical sequence to the torque settings specified at the beginning of the Chapter.

21 Turn the engine over. Clean the threads of the upper crankcase bolts and apply new engine oil to their threads. Insert them, not forgetting the copper washer with bolt 24 **(see illustration)**, earth lead with bolt 30 **(see**

23.19 Make sure the oil seals are correctly seated

23.20 The two 9 mm bolts on each end (arrowed) have steel washers

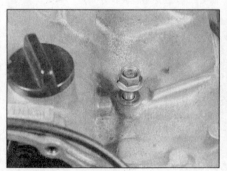

23.21a This bolt has a copper washer . . .

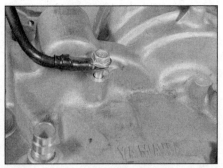

24.21b ... and this one secures the earth lead

illustration), and any leads and wiring guides, in their original locations (see illustration 23.7). Secure all bolts finger-tight at first, then tighten them evenly and a little at a time in the correct numerical sequence to

24.2a Unscrew the plate bolt ...

the torque settings specified at the beginning of the Chapter.

22 With all crankcase fasteners tightened, check that the crankshaft and transmission shafts rotate smoothly and easily. Check that the transmission shafts rotate freely and independently in neutral, then rotate the selector drum by hand and select each gear in turn whilst rotating the input shaft. Check that all gears can be selected and that the shafts rotate freely in every gear. If there are any signs of undue stiffness, tight or rough spots, or of any other problem, the fault must be rectified before proceeding further.

23 Apply a suitable non-permanent thread locking compound to the threads of the bearing retainer plate Torx screws, then fit the plate and tighten the screws to the specified torque setting (see illustration 23.6).

24 Fit the right-hand crankshaft end-cover using a new O-ring and tighten the screws to the specified torque setting (see illustration 23.5).

25 Install all other removed assemblies in the reverse of the sequences given in Steps 2, 3, and 4 according to your procedure.

24 Crankcase halves – inspection and servicing

1 After the crankcases have been separated, remove the crankshaft and bearings, cam chain tensioner blade, transmission shafts, selector drum and forks, Hy-Vo chain guide

blade, starter clutch and alternator drive shaft and bearings, and any other components or assemblies not already removed, referring to the relevant Sections of this and other Chapters (see Steps 2, 3, and 4 in Section 23).

2 Unscrew the bolt securing the oil nozzle plate and remove it and its gasket, then withdraw the nozzle, noting how it fits (see illustrations). Unscrew the bolts securing the oil spray pipe and withdraw it from the crankcase (see illustrations). Discard the O-rings as new ones should be used. Unscrew the bolts securing the oil baffle plates and remove them, noting which fits where (see illustration). Remove the circlip securing the clutch oil return pipe and remove the pipe and its mounting rubber (see illustration).

3 The crankcases should be cleaned thoroughly with new solvent and dried with compressed air. All oil passages, pipes and oil nozzles should be blown out with compressed air.

4 All traces of old gasket sealant should be removed from the mating surfaces. Minor damage to the surfaces can be cleaned up with a fine sharpening stone or grindstone.

Caution: Be very careful not to nick or gouge the crankcase mating surfaces or oil leaks will result. Check both crankcase halves very carefully for cracks and other damage.

5 Small cracks or holes in aluminium castings may be repaired with an epoxy resin adhesive as a temporary measure. Permanent repairs can only be effected by argon-arc welding, and only a specialist in this process is in a

24.2b ... and remove the plate and gasket ...

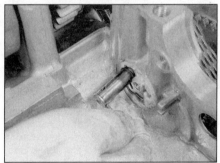

24.2c ... then withdraw the nozzle

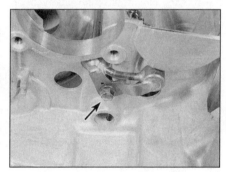

24.2d Unscrew the bolt (arrowed) ...

24.2e ... and withdraw the pipe

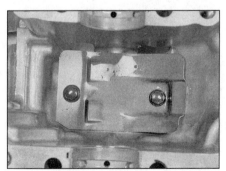

24.2f Remove the oil baffle plates

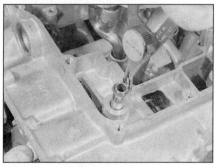

24.2g Remove the circlip and withdraw the oil return pipe

2

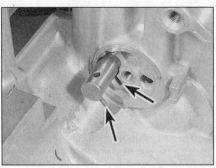

24.8a Align the pin on the nozzle with the slot in the crankcase (arrowed)

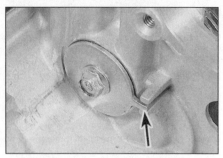

24.8b Make sure the tab on the plate (arrowed) locates between the lugs on the crankcase

position to advise on the economy or practical aspect of such a repair. If any damage is found that can't be repaired, renew the crankcase halves as a set.

6 Damaged threads can be economically reclaimed by using a diamond section wire insert, of the Heli-Coil type, which is easily fitted after drilling and re-tapping the affected thread.

7 Sheared studs or screws can usually be removed with screw extractors, which consist of a tapered, left thread screw of very hard steel. These are inserted into a pre-drilled hole in the stud, and usually succeed in dislodging the most stubborn stud or screw.

 HAYNES HiNT *Refer to Tools and Workshop Tips (Section 2) for details of installing a thread insert and using screw extractors.*

8 Install the clutch oil return pipe with its rubber mounting and secure it with the circlip **(see illustration 24.2g)**. Install the oil baffle plates, then apply a suitable non-permanent thread locking compound to the threads of the bolts and tighten them to the torque setting specified at the beginning of the Chapter **(see illustration 24.2f)**. Install the oil spray pipe using new O-rings and tighten the bolt to the specified torque setting **(see illustrations 24.2e and d)**. Align the pin on the head of the oil nozzle with the slot in the crankcase then push the nozzle into place **(see illustration)**. Fit the plate, using a new gasket if necessary **(see illustration 24.2b)**,

making sure the tab on the plate locates between the lugs on the crankcase, and tighten the bolt to the specified torque **(see illustration)**.

9 Install the crankshaft and bearings, cam chain and tensioner blade, transmission shafts, selector drum and forks, Hy-Vo chain, starter clutch and alternator drive shaft and bearings, before reassembling the crankcase halves.

25 Cam chain and tensioner blade – removal, inspection and installation

Removal

Cam chain

1 The original equipment cam chain has a staked-type split-link which can be disassembled using either a Yamaha service tool, or one of several commercially-available drive chain cutting/staking tools, so you don't have to remove the crankshaft. Such chains can be recognised by the split-link side plate's identification marks (and usually its different colour), as well as by the staked ends of the link's two pins which look as if they have been deeply centre-punched instead of peened over as with all the other pins **(see illustration)**. If a new chain is needed, or if you are removing the cylinder head with the camshafts in situ (see Section 11), check with your dealer as to whether the chain comes as a split-link type, or whole, and if it is a split-link type chain, whether it is supplied with the link split or

staked. If it is a split-link type and it comes split, then there is no need to disassemble the engine and remove the crankshaft to replace the chain, though the cylinder head must be removed (with the camshafts in situ) (see Section 11, taking note of all the information in **Note 2**) to avoid the possibility of a piston contacting a valve when the crankshaft is being turned without the chain attached to the camshafts. If the chain is being split to remove the cylinder head, and is not being replaced with a new one, you will need to obtain a new split-link from your dealer because you cannot re-use the old one. **Note:** *Due to the tricky nature of splitting and joining chains, and the need for special tools, and the fact that unless the job is done properly the consequences could be dire, it may be better to have the chain split and joined by a Yamaha dealer. If a new chain comes split, consider having it joined by the dealer when you buy it, and then fit it conventionally directly around the crankshaft and build the engine up as though the chain were endless. Although this involves more work, the repercussions of a badly staked chain coming apart when the engine is running should not be underestimated.*

⚠ *Warning: Use ONLY the correct service tools to disassemble the split-link – if you do not have access to such tools or do not have the skill to operate them correctly, have the chain removed by a dealer service department or bike repair shop.*

If you decide to split the chain and do the work yourself, remove the valve cover (see Section 8), the cam chain tensioner (see Section 9) and the cylinder head (see Section 11). Before splitting the cam chain, make a reference mark between a link on the chain and a tooth on the sprocket on each side of the split link so that it can be installed in exactly the same position, making the timing easier to set up. Split the existing chain at the split link using the chain cutter, following carefully the manufacturer's operating instructions (see also Section 8 in *Tools and Workshop Tips* in the Reference Section). Temporarily join the new chain to the rear run of the old one using the master link, then pull the new chain through using the old chain, turning the crankshaft anti-clockwise using the alternator rotor bolt at the same time, taking great care that the chain does not come off the sprocket on the crankshaft and become trapped between it and the crankcase – keep the chain taut on both runs at all times, with help from an assistant.

2 If the chain is not being split, remove the crankshaft (see Section 28).

3 Remove the cam chain from around its sprocket.

Tensioner blade

4 Remove the crankshaft (see Section 28).

5 Unscrew the bolts securing the tensioner blade base to the crankcase and remove the blade **(see illustration)**.

25.1 Note the difference between the split-link (arrowed) and the other links to identify it

25.5 The cam chain tensioner blade is secured by two bolts (arrowed)

Inspection

Cam chain

6 Check the chain for binding, kinks and any obvious damage and replace it with a new one if necessary. Check the camshaft and crankshaft sprocket teeth for wear and renew the cam chain, camshaft sprockets and crankshaft as a set if necessary.

Tensioner blade

7 Check the sliding surface and edges of the blade for excessive wear, deep grooves, cracking and other obvious damage, and replace it with a new one if necessary. Also check the condition of the pivot hardware on the base.

Installation

8 Installation of the chain and blade is the reverse of removal. Apply a suitable non-permanent thread locking compound to the tensioner blade bolts and tighten them to the torque setting specified at the beginning of the Chapter **(see illustration 25.5)**.

9 If the chain has been split, refer to Section 8 in *Tools and Workshop Tips* in the Reference Section when joining the chain, bearing in mind that it refers specifically to a final drive chain – a cam chain does not have O-rings. Stake the new link using the drive chain cutting/staking tool, following carefully the instructions of both the chain manufacturer and the tool manufacturer. DO NOT re-use old joining link components. After staking, check the joining link and staking for any signs of cracking. If there is any evidence of cracking, the joining link and side plate must be replaced with new ones. Measure the diameter of the staked ends in two directions and check that it is evenly staked.

26 Main and connecting rod bearings – general information

1 Even though main and connecting rod bearings are generally replaced with new ones during the engine overhaul, the old bearings should be retained for close examination as they may reveal valuable information about the condition of the engine.
2 Bearing failure occurs mainly because of lack of lubrication, the presence of dirt or other foreign particles, overloading the engine and/or corrosion. Regardless of the cause of bearing failure, it must be corrected before the engine is reassembled to prevent it from happening again.
3 When examining the connecting rod bearings, remove them from the connecting rods and caps and lay them out on a clean surface in the same general position as their location on the crankshaft journals **(see illustrations 27.10 and 28.3)**. This will enable you to match any noted bearing problems with the corresponding crankshaft journal.

4 Dirt and other foreign particles get into the engine in a variety of ways. It may be left in the engine during assembly or it may pass through filters or breathers. It may get into the oil and from there into the bearings. Metal chips from machining operations and normal engine wear are often present. Abrasives are sometimes left in engine components after reconditioning operations, especially when parts are not thoroughly cleaned using the proper cleaning methods. Whatever the source, these foreign objects often end up imbedded in the soft bearing material and are easily recognised. Large particles will not imbed in the bearing and will score or gouge the bearing and journal. The best prevention for this cause of bearing failure is to clean all parts thoroughly and keep everything spotlessly clean during engine reassembly. Frequent and regular oil and filter changes are also recommended.
5 Lack of lubrication or lubrication breakdown has a number of interrelated causes. Excessive heat (which thins the oil), overloading (which squeezes the oil from the bearing face) and oil leakage or throw off (from excessive bearing clearances, worn oil pump or high engine speeds) all contribute to lubrication breakdown. Blocked oil passages will also starve a bearing and destroy it. When lack of lubrication is the cause of bearing failure, the bearing material is wiped or extruded from the steel backing of the bearing. Temperatures may increase to the point where the steel backing and the journal turn blue from overheating.

> **Refer to Tools and Workshop Tips (Section 5) for bearing fault finding.**

6 Riding habits can have a definite effect on bearing life. Full throttle low speed operation, or labouring the engine, puts very high loads on bearings, which tend to squeeze out the oil film. These loads cause the bearings to flex, which produces fine cracks in the bearing face (fatigue failure). Eventually the bearing material will loosen in pieces and tear away from the steel backing. Short trip riding leads

to corrosion of bearings, as insufficient engine heat is produced to drive off the condensed water and corrosive gases produced. These products collect in the engine oil, forming acid and sludge. As the oil is carried to the engine bearings, the acid attacks and corrodes the bearing material.
7 Incorrect bearing installation during engine assembly will lead to bearing failure as well. Tight fitting bearings which leave insufficient bearing oil clearances result in oil starvation. Dirt or foreign particles trapped behind a bearing insert result in high spots on the bearing which lead to failure.
8 To avoid bearing problems, clean all parts thoroughly before reassembly, double check all bearing clearance measurements and lubricate the new bearings with clean engine oil during installation.

27 Connecting rods – removal, inspection and installation

Note: *To remove the connecting rods the engine must be removed from the frame and the crankcases separated.*

Removal

1 Remove the engine from the frame (see Section 5) and separate the crankcase halves (see Section 23). Remove the crankshaft (see Section 28).
2 Before removing the rods from the crankshaft, measure the side clearance on each rod with a feeler gauge **(see illustration)**. If the clearance between any rod is greater than the service limit listed in this Chapter's Specifications, replace that rod with a new one.
3 Using paint or a felt marker pen, mark the relevant cylinder identity on each connecting rod and cap. Mark across the cap-to-connecting rod join, and note the 'Y' mark on each connecting rod which must face to the left-hand side of the engine, to ensure that the cap and rod are fitted the correct way around on reassembly **(see illustration)**. Note that the number and letter already across the rod and cap indicate rod size and weight grade respectively, not cylinder number.

27.2 Measure the connecting rod side clearance using a feeler gauge

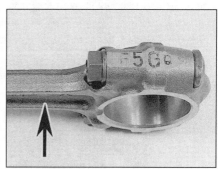

27.3 Note the marks across the rod and cap, and the 'Y' mark (arrowed) which must face the left-hand side of the engine

2

27.4 Unscrew the nuts (arrowed) and remove the connecting rods

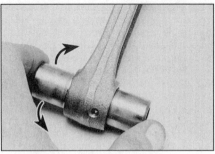

27.6 Slip the piston pin into the rod's small-end and rock it back and forth to check for looseness

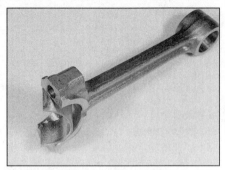

27.10 To remove a big-end bearing shell, push it sideways and lift it out

4 Unscrew the connecting rod cap nuts and separate the cap from the crankpin **(see illustration)**. Do not remove the bolts from the caps. Immediately install the relevant bearing shells (if removed), bearing cap, and nuts on each piston/connecting rod assembly so that they are all kept together as a matched set to ensure correct installation.

Inspection

5 Check the connecting rods for cracks and other obvious damage.

6 Apply clean engine oil to the piston pin, insert it into its connecting rod small-end and check for any freeplay between the two **(see illustration)**. If freeplay is excessive, measure the pin external diameter **(see illustration 15.13b)**. Compare the result to the specifications at the beginning of the Chapter. Replace the pin with a new one if it is worn beyond its specified limits. If the pin diameter is within specifications, replace the connecting rod with a new one. Repeat the measurements for all the rods.

7 Refer to Section 26 and examine the connecting rod bearing shells. If they are scored, badly scuffed or appear to have seized, new shells must be installed. Always renew the shells in the connecting rods as a set. If they are badly damaged, check the corresponding crankpin. Evidence of extreme heat, such as discoloration, indicates that lubrication failure has occurred. Be sure to thoroughly check the oil pump and pressure regulator as well as all oil holes and passages before reassembling the engine.

8 Have the rods checked for twist and bend

by a Yamaha dealer if you are in doubt about their straightness.

Oil clearance check

9 Whether new bearing shells are being fitted or the original ones are being re-used, the connecting rod (big-end) bearing oil clearance should be checked prior to reassembly. Obtain new bolts and nuts for the connecting rods and discard the old ones.

10 Remove the bearing shells from the rods and caps, keeping them in order **(see illustration)**. Clean the backs of the shells and the bearing locations in both the connecting rod and cap, and the crankpin journal.

11 Press the bearing shells into their locations, ensuring that the tab on each shell engages the notch in the connecting rod/cap **(see illustration)**. Make sure the bearings are fitted in the correct locations and take care not to touch any shell's bearing surface with your fingers.

12 Cut a length of the appropriate size Plastigauge (it should be slightly shorter than the width of the crankpin). Place a strand of Plastigauge on the crankpin journal.

13 Apply molybdenum disulphide grease to the bolt shanks and threads and to the seats of the nuts, then fit the bolts into the cap. Fit the connecting rod and cap onto the crankshaft **(see illustration 27.25)**. Make sure the cap is fitted the correct way around so the previously made markings align, and that the rod is facing the right way (see Step 3). Fit the nuts and tighten them finger-tight, making sure the connecting rod does not rotate on the crankshaft.

14 Tighten the cap nuts to the initial torque setting specified at the beginning of the Chapter, making sure the connecting rod does not rotate on the crankshaft **(see illustration 27.26)**. Now tighten each nut in turn and in one continuous movement to the final torque setting specified. If tightening is paused between the initial and final settings, slacken the nut to below the initial setting and repeat the procedure.

15 Slacken the cap nuts and remove the connecting rod, again taking great care not to rotate the rod or crankshaft.

16 Compare the width of the crushed Plastigauge on the crankpin to the scale printed on the Plastigauge envelope to obtain the connecting rod bearing oil clearance **(see illustration 28.20)**. Compare the reading to the specifications at the beginning of the Chapter.

17 On completion carefully scrape away all traces of the Plastigauge material from the crankpin and bearing shells using a fingernail or other object which is unlikely to score the shells.

18 If the clearance is within the range listed in this Chapter's Specifications and the bearings are in perfect condition, they can be reused. If the clearance is beyond the service limit, replace the bearing shells with new ones (see Steps 21 and 22). Check the oil clearance once again (the new shells may be thick enough to bring bearing clearance within the specified range). Always renew all of the shells at the same time.

19 If the clearance is still greater than the service limit listed in this Chapter's Specifications, the big-end bearing journal is worn and the crankshaft should be renewed.

20 Repeat the bearing selection procedure for the remaining connecting rods.

Bearing shell selection

21 Replacement bearing shells for the big-end bearings are supplied on a selected fit basis. Code numbers stamped on various components are used to identify the correct replacement bearings. The crankshaft journal size numbers are stamped on the outside of the crankshaft web on the left-hand end **(see illustration)**. The right-hand block of four numbers are for the big-end bearing journals (the left-hand block of five numbers are for the

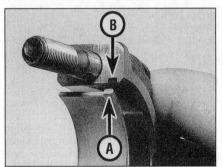

27.11 Make sure the tab (A) locates in the notch (B)

27.21 Big-end journal size numbers (A), main journal size numbers (B)

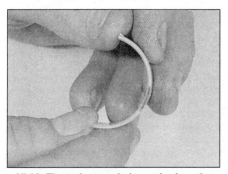

27.22 The colour code is marked on the side of each bearing

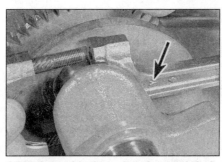

27.25 Assemble the rod on the crankshaft, making sure the 'Y' mark (arrowed) faces the left-hand end

27.26 Tighten the nuts as described, first to the initial torque, then to the final torque

main bearing journals). The first number of the four is for the left-hand (No. 1 cylinder) journal, and so on. Each connecting rod size number is marked in ink on the flat face of the connecting rod and cap **(see illustration 27.3)**.

22 A range of bearing shells is available. To select the correct bearing for a particular connecting rod, subtract the big-end bearing journal number (stamped on the crank web) from the connecting rod number (marked on the rod). Compare the bearing number calculated with the table below to find the colour coding of the replacement bearing required. The colour code is marked on the side of each bearing **(see illustration)**.

Number	Colour
1	Blue
2	Black
3	Brown
4	Green

Installation

23 Clean the backs of the bearing shells and the bearing locations in both the connecting rod and cap.

24 Press the bearing shells into their locations, making sure the tab on each shell locates in the notch in the connecting rod/cap **(see illustration 27.11)**. Make sure the bearings are fitted in their correct locations and take care not to touch any shell's bearing surface with your fingers. Lubricate the shells with clean engine oil.

25 Apply molybdenum disulphide grease to the bolt shanks and threads and to the seats of the nuts, then fit the bolts into the cap.

Assemble the connecting rod and cap on the crankpin **(see illustration)**. Make sure the cap is fitted the correct way around so the previously made markings align, and that the rod is facing the right way (see Step 3). Fit the nuts and tighten them finger-tight. Check again to make sure all components have been returned to their original locations using the marks made on disassembly.

26 Tighten the cap nuts to the initial torque setting specified at the beginning of the Chapter **(see illustration)**. Now tighten each nut in turn and in one continuous movement to the final torque setting specified. If tightening is paused between the initial and final settings, slacken the nut to below the initial setting and repeat the procedure.

27 Check that the rods rotate smoothly and freely on the crankpin. If there are any signs of roughness or tightness, remove the rods and re-check the bearing clearance. Sometimes tapping the bottom of the connecting rod cap will relieve tightness, but if in doubt, recheck the clearances.

28 Install the crankshaft (see Section 28).

28 Crankshaft and main bearings – removal, inspection and installation

Note: *To remove the crankshaft the engine must be removed from the frame and the crankcase halves separated.*

Removal

1 Remove the engine from the frame (see

Section 5) and separate the crankcase halves (see Section 23). Remove the alternator drive shaft and starter clutch (see Section 32).

2 Lift the crankshaft out of the upper crankcase half, taking care not to dislodge the main bearing shells, then remove the cam chain and Hy-Vo chain from it **(see illustration)**.

3 If required, remove the bearing shells from the crankcase halves by pushing their centres to the side, then lifting them out **(see illustration)**. Keep the shells in order. On YZF1000R models, note that the shells for the centre journal (J3) have no groove.

4 If required, separate the connecting rods from the crankshaft (see Section 27). **Note:** *If no work is to be carried out on the crankshaft or connecting rod assemblies, there is no need to separate them.*

Inspection

5 Clean the crankshaft with solvent, using a rifle-cleaning brush to scrub out the oil passages. If available, blow the crank dry with compressed air, and also blow through the oil passages. Check the primary drive gear, cam chain sprocket and Hy-Vo chain sprocket for wear or damage **(see illustration)**. If any of the teeth are excessively worn, chipped or broken, the crankshaft must be replaced with a new one. If wear or damage is found, check the driven gear on the clutch housing.

6 Refer to Section 26 and examine the main bearing shells. If they are scored, badly scuffed or appear to have been seized, new bearings must be installed. Always renew the main bearings as a set. If they are badly damaged, check the corresponding crank-

2

28.2 Carefully lift the crankshaft out of the crankcase

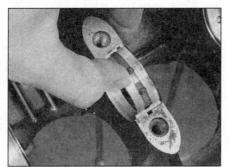

28.3 To remove a main bearing shell, push it sideways and lift it out

28.5 Check the gear and sprockets as described

28.13 Lay a strip of Plastigauge on each journal parallel to the crankshaft centreline

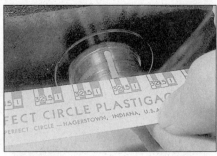

28.20 Measure the width of the crushed Plastigauge (be sure to use the correct scale – metric and imperial are included)

shaft journals. Evidence of extreme heat, such as discoloration, indicates that lubrication failure has occurred. Be sure to thoroughly check the oil pump and pressure regulator as well as all oil holes and passages before reassembling the engine.

7 Give the crankshaft journals a close visual examination, paying particular attention where damaged bearings have been discovered. If the journals are scored or pitted in any way a new crankshaft will be required. Note that undersizes are not available, precluding the option of re-grinding the crankshaft.

8 Place the crankshaft on V-blocks and check the runout at the main bearing journals using a dial gauge. Compare the reading to the maximum specified at the beginning of the Chapter. If the runout exceeds the limit, the crankshaft must be renewed.

Oil clearance check

9 Whether new bearing shells are being fitted or the original ones are being re-used, the main bearing oil clearance should be checked before the engine is reassembled. Main bearing oil clearance is measured with a product known as Plastigauge.

10 If not already done, remove the bearing shells from the crankcase halves (see Step 3). Clean the backs of the shells and the bearing housings in both crankcase halves, and the main bearing journals on the crankshaft.

11 Press the bearing shells into their cut-outs, ensuring that the tab on each shell engages in the notch in the crankcase **(see illustration 28.28)**. Make sure the bearings are fitted in the correct locations and take care not to touch any shell's bearing surface with your fingers.

12 Ensure the shells and crankshaft are clean and dry. Lay the crankshaft in position in the upper crankcase **(see illustration 28.2)**.

13 Cut several lengths of the appropriate size Plastigauge (they should be slightly shorter than the width of the crankshaft journals). Place a strand of Plastigauge on each journal, making sure it will be clear of the oil holes in the shells when the lower crankcase is installed **(see illustration)**. Make sure the crankshaft is not rotated.

14 If removed, fit the large locating dowel into its hole in the back of the crankcase, and the small dowel into the middle of the right-

hand side, using a new O-ring **(see illustrations 23.11a, b and c)**. Carefully install the lower crankcase half on to the upper half, making sure the dowel locates correctly **(see illustration 23.10)**. Check that the lower crankcase half is correctly seated. **Note:** *Do not tighten the crankcase bolts if the casing is not correctly seated.*

15 Clean the threads of the 9 mm lower crankcase bolts (Nos. 1 to 10) and apply molybdenum disulphide oil (a 50/50 mixture of molybdenum disulphide grease and new engine oil) to their threads. Insert them, with the washers on bolts 7 to 10 **(see illustration 23.20)**, in their original locations **(see illustration 23.7)**. Clean the threads of the 8 and 6 mm lower crankcase bolts and apply new engine oil to their threads. Insert them (with the radiator brackets where fitted) in their original locations **(see illustration 23.7)**. Secure all bolts finger-tight at first, then tighten them evenly and a little at a time in the correct numerical sequence to the torque settings specified at the beginning of the Chapter.

16 Turn the engine over, making sure the crankshaft does not rotate. Clean the threads of the upper crankcase bolts and apply new engine oil to their threads. Insert them, not forgetting the copper washer with bolt 24 **(see illustration 23.21a)**, earth lead with bolt 30 **(see illustration 23.21b)**, and any leads and wiring guides, in their original locations **(see illustration 23.7)**. Secure all bolts finger-tight at first, then tighten them evenly and a little at

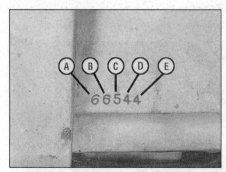

28.24 Main bearing housing numbers

A *No. 5 journal (J5)*   D *No. 2 journal (J2)*
B *No. 4 journal (J4)*   E *No. 1 journal (J1)*
C *No. 3 journal (J3)*

a time in the correct numerical sequence to the torque settings specified at the beginning of the Chapter.

17 Unscrew the upper crankcase bolts evenly and a little at a time in a reverse of the numerical sequence shown **(see illustration 23.7)** and as marked on the crankcase (the number of each bolt is cast into the crankcase), until they are finger-tight, then remove them, and place them back in the cardboard template, if used.

18 Turn the engine upside down so that it rests on the cylinder head studs, making sure the crankshaft does not rotate.

19 Unscrew the lower crankcase bolts evenly and a little at a time in a reverse of the numerical sequence shown **(see illustration 23.7)** and as marked on the crankcase (the number of each bolt is cast into the crankcase), until they are finger-tight, then remove them, and place them back in the cardboard template, if used. Carefully lift off the lower crankcase half, making sure the Plastigauge is not disturbed.

20 Compare the width of the crushed Plastigauge on each crankshaft journal to the scale printed on the Plastigauge envelope to obtain the main bearing oil clearance **(see illustration)**. Compare the reading to the specifications at the beginning of the Chapter.

21 On completion carefully scrape away all traces of the Plastigauge material from the crankshaft journal and bearing shells; use a fingernail or other object which is unlikely to score them.

22 If the oil clearance falls into the specified range, no bearing shell replacement is required (provided they are in good condition). If the clearance is beyond the service limit, refer to the marks on the case and the marks on the crankshaft and select new bearing shells (see Steps 24 and 25). Install the new shells and check the oil clearance once again (the new shells may bring bearing clearance within the specified range). Always renew all of the shells at the same time.

23 If the clearance is still greater than the service limit listed in this Chapter's Specifications (even with replacement shells), the crankshaft journal is worn and the crankshaft should be renewed.

Main bearing shell selection

24 Replacement bearing shells for the main bearings are supplied on a selective fit basis. Code numbers stamped on various components are used to identify the correct replacement bearings. The crankshaft journal size numbers are stamped on the outside of the crankshaft web on the left-hand end **(see illustration 27.21)**. The left-hand block of five numbers are for the main bearing journals (the right-hand block of four numbers are for the big-end bearing journals). The first number of the five is for the left-hand (No. 1) journal, and so on. The main bearing housing numbers are stamped into the back of the upper crankcase half **(see illustration)**. The first number of the five is for the right-hand (No. 5) journal, and so on. Note that if there is only one number stamped into the crankcase, it means that all the journals are the same number.

25 A range of bearing shells is available. To select the correct bearing for a particular journal, subtract the main bearing journal number (stamped on the crank web) from the main bearing housing number (stamped on the crankcase). Compare the bearing number calculated with the table below to find the colour coding of the replacement bearing required.

YZF750R and SP models:

Number	Colour
1	Blue
2	Black
3	Brown
4	Green
5	Yellow

YZF1000R models:

Note: *The bearing shells for journal 3 are identifiable by the lack of centre groove.*

Number	Colour – J1, J2, J4, J5	Colour – J3
1	Pink/Blue	Violet/Blue
2	Pink/Black	Violet/Black
3	Pink/Brown	Violet/Brown
4	Pink/Green	Violet/Green
5	Pink/Yellow	Violet/Yellow

Installation

26 If not already done, remove the bearing shells from the crankcase halves (see Step 3). Clean the backs of the shells and the bearing cut-outs in both crankcase halves, and the main bearing journals on the crankshaft. If new shells are being fitted, ensure that all traces of the protective grease are cleaned off using paraffin (kerosene). Wipe the shells and crankcase halves dry with a lint-free cloth. Make sure all the oil passages and holes are clear, and blow them through with compressed air if it is available.

28.28 Make sure the tabs on the shells locate in the notches in the cutouts

27 If removed, fit the connecting rods onto the crankshaft (see Section 27).

28 Press the bearing shells into their locations. Make sure the tab on each shell engages in the notch in the casing **(see illustration)**. Make sure the bearings are fitted in the correct locations and take care not to touch any shell's bearing surface with your fingers. Remember that on YZF1000R models, the shells for the centre journal (J3) have no centre groove, and are colour-coded differently (see table above). Lubricate each shell with clean engine oil.

29 Slip the cam chain and Hy-Vo chain around the sprockets on the crankshaft **(see illustration)**. Lower the crankshaft into position in the upper crankcase, making sure all bearings remain in place **(see illustration 28.2)**.

30 Reassemble the crankcase halves (see Section 23).

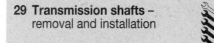

29 Transmission shafts – removal and installation

Note: *To remove the transmission shafts the engine must be removed from the frame and the crankcase halves separated.*

28.29 Loop the cam chain and Hy-Vo chain around the sprockets as shown

Removal

1 Remove the engine from the frame (see Section 5) and separate the crankcase halves (see Section 23).

2 Remove the clutch pushrod oil seal from the left-hand end of the input shaft **(see illustration)**. If required, remove the oil seal from the left-hand end of the output shaft.

3 Lift the input shaft and output shaft out of the crankcase, noting their relative positions in the crankcase and how they fit together **(see illustration)**. If they are stuck, use a soft-faced hammer and gently tap on the ends of the shafts to free them.

4 Remove the two bearing half-ring retainers from the crankcase, noting how they fit **(see illustration)**. If they are not in their slots in the crankcase, remove them from the bearings themselves on the output shaft.

5 If required, the shafts can be disassembled and inspected for wear or damage (see Section 30).

Installation

6 Fit the bearing half-ring retainers into their slots in the upper crankcase half **(see illustration 29.4)**.

7 Lower the output shaft into position in the upper crankcase, making sure the ball bearing locating pin faces back and locates in its

2

29.2 Remove the clutch pushrod oil seal (A) and if required the output shaft oil seal (B)

29.3 Lift the input shaft (A) and output shaft (B) out of the crankcase

29.4 Remove the half-ring retainers from the slots in the crankcase or the bearings themselves (arrowed)

29.7 Make sure the ball bearing locating pin faces back and locates in its recess (A), and the grooves in the bearings engage correctly with the half-ring retainers (B)

recess, and the grooves in the bearings engage correctly with the half-ring retainers (see illustration).

8 Lower the input shaft into position in the upper crankcase, making sure the locating pin on the ball bearing on the left-hand end of the shaft faces forward and locates in its recess.

9 Check the condition of the output shaft oil seal and renew if in any way damaged, worn or deteriorated, or if there were any signs of leakage from it. Smear the lips of the seal with grease. Slide the oil seal onto the left-hand end of the output shaft (see illustration 29.2). Also check the condition of the clutch pushrod oil seal and renew if in any way damaged, worn or deteriorated, or if there were any signs of leakage from it. Smear the lips of the seal with grease. Fit the seal against the left-hand end of the input shaft (see illustration 29.2).

10 Make sure both transmission shafts are correctly seated and their related pinions are correctly engaged (see illustration 29.3).
Caution: If the ball bearing locating pins and half-ring retainers are not correctly engaged, the crankcase halves will not seat correctly.

11 Position the gears in the neutral position and check the shafts are free to rotate easily and independently (ie the input shaft can turn whilst the output shaft is held stationary) before proceeding further.

12 Reassemble the crankcase halves (see Section 23).

30 Transmission shafts – disassembly, inspection and reassembly

YZF750R and SP models (six-speed transmission)

1 Remove the transmission shafts from the upper crankcase (see Section 29). Always disassemble the transmission shafts separately to avoid mixing up the components (see illustration).

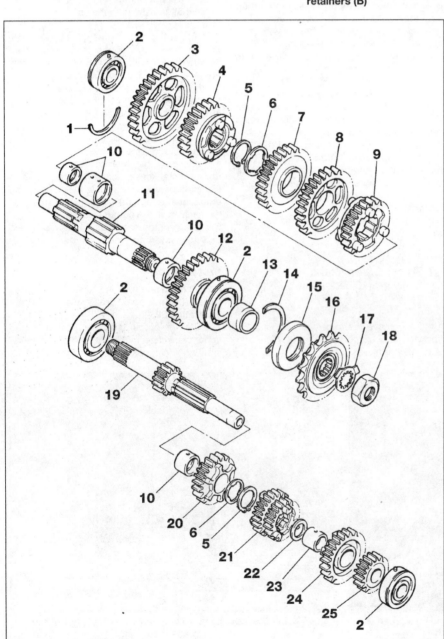

30.1 Transmission shaft components - six speed

1	Bearing half-ring retainer	14	Bearing half-ring retainer
2	Bearing	15	Oil seal
3	1st gear pinion	16	Front sprocket
4	5th gear pinion	17	Lockwasher
5	Circlip	18	Sprocket nut
6	Spline washer	19	Input shaft
7	4th gear pinion	20	5th gear pinion
8	3rd gear pinion	21	3rd/4th gear pinion
9	6th gear pinion	22	Thrust washer
10	Bush	23	Bush
11	Output shaft	24	6th gear pinion
12	2nd gear pinion	25	2nd gear pinion
13	Spacer		

Input shaft disassembly

 HAYNES HINT *When disassembling the transmission shafts, place the parts on a long rod or thread a wire through them to keep them in order and facing the proper direction.*

2 Remove the bearing from the left-hand end of the shaft. Do not remove the bearing from the right-hand end unless it or the shaft are being replaced with new ones.

3 Remove the 2nd gear pinion from the left-hand end of the shaft using a puller. It will be easier to set the puller up with the legs behind the 6th gear pinion, and draw the 2nd and 6th pinions off together. **Note:** *On the model stripped down, an hydraulic press was needed to remove the 2nd gear pinion as it was so tight on the shaft. Take the shaft to a properly equipped workshop if necessary.*

4 Slide the 6th gear pinion (if not already done), the 6th gear pinion bush, thrust washer and the combined 3rd/4th gear pinion off the shaft.

5 Remove the circlip securing the 5th gear pinion, then slide the spline washer and the pinion off the shaft.

6 The 1st gear pinion is integral with the shaft.

Input shaft inspection

7 Wash all of the components in clean solvent and dry them off.

8 Check the gear teeth for cracking, chipping, pitting and other obvious wear or damage. Any pinion that is damaged as such must be replaced with a new one.

9 Inspect the dogs and the dog holes in the gears for cracks, chips, and excessive wear especially in the form of rounded edges **(see illustrations)**. Make sure mating gears engage properly. Replace the paired gears with new ones as a set if necessary.

10 Check for signs of scoring or bluing on the pinions, bushes and shaft. This could be caused by overheating due to inadequate lubrication. Check that all the oil holes and passages are clear. Replace any damaged pinions or bushes with new ones. Some of the bushes are a press fit.

11 Check that each mobile pinion moves freely on the shaft but without undue freeplay.

12 The shaft is unlikely to sustain damage unless the engine has seized, placing an unusually high loading on the transmission, or the machine has covered a very high mileage. Check the surface of the shaft, especially where a pinion turns on it, and renew the shaft if it has scored or picked up, or if there are any cracks. Damage of any kind can only be cured by replacing the shaft with a new one. Check the shaft runout using V-blocks and a dial gauge and replace the shaft with a new one if the runout exceeds the limit specified at the beginning of the Chapter.

30.9a Check the edges of the dogs (arrowed) . . .

13 Check the washers and circlips and replace any that are bent or appear weakened or worn. Use new ones if in any doubt.

14 Referring to *Tools and Workshop Tips* (Section 5) in the Reference Section, check the bearings and replace them with new ones if necessary.

Input shaft reassembly

15 During reassembly, apply molybdenum disulphide oil (a 50/50 mixture of molybdenum disulphide grease and new engine oil) to the mating surfaces of the shaft and pinions. When installing the circlips, do not expand their ends any further than is necessary. Install the stamped circlips so that their chamfered side faces the pinion it secures (see *Correct fitting of a stamped circlip* in Section 2 of *Tools and Workshop Tips* in the Reference section).

16 Slide the 5th gear pinion, with the pinion dog holes facing away from the integral 1st gear onto the shaft. Slide the spline washer onto the shaft, then fit the circlip, making sure it locates correctly in the groove in the shaft.

17 Slide the combined 3rd/4th gear pinion onto the shaft with the larger 4th gear pinion facing the 5th gear pinion.

18 Slide the thrust washer, the 6th gear pinion bush and the 6th gear pinion onto the shaft.

19 Press the 2nd gear pinion onto the left-hand end of the shaft using a press or tubular drift, referring to *Tools and Workshop Tips* (Section 5) in the Reference Section if required. Set the pinion so that the distance between the outside edge of the 2nd gear

30.9b . . . and the edges of the dog holes (arrowed) for wear

pinion and the outside edge of the 1st gear pinion (which is integral with the shaft) is 116.6 mm **(see illustration)**.

20 Fit the bearing onto the left-hand end of the shaft. If removed, also fit the right-hand bearing, using a new one.

21 Check that all components have been correctly installed.

Output shaft disassembly

22 Remove the bearing from the right-hand end of the shaft.

23 Slide the 1st gear pinion and the 5th gear pinion off the right-hand end of the shaft.

24 Remove the circlip, then slide the spline washer, the 4th gear pinion, the 3rd gear pinion and the 6th gear pinion off the shaft.

25 Remove the spacer, bearing and 2nd gear pinion from the left-hand end of the shaft using a puller set up behind the 2nd gear pinion to draw them off, then remove the 2nd gear pinion bush.

Output shaft inspection

26 Refer to Steps 7 to 14 above.

Output shaft reassembly

27 During reassembly, apply molybdenum disulphide oil (a 50/50 mixture of molybdenum disulphide grease and new engine oil) to the mating surfaces of the shaft and pinions. When installing the circlips, do not expand their ends any further than is necessary. Install the stamped circlips so that their chamfered side faces the pinion it secures (see *Correct fitting of a stamped circlip* in Section 2 of *Tools and Workshop Tips* in the Reference section).

2

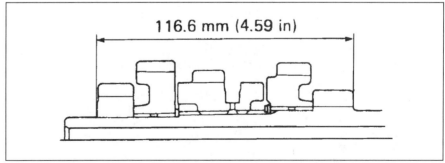

116.6 mm (4.59 in)

30.19 Set the distance between the 2nd and 1st gear pinions as specified

28 Slide the 2nd gear pinion bush onto the left-hand end of the shaft, then slide the 2nd gear pinion onto it. Fit the bearing and collar onto the end of the shaft using a tubular drift or press if necessary, referring to *Tools and Workshop Tips* (Section 5) in the Reference Section if required.

29 Slide the 6th gear pinion onto the right-hand end of the shaft, with its selector fork groove facing to the right. Slide the 3rd gear pinion, the 4th gear pinion and the spline washer onto the shaft and secure them with the circlip, making sure it locates correctly in its groove.

30 Slide the 5th gear pinion onto the shaft, with its selector fork groove facing the 4th gear pinion, then slide the 1st gear pinion onto the shaft.

31 Fit the bearing onto the right-hand end of the shaft.

32 Check that all components have been correctly installed.

YZF1000R models (five-speed transmission)

33 Remove the transmission shafts from the upper crankcase (see Section 29). Always disassemble the transmission shafts separately to avoid mixing up the components **(see illustration)**.

Input shaft disassembly

 When disassembling the transmission shafts, place the parts on a long rod or thread a wire through them to keep them in order and facing the proper direction.

34 Remove the bearing from the left-hand end of the shaft **(see illustration 30.52)**. Do not remove the bearing from the right-hand end unless it or the shaft are being replaced with new ones.

35 Remove the 2nd gear pinion from the left-hand end of the shaft using a puller. It will be easier to set the puller up with the legs behind the 5th gear pinion, and draw the 2nd and 5th pinions off together **(see illustration)**. **Note:** *On the model stripped down, an hydraulic press was needed to remove the 2nd gear pinion as it was so tight on the shaft. Take the shaft to a properly equipped workshop if necessary.*

36 Slide the 5th gear pinion (if not already done), the 5th gear pinion bush, thrust washer and the 3rd gear pinion off the shaft **(see illustrations 30.50c, b and a and 30.49)**.

37 Remove the circlip securing the 4th gear pinion, then slide the spline washer and the pinion off the shaft **(see illustrations 30.48c, b and a)**.

38 The 1st gear pinion is integral with the shaft.

Input shaft inspection

39 Wash all of the components in clean solvent and dry them off.

40 Check the gear teeth for cracking, chipping, pitting and other obvious wear or damage. Any pinion that is damaged as such must be replaced with a new one.

41 Inspect the dogs and the dog holes in the gears for cracks, chips, and excessive wear especially in the form of rounded edges **(see illustrations 30.9a and b)**. Make sure mating gears engage properly. Replace the paired gears with new ones as a set if necessary.

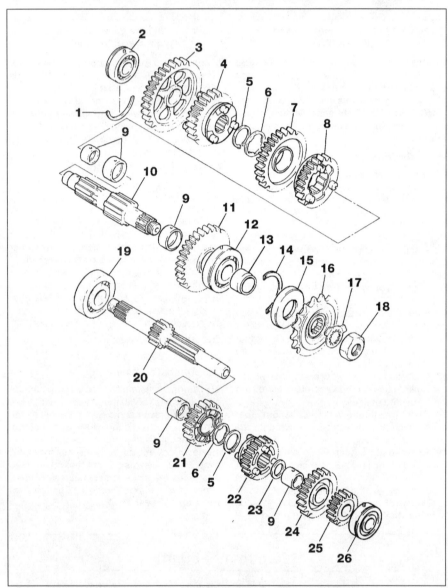

30.33 Transmission shaft components – five speed

1 Bearing half-ring retainer	10 Output shaft	18 Sprocket nut
2 Bearing	11 2nd gear pinion	19 Bearing
3 1st gear pinion	12 Bearing	20 Input shaft
4 4th gear pinion	13 Spacer	21 4th gear pinion
5 Circlip	14 Bearing half-ring	22 3rd gear pinion
6 Spline washer	retainer	23 Thrust washer
7 3rd gear pinion	15 Oil seal	24 5th gear pinion
8 5th gear pinion	16 Front sprocket	25 2nd gear pinion
9 Bush	17 Lockwasher	26 Bearing

30.35 Use a puller, or a press as shown, to remove the 2nd gear pinion

30.48a Slide the 4th gear pinion . . .

30.48b . . . . and the spline washer onto the shaft . . .

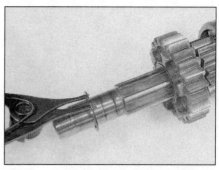

30.48c . . . then fit the circlip making sure it locates correctly in the groove

42 Check for signs of scoring or bluing on the pinions, bushes and shaft. This could be caused by overheating due to inadequate lubrication. Check that all the oil holes and passages are clear. Replace any damaged pinions or bushes with new ones. Some of the bushes are a press fit.

43 Check that each mobile pinion moves freely on the shaft but without undue freeplay.

44 The shaft is unlikely to sustain damage unless the engine has seized, placing an unusually high loading on the transmission, or the machine has covered a very high mileage. Check the surface of the shaft, especially where a pinion turns on it, and renew the shaft if it has scored or picked up, or if there are any cracks. Damage of any kind can only be cured by a new shaft. Check the shaft runout using V-blocks and a dial gauge and replace the shaft with a new one if the runout exceeds the limit specified at the beginning of the Chapter.

45 Check the washers and circlips and renew any that are bent or appear weakened or worn. Use new ones if in any doubt.

46 Referring to *Tools and Workshop Tips* (check Section 5) in the Reference Section, check the bearings and replace them with new ones if necessary.

Input shaft reassembly

47 During reassembly, apply molybdenum disulphide oil (a 50/50 mixture of molybdenum disulphide grease and new engine oil) to the mating surfaces of the shaft and pinions. When installing the circlips, do not expand their ends any further than is necessary. Install the stamped circlips so that their chamfered side faces the pinion it secures (see *Correct fitting of a stamped circlip* in Section 2 of *Tools and Workshop Tips* in the Reference section).

48 Slide the 4th gear pinion, with the pinion dog holes facing away from the integral 1st gear onto the shaft (see illustration). Slide

the spline washer onto the shaft, then fit the circlip, making sure it locates correctly in the groove in the shaft (see illustrations).

49 Slide the 3rd gear pinion onto the shaft with its selector fork groove facing the 4th gear pinion (see illustration).

50 Slide the thrust washer, the 5th gear pinion bush and the 5th gear pinion onto the shaft (see illustrations).

51 Press the 2nd gear pinion onto the left-hand end of the shaft using a press or tubular drift, referring to *Tools and Workshop Tips* (Section 5) in the Reference Section if required (see illustration). Set the pinion so that the distance between the outside edge of the 2nd gear pinion and the outside edge of the 1st gear pinion (which is integral with the shaft) is 116.6 mm (see illustration 30.19).

52 Fit the bearing onto the left-hand end of the shaft (see illustration). If removed, also fit the right-hand bearing, using a new one.

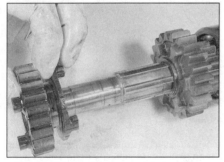

30.49 Slide the 3rd gear pinion onto the shaft . . .

30.50a . . . followed by the thrust washer . . .

30.50b . . . the 5th gear pinion bush . . .

30.50c . . . and the 5th gear pinion onto the shaft

30.51 . . . then press on the 2nd gear pinion as described

30.52 Fit the bearing onto the left-hand end of the shaft

2

30.53 The assembled shaft should be as shown

30.57 Remove the spacer, bearing and 2nd gear pinion using a puller or a press as shown

30.61a Slide the 5th gear pinion . . .

53 Check that all components have been correctly installed **(see illustration)**.

Output shaft disassembly

54 Remove the bearing from the right-hand end of the shaft **(see illustration 30.63)**.
55 Slide the 1st gear pinion and the 4th gear pinion off the right-hand end of the shaft **(see illustrations 30.62b and a)**.
56 Remove the circlip, then slide the spline washer, the 3rd gear pinion and the 5th gear pinion off the shaft **(see illustrations 30.61d, c, b and a)**.
57 Remove the spacer, bearing and 2nd gear pinion from the left-hand of the shaft using a puller set up behind the 2nd gear pinion, or a press, to draw them off, then remove the 2nd gear pinion bush **(see illustration)**.

Output shaft inspection

58 Refer to Steps 39 to 46 above.

Output shaft reassembly

59 During reassembly, apply molybdenum disulphide oil (a 50/50 mixture of molybdenum disulphide grease and new engine oil) to the mating surfaces of the shaft and pinions. When installing the circlips, do not expand their ends any further than is necessary. Install the stamped circlips so that their chamfered side faces the pinion it secures (see *Correct fitting of a stamped circlip* in Section 2 of *Tools and Workshop Tips* in the Reference section).
60 Slide the 2nd gear pinion bush onto the left-hand end of the shaft, then slide the 2nd gear pinion onto it. Fit the bearing and collar onto the end of the shaft using a tubular drift

or press if necessary, referring to *Tools and Workshop Tips* (Section 5) in the Reference Section if required **(see illustration 30.57)**.
61 Slide the 5th gear pinion onto the right-hand end of the shaft, with its selector fork groove facing to the right **(see illustration)**. Slide the 3rd gear pinion and the spline washer onto the shaft and secure them with the circlip, making sure it locates correctly in its groove **(see illustrations)**.
62 Slide the 4th gear pinion onto the shaft, with its selector fork groove facing the 3rd gear pinion, then slide the 1st gear pinion onto the shaft **(see illustrations)**.
63 Fit the bearing onto the right-hand end of the shaft **(see illustration)**.
64 Check that all components have been correctly installed.

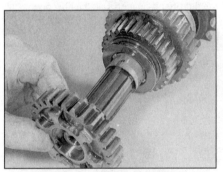

30.61b . . . the 3rd gear pinion . . .

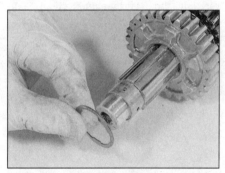

30.61c . . . and the spline washer onto the shaft . . .

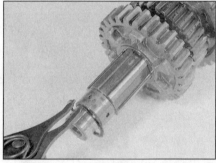

30.61d . . . and secure them with the circlip, making sure it locates correctly in its groove

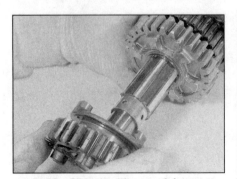

30.62a Slide the 4th gear pinion . . .

30.62b . . . and the 1st gear pinion onto the shaft . . .

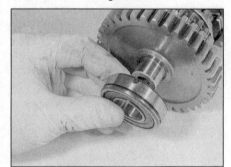

30.63 . . . then fit the bearing

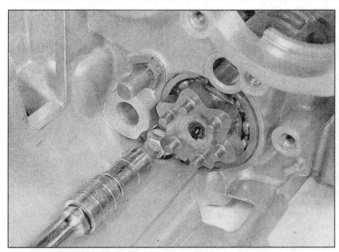

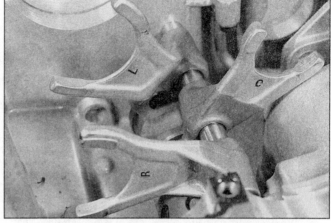

31.3 Unscrew the selector drum retainer bolt

31.4 Note the letter on each fork denoting its position

31 Selector drum and forks –
removal, inspection
and installation

Note: *To remove the selector drum and forks the engine must be removed from the frame and the crankcase halves separated.*

Removal

1 Remove the engine from the frame (see Section 5) and separate the crankcase halves (see Section 23).
2 If not already done, remove the gearchange mechanism (see Section 20).
3 Unscrew the bolt which acts as the selector drum retainer **(see illustration)**.
4 Before removing the selector forks, note that each fork is lettered for identification. The right-hand fork has an 'R', the centre fork a 'C', and the left-hand fork an 'L' **(see illustration)**. These letters face the right-hand side of the engine. If no letters are visible, mark them yourself using a felt pen.
5 Support the selector forks and withdraw the shaft from the casing, then remove the forks **(see illustration)**. Once removed from the case, slide the forks back onto their shaft in their correct order and the right way round.
6 Withdraw the selector drum from the right-hand side of the casing **(see illustration)**.

Inspection

7 Inspect the selector forks for any signs of wear or damage, especially around the fork ends where they engage with the groove in the pinion. Check that each fork fits correctly in its pinion groove. Check closely to see if the forks are bent. If the forks are in any way damaged they must be replaced with new ones.
8 Check that the forks fit correctly on their shaft. They should move freely with a light fit but no appreciable freeplay. Check that the fork shaft holes in the casing are not worn or damaged.
9 The selector fork shafts can be checked for trueness by rolling them along a flat surface. A bent rod will cause difficulty in selecting gears and make the gearchange action heavy. Replace the shafts with new ones if bent.
10 Inspect the selector drum grooves and selector fork guide pins for signs of wear or damage. If either show signs of wear or damage they must be replaced with new ones.
11 Check that the selector drum bearing rotates freely and has no signs of roughness or excessive freeplay between it and the drum or crankcase (when installed) (see *Tools and Workshop Tips* (Section 5) in the Reference Section for more information on bearings). Replace the selector drum with a new one if necessary – the bearing is not available separately, though it would be worth checking

with a bearing specialist before buying a new drum. Also check that the neutral switch contact plunger in the other end of the drum is free to move in and out under spring pressure. If required, remove the screw securing the contact plate and remove the plunger and spring for inspection or renewal.

Installation

12 Align the selector drum so that the neutral detent points to the bottom of the engine and slide the drum into the crankcase **(see illustration 31.6)**.
13 Refer to Step 4 for the correct location of each fork **(see illustration 31.4)**. Lubricate the selector fork shaft with clean engine oil, then slide it into the crankcase and through the forks and into the bore, making sure the forks are positioned according to their letter (Left, Centre and Right) and with the letters facing the right-hand side of the engine **(see illustration 31.5)** Locate the guide pin on the end of each fork in its groove in the drum **(see illustration)**.
14 Apply a suitable non-permanent thread locking compound to the selector drum retainer bolt and tighten it to the torque setting specified at the beginning of the Chapter **(see illustration 31.3)**.
15 Reassemble the crankcase halves (see Section 23).

2

31.5 Withdraw the shaft and remove the forks

31.6 Withdraw the selector drum from the crankcase

31.13 Locate the guide pin on each fork into its groove in the drum

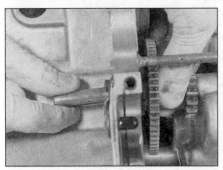

32.3 Withdraw the shaft and remove the gear

32.4a Unscrew the bolts . . .

32.4b . . . and remove the plate

32 Alternator/starter drive assembly – removal, inspection and installation

Note: *These components can only be accessed after separation of the crankcase halves.*

Removal

1 Remove the engine (see Section 5) and separate the crankcase halves (see Section 23). The alternator drive shaft, starter clutch and idle gear assembly are all located in the upper half of the crankcase.
2 Remove the transmission shafts (see Section 29). Also remove the oil nozzle and if required for improved access the oil spray pipe (see Section 24).

3 Withdraw the starter idle/reduction gear shaft and remove the gear **(see illustration)**.
4 Unscrew the three bolts securing the alternator drive shaft bearing retainer plate to the crankcase and remove the plate **(see illustrations)**.
5 Support the starter clutch, then withdraw the bearing and the drive shaft from the crankcase **(see illustrations)**. If the bearing is a tight fit, use a slide-hammer with suitable end-adapter to withdraw the shaft and bring the bearing with it.
6 Disengage the Hy-Vo chain from the starter clutch and remove the starter clutch from the crankcase **(see illustration)**.
7 If required, remove the crankshaft (see Section 28) and disengage the Hy-Vo chain. Unscrew the bolts securing the chain guide to the crankcase and remove the guide, noting which way round it fits.

Inspection

8 Withdraw the Hy-Vo chain sprocket from the starter clutch **(see illustration)**. With the clutch face down on a workbench, check that the gear rotates freely in a clockwise direction and locks against the rotor in an anti-clockwise direction **(see illustration)**. If it doesn't, replace the starter clutch with a new one. Withdraw the starter clutch gear from the starter clutch **(see illustration)**. If the gear appears stuck, rotate it anti-clockwise as you withdraw it.
9 Inspect the bearing surface of the starter clutch gear hub and the condition of the rollers inside the clutch body. If the bearing surface shows signs of excessive wear or the rollers are damaged, marked or flattened at any point, they should be renewed.

32.5a Remove the bearing . . .

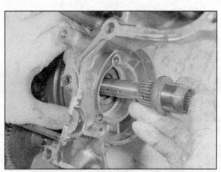

32.5b . . . and withdraw the shaft

32.6 Disengage the chain and remove the starter clutch

32.8a Withdraw the sprocket

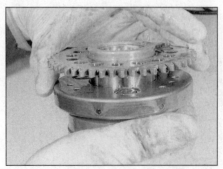

32.8b Check the operation of the clutch as described

32.8c Remove the gear and check the components as described

10 Remove the rollers and check the spring caps and springs for signs of deformation or damage. Make sure the pin moves freely in its socket.

11 Check that the three Allen bolts securing the starter clutch assembly together are tight. If any are loose, remove all the bolts, then apply a suitable non-permanent thread locking compound and tighten them to the torque setting specified at the beginning of the Chapter.

12 Examine the teeth of the starter idle/reduction gear and the corresponding teeth of the starter clutch gear and starter motor gear. Renew the gears as a set if worn or chipped teeth are discovered.

13 Inspect the alternator drive shaft and its bearings (one on the shaft, the other in the crankcase). If the bearings do not rotate freely or have rough spots or excessive play, they must be replaced with new ones. Heat the area around the bearing in the crankcase to ease its removal **(see illustration)**. If the shaft splines are worn or damaged the shaft must be replaced with a new one. Check also the corresponding splines in the starter clutch, and those on the Hy-Vo chain sprocket shaft.

14 The Hy-Vo chain and its guide in the crankcase can only be inspected properly after the crankshaft has been removed (see Section 31). Check the Hy-Vo chain and the chain guide for signs of wear or damage, and replace with a new one if necessary **(see illustration)**. Apply a suitable non-permanent thread locking compound to the bolt threads and tighten them to the torque setting specified at the beginning of the Chapter. Also check the Hy-Vo chain sprocket and the sprocket on the crankshaft for signs of wear or damage.

Installation

15 If removed, install the Hy-Vo chain guide in the crankcase, making sure it is the correct way round. Apply a suitable non-permanent thread locking compound to the bolts and tighten them securely. Install the crankshaft (see Section 28).

16 Insert the starter clutch in the crankcase and engage the Hy-Vo chain on the sprocket **(see illustration 32.6)**.

17 Supporting the starter clutch, insert the alternator drive shaft through the assembly from the outside of the crankcase until it seats fully into the bearing in the crankcase **(see illustration 32.5b)**. Fit the bearing onto the end of the shaft, making sure it is pressed fully into the crankcase **(see illustration 32.5a)**. Apply a suitable non-permanent thread locking compound to the retainer plate bolts and tighten them to the torque setting specified at the beginning of the Chapter **(see illustrations 32.4b and a)**.

18 Position the starter idler gear in the crankcase **(see illustration 32.3)**. Lubricate the idler gear shaft and slide it fully into place from the outside.

19 Install the oil nozzle and the oil spray pipe if removed (see Section 24). Check that the installed assembly is as shown **(see illustration)**. Install the transmission shafts (see Section 29).

33 Initial start-up after overhaul

1 Make sure the engine oil level and coolant level are correct (see *Daily (pre-ride) checks*).

2 Make sure there is fuel in the tank, then turn the fuel tap to the 'ON' position, and set the choke.

3 Start the engine and allow it to run at a moderately fast idle until it reaches normal operating temperature.

4 As no oil pressure warning light is fitted, an oil pressure check must be carried out (see Chapter 1).

5 Check carefully for oil and coolant leaks

32.13 Check the bearing that is housed in the crankcase

and make sure the transmission and controls, especially the brakes, function properly before road testing the machine. Refer to Section 34 for the recommended running-in procedure.

6 Upon completion of the road test, and after the engine has cooled down completely, recheck the valve clearances (see Chapter 1) and check the engine oil and coolant levels (see *Daily (pre-ride) checks*).

34 Recommended running-in procedure

1 Treat the machine gently for the first few miles to make sure oil has circulated throughout the engine and any new parts installed have started to seat.

2 Even greater care is necessary if the engine has been extensively overhauled – the bike will have to be run in as when new. This means greater use of the transmission and a restraining hand on the throttle until at least 600 miles (1000 km) have been covered. There's no point in keeping to any set speed limit – the main idea is to keep from labouring the engine and to gradually increase performance up to the 600 mile (1000 km) mark. These recommendations apply less

2

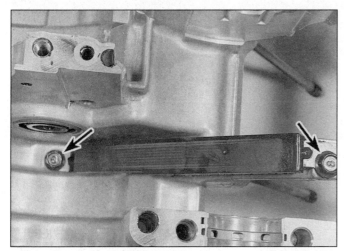

32.14 The Hy-Vo chain guide is secured by two bolts (arrowed)

32.19 The installed assembly should be as shown

when only a partial overhaul has been done, though it does depend to an extent on the nature of the work carried out and which components have been renewed. Experience is the best guide, since it's easy to tell when an engine is running freely. If in any doubt, consult a Yamaha dealer. The maximum engine speed limitations (see tables), which Yamaha provide for new motorcycles, can be used as a guide.

3 If a lubrication failure is suspected, stop the engine immediately and try to find the cause. If an engine is run without oil, even for a short period of time, severe damage will occur.

YZF750R and SP

Up to 100 miles (150 km)	6500 rpm max	Vary throttle position/speed. Do not use full throttle
100 to 300 miles (150 to 500 km)	7500 rpm max	Vary throttle position/speed. Do not use full throttle
300 to 600 miles (500 to 1000 km)	8500 rpm max	Vary throttle position/speed. Use full throttle for short bursts
Over 600 miles (1000 km)		Do not exceed tachometer red line

YZF1000R

Up to 100 miles (150 km)	5000 rpm max	Vary throttle position/speed. Do not use full throttle
100 to 300 miles (150 to 500 km)	6000 rpm max	Vary throttle position/speed. Do not use full throttle
300 to 600 miles (500 to 1000 km)	7000 rpm max	Vary throttle position/speed. Use full throttle for short bursts
Over 600 miles (1000 km)		Do not exceed tachometer red line

Chapter 3
Cooling system

Contents

Degrees of difficulty

Easy, suitable for novice with little experience	**Fairly easy,** suitable for beginner with some experience	**Fairly difficult,** suitable for competent DIY mechanic	**Difficult,** suitable for experienced DIY mechanic	**Very difficult,** suitable for expert DIY or professional 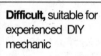

Specifications

Coolant
Mixture type and capacity .... see Chapter 1

Radiator
Cap valve opening pressure .... 13.5 to 17.8 psi (0.93 to 1.23 Bars)

Cooling fan switch
Cooling fan cut-in temperature .... 102 to 108°C
Cooling fan cut-out temperature .... 98°C

Coolant temperature gauge sender
Resistance
  YZF750R and SP models
    @ 80°C .... 47 to 53 ohms
    @ 100°C .... 26 to 30 ohms
  YZF1000R
    @ 80°C .... 47 to 56 ohms
    @ 100°C .... 26 to 29 ohms

Thermostat
Opening temperature .... 69 to 73°C
Valve lift .... 8 mm (min) @ 85°C

Torque wrench settings
Cooling fan bolts .... 10 Nm
Cooling fan switch .... 23 Nm
Coolant temperature sender .... 15 Nm
Thermostat cover bolts .... 10 Nm
Thermostat housing mounting bolts .... 10 Nm
Radiator mounting bolts .... 10 Nm
Water pump bolts .... 10 Nm
Water pump cover bolts .... 10 Nm
Coolant inlet union to cylinder block bolts .... 10 Nm
Coolant outlet union to cylinder head bolts .... 10 Nm

1 General information

The cooling system uses a water/antifreeze coolant to carry away excess energy in the form of heat. The cylinders are surrounded by a water jacket from which the heated coolant is circulated by thermo-syphonic action in conjunction with a water pump, driven by the oil pump. The hot coolant passes upwards to the thermostat and through to the radiator. The coolant then flows across the radiator core, where it is cooled by the passing air, to the water pump and back to the engine where the cycle is repeated.

A thermostat is fitted in the system to prevent the coolant flowing through the radiator when the engine is cold, therefore accelerating the speed at which the engine reaches normal operating temperature. A coolant temperature sender mounted in the radiator transmits to the temperature gauge on the instrument panel. Two thermostatically-controlled cooling fans are fitted to aid cooling in extreme conditions. The fan switch is also mounted in the radiator.

The complete cooling system is partially sealed and pressurised, the pressure being controlled by a valve contained in the spring-loaded radiator cap. By pressurising the coolant the boiling point is raised, preventing premature boiling in adverse conditions. The overflow pipe from the system is connected to a reservoir into which excess coolant is expelled under pressure. The discharged coolant automatically returns to the radiator when the engine cools.

⚠️ *Warning: Do not remove the pressure cap from the radiator when the engine is hot. Scalding hot coolant and steam may be blown out under pressure, which could cause serious injury. When the engine has cooled, place a thick rag, like a towel over the pressure cap; slowly rotate the cap anti-clockwise to the first stop. This procedure allows any residual pressure to escape. When the steam has stopped escaping, press down on the cap while turning it anti-clockwise and remove it. Do not allow antifreeze to come into contact with your skin or painted surfaces of the motorcycle. Rinse off any spills immediately with plenty of water. Antifreeze is highly toxic if ingested. Never leave antifreeze lying around in an open container or in puddles on the floor; children and pets are attracted by its sweet smell and may drink it. Check with the local authorities about disposing of used antifreeze. Many communities will have collection centres which will see that antifreeze is disposed of safely.*
Caution: At all times use the specified type of antifreeze, and always mix it with distilled water in the correct proportion.

The antifreeze contains corrosion inhibitors which are essential to avoid damage to the cooling system. A lack of these inhibitors could lead to a build-up of corrosion which would block the coolant passages, resulting in overheating and severe engine damage. Distilled water must be used as opposed to tap water to avoid a build-up of scale which would also block the passages.

2 Radiator pressure cap – check

1 If problems such as overheating or loss of coolant occur, check the entire system as described in Chapter 1. The radiator cap opening pressure should be checked by a Yamaha dealer with the special tester required to do the job. If the cap is defective, replace it with a new one.

3 Coolant reservoir – removal and installation

Removal

1 Remove the seat and the right-hand side cover (YZF1000R models), side covers (YZF750R models) or seat cowling (YZF750SP models) (see Chapter 8).
2 Release the clamp securing the breather/overflow hose (coming out of the top of the reservoir) and detach the hose (see illustration).
3 Place a suitable container underneath the reservoir, then release the clamp securing the radiator overflow hose to the base of the reservoir (see illustration 3.2). Detach the hose and allow the coolant to drain into the container.

4 Unscrew the reservoir mounting screws (see illustration 3.2) and remove the reservoir, noting how it fits.

Installation

5 Installation is the reverse of removal. Make sure the hoses are correctly installed and secured with their clamps. On completion refill the reservoir as described in Chapter 1.

4 Cooling fans and cooling fan switch – check and renewal

Cooling fan

Check

1 If the engine is overheating and the cooling fans aren't coming on, first check the cooling fan circuit fuse (see Chapter 9) and then the fan switch as described in Steps 8 to 12 below.
2 If the fans do not come on, (and the fan switch is good), or only one of them comes on, the fault lies in either the cooling fan motor or the relevant wiring. Test all the wiring and connections as described in Chapter 9.
3 To test the cooling fan motor, on 1993 and 1994 YZF750R and SP models, remove the fuel tank and air filter housing (see Chapter 4) – the fan motor wiring connectors are located between the coils, ahead of the carburettors. On all other models, remove the fairing side panels (see Chapter 8) – the wiring connector for each fan is located above the end of the radiator (see illustration). Trace the fan motor wiring and disconnect it at the connector for the fan being tested. Using a 12 volt battery and two jumper wires, connect the battery leads to the fan wiring connector. Once connected the fan should operate. If it does not, and the wiring is all good, then the fan is faulty. Individual components are available for the fan assembly.

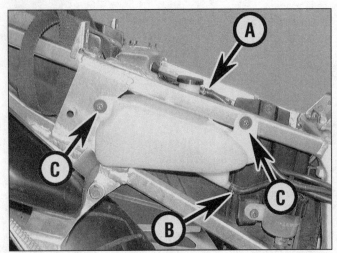

3.2 Breather/overflow hose (A), radiator overflow hose (B), mounting screws (C)

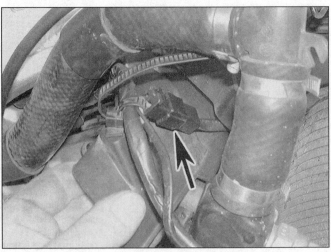

4.3 Fan motor wiring connector (arrowed)

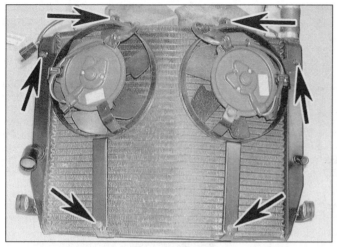

4.5 Fan assembly mounting bolts (arrowed) – YZF1000R model shown

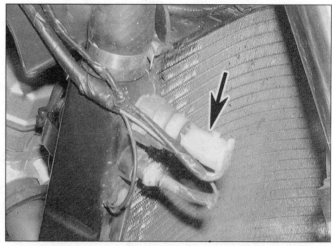

4.8 Disconnect the fan switch wiring connector (arrowed)

Renewal

> ⚠ **Warning: The engine must be completely cool before carrying out this procedure.**

4 Remove the radiator (see Section 7).

5 Unscrew the three bolts securing the relevant fan assembly to the radiator, noting any collars or clamps fitted with them, and remove the fan **(see illustration)**.

6 Installation is the reverse of removal. Tighten the bolts to the torque setting specified at the beginning of the Chapter.

Cooling fan switch

Check

7 If the engine is overheating and the cooling fans aren't coming on, first check the cooling fan circuit fuse (see Chapter 9). If the fuse is blown, check the fan circuit for a short to earth (see the wiring diagrams at the end of this book).

8 If the fuse is good, remove the right-hand fairing side panel (see Chapter 8). Disconnect

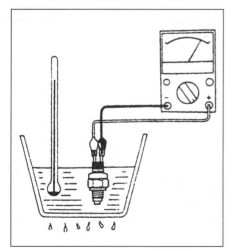

4.11 Fan switch testing set-up

the wiring connector from the fan switch, mounted in the front of the radiator above the gauge sender **(see illustration)**. Using a jumper wire, connect between the terminals in the wiring connector. The fan should come on. If it does, the fan switch is defective and must be replaced with a new one. If it does not come on, the fan should be tested (see Step 3).

9 If the fan stays on all the time, disconnect the wiring connector. The fan should stop. If it does, the switch is defective and must be replaced with a new one. If the fan doesn't stop, check the wiring between the switch and the fan, and the fan itself.

10 If the fan works but is suspected of cutting in at the wrong temperature, a more comprehensive test of the switch can be made as follows.

11 Remove the switch (see Steps 13 and 14). Fill a small heatproof container with coolant and place it on a stove. Connect the probes of an ohmmeter to the terminals of the switch, and using some wire or other support suspend the switch in the coolant so that just the sensing portion and the threads are submerged **(see illustration)**. Also place a thermometer capable of reading temperatures up to 110°C in the coolant so that its bulb is close to the switch. **Note:** *None of the components should be allowed to directly touch the container.*

12 Initially the ohmmeter reading should be very high indicating that the switch is open ('OFF'). Heat the coolant, stirring it gently.

> ⚠ **Warning: This must be done very carefully to avoid the risk of personal injury.**

When the temperature reaches around 102 to 108°C the meter reading should drop to around zero ohms, indicating that the switch has closed ('ON'). Now turn the heat off. As the temperature falls below 98°C the meter reading should show infinite (very high) resistance, indicating that the switch has opened ('OFF'). If the meter readings obtained

are different, or they are obtained at different temperatures, then the switch is faulty and must be replaced with a new one.

Renewal

> ⚠ **Warning: The engine must be completely cool before carrying out this procedure.**

13 Drain the cooling system (see Chapter 1).

14 Remove the right-hand fairing side panel (see Chapter 8). Disconnect the wiring connector from the fan switch, mounted in the front of the radiator **(see illustration 4.8)**. Unscrew the switch and remove it from the radiator **(see illustration)**.

15 Apply a suitable sealant to the switch threads, then install the switch and tighten it to the torque setting specified at the beginning of the Chapter. Take care not to overtighten the switch as it or the radiator could be damaged.

16 Reconnect the switch wiring and refill the cooling system (see Chapter 1).

3

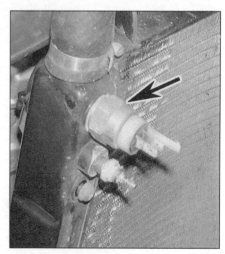

4.14 Unscrew the switch using a suitable spanner on the hex (arrowed)

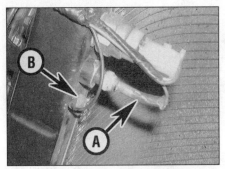

5.2 Temperature sender wiring connector (A), earth terminal (B)

5 Coolant temperature gauge and sender – check and renewal

Temperature gauge

Check

1 The circuit consists of the sender mounted in the radiator and the gauge assembly mounted in the instrument panel. If the system malfunctions check first that the battery is fully charged and that the fuses are all good. If they are, remove the right-hand fairing side panel (see Chapter 8).

2 Disconnect the wire from the sender and turn the ignition switch ON **(see illustration)**. The temperature gauge needle should be on the 'C' on the gauge. Now earth the sender wire on the engine. The needle should swing immediately over to the 'H' on the gauge. *Caution: Do not earth the wire for any longer than is necessary to take the reading, or the gauge may be damaged.*
If the needle moves as described above, the sender is proven defective and must be replaced with a new one (see below).

3 If the needle movement is still faulty, or if it does not move at all, the fault lies in the wiring or the gauge itself. Check all the relevant wiring and wiring connectors (see Chapter 9). If all appears to be well, the gauge is defective and must be renewed.

Renewal

4 See Chapter 9.

5.10 Unscrew the sender using a suitable spanner on the hex (arrowed)

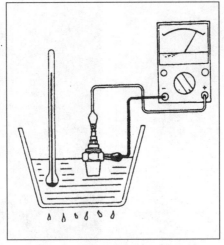

5.8 Temperature gauge sender testing set-up

Temperature gauge sender

Check

5 Drain the cooling system (see Chapter 1). The sender is mounted in the front of the radiator on the right-hand side, below the fan switch. Remove the right-hand fairing side panel (see Chapter 8).

6 Disconnect the sender wiring connector **(see illustration 5.2)**. Using a continuity tester, check for continuity between the sender body and earth (ground). There should be continuity. If there is no continuity, check that the sender mounting and the earth wire below it are secure, and that the earth terminal is clean **(see illustration 5.2)**.

7 Remove the sender (see Steps 14 and 15 below).

8 Fill a small heatproof container with water and place it on a stove. Using an ohmmeter, connect the positive (+ve) probe of the meter to the terminal on the sender, and the negative (–ve) probe to the body of the sender. Using some wire or other support suspend the sender in the coolant so that just the sensing portion and the threads are submerged. Also place a thermometer capable of reading temperatures up to 110°C in the water so that its bulb is close to the sender **(see illustration)**. **Note:** *None of the*

6.4a On YZF1000R models, slacken the clamps (arrowed) and detach the hoses from the thermostat housing . . .

components should be allowed to directly touch the container. Heat the coolant, stirring it gently.

> ⚠ **Warning: This must be done very carefully to avoid the risk of personal injury.**

When the temperature reaches around 80°C the meter reading should be as specified at the beginning of the Chapter. When the temperature reaches around 100°C the meter should again be as specified. If the meter readings obtained are different, or they are obtained at different temperatures, then the sender is faulty and must be renewed.

Renewal

> ⚠ **Warning: The engine must be completely cool before carrying out this procedure.**

9 Drain the cooling system (see Chapter 1). The sender is mounted in the front of the radiator on the right-hand side, below the fan switch. Remove the right-hand fairing side panel (see Chapter 8).

10 Disconnect the sender wiring connector **(see illustration 5.2)**. Unscrew the sender and remove it from the radiator **(see illustration)**.

11 Apply a suitable sealant to the switch threads, then install the switch and tighten it to the torque setting specified at the beginning of the Chapter. Take care not to overtighten the switch as it or the radiator could be damaged. Connect the sender wiring.

12 Refill the cooling system (see Chapter 1). Install the fairing side panel (see Chapter 8).

6 Thermostat housing and thermostat – removal, check and installation

1 The thermostat is automatic in operation and should give many years service without requiring attention. In the event of a failure, the valve will probably jam open, in which case the engine will take much longer than normal to warm up. Conversely, if the valve jams shut, the coolant will be unable to circulate and the engine will overheat. Neither condition is acceptable, and the fault must be investigated promptly.

Removal

> ⚠ **Warning: The engine must be completely cool before carrying out this procedure.**

Thermostat housing

2 Drain the cooling system (see Chapter 1).
3 Remove the carburettors (see Chapter 4).
4 Slacken the clamps securing the coolant hoses to the thermostat housing and the outlet union on the cylinder head and detach the hoses, noting which fits where **(see illustrations)**. Unscrew the bolts securing the union to the cylinder head and remove the union and housing together.

6.4b ... and the left-hand end of the outlet union (arrow) ...

6.4c ... then unscrew the union mounting bolts (arrowed)

5 If required, unscrew the bolts securing the housing to the union and separate them. Discard the O-ring.

Thermostat

6 Drain the cooling system (see Chapter 1).
7 Remove the fuel tank (see Chapter 4).
8 Unscrew the bolts securing the thermostat housing cover and separate it from the housing **(see illustration)**. Withdraw the thermostat, noting how it fits **(see illustration)**.

Check

9 Examine the thermostat visually before carrying out the test. If it remains in the open position at room temperature, it should be replaced with a new one.
10 Suspend the thermostat by a piece of wire in a container of cold water. Place a thermometer in the water so that the bulb is close to the thermostat **(see illustration)**. Heat the water, noting the temperature when the thermostat opens, and compare the result with the specifications given at the beginning of the Chapter. Also check the amount the valve opens after it has been heated at 85°C for a few minutes and compare the measurement to the specifications. If the readings obtained differ from those given, the thermostat is faulty and must be replaced with a new one.
11 In the event of thermostat failure, as an emergency measure only, it can be removed and the machine used without it. **Note:** *Take care when starting the engine from cold as it will take much longer than usual to warm up.* Ensure that a new unit is installed as soon as possible.

Installation

Thermostat housing

12 Installation is the reverse of removal. Use new O-rings and smear them with grease. Tighten the outlet union bolts to the torque setting specified at the beginning of the Chapter. Make sure the hoses are pushed fully on to their unions and are secured by the clamps **(see illustrations 6.4a, b and c, or 6.4d)**.
13 Refill the cooling system (see Chapter 1).

Thermostat

14 Fit the thermostat into the housing, making sure that it seats correctly and that the hole is at the top, aligned with the outlet hole in the housing **(see illustration 6.8b)**. Fit the cover onto the housing, then install the bolts and tighten them to the torque setting specified at the beginning of the Chapter **(see illustration)**.

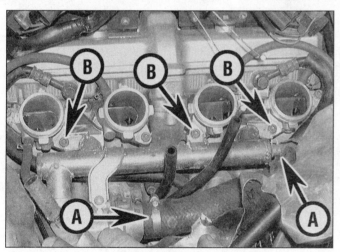
6.4d Hoses (A), union mounting bolts (B) – YZF750R and SP models

6.8a Unscrew the bolts (arrowed) ...

3

6.8b ... and remove the thermostat – YZF1000R model shown

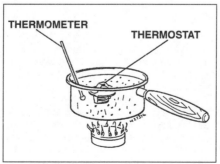
6.10 Thermostat testing set-up

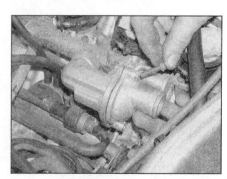
6.14 Installing the cover bolts

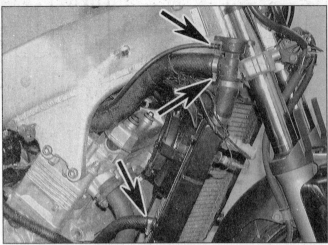

7.4a Release the clamps and detach the hoses (arrowed) from the right-hand side . . .

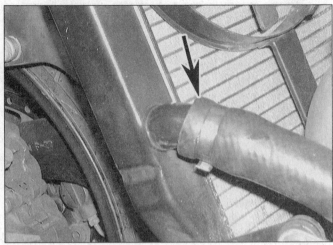

7.4b . . . and the left-hand side of the radiator – YZF1000R model shown

7 Radiator – removal and installation

Removal

⚠️ **Warning: The engine must be completely cool before carrying out this procedure.**

1 Remove the fairing side panels (see Chapter 8). On 1993 and 1994 YZF750R and SP models, also remove the fuel tank and air filter housing (see Chapter 4).
2 Drain the cooling system (see Chapter 1).
3 Trace the fan motor wiring and disconnect it at the connectors. On 1993 and 1994 YZF750R and SP models, they are located in front of the carburettors. On all other models, there is one on each end of the radiator **(see illustration 4.3)**.
4 Slacken the clamps securing all the radiator hoses and detach them from the radiator, noting which fits where **(see illustrations)**.
5 Unscrew the four bolts securing the radiator, noting the arrangement of the collars and rubber grommets, and carefully manoeuvre the radiator away from the machine, noting how it fits.
6 If necessary, remove the cooling fans from the radiator (see Section 4).
7 Check the radiator for signs of damage and clear any dirt or debris that might obstruct air flow and inhibit cooling. If the radiator fins are badly damaged or broken the radiator must be renewed. Also check the rubber mounting grommets, and replace them with new ones if necessary.

Installation

8 Installation is the reverse of removal, noting the following.
 a) Make sure the various collars and grommets are correctly installed with the mounting bolts. Tighten the bolts to the torque setting specified at the beginning of the Chapter.
 b) Make sure that the fan wiring is correctly connected.
 c) Ensure the coolant hoses are in good condition (see Chapter 1), and are securely retained by their clamps, using new ones if necessary.
 d) On completion refill the cooling system as described in Chapter 1.

8 Water pump – check, removal, seal and bearing renewal, and installation

Check

1 The water pump is located on the left-hand side of the engine. Visually check the area around the pump for signs of leakage.
2 To prevent leakage of water from the cooling system to the lubrication system and vice versa, two seals are fitted on the pump shaft. The seal on the water pump side is of the mechanical type which bears on the rear face of the impeller. The second seal, which is mounted behind the mechanical seal is of the normal feathered lip type. If on inspection there are signs of leakage, the seals must be removed and new ones installed. If you are not sure about their condition, remove the pump and check them visually, looking for signs of damage and leakage.
3 Remove the pump cover (see Step 7). Wiggle the water pump impeller back-and-forth and in-and-out, and spin it by hand. If there is excessive movement, or the pump is noisy or rough when turned, the drive shaft bearings must be renewed. If you are not sure about their condition, remove the pump and check them visually and mechanically, referring to *Tools and Workshop Tips* (Section 5) in the reference Section. Also check for corrosion or a build-up of scale in the pump body and clean or renew the pump as necessary.

Removal

4 Drain the coolant (see Chapter 1). Place a suitable container below the water pump to catch any residue as the water pump is removed.
5 Remove the front sprocket cover (see Chapter 6).
6 Slacken the clamp securing the coolant hose to the pump cover and detach the hose **(see illustration)**. Unscrew the bolt securing the coolant pipe to the engine **(see illustration)**.

8.6a Slacken the clamp (arrowed) and detach the hose

8.6b Unscrew the bolt (arrowed) securing the pipe

7 The pump can be removed complete by unscrewing the bolts that secure it to the crankcase, leaving the remaining bolts securing the cover untouched. To remove the cover, unscrew all the bolts. Note the position

8.7a Unscrew the pump bolts . . .

8.7b . . . and withdraw the pump from the crankcase, bringing the pipe with it

8.7c Remove the pump body O-ring and discard it

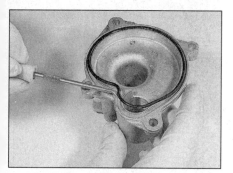

8.7d If the cover has been removed, discard its O-ring

of each bolt as they are different lengths, and some have washers. Carefully draw the pump from the crankcase, noting how it fits, bringing the pipe with it **(see illustrations)**. It may be necessary to lever it out to overcome the O-ring on the pump body. Separate the pipe from the pump. Remove the O-rings from the pipe and the rear of the pump body and discard them as new ones must be used **(see illustration)**. If the cover has been removed,

discard its O-ring, and also note the two locating pins **(see illustration)**.

Seal and bearing renewal

8 Remove the pump cover, then remove the pump (see above).
9 Remove the circlip on the impeller shaft and withdraw the impeller from the housing **(see illustration)**.

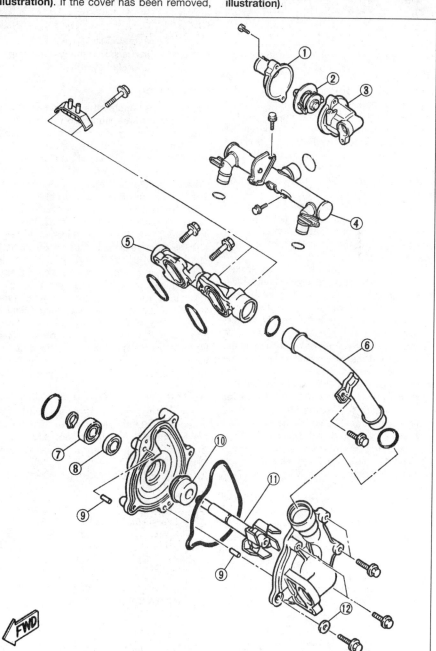

8.9 Water pump, inlet/outlet unions and thermostat components – there will be detail differences between models

1 Thermostat cover	5 Inlet union	9 Locating pin
2 Thermostat	6 Coolant pipe	10 Mechanical seal
3 Thermostat housing	7 Bearing	11 Impeller
4 Outlet union	8 Oil seal	12 Sealing washer

3

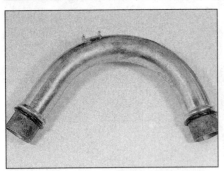

8.19a Fit a new O-ring onto each end of the pipe

8.19b Align the slot in the water pump shaft (arrowed) . . .

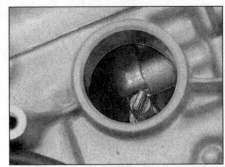

8.19c . . . with the tab on the oil pump shaft

10 To renew the bearing, tap it out from the inside of the housing using a bearing driver or suitable socket.

11 To renew the oil seal, first remove the bearing (see above). Tap the seal out from the inside of the housing using a bearing driver or suitable socket, noting which way round the seal fits. Discard it as a new one must be fitted.

12 To renew the mechanical seal, tap the seal out from the outside of the housing using a bearing driver or suitable socket, noting which way round the seal fits. Discard it as a new one must be fitted.

13 Smear Yamaha Bond 1215, Quick Gasket, or a suitable equivalent to the mechanical seal housing, then press or carefully drive the new mechanical seal into the front of the pump body using a suitable sized socket or seal driver.

14 Apply a smear of coolant to the lips of the new oil seal. Press or carefully drive the new oil seal into the rear of the pump body so that it fits against the back of the mechanical seal – use a suitable sized socket or seal driver and make sure the seal is the correct way round. Take care not dislodge the mechanical seal by driving the oil seal too far in.

15 Press or drive the new bearing into the rear of the pump body, using a suitable sized socket or bearing driver. Drive the bearing in until it is properly seated.

16 Check the condition of the rubber damper on the rear face of the impeller. If it is damaged or deteriorated, fit a new impeller as the damper is not available separately. Do not remove the damper from the shaft as it cannot be reused.

17 Slide the drive shaft and impeller into the housing and secure it with the circlip, making sure it is properly seated in its groove.

Installation

18 If removed, install the new cover O-ring into its groove **(see illustration 8.7d)**. Fit the cover, making sure it locates onto the pins, and tighten the bolts to the torque setting specified at the beginning of the Chapter.

19 Fit the new pump body O-ring **(see illustration 8.7c)** and pipe O-rings and smear them with grease **(see illustration)**. Press the pipe into the pump. Check the position of the tab on the end of the oil pump shaft, then turn the water pump shaft so that its slot will align with the tab on installation **(see illustrations)**. Slide the pump into the crankcase, making sure the slot locates correctly over the tab, and simultaneously fit the top end of the pipe into the union on the engine **(see illustration 8.7b)**. Install the bolts and tighten them to the torque setting specified at the beginning of the Chapter **(see illustration 8.7a)**. Make sure the different bolts are in their correct locations, with the washers where fitted. Install the pipe bolt and tighten it.

20 Attach the coolant hose to the pump cover and secure it with its clamp **(see illustration 8.6a)**. Also secure the coolant pipe with its bolt **(see illustration 8.6b)**.

21 Install the front sprocket cover (see Chapter 6).

22 Refill the cooling system (see Chapter 1).

9 Coolant hoses, pipes and unions – removal and installation

Removal

1 Before removing a hose, pipe or union, drain the coolant (see Chapter 1).

2 Use a screwdriver to slacken the larger-bore hose clamps, then slide them back along the hose and clear of the union spigot. The smaller-bore hoses are secured by spring clamps which can be expanded by squeezing their ears together with pliers.
Caution: The radiator unions are fragile. Do not use excessive force when attempting to remove the hoses.

3 If a hose proves stubborn, release it by rotating it on its union before working it off. If all else fails, cut the hose with a sharp knife then slit it at each union so that it can be peeled off in two pieces. Whilst this means renewing the hose, it is preferable to buying a new radiator.

4 Remove the coolant pipes and the unions on the cylinder head and block by detaching the hoses (see above), then unscrewing their retaining bolts. If they are removed, the O-rings must be renewed.

Installation

5 Slide the clamp onto the hose and then work it on to its respective union.

HAYNES HiNT *If the hose is difficult to push on its union, it can be softened by soaking it in very hot water, or alternatively a little soapy water can be used as a lubricant.*

6 Rotate the hose on its union to settle it in position before sliding the clamp into place and tightening it securely.

7 If the water pipes or unions on the engine have been removed, fit new O-rings and smear them with grease, then install them and tighten their mounting bolts to the torque setting specified at the beginning of the Chapter.

Chapter 4
Fuel and exhaust systems

Contents

Degrees of difficulty

Easy, suitable for novice with little experience	**Fairly easy,** suitable for beginner with some experience	**Fairly difficult,** suitable for competent DIY mechanic	**Difficult,** suitable for experienced DIY mechanic	**Very difficult,** suitable for expert DIY or professional

Specifications

Fuel

Grade	Unleaded, minimum 91 RON (Research Octane Number)
Fuel tank capacity (including reserve)	
YZF750R and SP models	19.0 litres
YZF1000R models	20.0 litres
Reserve	
YZF750R and SP models	3.5 litres
YZF1000R models	4.5 litres

Carburettors

Note: *Carburettor data is given for UK and US market models – specifications may differ for other markets.*

YZF750R – 1993 and 1994 UK models

Type	4 x Mikuni BDST38
Fuel level (see text)	6.8 to 7.8 mm above float chamber line
Idle speed	see Chapter 1
Pilot screw setting (turns out)	2
Main jet	
Cylinders 1 and 4	125
Cylinders 2 and 3	122.5
Main air jet	
Cylinders 1 and 4	45
Cylinders 2 and 3	60
Jet needle	
Cylinders 1 and 4	5CEX19
Cylinders 2 and 3	5CEX24
Needle jet	Y-2
Pilot air jet	125
Pilot jet	45
Starter jet 1	57.5
Starter jet 2	0.7

4

Carburettors (continued)

YZF750R – 1995-on UK models

Type	4 x Mikuni BDST38
Fuel level (see text)	6.8 to 7.8 mm above float chamber line
Idle speed	see Chapter 1
Pilot screw setting (turns out)	2½
Main jet	120
Main air jet	
Cylinders 1 and 4	60
Cylinders 2 and 3	110
Jet needle	
Cylinders 1 and 4	5CEX31
Cylinders 2 and 3	6CEZ11
Needle jet	Y-2
Pilot air jet	145
Pilot jet	45
Starter jet 1	57.5
Starter jet 2	0.7

YZF750R – US models

Type	4 x Mikuni BDST38
Fuel level (see text)	6.8 to 7.8 mm above float chamber line
Idle speed	see Chapter 1
Pilot screw setting (turns out)	
1994 models	3½
1995-on models	2
Main jet	122.5
Main air jet	
Cylinders 1 and 4	40
Cylinders 2 and 3	60
Jet needle	5CEX29
Needle jet	X-8
Pilot air jet	122.5
Pilot jet	35
Starter jet 1	57.5
Starter jet 2	0.7

YZF750SP – UK models

Type	4 x Keihin FCRD39
Fuel level (see text)	6.3 to 7.3 mm above dot mark
Idle speed	see Chapter 1
Pilot screw setting (turns out)	2 to 2½
Main jet	125
Main air jet	70
Jet needle	N1CB
Pilot air jet	120
Pilot jet	40

YZF1000R – UK models

Type	4 x Mikuni BDSR38
Fuel level (see text)	4.1 to 5.1 mm below line on float chamber
Idle speed	see Chapter 1
Pilot screw setting (turns out)	3
Main jet	
Cylinders 1 and 4	127.5
Cylinders 2 and 3	125
Main air jet	
Cylinders 1 and 4	60
Cylinders 2 and 3	45
Jet needle	6DEY1-53
Needle jet	P-0
Pilot air jet	127.5
Pilot jet	20
Starter jet 1	30
Starter jet 2	0.8

Carburettors (continued)

YZF1000R – US models

Type	4 x Mikuni BDSR38
Fuel level (see text)	4.1 to 5.1 mm below line on float chamber
Idle speed	see Chapter 1
Pilot screw setting (turns out)	pre-set
Main jet	
Cylinders 1 and 4	127.5
Cylinders 2 and 3	125
Main air jet	
Cylinders 1 and 4	60
Cylinders 2 and 3	45
Jet needle	6DJP15-53
Needle jet	P-0
Pilot air jet	122.5
Pilot jet	17.5
Starter jet 1	30
Starter jet 2	0.8

EXUP system

Servo motor static resistance	5.3 to 9.8 K-ohms
Servo motor variable resistance	zero to approx. 7.5 K-ohms

Fuel pump

Resistance	4.0 to 30 ohms @ 20°C

Torque wrench settings

Fuel tank mountings – YZF750R and SP models	
Front mounting bolt nut	7 Nm
Rear mounting bolt	16 Nm
Fuel tank mountings – YZF1000R models	
Front mounting bolt nut	10 Nm
Rear mounting bolt	10 Nm
Fuel tap screws	7 Nm
Carburettor joining bolts	
YZF750R	
Upper bolt	3.5 Nm
Lower bolt	5 Nm
YZF1000R	5 Nm
Silencer flange bolts (YZF1000R)	20 Nm
Silencer mounting bolt	
YZF750R and SP models	20 Nm
YZF1000R models	38 Nm
Downpipe assembly nuts	20 Nm
Downpipe assembly rear bolt	20 Nm
EXUP valve cover bolts	10 Nm
EXUP pulley cover bolts	10 Nm
Fuel pump mounting screws (YZF750R and SP models)	3 Nm
Fuel level sensor screws (YZF1000R models)	7 Nm

---

1 General information and precautions

General information

The fuel system consists of the fuel tank with internal level sensor, fuel tap, fuel filter, fuel pump, fuel hoses, carburettors and control cables. On YZF750R and SP models, the pump is housed inside the tank and has an integral filter. On YZF1000R models, the fuel tap has an integral strainer, and the fuel pump is mounted externally with an in-line filter.

The carburettors used on YZF750R and 1000R models are CV types, while the YZF750SP has standard slides. There is a carburettor for each cylinder. For cold starting, a choke lever is connected to the carburettors by a cable. On YZF750R and SP models, the lever is mounted behind the left-hand fairing side panel. On YZF1000R models, the lever is housed in the left-hand switch housing on the handlebar.

Air is drawn into the carburettors via an air filter which is housed under the fuel tank.

The exhaust system is a two-into-one design.

Many of the fuel system service procedures are considered routine maintenance items and for that reason are included in Chapter 1.

Precautions

⚠ **Warning: Petrol (gasoline) is extremely flammable, so take extra precautions when you work on any part of the fuel system. Don't smoke or allow open flames or bare light bulbs near the work area, and don't work in a garage where a natural gas-type appliance is present. If you spill any fuel on your skin, rinse it off immediately with soap and water. When you perform any kind of work on the fuel system, wear safety glasses and have a fire extinguisher suitable for a class B type fire (flammable liquids) on hand.**

Always perform service procedures in a well-ventilated area to prevent a build-up of fumes.

4

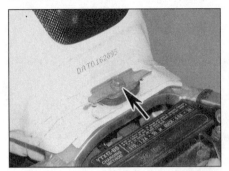

2.2 Unscrew the rear bolt (arrowed) and remove the plate

2.3a Place a rag over the front . . .

2.3b . . . then raise the rear and support it

Never work in a building containing a gas appliance with a pilot light, or any other form of naked flame. Ensure that there are no naked light bulbs or any sources of flame or sparks nearby.

Do not smoke (or allow anyone else to smoke) while in the vicinity of petrol (gasoline) or of components containing it. Remember the possible presence of vapour from these sources and move well clear before smoking.

Check all electrical equipment belonging to the house, garage or workshop where work is being undertaken (see the *Safety first!* section of this manual). Remember that certain electrical appliances such as drills, cutters etc. create sparks in the normal course of operation and must not be used near petrol (gasoline) or any component containing it. Again, remember the possible presence of fumes before using electrical equipment.

Always mop up any spilt fuel and safely

dispose of the rag used.

Any stored fuel that is drained off during servicing work must be kept in sealed containers that are suitable for holding petrol (gasoline), and clearly marked as such; the containers themselves should be kept in a safe place. Note that this last point applies equally to the fuel tank if it is removed from the machine; also remember to keep its filler cap closed at all times.

Read the *Safety first!* section of this manual carefully before starting work.

2 Fuel tank and fuel tap –
removal and installation

⚠️ **Warning: Refer to the precautions given in Section 1 before starting work.**

Fuel tank

Removal – YZF750R and SP models

1 Make sure the fuel cap is secure. Remove the rider's seat (see Chapter 8).
2 Unscrew the bolt and remove the plate securing the rear of the tank **(see illustration)**. Slacken the nut on the bolt at the front.
3 Place a rag over the front of the tank to protect it **(see illustration)**. Raise the tank at the rear and support it using a block of wood **(see illustration)**.
Caution: Do not raise the tank too high as the front could contact the fairing stay bolts and be damaged – place a rag between the tank and the stay as a precaution.
4 Release the clamp securing the drain hose to its union and detach the hose, then release it from the clip on the tank **(see illustration)**. Release the clamp securing the fuel hose to the fuel tap and detach the hose, being prepared to catch the residual fuel from the hose and the fuel filter with a rag **(see illustration)**. Also detach the vacuum hose from the tap **(see illustration)**. Disconnect the fuel pump and level sender wiring connector **(see illustration)**. On California models, also detach the EVAP hose from its union.
5 Remove the rag from the front of the tank. Unscrew the front mounting bolt nut and withdraw the bolt, then carefully lift the tank off the frame and remove it **(see illustrations)**.
6 Inspect the tank mounting rubbers for signs of damage or deterioration and replace them with new ones if necessary.

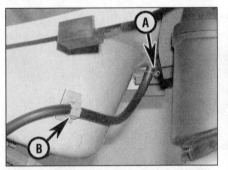

2.4a Detach the hose from its union (A) and release it from the clip (B)

2.4b Detach the fuel hose . . .

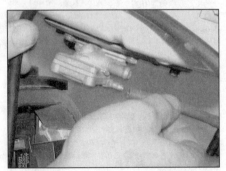

2.4c . . . and the vacuum hose . . .

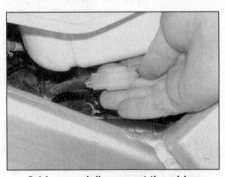

2.4d . . . and disconnect the wiring connector

2.5a Withdraw the front mounting bolt . . .

2.5b . . . and carefully remove the tank

2.8 Unscrew the nut and withdraw the front mounting bolt

2.9 Raise the front of the tank and support it

2.10a Turn the fuel tap OFF, and detach the fuel hose . . .

2.10b . . . and the drain hose . . .

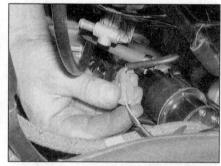

2.10c . . . and disconnect the wiring connector

Removal – YZF1000R models

7 Make sure the fuel cap is secure. Remove the side covers (see Chapter 8).
8 Slacken the bolt securing the rear of the tank, then unscrew the nut and withdraw the bolt securing the front of the tank **(see illustration)**.
9 Raise the tank at the front and support it using a block of wood **(see illustration)**. Turn the fuel tap off – it is located on the base of the tank **(see illustration 2.10a)**.
10 Release the clamp securing the fuel hose to the fuel tap and detach the hose, being prepared to catch any residual fuel with a rag **(see illustration)**. Release the clamp securing the drain hose to its union and detach the hose **(see illustration)**. Disconnect the fuel level sender wiring connector **(see illustration)**.
11 Remove the rear bolt and carefully lift the tank off the frame and remove it **(see illustration)**.
12 Inspect the tank mounting rubbers for signs of damage or deterioration and replace them with new ones if necessary.

Installation – all models

13 Installation is the reverse of removal, noting the following:
a) Make sure the hoses are properly attached and secured by their clamps. Make sure the wiring connector is securely connected.
b) On YZF1000R models, turn the fuel tap ON before lowering the tank.
c) Tighten the mounting bolts/nuts to the

torque settings specified at the beginning of the chapter.
d) Start the engine and check that there is no sign of fuel leakage, then shut if off.

Fuel tap

Removal – YZF750R and SP models

14 The tap should not be removed unnecessarily from the tank otherwise there is a possibility of damaging the O-ring or strainer.
15 Remove the fuel tank as described above.
16 Connect a drain hose to the fuel outlet union on the tap and insert its end in a container suitable and large enough for storing the fuel. Apply a vacuum to the tap using an auxiliary hose connected to the vacuum hose union and allow the tank to drain.

2.11 Carefully lift the tank off the bike

17 If the fuel tap has been leaking, tightening the assembly screws may help **(see illustration)**. Slacken all the screws a little first, then tighten them evenly a little at a time to ensure the cover seats properly on the tap body. If leakage persists, the tap should be replaced with a new one, however nothing is lost by dismantling the tap for further inspection. Remove the assembly screws and disassemble it, noting how the components fit. Inspect all components for wear or damage. If any of the components are worn or damaged beyond repair, a new tap must be fitted.
18 If no fuel has been flowing from the tap, it is likely that there is a split either in the vacuum hose or in the diaphragm. Replace the hose with a new one if necessary. If the diaphragm is split, a new tap must be fitted.
19 Remove the screws securing the tap to

4

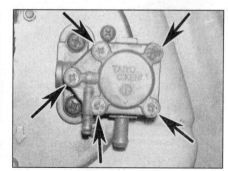

2.17 Fuel tap assembly screws (arrowed) – YZF750R and SP models

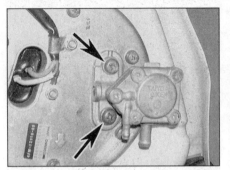

2.19 Fuel tap mounting screws (arrowed) – YZF750R and SP models

the tank and remove the tap assembly **(see illustration)**. Discard the O-ring as a new one must be used.

Removal – YZF1000R models

20 The tap should not be removed unnecessarily from the tank otherwise there is a possibility of damaging the O-ring or strainer.

21 Remove the fuel tank as described above.

22 Connect a drain hose to the fuel outlet union on the tap and insert its end in a container suitable and large enough for storing the fuel. Turn the fuel tap to the 'ON' position and allow the tank to drain. When the tank has drained, turn the tap to the 'OFF' position.

23 If the fuel tap has been leaking, tightening the assembly screws on the tap face may help. Slacken the screws a little first, then tighten them evenly and a little at a time to

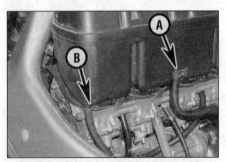

4.2 Detach the crankcase breather hose (A) and the drain hose (B) from the housing

4.3a Unscrew the bolt . . .

2.24 Fuel tap mounting screws (arrowed) – YZF1000R models

ensure the cover seats properly on the tap body. If leakage persists, the tap should be replaced with a new one, however nothing is lost by dismantling the tap for further inspection. Remove the screws on the face of the tap and disassemble it, noting how the components fit. Inspect all components for wear or damage, and replace them with new ones as necessary, if available. If any of the components are worn or damaged beyond repair and are not available individually, a new tap must be fitted.

24 Remove the screws securing the tap to the tank and withdraw the tap assembly **(see illustration)**. Discard the O-ring as a new one must be used.

25 Clean the gauze strainer to remove all traces of dirt and fuel sediment. Check the gauze for holes. If any are found, a new tap should be fitted as the strainer is not available individually.

Installation – all models

26 Installation is the reverse of removal.

27 Use a new O-ring on the tap, and tighten the screws to the torque setting specified at the beginning of the Chapter.

28 Install the fuel tank (see above).

3 Fuel tank –
cleaning and repair

1 All repairs to the fuel tank should be carried out by a professional who has experience in this critical and potentially dangerous work.

4.3b . . . then slacken the four carburettor clamp screws (arrowed) . . .

Even after cleaning and flushing of the fuel system, explosive fumes can remain and ignite during repair of the tank.

2 If the fuel tank is removed from the bike, it should not be placed in an area where sparks or open flames could ignite the fumes coming out of the tank. Be especially careful inside garages where a natural gas-type appliance is located, because the pilot light could cause an explosion.

4 Air filter housing –
removal and installation

Removal

1 Remove the fuel tank (see Section 2).

2 Release the clamps securing the crankcase breather hose and the drain hose to the air filter housing and detach the hoses **(see illustration)**.

3 Unscrew the bolt securing the front of the housing to the frame **(see illustration)**. Slacken the clamp screws securing the housing to the carburettor intakes on the underside **(see illustration)**.

4 Lift the housing up off the carburettors and remove it **(see illustration)**.

Installation

5 Installation is the reverse of removal. Check the condition of the various hoses and their clamps and replace them with new ones if necessary.

5 Air/fuel mixture adjustment –
general information

Adjustment – UK

1 If the engine runs extremely rough at idle or continually stalls, and if a carburettor overhaul does not cure the problem, the pilot screws probably require adjustment to achieve a smooth idle and restore low speed performance. It is worth noting at this point that unless you have the skill to carry this out on a multi-cylinder machine it is best to entrust the task to a motorcycle dealer, tuner

4.4 . . . and lift the housing off the carburettors

or fuel systems specialist. Note that you will need a long thin screwdriver with an angled end to access the pilot screws. Remove the fairing side panels (see Chapter 8).

2 Before adjusting the pilot screws, the engine must be warmed up to normal working temperature. Stop the engine and screw in all four pilot screws until they seat lightly, then back them out to the number of turns specified (see this Chapter's Specifications). This is the base position for adjustment.

3 Start the engine and reset the idle speed to the correct level (see Chapter 1). Working on one carburettor at a time, turn the pilot screw by a small amount either side of this position to find the point at which the highest consistent idle speed is obtained. When you've reached this position, reset the idle speed to the specified amount (see Chapter 1). Repeat on the other three carburettors in turn.

Other markets

4 Due to the increased emphasis on controlling exhaust emissions in certain world markets, regulations have been formulated which prevent adjustment of the air/fuel mixture. On such models the pilot screw positions are pre-set at the factory and in some cases have a limiter cap fitted to prevent tampering. Where adjustment is possible, it can only be made in conjunction with an exhaust gas analyser to ensure that the machine does not exceed the emissions regulations.

6 Carburettor overhaul – general information

1 Poor engine performance, hesitation, hard starting, stalling, flooding and backfiring are all signs that major carburettor maintenance may be required.

2 Keep in mind that many so-called carburettor problems are really not carburettor problems at all, but mechanical problems within the engine, or ignition system malfunctions. Try to establish for certain that the carburettors are in need of maintenance before beginning a major overhaul.

3 Check the fuel tap and filter, the fuel hoses, the fuel pump, the intake manifold joint clamps, the air filter, the ignition system, the spark plugs and carburettor synchronisation before assuming that a carburettor overhaul is required.

4 Most carburettor problems are caused by dirt particles, varnish and other deposits which build up in and block the fuel and air passages. Also, in time, gaskets and O-rings shrink or deteriorate and cause fuel and air leaks which lead to poor performance.

5 When overhauling the carburettors, disassemble them completely and clean the parts thoroughly with a carburettor cleaning solvent and dry them with filtered, unlubricated compressed air. Blow through

the fuel and air passages with compressed air to force out any dirt that may have been loosened but not removed by the solvent. Once the cleaning process is complete, reassemble the carburettor using new gaskets and O-rings.

6 Before disassembling the carburettors, make sure you have all necessary O-rings and other parts, some carburettor cleaner, a supply of clean rags, some means of blowing out the carburettor passages and a clean place to work. It is recommended that only one carburettor be overhauled at a time to avoid mixing up parts.

7 Carburettors – removal and installation

Warning: Refer to the precautions given in Section 1 before starting work.

Removal

1 Remove the fuel tank (see Section 2) and the air filter housing (see Section 4). On YZF750R and SP models, remove the left-hand fairing side panel (see Chapter 8).

2 On YZF750R models, detach the carburettor breather hoses, and on California models the emission system hoses, from their unions **(see illustration)**. Release the clamp securing the fuel supply hose to the carburettors and detach the hose **(see illustration)**. On 1995-on European models, disconnect the throttle position sensor wiring connector **(see illustration)**. Displace the ignition HT coils to provide access to the clamp bolts (see Chapter 5).

3 On YZF750SP models, detach the carburettor breather hoses from their unions. Release the clamp securing the fuel supply hose to the carburettors and detach the hose. Free the idle speed adjuster from its holder and feed it through to the base of the carburettors. Disconnect the throttle position sensor wiring connector. Displace the ignition HT coils and remove the rubber cover (see Chapter 5).

4 On YZF1000R models, drain the cooling system (see Chapter 1). Detach the carburettor breather hoses from the union on

7.2a Detach the breather hoses . . .

7.2b . . . and the fuel hose . . .

7.2c . . . and disconnect the throttle position sensor wiring connector (arrowed)

the back of the engine, and on California models detach the emission system hoses **(see illustration)**. Release the clamp securing the fuel supply hose to the carburettors and detach the hose **(see illustration)**. Free the

4

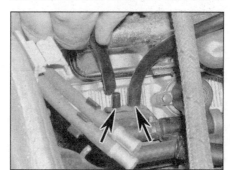

7.4a Detach the breather hoses (arrowed) . . .

7.4b . . . and the fuel hose

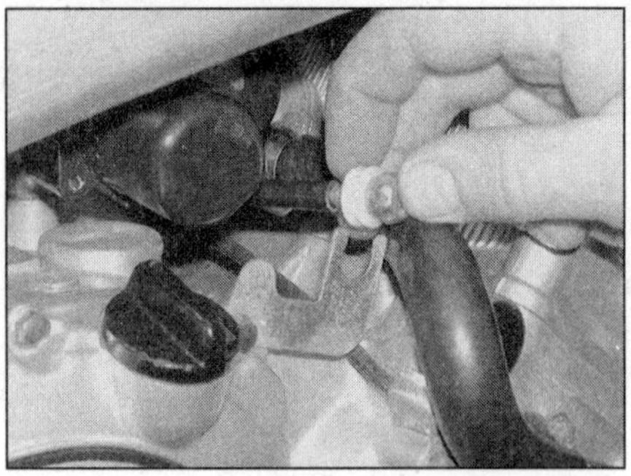

7.4c Free the idle speed adjuster from its holder

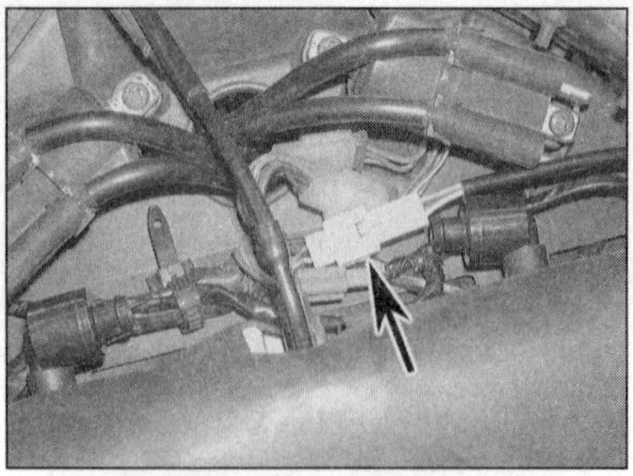

7.4d Disconnect the throttle position sensor wiring connector (arrowed)

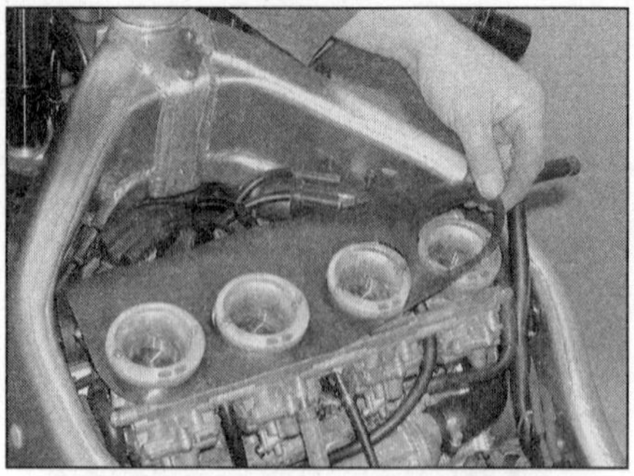

7.4e Pull back the rubber cover . . .

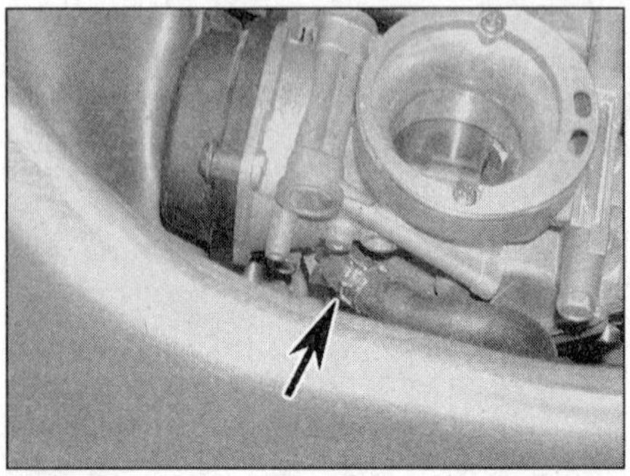

7.4f . . . and detach the heater system hose (arrowed) from each end of the carburettors

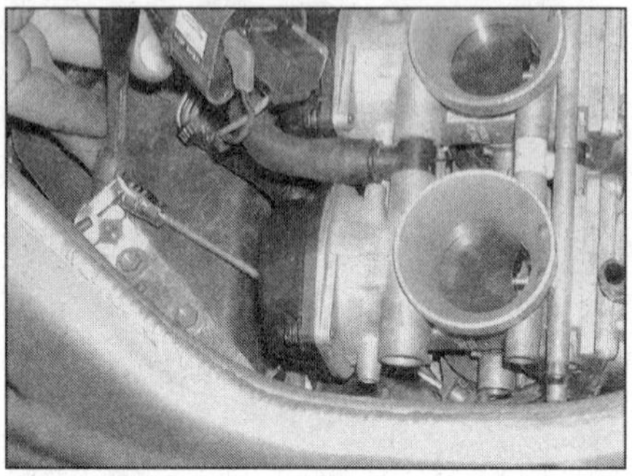

7.7 Access the clamp bolts from the front as shown

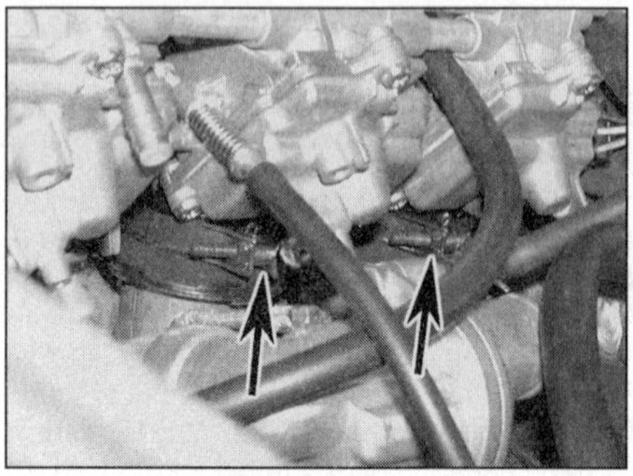

7.8a The clamp bolts (arrowed) are difficult to access . . .

idle speed adjuster from its holder and feed it through to the base of the carburettors **(see illustration)**. Disconnect the throttle position sensor wiring connector **(see illustration)**. Fold back the rubber cover, pulling the vent hose unions through at the same time **(see illustration)**. Release the clamps securing the heater system inlet and outlet hoses and detach the hoses **(see illustration)**.

5 Detach the choke cable from the carburettors (see Section 12).

6 Detach the throttle cables from the carburettors (see Section 11). If access is too restricted, detach them after the carburettors have been lifted off the cylinder head intakes.

7 On YZF750R and SP models, fully slacken the lower clamp bolts on the cylinder head intake rubbers using a suitable Allen key extension – access them from the front of the carburettors **(see illustration)**.

8 On YZF1000R models, fully slacken the upper clamp bolts on the cylinder head intake rubbers **(see illustration)**. The bolts are angled which makes access awkward – for easier access to the No. 4 bolt, detach the coolant hose from its union on the thermostat housing **(see illustration)**.

9 Ease the carburettors off the intakes and remove them **(see illustration)**. **Note:** *Keep the carburettors level to prevent fuel spillage from the float chambers and the possibility of the piston diaphragms being damaged.*

Caution: Stuff clean rag into each cylinder head intake after removing the carburettors to prevent anything from falling in.

10 Place a suitable container below the float chambers, then slacken the drain screw on each chamber in turn and drain all the fuel from the carburettors **(see illustration)**. Tighten the drain screws securely once all the fuel has been drained.

Installation

11 Installation is the reverse of removal, noting the following.

a) Check for cracks or splits in the cylinder head intake rubbers, and replace them with new ones if necessary.

b) On 1993 and 1994 YZF750R models and all SP models, if the carburettors are to be synchronised, prepare the gauges and hoses before installing the carburettors (see Chapter 1).

c) Make sure the carburettors are fully engaged with the air and cylinder head intake rubbers and the clamps are securely tightened.

d) Make sure all hoses are correctly routed and secured and not trapped or kinked.

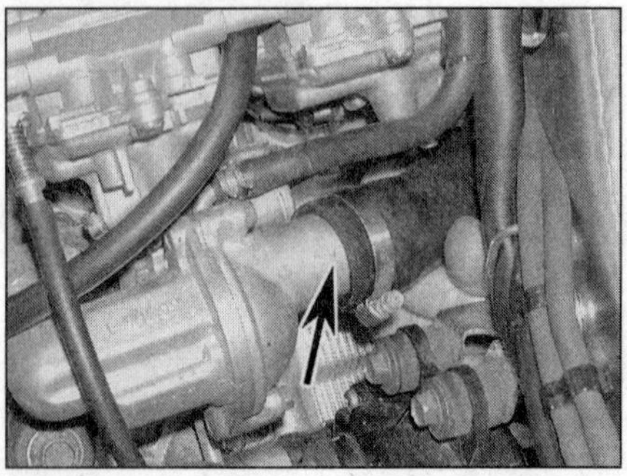

7.8b . . . detach the coolant hose from the thermostat housing (arrowed) to improve it

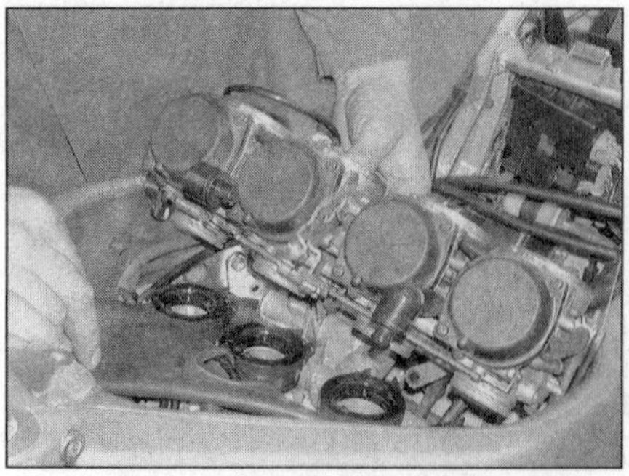

7.9 Lift the carburettors off the intakes and remove them

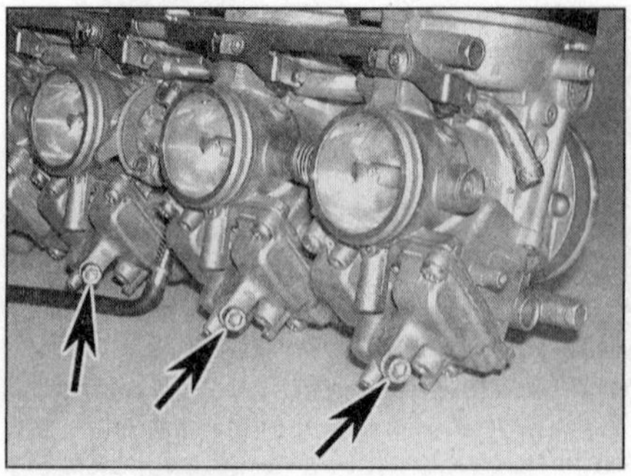

7.10 Carburettor drain screws (arrowed) – YZF1000R model shown

e) *Refer to Section 11 for installation of the throttle cables, and Section 12 for the choke cable. Check the operation of the cables and adjust them as necessary (see Chapter 1).*

f) *Check idle speed and carburettor synchronisation and adjust as necessary (see Chapter 1).*

g) *On YZF1000R models, do not forget to refill the cooling system (see Chapter 1).*

8 Carburettors –
disassembly, cleaning and inspection

Warning: Refer to the precautions given in Section 1 before starting work.

Disassembly

1 Remove the carburettors from the machine as described in the previous Section. **Note:** *Do not separate the carburettors unless absolutely necessary; each carburettor can be dismantled sufficiently for all normal cleaning and adjustments while in place on the mounting brackets. Dismantle the carburettors separately to avoid interchanging parts.*

YZF750R models

2 Unscrew and remove the top cover retaining screws and remove the cover **(see illustrations)**.

3 Remove the spring from inside the piston – the jet needle may well come away with it as it fits into a seat in the bottom of the spring **(see illustration)**. Carefully peel the diaphragm away from its sealing groove in the carburettor and withdraw the diaphragm and piston assembly **(see illustration)**. Remove the air passage O-ring **(see illustration 10.6)**. If the jet needle did not come out with the spring, push it up from the bottom of the piston and withdraw it from the top. If the E-clip and spacer are removed from the needle, note which notch the clip is fitted into. **Caution: Do not use a sharp instrument to displace the diaphragm as it is easily damaged.**

4 Remove the screws securing the float chamber to the base of the carburettor and remove the float chamber, noting how it fits

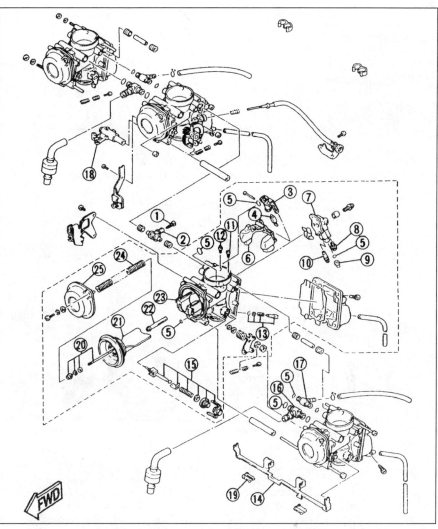

8.2a Carburettor assembly components – YZF750R models

1 Fuel filter	10 Pilot jet	18 Choke joint
2 Fuel T-piece	11 Pilot air jet	19 Clip
3 Needle valve seat	12 Main air jet	20 Jet needle assembly
4 Needle valve	13 Pilot screw	21 Throttle slide/diaphragm
5 O-ring	14 Choke linkage shaft	22 Needle jet
6 Float	15 Choke plunger assembly	23 Guide
7 Jet housing	16 Vacuum chamber vent	24 Spring
8 Starter jet	union	25 Top cover
9 Main jet	17 Float chamber vent union	

4

8.2b Remove the top cover . . .

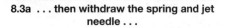

8.3a . . . then withdraw the spring and jet needle . . .

8.3b . . . and the piston/diaphragm assembly

8.4 Float chamber screws (arrowed)

8.5a Withdraw the pivot pin . . .

8.5b . . . and remove the float assembly

8.5c Remove the needle valve seat

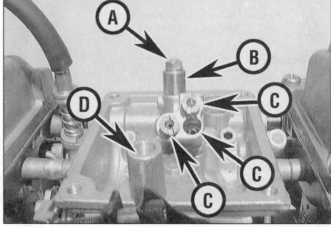

8.6a Unscrew the bolt (A) and remove the collar (B). Jets (C), idle mixture screw (D)

(see illustration). Remove the rubber gasket and discard it as a new one must be used. Note how the idle speed adjuster holder is secured on the left-hand carburettor.

5 Using a pair of thin-nose pliers, carefully withdraw the float pivot pin (see illustration). If necessary, carefully displace the pin using a small punch or a nail. Remove the float assembly, noting how it fits (see illustration). Unhook the needle valve from the tab on the float, noting how it fits (see illustration 10.4b). Remove the needle valve seat (see illustration). Discard its O-ring as a new one must be used.

6 Remove the jets from the holder if required, noting which fits where (see illustration).

Unscrew the bolt securing the jet holder and remove the collar. Lift the holder up off the needle jet, noting its O-ring (see illustration).

7 The pilot screw can be removed from the carburettor, but note that its setting will be disturbed (see Haynes Hint). Unscrew and remove the pilot screw along with its spring, washer and O-ring (see illustration 8.6a). Discard the O-ring as a new one must be used.

 HAYNES HiNT *To record the pilot screw's current setting, turn the screw in until it seats lightly, counting the number of turns necessary to achieve this, then*

fully unscrew it. On installation, the screw is simply backed out the number of turns you've recorded.

8 Release and push out the clips securing the choke linkage bar to the carburettors (see illustration). Lift off the bar, noting how it fits (see illustration). Release the choke plunger retainer clips, and withdraw the plunger assembly from the carburettor body.

9 On 1995-on European models, a throttle position sensor is mounted on the outside of the right-hand carburettor. Do not remove the sensor from the carburettor unless it is known to be faulty and is being replaced with a new

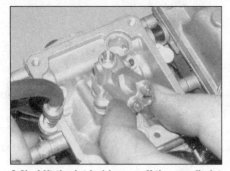

8.6b Lift the jet holder up off the needle jet

8.8a Push out the clips . . .

8.8b . . . and remove the linkage bar

YZF750SP models

10 Unscrew and remove the top cover retaining screws and remove the cover **(see illustration)**.

11 Carefully release the throttle slide from the throttle lever, noting how the rollers on the lever arms locate in the slits in the slide. It may be necessary to slacken the synchronisation screw locknut and back-off the screw to provide some clearance for the lever – if this is done, note exactly how many turns you back-off the screw as this will aid installation and set-up later on. The No. 2 carburettor is the base carburettor, and as such the position of its screw should not be altered. However if it is not possible to remove the slide without slackening it, note its current position well.

12 Remove the jet needle holder and withdraw the needle from the slide. If the E-clip is removed from the needle, note which notch it is fitted into.

13 Remove the screws securing the accelerator pump cover and remove the cover, spring, diaphragm and O-rings.

14 Remove the screws securing the float chamber to the base of the carburettor and remove the float chamber, noting how it fits. Remove the rubber gasket and discard it as a new one must be used.

15 Using a pair of thin-nose pliers, carefully withdraw the float pivot pin. If necessary, carefully displace the pin using a small punch or a nail. Remove the float assembly, noting how it fits. Unhook the needle valve from the tab on the float, noting how it fits. Remove the screw securing the needle valve seat and draw out the seat. Discard its O-ring as a new one must be used.

16 Unscrew and remove the main jet.

17 Unscrew and remove the pilot jet.

18 Unscrew and remove the starter jet.

19 Unscrew and remove the needle jet.

20 The pilot screw can be removed from the carburettor, but note that its setting will be disturbed **(see Haynes Hint)**. Unscrew and remove the pilot screw along with its spring, washer and O-ring. Discard the O-ring as a new one must be used.

 HAYNES HINT *To record the pilot screw's current setting, turn the screw in until it seats lightly, counting the number of turns necessary to achieve this, then fully unscrew it. On installation, the screw is simply backed out the number of turns you've recorded.*

21 Unhook the choke linkage bar return spring, noting how it fits. Remove the screws securing the choke linkage bar to the carburettors, noting the outer plastic washers. Lift off the bar, noting how it fits and remove the inner plastic washers. Unscrew the choke

plunger nut, using a pair of thin nosed pliers if access is too restricted for a spanner, and withdraw the plunger assembly from the carburettor body.

22 A throttle position sensor is mounted on the outside of the right-hand carburettor. Do not remove the sensor from the carburettor unless it is known to be faulty and is being replaced with a new one. Refer to Chapter 5 for check and adjustment of the sensor.

YZF1000R models

23 Unscrew and remove the top cover retaining screws and remove the cover **(see illustrations)**.

24 Remove the spring from inside the piston **(see illustration)**. Carefully peel the diaphragm away from its sealing groove in the carburettor and withdraw the diaphragm and piston assembly **(see illustration)**. Using a

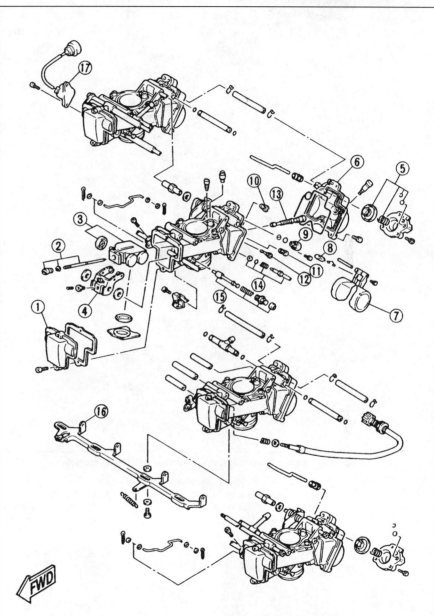

8.10 Carburettor assembly components – YZF750SP models

1 Top cover	6 Float chamber	12 Pilot jet
2 Jet needle	7 Float	13 Needle jet
3 Throttle slide	8 Needle valve	14 Pilot screw
4 Throttle lever	9 Needle valve seat	15 Choke plunger
5 Accelerator pump assembly	10 Main jet	16 Choke linkage bar
	11 Starter jet	17 Throttle position sensor

4

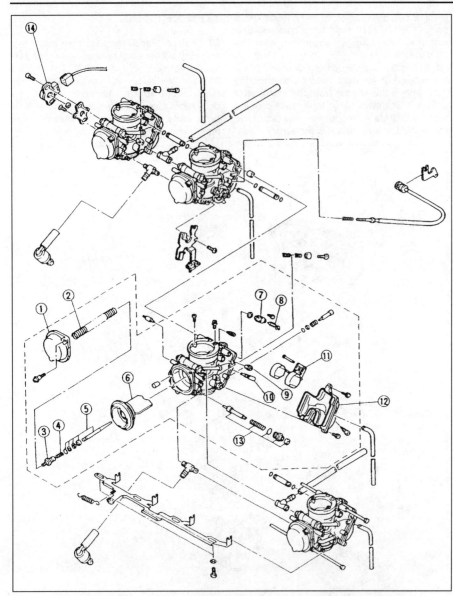

8.23a Carburettor assembly components – YZF1000R models

1 Top cover	6 Throttle slide/diaphragm	11 Float
2 Spring	7 Float valve seat	12 Float chamber
3 Jet needle holder	8 Float valve	13 Choke plunger assembly
4 Spring	9 Main jet	14 Throttle position sensor
5 Jet needle assembly	10 Pilot jet	

8.23b Remove the screws (arrowed) and lift off the cover

8.24a Withdraw the spring . . .

pair of thin-nosed pliers, carefully withdraw the jet needle holder from inside the piston – it is a press fit, held by an O-ring **(see illustration)**. Note the spring fitted into the bottom of the holder. Push the jet needle up from the bottom of the piston and withdraw it from the top, noting the washer on the top of the needle **(see illustration)**. If the E-clip and spacer are removed from the needle, note which notch the clip is fitted into.

Caution: Do not use a sharp instrument to displace the diaphragm as it is easily damaged.

25 Remove the screws securing the float chamber to the base of the carburettor and remove the float chamber, noting how it fits **(see illustration)**. Remove the rubber gasket and discard it as a new one must be used.

26 Using a pair of thin-nose pliers, carefully withdraw the float pivot pin **(see illustration)**.

8.24b . . . and the diaphragm/piston assembly

8.24c Pull the jet needle holder out of the piston

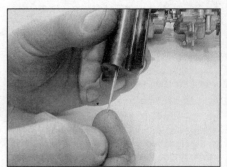

8.24d Push the needle up from the bottom and withdraw it from the top

8.25 Float chamber screws (arrowed)

8.26a Withdraw the pivot pin and remove the float

8.26b Remove the screw (arrowed) and pull out the needle valve seat

8.27 Remove the main jet (arrowed) . . .

8.28 . . . the needle jet (arrowed) . . .

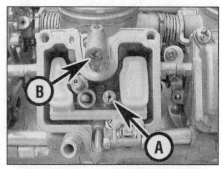

8.29 . . . and the pilot jet (A), and if necessary the pilot screw (B)

If necessary, carefully displace the pin using a small punch or a nail. Remove the float assembly, noting how it fits **(see illustration 10.24d)**. Unhook the needle valve from the tab on the float, noting how it fits

8.31a Unhook the return spring . . .

(see illustration 10.24c). Remove the screw securing the needle valve seat and draw out the seat **(see illustration)**. Discard its O-ring as a new one must be used.

27 Unscrew and remove the main jet **(see illustration)**.
28 Unscrew and remove the needle jet **(see illustration)**.
29 Unscrew and remove the pilot jet **(see illustration)**.
30 The pilot screw can be removed from the carburettor, but note that its setting will be disturbed **(see Haynes Hint)**. Unscrew and remove the pilot screw along with its spring, washer and O-ring **(see illustration 8.29)**. Discard the O-ring as a new one must be used.

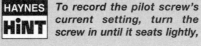

HAYNES HiNT *To record the pilot screw's current setting, turn the screw in until it seats lightly,*

counting the number of turns necessary to achieve this, then fully unscrew it. On installation, the screw is simply backed out the number of turns you've recorded.

31 Unhook the choke linkage bar return spring, noting how it fits **(see illustration)**. Remove the screws securing the choke linkage bar to the carburettors, noting the plastic washers **(see illustration)**. Lift off the bar, noting how it fits **(see illustration 10.22b)**. Unscrew the choke plunger nut, using a pair of thin nosed pliers if access is too restricted for a spanner **(see illustration)**, and withdraw the plunger assembly from the carburettor body **(see illustration 10.22a)**.
32 Carefully withdraw the fuel strainer from the fuel inlet union **(see illustration)**. Clean the strainer in new fuel.

4

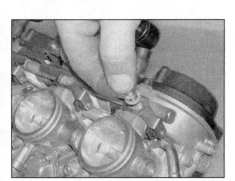

8.31b . . . then remove the screws and lift off the linkage bar . . .

8.31c . . . and unscrew the choke plunger nut

8.32 Withdraw the strainer from the union

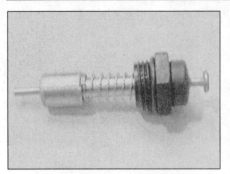

8.37 Choke plunger assembly – YZF1000R model shown

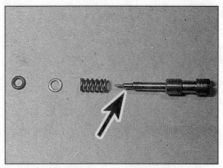

8.38 Check the tapered portion of the pilot screw (arrowed) for wear

33 A throttle position sensor is mounted on the outside of the right-hand carburettor. Do not remove the sensor from the carburettor unless it is known to be faulty and is being replaced with a new one. Refer to Chapter 5 for check and adjustment of the sensor.

Cleaning

Caution: Use only a petroleum based solvent for carburettor cleaning. Don't use caustic cleaners.

34 Submerge the metal components in the solvent for approximately thirty minutes (or longer, if the directions recommend it).

35 After the carburettor has soaked long enough for the cleaner to loosen and dissolve most of the varnish and other deposits, use a nylon-bristled brush to remove the stubborn deposits. Rinse it again, then dry it with compressed air.

36 Use a jet of compressed air to blow out all of the fuel and air passages in the main and upper body. Do not forget to blow through the air jets and passages in the intake side of the carburettor. The jets can be removed if required.

Caution: Never clean the jets or passages with a piece of wire or a drill bit, as they will be enlarged, causing the fuel and air metering rates to be upset.

Inspection

Note: *On YZF750SP models, individual carburettor bodies are not available – if there is a problem with one of the bodies, it is necessary to renew all four bodies as a set. Internal components are available individually.*

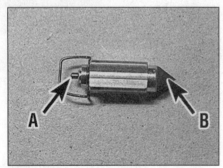

8.44 Check the valve's spring loaded rod (A) and tip (B) for wear or damage

37 Check the operation of the choke plunger assembly. If it doesn't move smoothly, inspect the needle on the end of the choke plunger, the spring and the plunger linkage bar **(see illustration)**. Replace the assembly with a new one if any component is worn, damaged or bent – individual parts are not available.

38 If removed from the carburettor, check the tapered portion of the pilot screw and the spring and O-ring for wear or damage **(see illustration)**. Replace the assembly with a new one if necessary – individual parts are not available.

39 Check the carburettor body, float chamber and top cover for cracks, distorted sealing surfaces and other damage. If any defects are found, replace the faulty component with a new one, although replacement of the entire carburettor may be necessary (check with a Yamaha dealer on the availability of separate components).

40 On YZF750R and YZF1000R models, check the piston diaphragm for splits, holes and general deterioration. Holding it up to a light will help to reveal problems of this nature.

41 On YZF750SP models, check the accelerator pump diaphragm for splits, holes and general deterioration. Holding it up to a light will help to reveal problems of this nature. Also check the spring for distortion.

42 Insert the piston or slide in the carburettor body and check that it moves up-and-down smoothly. Check the surface of the piston or slide for wear. If it's worn excessively or doesn't move smoothly in the guide, replace the components with new ones as necessary.

43 Check the jet needle for straightness by rolling it on a flat surface such as a piece of glass. Replace it with a new one if it's bent or if the tip is worn.

44 Check the tip of the float needle valve and the valve seat. If either has grooves or scratches in it, or is in any way worn, they must be renewed as a set **(see illustration)**.

45 Operate the throttle shaft to make sure the throttle butterfly valve (R models) or lever (SP models) opens and closes smoothly. If it doesn't, clean the throttle linkage, and also check the butterfly for distortion, or for any debris caught between its edge and the

carburettor. Also check that the butterfly is central on the shaft – if the screws securing it to the shaft have come loose it may be catching. On YZF750SP models, check the rollers on the ends of the lever arms and the slots in the slides. Otherwise, replace the carburettor with a new one.

46 Check the float for damage. This will usually be apparent by the presence of fuel inside the float. If it is damaged, replace it with a new one.

9 Carburettors – separation and joining (YZF750R and YZF1000R models only)

⚠️ *Warning: Refer to the precautions given in Section 1 before proceeding.*
Caution: Do not separate the carburettors on YZF750SP models.

Separation

1 The carburettors do not need to be separated for normal overhaul. If you need to separate them (to replace a carburettor body with a new one, for example), refer to the following procedure.

2 Remove the carburettors from the machine (see Section 7). Mark the body of each carburettor with its cylinder location to ensure that it is positioned correctly on reassembly **(see illustration 8.2a or 8.23a)**.

3 Make a note of how the throttle return springs, linkage assembly and carburettor synchronisation springs are arranged to ensure that they are fitted correctly on reassembly **(see illustrations)**. Also note the arrangement of the various hoses, unions, joint pieces and collars, and of the cable brackets **(see illustrations)**.

4 On YZF750R models, release and push out the clips securing the choke linkage bar to the carburettors **(see illustration 8.8a)**. Lift off the bar, noting how it fits **(see illustration 8.8b)**.

5 On YZF1000R models, unhook the choke linkage bar return spring, noting how it fits **(see illustration 8.31a)**. Remove the screws securing the choke linkage bar to the carburettors, noting the plastic washers **(see illustration 8.31b)**. Lift off the bar, noting how it fits **(see illustration 10.22b)**.

6 The carburettors are joined by two long bolts which pass through them **(see illustrations)**. Remove the bolts and any spacing collars, on YZF750R models noting how the choke cable lever fits on the top bolt.

7 Mark the position of each carburettor and gently separate them, noting how the throttle linkage is connected, and being careful not to lose any springs or fuel and vent fittings that are present between the carburettors, noting any O-rings fitted with them.

Joining

8 Where fitted, install new O-rings on the fuel and vent fittings. Lubricate the O-rings with a

9.3a Carburettor assembly –
YZF750R models

9.3b Carburettor assembly –
YZF1000R models

9.3c Carburettor assembly –
YZF750R models

9.3d Carburettor assembly –
YZF1000R models

9.6a Carburettor joining bolts (arrowed) –
YZF750R models

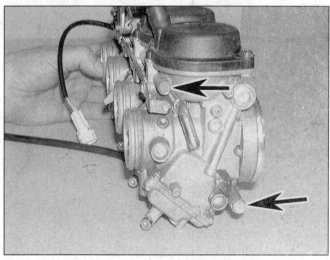

9.6b Carburettor joining bolts (arrowed) –
YZF1000R models

4

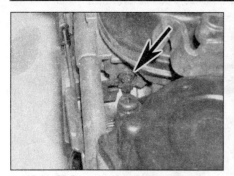

10.1a Make sure the slot in each arm locates correctly behind the nipple on the end of each choke plunger (arrowed)

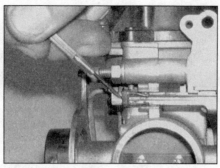

10.1b Secure the arm with the clips, making sure they locate correctly

light film of oil and install the fittings into their respective holes, making sure they seat completely **(see illustration 8.2a or 8.23a)**.

9 Position the coil springs between the carburettors, gently push the carburettors together, then make sure the throttle linkages are correctly engaged **(see illustration 8.3a or b)**. Check the fuel and vent fittings to make sure they engage properly also.

10 Install the two long through-bolts with their collars, on YZF750R models not forgetting the choke cable lever with the top bolt, but do not yet tighten them. Set the carburettors on a sheet of glass, then align them with a straight-edge placed along the edges of the bores. When the centrelines of the carburettors are all in horizontal and vertical alignment, tighten the bolts to the torque setting specified at the beginning of the Chapter.

11 On YZF750R models, fit the choke linkage bar onto the plungers **(see illustration 8.8b)**, making sure the slots locate correctly behind the nipple on the end of each choke plunger **(see illustration 10.1a)**. Secure the linkage bar in place with the clips, making sure their ends locate over the ends of the slide guide **(see illustration 10.1b)**.

12 On YZF1000R models, fit the choke linkage bar onto the plungers, making sure the slots locate correctly behind the nipple on the end of each choke plunger **(see illustration 10.1a)**. Fit the plastic washers and secure the linkage bar in place with the screws **(see illustration 8.31b)**. Make sure the choke linkage operates smoothly and returns quickly under spring pressure.

13 Install the throttle synchronisation springs **(see illustration 8.3a or b)**. Visually synchronise the throttle butterfly valves,

turning the adjusting screws on the throttle linkage, if necessary, to equalise the clearance between the butterfly valve and throttle bore of each carburettor. Make sure the throttle operates smoothly and returns quickly under spring pressure.

14 Install the carburettors (see Section 7) and check carburettor synchronisation and idle speed (see Chapter 1).

10 Carburettors – reassembly and fuel level check

> ⚠ **Warning: Refer to the precautions given in Section 1 before proceeding.**

Note: *When reassembling the carburettors, be sure to use the new O-rings, seals and other parts supplied in the rebuild kit. Do not overtighten the carburettor jets and screws as they are easily damaged.*

Reassembly

YZF750R models

1 Fit the choke plunger assembly into the carburettor body, making sure the clips locate correctly in their holes. Fit the choke linkage bar onto the plungers **(see illustration 8.8b)**, making sure the slots locate correctly behind the nipple on the end of each choke plunger **(see illustration)**. Secure the linkage bar in place with the clips, making sure their ends locate over the ends of the slide guide **(see illustration)**.

2 Install the pilot screw (if removed) along with its spring, washer and O-ring, turning it in until it seats lightly **(see illustration 8.6a)**. Now, turn the screw out the number of turns previously recorded, or as specified at the beginning of the Chapter.

3 Check the condition of the jet holder O-ring and use a new one if it is damaged or deteriorated **(see illustration)**. Fit the O-ring into the base of the holder, then install the holder **(see illustration)**. Fit the collar and tighten the bolt **(see illustrations)**. If removed, install the jets in the jet holder **(see illustration 8.6a)**.

4 Fit a new O-ring onto the needle valve seat, then press it into place **(see illustration)**.

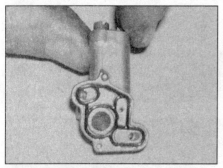

10.3a Make sure the O-ring is correctly located in the base of the jet holder . . .

10.3b . . . then install the holder . . .

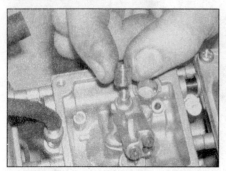

10.3c . . . and fit the collar . . .

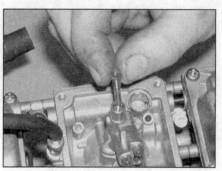

10.3d . . . and the bolt . . .

10.3e . . . and tighten the bolt

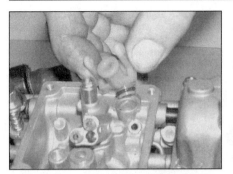

10.4a Press the needle valve seat into place

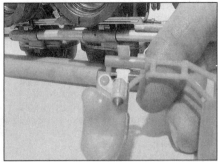

10.4b Hook the needle valve onto the tab on the float

10.6 Make sure the diaphragm rim is correctly seated. Do not forget the air passage O-ring (arrowed)

Hook the float needle valve onto the tab on the float assembly **(see illustration)**. Position the float assembly in the carburettor, making sure the needle valve locates in the seat, and install the pin, making sure it is secure **(see illustrations 8.5b and a)**.

5 Fit a new gasket onto the float chamber, making sure it is seated properly in its groove, then install the chamber on the carburettor and tighten its screws securely **(see illustration 8.4)**.

6 Fit the piston/diaphragm assembly into the carburettor and lightly push the piston down **(see illustration 8.3b)**. Press the diaphragm outer edge into its groove, making sure it is correctly seated **(see illustration)**. Check the diaphragm is not creased, and that the piston moves smoothly up and down in the guide. Fit a new O-ring around the air passage.

7 If removed, fit the spacer and E-clip onto the jet needle, making sure the clip is in the same groove from which it was removed. If removed, fit the needle seat into the bottom of the spring, then fit the needle into the seat **(see illustration)**. Fit the spring into the diaphragm assembly, making sure the needle is correctly aligned with the needle jet **(see illustration)**. Fit the top cover onto the carburettor, locating the peg into the top of the spring, and tighten its screws securely **(see illustration 8.2b)**.

8 Install the carburettors, but if the fuel level (float height) is to be checked do not yet install the air filter housing or fuel tank (see Section 7).

YZF750SP models

9 Fit the choke plunger assembly into the carburettor body and tighten the nut to secure it **(see illustration 8.10)**. Fit the choke linkage bar onto the plungers, not forgetting the inner plastic washers, and making sure the slots locate correctly behind the nipple on the end of each choke plunger. Fit the outer plastic washers and secure the linkage bar in place with the screws.

10 Install the pilot screw (if removed) along with its spring, washer and O-ring, turning it in until it seats lightly. Now, turn the screw out the number of turns previously recorded, or as specified at the beginning of the Chapter.

11 Install the needle jet.

12 Install the starter jet.

13 Install the pilot jet.

14 Install the main jet.

15 If removed, fit a new O-ring onto the needle valve seat, then press it into place and secure it with the screw. Hook the float needle valve onto the tab on the float assembly, then position the float assembly in the carburettor, making sure the needle valve locates in the seat, and install the pin, making sure it is secure.

16 Fit a new gasket onto the float chamber, making sure it is seated properly in its groove, then install the chamber on the carburettor and tighten its screws securely.

17 Fit the accelerator pump diaphragm, spring and O-rings, then fit the cover and tighten its screws securely.

18 If removed, fit the E-clip onto the needle, making sure the clip is in the same groove from which it was removed. Fit the needle into the slide and secure it with the holder. Fit the slide into the carburettor and lightly push it down, making sure the needle is correctly aligned with the needle jet. Locate the rollers on the throttle lever arms into the slots in the top of the slide. Check the slide moves smoothly up and down when the throttle shaft is turned. If slackened, adjust the synchronisation screws to the position they were previously set to, then lightly tighten the locknuts.

19 Fit the top cover onto the carburettor and tighten its screws securely.

20 Refer to Chapter 1, Section 4, Step 4 and prepare the carburettors for synchronisation. Install the carburettors, then check the fuel level (float height) if required (see below), and synchronise the carburettors.

YZF1000R models

21 Fit the fuel strainer back into the fuel inlet union **(see illustration 8.32)**.

22 Fit the choke plunger assembly into the carburettor body and tighten the nut to secure it **(see illustration)**. Fit the choke linkage bar onto the plungers, making sure the slots locate correctly behind the nipple on the end of each choke plunger **(see illustration)**. Fit the plastic washers and secure the linkage bar in place with the screws **(see illustration 8.31b)**. Hook up the linkage bar return spring **(see illustration 8.31a)**.

4

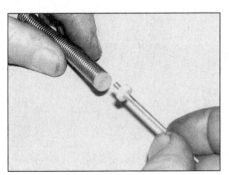

10.7a Fit the needle into the seat in the bottom of the spring . . .

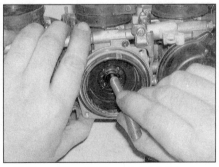

10.7b . . . then fit the needle and spring into the piston

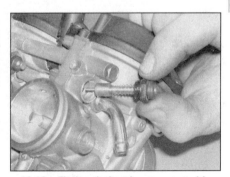

10.22a Fit the choke plunger assembly into the carburettor . . .

10.22b ... and install the linkage bar, making sure the slots in the arms locate behind the nipples on the plungers

23 Install the pilot screw (if removed) along with its spring, washer and O-ring, turning it in until it seats lightly **(see illustration 8.29)**.

Now, turn the screw out the number of turns previously recorded, or as specified at the beginning of the Chapter.
24 If removed, fit a new O-ring onto the needle valve seat, then press it into place and secure it with the screw **(see illustrations)**. Hook the float needle valve onto the tab on the float assembly, then position the float assembly in the carburettor, making sure the needle valve locates in the seat, and install the pin, making sure it is secure **(see illustrations)**.
25 Install the pilot jet **(see illustration)**.
26 Install the needle jet **(see illustration)**.
27 Install the main jet **(see illustration)**.
28 Fit a new gasket onto the float chamber, making sure it is seated properly in its groove, then install the chamber on the carburettor and tighten its screws securely **(see illustration)**.

29 If removed, fit the spacer and E-clip onto the needle, making sure the clip is in the same groove from which it was removed, then fit the washer on top of the clip **(see illustration)**. Check that the spring and O-ring are fitted to the needle holder – use a new O-ring if necessary. Fit the jet needle into the piston, then fit the needle holder onto it and press it gently down until it is secure **(see illustrations)**. Fit the piston/diaphragm assembly into the carburettor and lightly push the piston down, making sure the needle is correctly aligned with the needle jet **(see illustration)**. Press the diaphragm outer edge into its groove, making sure it is correctly seated with the tab on the diaphragm locating correctly into the recess in the carburettor. Check the diaphragm is not creased, and that the piston moves smoothly up and down in the guide.

10.24a Fit the valve seat using a new O-ring ...

10.24b ... and secure it with the screw

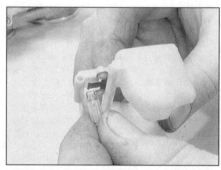

10.24c Hook the needle valve onto the tab on the float ...

10.24d ... then install the float assembly ...

10.24e ... and fit the pivot pin

10.25 Install the pilot jet ...

10.26 ... the needle jet ...

10.27 ... and the main jet

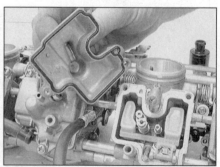

10.28 Fit a new gasket into the groove and install the float chamber

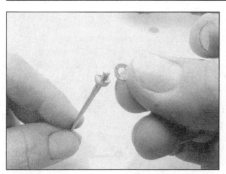

10.29a Fit the washer onto the E-clip . . .

10.29b . . . then fit the needle into the piston . . .

10.29c . . . and secure it with the holder

10.29d Install the piston/diaphragm assembly . . .

10.29e . . . making sure the diaphragm locates correctly . . .

10.29f . . . then fit the top cover

30 Fit the spring into the diaphragm assembly, making sure it locates correctly onto the needle holder, then fit the top cover onto the carburettor, locating the peg into the top of the spring, and tighten its screws securely.

31 Install the carburettors, but if the fuel level (float height) is to be checked do not yet install the air filter housing or fuel tank (see Section 7).

Fuel level check

32 To check the fuel level, position the motorcycle on level ground and support it using an auxiliary stand so that it is vertical.

33 Arrange a temporary fuel supply, either by

using a small temporary tank or by using an extra long fuel pipe to the now remote fuel tank. Alternatively, position the tank on a suitable base on the motorcycle, taking care not to scratch any paintwork, and making sure that the tank is safely and securely supported. Connect the fuel line to the carburettors.

34 Yamaha provide a fuel level gauge (Pt. No. 90890-01312), or alternatively a suitable length of clear plastic tubing can be used. Attach the gauge or tubing to the drain hose union on the bottom of the float chamber on the first carburettor and position its open end vertically alongside the carburettors **(see illustrations)**.

35 Slacken the drain screw and allow the fuel

to flow into the tube. The level at which the fuel stabilises in the tubing indicates the level of the fuel in the float chamber. Refer to the Specifications at the beginning of the Chapter and measure the level relative to the correct reference point on the carburettor for your model **(see illustrations 34a, b or c)**.

36 If it is incorrect, detach the fuel supply and drain the carburettors, then remove the float from the chamber (see Section 8), and adjust the float height by carefully bending the float tab a little at a time until the correct height is obtained. Repeat the procedure for the other carburettors. **Note:** *Bending the tab up lowers the fuel level – bending it down raises the fuel level.*

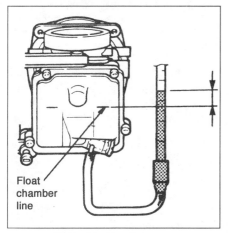

Float chamber line

10.34a Fuel level gauge – YZF750R models

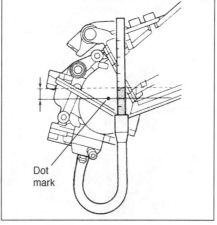

Dot mark

10.34b Fuel level gauge – YZF750SP models

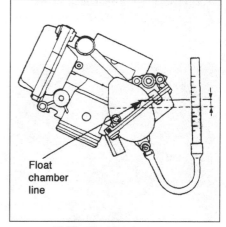

Float chamber line

10.34c Fuel level gauge – YZF1000R models

4

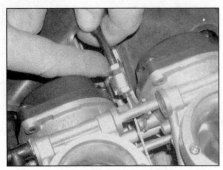

11.3a Slacken the locknut . . .

11.3b . . . then free the cable from the bracket . . .

11.3c . . . and detach the cable end from the carburettor

11.3d Slacken the hex . . .

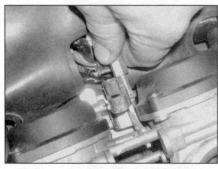

11.3e . . . then free the cable from the bracket . . .

11.3f . . . and detach the cable end from the carburettor

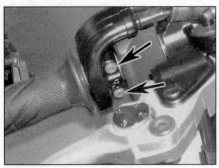

11.4a Pull the boot back off the housing . . .

11 Throttle cables – removal and installation

⚠ **Warning: Refer to the precautions given in Section 1 before proceeding.**

Removal

1 Remove the fuel tank and the air filter housing (see Sections 2 and 4).

2 Mark each cable according to its location at both ends. If new cables are being fitted, match them to the old cables to ensure they are correctly installed.

3 Slacken the accelerator (opening) cable top nut and thread it up the elbow, then slide the cable down in the bracket until the bottom nut is clear of the small lug on the bracket **(see illustration)**. Slip the cable out of the bracket and detach the nipple from the carburettors **(see illustrations)**. Slacken the decelerator (closing) cable hex, then slide the cable down in the bracket until the bottom nut is clear of the small lug on the bracket **(see illustrations)**. Slip the cable out of the bracket and detach the nipple from the carburettors **(see illustration)**. Withdraw the cables from the machine noting the correct routing of each cable.

4 Pull the rubber boot back off the throttle housing on the handlebar **(see illustration)**. Remove the throttle housing screws and separate the halves **(see illustrations)**. Displace the cable elbows from the housing, noting how they fit, and detach the cable nipples from the pulley **(see illustrations)**. Mark each cable to ensure it is connected correctly on installation.

11.4b . . . and remove the housing screws (arrowed)

11.4c Separate the housing halves . . .

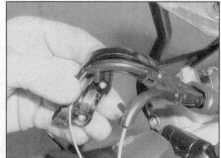

11.4d . . . then detach the cable elbows . . .

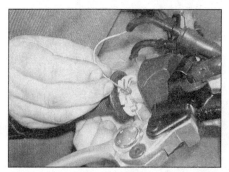

11.4e ... and free the cable ends from the throttle pulley

Installation

5 Lubricate the cable nipples with multi-purpose grease and install them into the throttle pulley at the handlebar **(see illustration 11.4e)**. Fit the cable elbows into the housing, making sure they locate correctly **(see illustration 11.4d)**. Join the housing halves, making sure the pin locates in the hole in the handlebar, and tighten the screws **(see illustrations 11.4c and b)**. Fit the rubber boot **(see illustration)**.

6 Feed the cables through to the carburettors, making sure they are correctly routed. The cables must not interfere with any other component and should not be kinked or bent sharply.

7 Lubricate the decelerator cable nipple with multi-purpose grease and fit it into the lower

socket on the carburettor throttle cam **(see illustration 11.3f)**. Fit the decelerator cable into the bracket and draw it up into the bracket so that the bottom nut becomes captive against the small lug **(see illustration 11.3e)**. Tighten the hex down onto the bracket **(see illustration 11.3d)**. Lubricate the accelerator cable nipple with multi-purpose grease and fit it into the upper socket on the carburettor throttle cam **(see illustration 11.3c)**. Fit the accelerator cable into the upper bracket and adjust as described in Chapter 1 to obtain the correct amount of freeplay **(see illustration 11.3b)**.

8 Operate the throttle to check that it opens and closes freely. Turn the handlebars back and forth to make sure the cable doesn't cause the steering to bind.

9 Install the air filter housing and the fuel tank (see Sections 4 and 2).

10 Start the engine and check that the idle speed does not rise as the handlebars are turned. If it does, the throttle cable is routed incorrectly. Correct the problem before riding the motorcycle.

12 Choke cable – removal and installation

Removal

1 Remove the fuel tank and the air filter housing (see Sections 2 and 4). On YZF750R and SP models, remove the left-hand fairing side panel (see Chapter 8).

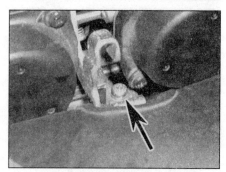

12.2a Slacken the clamp screw (arrowed) ...

2 Slacken the choke outer cable bracket screw and free the cable from the bracket on the front of the carburettors, then detach the inner cable nipple from the choke linkage bar arm **(see illustrations)**.

3 On YZF750R and SP models, unscrew the bolt securing the choke lever housing bracket and displace it **(see illustration)**. Draw the outer cable end from its socket and free the nipple from the lever **(see illustrations)**.

4 On YZF1000R models, unscrew the two handlebar switch/choke lever housing screws and separate the two halves **(see illustration)**. Lift the cable elbow and lever out of the housing, noting how they fit, and detach the cable nipple from the lever **(see illustrations)**.

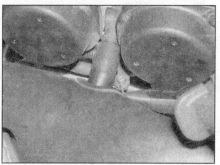

12.2b ... and free the outer cable from the clamp ...

12.2c ... and the cable nipple from the linkage bar

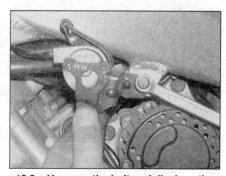

12.3a Unscrew the bolt and displace the housing ...

4

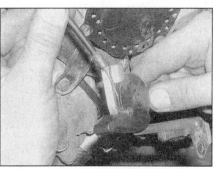

12.3b ... then draw the cable from the housing ...

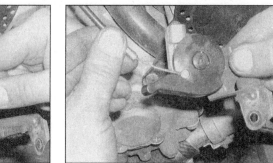

12.3c ... and free the nipple from the lever

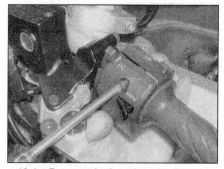

12.4a Remove the housing screws and separate the halves

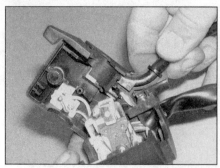

12.4b Remove the choke lever and cable elbow from the housing . . .

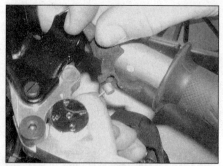

12.4c . . . and free the cable end from the lever

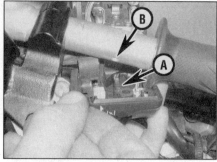

12.7 Make sure the pin (A) in the housing locates in the hole (B) in the handlebar

Installation

5 Install the cable making sure it is correctly routed. The cable must not interfere with any other component and should not be kinked or bent sharply.

6 On YZF750R and SP models, lubricate the cable nipple with multi-purpose grease and fit it into the lever, then fit the outer cable end into its socket (see illustrations 12.3c and b). Mount the bracket onto the frame and tighten the bolt securely (see illustration 12.3a).

7 On YZF1000R models, lubricate the cable nipple with multi-purpose grease and attach it to the choke lever (see illustrations 12.4c). Fit the lever and cable elbow into the housing (see illustration 12.4b), then fit the two halves of the housing onto the handlebar, making sure the lever fits correctly, and the pin in the front half locates in the hole in the front of the handlebar (see illustration). Install the screws and tighten them securely (see illustration 12.4a).

8 Lubricate the cable nipple with multi-purpose grease and attach it to the choke linkage bar on the carburettor (see illustration 12.2c). Fit the outer cable into its bracket, making sure there is a small amount of freeplay in the inner cable, and tighten the screw (see illustrations 12.2b and a).

9 Check the operation of the choke cable (see Chapter 1).

10 Install the air filter housing and the fuel tank (see Sections 4 and 2). On YZF750R and SP models, install the left-hand fairing side panel (see Chapter 8).

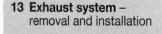

13 Exhaust system – removal and installation

 Warning: If the engine has been running the exhaust system will be very hot. Allow the system to cool before carrying out any work.

Silencer

Removal

1 On YZF750R and SP models, for improved clearance and to avoid the possibility of damage, remove the lower fairing (see Chapter 8). Slacken the clamp bolt securing the silencer pipe to the downpipe assembly. Unscrew and remove the silencer mounting bolt, then release the silencer pipe from the downpipe assembly. Remove the sealing ring from the end of the silencer or downpipe assembly and discard it as a new one should be used.

2 On YZF1000R models, unscrew the three flange bolts securing the silencer to the downpipe assembly, noting the guard where fitted (see illustration). Unscrew the nut on the silencer mounting bolt, then withdraw the bolt and remove the silencer (see illustration). Remove the sealing ring from the end of the silencer or downpipe assembly and discard it as a new one should be used.

Installation

3 On YZF750R and SP models, fit the new

sealing ring into the silencer pipe. Fit the silencer onto the downpipe assembly, making sure it is pushed fully home. Align the silencer mounting bracket at the rear and install the bolt, but do not yet tighten it. Tighten the clamp bolt securely, but not overtight, then tighten the silencer mounting bolt to the torque setting specified at the beginning of the Chapter.

4 On YZF1000R models, fit the new sealing ring into the silencer. Fit the silencer onto the downpipe assembly, making sure it locates correctly against the flange, not forgetting the guard where fitted. Align the silencer mounting bracket at the rear and install the bolt, but do not yet tighten it. Tighten the silencer flange bolts to the torque setting specified at the beginning of the Chapter, then tighten the silencer mounting bolt nut to the specified torque (see illustrations 13.2a and b).

5 Run the engine and check the system for leaks.

Complete system

Removal

6 Remove the lower fairing and the fairing side panels (see Chapter 8).

7 Detach the cables from the EXUP valve (see Section 14).

8 Slacken the silencer mounting bolt but do not yet remove it (see illustration 13.2b). Unscrew the bolt securing the rear of the downpipe assembly to the frame (see illustration).

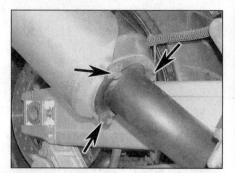

13.2a Remove the bolts (arrowed) and the guard (where fitted)

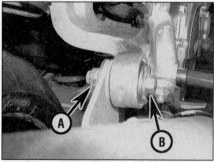

13.2b Unscrew the nut (A), withdraw the bolt (B) and remove the silencer

13.8 Unscrew the bolt (arrowed) . . .

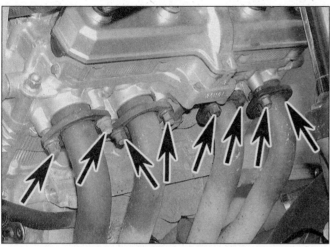

13.9 . . . and the nuts (arrowed) . . .

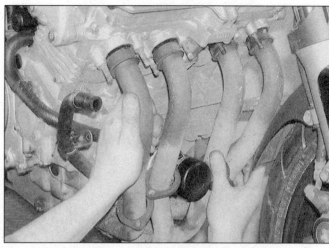

13.10 . . . and remove the exhaust

9 Unscrew the eight downpipe flange nuts and draw the flanges off the studs **(see illustration)**.

10 Supporting the system, remove the silencer mounting bolt, then detach the downpipes from the cylinder head and remove the system **(see illustration)**.

11 Remove the gasket from each port in the cylinder head and discard them as new ones must be fitted.

Installation

12 Fit a new gasket into each of the cylinder head ports **(see illustration)**. Apply a smear of grease to the gaskets to keep them in place whilst fitting the downpipe if necessary.

13 Manoeuvre the assembly into position so that the head of each downpipe is located in its port in the cylinder head **(see illustration 13.10)**, then install the silencer mounting bolt and the downpipe assembly rear bolt, but do not yet tighten them **(see illustrations 13.2b and 13.8)**.

14 Locate the downpipe flanges onto the studs, then fit the nuts and tighten them to the torque setting specified at the beginning of the Chapter **(see illustration)**. Now tighten the other bolts to the specified torque.

15 Attach the cables to the EXUP valve (see Section 14).

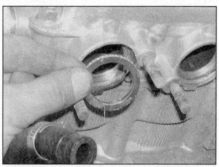

13.12 Fit a new gasket into each port

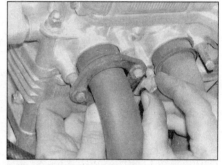

13.14 Fit the flanges onto the studs and secure them with the nuts

16 Run the engine and check the system for leaks.

---

14 EXUP system –
cable renewal, check, removal and installation

Cable renewal

1 Remove the fuel tank (see Chapter 4) and the lower fairing (see Chapter 8).

2 Unscrew the bolts securing the EXUP pulley cover on the exhaust and remove the cover **(see illustration)**.

3 Unscrew the bolt securing the cable pulley and remove the washer, using a suitable bolt or screw located as shown to stop the pulley turning **(see illustration)**. Draw the pulley off the shaft and detach the cable ends from it, noting which fits where **(see illustration)**. Draw the cables out of the bracket, noting which fits where **(see illustration)**. Note the spring and washer fitted on the valve shaft and remove them for safekeeping if required **(see illustration 14.7a)**.

4

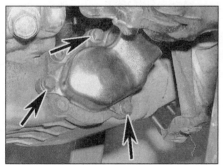

14.2 Unscrew the bolts (arrowed) and remove the cover

14.3a Unscrew the bolt, securing the pulley as shown

14.3b Draw the pulley off the shaft and detach the cable nipples . . .

14.3c . . . then free the cables from the bracket

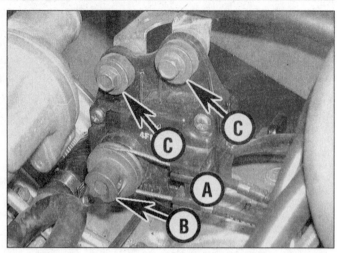

14.4 Draw the cables from their holders (A) and release the ends from the pulley (B). Servo mounting bolts (C)

4 Free the top ends of the outer cables from their holders on the servo housing, noting their location, and detach the cable nipples from the pulley **(see illustration)**. Withdraw the cables from the machine noting the correct routing of each cable.

5 Lubricate the cable nipples with multi-purpose grease and install them into the servo pulley **(see illustration 14.4)**. Fit the outer cable ends into their holders, making sure they locate correctly.

6 Feed the cables through to the exhaust, making sure they are correctly routed. The cables must not interfere with any other component and should not be kinked or bent sharply.

14.7a Fit the washer and spring if removed

7 Fit the outer cable ends into the bracket, then fit the nipples into the pulley **(see illustrations 14.3c and b)**. If removed, slide the washer and spring onto the shaft, then locate the pulley and secure it with the bolt, not forgetting its washer **(see illustrations)**. Check and adjust cable freeplay (see Chapter 1), then install the cover and tighten the bolts to the torque setting specified at the beginning of the Chapter.

Check

8 Trace the wiring from the EXUP system servo motor and disconnect it at the connectors **(see illustration)**. Using a fully charged 12V battery and some jumper leads, connect the positive (+ve) terminal of the battery to the black/yellow wire terminal on the servo side of the connector, and the negative (–ve) terminal to the black/red wire terminal. When the battery is connected, the servo should operate. Disconnect the battery immediately after the test.

Caution: Disconnect the battery immediately after the test to prevent possible damage to the servo motor.

9 If the servo now operates, yet did not beforehand, check for voltage at the wiring connector using a voltmeter – connect the positive (+ve) probe of the meter to the

black/red wire terminal on the loom side of the connector, and the negative (–ve) terminal to the black/yellow wire terminal. Battery voltage should be present. If not, check the connector for loose or corroded terminals, then check the fuse and the battery, and then the wiring between the connector and the ignition control unit, referring to the test procedures and *Wiring Diagrams* in Chapter 9.

10 If the servo does not operate, check the static resistance between the white/black wire terminal and the yellow/blue wire terminal on the servo side of the connector using an ohmmeter or multimeter set to the K-ohms scale. Compare the reading to that specified at the beginning of the Chapter. Disconnect the single white/red wire bullet connector **(see illustration 14.8)**. Now check the variable resistance between the white/black wire terminal and the white/red wire terminal on the servo side of the connectors while turning the servo pulley by hand. Compare the reading to that specified at the beginning of the Chapter. If either reading is not within the range specified, replace the servo with a new one.

11 If the operation of the valve has been sticky, remove it as described below, then check the valve shaft, face, cover and housing for any corrosion or dirt which may be causing

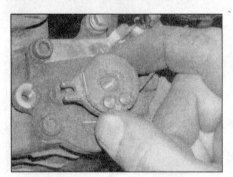

14.7b Fit the pulley onto the shaft . . .

14.7c . . . and secure it with the bolt

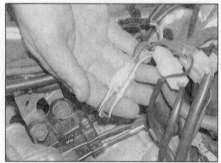

14.8 EXUP system wiring connectors

the problem. Also check the shaft collars in which the valve turns – one in the housing and one in the cover. Clean of all dirt and corrosion and check the operation of the valve. If the shaft ends or collars are worn, replace them with new ones.

Removal

12 To access the servo, remove the fuel tank (see Chapter 4). To access the valve, remove the lower fairing (see Chapter 8). Before removing either the servo or the valve, detach the cables (see above). If only the servo is being removed, it may be necessary to detach the cables from the valve as well to create enough slack.

13 To remove the servo, detach the cables as described above then unscrew its mounting bolts, noting the rubber grommets and collars **(see illustration 14.4)**.

14 To remove the valve, detach the cables as described above and remove the spring and washer. Unscrew the bolts securing the valve cover and remove the cable bracket and cover. Draw out the valve, noting how it fits.

Installation

15 Installation is the reverse of removal. Tighten the valve cover bolts to the torque setting specified at the beginning of the Chapter.

16 Check the operation of the system and the cable freeplay (see Chapter 1). Install the pulley cover and tighten the bolts to the specified torque.

---

15 Fuel pump and relay –
check, removal and installation

 Warning: Refer to the precautions given in Section 1 before starting work.

Check

1 The fuel pump is located inside the fuel tank on YZF750R and SP models, and is mounted on the frame cross-member below the fuel tank on YZF1000R models. The fuel pump relay is contained within the relay assembly mounted on the front of the battery box below the tank rear mounting on YZF750R and SP models, and on top of the fuel filter, which is just behind the fuel pump, on YZF1000R models **(see illustrations)**. Remove the fuel tank to access all components (see Chapter 4).

2 The fuel pump is controlled through the relay so that it runs whenever the ignition is switched ON and the ignition is operative (ie only when the engine is turning over). As soon as the ignition is killed, the relay will cut off the fuel pump's electrical supply (so that there is no risk of fuel being sprayed out under pressure in the event of an accident).

3 It should be possible to hear or feel the fuel pump running whenever the engine is turning over – either place your ear close beside the fuel tank or pump or feel it with your fingertips. If you can't hear or feel anything, check that the battery is fully charged and the circuit fuse is good (see Chapter 9). Then check the pump and relay for loose or corroded connections or physical damage and rectify as necessary.

4 If the circuit is fine so far, switch the ignition OFF. Unplug the relay's wiring connector. Using an ohmmeter or continuity tester, connect the positive (+ve) probe to the relay's red/black terminal, and the negative (–ve) probe to the relay's blue/black terminal. There should be no continuity. Leaving the meter connected, now connect a fully charged 12 volt battery and two insulated jumper wires, connect the positive (+ve) terminal of the battery to the relay's red/black terminal, and the negative (–ve) terminal of the battery

15.1a Relay assembly (arrowed) – YZF750R and SP models

to the relay's blue/red terminal. There should now be continuity. If the relay assembly does not behave as described, replace it with a new one.

5 If the pump still does not work, on YZF1000R models trace the wiring from the pump and disconnect it at the connector **(see illustration 15.1b)**. On YZF750R and SP models, the connector is on the end of the wiring from the base of the fuel tank **(see illustration 15.7)**. Using an ohmmeter, connect the positive (+ve) probe to the pump's blue (YZF750R and SP) or black/blue (YZF1000R models) terminal, and the negative (–ve) probe to the black terminal, and measure the resistance. If the reading is not as specified at the beginning of the Chapter, replace the pump with a new one.

Removal

6 Make sure the ignition is switched OFF. Remove the fuel tank (see Section 2).

7 On YZF750R and SP models, remove the fuel tap (see Section 2), then remove the screws securing the pump assembly to the base of the tank and withdraw the pump **(see illustration)**. Discard the seal as a new one must be used.

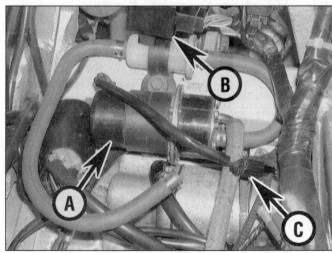

15.1b Fuel pump (A), relay assembly (B), fuel pump wiring connector (C) – YZF1000R models

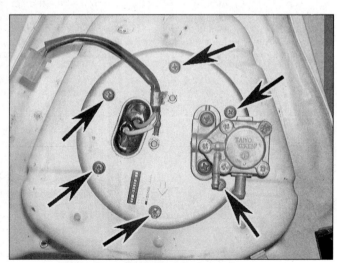

15.7 Fuel pump mounting screws (arrowed) – YZF750R and SP models

15.8a Displace the relay . . .

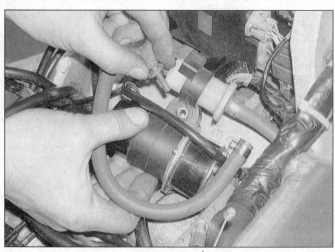

15.8b . . . then unscrew the bolt and remove the pump

8 On YZF1000R models, trace the wiring from the fuel pump and disconnect it at the connector (see illustration 15.1b). Make a note or sketch of which fuel hose fits where as an aid to installation. Using a rag to mop up any spilled fuel, disconnect the two fuel hoses from the fuel pump (see illustration 15.1b). Displace the relay from its mounting (see illustration). Unscrew the bolt securing the pump/filter sleeve to the frame and remove the pump and filter with its rubber mounting sleeve (see illustration). Separate the pump from the sleeve.

9 To remove the relay assembly, disconnect the relay wiring connector and remove the relay from its mounting (see illustration 15.8a).

Installation

10 Installation is a reverse of the removal procedure. On YZF750R and SP models use a new seal and fit the pump with the arrow on the base pointing forward. Tighten the screws to the torque setting specified at the beginning of the Chapter. On YZF1000R models, make sure the fuel hoses are correctly and securely fitted to the pump – the hose from the in-line filter attaches to the

16.6 Fuel level sensor screws (arrowed) – YZF1000R models

union marked 'INLET' ; the hose to the carburettors attaches to the other union (see illustration 15.1b). Start the engine and check carefully that there are no leaks at the pipe connections.

16 Fuel warning light and sensor – check and renewal

Check

1 The circuit consists of the sensor mounted in the fuel tank and the warning light mounted in the instrument panel. If the system malfunctions check first that the battery is fully charged and that the bulb and fuses are good (see Chapter 9). If they are, remove the fuel tank and drain it (see Section 2).

2 Using an ohmmeter or continuity tester, check for continuity between the green and black wire terminals on the sensor side of the wiring connector coming from the fuel tank, with the tank the right way up. There should be continuity. If not, replace the sensor with a new one (see below).

3 If the sensor is good, install the fuel tank, but do not fill it with the fuel. With the ignition ON, check for voltage at the warning light bulbholder by connecting the positive (+ve) probe of a voltmeter to the brown (YZF750R and SP models) or green/yellow (YZF1000R models) terminal on the loom side of the instrument cluster wiring connector, and the negative (–ve) probe to the green/white terminal. If no voltage is present, the fault lies in the wiring. Check all the relevant wiring and wiring connectors (see Chapter 9), referring to the *Wiring Diagrams* at the end of Chapter 9.

Renewal

4 See Chapter 9 for renewal of the warning light bulb.

5 To renew the sensor on YZF750R and SP models, remove the fuel pump (see Section 15) – the pump and sensor come as an assembly and must be renewed as such. Follow the installation procedure as described in that Section.

6 To renew the sensor on YZF1000R models, remove the fuel tank (see Section 2) and drain it. Free the wiring from its clip on the tank. Remove the screws securing the sensor and draw it out of the tank (see illustration). Discard the O-ring. Fit a new O-ring onto the sensor and install it in the tank. Tighten the screws to the torque setting specified at the beginning of the Chapter.

7 Install the tank (see Section 2), and check carefully that there are no leaks before using the bike.

17 Fuel reserve switch – 1993 and 1994 YZF750 models

1 The fuel reserve switch is set in the left-hand fairing side panel. In normal use the switch should be in the ON position, and should only be moved to RES when the fuel level warning light illuminates, indicating that there is just 3.5 litres of fuel remaining in the tank. The switch should be moved back to ON after refuelling.

2 If the fuel supply fails to switch over to reserve, refer to the wiring diagrams and check the reserve circuit wiring for breaks and bad connections. To test the switch, trace the wiring from the back of the switch and disconnect the wiring connector. Connect a continuity tester across the two wire terminals on the switch side of the connector. Continuity should be shown in one position and no continuity (infinite resistance) with the switch moved to the other position.

Chapter 5
Ignition system

Contents

Degrees of difficulty

Easy, suitable for novice with little experience	Fairly easy, suitable for beginner with some experience	Fairly difficult, suitable for competent DIY mechanic	Difficult, suitable for experienced DIY mechanic	Very difficult, suitable for expert DIY or professional

Specifications

General information
Cylinder numbering .... 1 to 4 from left to right
Spark plugs .... see Chapter 1

Ignition timing
At idle
  YZF750R models .... 10° BTDC @ 1200 rpm
  YZF750SP models .... 5° BTDC @ 1200 rpm
  YZF1000R models .... 5° BTDC @ 1100 rpm

Pick-up coil
Resistance .... 135 to 165 ohms @ 20°C

Ignition HT coils
Primary winding resistance
  YZF750R and SP models .... 1.8 to 2.2 ohms @ 20°C
  YZF1000R models .... 1.9 to 2.5 ohms @ 20°C
Secondary winding resistance (without plug cap)
  YZF750R and SP models .... 9.6 to 14.4 K-ohms @ 20°C
  YZF1000R models .... 12 to 18 K-ohms @ 20°C
Spark plug cap resistance .... 10 K-ohms @ 20°C
Minimum spark gap (see Section 2) .... 6 mm

Throttle position sensor
Maximum resistance
  1995-on YZF750R and all SP models .... 5.0 ± 1.5 K-ohms
  YZF1000R models .... 5.0 ± 1.0 K-ohms
Resistance range
  1995-on YZF750R and all SP models .... Zero to 5.0 ± 1.5 K-ohms
  YZF1000R models .... Zero to 5.0 ± 1.0 K-ohms

Torque wrench setting
Pick-up coil and clamp bolts .... 10 Nm

5

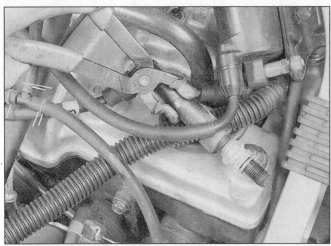

2.2 Ground (earth) the spark plug and operate the starter – bright blue sparks should be visible

2.5 Connect the tester as shown – when the starter is operated sparks should jump between the nails

1 General information

All models are fitted with a fully transistorised electronic ignition system, which due to its lack of mechanical parts is totally maintenance free. The system comprises a trigger, pick-up coil, ignition control unit and ignition HT coils (refer to the wiring diagrams at the end of Chapter 9 for details). All models are fitted with two HT coils. A throttle position sensor provides information for the ignition control unit (not fitted on 1993 and 1994 YZF750R models).

The ignition trigger, which is on the right-hand end of the crankshaft, magnetically operates the pick-up coil as the crankshaft rotates. The pick-up coil sends a signal to the ignition control unit which then supplies the ignition HT coils with the power necessary to produce a spark at the plugs.

The system incorporates an electronic advance system controlled by signals from the ignition triggers, the pick-up coil and the throttle position sensor (where fitted).

The system also incorporates a safety interlock circuit which will cut the ignition if the sidestand is extended whilst the engine is running and in gear, or if a gear is selected whilst the engine is running and the sidestand is extended. It also prevents the engine from being started if the engine is in gear unless the clutch lever is pulled in.

Because of their nature, the individual ignition system components can be checked but not repaired. If ignition system troubles occur, and the faulty component can be isolated, the only cure for the problem is to replace the part with a new one. Keep in mind that most electrical parts, once purchased, cannot be returned. To avoid unnecessary expense, make very sure the faulty component has been positively identified before buying a replacement part.

Note that there is no provision for adjusting the ignition timing on these models.

2 Ignition system – check

⚠ **Warning: The energy levels in electronic systems can be very high. On no account should the ignition be switched on whilst the plugs or plug caps are being held. Shocks from the HT circuit can be most unpleasant. Secondly, it is vital that the engine is not turned over or run with any of the plug caps removed, and that the plugs are soundly earthed (grounded) when the system is checked for sparking. The ignition system components can be seriously damaged if the HT circuit becomes isolated.**

A simple spark gap testing tool can be made from a block of wood, a large alligator clip and two nails, one of which is fashioned so that a spark plug cap or bare HT lead end can be connected to its end. Make sure the gap between the two nail ends is the same as specified

1 As no means of adjustment is available, any failure of the system can be traced to failure of a system component or a simple wiring fault. Of the two possibilities, the latter is by far the most likely. In the event of failure, check the system in a logical fashion, as described below.

2 Disconnect the HT lead from one spark plug. Connect the lead to a spare spark plug and lay the plug on the engine with the threads contacting the engine **(see illustration)**. If necessary, hold the spark plug with an insulated tool.

⚠ **Warning: Do not remove any of the spark plugs from the engine to perform this check – atomised fuel being pumped out of the open spark plug hole could ignite, causing severe injury!**

3 Check that the kill switch is in the 'RUN' position and the transmission is in neutral, then turn the ignition switch ON and turn the engine over on the starter motor. If the system is in good condition a regular, fat blue spark should be evident at the plug electrodes. If the spark appears thin or yellowish, or is non-existent, further investigation will be necessary. Turn the ignition off and repeat the test for each spark plug in turn.

4 The ignition system must be able to produce a spark which is capable of jumping a particular size gap. Yamaha specify that a healthy system should produce a spark capable of jumping at least 6 mm. A simple testing tool can be made to test the minimum gap across which the spark will jump **(see Tool Tip)** or alternatively it is possible to buy an ignition spark gap tester tool and some of these are adjustable to alter the spark gap.

5 Connect one of the spark plug HT leads from one coil to the protruding electrode on the test tool, and clip the tool to a good earth (ground) on the engine or frame **(see illustration)**. Check that the kill switch is in the 'RUN' position, turn the ignition switch ON and turn the engine over on the starter motor.

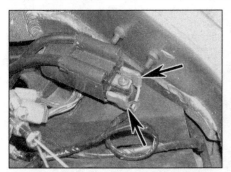

3.5a Disconnect the primary circuit connectors (arrowed) from the coil . . .

3.5b . . . and the caps from the spark plugs

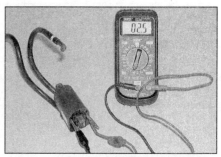

3.6 To test the coil primary resistance, connect the multimeter leads between the primary circuit terminals

If the system is in good condition a regular, fat blue spark should be seen to jump the gap between the nail ends. Repeat the test for the other coil. If the test results are good the entire ignition system can be considered good. If the spark appears thin or yellowish, or is non-existent, further investigation will be necessary.

6 Ignition faults can be divided into two categories, namely those where the ignition system has failed completely, and those which are due to a partial failure. The likely faults are listed below, starting with the most probable source of failure. Work through the list systematically, referring to the subsequent sections for full details of the necessary checks and tests. **Note:** *Before checking the following items ensure that the battery is fully charged and that all fuses are in good condition.*

a) *Loose, corroded or damaged wiring connections, broken or shorted wiring between any of the component parts of the ignition system (see Chapter 9).*
b) *Faulty HT lead or spark plug cap, faulty spark plug, dirty, worn or corroded plug electrodes, or incorrect gap between electrodes.*
c) *Faulty ignition (main) switch or engine kill switch (see Chapter 9).*

d) *Faulty neutral, clutch or sidestand switch, or diode (see Chapter 9).*
e) *Faulty pick-up coil or damaged trigger.*
f) *Faulty ignition HT coil(s).*
g) *Faulty ignition control unit.*

7 If the above checks don't reveal the cause of the problem, have the ignition system tested by a Yamaha dealer.

3 Ignition HT coils – check, removal and installation

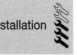

Check

1 Check the coil visually for cracks and other damage.
2 The primary and secondary coil resistances can be measured with a multimeter as follows.
3 Remove the rider's seat (see Chapter 8). Disconnect the battery negative (–ve) lead.
4 The coils are mounted on the inside of the frame behind the steering head – remove the fuel tank and the air filter housing for access (see Chapter 4).
5 On 1993 and 1994 YZF750R and SP models, trace the wiring from the coil and disconnect it at the connector. On all other models, disconnect the primary circuit electrical connectors from the coil (see

illustration). On all models disconnect the HT leads from the spark plugs (see illustration). Mark the locations of all wires and leads before disconnecting them.

6 Set the meter to the ohms x 1 scale and measure the resistance between the primary circuit terminals in the coil side of the wiring connector (1993 and 1994 YZF750R and SP models) or on the coil terminals (all other models) (see illustration). This will give a resistance reading of the primary windings of the coil and should be consistent with the value given in the Specifications at the beginning of the Chapter.

7 To check the condition of the secondary windings, unscrew the spark plug caps from the HT leads and set the meter to the K-ohm scale. Connect one meter probe to one HT lead end and the other probe to the other lead end (see illustration). If the reading obtained is not within the range shown in the Specifications, it is likely that the coil is defective.

8 If the reading is as specified, measure the resistance of the spark plug cap by connecting the meter probes between the HT lead socket in the cap and the spark plug contact in the cap (see illustration). If the reading obtained is not as specified, replace the spark plug caps with new ones.

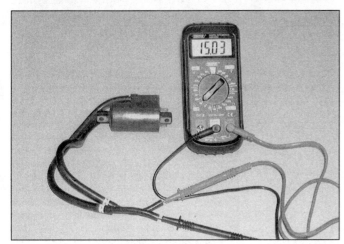

3.7 To test the coil secondary resistance, connect the multimeter leads between the spark plug leads

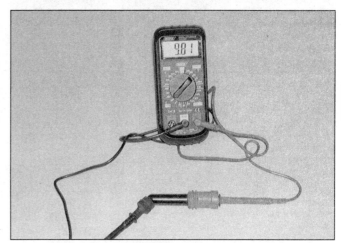

3.8 Measuring the resistance of the spark plug cap

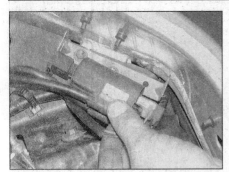

3.13a Draw the coil off its bracket

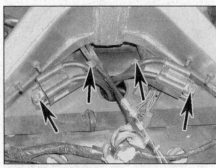

3.13b Each coil is secured by two screws (arrowed)

9 If either coil is confirmed to be faulty, it must be replaced with a new one: the coils are sealed units and cannot therefore be repaired.

Removal

10 Remove the seat (see Chapter 8). Disconnect the battery negative (–ve) lead.
11 The coils are mounted on the inside of the frame behind the steering head – remove the fuel tank and the air filter housing for access (see Chapter 4).
12 On 1993 and 1994 YZF750R and SP models, trace the wiring from the coil and disconnect it at the connector. On all other models, disconnect the primary circuit electrical connectors from the coil **(see illustration 3.5a)**. On all models disconnect the HT leads from the spark plugs **(see illustration 3.5b)**. Mark the locations of all wires and leads before disconnecting them.
13 On 1993 and 1994 YZF750R and SP models, release the strap securing the coil and remove the coil. On all other YZF750R and SP models, draw the coil off its mounting bracket **(see illustration)**. On YZF1000R models, remove the screws securing the coil and remove the coil **(see illustration)**. Note the routing of the HT leads.

Installation

14 Installation is the reverse of removal.

Make sure the wiring connectors and HT leads are securely connected.

4 Pick-up coil – check and renewal

Check

1 Remove the rider's seat (see Chapter 8). Disconnect the battery negative (–ve) lead.
2 Remove the fuel tank (see Chapter 4).
3 Trace the wiring from the pick-up coil on the right-hand side of the engine and disconnect it at the white 2-pin connector inside the rubber boot above the crankcase **(see illustration)**. Using a multimeter set to the ohms x 100 scale, measure the resistance between the terminals on the pick-up coil side of the connector.
4 Compare the reading obtained with that given in the Specifications at the beginning of this Chapter. The pick-up coil must be replaced with a new one if the reading obtained differs greatly from that given, particularly if the meter indicates a short circuit (no measurable resistance) or an open circuit (infinite, or very high resistance).
5 If the pick-up coil is thought to be faulty, first remove the lower fairing and the right-hand

fairing side panel (see Chapter 8), and check that this is not due to a damaged or broken wire from the coil to the connector: pinched or broken wires can usually be repaired.

Renewal

6 Remove the rider's seat (see Chapter 8). Disconnect the battery negative (–ve) lead.
7 Remove the fuel tank (see Chapter 4), the lower fairing and the right-hand fairing side panel (see Chapter 8).
8 Trace the wiring from the pick-up coil on the right-hand side of the engine and disconnect it at the white 2-pin connector inside the rubber boot above the crankcase **(see illustration 4.3)**. Feed the wiring back to the coil, noting its routing and releasing it from any clips or ties.
9 Unscrew the bolts securing the pick-up coil and its wiring clamp and withdraw the coil from the engine **(see illustration)**. Discard the O-ring.
10 Apply some clean engine oil to the new O-ring and fit it onto the pick-up coil. Fit the coil into the engine and tighten the bolts and the wiring clamp bolt to the torque setting specified at the beginning of the chapter. Feed the wiring through to the connector, securing it with any clips or ties and making sure it is correctly routed, and reconnect it.
11 Install the fuel tank (see Chapter 4) and the fairing panels (see Chapter 8).

5 Ignition control unit – check, removal and installation

Check

1 If the tests shown in the preceding or following Sections have failed to isolate the cause of an ignition fault, it is possible that the ignition control unit itself is faulty. No test details are available with which the unit can be tested.

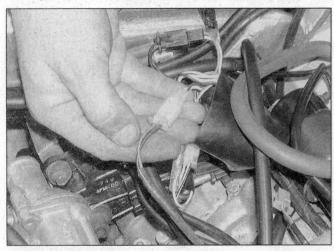

4.3 Disconnect the pick-up coil wiring connector

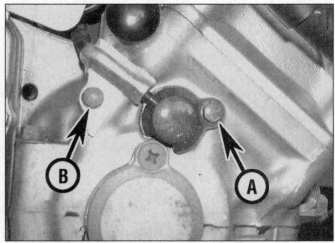

4.9 Pick-up coil bolt (A) and wiring clamp bolt (B)

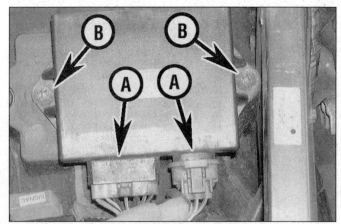

5.3a ICU wiring connectors (A) and mounting screws (B) –
YZF750R and SP models

5.3b ICU wiring connectors (arrowed) . . .

Removal

2 Remove the rider's seat (see Chapter 8). Disconnect the battery negative (–ve) lead. On YZF1000R models, remove the fuel tank (see Chapter 4).

3 Disconnect the wiring connectors from the ignition control unit **(see illustrations)**.

4 Remove the screw(s) securing the ignition control unit and remove the unit **(see illustration)**.

Installation

5 Installation is the reverse of removal. Make sure the wiring connectors are correctly and securely connected.

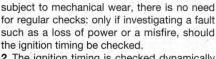

6 Ignition timing –
general information and check

General information

1 Since no provision exists for adjusting the ignition timing and since no component is subject to mechanical wear, there is no need for regular checks: only if investigating a fault such as a loss of power or a misfire, should the ignition timing be checked.

2 The ignition timing is checked dynamically (engine running) using a stroboscopic lamp. The inexpensive neon lamps should be adequate in theory, but in practice may produce a pulse of such low intensity that the timing mark remains indistinct. If possible, one of the more precise xenon tube lamps should be used, powered by an external source of the appropriate voltage. **Note:** *Do not use the machine's own battery as an incorrect reading may result from stray impulses within the machine's electrical system.*

Check

3 Warm the engine up to normal operating temperature then stop it. Remove the lower fairing (see Chapter 8).

4 Unscrew the timing inspection plug from the left-hand side of the engine **(see illustration)**.

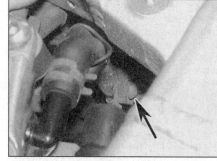

5.4 . . . and mounting screw (arrowed) –
YZF1000R models

5 The mark on the crankshaft which indicates the firing point at idle speed for the No. 1 cylinder is an 'H' mark **(see illustration)**. The static timing mark with which this should align is the triangular pointer in the inspection hole.

 HAYNES HiNT *The timing marks can be highlighted with white paint to make them more visible under the stroboscope light.*

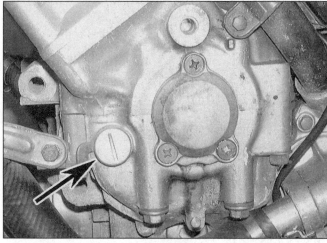

6.4 Unscrew the timing inspection plug (arrowed)

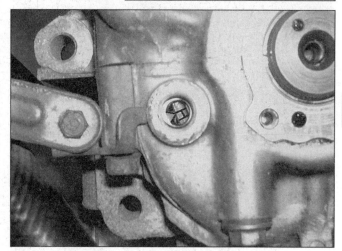

6.5 Timing marks

5

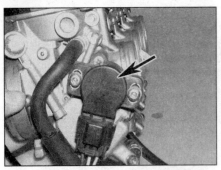

7.3 Throttle position sensor (arrowed) – YZF1000R model shown

6 Connect the timing light to the No. 1 cylinder HT lead as described in the manufacturer's instructions.

7 Start the engine and aim the light at the static timing mark.

8 With the machine idling at the specified speed, the static timing mark should point between the uprights of the 'H'.

9 Slowly increase the engine speed whilst observing the 'H' mark. The mark should move clockwise, increasing in relation to the engine speed until it reaches full advance (no identification mark).

10 As already stated, there is no means of adjustment of the ignition timing on these machines. If the ignition timing is incorrect, or suspected of being incorrect, one of the ignition system components is at fault, and the system must be tested as described in the preceding Sections of this Chapter.

11 When the check is complete, install the timing inspection plug and tighten it securely.

7 Throttle position sensor – check, adjustment and renewal

Note: *The throttle position sensor is fitted to 1995-on European YZF750R, all YZF750SP and all YZF1000R models .*

1 The throttle position sensor (TPS) is mounted on the outside of the right-hand carburettor and is keyed to the throttle shaft. The sensor provides the ignition control unit with information on throttle position and rate of opening or closing.

7.4 Disconnect the TPS wiring connector (arrowed)

2 When the ignition is first switched ON, or while the engine is running, the throttle position sensor performs its own self-diagnosis in the event of failure or faulty wiring. When a fault occurs, the tachometer will be seen to display zero rpm for 3 seconds, then 10,000 rpm (YZF750R and SP models) or 3000 rpm (YZF1000R models) for 2.5 seconds, then the actual engine speed for 3 seconds, whereupon it will repeat the cycle until the engine is switched off.

Check

3 Remove the fuel tank and the air filter housing (see Chapter 4). The throttle sensor is mounted on the outside of the right-hand carburettor (see illustration).

4 Make sure the ignition is switched OFF, then disconnect the sensor's wiring connector (see illustration). Using an ohmmeter or multimeter set to the K-ohms range, measure the sensor maximum resistance by connecting the meter probes between the blue and black (YZF750R and SP models) or black/blue (YZF1000R models) wire terminals on the sensor side of the connector. Now measure the resistance range by connecting the meter probes between the yellow and black (YZF750R and SP models) or black/blue (YZF1000R models) wire terminals on the connector, and slowly opening the throttle from fully closed to fully open. If the readings obtained differ from those specified at the beginning of the Chapter, replace the sensor with a new one.

5 If the readings were as specified, using a multimeter set to resistance or a continuity tester, check for continuity between the terminals on the wiring loom side of the sensor wiring connector and the corresponding terminals on the ignition control unit connector, referring to the *Wiring Diagrams* at the end of Chapter 9 (first disconnect it). There should be continuity between each terminal. If not, this is probably due to a damaged or broken wire between the connectors: pinched or broken wires can usually be repaired. Also check the connectors for loose or corroded terminals, and check the sensor itself for cracks and other damage. If the wiring and connectors are good, check the adjustment of the sensor as described below.

6 If the sensor is suspected of being faulty, take it to a Yamaha dealer for further testing. If it is confirmed to be faulty, it must be replaced with a new one: the sensor is a sealed unit and cannot therefore be repaired.

Adjustment

1993 and 1994 YZF750SP models

7 Before adjusting the sensor, check the idle speed and carburettor synchronisation (see Chapter 1).

8 Remove the fuel tank and the air filter housing (see Chapter 4). Turn the ignition switch ON, then disconnect the sensor wiring connector (see illustration 7.4). Using an ohmmeter or multimeter set to the K-ohms

range, connect the meter probes between the yellow and black wire terminals on the sensor side of the connector. The sensor must be adjusted so that the minimum resistance reading, ie with the throttle fully closed (idle position), is between 0.122 and 0.128 x the maximum reading obtained in Step 4. For example, if the maximum reading was 5.0 K-ohms, then the minimum reading required is between 5 x 0.122 and 5 x 0.128, which is 610 to 640 ohms.

9 Slacken the sensor mounting screws and rotate the sensor until the reading is as calculated above, then tighten the screws evenly and a little at a time (see illustration 7.3). Unless an angled tool is available, it may be necessary to displace the carburettors to access the screws (see Chapter 4). If it cannot be adjusted to within the range, or if no reading is obtained, check it as described above.

All other models

10 Before adjusting the sensor, check the idle speed and carburettor synchronisation (see Chapter 1).

11 Remove the fuel tank and the air filter housing (see Chapter 4). Turn the ignition switch ON, then disconnect and reconnect the sensor wiring connector (see illustration 7.4). This sets the ignition control unit to 'sensor adjustment mode'.

12 Slacken the sensor mounting screws and rotate the sensor until the tachometer needle reads 5000 rpm (see illustration 7.3). If the tachometer reads either 0 rpm or 10000 rpm, the angle of the sensor is either too narrow or too wide. Adjust it as required until the reading is 5000 rpm, then tighten the screws evenly and a little at a time. Unless an angled tool is available, it may be necessary to displace the carburettors to access the screws (see Chapter 4). If it cannot be adjusted to within the range, or if no reading is obtained, check it as described above. Start the engine or turn the ignition switch OFF to reset the mode.

Renewal

13 Remove the fuel tank and the air filter housing (see Chapter 4). The throttle sensor is mounted on the outside of the right-hand carburettor (see illustration 7.3).

14 Disconnect the wiring connector, then unscrew the sensor mounting screws and remove the sensor, noting how it fits (see illustration 7.4). Unless an angled screwdriver is available, it may be necessary to displace the carburettors to access the screws (see Chapter 4).

15 Install the sensor and lightly tighten the screws, then connect the wiring connector and adjust the sensor as described above until the correct reading is obtained. On completion, tighten the screws evenly and a little at a time.

16 Install the air filter housing and fuel tank (see Chapter 4).

Chapter 6
Frame, suspension and final drive

Contents

Degrees of difficulty

Easy, suitable for novice with little experience 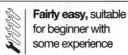	Fairly easy, suitable for beginner with some experience 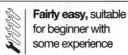	Fairly difficult, suitable for competent DIY mechanic 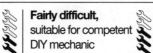	Difficult, suitable for experienced DIY mechanic 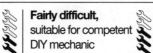	Very difficult, suitable for expert DIY or professional 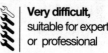

Specifications

Front forks

Fork oil type . . . . Yamaha suspension oil '01' or equivalent
Fork oil capacity
  1993 YZF750R models . . . . 469 cc
  1994 YZF750R models . . . . 466 cc
  1995-on YZF750R models . . . . 468 cc
  1993 and 1994 YZF750SP models . . . . 464 cc
  1995-on YZF750SP models . . . . 471 cc
  1996 YZF1000R models . . . . 590 cc
  1997-on YZF1000R models . . . . 620 cc
Fork oil level*
  1993 YZF750R models . . . . 93 mm
  1994 YZF750R models . . . . 99 mm
  1995-on YZF750R models . . . . 98 mm
  1993 and 1994 YZF750SP models . . . . 93 mm
  1995-on YZF750SP models . . . . 94 mm
  1996 YZF1000R models . . . . 123 mm
  1997-on YZF1000R models . . . . 103 mm
Fork spring free length
  YZF750R models
    Standard . . . . 269 mm
    Service limit . . . . 264 mm
  YZF750SP models
    Standard . . . . 269 mm
    Service limit . . . . 264 mm
  1996 YZF1000R models
    Standard . . . . 297 mm
    Service limit . . . . 294 mm
  1997-on YZF1000R models
    Standard . . . . 287 mm
    Service limit . . . . 284 mm

*Oil level is measured from the top of the tube with the fork spring removed and the leg fully compressed.

6

Rear suspension

Shock absorber spring free length

1993 and 1994 YZF750R models

Standard	216 mm
Service limit	211.5 mm

1995-on YZF750R models

Standard	200 mm
Service limit	196 mm

1993 and 1994 YZF750SP models

Standard	220 mm
Service limit	215.5 mm

1995-on YZF750SP models

Standard	160 mm
Service limit	157 mm

YZF1000R models

Standard	196 mm
Service limit	184 mm

Final drive

Chain type

YZF750R models	KAI/DAIDO 532ZLV (106 links)
YZF750SP models	KAI/DAIDO 532ZLV (104 links)
YZF1000R models	KAI/DAIDO 532ZLV (110 links)

Torque wrench settings

Footrest bracket bolts	28 Nm
Steering stem nut	110 Nm
Handlebar positioning bolts	13 Nm
Handlebar to holder bolt (1996 YZF1000R models)	28 Nm

Handlebar holder clamp bolts

YZF750R and SP models	13 Nm
YZF1000R models	17 Nm

Handlebar end-weights

YZF750R and SP models	23 Nm
YZF1000R models	21 Nm

Fork clamp bolts (top yoke)

YZF750R and SP models	25 Nm
YZF1000R models	26 Nm

Fork clamp bolts (bottom yoke)

YZF750R and SP models	23 Nm
YZF1000R models	23 Nm

Damper cartridge Allen bolt

YZF750R and SP models	40 Nm
YZF1000R models	35 Nm
Damper cartridge to top bolt locknut (YZF750R and SP models)	15 Nm

Fork top bolt

YZF750R and SP models	23 Nm
YZF1000R models	25 Nm
Steering stem nut	110 Nm
Rear shock absorber nuts	40 Nm
Rear suspension linkage arm and linkage rod nuts	48 Nm
Swingarm pivot bolt nut	125 Nm
Rear brake torque arm nuts	30 Nm

Front sprocket nut

YZF750R and SP models	70 Nm
YZF1000R models	80 Nm
Front sprocket cover bolts	10 Nm
Rear sprocket nuts	60 Nm

1 General information

All models use a twin spar box-section aluminium frame which uses the engine as a stressed member.

Front suspension is by a pair of oil-damped telescopic forks which use a cartridge-type damper. YZF750R and SP models have upside-down forks. On all models the forks are adjustable for spring pre-load and both rebound and compression damping.

At the rear, an aluminium alloy swingarm acts on a single shock absorber via a three-way linkage. The shock absorber is adjustable for spring pre-load and for both rebound and compression damping.

The drive to the rear wheel is by chain and sprockets.

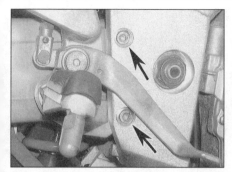

3.1a Unscrew the two bolts (arrowed) and displace the bracket . . .

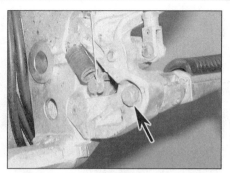

3.1b . . . to access the nut (arrowed) securing the footrest

3.2 Unscrew the nut (arrowed) and remove the footrest

2 Frame –
inspection and repair

1 The frame should not require attention unless accident damage has occurred. In most cases, frame renewal is the only satisfactory remedy for such damage. A few frame specialists have the jigs and other equipment necessary for straightening the frame to the required standard of accuracy, but even then there is no simple way of assessing to what extent the frame may have been over stressed.
2 After the machine has accumulated a lot of miles, the frame should be examined closely for signs of cracking or splitting at the welded joints. Loose engine mount bolts can cause ovaling or fracturing of the mounts themselves. Minor damage can often be repaired by welding, depending on the extent and nature of the damage, but this is a task for an expert.
3 Remember that a frame which is out of alignment will cause handling problems. If misalignment is suspected as the result of an accident, it will be necessary to strip the machine completely so the frame can be thoroughly checked.

3 Footrests, brake pedal and gearchange lever –
removal and installation

Footrests

Removal – rider's footrests

1 To remove the right-hand footrest, unscrew the bolts securing the footrest bracket and displace it just enough to provide access to the footrest nut on the back (see illustration). Make sure no strain is placed on the wiring or brake hoses. Unscrew the nut and separate the footrest from the bracket (see illustration). The footrest rubber can be detached from the footrest by removing the screws that secure it to the footrest.
2 To remove the left-hand footrest, unscrew the nut from the back of the footrest bracket and separate the footrest from the bracket (see illustration). The footrest rubber can be replaced by removing the screws that secure it to the footrest.

Removal – passenger footrests

3 On 1993 YZF750R models, remove the split pin from the bottom of the pivot pin, then withdraw the pivot pin and remove the

footrest, noting the fitting of the detent plate ball and spring – take care that they do not spring out when removing the footrest.
4 On all other YZF750R models and YZF1000R models, unscrew the nut from the bottom of the footrest pivot bolt, then withdraw the bolt and remove the footrest, noting the fitting of the detent plates, ball and spring – take care that they do not spring out when removing the footrest (see illustration). Also note the collar for the pivot bolt on YZF750R models.

Installation

5 Installation is the reverse of removal. When installing the right-hand front footrest, tighten the bracket bolts to the torque setting specified at the beginning of the Chapter.

Brake pedal

Removal

6 Remove the split pin and washer from the clevis pin securing the brake pedal to the master cylinder pushrod (see illustration). Remove the clevis pin and separate the pushrod from the pedal. Unscrew the pedal pivot bolt and remove the pedal, freeing the brake pedal return spring and the brake light switch spring from the lug on the pedal, and

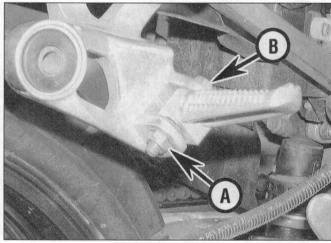

3.4 Unscrew the nut (A) and withdraw the bolt (B)

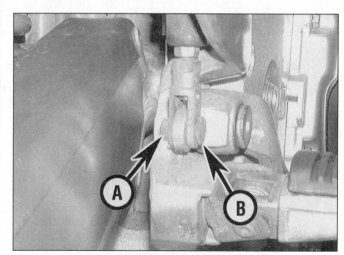

3.6a Remove the split and washer (A) and withdraw the clevis pin (B)

6

3.6b Brake pedal pivot bolt (arrowed)

3.8a Slacken the locknuts (arrowed) and thread the rod out of the lever and arm

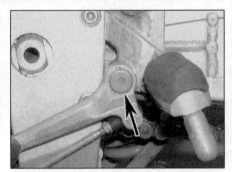

3.8b Unscrew the pivot bolt (arrowed) and remove the lever, noting the washers

noting the wave washer on the outside and the plain washer on the inside **(see illustration)**.

Installation

7 Installation is the reverse of removal, noting the following:
  a) *Apply grease to the brake pedal pivot.*
  b) *Tighten the pedal pivot bolt securely.*
  c) *Use a new split pin on the clevis pin securing the brake pedal to the master cylinder pushrod.*
  d) *Check the operation of the rear brake light switch (see Chapter 1).*

Gearchange lever

Removal

8 To remove the lever on its own, slacken the gearchange lever linkage rod locknuts, then unscrew the rod and separate it from the lever and the arm (the rod is reverse-threaded on one end and so will simultaneously unscrew from both lever and arm when turned in the one direction) **(see illustration)**. Note how far the rod is threaded into the lever and arm as this determines the height of the lever relative

to the footrest. Unscrew the lever pivot bolt and remove the lever, noting the washers on the outside and the inside **(see illustration)**.
9 To remove the lever with the linkage rod and arm as an assembly, first unscrew the gearchange lever linkage arm pinch bolt and slide the arm off the shaft, noting any alignment marks **(see illustration)**. If no marks are visible, make your own before removing the arm so that it can be correctly aligned with the shaft on installation. Unscrew the lever pivot bolt and remove the lever, noting the washer on the outside and the inside **(see illustration 3.8b)**.

Installation

10 Installation is the reverse of removal, noting the following:
  a) *Apply grease to the gear lever pivot.*
  b) *If removed, align the gearchange linkage arm with the shaft as noted on removal (see illustration 3.9).*
  c) *Tighten the lever pivot bolt securely.*
  d) *Adjust the gear lever height as required by screwing the rod in or out of the lever and arm. Tighten the locknuts securely (see illustration 3.8a).*

4 Sidestand – removal and installation

1 Support the motorcycle securely in an upright position using an auxiliary stand.
2 Unhook the stand springs and remove the link plate for the sidestand switch, noting how it fits **(see illustration)**. Counter-hold the pivot bolt and unscrew the nut on the inside of the bracket. Remove the pivot bolt and the stand.
4 On installation apply grease to the pivot and to the contact surfaces of the stand and bracket. Apply a suitable non-permanent thread locking compound to the bolt threads. Tighten the bolt securely, then tighten the nut. Fit the link plate and reconnect the sidestand springs. Check that the springs hold the stand securely up when not in use – an accident is almost certain to occur if the stand extends while the machine is in motion.
5 Check the operation of the sidestand switch (see Chapter 1).

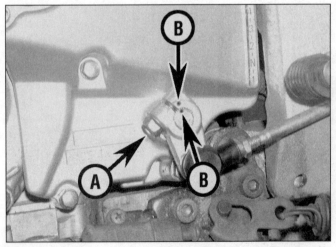

3.9 Unscrew the bolt (A) and slide the arm off the shaft, noting the alignment marks (B)

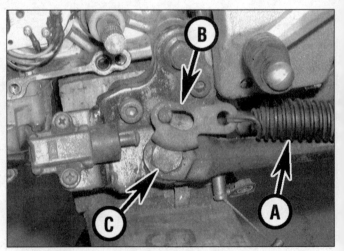

4.2 Sidestand springs (A), link plate (B) and pivot bolt (C)

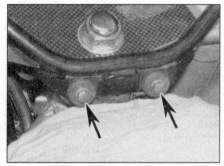

5.1a Fairing stay bolts (arrowed) –
YZF750R and SP models

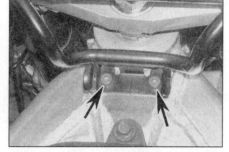

5.1b Fairing stay bolts (arrowed) –
YZF1000R models

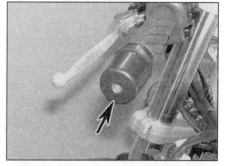

5.4 Handlebar end-weight (arrowed)

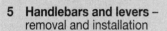

5 Handlebars and levers –
removal and installation

Handlebars

Removal

Note: *The handlebars can be displaced from the top yoke without having to remove any of the lever or switch assemblies.*

1 Remove the fairing (see Chapter 8), and on YZF1000R models the fuel tank (see Chapter 4). Unscrew the bolts securing the stay to the tank bracket (YZF750R and SP models) or frame (YZF1000R models) and remove the stay **(see illustrations)**. **Note:** *The fairing can remain on the bike if required, though it is advisable to remove it to prevent the possibility of damaging it. If you aren't removing the fairing, remove the rear view mirrors (see Chapter 8), then remove the fairing stay as described.*

2 If removing the right handlebar, displace the front brake master cylinder and reservoir (see Chapter 7). There is no need to disconnect the hydraulic hose. Keep the reservoir upright to prevent possible fluid leakage and make sure no strain is placed on the hydraulic hose(s). Displace the throttle cable housing from the handlebars (see Chapter 4). There is no need

5.5a Remove the blanking caps . . .

to detach the cables from the carburettors. Displace the handlebar switch (see Chapter 9). There is no need to disconnect the loom wiring connector.

3 If removing the left handlebar, displace the clutch master cylinder and reservoir (see Chapter 2). There is no need to disconnect the hydraulic hose. Keep the reservoir upright to prevent possible fluid leakage and make sure no strain is placed on the hydraulic hose(s). Displace the handlebar switch (see Chapter 9) and the choke cable (see Chapter 4). There is no need to disconnect the wiring connector.

4 If necessary, remove the handlebar end-weight from the end of the handlebar and remove the grip – the weights themselves

5.5b . . . and unscrew the positioning bolts

thread into the handlebars **(see illustration)**. It may be necessary to slit open the left-hand grip using a sharp blade in order to remove it as they are sometimes stuck in place, though a screwdriver between the grip and the handlebar and some compressed air or spray lubricant directed into the grip will usually work. Depending on your removal method and its success, a new grip may be required on assembly.

5 Remove the blanking caps from the heads of the handlebar positioning bolts using a small flat-bladed screwdriver, then unscrew the bolts **(see illustrations)**. Also slacken the fork clamp bolts in the top yoke **(see illustrations)**. Unscrew the steering stem nut

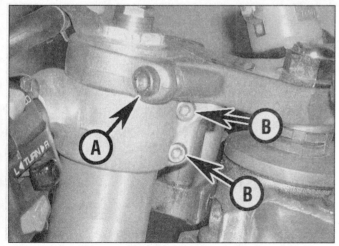

5.5c Fork clamp bolt (A), handlebar clamp bolts (B) –
YZF750R and SP models

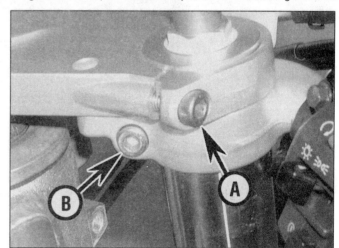

5.5d Fork clamp bolt (A), handlebar clamp bolt (B) –
YZF1000R models

5.5e Unscrew the steering stem nut (arrowed) . . .

5.5f . . . and lift the yoke off the stem and forks

5.7 Draw the handlebar up and off the fork

and remove it along with its washer, where fitted **(see illustration)**. Gently ease the top yoke upwards off the fork tubes and position it clear, using a rag to protect the tank or other components **(see illustration)**.

6 On 1996 YZF1000R models, if removing the handlebar leaving the holder in place, remove the blanking cap from the inner end of the handlebar, then unscrew the retaining bolt and slide the bar out of the holder, noting how it locates.

7 On all other models (and on 1996 YZF1000R models if removing the handlebar and holder together) slacken the handlebar holder clamp bolt(s) **(see illustration 5.5c or d)**. Ease the handlebar holder up and off the fork **(see illustration)**.

Installation

8 Installation is the reverse of removal, noting the following.

 a) *On 1996 YZF1000R models, if separated, make sure the flat on the inner end of the handlebar aligns correctly with the corresponding flat in the holder. Tighten the handlebar to holder bolt to the torque setting specified at the beginning of the Chapter.*
 b) *Tighten the steering stem nut, fork clamp bolts, handlebar positioning bolt,*

 handlebar clamp bolts, and the end-weights if removed, to the torque settings specified at the beginning of the Chapter, in that order.
 c) *Refer to the relevant Chapters as directed for the installation of the handlebar mounted assemblies.*
 d) *Do not forget to reconnect the front brake light switch and clutch switch wiring connectors.*
 e) *Adjust throttle cable freeplay (see Chapter 1).*
 f) *Check the operation of all switches and the front brake and clutch before taking the machine on the road.*

Front brake lever and clutch lever

Removal

9 Unscrew the lever pivot screw locknut, then remove the pivot screw and slide the lever out **(see illustration)**. Take care not to lose the pushrod bush from its socket in the clutch lever.

Installation

10 Installation is the reverse of removal. Apply grease to the pivot bolt shaft and the contact areas between the lever and its

bracket. When installing the clutch lever, make sure the end of the pushrod locates in the hole in the bush housed in the lever **(see illustration)**.

6 Forks – removal and installation

Removal

Caution: Although not strictly necessary, before removing the forks it is recommended that the fairing side panels and/or fairing are removed (see Chapter 8). This will prevent accidental damage to the paintwork.

1 Remove the fairing and the fairing side panels (see Chapter 8).

2 Displace the front brake calipers (see Chapter 7). There is no need to disconnect the hydraulic hoses from the calipers.

3 Remove the front wheel (see Chapter 7).

4 Remove the front mudguard (see Chapter 8).

5 Work on each fork individually. Slacken the handlebar holder clamp bolt(s) **(see illustration 5.5c or d)**. Release the cable tie

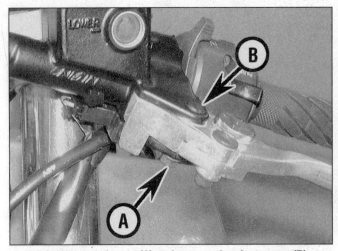

5.9 Unscrew the nut (A) and remove the pivot screw (B)

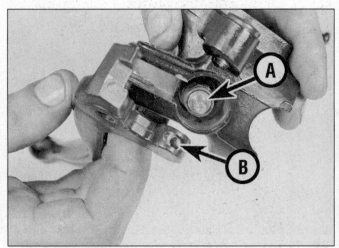

5.10 When installing the clutch lever, fit the pushrod (A) into the hole in the bush (B)

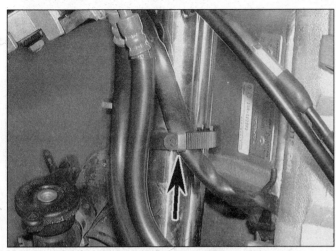

6.5 Release the wiring tie (arrowed)

6.7a Slacken the clamp bolts (arrowed) in the bottom yoke . . .

around the top of the fork tube, noting the routing of the wire **(see illustration)**. Also note the routing of the various cables and hoses around the forks.

6 Slacken the fork clamp bolt in the top yoke **(see illustration 5.5c or d)**. If the forks are to be disassembled, or if the fork oil is being changed, it is advisable to slacken the fork top bolt at this stage.

7 Note the alignment or amount of protrusion of the tops of the fork tube with the top yoke. Slacken but do not remove the fork clamp bolts in the bottom yoke, and remove the fork

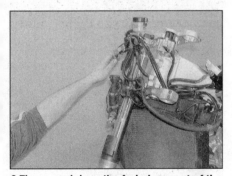

6.7b . . . and draw the fork down out of the yokes

by twisting it and pulling it downwards **(see illustrations)**. Secure the handlebar assembly so that the master cylinder reservoir remains upright, making sure there is no strain on the hose or wiring.

 HAYNES HiNT *If the fork legs are seized in the yokes, spray the area with penetrating oil and allow time for it to soak in before trying again.*

Installation

8 Remove all traces of corrosion from the fork tubes and the yokes. Slide the fork up through the bottom yoke and the handlebars and up into the top yoke, making sure the wiring, cables and hoses are the correct side of the fork as noted on removal **(see illustration 6.7b)**. Check that the amount of protrusion of the fork tube above the top yoke is as noted on removal and equal on both sides – the tops of the tubes should be flush with the top of the top yoke **(see illustration 5.5c or d)**.

9 Tighten the fork clamp bolts in the bottom yoke to the torque setting specified at the

beginning of the Chapter **(see illustration 6.7a)**. If the fork leg has been dismantled or if the fork oil has been changed, the fork top bolt should now be tightened to the specified torque setting **(see illustration)**. Now tighten the fork clamp bolt in the top yoke, and the handlebar holder clamp bolt(s), to the specified torque settings **(see illustrations)**. Secure the wiring to the fork using the cable tie **(see illustration 6.5)**. **Note:** *Depending on the tools available, it may be necessary to remove the handlebar positioning bolt and slide the handlebar down the fork in order to gain clearance for a torque wrench. Refer to Section 5 for details and illustrations. If this is done, tighten the handlebar positioning bolt before the handlebar clamp bolt.*

10 Install the front wheel (see Chapter 7), the front mudguard (see Chapter 8), and the brake calipers (see Chapter 7). Make sure the speedometer cable is correctly routed.

11 Install the fairing and the fairing side panels (see Chapter 8).

12 Check the operation of the front forks and brakes before taking the machine out on the road.

6.9a If slackened, tighten the fork top bolt to the specified torque

6.9b Tighten the fork clamp bolt . . .

6.9c . . . and the handlebar clamp bolt(s) to the specified torque

 6

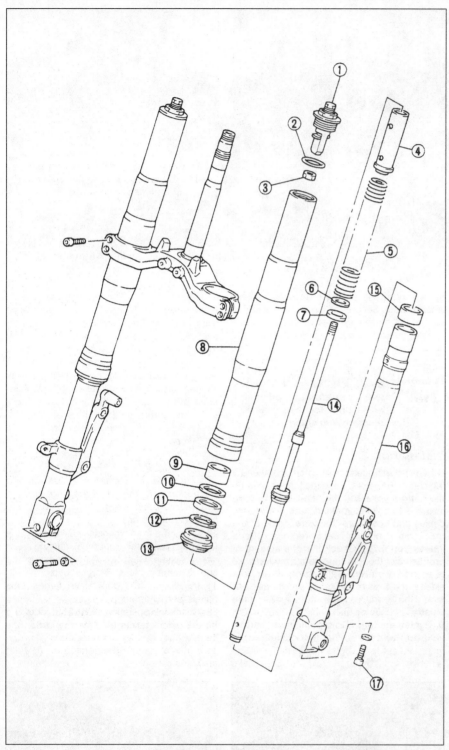

**7.1 Front fork components –
YZF750R and SP models**

1 Top bolt assembly
2 O-ring
3 Locknut
4 Spacer
5 Spring
6 Felt washer
   (1993 and 1994 models)

7 Slide washer
   (1993 and 1994 models)
8 Outer tube
9 Bottom bush
10 Washer
11 Oil seal
12 Retaining clip

13 Dust seal
14 Damper cartridge
15 Top bush
16 Inner tube
17 Damper cartridge bolt
   and sealing washer

7 Forks –
disassembly, inspection
and reassembly

YZF750R and SP models

Disassembly

1 Always dismantle the fork legs separately to avoid interchanging parts and thus causing an accelerated rate of wear. Store all components in separate, clearly marked containers **(see illustration)**. Due to the construction of these forks, an assistant and a special tool are required (see Step 5).

2 Before dismantling the fork, it is advised that the damper cartridge bolt be slackened at this stage. Compress the outer fork tube over the inner tube so that the spring exerts maximum pressure on the damper cartridge head, then have an assistant slacken the damper cartridge bolt in the base of the inner tube **(see illustration)**. If an assistant is not available, clamp the brake caliper lugs on the inner tube between the padded jaws of a vice.

3 If the fork top bolt was not slackened with the fork in situ, carefully clamp the outer tube in a vice equipped with soft jaws, taking care not to overtighten or score its surface.

4 Unscrew the fork top bolt from the top of the outer tube **(see illustration)**. The bolt will remain threaded on the damper cartridge.

5 Carefully clamp the brake caliper lugs on the inner tube between the padded jaws of a vice and slide the outer tube fully down onto the inner tube (wrap a rag around the top of the outer tube to minimise oil spillage) while, with

7.2 Slacken the damper rod Allen bolt

7.4 Unscrew the top bolt from the outer tube

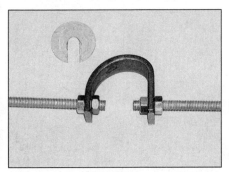

7.5a A home-made tool can be made as shown

7.5b Fit the tool into the holes in the spacer as shown

7.5c Press down on the tool and slide a slotted washer between the top of the spacer and the locknut

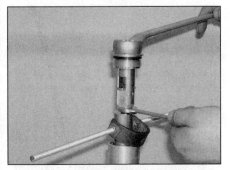

7.6 Remove the top bolt assembly as described

7.7a Withdraw the spring . . .

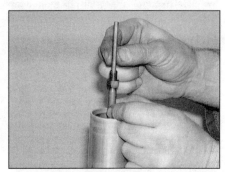

7.7b . . . then withdraw the adjusting rod from the centre of the damper cartridge

the aid of an assistant if necessary, keeping the damper cartridge fully extended. Obtain either the Yamaha service tool (Pt. No. 90890-01441), or construct a home-made equivalent from a piece of steel strap bent into a U-shape, some threaded rod and nuts, as shown (see illustration). Fit the tool onto the spacer, locating it into the holes (see illustration). Push down on the spacer using the tool and have an assistant insert a suitably sized washer with a slot cut into it between the top of the spacer and the base of the locknut on the damper cartridge (see illustration). This will keep the spacer and spring compressed while removing the top bolt assembly.

6 Using two spanners, one on the locknut and one on the fork top bolt, counter-hold the top bolt and slacken the locknut, and thread it to the base of its threads (see illustration). Now counter-hold the locknut and thread the damping adjuster/pre-load adjuster/top bolt

assembly off the damper cartridge.

7 Push down on the spacer using the tool and have an assistant remove the fabricated slotted washer (see illustration 7.5c), then slowly release the spring pressure and remove the spacer (see illustration 7.28c). Withdraw the spring from the tube, noting which way up it fits (see illustration). Withdraw the damping adjuster rod from inside the damper cartridge – if the damper has sunk into the fork, draw it out using a pair of thin-nosed pliers (see illustration). Remove the holding tool from the spacer if required, but note that it will be needed for installation.

8 On 1993 and 1994 YZF750R and SP models, two washers are fitted between the bottom of the spring and the top of the damper cartridge. It is unlikely that they will come out with the spring, and it is difficult to retrieve them from the fork with the oil still in it. When draining the oil (see next Step), take

care to retrieve the washers from the oil if they fall out. Otherwise, pick them off the top of the damper when it is removed.

9 Invert the fork leg over a suitable container and pump the fork and damper cartridge vigorously to expel as much fork oil as possible.

10 Remove the previously slackened damper cartridge bolt and its sealing washer from the bottom of the inner tube (see illustration). Discard the sealing washer as a new one must be used on reassembly. Invert the fork and withdraw the damper cartridge from inside the fork.

11 Carefully prise out the dust seal from the bottom of the outer tube to gain access to the oil seal retaining clip (see illustration). Discard the dust seal as a new one must be used.

12 Carefully remove the retaining clip, taking care not to scratch the surface of the tube (see illustration).

7.10 Unscrew and remove the damper cartridge bolt

7.11 Prise off the dust seal . . .

7.12 . . . then lever out the retaining clip using a flat-bladed screwdriver

6

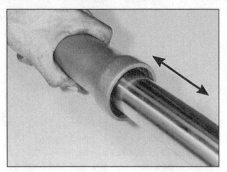

7.13 To separate the inner and outer fork tubes, pull them apart firmly several times – the slide-hammer effect will pull them apart

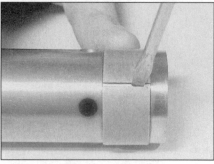

7.14a Carefully lever apart the ends of the top bush and remove it from the inner tube

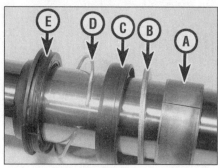

7.14b Bottom bush (A), oil seal washer (B), oil seal (C), retaining clip (D), dust seal (E)

13 To separate the inner tube from the outer tube it is necessary to displace the bottom bush and oil seal. The top bush should not pass through the bottom bush, and this can be used to good effect. Push the inner tube gently inwards until it stops. Take care not to do this forcibly. Then pull the inner tube sharply outwards until the top bush strikes the bottom bush (see illustration). Repeat this operation until the bottom bush and seal are tapped out of the outer tube.

14 With the tubes separated, remove the top bush from the inner tube by carefully levering its ends apart using a screwdriver (see illustration). Slide the bottom bush, the oil seal washer, the oil seal, the retaining clip and the dust seal off the inner tube, noting which

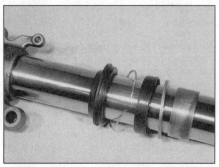

7.20a Slide the dust seal, the retaining clip, the oil seal, the oil seal washer and the bottom bush onto the inner tube as shown

way up they fit (see illustration). Discard the oil seal and the dust seal as new ones must be used.

Inspection

15 Clean all parts in solvent and blow them dry with compressed air, if available. Check the inner tube for score marks, scratches, flaking of the chrome finish and excessive or abnormal wear. Renew the inner tube in both forks if any dents are found. Check the fork seal seat in the bottom of the outer tube for nicks, gouges and scratches. If damage is evident, leaks will occur. Also check the oil seal washer for damage or distortion and renew it if necessary.

16 Check the spring for cracks and other damage. Measure the spring free length and compare the measurement to the specifications at the beginning of the Chapter. If it is defective or sagged below the service limit, replace the springs in both forks with new ones. Never renew only one spring.

17 Examine the working surfaces of the two bushes; if worn or scuffed they must be renewed. Yamaha recommend new ones are fitted as a matter of course.

18 Check the damper cartridge assembly for damage and wear, and renew it if necessary. Holding the outside of the damper, pump the rod in and out of the damper. If the rod does not move smoothly in the damper it must be replaced with a new one.

Reassembly

19 Wrap some insulating tape over the ridges on the top of the inner tube to protect the lips of the new oil seal as it is installed.

20 Apply a smear of the specified clean fork oil to the lips of the oil seal and the inner surface of each bush, then slide the new dust seal, the retaining clip, the oil seal, the oil seal washer and the bottom bush onto the inner tube, making sure that the marked side of the oil seal faces the dust seal (see illustration). Remove the insulating tape and fit the top bush into its recess in the tube (see illustration).

21 Apply a smear of the specified clean fork oil to the outer surface of each bush, then carefully insert the inner tube fully into the outer tube (see illustration).

22 Support the fork upside down, then press the bottom bush squarely into its recess in the outer tube as far as possible (see illustration). Slide the oil seal washer on top of the bush, and keep the oil seal, the retaining clip and the dust seal out of the way by sliding them up the inner tube. If necessary, tape them to the tube to prevent them from falling down and interfering as the bush is drifted into place.

23 Using either the special service tool (Pt. No. 09940-01442) or a suitable drift, carefully drive the bottom bush fully into its recess using the oil seal washer to prevent damaging

7.20b Make sure the top bush seats properly in its recess

7.21 Fit the inner tube into the bottom of the outer tube

7.22 Make sure the bottom bush enters the outer tube squarely

7.24 Drive the oil seal into the bottom of the outer tube . . .

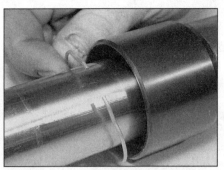

7.25a . . . and fit its retaining clip, making sure it is properly seated . . .

7.25b . . . then press the dust seal into place

7.26 Apply a thread locking compound to the damper cartridge bolt and use a new sealing washer

7.28a Grasp the damper cartridge and draw it out of the fork

7.28b Tie a piece of wire around the damper cartridge as shown and use it to keep the cartridge extended

the edges of the bush. Make sure the bush enters the recess squarely, and take care not to scratch or gouge the inner tube.

24 When the bush is seated fully and squarely in its recess in the tube (remove the washer to check, wipe the recess clean, then reinstall the washer), drive the oil seal into place as described in Step 23 until the retaining clip groove is visible above the seal (see illustration).

25 Once the oil seal is correctly seated, fit the retaining clip, making sure it is correctly located in its groove, then press the dust seal into position (see illustrations).

26 Lay the fork flat and push the inner tube fully into the outer tube. On 1993 and 1994 YZF750R and SP models, fit the slide washer and the felt washer onto the top of the damper cartridge, with the felt washer uppermost (see illustration 7.1). Insert the damper cartridge into the top of the fork until it seats on the bottom of the inner tube. Fit a new sealing washer onto the damper cartridge bolt and apply a few drops of a suitable non-permanent thread locking compound, then install the bolt into the bottom of the inner tube and tighten it to the torque setting specified at the beginning of the Chapter (see illustration). If the damper cartridge rotates inside the tube, wait until the fork is fully reassembled before tightening the bolt.

27 Stand the fork upright. Slowly pour in the specified quantity and grade of fork oil and pump the fork and damper cartridge slowly at

least ten times each to distribute it evenly and expel all the air (see illustration 7.59a). Be careful not to extend the outer tube by more than 120 mm when pumping it as this can cause air to enter the system, in which case the process must be repeated. Wait ten minutes, then fully compress the fork and measure the fork oil level from the top of the tube (see illustration 7.59b). Add or subtract fork oil until it is at the level specified at the beginning of the Chapter.

28 Fit the adjuster rod into the damper cartridge (see illustration 7.7b). Install the spring, with its tapered end upwards, into the fork tube (see illustration 7.7a). Withdraw the damper cartridge fully from the fork, using a pair of thin-nosed pliers to grab it if necessary (see illustration). As the damper cartridge will have to be kept extended out of the tube, tie a

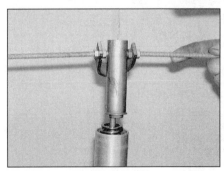

7.28c Fit the spacer into the top of the spring . . .

piece of wire around the base of the locknut on the top of the rod to use as a holder (see illustration). If the holding tool used on disassembly was removed from the spacer, fit it back on. Install the spacer, making sure the lip on the bottom fits into the top of the spring (see illustration). Push down on the spacer using the tool and insert a suitably sized washer with a slot cut into it (as used on removal) between the top of the spacer and the base of the locknut on the damper cartridge (see illustration). This will keep the spacer and spring compressed while installing the top bolt assembly. You can now remove the piece of wire.

29 Thread the locknut up the damper cartridge so that the distance between the top of the nut and the top of the rod is 12 mm (see illustration).

7.28d . . . then push down on the spacer to compress the spring and insert the slotted washer as shown

6

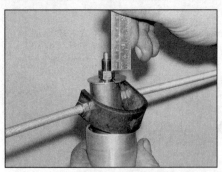
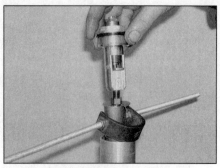
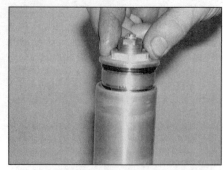

7.29 Set the locknut at the specified depth on the cartridge . . .

7.30 . . . then thread the top bolt assembly onto it

7.32 Thread the top bolt into the fork

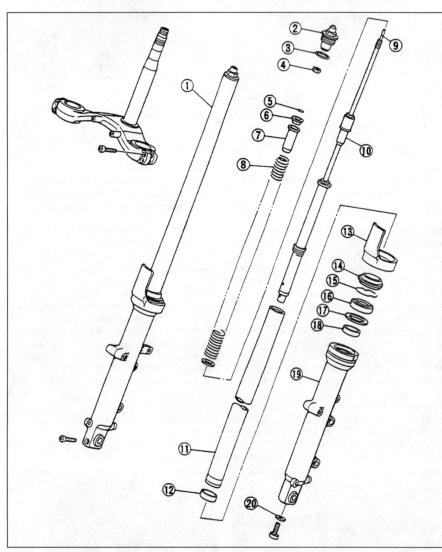

7.34 Front fork components – YZF1000R models

1	Fork assembly	9	Rebound damping	15	Retaining clip
2	Top bolt		adjuster rod	16	Oil seal
3	O-ring	10	Damper cartridge and	17	Washer
4	Locknut		rebound spring	18	Top bush
5	Circlip	11	Fork tube	19	Fork slider
6	Collar	12	Bottom bush	20	Damper cartridge bolt
7	Spacer	13	Fork protector		and sealing washer
8	Spring	14	Dust seal		

30 Fit a new O-ring onto the damping adjuster/pre-load adjuster/top bolt assembly and thread it down onto the damper cartridge until it seats against the locknut, holding the rod to prevent it from turning **(see illustration)**. Counter-hold the top bolt and tighten the locknut securely against it, to the specified torque if the correct tools are available **(see illustration 7.6)**.

31 Push down on the spacer using the tool and have an assistant remove the fabricated slotted washer, then slowly release the spring pressure and allow the spacer to settle against the pre-load adjuster arms **(see illustrations 7.5c and b)**. Remove the holding tool from the spacer.

32 Apply a smear of the specified clean oil to the top bolt O-ring. Fully extend the outer tube and carefully screw the top bolt into the tube making sure it is not cross-threaded **(see illustration)**. **Note:** *The top bolt can be tightened to the specified torque setting at this stage if the tube is held between the padded jaws of a vice, but do not risk distorting the tube by doing so. A better method is to tighten the top bolt when the fork leg has been installed and is securely held in the yokes.*

> **TOOL TIP** *Use a ratchet-type tool when installing the fork top bolt. This makes it unnecessary to remove the tool from the bolt whilst threading it in.*

If the damper cartridge Allen bolt requires tightening, clamp the fork between the padded jaws of a vice and have an assistant compress the fork so that maximum spring pressure is placed on the damper cartridge head – tighten the boit to the specified torque setting **(see illustration 7.2)**.

33 Install the forks as described in Section 6. Set the spring pre-load and rebound damping as required (see Section 11).

YZF1000R models

Disassembly

34 Always dismantle the fork legs separately to avoid interchanging parts and thus causing an accelerated rate of wear. Store all components in separate, clearly marked containers **(see illustration)**.

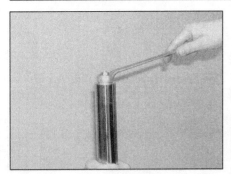

7.37 Unscrew the top bolt from the fork tube

7.38a Remove the top bolt assembly as described

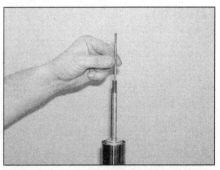

7.38b Withdraw the adjusting rod from the centre of the damper cartridge

35 Before dismantling the fork, it is advised that the damper cartridge bolt be slackened at this stage. Turn the fork upside down and compress the slider so that the spring exerts maximum pressure on the damper cartridge head, then have an assistant slacken the damper cartridge bolt in the base of the fork slider **(see illustration 7.2)**. If an assistant is not available, clamp the brake caliper mounting lugs between the padded jaws of a vice to support the fork.

36 If the fork top bolt was not slackened with the fork in situ, carefully clamp the fork tube in a vice equipped with soft jaws, taking care not to overtighten or score its surface.

37 Unscrew the fork top bolt from the top of the fork tube **(see illustration)**. The bolt will remain threaded on the damper cartridge.

38 Carefully clamp the fork slider between the padded jaws of a vice and slide the fork tube down into the slider a little way (wrap a rag around the top of the tube to minimise oil spillage) while, with the aid of an assistant if necessary, keeping the damper cartridge fully extended. Counter-hold the pre-load adjuster, then slacken the locknut and thread it to the base of the threads on the damper cartridge **(see illustration)**. Now counter-hold the locknut and thread the top bolt assembly off the damper cartridge, then thread the locknut off the rod. Remove the adjuster rod from the centre of the damper cartridge **(see illustration)**.

39 Slide the fork tube fully down into the slider and fully extend the damper cartridge

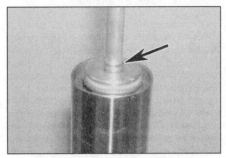

7.39a Compress the fork tube and withdraw the damper cartridge to expose the circlip (arrowed) . . .

so that the circlip is exposed **(see illustration)**. Keep the damper cartridge extended with the aid of an assistant, then remove the circlip **(see illustration)**.

 Make hole in a piece of paper and slide it down the damper cartridge so that it is below the circlip. This will prevent the circlip from falling into the fork as you remove it.

40 Remove the collar and the spacer and withdraw the spring from the tube, noting which way up it fits **(see illustration)**.

41 Invert the fork leg over a suitable container and pump the fork and the damper cartridge vigorously to expel as much fork oil as possible.

42 Remove the previously slackened damper

7.39b . . . then remove the circlip, using a piece of paper as shown to prevent it falling into the fork

cartridge bolt and its copper sealing washer from the bottom of the slider **(see illustration 7.10)**. Discard the sealing washer as a new one must be used on reassembly.

43 Invert the fork and withdraw the damper cartridge from inside the fork tube **(see illustration)**.

44 Carefully prise out the dust seal from the top of the slider to gain access to the oil seal retaining clip **(see illustration)**. Discard the dust seal as a new one must be used. Note that the fork protector should not be removed from the top of the slider unless necessary, and if it is removed, it should be replaced with a new one.

45 Carefully remove the retaining clip, taking care not to scratch the surface of the tube **(see illustration)**.

46 To separate the tube from the slider it is necessary to displace the top bush and oil

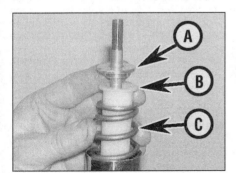

7.40 Remove the collar (A) and spacer (B), then withdraw the spring (C)

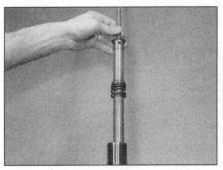

7.43 Withdraw the damper cartridge

7.44 Prise off the dust seal . . .

6

7.45 ... then lever out the retaining clip using a flat-bladed screwdriver

7.47 The oil seal (1), washer (2), top bush (3) and bottom bush (4) will come out with the fork tube

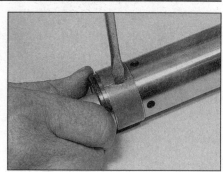

7.51 Prise off the bottom bush using a flat-bladed screwdriver

seal. The bottom bush should not pass through the top bush, and this can be used to good effect. Push the tube gently inwards until it stops against the damper cartridge seat. Take care not to do this forcibly or the seat may be damaged. Then pull the tube sharply outwards until the bottom bush strikes the top bush. Repeat this operation until the top bush and seal are tapped out of the slider **(see illustration 7.13)**.

47 With the tube removed, slide off the oil seal, washer and top bush, noting which way up they fit **(see illustration)**. Discard the oil seal as a new one must be used.

Caution: Do not remove the bottom bush from the tube unless it is to be renewed.

Inspection

48 Clean all parts in solvent and blow them dry with compressed air, if available. Check the fork tube for score marks, scratches, flaking of the chrome finish and excessive or abnormal wear. Look for dents in the tube and replace the tube in both forks with new ones if any are found. Check the fork seal seat for nicks, gouges and scratches. If damage is evident, leaks will occur. Also check the oil seal washer for damage or distortion and replace it with a new one if necessary.

49 Check the fork tube for runout (bending) using V-blocks and a dial gauge, or have it done by a Yamaha dealer or suspension specialist **(see illustration 7.16)**. Yamaha do not specify a runout limit, but if the tube is bent beyond the generally accepted limit specified, it should be replaced with a new one.

⚠️ *Warning: If the tube is bent, it should not be straightened; replace it with a new one.*

50 Check the spring for cracks and other damage. Measure the spring free length and compare the measurement to the specifications at the beginning of the Chapter. If it is defective or sagged below the service limit, replace the springs in both forks with new ones. Never replace only one spring. Also check the rebound spring on the damper cartridge.

51 Examine the working surfaces of the two bushes; if worn or scuffed they must be replaced with new ones. To remove the bottom bush from the fork tube, prise it apart at the slit using a flat-bladed screwdriver and slide it off **(see illustration)**. Make sure the new one seats properly.

52 Check the damper cartridge assembly for damage and wear, and replace it with a new one if necessary. Holding the outside of the damper, pump the rod in and out of the damper. If the rod does not move smoothly in the damper it must be replaced with a new one.

Reassembly

53 Insert the damper cartridge into the fork tube and slide it into place so that it projects fully from the bottom of the tube **(see illustration 7.43)**.

54 Oil the fork tube and bottom bush with the specified fork oil and insert the assembly into the slider **(see illustration)**. Make sure that the bottom of the damper cartridge locates

correctly into the bottom of the slider, otherwise the damper cartridge Allen bolt will not thread into the rod. Look up into the bottom of the fork via the bolt hole to check. Fit a new copper sealing washer onto the damper cartridge bolt and apply a few drops of a suitable non-permanent thread locking compound, then install the bolt into the bottom of the slider **(see illustration 7.26)**. Tighten the bolt to the specified torque setting. If the damper cartridge rotates inside the tube, wait until the fork is fully reassembled before tightening the bolt.

55 Push the fork tube fully into the slider, then oil the top bush and slide it down over the tube **(see illustration)**. Press the bush squarely into its recess in the slider as far as possible, then install the oil seal washer with its flat side facing up **(see illustration)**. Either use the Yamaha service tool or a suitable piece of tubing to tap the bush fully into place; the tubing must be slightly larger in diameter than the fork tube and slightly smaller in diameter than the bush recess in the slider. Take care not to scratch the fork tube during this operation; it is best to make sure that the fork tube is pushed fully into the slider so that any accidental scratching is confined to the area above the oil seal.

56 When the bush is seated fully and squarely in its recess in the slider (remove the washer to check, wipe the recess clean, then reinstall the washer), install the new oil seal. Smear the seal's lips with lithium-based grease and slide it over the tube so that its

7.54 Slide the fork tube into the slider

7.55a Install the top bush ...

7.55b ... followed by the washer

7.56 Make sure the oil seal is the correct way up

7.57 Install the retaining clip . . .

7.58 . . . followed by the dust seal. . .

markings face upwards and drive the seal into place as described above until the retaining clip groove is visible above the seal **(see illustration)**.

HAYNES HiNT *Place the old oil seal on top of the new one to protect it when driving the seal into place.*

57 Once the seal is correctly seated, fit the retaining clip, making sure it is correctly located in its groove **(see illustration)**.
58 Lubricate the lips of the new dust seal then slide it down the fork tube and press it into position **(see illustration)**.
59 Slowly pour in the specified quantity and grade of fork oil, then pump the damper cartridge first, then the fork tube, at least ten

times each to distribute the oil evenly and remove any air bubbles **(see illustration)**. Be careful not to extend the tube by more than 130 mm when pumping it as this can cause air to enter the system, in which case the process must be repeated. Wait ten minutes, then fully compress the fork tube and damper cartridge into the slider and measure the fork oil level from the top of the tube **(see illustration)**. Add or subtract fork oil until it is at the level specified at the beginning of the Chapter.
60 Clamp the slider in a vice via the brake caliper mounting lugs, taking care not to overtighten and damage them. Pull the fork tube and damper cartridge out of the slider as far as possible then install the spring with its tapered end at the top **(see illustration)**. Fit the spacer, with its tapered end fitting into the

top of the spring, then fit the collar into the top of the spacer **(see illustrations)**. Fit a piece of paper around the damper cartridge as on disassembly **(see Haynes Hint above)**, then fit the circlip, making sure it locates correctly into its groove **(see illustration)**. Fit the damping adjuster rod into the damper cartridge **(see illustration 7.38b)**.
61 Thread the locknut onto the damper cartridge and set it so that there is 16 mm of damper cartridge thread above it **(see illustrations)**. Fit a new O-ring onto the fork top bolt. Thread the top bolt assembly onto the damper cartridge until it contacts the locknut, then counter-hold the pre-load adjuster and tighten the locknut securely against it **(see illustration and 7.38a)**.
62 Withdraw the tube fully from the slider and carefully screw the top bolt into the fork tube

7.59a Pour the oil into the top of the tube

7.59b Measure the oil level with the fork held vertical

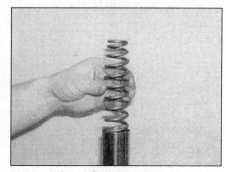

7.60a Install the spring . . .

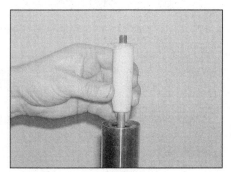

7.60b . . . followed by the spacer . . .

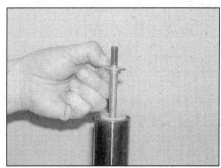

7.60c . . . and the collar

7.60d Fit the circlip into its groove

6

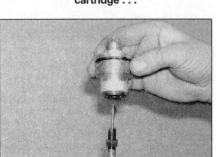

7.61a Thread the locknut onto the damper cartridge . . .

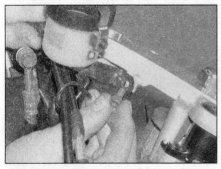

7.61c Thread the top bolt assembly onto the damper cartridge and tighten it against the locknut

making sure it is not cross-threaded (see illustration). Note: *The top bolt can be tightened to the specified torque setting at this stage if the tube is held between the padded jaws of a vice, but do not risk distorting the tube*

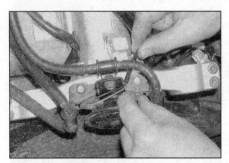

8.3 Displace the reservoir(s) from the top yoke . . .

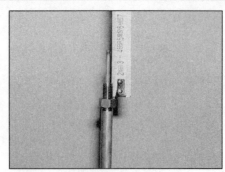

7.61b . . . and set it at the correct position as described

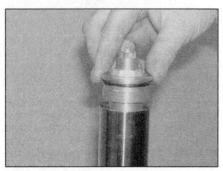

7.62 Thread the top bolt into the fork tube

by doing so. A better method is to tighten the top bolt when the fork leg has been installed and is securely held in the triple clamps.

 TOOL TiP *Use a ratchet-type tool when installing the fork top bolt. This makes it unnecessary to remove the tool from the bolt whilst threading it in.*

If the damper cartridge Allen bolt requires tightening, clamp the fork slider between the padded jaws of a vice and have an assistant compress the tube into the slider so that maximum spring pressure is placed on the damper cartridge head – tighten the damper cartridge Allen bolt to the specified torque setting (see illustration 7.2).
63 Install the forks (see Section 6). Set the spring pre-load and damping adjusters as required (see Section 12).

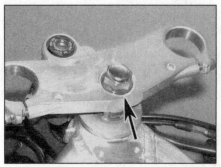

8.4 . . . and the horn/brake hose assembly from the bottom yoke – YZF1000R model shown

8 Steering stem – removal and installation

Removal

1 Remove the fairing and the fairing side panels (see Chapter 6). It is also advisable to remove the fuel tank to avoid the possibility of scratching it (see Chapter 4).
2 Remove the front forks (see Section 6).
3 Unscrew the bolt securing the front brake master cylinder reservoir bracket, and on YZF750R and SP models, the clutch reservoir bracket, to the top yoke (see illustration). Keep the reservoir(s) upright.
4 Disconnect the horn wiring connectors, then unscrew the bolts securing the front brake hose/horn bracket to the bottom yoke (see illustration). If the top yoke is being removed from the bike rather than just being displaced, trace the wiring from the ignition switch and disconnect it at the connector.
5 Remove the blanking caps from the heads of the handlebar positioning bolts using a small flat-bladed screwdriver, then unscrew the bolts and displace the handlebars (see illustrations 5.5a and b). Secure the handlebar assemblies so that the master cylinders are upright, making sure there is no strain on the hoses or wiring.
6 Unscrew the steering stem nut and remove it along with its washer, where fitted (see illustration). Lift the top yoke up off the steering stem and position it clear, using a rag to protect the tank or other components (see illustration).
7 Remove the tabbed lockwasher, noting how it fits, then unscrew and remove the locknut using either a C-spanner, a peg spanner or a drift located in one of the notches (see illustrations). Remove the rubber washer (see illustration).
8 Supporting the bottom yoke, unscrew the adjuster nut using either a C-spanner, a peg-spanner or a drift located in one of the notches, then remove the adjuster nut and the bearing cover from the steering stem (see illustrations).
9 Gently lower the bottom yoke and steering stem out of the frame (see illustration).

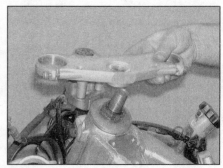

8.6a Unscrew the steering stem nut (arrowed) . . .

8.6b . . . and lift the yoke up off the steering stem

8.7a Remove the lockwasher . . .

8.7b . . . the locknut . . .

8.7c . . . and the rubber washer

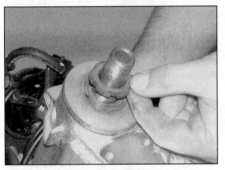

8.8a Unscrew the adjuster nut . . .

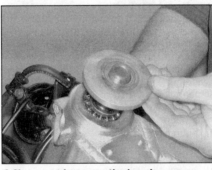

8.8b . . . and remove the bearing cover . . .

8.9 . . . then gently lower the steering stem out of the head

10 Remove the inner race and bearing from the top of the steering head **(see illustrations 8.12b and a)**. Remove the washer, bearing and rubber dust seal from the base of the steering stem **(see**

illustrations **8.11c, b and a)**. Remove all traces of old grease from the bearings and races and check them for wear or damage as described in Section 9. **Note:** *Do not attempt to remove the races from the steering head or*

the steering stem unless they are to be replaced with new ones.

Installation

11 Smear a liberal quantity of lithium-based grease onto the bearing races. Also work some grease well into both the upper and lower bearings. Fit the rubber dust seal over the lower bearing inner race on the steering stem, then fit the bearing and the washer **(see illustrations)**.
12 Carefully lift the steering stem/bottom yoke up through the steering head **(see illustration 8.9)**. Fit the upper bearing and the inner race into the top of the steering head, then install the bearing cover **(see illustrations and 8.8b)**. Thread the adjuster nut onto the steering stem and adjust the bearings as described in Chapter 1 **(see illustration 8.8a)**.

8.11a Fit the dust seal . . .

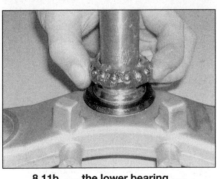

8.11b . . . the lower bearing . . .

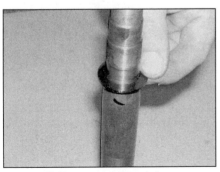

8.11c . . . and the washer

8.12a Fit the upper bearing . . .

8.12b . . . and its inner race into the steering head

6

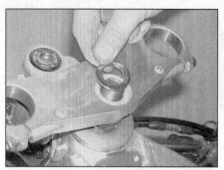

8.14a Install the washer (if fitted) . . .

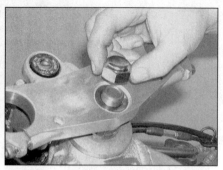

8.14b . . . and the steering stem nut

13 Install the rubber washer and the locknut **(see illustrations 8.7c and b)**. Tighten the locknut finger-tight, then tighten it further until its notches align with those in the adjuster nut. If necessary, counter-hold the adjuster nut and tighten the locknut using a C-spanner or drift until the notches align, but make sure the

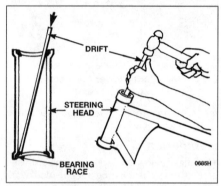

9.4 Drive the bearing races out with a brass drift as shown

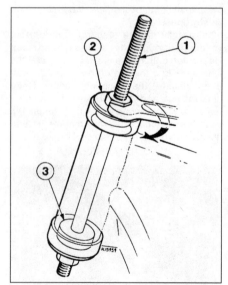

9.6 Drawbolt arrangement for fitting steering stem bearing races

1 Long bolt or threaded bar
2 Thick washer
3 Guide for lower race

adjuster nut does not turn as well. Install the tabbed lockwasher so that the tabs fit into the notches in both the locknut and adjuster nut **(see illustration 8.7a)**.
14 Fit the top yoke onto the steering stem **(see illustration 8.6b)**, then install the washer (where fitted) and steering stem nut and tighten it finger-tight **(see illustrations)**. Temporarily install one of the forks to align the top and bottom yokes, and secure it by tightening the bottom yoke clamp bolts only. Now tighten the steering stem nut to the torque setting specified at the beginning of the Chapter.
15 Install the remaining components in a reverse of the removal procedure, referring to the relevant Sections or Chapters, and to the torque settings specified at the beginning of the Chapter.
16 Carry out a check of the steering head bearing freeplay as described in Chapter 1, and if necessary re-adjust.

9 Steering head bearings – inspection and renewal

Inspection

1 Remove the steering stem (see Section 8).
2 Remove all traces of old grease from the bearings and races and check them for wear or damage.
3 The outer races should be polished and free from indentations. Inspect the bearing balls for signs of wear, damage or discoloration, and examine their retainer cage for signs of cracks

9.7a Remove the lower bearing inner race as described . . .

or splits. Spin the bearing balls by hand. They should spin freely and smoothly. If there are any signs of wear on any of the above components both upper and lower bearing assemblies must be renewed as a set. Only remove the outer races in the steering head and the lower bearing inner race on the steering stem if they need to be renewed – do not re-use them once they have been removed.

Renewal

4 The outer races are an interference fit in the steering head and can be tapped from position with a suitable drift **(see illustration)**. Tap firmly and evenly around each race to ensure that it is driven out squarely. It may prove advantageous to curve the end of the drift slightly to improve access.
5 Alternatively, the races can be removed using a slide-hammer type bearing extractor; these can often be hired from tool shops.
6 The new outer races can be pressed into the head using a drawbolt arrangement **(see illustration)**, or by using a large diameter tubular drift. Ensure that the drawbolt washer or drift (as applicable) bears only on the outer edge of the race and does not contact the working surface. Alternatively, have the races installed by a Yamaha dealer equipped with the bearing race installing tools.

 HAYNES HiNT *Installation of new bearing outer races is made much easier if the races are left overnight in the freezer. This causes them to contract slightly making them a looser fit. Alternatively, use a freeze spray.*

7 The lower bearing inner race should only be removed from the steering stem if a new one is being fitted. To remove the race from the steering stem, use two screwdrivers placed on opposite sides of the race to work it free, using blocks of wood to improve leverage and protect the yoke, or tap under it using a cold chisel **(see illustration)**. If the race is firmly in place it will be necessary to use a puller, or in extreme circumstances to split the race using an angle grinder **(see illustration)**. Take the steering stem to a Yamaha dealer if required.

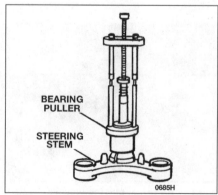

9.7b . . . you may have to use a puller

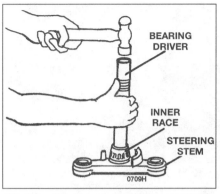

9.8 Drive the new race on using a suitable driver or a length of pipe

8 Fit the new lower race onto the steering stem. A length of tubing with an internal diameter slightly larger than the steering stem will be needed to tap the new race into position (see illustration).

9 Install the steering stem (see Section 8).

10 Rear shock absorber – removal, inspection and installation

⚠ **Warning: Do not attempt to disassemble this shock absorber. It is nitrogen-charged under high pressure. Improper disassembly could result in serious injury. Instead, take the shock to a Yamaha dealer or suspension specialist to do the job.**

10.3c Slacken the reservoir clamp screw (arrowed) – YZF1000R model shown

10.5a Unscrew the nut and remove the upper mounting bolt . . .

10.3a On YZF1000R models, disconnect the relay wiring connector and displace the relay

Removal

1 Support the motorcycle securely in an upright position using an auxiliary stand. Position a support under the rear wheel so that it does not drop when the shock absorber is removed, but also making sure that the weight of the machine is off the rear suspension so that the shock is not compressed.

2 Remove the seat, side covers or seat cowling, and lower fairing (see Chapter 8), and the fuel tank (see Chapter 4).

3 Remove the battery (see Chapter 9). On YZF1000R models, disconnect the starter relay wiring connector then displace the relay from its mount (see illustration). Unscrew the two bolts securing the battery box (see illustration). Slacken the clamp screw securing the reservoir to its holder (see illustration).

4 Unscrew the nut, remove the washer and

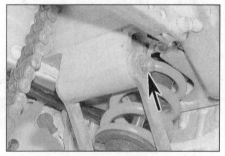

10.4a Unscrew the nut (arrowed), withdraw the bolt and separate the linkage rods to the swingarm

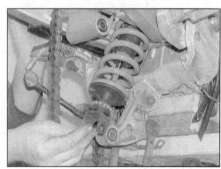

10.5b . . . then lower the shock . . .

10.3b Unscrew the battery box bolts (arrowed)

withdraw the bolt securing the linkage rods to the swingarm (see illustration). Unscrew the nut, remove the washer and withdraw the bolt securing the bottom of the shock absorber to the linkage arm, then swing the rods and the arm down to provide clearance for the shock (see illustration). On YZF750SP models, note the collars that fit between the shock and the arm and remove them for safekeeping if required.

5 Unscrew the nut on the shock absorber upper mounting bolt, then support the shock absorber and withdraw the bolt (see illustration). Lift the swingarm and lower the shock out of the frame, feeding the reservoir down between the upper mudguard and the frame, taking care not to scratch anything – it is necessary to push the mudguard in to provide clearance, and even then it is a tight fit (see illustrations). The alternative to the above

10.4b Unscrew the nut and remove the lower mounting bolt

10.5c . . . feeding the reservoir between the frame and the battery box . . .

6

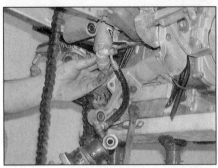

10.5d ... and remove the assembly out from the bottom

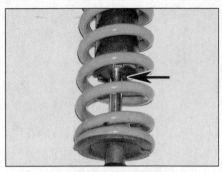

10.7 Look for cracks, pitting and oil leakage on the damper rod (arrowed)

10.11 Tighten the nuts to the specified torque settings

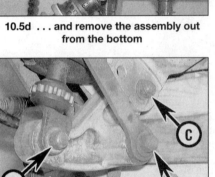

11.3 Remove the shock lower bolt (A), the linkage rods-to-arm bolt (B), and the linkage arm-to-frame bolt (C), and remove the arm

procedure is to displace all components from the upper mudguard, remove its bolts and draw it back off the machine to provide the clearance for the reservoir.

Inspection

6 Inspect the shock absorber for obvious physical damage and the coil spring for looseness, cracks or signs of fatigue.
7 Inspect the damper rod for signs of bending, pitting and oil leakage **(see illustration)**.
8 Inspect the pivot hardware at the top and bottom of the shock for wear or damage.
9 Check the reservoir, hose and hose connections for damage, cracks or leakage.
10 Individual components are not available for the shock absorber. If it is worn or damaged, it must be replaced with a new one.

Installation

11 Installation is the reverse of removal. Apply molybdenum disulphide grease to the shock absorber and linkage rod pivot points. Install the bolts and nuts finger-tight only until all components are in position, then tighten the nuts to the torque settings specified at the beginning of the Chapter **(see illustration)**.

---

11 Rear suspension linkage – removal, inspection and installation

Removal

1 Support the motorcycle securely in an upright position using an auxiliary stand. Position a support under the rear wheel so that it does not drop when the shock absorber lower mounting bolt is removed, but also making sure that the weight of the machine is off the rear suspension so that the shock is not compressed.
2 Remove the seat, side covers and lower fairing (see Chapter 8).
3 Unscrew the nuts, remove the washers and withdraw the bolts securing the shock absorber and the linkage rods to the linkage arm **(see illustration)**. Note which bolts fit where. On YZF750SP models, note the collars that fit between the shock and the arm and remove them for safekeeping if required.
4 Unscrew the nut, remove the washer and withdraw the bolt securing the linkage rods to the swingarm and remove the rods **(see illustration 10.4a)**.
5 Unscrew the nut and withdraw bolt securing the linkage arm to the frame and remove the linkage arm, noting which way round it fits **(see illustration 11.3)**.

Inspection

6 Withdraw all the spacers from the linkage arm and swingarm, noting their different sizes **(see illustrations)**. Lever the grease seals out of the linkage arm. Thoroughly clean all components, removing all traces of dirt, corrosion and grease.
7 Inspect all components closely, looking for obvious signs of wear such as heavy scoring, or for damage such as cracks or distortion.

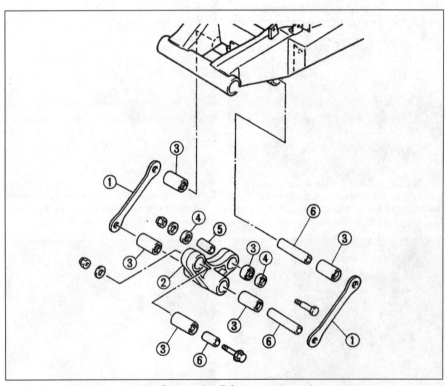

11.6a Suspension linkage components

1 Linkage rods	3 Bearings	5 Spacer
2 Linkage arm	4 Grease seals	6 Spacers

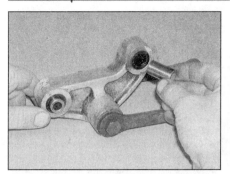

11.6b Withdraw the spacers, noting which fits where

Slip each spacer back into its bearing and check that there is not an excessive amount of freeplay between the two components. Renew any components as required.

8 Check the condition of the needle roller bearings in the linkage arm and in the bottom of the swingarm. Refer to *Tools and Workshop Tips* (Section 5) in the Reference section for more information on bearings. If the linkage rod bearings in the swingarm need to be renewed, remove the swingarm (see Section 13).

9 Worn bearings can be drifted out of their bores, but note that removal will destroy them; new bearings should be obtained before work commences. The new bearings should be pressed or drawn into their bores rather than driven into position. In the absence of a press, a suitable drawbolt tool can be made up as described in *Tools and Workshop Tips* (Section 5) in the Reference section.

10 Lubricate the needle roller bearings and the spacers with molybdenum disulphide grease and install the spacers.

11 Check the condition of the grease seals for the shock absorber mounting in the linkage arm and renew them if they are damaged or deteriorated. Press the seals squarely into place.

Installation

12 Installation is the reverse of removal. Apply molybdenum disulphide grease to the pivot points. Install the bolts and nuts finger-tight only until all components are in position, then tighten the nuts to the torque settings

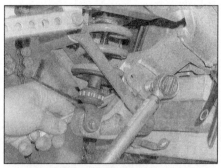

11.12 Tighten the nuts to the specified torque settings

specified at the beginning of the Chapter (see illustration).

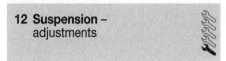

12 Suspension – adjustments

Note: *Refer to the owners handbook supplied with the machine for recommended front and rear suspension settings to suit loading.*

Front forks

1 On 1993 YZF750R models, the forks are adjustable for spring pre-load. On all other models, the front forks are adjustable for spring pre-load, rebound damping, and compression damping.

2 Spring pre-load is adjusted using a suitable spanner on the adjuster flats on the top of the forks (see illustration). The amount of pre-load is indicated by lines on the adjuster. On YZF750R and SP models, there are eight lines. On 1996 and 1997 YZF1000R models, there are four lines, on 1998-on YZF1000R models there are five. The standard position is with the 4th (YZF750R models) or 6th (YZF750SP models) or 3rd (1996 and 1997 YZF1000R models) or 4th (1998-on YZF1000R models) line just visible above the top bolt hex. Turn the adjuster clockwise to increase pre-load and anti-clockwise to decrease it. Always make sure both adjusters are set equally.

3 Rebound damping is adjusted using a screwdriver in the slot in the adjuster protruding from the pre-load adjuster (see illustration). The amount of damping is

indicated by the number of clicks when turned anti-clockwise from the fully screwed-in position. There are twelve positions on YZF750R and SP models, seventeen on 1996 and 1997 YZF1000R models, and twenty-five on 1998-on models. The standard position is four or five (YZF750R models), five or six (YZF750SP models) or nine (YZF1000R models) clicks out. Turn the adjuster clockwise to increase damping and anti-clockwise to decrease it. To establish the current setting, turn the adjuster in (clockwise) until it stops, counting the number of clicks, then reset it as required by turning it out. Always make sure both adjusters are set equally.

4 Compression damping is adjusted using a screwdriver in the slot in the adjuster on the base of each fork (see illustration). The amount of damping is indicated by the number of clicks when turned anti-clockwise from the fully screwed-in position. There are ten positions on YZF750R and SP models, twenty-one on 1996 and 1997 YZF1000R models, and twenty-five on 1998-on models. The standard position is seven (YZF750R models), six (YZF750SP models) or twelve (YZF1000R models) clicks out. Turn the adjuster clockwise to increase damping and anti-clockwise to decrease it. To establish the current setting, turn the adjuster in (clockwise) until it stops, counting the number of clicks, then reset it as required by turning it out. Always make sure both adjusters are set equally.

Rear shock absorber

5 On 1993 YZF750R models the rear shock absorber is adjustable for spring pre-load and rebound damping. On all other models the rear shock absorber is adjustable for spring pre-load, rebound damping and compression damping.

YZF750R models – spring pre-load

6 On 1993 and UK 1994 YZF750R models, pre-load adjustment is made using a suitable C-spanner (one is provided in the toolkit) to turn the spring seat on the top of the shock absorber (see illustration 12.19). There are seven positions. Position 1 is the softest setting, position 3 is the standard, position 7 is the hardest. Align the setting required with the adjustment stopper.

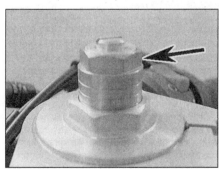

. **12.2 Spring pre-load adjuster (arrowed)**

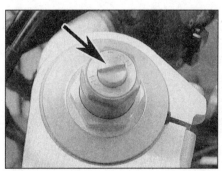

12.3 Rebound damping adjuster (arrowed)

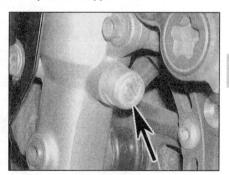

12.4 Compression damping adjuster (arrowed)

6

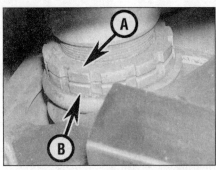

12.7 Slacken the locknut (A) and turn the adjuster (B) as required

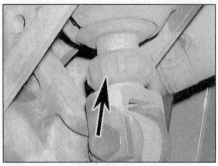

12.8 Rebound damping adjuster (arrowed)

7 On US 1994 YZF750R models and all 1995-on YZF750R models, spring pre-load is adjusted by turning the adjuster nut on the threads of the shock absorber body. Slacken the locknut, then turn the adjuster nut clockwise to increase pre-load and anti-clockwise to decrease it **(see illustration)**. Tighten the locknut securely after adjustment. Measure the distance between the top of the spring and the middle of the upper mounting bore to obtain the amount of pre-load set. The minimum amount is with a distance of 51.5 mm, the standard amount with 55.5 mm, and the maximum amount with 61.5 mm.

YZF750R models – rebound damping

8 On 1993 and 1994 YZF750R models, rebound damping adjustment is made by turning the adjuster on the bottom of the shock absorber **(see illustration)**. Turn the adjuster anti-clockwise (as you look down at it from the top) to increase damping and clockwise to decrease it. To establish the current setting, turn the adjuster anti-clockwise until it stops, counting the number of clicks, then reset it as required by turning it out. There are eleven positions. The standard position is nine clicks out. The hardest is three clicks out, and the softest is eleven clicks out.
9 On all other UK YZF750R models, rebound damping adjustment is made by turning the adjuster on the bottom of the shock absorber **(see illustration 12.8)**. Turn the adjuster anti-clockwise (as you look down at it from the top) to increase damping and clockwise to decrease it. To establish the current setting, turn the adjuster anti-clockwise until it stops,

counting the number of clicks, then reset it as required by turning it out. There are twenty positions. The standard position is ten clicks out. The hardest is six clicks out, and the softest is twenty clicks out.
10 On all other US YZF750R models, rebound damping adjustment is made by turning the adjuster on the bottom of the shock absorber **(see illustration 12.8)**. Turn the adjuster anti-clockwise (as you look down at it from the top) to increase damping and clockwise to decrease it. To establish the current setting, turn the adjuster anti-clockwise until it stops, counting the number of clicks, then reset it as required by turning it out. There are thirteen positions. The standard position is ten clicks out. The hardest is one click out, and the softest is thirteen clicks out.

YZF750R models – compression damping

11 Compression damping adjustment is made by turning the adjuster on the shock absorber reservoir **(see illustration)**. Turn the adjuster clockwise to increase damping and anti-clockwise to decrease it. To establish the current setting, turn the adjuster in (clockwise) until it stops, counting the number of clicks, then reset it as required by turning it out.
12 There are twenty positions. The standard position is ten clicks out. The hardest is one click out, and the softest is twenty clicks out.

YZF750SP models – spring pre-load

13 On 1993 and 1994 YZF750SP models, spring pre-load is adjusted by turning the adjuster nut on the threads on the shock

absorber body. Slacken the locknut, then turn the adjuster nut clockwise to increase pre-load and anti-clockwise to decrease it **(see illustration 12.7)**. Tighten the locknut securely after adjustment. Measure the distance between the top of the spring and the middle of the upper mounting bore. The minimum amount is with a spring length of 65.5 mm, the standard amount with 55.5 mm, and the maximum amount with 35.5 mm.
14 On 1995-on YZF750SP models, spring pre-load is adjusted by turning the ring on the remote adjuster. Turn the adjuster in to increase pre-load, and turn it out to decrease it. There are twelve settings as indicated on the body of the adjuster. The minimum is 0, the standard 3 and the hardest 12. Do not turn the adjuster beyond the minimum or maximum settings.

YZF750SP models – rebound damping

15 On 1993 and 1994 YZF750SP models, rebound damping adjustment is made by turning the adjuster on the bottom of the shock absorber **(see illustration 12.8)**. Turn the adjuster anti-clockwise (as you look down at it from the top) to increase damping and clockwise to decrease it. To establish the current setting, turn the adjuster anti-clockwise until it stops, counting the number of clicks, then reset it as required by turning it out. There are thirteen positions. The standard position is nine clicks out. The hardest is one click out, and the softest is thirteen clicks out.
16 On 1995-on YZF750SP models, rebound damping adjustment is made by turning the adjuster on the bottom of the shock absorber **(see illustration 12.8)**. Turn the adjuster anti-clockwise (as you look down at it from the top) to increase damping and clockwise to decrease it. To establish the current setting, turn the adjuster anti-clockwise until it stops, counting the number of clicks, then reset it as required by turning it out. There are twenty-two positions. The standard position is ten clicks out. The hardest is one click out, and the softest is twenty-two clicks out.

YZF750SP models – compression damping

17 Compression damping adjustment is made by turning the adjuster on the shock absorber reservoir **(see illustration 12.11)**. Turn the adjuster clockwise to increase damping and anti-clockwise to decrease it. To establish the current setting, turn the adjuster in (clockwise) until it stops, counting the number of clicks, then reset it as required by turning it out.
18 There are twenty positions. The standard position is ten clicks out. The hardest is one click out, and the softest is twenty clicks out.

YZF1000R models

19 Spring pre-load adjustment is made using a suitable C-spanner (one is provided in the toolkit) to turn the spring seat on the top of the shock absorber **(see illustration)**. There are nine positions. Position 1 is the softest setting, position 4 is the standard, position 9

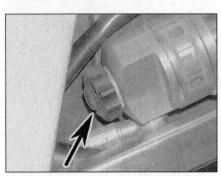

12.11 Compression damping adjuster (arrowed)

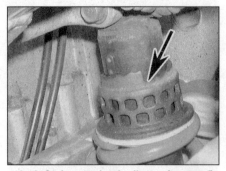

12.19 Spring pre-load adjuster (arrowed)

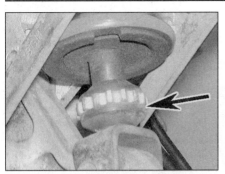

12.20 Rebound damping adjuster (arrowed)

is the hardest. Align the setting required with the adjustment stopper. Turn the spring seat clockwise to increase pre-load and anticlockwise to decrease it.

20 Rebound damping adjustment is made by turning the adjuster on the bottom of the shock absorber **(see illustration)**. Turn the adjuster anti-clockwise (as you look down at it from the top) to increase damping and clockwise to decrease it. To establish the current setting, turn the adjuster anti-clockwise until it stops, counting the number of clicks, then reset it as required by turning it out. There are twenty positions. The standard position is ten clicks out. The hardest is zero clicks out, and the softest is twenty clicks out.

21 Compression damping adjustment is made by turning the adjuster on the shock absorber reservoir using a screwdriver **(see illustration)**. Turn the adjuster clockwise to increase damping and anti-clockwise to

decrease it. To establish the current setting, turn the adjuster in (clockwise) until it stops, counting the number of clicks, then reset it as required by turning it out. There are twenty-four positions. The standard position is ten clicks out. The hardest is zero clicks out, and the softest is twenty-four clicks out.

13 Swingarm – removal and installation

Removal

Note: *Before removing the swingarm, it is advisable to perform the rear suspension checks described in Chapter 1 to assess the extent of any wear.*

1 Remove the rear wheel (see Chapter 7) and the shock absorber (see Section 10). On YZF750R and SP models, free the brake hose from the guide on the torque arm **(see illustration)**.

2 Unscrew the bolts securing the chainguard to the swingarm and remove it, noting how it fits **(see illustrations)**. Remove the split pin from the bolt securing the brake torque arm to the swingarm, then unscrew the nut, withdraw the bolt and detach the arm along with the brake caliper bracket **(see illustration)**.

3 Unscrew the bolts securing the brake hose guides/clamps to the swingarm **(see illustrations)**. Loop the caliper over the swingarm and position it clear, making sure no strain is placed on the brake hose.

4 Before removing the swingarm it is

12.21 Compression damping adjuster (arrowed)

advisable to re-check for play in the bearings (see Chapter 1). Any problems which may have been overlooked with the other suspension components attached to the frame are highlighted with them loose.

5 On YZF750R and SP models, remove the front sprocket (see Section 16).

6 Unscrew the nut on the end of the swingarm pivot bolt and remove the washer **(see illustration)**. Support the swingarm, then withdraw the pivot bolt and remove the swingarm, along with the drive chain on YZF750R and SP models **(see illustration)**. Knock the pivot bolt through using a drift if required.

7 Remove the chain slider from the front of the swingarm if necessary, noting how it fits **(see illustration)**. If it is badly worn or damaged, it should be replaced with a new one.

8 Inspect all components for wear or damage as described in Section 14.

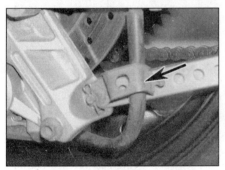

13.1 Free the hose from its guide (arrowed)

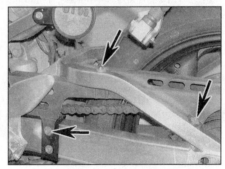

13.2a Chainguard bolts (arrowed) – YZF750R and SP models

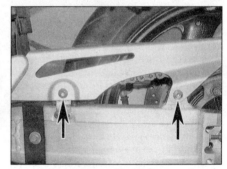

13.2b Chainguard bolts (arrowed) – YZF1000R models

13.2c Unscrew the bolt (arrowed) and detach the torque arm from the swingarm

13.3a Brake hose clamp bolt (arrowed) – YZF750R and SP models

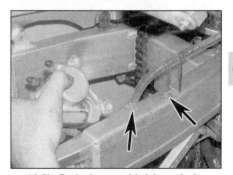

13.3b Brake hose guide/clamp bolts (arrowed) – YZF1000R models

6

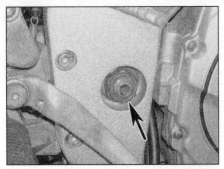

13.6a Unscrew the nut (arrowed) and remove the washer . . .

13.6b . . . then withdraw the bolt and remove the swingarm

13.7 Remove the chain slider if required – YZF1000R model shown

13.11a Locate the swingarm and install the pivot bolt . . .

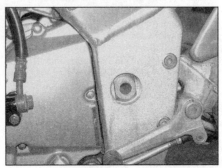

13.11b . . . making sure the bolt head flats locate correctly in the frame

13.11c Install the washer . . .

Installation

9 If removed, install the chain slider and tighten its bolt(s) securely **(see illustration 13.7)**.

10 If not already done, remove the cap and washer(s) (where fitted) from each side of the swingarm (Section 14) and withdraw the collar **(see illustrations 14.2a and b)**. Lubricate the bearings with molybdenum disulphide grease. Also grease the swingarm pivot, the washers and caps, and the linkage rod bearings in the bottom of the swingarm – remove the collar first and grease that as well. Check the condition of the seal in each cap and replace it with a new one if necessary. Re-install the collars, washers (where fitted) and caps.

11 Offer up the swingarm and have an assistant hold it in place. Make sure the drive chain is looped over the front of the swingarm. Slide the pivot bolt through from the left-hand

side, locating the hex head correctly in the frame **(see illustrations)**. Install the nut with its washer, and tighten the nut to the torque setting specified at the beginning of the Chapter **(see illustrations)**.

12 On YZF750R and SP models, install the front sprocket (see Section 16).

13 Install the rear shock absorber (see Section 10).

14 Fit the brake torque arm onto the swingarm, then install the bolt and tighten the nut to the specified torque setting **(see illustration 13.2c)**. Fit a new split pin onto the bolt. Loop the caliper over the swingarm, then fit the brake hose guides/clamps onto the swingarm **(see illustration 13.3a or b)**. On YZF750R and SP models, fit the brake hose into the guide on the torque arm **(see illustration 13.1)**.

15 Install the chainguard **(see illustrations 13.2a or b)**.

16 Install the rear wheel (see Chapter 7).

17 Check and adjust the drive chain slack (see Chapter 1). Check the operation of the rear suspension before taking the machine on the road.

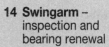

14 Swingarm –
inspection and
bearing renewal

Inspection

1 Thoroughly clean the swingarm, removing all traces of dirt, corrosion and grease **(see illustration)**.

2 Remove the cap and washer(s) (where fitted) from each side of the swingarm, then withdraw the collar **(see illustrations)**. Check the condition of the seal in each cap and replace it with a new one if necessary.

3 Inspect all components closely, looking for

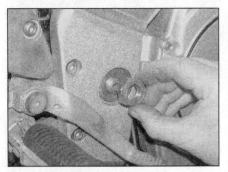

13.11d . . . and the nut . . .

13.11e . . . and tighten the nut to the specified torque

14.1 Clean off all accumulated chain lube and road dirt using a suitable degreaser

14.2a Remove the cap and washer(s) . . .

14.2b . . . then withdraw the collar

obvious signs of wear such as heavy scoring, and cracks or distortion due to accident damage. Check the bearings for roughness, looseness and any other damage, referring to *Tools and Workshop Tips* (Section 5) in the Reference section **(see illustration)**. Any damaged or worn component must be renewed.

4 Check the swingarm pivot bolt for straightness by rolling it on a flat surface such as a piece of plate glass (first wipe off all old grease and remove any corrosion using fine emery cloth). If the equipment is available, place the axle in V-blocks and measure the runout using a dial indicator. If the axle is bent, replace it with a new one.

Bearing renewal

5 Remove the cap and washer(s) (where fitted) from each side of the swingarm, then withdraw the collar **(see illustrations 14.2a and b)**. Refer to *Tools and Workshop Tips* (Section 5) in the Reference section for more information on bearing checks and replacement methods.

6 Needle bearings can be drawn or drifted out of their bores, but note that removal will destroy them; new bearings should be obtained before work commences. Pass a long drift with a hooked end through one side of the swingarm and locate it on the inner edge of the bearing on the other side. Tap the drift around the bearing's inner edge to ensure that it leaves its bore squarely. Use the same method to extract the other bearing. If available, a slide-hammer with knife-edged bearing puller can be used, and is better than

14.3 Check the needle bearing in each side as described

using a drift, to extract the bearings.

7 The new bearings should be pressed or drawn into their bores rather than driven into position. In the absence of a press, a suitable drawbolt arrangement can be made up as described in *Tools and Workshop Tips* (Section 5) in the Reference section. Lubricate the bearings with molybdenum disulphide grease. Install the collar, then fit the washer(s) and cap onto each side **(see illustrations 14.2b and a)**.

15 Drive chain – removal, cleaning and installation

Removal

Riveted link chain

Note: *Chains with a staked-type master (joining) link can be disassembled using one of several commercially-available drive chain cutting/staking tools. Such chains can be recognised by the master link side plate's identification marks (and usually its different colour), as well as by the staked ends of the link's two pins which look as if they have been deeply centre-punched, instead of peened over as with all the other pins. The YZF750R and SP models are fitted with a riveted link chain as standard.*

Warning: Use ONLY the correct service tools to disassemble the staked-type of master link – if you do not have access to such tools or do not have the skill to operate them correctly, have the chain removed by a dealer service department or bike repair shop.

1 Remove the front sprocket cover (see Section 16).

2 Locate the joining link in a suitable position to work on by rotating the back wheel.

3 Slacken the drive chain as described in Chapter 1.

4 Split the chain at the joining link using the chain cutter, following carefully the manufacturer's operating instructions (see also Section 8 in *Tools and Workshop Tips* in the Reference Section). Remove the chain from the bike, noting its routing through the swingarm.

Endless chain

Note: *Removal requires the removal of the swingarm as detailed below. The original equipment drive chain fitted to all 1000R models is an endless chain.*

Warning: NEVER install a drive chain which uses a clip-type master (split) link.

5 Remove the swingarm (see Section 13).
6 Remove the front sprocket (see Section 16).
7 Remove the chain from the bike.

Cleaning

8 Soak the chain in paraffin (kerosene) for approximately five or six minutes.

Caution: Don't use gasoline (petrol), solvent or other cleaning fluids. Don't use high-pressure water. Remove the chain, wipe it off, then blow dry it with compressed air immediately. The entire process shouldn't take longer than ten minutes – if it does, the O-rings in the chain rollers could be damaged.

Installation

Riveted link chain

Warning: NEVER install a drive chain which uses a clip-type master (split) link. Use ONLY the correct service tools to secure the staked-type of master link – if you do not have access to such tools or do not have the skill to operate them correctly, have the chain installed by a dealer service department or bike repair shop to be sure of having it securely installed.

9 Slip the drive chain through the swingarm sections and around the front sprocket, leaving the two ends in a convenient position to work on.

10 Refer to Section 8 in *Tools and Workshop Tips* in the Reference Section. Install the new joining link from the inside. Fit an O-ring onto each pin, then slide the link through and fit the other two O-rings. Install the new side plate with its identification marks facing out. Stake the new link using the drive chain cutting/staking tool, following carefully the instructions of both the chain manufacturer and the tool manufacturer. DO NOT re-use old joining link components.

11 After staking, check the joining link and staking for any signs of cracking. If there is any evidence of cracking, the joining link, O-rings and side plate must be renewed. Measure the diameter of the staked ends in two directions and check that it is evenly staked.

12 Install the sprocket cover (see Section 16).
13 On completion, adjust and lubricate the chain following the procedures described in Chapter 1.

Caution: Use only the recommended lubricant.

6

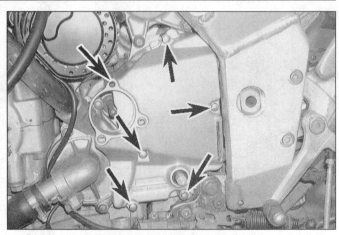

16.2a Unscrew the bolt (A) and slide the arm off the shaft, noting the alignment marks (B)

16.2b Sprocket cover bolts (arrowed)

Endless chain

14 Installation is the reverse of removal. On completion adjust and lubricate the chain following the procedures described in Chapter 1.

Caution: Use only the recommended lubricant.

16 Sprockets –
check and renewal

Check

1 Remove the lower fairing, and if required for

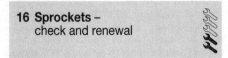

16.7a Bend back the lockwasher tab(s) ...

improved clearance and to prevent the possibility of damage, remove the left-hand fairing side panel (see Chapter 8).

2 Unscrew the gearchange lever linkage arm pinch bolt and slide the arm off the shaft, noting any alignment marks **(see illustration)**. If no marks are visible, make your own before removing the arm so that it can be correctly aligned with the shaft on installation. Unscrew the bolts securing the front sprocket cover and displace the cover **(see illustration)**. There is no need to fully detach the clutch release cylinder from the cover unless you want to (see Chapter 2). Note the position of the dowels and remove them if loose. Discard the gasket as a new one must be used.

3 Check the wear pattern on both sprockets **(see illustration 1.7 in Chapter 1)**. Whenever the sprockets are inspected the drive chain should also be inspected. If the sprocket teeth are worn excessively, or you are fitting a new chain, renew the chain and sprockets as a set.

4 Adjust and lubricate the chain following the procedures described in Chapter 1.

Caution: Use only the recommended lubricant.

Renewal

Front sprocket

5 Remove the lower fairing, and if required for improved clearance and to prevent the

possibility of damage, remove the left-hand fairing side panel (see Chapter 8).

6 Unscrew the gearchange lever linkage arm pinch bolt and slide the arm off the shaft, noting any alignment marks **(see illustration 16.2a)**. If no marks are visible, make your own before removing the arm so that it can be correctly aligned with the shaft on installation. Unscrew the bolts securing the front sprocket cover and displace the cover **(see illustration 16.2b)**. There is no need to detach the clutch release cylinder from the cover unless you want to (see Chapter 2). Note the position of the dowels and remove them if loose. Discard the gaskets as new ones must be used.

7 Bend down the tab(s) on the sprocket nut lockwasher **(see illustration)**. Have an assistant apply the rear brake hard, then unscrew the nut and remove the washer **(see illustration)**. Discard the washer as a new one should be used. Refer to Chapter 1 and adjust the chain so that it is fully slack.

8 Slide the sprocket and chain off the shaft and slip the sprocket out of the chain **(see illustration)**. If there is not enough slack on the chain to remove the sprocket, disengage the chain from the rear wheel.

9 Engage the new sprocket with the chain and slide it on the shaft **(see illustration)**. Take up the slack in the chain (see Chapter 1).

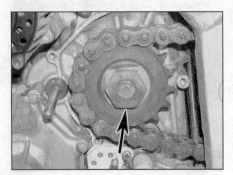

16.7b ... then unscrew the nut (arrowed)

16.8 Slide the sprocket off the shaft and remove it

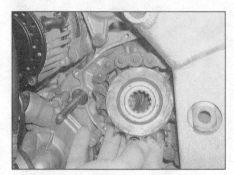

16.9 Fit the sprocket into the chain and slide it onto the shaft

16.10a Fit the new lockwasher . . .

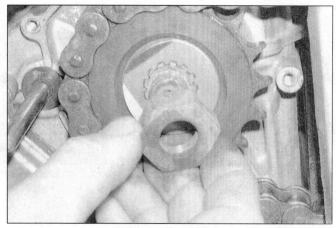

16.10b . . . and the nut . . .

16.10c . . . and tighten it to the specified torque

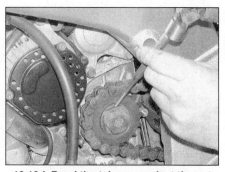

16.10d Bend the tabs up against the nut

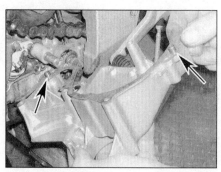

16.11a Fit the main gasket, locating it onto the dowels (arrowed) . . .

10 Slide on the new lockwasher, then fit the nut and tighten it to the torque setting specified at the beginning of the Chapter, applying the rear brake to prevent the sprocket from turning **(see illustrations)**. Bend up the tabs of the lockwasher against the nut **(see illustration)**.

11 If removed, fit the sprocket cover dowels into the crankcase. Install the cover using new gaskets and tighten its bolts to the specified torque setting **(see illustrations)**. A smear of grease will hold the gaskets in place while you fit the cover if necessary. Slide the gearchange linkage arm onto the shaft,

aligning the marks, and tighten the pinch bolt **(see illustration 16.2a)**.

Rear sprocket

12 Remove the rear wheel (see Chapter 7).
13 Unscrew the nuts securing the sprocket to the hub assembly **(see illustration)**. Remove the sprocket, noting which way round it fits.
14 Install the sprocket onto the hub with the stamped mark facing out. Tighten the nuts evenly and in a criss-cross sequence to the torque setting specified at the beginning of the Chapter.
15 Install the rear wheel (see Chapter 7).

17 Rear sprocket coupling/rubber dampers – check and renewal

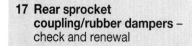

1 Remove the rear wheel (see Chapter 7).
Caution: Do not lay the wheel down on the disc as it could become warped. Lay the wheel on wooden blocks so that the disc is off the ground.
2 Lift the sprocket coupling away from the wheel leaving the rubber dampers in position in the wheel **(see illustration)**. Note the spacer inside the coupling – it should be a

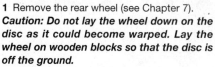

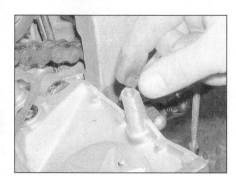

16.11b . . . and the small gasket, using a dab of grease to hold it . . .

16.11c . . . then fit the cover

16.13 Unscrew the nuts (arrowed) and remove the sprocket

6

17.2 Lift the sprocket coupling out of the wheel . . .

17.3 . . . and remove the rubber dampers

tight fit but remove it if it is likely to drop out. Check the coupling for cracks or any obvious signs of damage. Also check the sprocket studs for wear or damage.

3 Lift the rubber damper segments from the wheel and check them for cracks, hardening and general deterioration **(see illustration)**. Renew the rubber dampers as a set if necessary.

4 Checking and replacement procedures for the sprocket coupling bearing are described in Chapter 7.

5 Installation is the reverse of removal. Make sure the spacer is still correctly installed in the coupling, or install it if it was removed.

6 Install the rear wheel (see Chapter 7).

Chapter 7
Brakes, wheels and tyres

Contents

Degrees of difficulty

| Easy, suitable for novice with little experience | Fairly easy, suitable for beginner with some experience 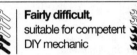 | Fairly difficult, suitable for competent DIY mechanic 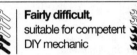 | Difficult, suitable for experienced DIY mechanic 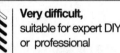 | Very difficult, suitable for expert DIY or professional 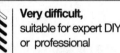 |

Specifications

Brakes

Brake fluid type . . . . DOT 4
Front caliper bore ID
  YZF750R and SP models
    Upper and centre bores . . . . 27.00 mm
    Lower bore . . . . 25.48 mm
  YZF1000R models
    Upper bore . . . . 30.20 mm
    Lower bore . . . . 27.00 mm
Front disc thickness
  Standard . . . . 5.0 mm
  Service limit . . . . 4.5 mm
Front disc maximum runout . . . . 0.2 mm
Front master cylinder bore ID
  YZF750R and SP models . . . . 15.875 mm
  YZF1000R models . . . . 14.00 mm
Rear caliper bore ID . . . . 42.80 mm
Rear disc thickness
  Standard . . . . 6.0 mm
  Service limit . . . . 5.5 mm
Rear disc maximum runout . . . . 0.15 mm
Rear master cylinder bore ID . . . . 14.00 mm

Wheels

Rim size
  Front . . . . 17 x MT3.50
  Rear . . . . 17 x MT5.50
Wheel runout (max)
  Axial (side-to-side) . . . . 0.5 mm
  Radial (out-of-round) . . . . 1.0 mm

Tyres

Tyre pressures . . . . see *Daily (pre-ride) checks*
Tyre sizes*
  Front 120/70-ZR17
  Rear 180/55-ZR17
*Refer to the owners handbook, the tyre information label on the swingarm, or your dealer for approved tyre brands.

7

Torque wrench settings

Front brake caliper mounting bolts
   YZF750R and SP models . . . . 35 Nm
   YZF1000R models . . . . 40 Nm
Brake hose banjo bolts
   YZF750R and SP models . . . . 26 Nm
   YZF1000R models . . . . 30 Nm
Front brake disc bolts . . . . 23 Nm
Front brake master cylinder clamp bolts
   YZF750R and SP models . . . . 10 Nm
   YZF1000R models . . . . 13 Nm
Rear brake caliper mounting bolts
   YZF750R and SP models . . . . 35 Nm
   YZF1000R models . . . . 40 Nm
Rear brake disc bolts . . . . 23 Nm
Rear brake master cylinder mounting bolts . . . . 23 Nm
Bleed valve . . . . 6 Nm
Front wheel axle
   YZF750R and SP models . . . . 72 Nm
   YZF1000R models . . . . 70 Nm
Front axle clamp bolt . . . . 23 Nm
Rear axle nut
   1993 and 1994 YZF750R and SP models . . . . 203 Nm
   1995-on YZF750R and SP models . . . . 150 Nm
   YZF1000R models . . . . 150 Nm

1 General information

All models are fitted with cast alloy wheels designed for tubeless tyres only. Both front and rear brakes are hydraulically operated disc brakes.

The front brakes are triple opposed-piston calipers on YZF750R and SP models, and twin opposed-piston calipers on YZF1000R models. The rear brake is a single opposed-piston caliper on all models.

Caution: Disc brake components rarely require disassembly. Do not disassemble components unless absolutely necessary. If a hydraulic brake line is loosened, the entire system must be disassembled, drained, cleaned and then properly filled and bled upon reassembly. Do not use solvents on internal brake components. Solvents will cause the seals to swell and distort. Use only clean brake fluid or denatured alcohol for cleaning. Use care when working with brake fluid as it can injure your eyes and it will damage painted surfaces and plastic parts.

2 Front brake pads – renewal

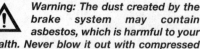

Warning: The dust created by the brake system may contain asbestos, which is harmful to your health. Never blow it out with compressed air and don't inhale any of it. An approved filtering mask should be worn when working on the brakes.

1 On YZF750R and SP models, remove the retaining clip from each pad retaining pin, then withdraw the pad pins, noting how they locate through the pad spring (see illustrations). Remove the pad spring, noting which way round it fits (see illustration). Withdraw the pads from the top of the caliper, noting how they fit (see illustration). Remove the shim from the back of each pad, noting how it fits (see illustration).

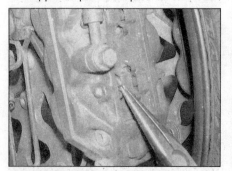

2.1a Remove the retaining clips . . .

2.1b . . . then withdraw the pad pins . . .

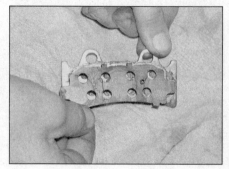

2.1e . . . and remove the shim, where fitted

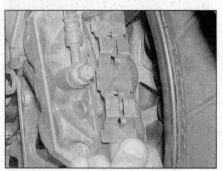

2.1c . . . and remove the pad spring

2.1d Lift the pads out of the caliper . . .

2.2a Remove the retaining clips . . .

2.2b . . . then withdraw the pad pin and remove the pad spring

2.2c Lift the pads out of the caliper . . .

2 On YZF1000R models, remove the retaining clip from each end of the pad retaining pin, then withdraw the pad pin, noting how it locates through the pad spring, and remove the pad spring, noting which way round it fits **(see illustrations)**. Withdraw the pads from the top of the caliper, noting how they fit **(see illustration)**. Remove the shim from the back of each pad, noting how it fits **(see illustration)**.

3 Inspect the surface of each pad for contamination and check that the friction material has not worn beyond its service limit (see Chapter 1, Section 8). If either pad is worn down to or beyond the service limit wear indicator, is fouled with oil or grease, or is heavily scored or damaged by dirt and debris, both pads in each caliper must be renewed. Note that it is not possible to degrease the friction material; if the pads are contaminated in any way new ones must be fitted.

4 If the pads are in good condition clean them carefully, using a fine wire brush which is completely free of oil and grease to remove all traces of road dirt and corrosion. Using a pointed instrument, clean out the grooves in the friction material and dig out any embedded particles of foreign matter. Any areas of glazing may be removed using emery cloth. Spray with a dedicated brake cleaner to remove any dust.

5 Check the condition of the brake disc (see Section 4).

6 Remove all traces of corrosion from the pad pin. Check it for signs of damage and renew it if necessary.

7 Push the pistons as far back into the caliper as possible using hand pressure or a piece of

wood as leverage. Due to the increased friction material thickness of new pads, it may be necessary to remove the fluid reservoir cap, plate and diaphragm and siphon out some fluid. If access to the piston heads is too restricted with the calipers in place, unbolt the caliper from the forks (see Section 3). If the pistons are difficult to push back, attach a length of clear hose to the bleed valve and place the open end in a suitable container, then open the valve and try again. Take great care not to draw any air into the system. If in doubt, bleed the brakes afterwards (see Section 11).

8 Smear the backs of the pads and the shank of the pad pin(s) with copper-based grease, making sure that none gets on the front or sides of the pads.

9 On YZF750R and SP models, fit the shim (where fitted) onto the back of each pad, making sure the arrow, where present, points in the direction of normal disc rotation **(see illustration 2.1e)**. Insert the pads into the caliper so that the friction material of each pad faces the disc **(see illustration 2.1d)**. Fit the pad spring onto the pads, making sure the arrow (where marked) points forward, in the direction of normal disc rotation **(see illustration 2.1c)**. Insert the pad retaining pins through the holes in the outer pad, then press down on the pad spring and push the pins through the spring and the holes in the inner pad **(see illustration)**. Install the retaining clips, using new ones if necessary **(see illustration)**.

10 On YZF1000R models, fit the shim (where fitted) onto the back of each pad, making sure the arrow, where present, points in the

2.2d . . . and remove the shim, where fitted

direction of normal disc rotation **(see illustration 2.2d)**. Insert the pads into the caliper so that the friction material of each pad faces the disc **(see illustration 2.2c)**. Fit the pad spring onto the pads, making sure the arrow (where marked) points forward, in the direction of normal disc rotation **(see illustration 2.2b)**. Insert the pad retaining pin through the hole in the outer pad, then press down on the pad spring and push the pin through the spring and the hole in the inner pad **(see illustration 2.2b)**. Install the retaining clips, using new ones if necessary **(see illustration)**.

11 Top up the master cylinder reservoir if necessary (see *Daily (pre-ride) checks*), and refit the diaphragm, plate and reservoir cap.

12 Operate the brake lever several times to bring the pads into contact with the disc. Check the operation of the brake before riding the motorcycle.

2.9a Insert the pad pins . . .

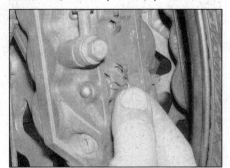

2.9b . . . and secure them with the clips

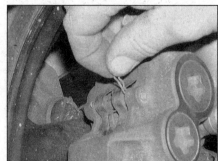

2.10 Secure the pin with the clips

7

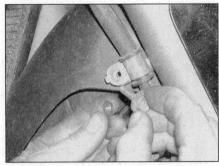

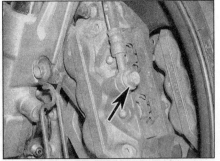

3.1a On YZF750R and SP models, unscrew the bolt (arrowed) securing the hose clamp to the caliper bracket

3.1b On YZF1000R models, unscrew the nut and withdraw the bolt securing the brake hose clamp to the mudguard

3 Front brake calipers – removal, overhaul and installation

⚠️ **Warning: If a caliper indicates the need for an overhaul (usually due to leaking fluid or sticky operation), all old brake fluid should be flushed from the system. Also, the dust created by the brake system may contain asbestos, which is harmful to your health. Never blow it out with compressed air and**

don't inhale any of it. An approved filtering mask should be worn when working on the brakes. Do not, under any circumstances, use petroleum-based solvents to clean brake parts. Use the specified clean brake fluid, dedicated brake cleaner or denatured alcohol only, as described.

Removal

1 If the calipers are being overhauled, remove the brake pads (see Section 2). If the calipers are just being displaced or removed, the pads can be left in place. Remove the bolt securing

the brake hose to the mudguard **(see illustrations)**.

2 If the calipers are just being displaced and not completely removed or overhauled, do not disconnect the brake hose. If the calipers are being completely removed or overhauled, remove the brake hose banjo bolt and detach the hose, noting its alignment with the caliper **(see illustrations)**. Plug the hose end or wrap a plastic bag tightly around to minimise fluid loss and prevent dirt entering the system. Discard the sealing washers as new ones must be used on installation. **Note:** *If you are planning to overhaul the caliper and don't have a source of compressed air to blow out the pistons, just loosen the banjo bolt at this stage and retighten it lightly. The bike's hydraulic system can then be used to force the pistons out of the body once the pads have been removed. Disconnect the hose once the pistons have been sufficiently displaced.*

3 Unscrew the caliper mounting bolts and slide the caliper off the disc; on YZF750R and SP models note the speedometer cable guide secured by the lower bolt on the left-hand caliper **(see illustrations)**.

Overhaul

4 Clean the exterior of the caliper with denatured alcohol or brake system cleaner **(see illustrations)**.

5 Using a flat piece of wood, block the pistons on one side of the caliper in their bores and displace the opposite pistons either by pumping them out by operating the front brake lever, or by forcing them out using compressed air. Remove the seals (see below) from the bore of the displaced pistons, then reinstall the pistons and block them using the wood. Now displace the pistons from the other side using the same method. Remove the wood and all the pistons. Mark each piston head and caliper body with a felt marker to ensure that the pistons can be matched to their original bores on reassembly. If the compressed air method is used, direct the air

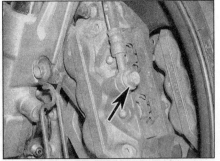

3.2a Brake hose banjo bolt (arrowed) – YZF750R and SP models

3.2b Brake hose banjo bolt (arrowed) – YZF1000R models

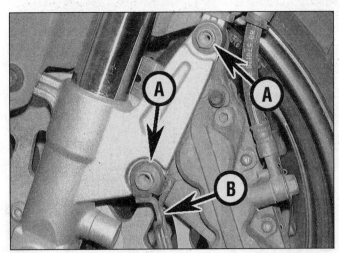

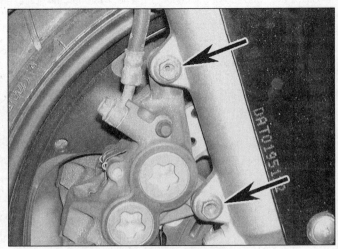

3.3a Caliper mounting bolts (A) – YZF750R and SP models. Note the cable guide (B)

3.3b Caliper mounting bolts (arrowed) – YZF1000R models

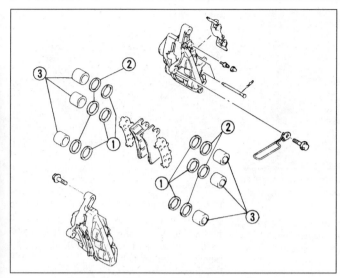

**3.4a Front brake caliper components –
YZF750R and SP models**

1 Dust seal   2 Piston seal   3 Piston

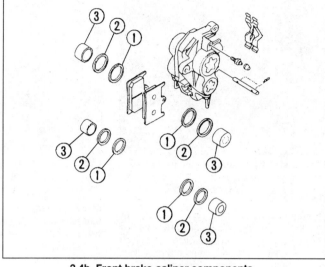

**3.4b Front brake caliper components –
YZF1000R models**

1 Dust seal   2 Piston seal   3 Piston

into the fluid inlet to force the pistons out of the body. Use only low pressure to ease the pistons out and make sure both pistons on the side concerned are displaced at the same time. If the air pressure is too high and the pistons are forced out, the caliper and/or pistons may be damaged.

⚠️ *Warning: Never place your fingers in front of the pistons in an attempt to catch or protect them when applying compressed air, as serious injury could result.*

Caution: Do not try to remove the pistons by levering them out, or by using pliers or any other grips. On YZF1000R models, do not attempt to remove the caliper bore plugs on the outside of the caliper, or the brake pipe linking the two sides of the caliper.

6 Using a wooden or plastic tool, remove the dust seals from the caliper bores **(see**

illustration). Discard them as new ones must be used on installation. If a metal tool is being used, take great care not to damage the caliper bores.

7 Remove and discard the piston seals in the same way.

8 Clean the pistons and bores with clean brake fluid of the specified type. If compressed air is available, use it to dry the parts thoroughly (make sure it's filtered and unlubricated).

Caution: Do not, under any circumstances, use a petroleum-based solvent to clean brake parts.

9 Inspect the caliper bores and pistons for signs of corrosion, nicks and burrs and loss of plating. If surface defects are present, the caliper assembly must be renewed. If the necessary measuring equipment is available, compare the dimensions of the caliper bores

to those specified at the beginning of the Chapter, and install a new caliper if necessary. If the caliper is in bad shape the master cylinder should also be checked.

10 Lubricate the new piston seals with clean brake fluid and install them in their grooves in the caliper bores. Note that two sizes of bore and piston are used (see Specifications), and care must therefore be taken to ensure that the correct size seals are fitted to the correct bores. The same applies when fitting the new dust seals and pistons.

11 Lubricate the new dust seals with clean brake fluid and install them in their grooves in the caliper bores.

12 Lubricate the pistons with clean brake fluid and install them closed-end first into the caliper bores. Using your thumbs, push the pistons all the way in, making sure they enter the bore squarely.

3.6 Use a plastic or wooden tool (such as a pencil) to remove the seals

3.13 Slide the caliper onto the disc

7

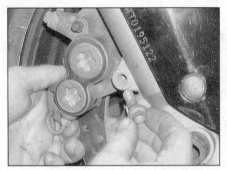

3.14a Install the caliper mounting bolts . . .

3.14b . . . and tighten them to the specified torque

Installation

13 If necessary, push the pistons a little way back into the caliper using hand pressure or a piece of wood as leverage. Slide the caliper onto the brake disc, making sure the pads sit squarely either side of the disc if they weren't removed **(see illustration)**.

14 Install the caliper mounting bolts, on YZF750R and SP models, not forgetting to secure the speedometer cable guide with the lower bolt on the left-hand caliper **(see illustration 3.3a)**, and tighten them to the torque setting specified at the beginning of the Chapter **(see illustrations)**.

15 If removed, connect the brake hose to the caliper, using new sealing washers on each side of the fitting. Align the hose as noted on removal **(see illustration 3.2a or b)**. Tighten the banjo bolt to the torque setting specified

4.2 Set up a dial indicator with the probe contacting the brake disc, then rotate the wheel to check for runout

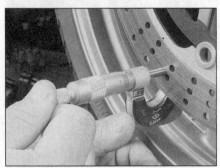

4.3 Using a micrometer to measure disc thickness

at the beginning of the Chapter. Top up the master cylinder reservoir with DOT 4 brake fluid (see *Daily (pre-ride) checks*) and bleed the hydraulic system as described in Section 11.

16 If removed, install the brake pads (see Section 2). Secure the brake hose in its clamp **(see illustration 3.1a or b)**.

17 Check for leaks and thoroughly test the operation of the brake before riding the motorcycle.

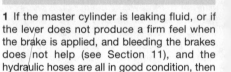

4 Front brake discs – inspection, removal and installation

Inspection

1 Visually inspect the surface of the disc for score marks and other damage. Light scratches are normal after use and won't affect brake operation, but deep grooves and heavy score marks will reduce braking efficiency and accelerate pad wear. If a disc is badly grooved it must be machined or a new one fitted.

2 To check disc runout, position the bike on an auxiliary stand and support it so that the front wheel is raised off the ground. Mount a dial gauge to a fork leg, with the plunger on the gauge touching the surface of the disc about 10 mm (1/2 in) from the outer edge **(see illustration)**. Rotate the wheel and watch the gauge needle, comparing the reading with the limit listed in the Specifications at the beginning of the Chapter. If the runout is greater than the service limit, check the wheel bearings for play (see Chapter 1). If the bearings are worn, install new ones (see Section 16) and repeat this check. If the disc runout is still excessive, a new one will have to be fitted, although machining by an engineer may be possible.

3 The disc must not be machined or allowed to wear down to a thickness less than the service limit as listed in this Chapter's Specifications. The thickness of the disc can be checked with a micrometer or any other measuring tool **(see illustration)**. If the thickness of the disc is less than the service limit, a new one must be fitted.

Removal

4 Remove the wheel (see Section 14).

Caution: Do not lay the wheel down and allow it to rest on the disc – the disc could become warped. Set the wheel on wood blocks so the disc doesn't support the weight of the wheel.

5 Mark the relationship of the disc to the wheel, so it can be installed in the same position. Unscrew the disc retaining bolts, loosening them evenly and a little at a time in a criss-cross pattern to avoid distorting the disc, then remove the disc from the wheel **(see illustration)**.

Installation

6 Mount the disc on the wheel with its marked side facing out, aligning the previously applied matchmarks (if you're reinstalling the original disc).

7 Clean the threads of the disc mounting bolts, then apply a suitable non-permanent thread locking compound. Install the bolts and tighten them evenly and a little at a time in a criss-cross pattern to the torque setting specified at the beginning of the Chapter. Clean off all grease from the brake disc using acetone or brake system cleaner. If a new brake disc has been installed, remove any protective coating from its working surfaces.

8 Install the front wheel (see Section 14).

9 Operate the brake lever several times to bring the pads into contact with the disc. Check the operation of the brakes carefully before riding the bike.

5 Front brake master cylinder – removal, overhaul and installation

1 If the master cylinder is leaking fluid, or if the lever does not produce a firm feel when the brake is applied, and bleeding the brakes does not help (see Section 11), and the hydraulic hoses are all in good condition, then master cylinder overhaul is recommended.

2 Before disassembling the master cylinder, read through the entire procedure and make sure that you have the correct rebuild kit. Also, you will need some new DOT 4 brake fluid, some clean rags and internal circlip

4.5 Unscrew the bolts (arrowed) and remove the disc

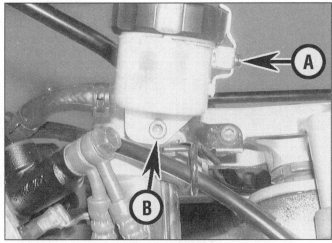

5.3 Reservoir cap clamp screw (A), reservoir mounting bolt (B)

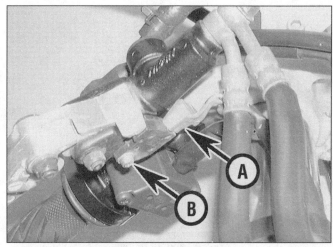

5.4 Brake light switch wiring connectors (A), switch mounting screw (B)

pliers. **Note:** *To prevent damage to the paint from spilled brake fluid, always cover the fuel tank when working on the master cylinder.*
Caution: Disassembly, overhaul and reassembly of the brake master cylinder must be done in a spotlessly clean work area to avoid contamination and possible failure of the brake hydraulic system components.

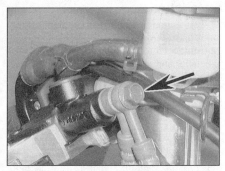

5.6 Brake hose banjo bolt (arrowed)

Removal

3 Remove the reservoir cap clamp and partially unscrew the cap **(see illustration)**.
4 Disconnect the brake light switch wiring connectors **(see illustration)**.
5 If the master cylinder is being overhauled, remove the front brake lever (see Chapter 6). If it is just being displaced it can remain in situ.
6 If the master cylinder is being completely removed or overhauled, unscrew the brake hose banjo bolt and separate the hoses from the master cylinder, noting the alignment **(see illustration)**. Discard the sealing washers as they must be replaced with new ones. Wrap the end(s) of the hose(s) in a clean rag and suspend them in an upright position or bend them down carefully and place the open end(s) in a clean container. The objective is to prevent excessive loss of brake fluid, fluid spills and system contamination. If the master cylinder is just being displaced and not completely removed or overhauled, do not disconnect the brake hoses.

7 Unscrew the bolt securing the reservoir to its bracket, then remove the reservoir cap and lift off the diaphragm plate and the rubber diaphragm **(see illustration 5.3)**. Drain the brake fluid from the reservoir into a suitable container. Release the clamp securing the reservoir hose to the union on the master cylinder, then detach the hose **(see illustration)**. Wipe any remaining fluid out of the reservoir with a clean rag.
8 Unscrew the master cylinder clamp bolts, then lift the master cylinder away from the handlebar **(see illustration)**.
9 If required, remove the screw securing the brake light switch and remove the switch **(see illustration 5.4)**.
Caution: Do not tip the master cylinder upside down or brake fluid will run out.

Overhaul

10 Carefully remove the dust boot from the master cylinder **(see illustrations)**.
11 Using circlip pliers, remove the circlip and

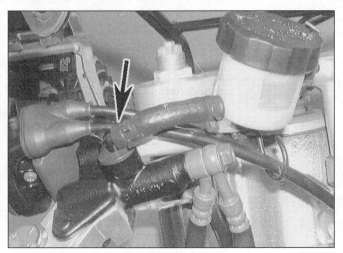

5.7 Release the clamp and detach the hose from its union (arrowed)

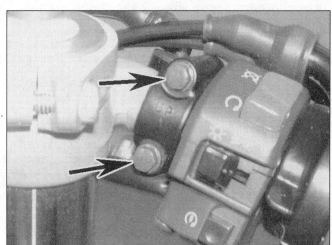

5.8 Front brake master cylinder clamp bolts (arrowed)

7

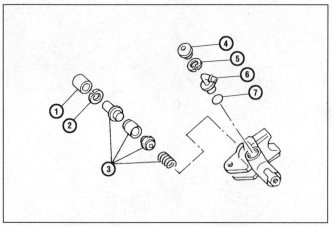

5.10a Front master cylinder components – YZF750R and SP models

1	Rubber boot	4	Rubber cap
2	Circlip	5	Circlip
3	Piston assembly and	6	Reservoir hose union
	spring	7	O-ring

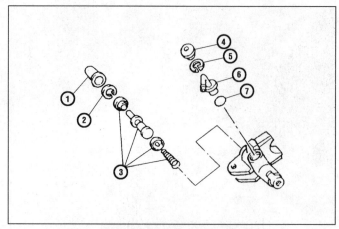

5.10b Front master cylinder components – YZF1000R models

1	Rubber boot	4	Rubber cap
2	Circlip	5	Circlip
3	Piston assembly and	6	Reservoir hose union
	spring	7	O-ring

slide out the piston assembly and the spring, noting how they fit **(see illustration)**. Lay the parts out in the proper order to prevent confusion during reassembly.

12 Remove the fluid reservoir hose union rubber cap, then remove the circlip and detach the union from the master cylinder. Discard the O-ring as a new one must be used. Inspect the reservoir hose for cracks or splits and renew if necessary.

13 Clean all parts with clean brake fluid. If compressed air is available, use it to dry the parts thoroughly (make sure it's filtered and unlubricated).

Caution: Do not, under any circumstances, use a petroleum-based solvent to clean brake parts.

14 Check the master cylinder bore for corrosion, scratches, nicks and score marks. If the necessary measuring equipment is available, compare the diameter of the bore to that given in the Specifications Section of this Chapter. If damage or wear is evident, the master cylinder must be replaced with a new one. If the master cylinder is in poor condition, then the calipers should be checked as well.

Check that the fluid inlet and outlet ports in the master cylinder are clear.

15 The dust boot, circlip, piston assembly and spring are included in the rebuild kit. Use all of the new parts, regardless of the apparent condition of the old ones. Fit them according to the layout of the old piston assembly.

16 Fit the spring into the master cylinder. On YZF1000R models its narrow end should face out.

17 Lubricate the piston assembly with clean brake fluid. Fit the assembly into the master cylinder, making sure it is the correct way round. Make sure the lips on the cup do not turn inside out when they are slipped into the bore. Depress the piston and install the new circlip, making sure that it locates in the groove **(see illustration 5.11)**.

18 Install the rubber dust boot, making sure the lip is seated correctly in the groove **(see illustration 5.10c)**.

19 Fit a new O-ring onto the reservoir hose union, then press the union into the master cylinder and secure it with the circlip. Fit the rubber cap over the circlip.

20 Inspect the reservoir cap rubber diaphragm and renew it if it is damaged or deteriorated.

Installation

21 If removed, install the brake light switch **(see illustration 5.4)**.

22 Attach the master cylinder to the handlebar and fit the clamp with its 'UP' mark facing up, aligning the top mating surfaces of the clamp with the punchmark on the handlebar **(see illustration 5.8)**. Tighten the upper bolt first, then the lower bolt to the torque setting specified at the beginning of the Chapter.

23 If detached, connect the brake hoses to the master cylinder, using new sealing washers on each side of the unions, and aligning the hoses as noted on removal **(see illustration 5.6)**. Tighten the banjo bolt to the torque setting specified at the beginning of this Chapter.

24 If removed, install the brake lever (see Chapter 6).

25 Mount the reservoir and tighten the bolt securely **(see illustration 5.3)**. Connect the reservoir hose to the union and secure it with the clamp **(see illustration 5.7)**.

26 Connect the brake light switch wiring connectors **(see illustration 5.4)**.

27 Fill the fluid reservoir with new DOT 4 brake fluid as described in *Daily (pre-ride) checks*. Refer to Section 11 of this Chapter and bleed the air from the system.

28 Fit the rubber diaphragm, making sure it is correctly seated, the diaphragm plate and the cap onto the master cylinder reservoir, then fit the cap clamp **(see illustration 5.3)**.

29 Check the operation of the front brake before riding the motorcycle.

5.10c Remove the rubber boot from the end of the master cylinder piston . . .

5.11 . . . then depress the piston and remove the circlip using a pair of internal circlip pliers

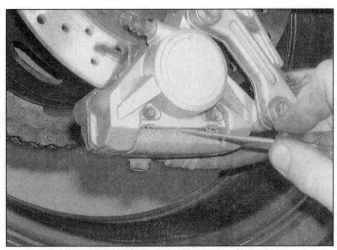

6.1a Remove the caliper cover . . .

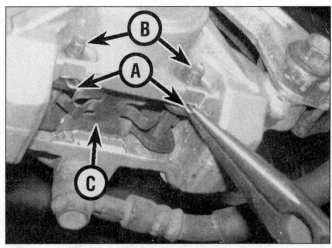

6.1b . . . then remove the retaining clips (A), withdraw the pad pins (B) and remove the spring (C), noting how it fits

6 Rear brake pads – renewal

Warning: The dust created by the brake system may contain asbestos, which is harmful to your health. Never blow it out with compressed air and don't inhale any of it. An approved filtering mask should be worn when working on the brakes.

1 Press in the edges of the brake pad cover to release its clips and remove it – use a flat-bladed screwdriver if necessary **(see illustration)**. Remove the pad pin retaining clips, then withdraw the pad pins from the caliper using a suitable pair of pliers and remove the pad spring, noting how it fits **(see illustration)**. Withdraw the pads from the caliper body **(see illustration)**. If required, remove the anti-chatter shim from the back of each pad, noting how it fits **(see illustration 6.7)**.

2 Inspect the surface of each pad for contamination and check that the friction material has not worn beyond its service limit (see Chapter 1, Section 8). If either pad is worn down to or beyond the service limit wear indicator, is fouled with oil or grease, or is

heavily scored or damaged by dirt and debris, both pads must be renewed as a set. Note that it is not possible to degrease the friction material; if the pads are contaminated in any way new ones must be fitted.

3 If the pads are in good condition clean them carefully, using a fine wire brush which is completely free of oil and grease to remove all traces of road dirt and corrosion. Using a pointed instrument, clean out the grooves in the friction material and dig out any embedded particles of foreign matter. Any areas of glazing may be removed using emery cloth. Spray with a dedicated brake cleaner to remove any dust.

4 Check the condition of the brake disc (see Section 8).

5 Remove all traces of corrosion from the pad pins. Check them for signs of damage and renew them if necessary.

6 Push the pistons as far back into the caliper as possible using hand pressure or a piece of wood as leverage. Due to the increased friction material thickness of new pads, it may be necessary to remove the fluid reservoir cap, plate and diaphragm and siphon out some fluid. If access to the piston heads is too restricted with the caliper in place, remove the caliper from its bracket (see Section 7). If the pistons are difficult to push back, attach a

6.1c Remove the pads from the caliper

length of clear hose to the bleed valve and place the open end in a suitable container, then open the valve and try again. Take great care not to draw any air into the system. If in doubt, bleed the brakes afterwards (see Section 11).

7 Smear the backs of the pads and the shank of each pad pin with copper-based grease, making sure that none gets on the front or sides of the pads. Fit the anti-chatter shim onto the back of each pad, making sure the arrow points in the direction of normal disc rotation **(see illustration)**.

8 Insert the pads into the caliper so that the friction material of each pad is facing the disc **(see illustration)**. Insert one of the pad pins, making sure it passes through the hole in each

6.7 Fit the shim with arrow pointing in the direction of disc rotation

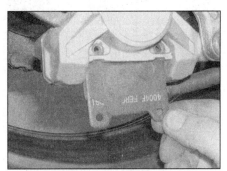

6.8a Install the pads . . .

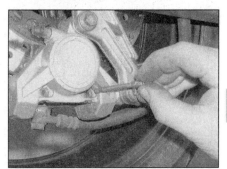

6.8b . . . then insert the front pad pin

7

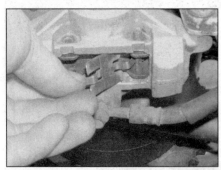

6.8c Hook the spring end under the pin . . .

6.8d . . . then press the spring onto the pads and insert the other pin

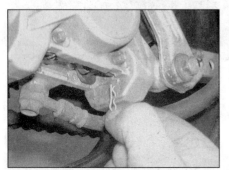

6.8e Secure the pins with the clips . . .

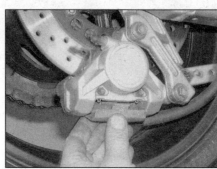

6.8f . . . then fit the caliper cover

pad, then hook the end of the pad spring under the pin, making sure the longer outer tabs of the spring point in the direction of normal disc rotation (see illustrations). Insert the other pad pin, pressing down on the spring end so that the pin fits over it (see illustration). Fit the retaining clips (see illustration). Install the caliper cover (see illustration).

9 Top up the master cylinder reservoir if necessary (see *Daily (pre-ride) checks*).

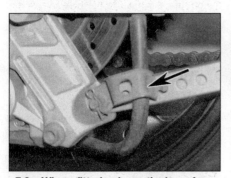

7.2a Where fitted, release the hose from its guide (arrowed)

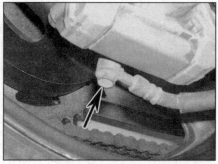

7.2b Brake hose banjo bolt (arrowed)

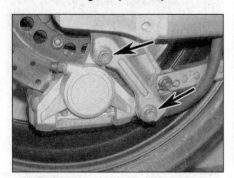

7.3a Unscrew the bolts (arrowed) . . .

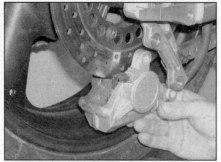

7.3b . . . and slide the caliper off the disc

10 Operate the brake pedal several times to bring the pads into contact with the disc. Check the operation of the brake before riding the motorcycle.

7 Rear brake caliper – removal, overhaul and installation

⚠ Warning: *If a caliper indicates the need for an overhaul (usually due to leaking fluid or sticky operation), all old brake fluid should be flushed from the system. Also, the dust created by the brake system may contain asbestos, which is harmful to your health. Never blow it out with compressed air and don't inhale any of it. An approved filtering mask should be worn when working on the brakes. Do not, under any circumstances, use petroleum-based solvents to clean brake parts. Use the specified clean brake fluid, dedicated brake cleaner or denatured alcohol only, as described.*

Removal

1 If the caliper is being overhauled, remove the brake pads (see Section 6). If the caliper is only being displaced or removed, the pads can be left in place.

2 If the caliper is just being displaced and not completely removed or overhauled, do not disconnect the brake hose. If this is the case, release the brake hose from its guide (where fitted) on the torque arm – this will provide a bit more slack in the hose (see illustration). If the caliper is being overhauled, unscrew the brake hose banjo bolt and separate the brake hose from the caliper, noting its alignment (see illustration). Plug the hose end or wrap a plastic bag tightly around it to minimise fluid loss and prevent dirt entering the system. Discard the two sealing washers as they must be replaced with new ones. **Note:** *If you are planning to overhaul the caliper and don't have a source of compressed air to blow out the pistons, just loosen the banjo bolt at this stage and retighten it lightly. The bike's hydraulic system can then be used to force the pistons out of the body once the pads have been removed. Disconnect the hose once the pistons have been sufficiently displaced.*

3 Unscrew the caliper mounting bolts, and slide the caliper off the disc (see illustrations).

Overhaul

4 Clean the exterior of the caliper with denatured alcohol or brake system cleaner (see illustration).

5 Using a flat piece of wood, block the piston on one side of the caliper in its bore and displace the opposite piston either by pumping it out by operating the brake pedal, or by forcing it out using compressed air.

Remove the seals (see below) from the bore of the displaced piston, then reinstall the piston and block it using the wood. Now displace the piston from the other side using the same method. Remove the wood and both pistons. Mark each piston head and caliper body with a felt marker to ensure that the pistons can be matched to their original bores on reassembly. If the compressed air method is used, direct the air into the fluid inlet to force the piston out of the body. Use only low pressure to ease the piston out. If the air pressure is too high and the piston is forced out, the caliper and/or piston may be damaged.

⚠ **Warning: Never place your fingers in front of the piston in an attempt to catch or protect it when applying compressed air, as serious injury could result.**
Caution: Do not try to remove the pistons by levering them out, or by using pliers or any other grips.

6 Using a wooden or plastic tool, remove the dust seals from the caliper bores **(see illustration 3.6)**. Discard them as new ones must be used on installation. If a metal tool is being used, take great care not to damage the caliper bores.
7 Remove and discard the piston seals in the same way.
8 Clean the pistons and bores with clean brake fluid of the specified type. If compressed air is available, use it to dry the parts thoroughly (make sure it's filtered and unlubricated).
Caution: Do not, under any circumstances, use a petroleum-based solvent to clean brake parts.
9 Inspect the caliper bores and pistons for signs of corrosion, nicks and burrs and loss of plating. If surface defects are present, the caliper assembly must be renewed. If the necessary measuring equipment is available, compare the dimensions of the caliper bores to those specified at the beginning of the Chapter, and install a new caliper if necessary. If the caliper is in bad shape the master cylinder should also be checked.
10 Lubricate the new piston seals with clean brake fluid and install them in their grooves in the caliper bores.
11 Lubricate the new dust seals with clean

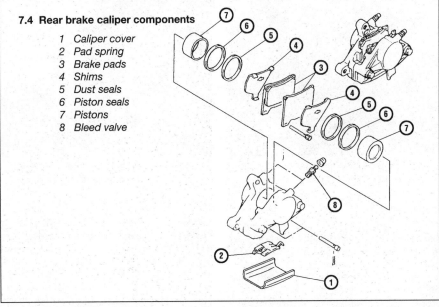

7.4 Rear brake caliper components

1 Caliper cover
2 Pad spring
3 Brake pads
4 Shims
5 Dust seals
6 Piston seals
7 Pistons
8 Bleed valve

brake fluid and install them in their grooves in the caliper bores.
12 Lubricate the pistons with clean brake fluid and install them closed-end first into the caliper bores. Using your thumbs, push the pistons all the way in, making sure they enter the bore squarely.

Installation

13 Push the pistons a little way back into the caliper using hand pressure or a piece of wood as leverage. Slide the caliper onto the brake disc, making sure the pads sit squarely either side of the disc if they weren't removed **(see illustration 7.3b)**.
14 Install the caliper mounting bolts, and tighten them to the torque setting specified at the beginning of the Chapter **(see illustrations)**.
15 If detached, connect the brake hose to the caliper, making sure it is correctly routed round the torque arm. Use new sealing washers on each side of the union, and align the hose as noted on removal **(see illustration 7.2b)**. Tighten the banjo bolt to the torque setting specified at the beginning of the Chapter. Top up the master cylinder reservoir with DOT 4 brake fluid (see *Daily*

(pre-ride) checks) and bleed the hydraulic system as described in Section 11.
16 If removed, install the brake pads (see Section 2). Also fit the hose into its clamp if necessary **(see illustration 7.2a)**.
17 Check for leaks and thoroughly test the operation of the brake before riding the motorcycle.

8 Rear brake disc – inspection, removal and installation

Inspection

1 Refer to Section 4 of this Chapter, noting that the dial gauge should be attached to the swingarm.

Removal

2 Remove the rear wheel (see Section 15).
3 Mark the relationship of the disc to the wheel so it can be installed in the same position. Unscrew the disc retaining bolts, loosening them evenly and a little at a time in a criss-cross pattern to avoid distorting the disc, and remove the disc **(see illustration)**.

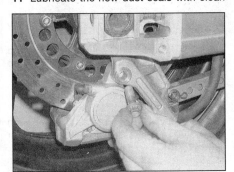

7.14a Install the caliper mounting bolts . . .

7.14b . . . and tighten them to the specified torque

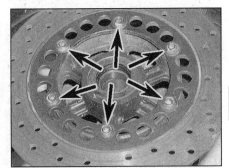

8.3 Rear brake disc bolts (arrowed)

7

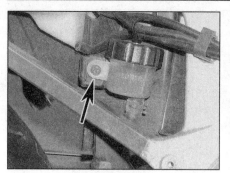

9.4a Remove the screw (arrowed) and drain the reservoir ...

9.4b ... and detach the hose (arrowed) from the master cylinder

9.5 Brake hose banjo bolt (arrowed)

Installation

4 Install the disc on the wheel with its marked side facing out, aligning the previously applied matchmarks (if you're reinstalling the original disc).

5 Clean the threads of the disc mounting bolts, then apply a suitable non-permanent thread locking compound. Install the bolts and tighten them evenly and a little at a time in a criss-cross pattern to the torque setting specified at the beginning of the Chapter. Clean off all grease from the brake disc using acetone or brake system cleaner. If a new brake disc has been installed, remove any protective coating from its working surfaces.

6 Install the rear wheel (see Section 15).

7 Operate the brake pedal several times to bring the pads into contact with the disc. Check the operation of the brake carefully before riding the motorcycle.

9 Rear brake master cylinder – removal, overhaul and installation

1 If the master cylinder is leaking fluid, or if the lever does not produce a firm feel when the brake is applied, and bleeding the brakes

does not help (see Section 11), and the hydraulic hose is in good condition, then master cylinder overhaul is recommended.

2 Before disassembling the master cylinder, read through the entire procedure and make sure that you have the correct rebuild kit. Also, you will need some new DOT 4 brake fluid, some clean rags and internal circlip pliers. **Note:** *To prevent damage to the paint from spilled brake fluid, always cover the surrounding components when working on the master cylinder.*

Caution: Disassembly, overhaul and reassembly of the brake master cylinder must be done in a spotlessly clean work area to avoid contamination and possible failure of the brake hydraulic system components.

Removal

3 Remove the right-hand side cover (YZF1000R), side covers (YZF750R) or seat cowling (YZF750SP) (see Chapter 8).

4 Remove the screw securing the master cylinder fluid reservoir to the frame, then remove the reservoir cap clamp (YZF750R and SP only), cap, diaphragm plate and diaphragm and pour the fluid into a container **(see illustration)**. Release the clamp securing

the reservoir hose to the union on the master cylinder and detach the hose, being prepared to catch any residual fluid **(see illustration)**.

5 Unscrew the brake hose banjo bolt and separate the brake hose from the master cylinder, noting its alignment **(see illustration)**. Discard the two sealing washers as they must be replaced with new ones. Wrap the end of the hose in a clean rag and suspend the hose in an upright position or bend it down carefully and place the open end in a clean container. The objective is to prevent excessive loss of brake fluid, fluid spills and system contamination.

6 Remove the split pin and washer from the clevis pin securing the brake pedal to the master cylinder pushrod **(see illustration)**. Withdraw the clevis pin and separate the pedal from the pushrod. Discard the split pin as a new one must be used.

7 Unscrew the two bolts securing the master cylinder to the footrest bracket and remove the master cylinder **(see illustration)**.

Overhaul

8 If required, mark the position of the clevis locknut on the pushrod, then slacken the locknut and thread the clevis off the pushrod **(see illustration)**.

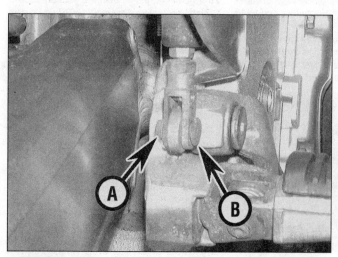

9.6 Remove the split pin (A) and withdraw the clevis pin (B)

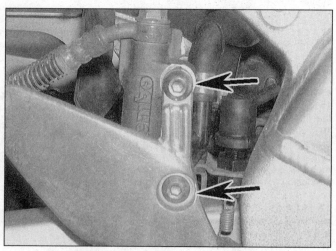

9.7 Master cylinder mounting bolts (arrowed)

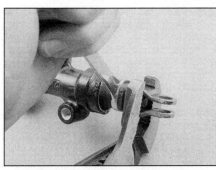

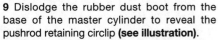

9.8 Hold the clevis and slacken the locknut

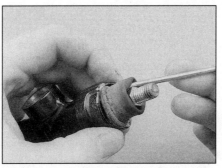

9.9 Remove the dust boot from the bottom of the master cylinder

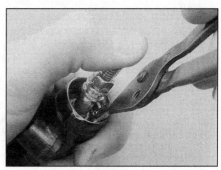

9.10a Depress the pushrod and remove the circlip

9 Dislodge the rubber dust boot from the base of the master cylinder to reveal the pushrod retaining circlip **(see illustration)**.

10 Depress the pushrod and, using circlip pliers, remove the circlip **(see illustration)**. Slide out the piston assembly and spring **(see illustrations)**. If they are difficult to remove, apply low pressure compressed air to the fluid outlet. Lay the parts out in the proper order to prevent confusion during reassembly.

11 Clean all of the parts with clean brake fluid.

Caution: Do not, under any circumstances, use a petroleum-based solvent to clean brake parts. If compressed air is available, use it to dry the parts thoroughly (make sure it's filtered and unlubricated).

12 Check the master cylinder bore for corrosion, scratches, nicks and score marks. If the necessary measuring equipment is available, compare the diameter of the bore to that given in the Specifications Section of this Chapter. If damage is evident, the master cylinder must be replaced with a new one. If the master cylinder is in poor condition, then the caliper should be checked as well.

13 Inspect the reservoir hose for cracks or splits and replace it with a new one if necessary. If required, pull the union from the master cylinder. Discard the bush as a new one must be used.

14 The dust boot, circlip, piston assembly and spring are included in the rebuild kit. Use all of the new parts, regardless of the apparent condition of the old ones. Fit them according to the layout of the old piston assembly.

15 Fit the spring in the master cylinder so that its tapered end faces the piston.

16 Lubricate the piston assembly with clean brake fluid. Fit the assembly into the master cylinder, making sure it is the correct way round. Make sure the lips on the cup do not turn inside out when they are slipped into the bore.

17 Install and depress the pushrod, then fit a new circlip, making sure it is properly seated in the groove **(see illustration 9.10a)**.

18 Install the rubber dust boot, making sure the lip is seated properly in the groove **(see illustration 9.9)**.

19 If removed, fit a new reservoir hose union bush, then push the union into the master cylinder.

20 If removed, thread the clevis locknut and the clevis onto the master cylinder pushrod end. Position the clevis as noted on removal, then tighten the locknut securely **(see illustration 9.8)**.

Installation

21 Fit the master cylinder onto the footrest bracket and tighten its mounting bolts to the torque setting specified at the beginning of the Chapter **(see illustration 9.7)**.

22 Align the brake pedal with the master cylinder pushrod clevis, then slide in the clevis pin and secure it using a new split pin, not forgetting the washer **(see illustration 9.6)**.

23 Connect the brake hose banjo bolt to the master cylinder, using a new sealing washer on each side of the banjo union. Ensure that the hose is positioned so that it butts against the lug and tighten the banjo bolt to the specified torque setting **(see illustrations 9.5)**.

24 On YZF1000R models, install the fluid reservoir and tighten its screw **(see illustration 9.4a)**. On YZF750R and SP models, locate the reservoir in position but do not fix it to the bracket because of the cap clamp. Ensure that the hose is correctly routed, then connect it to the union on the master cylinder and secure it with the clamp **(see illustration 9.4b)**. Check that the hose is secure and clamped at the reservoir end as well. If the clamps have weakened, use new ones.

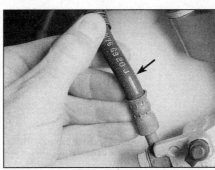

10.2 Flex the brake hoses and check for cracks, bulges and leaking fluid

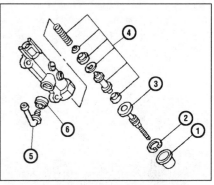

9.10b Master cylinder components

1 Rubber boot
2 Circlip
3 Pushrod
4 Piston assembly and spring
5 Reservoir hose union
6 Bush

25 Fill the fluid reservoir with new DOT 4 brake fluid (see *Daily (pre-ride) checks*) and bleed the system following the procedure in Section 11. On YZF750R and SP models, on completion install the reservoir cap clamp and tighten the screw.

26 Install the right-hand side cover (YZF1000R), side covers (YZF750R) or seat cowling (YZF750SP) (see Chapter 8).

27 Check the operation of the brake carefully before riding the motorcycle.

10 Brake hoses, pipes and unions – inspection and renewal

Inspection

1 Brake hose and pipe condition should be checked regularly and the hoses renewed at the specified interval (see Chapter 1).

2 Twist and flex the rubber hoses while looking for cracks, bulges and seeping fluid **(see illustration)**. Check extra carefully around the areas where the hoses connect with the banjo fittings, as these are common areas for hose failure.

7

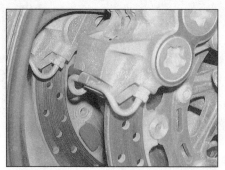

10.3 On YZF1000R models, check the condition of the metal pipe on each front caliper

3 On YZF1000R models, inspect the metal brake pipe on each front caliper, and on all models check the banjo union fittings connected to the brake hoses **(see illustration)**. If the pipe is damaged or rusted or cracked, a new caliper must be installed as the pipe is not available separately (though it would be worth checking with a brake or hydraulic hose/pipe specialist). If the union fittings are rusted, scratched or cracked, fit new hoses.

Renewal

4 The brake hoses have banjo union fittings on each end. Cover the surrounding area with plenty of rags and unscrew the banjo bolt at each end of the hose or pipe, noting its alignment **(see illustration)**. Free the hose from any clips or guides and remove it. Discard the sealing washers on the hose unions.

5 Position the new hose, making sure it isn't twisted or otherwise strained, and abut the tab on the hose union with the lug on the component casting, where present. Otherwise align the hose as noted on removal. Install the hose banjo bolts using new sealing washers on both sides of the unions. Tighten the banjo bolts to the torque setting specified at the beginning of this Chapter. Make sure the hoses are correctly aligned and routed clear of all moving components.

6 Flush the old brake fluid from the system, refill with new DOT 4 brake fluid (see *Daily*

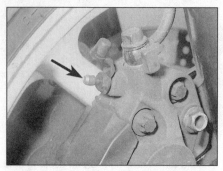

11.6a Brake caliper bleed valve (arrowed) – typical example shown

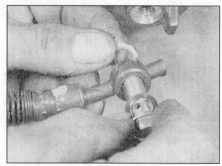

10.4 Remove the banjo bolt and separate the hose from the caliper ; there is a sealing washer on each side of the fitting

(pre-ride) checks) and bleed the air from the system (see Section 11). Check the operation of the brakes carefully before riding the motorcycle.

11 Brake system bleeding

1 Bleeding the brakes is simply the process of removing all the air bubbles from the brake fluid reservoirs, the hoses and the brake calipers. Bleeding is necessary whenever a brake system hydraulic connection is loosened, when a component or hose is replaced or renewed, or when the master cylinder or caliper is overhauled. Leaks in the system may also allow air to enter, but leaking brake fluid will reveal their presence and warn you of the need for repair.

2 To bleed the brakes, you will need some new DOT 4 brake fluid, a length of clear vinyl or plastic tubing, a small container partially filled with clean brake fluid, some rags and a spanner to fit the brake caliper bleed valves.

3 Cover the fuel tank and other painted components to prevent damage in the event that brake fluid is spilled.

4 When bleeding the rear brake, remove the right-hand side cover (YZF1000R), side covers (YZF750R) or seat cowling (YZF750SP) (see Chapter 8) for access to the fluid reservoir.

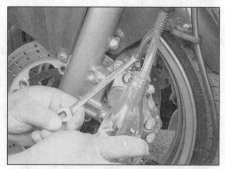

11.6b To bleed the brakes, you need a spanner, a short section of clear tubing, and a clear container half-filled with brake fluid

5 Remove the reservoir cap or cover, diaphragm plate and diaphragm and slowly pump the brake lever or pedal a few times, until no air bubbles can be seen floating up from the holes in the bottom of the reservoir. This bleeds the air from the master cylinder end of the line. Loosely refit the reservoir cap or cover.

6 Pull the dust cap off the bleed valve **(see illustration)**. Attach one end of the clear vinyl or plastic tubing to the bleed valve and submerge the other end in the brake fluid in the container **(see illustration)**.

7 Remove the reservoir cap or cover and check the fluid level. Do not allow the fluid level to drop below the lower mark during the bleeding process.

8 Carefully pump the brake lever or pedal three or four times and hold it in (front) or down (rear) while opening the caliper bleed valve. When the valve is opened, brake fluid will flow out of the caliper into the clear tubing and the lever will move toward the handlebar or the pedal will move down.

9 Retighten the bleed valve, then release the brake lever or pedal gradually. Repeat the process until no air bubbles are visible in the brake fluid leaving the caliper, or if the fluid is being changed until new fluid is coming out, and the lever or pedal is firm when applied. On completion, disconnect the bleeding equipment, then tighten the bleed valve to the torque setting specified at the beginning of the Chapter and install the dust cap.

> **HAYNES HiNT** *Old brake fluid is invariably much darker in colour than new fluid, making it easy to see when all old fluid has been expelled from the system.*

10 Install the diaphragm and cap or cover assembly, wipe up any spilled brake fluid and check the entire system for leaks.

> **HAYNES HiNT** *If it's not possible to produce a firm feel to the lever or pedal the fluid may be aerated. Let the brake fluid in the system stabilise for a few hours and then repeat the procedure when the tiny bubbles in the system have settled out.*

12 Wheels – inspection and repair

1 In order to carry out a proper inspection of the wheels, it is necessary to support the bike upright so that the wheel being inspected is raised off the ground. Position the motorcycle on an auxiliary stand. Clean the wheels thoroughly to remove mud and dirt that may interfere with the inspection procedure or mask defects. Make a general check of the wheels (see Chapter 1) and tyres (see *Daily (pre-ride) checks*).

2 Attach a dial gauge to the fork or the swingarm and position its tip against the side of the rim **(see illustration)**. Spin the wheel slowly and check the axial (side-to-side) runout of the rim. In order to accurately check radial (out of round) runout with the dial gauge, the wheel would have to be removed from the machine, and the tyre from the wheel. With the axle clamped in a vice and the dial gauge positioned on the top of the rim, the wheel can be rotated to check the runout.

3 An easier, though slightly less accurate, method is to attach a stiff wire pointer to the fork or the swingarm and position the end a fraction of an inch from the wheel (where the wheel and tyre join). If the wheel is true, the distance from the pointer to the rim will be constant as the wheel is rotated. **Note:** *If wheel runout is excessive, check the wheel bearings very carefully before renewing the wheel.*

4 The wheels should also be visually inspected for cracks, flat spots on the rim and other damage. Look very closely for dents in the area where the tyre bead contacts the rim. Dents in this area may prevent complete sealing of the tyre against the rim, which leads to deflation of the tyre over a period of time. If damage is evident, or if runout in either direction is excessive, the wheel will have to be replaced with a new one. Never attempt to repair a damaged cast alloy wheel.

13 Wheels – alignment check

1 Misalignment of the wheels, which may be due to a cocked rear wheel or a bent frame or fork yokes, can cause strange and possibly serious handling problems. If the frame or yokes are at fault, repair by a frame specialist or replacement with new parts are the only alternatives.

2 To check the alignment you will need an assistant, a length of string or a perfectly straight piece of wood and a ruler. A plumb bob or other suitable weight will also be required.

3 In order to make a proper check of the wheels it is necessary to support the bike in

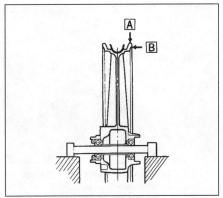

12.2 Check the wheel for radial (out-of-round) runout (A) and axial (side-to-side) runout (B)

an upright position, using an auxiliary stand. Measure the width of both tyres at their widest points. Subtract the smaller measurement from the larger measurement, then divide the difference by two. The result is the amount of offset that should exist between the front and rear tyres on both sides.

4 If a string is used, have your assistant hold one end of it about halfway between the floor and the rear axle, touching the rear sidewall of the tyre.

5 Run the other end of the string forward and pull it tight so that it is roughly parallel to the floor **(see illustration)**. Slowly bring the string into contact with the front sidewall of the rear tyre, then turn the front wheel until it is parallel with the string. Measure the distance from the front tyre sidewall to the string.

6 Repeat the procedure on the other side of the motorcycle. The distance from the front tyre sidewall to the string should be equal on both sides.

7 As previously mentioned, a perfectly straight length of wood or metal bar may be substituted for the string **(see illustration)**. The procedure is the same.

8 If the distance between the string and tyre is greater on one side, or if the rear wheel appears to be cocked, refer to Chapter 1, Section 1 and check that the chain adjuster markings coincide on each side of the swingarm.

9 If the front-to-back alignment is correct, the wheels still may be out of alignment vertically.

10 Using a plumb bob, or other suitable weight, and a length of string, check the rear wheel to make sure it is vertical. To do this, hold the string against the tyre upper sidewall and allow the weight to settle just off the floor. When the string touches both the upper and lower tyre sidewalls and is perfectly straight, the wheel is vertical. If it is not, place thin spacers under one leg of the stand until it is.

11 Once the rear wheel is vertical, check the front wheel in the same manner. If both wheels are not perfectly vertical, the frame and/or major suspension components are bent.

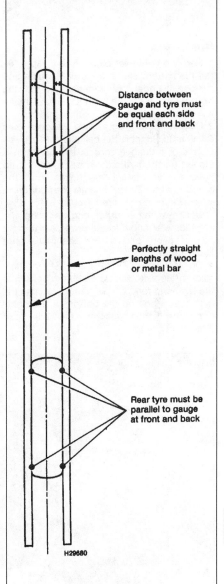

Distance between gauge and tyre must be equal each side and front and back

Perfectly straight lengths of wood or metal bar

Rear tyre must be parallel to gauge at front and back

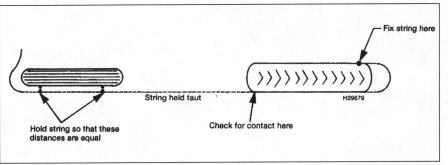

13.5 Wheel alignment check using string

13.7 Wheel alignment check using a straight edge

7

14.3 Unscrew the ring (arrowed) and detach the cable

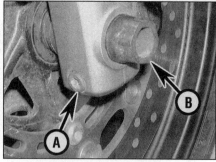

14.4 Slacken the clamp bolt (A) and unscrew the axle (B)

14.5 Withdraw the axle and remove the wheel

14 Front wheel – removal and installation

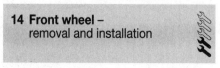

Removal

1 Remove the lower fairing (see Chapter 8). Put the motorcycle on an auxiliary stand and support it under the crankcase so that the front wheel is off the ground. Always make sure the motorcycle is properly supported.
2 Displace the front brake calipers (see Section 3). Support the calipers with a piece of wire or a bungee cord so that no strain is placed on the hydraulic hoses. There is no need to disconnect the hoses from the calipers. **Note:** *Do not operate the front brake lever with the calipers removed.*
3 Unscrew the knurled ring securing the speedometer cable to the drive gear using a pair of pliers and detach the cable **(see illustration)**.
4 On 1994-on YZF750R and SP models, slacken the axle clamp bolt on the bottom of the left-hand fork. On all models, slacken the axle clamp bolt on the bottom of the right-hand fork, then unscrew the axle **(see illustration)**.

5 Support the wheel, then withdraw the axle from the right-hand side **(see illustration)**. Carefully lower the wheel from between the forks, noting how the speedometer drive gear locates against the fork. Use a drift to drive out the axle if required.
6 Remove the spacer from the right-hand side of the wheel and the speedometer drive gear from the left-hand side, noting how they fit **(see illustrations)**.
Caution: Don't lay the wheel down and allow it to rest on a disc – the disc could become warped. Set the wheel on wood blocks so the disc doesn't support the weight of the wheel, or keep it upright.
7 Check the axle for straightness by rolling it on a flat surface such as a piece of plate glass (first wipe off all old grease and remove any corrosion using fine emery cloth). If the equipment is available, place the axle in V-blocks and check for runout using a dial gauge. If the axle is bent, replace it with a new one.
8 Check the condition of the wheel bearings (see Section 16).

Installation

9 Apply lithium based grease to the wheel spacer, the lips of the grease seals, and to the

14.6a Remove the spacer . . .

speedometer drive gear. Fit the spacer into the right-hand side of the wheel **(see illustration 14.6a)**. Fit the drive gear into the left-hand side, making sure the drive plate tabs locate in the slots **(see illustration)**.
10 Manoeuvre the wheel into position. Apply a thin coat of grease to the axle.
11 Lift the wheel into place between the forks, making sure the spacer and drive gear remain in position, and that the slot in the drive gear locates over the tab on the inside of the fork **(see illustration)**. Slide the axle in from the right-hand side and tighten it to the

14.6b . . . and the speedometer drive gear housing

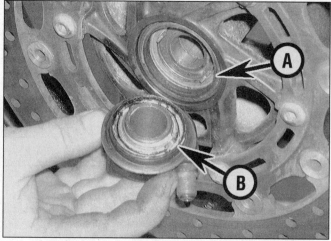

14.9 Make sure the drive tabs (A) locate in the slots (B)

14.11a Locate the tab on the inside of the fork in the slot in the top of the housing (arrowed)

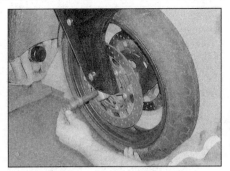

14.11b ... and insert the axle

14.11c Tighten the axle to the specified torque, then tighten the clamp bolt

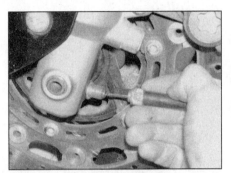

14.13a Insert the cable ...

14.13b ... and tighten the ring securely

torque setting specified at the beginning of the Chapter (see illustrations). Now tighten the axle clamp bolt on the bottom of the right-hand fork to the specified torque setting (see illustration 14.4), and on 1994-on YZF750R and SP models also tighten the left-hand clamp bolt. On YZF750R and SP models that don't have a circlip fitted in the groove in the axle head, make sure that the groove is visible. If it isn't, repeat the installation procedure.

12 Install the brake calipers, making sure the pads sit squarely on each side of the discs (see Section 3). Tighten the caliper mounting bolts to the specified torque setting.

13 Fit the speedometer cable into the drive housing and tighten the knurled ring securely (see illustrations). Take the bike off its auxiliary stand and install the lower fairing (see Chapter 8).

14 Apply the front brake a few times to bring the pads back into contact with the discs. Take the bike off the stand, apply the front brake and pump the front forks a few times to settle all components in position.

15 Check for correct operation of the front brake before riding the motorcycle.

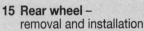

15 Rear wheel –
removal and installation

Removal

1 Support the motorcycle securely in an upright position using an auxiliary stand.

2 Displace the rear brake caliper (see Section 7). Make sure no strain is placed on the hydraulic hose. There is no need to disconnect the hose from the caliper. **Note:** *Do not operate the brake pedal with the caliper removed.*

3 Slacken the adjuster locknut on each side of the swingarm, then turn the adjusters in to provide some slack in the chain (see illustration). Where fitted, remove the split pin from the end of the axle. Unscrew the axle nut and remove the washer (see illustration). Remove the adjustment position marker from the left-hand side (see illustration).

4 Note how the caliper bracket locates

between the wheel and the swingarm. Support the wheel then withdraw the axle along with the other adjustment position marker and lower the wheel to the ground, bringing the

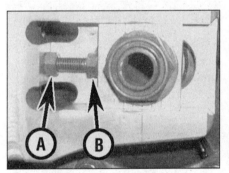

15.3a Slacken the locknut (A) on each side and turn each adjuster (B) in

15.3c ... and remove the position marker

caliper bracket with it (see illustrations).

5 Disengage the chain from the sprocket and remove the wheel from between the swingarm ends (see illustration 15.10).

15.3b Unscrew the axle nut (arrowed) ...

15.4a Withdraw the axle ...

7

15.4b . . . and lower the wheel with the caliper bracket to the ground

15.7a Remove the collar from the right-hand side . . .

15.7b . . . and from the left-hand side, noting which fits where

Caution: Do not lay the wheel down and allow it to rest on the disc or the sprocket – they could become warped. Set the wheel on wood blocks so the disc or the sprocket doesn't support the weight of the wheel. Do not operate the brake pedal with the wheel removed.

6 Check the axle for straightness by rolling it on a flat surface such as a piece of plate glass (first wipe off all old grease and remove any corrosion using fine emery cloth). If the equipment is available, place the axle in V-blocks and check for runout using a dial gauge. If the axle is bent, replace it with a new one.

7 Remove the collar from each side of the wheel, noting which fits where **(see illustrations)**. Check the condition of the grease seals and wheel bearings (see Section 16).

Installation

8 Apply a thin coat of lithium based grease to the lips of each grease seal, and also to the collars and the axle. Slide the right-hand adjustment position marker onto the axle, making sure it is the correct way round.

9 Install the collar with the small groove into the right-hand side of the wheel and the collar with the large groove into the left-hand side **(see illustrations 15.7a and b)**. Manoeuvre the wheel into place between the ends of the swingarm. Align the brake caliper bracket with the wheel.

10 Engage the drive chain with the sprocket **(see illustration)**. Lift the wheel into position, bringing the caliper bracket with it, making sure it locates correctly between the wheel and the swingarm **(see illustration 15.4b)**. Make sure the collars remain in place.

11 Slide the axle, with the adjustment

marker, through from the right-hand side **(see illustration 15.4a)**. Make sure it passes through the caliper bracket. Align the flats on the axle head between the raised sections on the adjustment marker **(see illustration)**. Check that everything is correctly aligned, then fit the left-hand adjustment position marker with the 'FWD' mark at the front **(see illustration)**. Fit the washer and the axle nut **(see illustration)**.

12 Adjust the chain slack as described in Chapter 1, then tighten the axle nut to the torque setting specified at the beginning of the Chapter **(see illustration)**. Where applicable, fit a new split pin into the hole in the end of the axle – if the hole is not aligned with slots in the nut, tighten the nut until they align – do not slacken the nut.

13 Install the brake caliper, making sure the pads sit squarely on each side of the disc (see Section 7).

14 Operate the brake pedal several times to bring the pads into contact with the disc. Check the operation of the rear brake carefully before riding the bike.

16 Wheel bearings – removal, inspection and installation

Front wheel bearings

Note: *Always renew the wheel bearings in pairs, never individually. Avoid using a high pressure cleaner on the wheel bearing area.*

1 Remove the wheel (see Section 14).

15.10 Manoeuvre the wheel into position and fit the chain onto the sprocket

15.11a Locate the flats on the axle head between the raised sections on the position marker

15.11b Fit the left-hand position marker with the 'FWD' mark at the front . . .

15.11c . . . then fit the washer and nut

15.12 Tighten the axle nut to the specified torque

16.3 Lever out the grease seal on each side

16.4a . . . then lever out the retainer plate from the left-hand side . . .

16.4b . . . and remove the drive plate

2 Set the wheel on blocks so as not to allow the weight of the wheel to rest on either brake disc.

3 Lever out the grease seal on each side of the wheel using a large flat-bladed screwdriver, taking care not to damage the rim **(see illustration)**. Discard the seals if they are damaged or deteriorated.

 HAYNES HINT *Position a piece of wood against the wheel to prevent the screwdriver shaft damaging it when levering the grease seal out.*

4 Remove the retainer plate from the left-hand side of the wheel and remove the speedometer drive plate, noting how it fits **(see illustrations)**.

5 Using a metal rod (preferably a brass drift punch) inserted through the centre of the one bearing, tap evenly around the inner race of the other bearing to drive it from the hub **(see illustrations)**. The bearing spacer will also come out.

6 Lay the wheel on its other side so that the remaining bearing faces down. Drive the bearing out of the wheel using the same technique as above.

7 If the bearings are of the unsealed type or are only sealed on one side, clean them with a high flash-point solvent (one which won't leave any residue) and blow them dry with compressed air (don't let the bearings spin as you dry them). Apply a few drops of oil to the bearing. **Note:** *If the bearing is sealed on both sides don't attempt to clean it.*

16.5a Knock out the bearings using a drift . . .

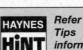 **HAYNES HINT** *Refer to Tools and Workshop Tips (Section 5) for more information about bearings.*

8 Hold the outer race of the bearing and rotate the inner race – if the bearing doesn't turn smoothly, has rough spots or is noisy, replace it with a new one.

9 If the bearing is good and can be re-used, wash it in solvent once again and dry it, then pack the bearing with lithium based grease.

10 Thoroughly clean the hub area of the wheel. Install the right-hand bearing into its recess in the hub, with the marked or sealed side facing outwards. Using the old bearing (if new ones are being fitted), a bearing driver or a socket large enough to contact the outer race of the bearing, drive it in until it's completely seated **(see illustration)**.

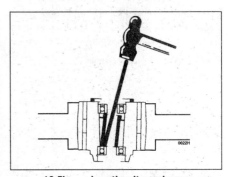

16.5b . . . locating it as shown

11 Turn the wheel over and install the bearing spacer. Drive the left-hand bearing into place as described above.

12 Fit the speedometer drive plate into the left-hand side of the wheel, with the drive tabs facing out and aligning the flat tabs with the cutouts in the hub **(see illustration 16.4b)**. Press the retainer plate onto the drive plate **(see illustration 16.4a)**. Apply a smear of lithium based grease to the lips of one seal, then press it into the wheel, using a seal or bearing driver or a suitable socket to drive it into place if necessary **(see illustrations)**. Drive the seal in until it sits against the retainer plate.

13 Apply a smear of lithium based grease to the lips of the other seal, then press it into the right-hand side of the wheel. As this seal sits flush with the hub, it is best to knock it into place using a flat piece of wood **(see illustration)**.

16.10 A socket can be used to drive in the bearing

16.12a Fit the grease seal . . .

16.12b . . . and tap it into place

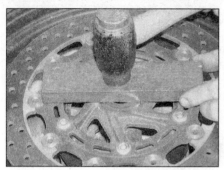

16.13 Using a piece of wood ensures the seal sits flush with the rim

14 Clean off all grease from the brake discs using acetone or brake system cleaner then install the wheel (see Section 14).

Rear wheel bearings

15 Remove the rear wheel (see Section 15). Lift the sprocket coupling out of the wheel, noting how it fits, and remove the rubber dampers **(see illustrations)**.
16 Set the wheel on blocks so as not to allow the weight of the wheel to rest on the brake disc.
17 Lever out the grease seal on the right-hand side of the wheel using a large flat-bladed screwdriver, taking care not to damage the rim of the hub **(see Haynes Hint above) (see illustration)**. Discard the seal if it is damaged or deteriorated.
18 Using a metal rod (preferably a brass drift punch) inserted through the centre of the right-hand bearing, tap evenly around the inner race of the left-hand bearing to drive it from the hub **(see illustrations 16.5a and b)**.

16.17 Lever out the grease seal

16.26b Use a socket to drive out the spacer

16.15a Lift the sprocket coupling out of the wheel . . .

The bearing spacer will also come out.
19 Lay the wheel on its other side so that the right-hand bearing faces down. Drive the bearing out of the wheel using the same technique as above.
20 Refer to Steps 7 to 9 above and check the bearings.
21 Thoroughly clean the hub area of the wheel. First install the left-hand bearing into its recess in the hub, with the marked or sealed side facing outwards. Using the old bearing (if new ones are being fitted), a bearing driver or a socket large enough to contact the outer race of the bearing, drive it in squarely until it's completely seated **(see illustration 16.10)**.
22 Turn the wheel over and install the bearing spacer. Drive the right-hand side bearing into place as described above.
23 Apply a smear of grease to the lips of the new grease seal, and press it into the right-hand side of the wheel, using a seal or bearing driver, a suitable socket or a flat piece of

16.26a Lever out the grease seal

16.27 Drive the bearing out from the inside

16.15b . . . and remove the rubber damper segments

wood to drive it into place if necessary **(see illustrations 16.12a and b and 6.13)**.
24 Clean off all grease from the brake disc using acetone or brake system cleaner. Fit the rubber dampers into the wheel, then install the sprocket coupling assembly **(see illustrations 16.15b and a)**. Install the wheel (see Section 15).

Sprocket coupling bearing

25 Remove the rear wheel (see Section 15). Lift the sprocket coupling out of the wheel, noting how it fits **(see illustration 16.15a)**.
26 Using a large flat-bladed screwdriver lever out the grease seal from the outside of the coupling, taking care not to damage the rim of the coupling **(see Haynes Hint above) (see illustration)**. Discard the seal if it is damaged or deteriorated. Remove the spacer from the inside of the coupling bearing, noting which way round it fits, using a suitable socket to drive it out from the outside if it is tight **(see illustration)**.
27 Support the coupling on blocks of wood and drive the bearing out from the inside using a bearing driver or socket **(see illustration)**.
28 Refer to Steps 7 to 9 above and check the bearings.
29 Thoroughly clean the bearing recess in the coupling then fit the bearing into the outside of the coupling, with the marked or sealed side facing out. Using the old bearing (if a new one is being fitted), a bearing driver or a socket large enough to contact the outer race of the bearing, drive it in until it is completely seated **(see illustration)**.

16.29 A socket can be used to drive in the bearing

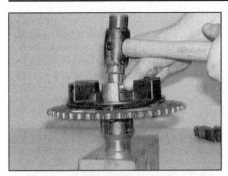

16.30 Support the bearing as shown when driving in the spacer

16.31a Press or drive the seal into the coupling . . .

16.31b . . . using a piece of wood as shown automatically sets the seal flush with the rim

30 Fit the spacer into the inside of the coupling, making sure it is the correct way round and fits squarely into the bearing. Drive it into place if it is tight – support the bearing on a suitable socket to prevent it from being driven out at the same time **(see illustration)**.
31 Apply a smear of grease to the lips of the new seal, and press it into the coupling, using a seal or bearing driver, a suitable socket or a flat piece of wood to drive it into place if necessary **(see illustrations)**. The seal should sit flush with the rim.
32 Check the sprocket coupling/rubber dampers (see Chapter 6).
33 Clean off all grease from the brake disc using acetone or brake system cleaner. Fit the sprocket coupling into the wheel **(see illustration 16.15a)**, then install the wheel (see Section 15).

17 Tyres –
general information and fitting

General information

1 The wheels fitted on all models are designed to take tubeless tyres only. Tyre sizes are given in the Specifications at the beginning of this chapter.
2 Refer to the Daily (pre-ride) checks listed at the beginning of this manual for tyre maintenance.

Fitting new tyres

3 When selecting new tyres, refer to the tyre information label on the swingarm and the tyre options listed in the owners handbook. Ensure that front and rear tyre types are compatible, the correct size and correct speed rating; if necessary seek advice from a Yamaha dealer or tyre fitting specialist **(see illustration)**.
4 It is recommended that tyres are fitted by a motorcycle tyre specialist rather than attempted in the home workshop. This is particularly relevant in the case of tubeless tyres because the force required to break the seal between the wheel rim and tyre bead is substantial, and is usually beyond the capabilities of an individual working with normal tyre levers. Additionally, the specialist will be able to balance the wheels after tyre fitting.
5 Note that punctured tubeless tyres can in some cases be repaired. Seek the advice of a Yamaha dealer or a motorcycle tyre fitting specialist concerning tyre repairs.

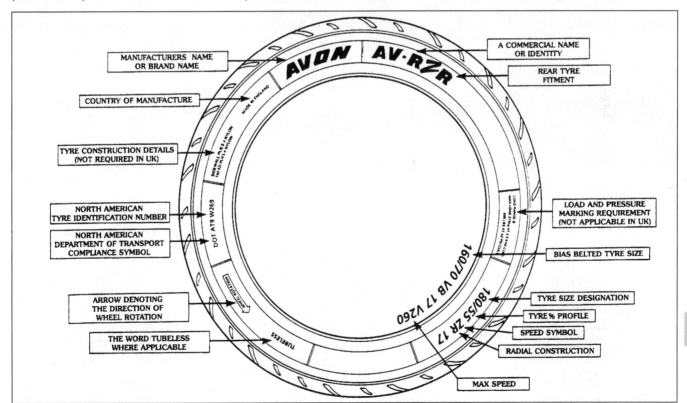

17.3 Common tyre sidewall markings

7

Notes

Chapter 8
Bodywork

Contents

Degrees of difficulty

Easy, suitable for novice with little experience	Fairly easy, suitable for beginner with some experience	Fairly difficult, suitable for competent DIY mechanic	Difficult, suitable for experienced DIY mechanic	Very difficult, suitable for expert DIY or professional

1 General information

This Chapter covers the procedures necessary to remove and install the body parts. Since many service and repair operations on these motorcycles require the removal of the body parts, the procedures are grouped here and referred to from other Chapters.

In the case of damage to the body parts, it is usually necessary to remove the broken component and replace it with a new (or used) one. The material that the body panels are composed of doesn't lend itself to conventional repair techniques. There are however some shops that specialise in 'plastic welding', so it may be worthwhile seeking the advice of one of these specialists before consigning an expensive component to the bin.

When attempting to remove any body panel, first study it closely, noting any fasteners and associated fittings, to be sure of returning everything to its correct place on installation. In some cases the aid of an assistant will be required when removing panels, to help avoid the risk of damage to paintwork. Once the evident fasteners have been removed, try to withdraw the panel as described but DO NOT FORCE IT – if it will not release, check that all fasteners have been removed and try again. Where a panel engages another by means of tabs, be careful not to break the tab or its mating slot or to damage the paintwork. Remember that a few moments of patience at this stage will save you a lot of money in replacing broken fairing panels !

When installing a body panel, first study it closely, noting any fasteners and associated fittings removed with it, to be sure of returning everything to its correct place. Check that all fasteners are in good condition, including all trim nuts or clips and damping/rubber mounts; any of these must be replaced with new ones if faulty before the panel is reassembled. Check also that all mounting brackets are straight and repair or renew them if necessary before attempting to install the panel. Where assistance was required to remove a panel, make sure your assistant is on hand to install it.

Tighten the fasteners securely, but be careful not to overtighten any of them or the panel may break (not always immediately) due to the uneven stress.

2 Seats – removal and installation

Removal

1 On YZF750R models, to remove the passenger seat, insert the ignition key into the seat lock located below the tail light, and turn it clockwise to unlock the seat (see illustration). Lift up the back of the seat and draw it rearwards, noting how the hooks locate under the pegs (see illustration). To remove the rider's seat, first remove the passenger seat. Now pull the release lever back, then lift up the back of the seat and draw it rearwards, noting how the tabs locate under the plate (see illustrations).

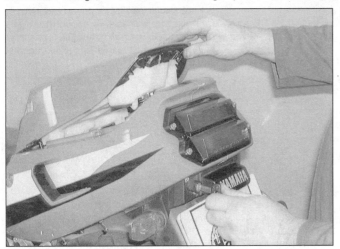

2.1a Turn the key and draw the seat up and back . . .

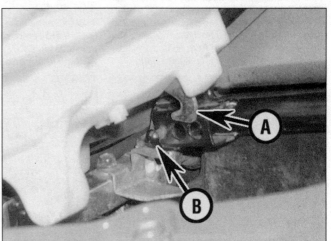

2.1b . . . noting how the hooks (A) locate under the pegs (B)

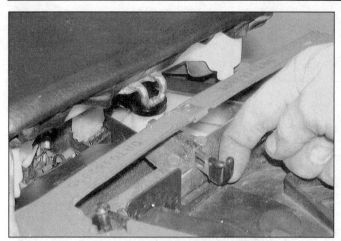

2.1c Pull the lever back to release the seat ...

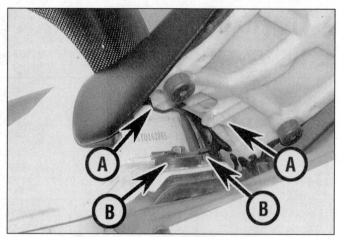

2.1d ... noting how the tab (A) locates under the ends of the plate (B)

2.3a Turn the key and draw the seat up and back ...

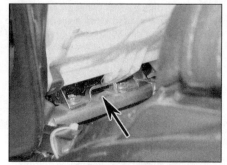

2.3b ... noting how the tab locates in the bracket (arrowed)

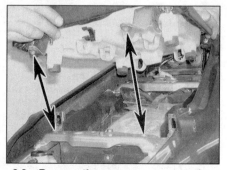

2.3c Remove the passenger seat, noting how it fits (arrowed)

2 On YZF750SP models, remove the seat cowling (see Section 3). If required, remove the screws securing the seat to the cowling and separate them.

3 On YZF1000R models, to remove the rider's seat, insert the ignition key into the seat lock located in the left-hand side cover, and turn it clockwise to unlock the seat (see illustration). Lift up the back of the seat and draw it rearwards, noting how the tab locates into the tank bracket (see illustration). To remove the passenger seat, first remove the rider's seat. Now lift up the front of the passenger seat and draw it forwards, noting how it locates onto the frame cross-piece at the front and how it slots over the tab at the back (see illustration).

Installation

4 Installation is the reverse of removal.

---

3 Fairing and body panels – removal and installation

YZF750R models

Side covers

1 Remove the seats (see Section 2). The side covers are removed as an assembly rather than individually.

2 Remove the bulbholders from the tail light

by turning them anti-clockwise (see illustration).

3 Unscrew the two bolts and the screw on each side and the screw joining the middle section (see illustration). Carefully draw the side covers apart at the front and middle, then draw the assembly back off the bike (see illustration).

4 Installation is the reverse of removal.

Fairing side panels

5 Each panel can be removed individually. Remove the four screws securing the side panel to the lower fairing, and the four screws securing the side panel to the fairing (see illustrations).

3.2 Remove the bulbholders ...

3.3a ... then unscrew the bolts and screws (arrowed) ...

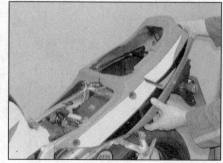

3.3b ... and remove the side cover assembly

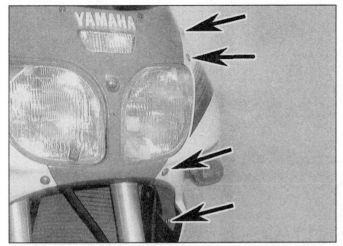

3.5a Side panel to fairing screws (arrowed)

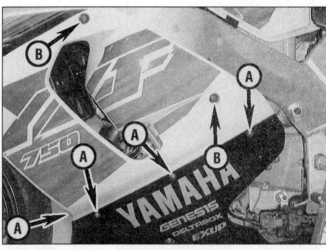

3.5b Side panel to lower fairing screws (A), side panel to frame bolts (B)

6 Disconnect the turn signal wiring connectors **(see illustration)**. If removing the left-hand panel, unscrew the knurled ring securing the speedometer cable to the front wheel and draw the cable out of its guide below the brake caliper **(see illustration)**. On 1993 and 1994 YZF750 models, disconnect the fuel reserve switch wiring connector if removing the left-hand side panel.
7 Remove the two bolts securing the side panel to the frame **(see illustration 3.5a)**.
8 Carefully draw the panel away, noting how it engages with the fairing along its top edge and the lower fairing along its bottom edge. If

removing the left-hand panel, draw the speedometer cable out of its guides on the inside as you remove it **(see illustration)**.
9 Installation is the reverse of removal. Make sure the panel locates correctly with the fairing and lower fairing.

Lower fairing

10 Remove the four screws securing each side of the lower fairing to each side panel, and the two screws securing each side of the lower fairing to the frame **(see illustration)**.
11 Carefully lower the panel and remove it, noting how it engages with the fairing side panels along its top edges **(see illustration)**.

12 Installation is the reverse of removal. Make sure the panel locates correctly with the side panels.

Fairing

13 Remove the fairing side panels (see above).
14 Disconnect the headlight/sidelight and instrument cluster wiring connectors **(see illustration)**.
15 Remove the two bolts securing the front stay to the steering head, and the two bolts securing the rear stay to the tank bracket – use a rag to protect the tank **(see illustrations)**.
16 Carefully draw the fairing assembly to the

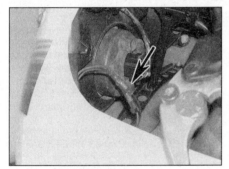

3.6a Disconnect the turn signal wiring connectors (arrowed)

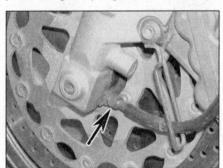

3.6b Unscrew the ring (arrowed) and detach the cable

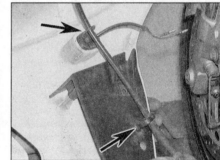

3.8 Draw the cable out of the guides (arrowed)

3.10 Lower fairing fasteners (arrowed)

3.11 Note how it engages with the side panel

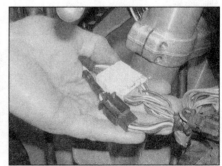

3.14 Disconnect the headlight/sidelight and instrument cluster wiring connectors

8

3.15a Unscrew the front stay bolts (arrowed) . . .

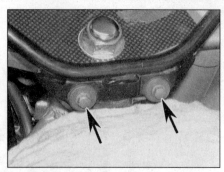

3.15b . . . and the rear stay bolts (arrowed) . . .

3.16 . . . and remove the fairing as described

3.24a Remove the screws (arrowed) . . .

right to disengage it from the steering head and remove it – the headlight and instrument cluster come with the fairing **(see illustration)**. Separate them if required (see Chapter 9).

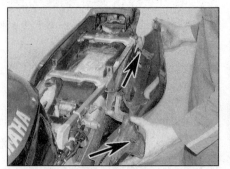

3.24b . . . and release the pegs (arrowed) from the grommets . . .

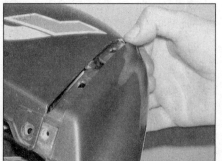

3.24c . . . noting how the back engages

17 Installation is the reverse of removal. Make sure the wiring connectors are correctly and securely connected.

YZF750SP models

Seat cowling

18 Remove the two screws securing each side of the seat cowling and carefully lift it up at the front until the tail light wiring connector becomes accessible, then disconnect it and free the wiring from its tie, and remove the seat cowling.
19 Installation is the reverse of removal.

Fairing side panels

20 The procedure is the same as that for YZF750R models (see above).

Lower fairing

21 The procedure is the same as that for YZF750R models (see above).

Fairing

22 The procedure is the same as that for YZF750R models (see above).

YZF1000R models

Side covers

23 Remove the seats (see Section 2). The side covers are removed individually rather than as an assembly.
24 Remove the three screws securing the side cover, then carefully pull the cover away from the bike to release the two pegs from their rubber grommets **(see illustrations)**. Note how the back of the cover engages with the tail light cover **(see illustration)**.
25 Installation is the reverse of removal.

Fairing side panels

26 Each panel can be removed individually. If removing the left-hand panel, unscrew the knurled ring securing the speedometer cable to the front wheel **(see illustration)**. Remove the screws securing the side panel to the lower fairing, and the screws securing the side panel to the fairing and its trim panel **(see illustration)**.
27 Remove the bolt securing the side panel to the frame **(see illustration 3.26b)**. Carefully

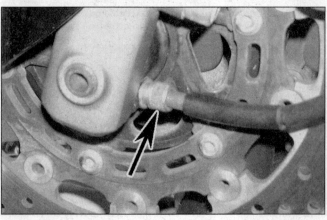

3.26a Unscrew the ring (arrowed) and detach the cable

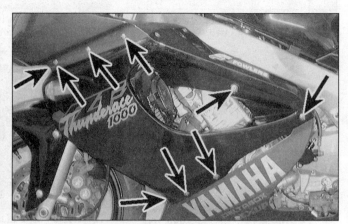

3.26b Fairing side panel fasteners (arrowed)

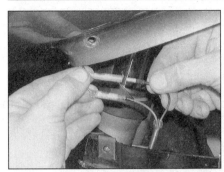

3.27a Disconnect the turn signal wiring connectors

3.27b Draw the cable out of its guide (arrowed)

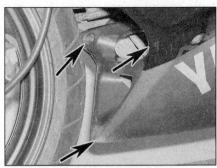

3.29a Remove the screws (arrowed) . . .

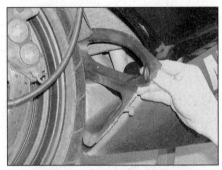

3.29b . . . and the front section

draw the panel away, noting how it engages with the fairing along its top edge and the lower fairing along its bottom edge, and disconnect the turn signal wiring connectors as they become accessible **(see illustration)**. If removing the left-hand panel, draw the speedometer cable out of its guide on the inside as you remove it **(see illustration)**.

28 Installation is the reverse of removal. Make sure the panel locates correctly with the fairing and lower fairing.

Lower fairing

29 Remove the three screws securing the front section of the lower fairing and lift it away, noting how it engages **(see illustrations)**. Remove the three screws securing each side of the lower fairing to each side panel, and the two screws securing each side of the lower fairing to the frame **(see illustrations)**.

30 Carefully lower the panel and remove it, noting how it engages with the fairing side panels along its top edges.

31 Installation is the reverse of removal.

Fairing

32 Remove the fairing side panels (see above).
33 Remove the rear view mirrors (see Section 4).
34 Remove the single screw on each side securing the rear of the fairing trim panel **(see illustration)**.
35 Disconnect the headlight/sidelight and instrument cluster wiring connectors **(see illustration)**.
36 Remove the two nuts securing the stay to the steering head **(see illustration)**.
37 Carefully draw the fairing assembly to the left to disengage the stay bolts from the steering head and remove it – the headlight and instrument cluster come with the fairing

(see illustration). Separate them if required (see Chapter 9).
38 Installation is the reverse of removal. Make sure the wiring connectors are correctly and securely connected.

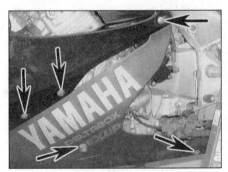

3.29c Remove the screws (arrowed) . . .

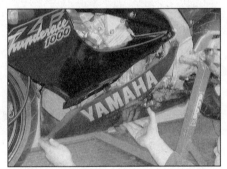

3.29d . . . and remove the lower fairing, noting how it fits

3.34 Remove the trim panel screw (arrowed) on each side

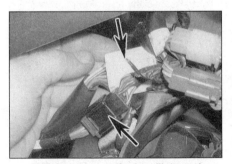

3.35 Disconnect the headlight and instrument cluster wiring connectors (arrowed)

3.36 Unscrew the nuts (arrowed)

3.37 Draw the fairing sideways until the bolts are clear

8

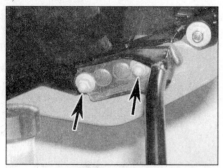

4.1 Unscrew the nuts (arrowed) and remove the mirror

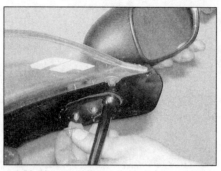

4.2a Unscrew the nuts and remove the mirror . . .

4.2b . . . and the rubber pad if required

5.1 Windshield screws (arrowed) – YZF1000R model shown

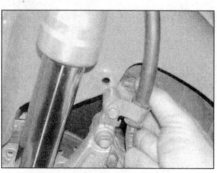

6.1a Unscrew the bolts . . .

6.1b . . . and draw the mudguard forwards

4 Rear view mirrors – removal and installation

Removal

1 On YZF750R and SP models, unscrew the nuts securing each mirror and remove the mirror along with its rubber insulator pad **(see illustration)**.

2 On YZF1000R models, unscrew the two nuts securing each mirror and remove the mirror **(see illustration)**. If required, remove the rubber insulator pad from between the fairing and the stay **(see illustration)**.

Installation

3 Installation is the reverse of removal.

5 Windshield – removal and installation

Removal

1 Remove the six screws securing the windshield to the fairing, taking careful note of the exact location of the washer, nut and protector pieces on the inside of the fairing **(see illustration)**.

Installation

2 Installation is the reverse of removal. Do not overtighten the screws.

6 Front mudguard – removal and installation

Removal

1 On YZF750R and SP models, remove the four bolts securing the mudguard and draw it forward – the rear bolts are accessed from the inside of the mudguard **(see illustrations)**.

2 On YZF1000R models, unscrew the nut and remove the bolt securing the brake hose clamp on each side **(see illustration)**. Remove the four bolts securing the front section of the mudguard and draw it forward **(see illustration)**. Unscrew the four bolts securing the rear section and draw it backwards, noting how it fits **(see illustration)**.

Installation

3 Installation is the reverse of removal.

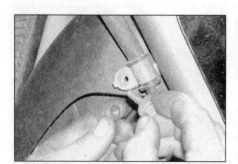

6.2a Detach the brake hose clamp from the mudguard . . .

6.2b . . . then remove the front section . . .

6.2c . . . followed by the rear section

Chapter 9
Electrical system

Contents

Degrees of difficulty

Easy, suitable for novice with little experience	**Fairly easy**, suitable for beginner with some experience	**Fairly difficult**, suitable for competent DIY mechanic	**Difficult**, suitable for experienced DIY mechanic	**Very difficult**, suitable for expert DIY or professional

Specifications

Battery
Capacity
 YZF750R and SP models 12V, 10Ah
 YZF1000R models 12V, 12Ah
Type
 YZF750R and SP models .... YTX12-BS or GTX12-BS
 YZF1000R models YTX14-BS
Charge condition
 Fully charged 12.8V
 Half-charged 12.3V
 Discharged .... 12V or less
Charging time .... until fully charged (12.8V) (see Text)
Current leakage .... 1 mA (max)

Alternator
Nominal output
 YZF750R and SP models .... 12V, 34A @ 3000 rpm
 YZF1000R models .... 12V, 28A @ 5000 rpm
Brush length
 Standard .... 13.7 mm
 Service limit (min) .... 4.7 mm
Stator coil resistance
 YZF750R and SP models .... 0.13 to 0.15 ohms @ 20°C
 YZF1000R models .... 0.19 to 0.21 ohms @ 20°C
Rotor coil resistance .... 2.7 to 3.1 ohms @ 20°C

Regulator/rectifier
Regulated voltage output (no load) .... 14.2 to 14.8V @ 5000 rpm

Oil level sensor resistor
YZF750R and SP models . . . . 6.4 to 9.6 ohms
YZF1000R models . . . . 8.0 ohms

Starter circuit cut-off relay
Resistance
  YZF750R and SP models . . . . 203 to 247 ohms @ 20°C (red/black – black/yellow)

Starter relay
Resistance . . . . 4.2 to 4.6 ohms @ 20°C

Starter motor
Brush length
  Standard . . . . 12.5 mm
  Service limit (min) . . . . 4 mm
Commutator diameter
  Standard . . . . 28 mm
  Service limit (min) . . . . 27 mm
Mica depth . . . . 0.7 mm

Fuses
YZF750R and SP models
  Main 30A
  Headlight 20A
  Signal 15A
  Ignition
    1993 and 1994 models 7.5A
    1995-on models 20A
  Cooling fan . . . . 7.5A x 1 (1993/94), 7.5A x 2 (1995-on)
YZF1000R models
  Main 30A
  Headlight 20A
  Signal 15A
  Ignition 15A
  Cooling fan . . . . 7.5A x 2

Bulbs
Headlight . . . . 35/35W halogen x 2
Sidelight (UK models) . . . . 5W x 1
Brake/tail light
  UK models . . . . 21/5W x 2
  US models . . . . 27/8W x 1
Licence plate light (YZF750R and SP models)
  UK models . . . . 5W x 2
  US models . . . . 3.8W x 1
Turn signal lights
  UK models . . . . 21W x 4
  US models . . . . 27/8W x 2 (front with running light), 27W x 2 (rear)
Instrument lights . . . . 1.7W x 4
Turn signal indicator light 3.4W
Neutral indicator light 3.4W
High beam indicator light 3.4W
Oil level warning light 3.4W
Fuel level warning light 3.4W

Torque wrench settings
Oil level sensor bolts . . . . 7 Nm
Starter motor bolts . . . . 10 Nm
Alternator assembly bolts . . . . 25 Nm

1 General information

All models have a 12 volt electrical system charged by a three-phase alternator with an integral regulator/rectifier.

The regulator maintains the charging system output within the specified range to prevent overcharging, and the rectifier converts the ac (alternating current) output of the alternator to dc (direct current) to power the lights and other components and to charge the battery. The alternator rotor is mounted in the top of the crankcase and is driven off the crankshaft by a Hy-Vo chain.

The starter motor is mounted on the top of the crankcase. The starting system includes the motor, the battery, the relay and the various wires and switches. If the engine kill switch is in the 'RUN' position and the ignition (main) switch is ON, the starter relay allows the starter motor to operate only if the transmission is in neutral (neutral switch on) or, if the transmission is in gear, with the clutch lever pulled into the handlebar and the sidestand up.

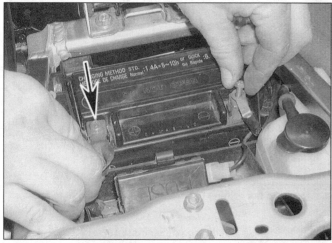

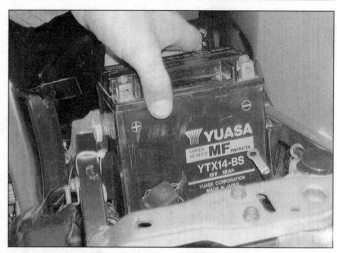

3.2a Disconnect the negative terminal first, then the positive (arrowed)

3.2b Lift the battery out of its box

Note: *Keep in mind that electrical parts, once purchased, cannot be returned. To avoid unnecessary expense, make very sure the faulty component has been positively identified before buying a replacement part.*

2 Electrical system – fault finding

⚠️ *Warning: To prevent the risk of short circuits, the ignition (main) switch must always be OFF and the battery negative (–ve) terminal should be disconnected before any of the bike's other electrical components are disturbed. Don't forget to reconnect the terminal securely once work is finished or if battery power is needed for circuit testing.*

1 A typical electrical circuit consists of an electrical component, the switches, relays, etc. related to that component and the wiring and connectors that hook the component to both the battery and the frame. To aid in locating a problem in any electrical circuit, refer to the *Wiring Diagrams* at the end of this Chapter.

2 Before tackling any troublesome electrical circuit, first study the wiring diagram (see end of Chapter) thoroughly to get a complete picture of what makes up that individual circuit. Trouble spots, for instance, can often be narrowed down by noting if other components related to that circuit are operating properly or not. If several components or circuits fail at one time, chances are the fault lies in the fuse or earth (ground) connection, as several circuits are often routed through the same fuse and earth (ground) connections.

3 Electrical problems often stem from simple causes, such as loose or corroded connections or a blown fuse. Prior to any electrical fault finding, always visually check the condition of the fuse, wires and connections in the problem circuit. Intermittent failures can be especially frustrating, since you can't always duplicate the failure when it's convenient to test. In such situations, a good practice is to clean all connections in the affected circuit, whether or not they appear to be good. All of the connections and wires should also be wiggled to check for looseness which can cause intermittent failure.

4 If testing instruments are going to be utilised, use the wiring diagram to plan where you will make the necessary connections in order to accurately pinpoint the trouble spot.

5 The basic tools needed for electrical fault finding include a battery and bulb test circuit, a continuity tester, a test light, and a jumper wire. A multimeter capable of reading volts, ohms and amps is also very useful as an alternative to the above, and is necessary for performing more extensive tests and checks.

> **HAYNES HINT** *Refer to Fault Finding Equipment in the Reference section for details of how to use electrical test equipment.*

3 Battery – removal, installation, inspection and maintenance

Caution: Be extremely careful when handling or working around the battery. The electrolyte is very caustic and an explosive gas (hydrogen) is given off when the battery is charging.

Removal and installation

1 Remove the rider's seat (see Chapter 8).

2 Unscrew the negative (–ve) terminal bolt first and disconnect the lead from the battery **(see illustration)**. Lift up the insulating cover to access the positive (+ve) terminal, then unscrew the bolt and disconnect the lead. Release the battery strap or holder, where fitted, and remove the battery from the bike **(see illustration)**.

3 On installation, clean the battery terminals and lead ends with a wire brush or knife and emery paper. Reconnect the leads, connecting the positive (+ve) terminal first.

> **HAYNES HINT** *Battery corrosion can be kept to a minimum by applying a layer of petroleum jelly to the terminals after the cables have been connected.*

4 Install the seat (see Chapter 8).

Inspection and maintenance

5 The battery fitted on all models is of the maintenance-free (sealed) type, therefore requiring no specific maintenance. However, the following checks should still be regularly performed.

6 Check the battery terminals and leads for tightness and corrosion. If corrosion is evident, unscrew the terminal bolts and disconnect the leads from the battery, disconnecting the negative (–ve) terminal first, and clean the terminals and lead ends with a wire brush or knife and emery paper. Reconnect the leads, connecting the negative (–ve) terminal last, and apply a thin coat of petroleum jelly to the connections to slow further corrosion.

7 The battery case should be kept clean to prevent current leakage, which can discharge the battery over a period of time (especially when it sits unused). Wash the outside of the case with a solution of baking soda and water. Rinse the battery thoroughly, then dry it.

8 Look for cracks in the case and renew the battery if any are found. If acid has been spilled on the frame or battery box, neutralise it with a baking soda and water solution, dry it thoroughly, then touch up any damaged paint.

9 If the motorcycle sits unused for long periods of time, disconnect the leads from the battery terminals, negative (–ve) terminal first.

9

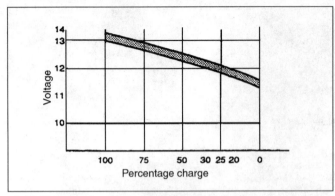

3.10 Measure the voltage to assess the condition of the battery from the chart

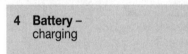

4.1 Measure the voltage to determine the charging time required

Refer to Section 4 and charge the battery once every month to six weeks.

10 The condition of the battery can be assessed by measuring the voltage present at the battery terminals, and comparing the figure against the chart **(see illustration)**. Connect the voltmeter positive (+ve) probe to the battery positive (+ve) terminal, and the negative (–ve) probe to the battery negative (–ve) terminal. When fully charged there should be 12.8 volts (or more) present. If the voltage falls below 12.3 volts the battery must be removed, disconnecting the negative (–ve) terminal first, and recharged as described in Section 4.

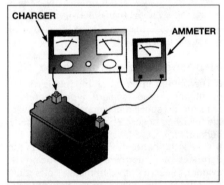

4.2 If the charger doesn't have an ammeter built in, connect one in series as shown. DO NOT connect the ammeter between the battery terminals or it will be ruined

4 Battery – charging

Caution: Be extremely careful when handling or working around the battery. The electrolyte is very caustic and an explosive gas (hydrogen) is given off when the battery is charging.

1 Remove the battery (see Section 3). If not already done, refer to Section 3, Step 10, and check the open circuit voltage of the battery. Refer to the chart and read off the charging time required according to the voltage reading taken **(see illustration)**.

2 Connect the charger to the battery, making sure that the positive (+ve) lead on the charger is connected to the positive (+ve) terminal on the battery, and the negative (–ve) lead is connected to the negative (–ve) terminal. The battery should be charged for the specified time, or until the voltage across the terminals reaches 12.8V (allow the battery to stabilise for 30 minutes after charging before taking a voltage reading). Exceeding this can cause the battery to overheat, buckling the plates and rendering it useless. Few owners will have access to an expensive current controlled charger, so if a normal domestic charger is used check that after a possible initial peak, the charge rate falls to a safe level **(see illustration)**. If the battery becomes hot

during charging **stop**. Further charging will cause damage. **Note:** *In emergencies the battery can be charged at a higher rate of around 3.0 amps for a period of 1 hour. However, this is not recommended and the low amp charge is by far the safer method of charging the battery.*

3 If the recharged battery discharges rapidly when left disconnected it is likely that an internal short caused by physical damage or sulphation has occurred. A new battery will be required. A sound item will tend to lose its charge at about 1% per day.

4 Install the battery (see Section 3).

5 If the motorcycle sits unused for long periods of time, charge the battery once every month to six weeks and leave it disconnected.

5 Fuses – check and renewal

1 The electrical system is protected by fuses of different ratings. All except the main fuse are housed in the fusebox, which is located under the rider's seat **(see illustrations)**. On YZF750R and SP models, the main fuse is mounted on the front of the battery box below the fuel tank **(see illustration)**. On YZF1000R models, the main fuse is integral with the starter relay, which is located behind the left-hand side cover **(see illustration)**.

5.1a Fusebox – YZF750R and SP models

5.1b Fusebox – YZF1000R models

5.1c Main fuse (arrowed) – YZF750R and SP models

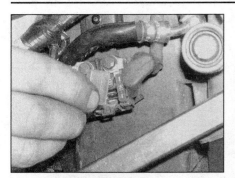

5.1d Main fuse – YZF1000R models

5.2 Unclip the lid to access the fusebox fuses

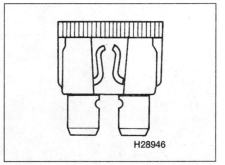

5.3 A blown fuse can be identified by a break in its element

2 To access the fusebox fuses, remove the rider's seat (see Chapter 8) and unclip the fusebox lid **(see illustration)**. To access the main fuse on YZF750R and SP models remove the fuel tank (see Chapter 4) **(see illustration 5.1c)**. On YZF1000R models remove the left-hand side cover (see Chapter 8), then remove the fuse cover from the relay **(see illustration 5.1d)**.

3 The fuses can be removed and checked visually. If you can't pull the fuse out with your fingertips, use a suitable pair of pliers. A blown fuse is easily identified by a break in the element **(see illustration)**, or can be tested for continuity using an ohmmeter or continuity tester – if there is no continuity, it has blown. Each fuse is clearly marked with its rating and must only be replaced by a fuse of the same rating. Spare fuses are housed in the fusebox, and on YZF1000R models a spare main fuse is housed in the starter relay. If a spare fuse is used, always replace it with a new one so that a spare of each rating is carried on the bike at all times.

⚠ **Warning: Never put in a fuse of a higher rating or bridge the terminals with any other substitute, however temporary it may be. Serious damage may be done to the circuit, or a fire may start.**

4 If a fuse blows, be sure to check the wiring circuit very carefully for evidence of a short-circuit. Look for bare wires and chafed, melted or burned insulation. If the fuse is renewed before the cause is located, the new fuse will blow immediately.

5 Occasionally a fuse will blow or cause an open-circuit for no obvious reason. Corrosion of the fuse ends and fusebox terminals may occur and cause poor fuse contact. If this happens, remove the corrosion with a wire brush or emery paper, then spray the fuse end and terminals with electrical contact cleaner.

6 Lighting system –
check

1 The battery provides power for operation of the headlight, tail light, brake light, turn signals and instrument cluster lights. If none of the lights operate, always check battery voltage before proceeding. Low battery voltage indicates either a faulty battery or a defective charging system. Refer to Section 3 for battery checks and Sections 30 and 31 for charging system tests. Also, check the condition of the fuses (see Section 5). When checking for a blown filament in a bulb, it is advisable to back up a visual check with a continuity test of the filament as it is not always apparent that a bulb has blown. When testing for continuity, remember that on tail light and turn signal bulbs it is often the metal body of the bulb which is the ground or earth.

Headlight

2 If the headlight fails to work, check the bulbs first (see Section 7), then the fuse (see Section 5), and the wiring connector, then check for battery voltage at the yellow (HI beam) and/or green (LO beam) wire terminal on the supply side of the headlight wiring connector. If voltage is present, check the earth (ground) circuit for an open or poor connection.

3 If no voltage is indicated, check the wiring between the headlight, the dimmer switch, lighting switch (European models) and the ignition switch, then check the switches themselves.

Tail light

4 If the tail light fails to work, check the bulb(s) and the bulb terminals and wiring connector first (see Section 9), then the headlight fuse, then check for battery voltage at the blue/red wire terminal on the supply side of the tail light wiring connector, with the ignition switch and lighting switch ON. If voltage is present, check for continuity between the wiring connector terminals on the tail light side of the wiring connector and the corresponding terminals in the bulbholder. If voltage and continuity are present, check the earth (ground) circuit for an open or poor connection.

5 If no voltage is indicated, check the wiring between the tail light, the lighting switch (European models) and the ignition switch, then check the switches themselves.

Brake light

6 If the brake light fails to work, check the bulb(s) and the bulb terminals and wiring connector first (see Section 9), then the signal fuse, then check for battery voltage at the yellow wire terminal on the supply side of the tail light wiring connector, with the ignition switch ON and the brake lever or pedal applied. If voltage is present, check the earth (ground) circuit for an open or poor connection.

7 If no voltage is indicated, check the brake light switches (see Section 14), then the wiring between the tail light and the switches.

Instrument and warning lights

8 See Section 17 for instrument and warning light bulb renewal.

Turn signal lights

9 If one light fails to work, check the bulb and the bulb terminals first, then the wiring connectors. If none of the turn signals work, first check the signal fuse.

10 If the fuse is good, see Section 11 for the turn signal circuit check.

7 Headlight bulb
and sidelight bulb –
renewal

Note: *The headlight bulb is of the quartz-halogen type. Do not touch the bulb glass as skin acids will shorten the bulb's service life. If the bulb is accidentally touched, it should be wiped carefully when cold with a rag soaked in methylated spirit and dried before fitting.*

⚠ *Warning: Allow the bulb time to cool before removing it if the headlight has just been on.*

Headlight

1 On YZF1000R models, for best access to the headlight bulbs, remove the fairing side panel on the relevant side (see Chapter 8), but note that access is possible, albeit fiddly, with it in place.

7.2a Disconnect the wiring connector . . .

7.2b . . . and remove the dust cover

2 Disconnect the relevant wiring connector from the back of the headlight assembly and remove the rubber dust cover, noting how it fits (see illustrations).
3 Release the bulb retaining clip, noting how it fits, then remove the bulb (see illustrations).
4 Fit the new bulb, bearing in mind the information in the Note above. Make sure the tabs on the bulb fit correctly in the slots in the bulb housing, and secure it in position with the retaining clip.
5 Install the dust cover, making sure it is correctly seated and with the 'TOP' mark at the top, and connect the wiring connector (see illustrations 7.2b and a).
6 Check the operation of the headlight.

> **HAYNES HiNT** *Always use a paper towel or dry cloth when handling new bulbs to prevent injury if the bulb should break and to increase bulb life.*

Sidelight

7 On YZF750R and SP models, remove the screws securing the lens and remove the lens (see illustrations). Carefully pull the bulb from the bulbholder (see illustrations). Install the new bulb in the holder, then install the lens and tighten the screws – do not overtighten them as the lens or threads could be damaged.
8 On YZF1000R models, the bulbholder is accessed via the underside of the fairing. Turn it anti-clockwise to release it and draw it out of the headlight (see illustration).

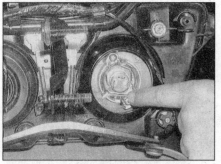

7.3a Release the clip . . .

7.3b . . . and remove the bulb

7.7a Remove the screws (arrowed) . . .

7.7b . . . and detach the lens

7.7c Pull the bulb out of the bulbholder

7.8a Release the bulbholder from the base of the headlight

Carefully pull the bulb out of the holder **(see illustration)**. Install the new bulb, then install the bulbholder and turn it clockwise to lock it in place.

9 Check the operation of the sidelight.

8 Headlight assembly – removal and installation

Removal

1 Remove the fairing (see Chapter 8), then remove the instrument cluster from the fairing (see Section 15).

2 On YZF1000R models, release the turn signal wiring from the clips on the fairing **(see illustration)**. Disconnect the headlight wiring connectors and release the sidelight bulbholder from the headlight **(see illustration)**. Remove the four screws securing the fairing stay and remove the stay along with the wiring **(see illustration)**.

3 Remove the four screws securing the headlight assembly and lift it out of the fairing **(see illustrations)**.

Installation

4 Installation is the reverse of removal. Make sure all the wiring is correctly connected and secured. Check the operation of the headlight and sidelight. Check the headlight aim (see Chapter 1).

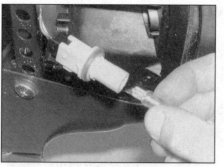

7.8b ... then remove the bulb from the holder

9 Brake/tail light/ licence plate bulb – renewal

1 On YZF750R and YZF1000R models, remove the passenger seat (see Chapter 8). On YZF750SP models, remove the seat cowling (see Chapter 8). On YZF750R and SP models there is a separate licence plate light, while on YZF1000R models the tail light bulbs also illuminate the licence plate.

Brake/tail light bulbs

2 Turn the bulbholder anti-clockwise and withdraw it from the tail light **(see illustration)**. Push the bulb into the holder and twist it anti-clockwise to remove it **(see illustration)**.

3 Check the socket terminals for corrosion

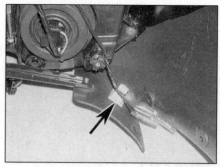

8.2a Release the wiring from the clip (arrowed) on each side

and clean them if necessary. Line up the pins of the new bulb with the slots in the socket, then push the bulb in and turn it clockwise until it locks into place. **Note:** *The pins on the bulb are offset so it can only be installed one way. It is a good idea to use a paper towel or dry cloth when handling the new bulb to prevent injury if the bulb should break and to increase bulb life.*

4 Fit the bulbholder into the tail light and turn it clockwise to secure it, then install the seat or cowling (see Chapter 8).

Licence plate bulb

5 To renew the licence plate light on YZF750R and SP models, first remove the tail light assembly (see Section 10). Unscrew the nuts securing the licence plate light and draw it off the back, then remove the backing plate,

8.2b Disconnect the headlight wiring connectors (arrowed) and remove the sidelight bulbholder

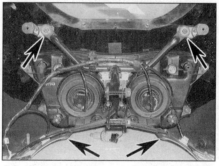

8.2c Remove the screws (arrowed) and lift the stay out of the fairing

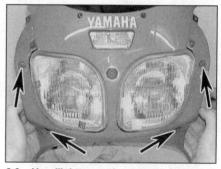

8.3a Headlight mounting screws (arrowed) – YZF750R and SP models

8.3b Headlight mounting screws (arrowed) – YZF1000R models

9.2a Release the bulbholder from the taillight ...

9.2b ... then release the bulb from the holder

9.5a Unscrew the nuts (arrowed) . . .

9.5b . . . and detach the licence plate light

9.5c Draw out the bulbholder . . .

noting how it fits **(see illustrations)**. Draw out the bulbholders, then pull the relevant bulb out of the holder **(see illustrations)**. Fit the new bulb, then install the light and the tail light assembly.

10 Tail light assembly – removal and installation

Removal

1 On YZF750R models, remove the pillion seat, and on YZF750SP models, remove the seat cowling (see Chapter 8). Remove the bulbholders from the tail light by turning them anti-clockwise **(see illustration)**. Unscrew the bolts securing the tail light and draw it out the back **(see illustrations)**.

2 On YZF1000R models, remove the left-hand side cover (see Chapter 8). Either remove the bulbholders from the tail light by turning them anti-clockwise **(see illustration 9.2a)** or disconnect the tail light assembly wiring connector **(see illustration)**. Remove the screw securing the top cover to

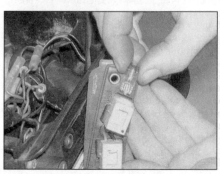

9.5d . . . and fit the new bulb

the right-hand side cover, and the two bolts securing the tail light bracket, then remove the tail light, bracket and top cover as an assembly **(see illustrations)**. Remove the bolts securing the tail light to the bracket and separate them **(see illustration)**.

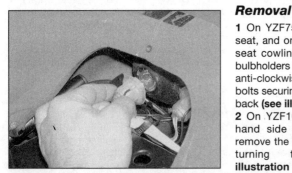

10.1a Release the bulbholders from the taillight . . .

10.1b . . . then unscrew the bolts (arrowed) . . .

10.1c . . . and remove the taillight

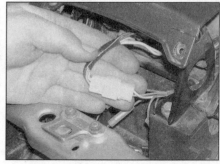

10.2a Taillight wiring connector

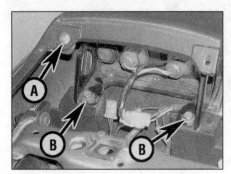

10.2b Remove the screw (A) and the bolts (B) . . .

10.2c . . . then remove the taillight/bracket/top cover assembly, noting how it fits

10.2d Unscrew the bolts (arrowed) and separate the taillight from the bracket/top cover

Installation

3 Installation is the reverse of removal. Check the operation of the tail light and the brake light.

11 Turn signal circuit – check

1 Most turn signal problems are the result of a burned out bulb or corroded socket. This is especially true when the turn signals function properly in one direction, but fail to flash in the other direction. Check the bulbs and the sockets (see Section 12) and the wiring connectors. Also, check the signal fuse (see Section 5) and the switch (see Section 20).
2 The battery provides power for operation of the turn signal lights, so if they do not operate, also check the battery voltage. Low battery voltage indicates either a faulty battery or a defective charging system. Refer to Section 3 for battery checks and Sections 30 and 31 for charging system tests.
3 If the bulbs, sockets, connectors, fuse, switch and battery are good, check the turn signal relay, which is mounted under the fuel tank **(see illustrations)**. Remove the fuel tank for access (see Chapter 4).
4 Check for voltage at the brown wire in the relay wiring connector with the ignition ON. If no voltage is present, using the appropriate wiring diagram at the end of this Chapter check the wiring between the relay and the ignition (main) switch. If voltage was present,

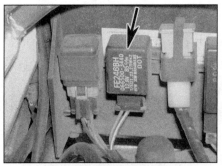

11.3a Turn signal relay – YZF750R and SP models

check for voltage at the brown/white wire with the ignition ON, and with the switch turned to either LEFT or RIGHT. If no voltage is present, renew the relay. If voltage was present, check the wiring between the relay, turn signal switch and turn signal lights for continuity. Turn the ignition OFF when the check is complete.

12 Turn signal bulbs – renewal

1 Remove the screw securing the turn signal lens and remove the lens, noting how it fits **(see illustration)**.
2 Push the bulb into the holder and twist it anti-clockwise to remove it **(see illustration)**. Check the socket terminals for corrosion and clean them if necessary. Line up the pins of

11.3b Turn signal relay – YZF1000R models

the new bulb with the slots in the socket, then push the bulb in and turn it clockwise until it locks into place.
3 Fit the lens onto the holder, making sure the tab locates correctly **(see illustration)**. Do not overtighten the screw as the lens or threads could be damaged.

13 Turn signal assemblies – removal and installation

Front

Removal

1 Remove the fairing side panel (see Chapter 8). On YZF1000R models, remove the inner panel from the side panel – it is secured by four screws **(see illustration)**.
2 Remove the screw securing the turn signal to the inside of the fairing and remove the mounting plate **(see illustration)**. Remove the turn signal from the fairing, noting how it fits. Take care not to snag the wiring as you pull it through.

Installation

3 Installation is the reverse of removal. Make sure the wiring is correctly routed and securely connected. Check the operation of the turn signals.

Rear

Removal

4 On YZF1000R models, remove the pillion

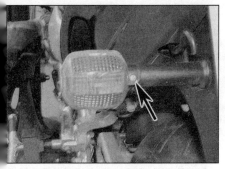

12.1 Remove the screw (arrowed) and detach the lens . . .

12.2 . . . and remove the bulb

13.2 Remove the mounting plate screw (arrowed) and withdraw the signal

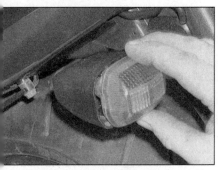

12.3 Make sure the tab locates correctly when fitting the lens

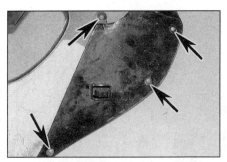

13.1 On YZF1000R models, undo the screws (arrowed) and remove the inner panel

9

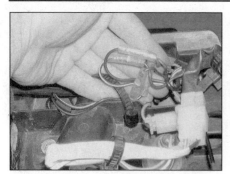

13.5a Rear turn signal wiring connectors – YZF750R and SP models

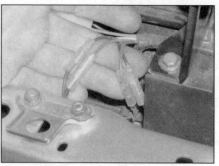

13.5b Rear turn signal wiring connectors – YZF1000R models

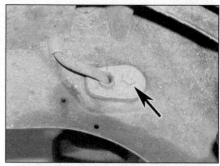

13.6 The turn signal is secured by a nut (arrowed) on the inside of the mudguard

seat, on YZF750R models remove the side covers, and on YZF750SP models remove the seat cowling (see Chapter 8).

5 Trace the wiring back from the turn signal and disconnect it at the connectors **(see illustrations)**.

6 Unscrew the nut securing the turn signal to the inside of the mudguard and remove the mounting plate **(see illustration)**. Remove the turn signal from the mudguard, taking care not to snag the wiring as you pull it through.

Installation

7 Installation is the reverse of removal. Make sure the wiring is correctly routed and securely connected. Check the operation of the turn signals.

14 Brake light switches – check and renewal

Circuit check

1 Before checking the switches, check the brake light circuit (see Section 6, Step 6).

2 The front brake light switch is mounted on the underside of the brake master cylinder. Disconnect the wiring connectors from the switch **(see illustration)**. Using a continuity tester, connect the probes to the terminals of the switch. With the brake lever at rest, there should be no continuity. With the brake lever applied, there should be continuity. If the switch does not behave as described, replace it with a new one.

3 The rear brake light switch is mounted on the inside of the frame on the right-hand side, above the brake pedal **(see illustration)**. Remove the fuel tank to access the wiring connector (see Chapter 4). Trace the wiring from the switch and disconnect it at the connector **(see illustrations)**. Using a continuity tester, connect the probes to the terminals on the switch side of the wiring connector. With the brake pedal at rest, there should be no continuity. With the brake pedal applied, there should be continuity. If the switch does not behave as described, replace it with a new one.

4 If the switches are good, check for voltage at the brown wire terminal on the connector with the ignition switch ON – there should be

battery voltage. If there's no voltage present, check the wiring between the switch and the ignition switch (see the *Wiring Diagrams* at the end of this Chapter).

Switch renewal

Front brake light switch

5 The switch is mounted on the underside of the brake master cylinder. Disconnect the wiring connectors from the switch **(see illustration 14.2)**.

6 Remove the single screw and washers securing the switch to the bottom of the master cylinder and remove the switch.

7 Installation is the reverse of removal. The switch isn't adjustable.

Rear brake light switch

8 The switch is mounted on the inside of the frame on the right-hand side, above the brake pedal **(see illustration 14.3a)**. Remove the fuel tank to access the wiring connector (see Chapter 4). Trace the wiring from the switch and disconnect it at the connector **(see illustration 14.3b or c)**. Free the wiring from any clips or ties and feed it through to the switch.

9 Detach the lower end of the switch spring from the brake pedal, then unscrew and remove the switch.

10 Installation is the reverse of removal. Make sure the brake light is activated just before the rear brake pedal takes effect. If adjustment is necessary, hold the switch and turn the adjusting ring on the switch body until the brake light is activated when required.

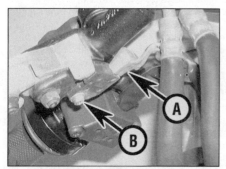

14.2 Front brake switch wiring connectors (A) and mounting screw (B)

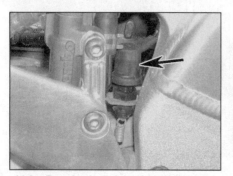

14.3a Rear brake light switch (arrowed) – YZF1000R model shown

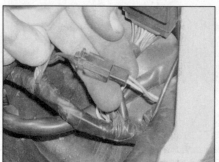

14.3b Rear brake switch wiring connector – YZF750R and SP models

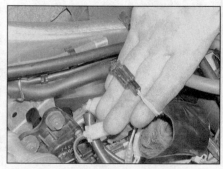

14.3c Rear brake switch wiring connector – YZF1000R models

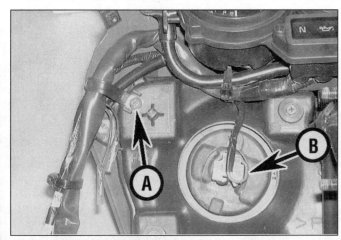

15.2a Release the wiring from the clip (A) and disconnect each headlight wiring connector (B)

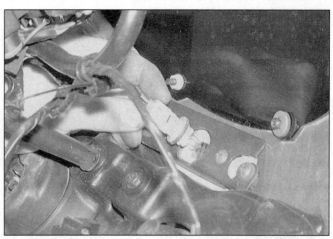

15.2b Release the sidelight bulbholder from the light

15.2c Remove the four screws (arrowed) on the inside of the fairing . . .

15.2d . . . and the screw on the front (arrowed) . . .

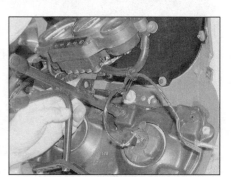

15.2e . . . and remove the stay and instrument cluster together

15 Instrument cluster and speedometer cable –
removal and installation

Instrument cluster

Removal

1 Remove the fairing (see Chapter 8).

2 On YZF750R and SP models, release the instrument cluster and headlight wiring from its clip on the fairing and disconnect the headlight wiring connectors (see illustration). Also release the sidelight bulbholder from the light (see illustration). Remove the five screws securing the fairing stay to the fairing and remove it along with the instrument cluster (see illustrations). Unscrew the

knurled ring securing the speedometer cable to the back of the speedometer and detach the cable (see illustration). Free the instrument cluster wiring from any ties, then unscrew the two nuts securing the cluster to the stay and remove it.

3 On YZF1000R models, free the instrument cluster wiring from any clips and ties (see illustration). Remove the screws securing the

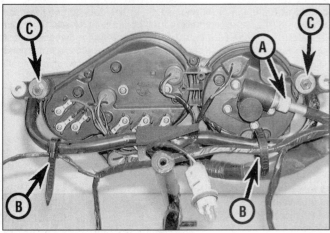

15.2f Unscrew the ring (A) and detach the cable, then free the wiring from its ties (B), unscrew the nuts (C) and remove the instruments

15.3a Release the wiring from its clips and ties (arrowed) . . .

9

15.3b . . . then remove the trim panel screws (arrowed) . . .

15.3c . . . and the lower windshield screws (arrowed) . . .

15.3d . . . and lift the instrument cluster and trim panel out of the fairing

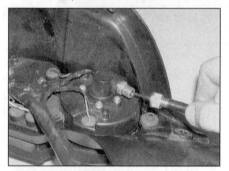

15.3e Detach the speedometer cable . . .

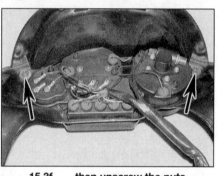

15.3f . . . then unscrew the nuts (arrowed) . . .

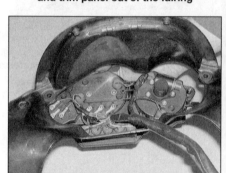

15.3g . . . and remove the instruments from the front of the panel

fairing trim panel to the fairing, and the two screws securing the bottom of the windshield **(see illustrations)**. Lift the instrument cluster along with the trim panel out of the fairing **(see illustration)**. Unscrew the knurled ring securing the speedometer cable to the back of the speedometer and detach the cable **(see illustration)**. Unscrew the two nuts securing the instrument cluster to the trim panel and draw the cluster out of the front **(see illustrations)**.

Installation

4 Installation is the reverse of removal. On YZF1000R models, make sure the trim panel locates correctly in the fairing **(see illustration)**. Make sure that the speedometer cable and wiring connectors are correctly routed and secured.

Speedometer cable

Removal

5 Remove the fairing (see Chapter 8), then separate the instrument cluster from it (see above) – there is no need to separate the instrument cluster from either the fairing stay (YZF750R and SP) or trim panel (YZF1000R).
6 Unscrew the knurled ring securing the speedometer cable to the back of the speedometer and detach the cable **(see illustration 15.2f or 15.3e)**.

Installation

7 Connect the cable upper end to the speedometer and tighten the retaining ring securely **(see illustration 15.2f or 15.3e)**.
8 Install the fairing (see Chapter 8).
9 Check that the cable doesn't restrict steering movement or interfere with any other components.

16 Instruments –
check and renewal

Speedometer

Check

1 Special instruments are required to properly check the operation of this meter. If it is believed to be faulty, take the motorcycle to a Yamaha dealer for assessment. Before doing this, make sure that the fault is not due to a faulty cable or drive gear, either at the front wheel or at the instruments (see Step 2).

2 Remove the speedometer cable (see Section 15), and check that it is not seized or broken. Replace it with a new one if necessary. Remove the front wheel (see Chapter 7), and check that the drive gear rotates freely. Clean and re-grease it. Replace it with a new one if necessary. Similarly check the driven gear on the back of the instrument cluster.

Renewal

3 Remove the instrument cluster (see Section 15).
4 Remove the casing screws from the back of the cluster and lift off the front cover assembly **(see illustration)**. Unscrew the odometer trip knob **(see illustration)**. Remove the two screws securing the speedometer gearbox and lift off the box **(see illustration)**. Remove the two screws securing the speedometer to the casing. Carefully withdraw the speedometer from the front.

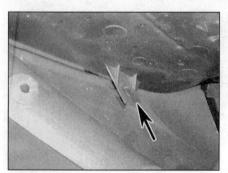

15.4 Make sure the trim panel engages correctly with the fairing (arrowed)

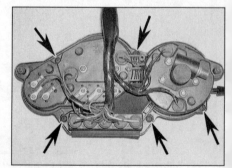

16.4a Remove the screws (arrowed) and lift off the front cover

16.4b Unscrew the trip knob (arrowed)

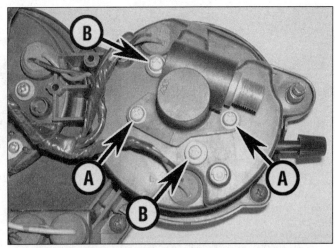

16.4c Remove the gearbox housing screws (A) and the
instrument screws (B) and remove the speedometer

5 Installation is the reverse of removal.

Tachometer

Check

6 Special instruments are required to properly check the operation of this meter. If it is believed to be faulty, take the motorcycle to a Yamaha dealer for assessment.

Renewal

7 Remove the instrument cluster (see Section 15).

8 Remove the casing screws from the back of the cluster and lift off the front cover assembly **(see illustrations 16.4a)**. Remove the screws securing the three tachometer wires and detach the wires, noting which fits where **(see illustration)**. Remove the two screws securing the tachometer to the casing. Carefully withdraw the tachometer from the front.

9 Installation is the reverse of removal. Make

sure the wiring is correctly connected. As you look at the back of the cluster, the brown wire is for the left-hand terminal, the black for the middle terminal, and the grey for the right-hand terminal **(see illustration 16.8)**.

Coolant temperature gauge

Check

10 See Chapter 3.

Renewal

11 Remove the instrument cluster (see Section 15).

12 Remove the casing screws from the back of the cluster and lift off the front cover assembly **(see illustrations 16.4a)**.

13 Remove the screws securing the three temperature gauge wires and detach the wires, noting which fits where **(see illustration)**.

14 Carefully withdraw the temperature gauge from the front.

15 Installation is the reverse of removal. Make sure the wiring is correctly connected. As you look at the back of the cluster, the green/red wire is for the top terminal, the black for the left-hand terminal, and the brown for the right-hand terminal **(see illustration 16.13)**.

17 Instrument and warning light bulbs – renewal

1 Remove the fairing (see Chapter 8). Some of the bulbs are accessible with the instrument cluster in situ in the fairing, while others can only be accessed after separating the instrument cluster and either the fairing stay (YZF750R and SP) or trim panel (YZF1000R) from it (see Section 15).

2 Carefully pull the bulbholder out of the instrument casing, then pull the bulb out of

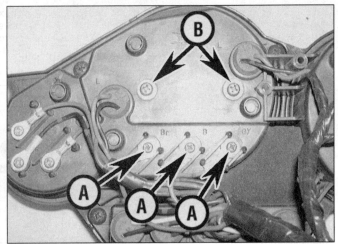

16.8 Remove the screws (A) and detach the wires, then remove
the instrument screws (B)

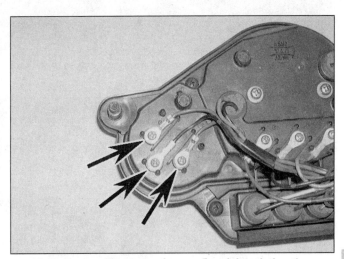

16.13 Remove the screws (arrowed) and detach the wires

9

17.2a Pull out the bulbholder . . .

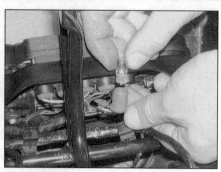

17.2b . . . and remove the bulb

the bulbholder **(see illustrations)**. If the socket contacts are dirty or corroded, scrape them clean and spray with electrical contact cleaner before a new bulb is installed. Carefully push the new bulb into the holder and push the holder into the casing.

18.1 Disconnect the ignition switch wiring connectors

3 Install the instrument cluster and/or fairing as required (see Section 15 and/or Chapter 8).

18 Ignition (main) switch –
check, removal and installation

⚠️ **Warning: To prevent the risk of short circuits, remove the seat and disconnect the battery negative (–ve) lead before making any ignition (main) switch checks.**

Check

1 Remove the fairing (see Chapter 8). Trace the ignition (main) switch wiring back from the base of the switch and disconnect it at the connectors **(see illustration)**. Make the checks on the switch side of the connector.
2 Using an ohmmeter or a continuity tester,

check the continuity of the connector terminal pairs (see the *Wiring Diagrams* at the end of this Chapter). Continuity should exist between the terminals connected by a solid line on the diagram when the switch key is turned to the indicated position.
3 If the switch fails any of the tests, replace it with a new one.

Removal

4 Position the motorcycle on an auxiliary stand so that its weight is off the front end. Remove the fairing (see Chapter 8). Trace the ignition (main) switch wiring back from the base of the switch and disconnect it at the connectors **(see illustration 18.1)**. Draw the wiring through to the switch, freeing it from any clips or ties and noting its routing.
5 Unscrew the bolt securing the front brake master cylinder, and on YZF750R and SP models the clutch master cylinder, to the top yoke and displace it/them **(see illustration)**. Keep the master cylinder(s) upright to prevent fluid leakage.
6 Remove the blanking caps from the heads of the handlebar positioning bolts using a small flat-bladed screwdriver, then unscrew the bolts **(see illustrations)**.
7 Slacken the fork clamp bolts in the top yoke and the handlebar clamp bolts **(see illustration)**. Unscrew the steering stem nut and remove it along with its washer, where fitted **(see illustration)**. Gently ease the top yoke upwards off the fork tubes and remove it **(see illustration)**.
8 Two shear-head bolts mount the ignition

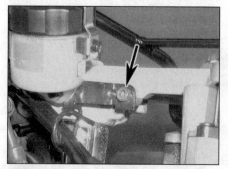

18.5 Displace the master cylinder(s) from the top yoke by removing the bolt

18.6a Remove the blanking caps . . .

18.6b . . . and unscrew the positioning bolts

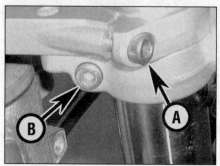

18.7a Slacken the fork clamp bolts (A) and the handlebar clamp bolts (B) . . .

18.7b . . . then unscrew the steering stem nut (arrowed) . . .

18.7c . . . and ease the yoke up off the steering stem and forks

switch to the underside of the top yoke (see illustration). The heads of the bolts must be drifted round using a suitable punch or drift, or drilled off, before the switch can be removed. Mount the yoke in a vice equipped with soft jaws and padded out with rags to do this. Remove the bolts and withdraw the switch from the top yoke.

Installation

9 Installation is the reverse of removal. Tighten the new bolts until the heads shear off. Make sure wiring connectors are securely connected and correctly routed. Tighten the steering stem nut, the fork clamp bolts, the handlebar positioning bolts and the handlebar clamp bolts, in that order, to the torque settings specified at the beginning of Chapter 6.

19 Handlebar switches – check

1 Generally speaking, the switches are reliable and trouble-free. Most troubles, when they do occur, are caused by dirty or corroded contacts, but wear and breakage of internal parts is a possibility that should not be overlooked. If breakage does occur, the entire switch and related wiring harness will have to be replaced with a new one, as individual parts are not available.
2 The switches can be checked for continuity using an ohmmeter or a continuity test light.
3 Remove the left-hand fairing side panel to access the left-hand switch wiring connectors and/or the air filter housing to access the right-hand switch wiring connectors (see Chapters 8 and/or 4). Trace the wiring harness of the switch in question back to its connectors and disconnect them (see illustrations).
4 Check for continuity between the terminals of the switch harness with the switch in the various positions (ie switch off – no continuity, switch on – continuity) – see the *Wiring Diagrams* at the end of this Chapter.
5 If the continuity check indicates a problem exists, refer to Section 20, remove the switch and spray the switch contacts with electrical contact cleaner. If they are accessible, the contacts can be scraped clean with a knife or polished with crocus cloth. If switch components are damaged or broken, it should be obvious when the switch is disassembled.

20 Handlebar switches – removal and installation

Removal

1 If the switch is to be removed from the bike, rather than just displaced from the handlebar, trace the wiring harness of the switch in question back to its connectors and disconnect them. Remove the left-hand fairing

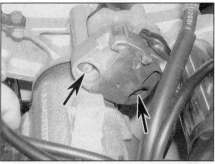
18.8 Ignition switch bolts (arrowed)

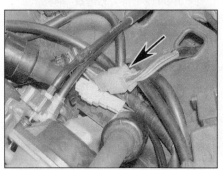
19.3b Right-hand switch connector (arrowed) – YZF750R and SP models

side panel to access the left-hand switch wiring connectors and/or the air filter housing to access the right-hand switch wiring connectors (see Chapters 8 and/or 4) (see illustrations 19.3a, b or c). Work back along the harness, freeing it from all the relevant clips and ties, whilst noting its correct routing.

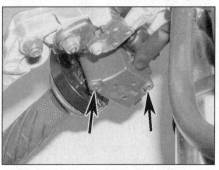
20.3a Right-hand switch housing screws (arrowed) – YZF1000R models

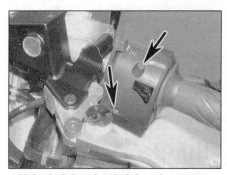
20.3c Left-hand switch housing screws (arrowed) – YZF1000R models

19.3a Left-hand switch wiring connectors – YZF1000R model shown

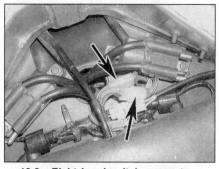
19.3c Right-hand switch connectors (arrowed) – YZF1000R models

2 Disconnect the wiring connectors from the brake light switch (if removing the right-hand switch) or the clutch switch (if removing the left-hand switch) (see illustration 14.2 or 23.2).
3 Unscrew the handlebar switch screws and free the switch from the handlebar by separating the halves (see illustrations). On

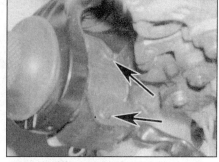
20.3b Right-hand switch housing screws (arrowed) – YZF750R and SP models

20.3d Left-hand switch housing screws (arrowed) – YZF750R and SP models

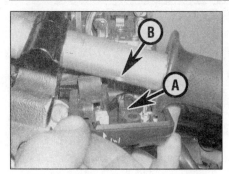

20.4 Locate the pin (A) in the hole (B)

21.2 Disconnect the neutral switch/oil level sensor wiring connector

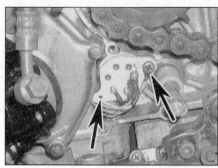

21.10 Neutral switch screws (arrowed)

YZF1000R models, if removing the left-hand switch, remove the choke cable lever, noting how it fits.

Installation

4 Installation is the reverse of removal. On YZF1000R models, refer to Chapter 4 for installation of the choke cable, if required. Make sure the locating pin in the switch housing locates in the hole in the handlebar **(see illustration)**. Make sure the wiring connectors are correctly routed and securely connected.

21 Neutral switch – check, removal and installation

Check

Note: *1995-on YZF750 models and all YZF1000 models have a second and third gear position sensor combined in the neutral switch. These sensors are linked to the ignition control unit (see Wiring diagrams) and allow the ignition timing characteristics to be changed to suit gearing.*

1 Before checking the electrical circuit, check the bulb (see Section 17) and fuse (see Section 5).
2 The switch is located in the left-hand side of the transmission casing below the front sprocket. Make sure the transmission is in neutral. To access the neutral switch/oil level sensor wiring connector, remove the fuel tank (see Chapter 4). Trace the wiring from the

switch and disconnect it at the connector **(see illustration)**.
3 With the connector disconnected and the ignition switched ON, the neutral light should be out. If not, the wire between the connector and instrument cluster must be earthed (grounded) at some point.
4 Check for continuity between the light blue wire terminal on the switch side of the wiring connector and the crankcase. With the transmission in neutral, there should be continuity. With the transmission in gear, there should be no continuity. If the tests prove otherwise, then the switch is faulty.
5 If the continuity tests prove the switch is good, check for voltage (ignition ON) at the brown terminal on the wiring loom side of the instrument cluster wiring connector – remove the left-hand fairing side panel to access the connector. If there's no voltage present, check the wire between the connector and signal fuse (see the *Wiring Diagrams* at the end of this Chapter). If the voltage is good, check the wiring between the connector and the bulbholder, then check the starter circuit cut-off relay and other components in the starter circuit as described in the relevant sections of this Chapter. If all components are good, check the wiring between the various components (see the *Wiring Diagrams* at the end of this Chapter).

Removal

6 Remove the left-hand fairing side panel (see Chapter 8). To access the wiring connector, remove the fuel tank (see Chapter 4). Trace the wiring from the switch and disconnect it at

the connector, then release it from any ties **(see illustration 21.2)**.
7 Make sure the transmission is in neutral. The switch is located in the left-hand side of the transmission casing below the front sprocket.
8 Remove the front sprocket cover (see Chapter 6, Section 16, following the relevant Steps).
9 Disconnect the wire from the oil level sensor at the single bullet connector.
10 Remove the screws securing the switch and detach it from the casing **(see illustration)**. Discard the O-ring, as a new one must be used. Note the routing of the wiring as you draw it through.

Installation

11 Fit a new O-ring onto the switch, then install the switch and tighten its screws securely **(see illustration 21.10)**.
12 Feed the wiring up to the connector, making sure it is correctly routed, and connect it **(see illustration 21.2)**. Secure the wiring in any ties. Connect the oil level sensor wiring bullet connector. Check the operation of the neutral light.
13 Install the front sprocket cover (see Chapter 6, Section 16, following the relevant Steps).
14 Install the fuel tank and the left-hand fairing side panel (see Chapters 4 and 8).

22 Sidestand switch – check and renewal

Check

1 The sidestand switch is mounted on the sidestand. The switch is part of the safety circuit which prevents or stops the engine running if the transmission is in gear whilst the sidestand is down, and prevents the engine from starting if the transmission is in gear unless the sidestand is up, and unless the clutch is pulled in. Before checking the electrical circuit, check the fuse (see Section 5).
2 To access the wiring connector, remove the fuel tank (see Chapter 4). Trace the wiring from the switch and disconnect it at the connector(s) **(see illustrations)**.

22.2a Sidestand switch wiring connectors – YZF750R and SP models

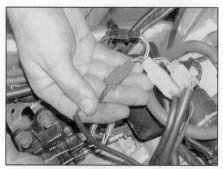

22.2b Sidestand switch wiring connector – YZF1000R models

3 Check the operation of the switch using an ohmmeter or continuity test light. Connect the meter probes to the terminals on the switch side of the connector. With the sidestand up there should be continuity (zero resistance) between the terminals, and with the stand down there should be no continuity (infinite resistance).
4 If the switch does not perform as expected, it is defective and must be renewed.
5 If the switch is good, check the starter circuit cut-off relay and other components in the starter circuit as described in the relevant sections of this Chapter. If all components are good, check the wiring between the various components (see the *Wiring Diagrams* at the end of this Chapter).

Renewal

6 The sidestand switch is mounted on the sidestand. Remove the fuel tank (see Chapter 4) to access the wiring connector(s). Trace the wiring from the switch and disconnect it at the connector(s) **(see illustration 22.2a or b)**. Work back along the switch wiring, freeing it from any relevant retaining clips and ties, noting its correct routing.
7 Remove the screws securing the switch and remove the switch, noting how it fits **(see illustration)**.
8 Fit the new switch, making sure the plunger locates correctly, and tighten the screws securely.
9 Make sure the wiring is correctly routed up to the connector(s) and retained by all the necessary clips and ties.
10 Reconnect the wiring connector(s) and check the operation of the sidestand switch.
11 Install the fuel tank (see Chapter 4).

23 Clutch switch –
check and renewal

Check

1 The clutch switch is mounted on the underside of the clutch lever bracket. The switch is part of the safety circuit which prevents or stops the engine running if the transmission is in gear whilst the sidestand is down, and prevents the engine from starting if the transmission is in gear unless the sidestand is up and the clutch lever is pulled in. The switch isn't adjustable.
2 To check the switch, disconnect the wiring connector **(see illustration)**. Connect the probes of an ohmmeter or a continuity test light to the two switch terminals. With the clutch lever pulled in, continuity should be indicated. With the clutch lever out, no continuity (infinite resistance) should be indicated.
3 If the switch is good, check the starter circuit cut-off relay and other components in the starter circuit as described in the relevant sections of this Chapter. If all components are

22.7 The sidestand switch is secured by two screws (arrowed)

good, check the wiring between the various components (see the *Wiring Diagrams* at the end of this Chapter).

Renewal

4 The clutch switch is mounted on the underside of the clutch lever bracket.
5 Disconnect the wiring connector **(see illustration 23.2)**, then remove the screw and detach the switch.
6 Installation is the reverse of removal.

24 Relay assembly –
check and renewal

Starter circuit cut-off relay
Check

1 The starter circuit cut-off relay is part of the safety circuit which prevents or stops the engine running if the transmission is in gear whilst the sidestand is down, and prevents the engine from starting if the transmission is in gear unless the sidestand is up and the clutch lever is pulled in.
2 The starter circuit cut-off relay and its diodes are contained within the relay assembly mounted on the front of the battery box below the tank rear mounting on YZF750R and SP models, and on top of the fuel filter, which is just behind the fuel pump, on YZF1000R models **(see illustrations)**. Remove the fuel tank for access (see Chapter 4).

24.2a Relay assembly (arrowed) – YZF750R and SP models

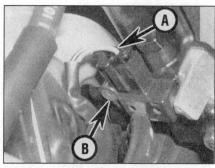
23.2 Clutch switch wiring connector (A) and mounting screw (B)

3 Disconnect the relay wiring connector and remove the relay. Refer to the wiring diagram for your model (see end of chapter) and the following procedures:
4 To check the operation of the relay, connect a meter set to the ohms x 100 range, or a continuity tester, between the blue and blue/white wire terminals of the relay. No continuity should be shown. Now using jumper wires connect a fully charged 12V battery to the relay's black/yellow and red/black wire terminals (positive (+ve) lead to red/black and negative (–ve) lead to black/yellow). The meter should show continuity with battery voltage applied.
5 On YZF750R and SP models a figure is provided for the cut-off relay resistance. Connect a meter set to the ohms x 100 range between the black/yellow and red/black wire terminals of the relay. The figure given in the Specifications at the beginning of this chapter should be obtained.
6 The diodes contained within the relay assembly can be checked by performing a continuity test. Refer to the appropriate wiring diagram at the end of this chapter and connect the meter (set to the ohms function) or continuity tester across the wire terminals for the diode being tested. The diode should show continuity in one direction and no continuity when the meter or tester probes are reversed. If the diode shows the same condition in both directions it should be considered faulty.
7 If the cut-out relay and diodes are proved good, yet the starting system fault still exists check all other components in the starting

24.2b Relay assembly – YZF1000R models

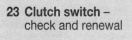

9

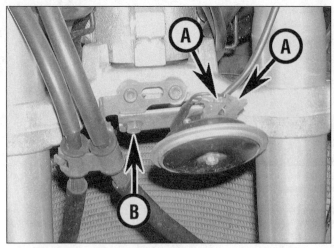

25.3a Horn wiring connectors (A) and mounting bolt (B) – YZF750R and SP models

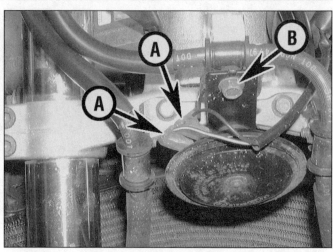

25.3b Horn wiring connectors (A) and mounting bolt (B) – YZF1000R models

circuit (ie the neutral switch, side stand switch, clutch switch, starter switch and starter relay) as described in the relevant sections of this Chapter. If all components are good, check the wiring between the various components (see *Wiring Diagrams* at the end of this Chapter).

Renewal

8 The relay assembly is mounted on the front of the battery box below the tank rear mounting on YZF750R and SP models, and on top of the fuel filter, which is just behind the fuel pump, on YZF1000R models **(see illustration 24.2a or b)**. Remove the fuel tank for access (see Chapter 4).
9 Installation is the reverse of removal.

Fuel pump relay

10 The fuel pump relay is housed within the relay assembly. Refer to Chapter 4, Section 15 for test details.

Oil level sensor resistor

11 The oil level sensor resistor is housed within the relay assembly. Refer to Section 26 of this chapter for test details.

25 Horn –
check and renewal

Check

1 If the horn, doesn't work, first check the fuse (see Section 5) and the battery (see Section 3).
2 The horn is mounted on the bottom yoke. Remove the fairing for best access to it (see Chapter 8).
3 Unplug the wiring connectors from the horn **(see illustrations)**. Using two jumper wires, apply battery voltage directly to the terminals on the horn. If the horn sounds, check the switch (see Section 19) and the wiring between the switch and the horn (see *Wiring Diagrams* at the end of this Chapter).

4 If the horn doesn't sound, replace it with a new one.

Renewal

5 The horn is mounted on the bottom yoke. Remove the fairing for best access to it (see Chapter 8).
6 Unplug the wiring connectors from the horn **(see illustration 25.3a or b)**. Unscrew the bolt securing the horn and remove it from the bike **(see illustration or 25.3a or b)**.
7 Install the horn and securely tighten the bolt. Connect the wiring connectors to the horn. Install the fairing (see Chapter 8).

26 Oil level sensor and relay –
check, removal and installation

Check

1 With the ignition switch ON and the kill switch in the 'RUN' position, the oil level warning light should not come on, indicating that the oil level is good. If the light does come on, check the oil level (see *Daily (pre-ride) checks*). If the oil level is good, check the sensor and relay (see Steps 3 and 4).
2 Start the engine. The oil level warning light

should come on, indicating that the oil level has dropped as it is being pumped round the engine. If the light does not come on, stop the engine and check the bulb (see Section 17). If the bulb is good, check for continuity in the wire between the sensor bullet connector and the loom side of the instrument cluster wiring connector. Also check for continuity between the cluster side of the connector and the bulb holder.
3 To check the sensor, remove it from the sump (see Steps 5 and 6 below). Connect one probe of an ohmmeter or continuity tester to the sensor wire and the other probe to its base. With the sensor in its normal installed position (wiring at the bottom), there should be continuity. Turn the sensor upside down. There should be no continuity. If either condition does not occur, replace the sensor with a new one.
4 To check the relay, remove the fuel tank (see Chapter 4), then disconnect the relay wiring connector and release it from its holder **(see illustrations)**. Set a multimeter to the ohms x 1 scale and connect the positive (+ve) probe to the red/blue wire terminal, and the negative (–ve) probe to the black terminal. There should be no continuity. Leaving the meter connected, and using a fully-charged 12 volt battery and two insulated jumper

26.4a Oil level sensor relay (arrowed) – YZF750R and SP models

26.4b Oil level sensor relay (arrowed) – YZF1000R models

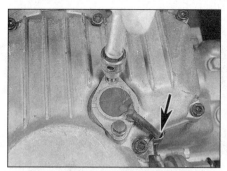

26.8 Free the wiring from its clamp (arrowed) then unscrew the bolts and remove the sensor

26.10 Use a new O-ring when installing the sensor

27.2a Starter relay (arrowed) – YZF750R and SP models

wires, connect the battery positive (+ve) lead to the brown wire terminal, and the negative (–ve) lead to the black/red wire terminal. There should now be continuity shown on the meter. If the relay doesn't behave as stated, replace it with a new one.

5 A resistor is fitted inside the relay assembly (see Sec 24) to stabilise the signals to the oil level warning light, thus preventing it flickering when cornering or braking hard. If there is a fault in the warning light operation which is not due to a faulty bulb or relay, the resistor value can be checked as follows.

6 Refer to Section 24 and disconnect the relay assembly from the machine. Using a multimeter set to the ohms x 100 range, connect its positive probe (+ve) to the black/red wire terminal and the negative (–ve) probe to the red/blue wire terminal on the relay. The value obtained should be similar to that given in the Specifications at the beginning of this chapter. If no continuity (infinite resistance) is indicated the resistor is open-circuit and the relay assembly should be renewed.

Removal

7 Drain the engine oil (see Chapter 1).

8 Trace the wiring back from the sensor and disconnect it at the single bullet connector. Free it from its clamp. Unscrew the two bolts securing the sensor to the bottom of the sump and withdraw it from the sump, being prepared to catch any residue oil **(see illustration)**. Discard the O-ring as a new one must be used.

9 To remove the relay, remove the fuel tank (see Chapter 4), then disconnect the relay wiring connector and release it from its holder **(see illustration 26.4a or b)**.

Installation

10 Install a new O-ring onto the oil level sensor, then fit the sensor into the sump **(see illustration)**. Tighten its bolts to the torque setting specified at the beginning of the Chapter.

11 Connect the wiring at the connector and check the operation of the sensor (see Steps 1 to 4 above). Secure the wiring in its clamp.

12 Fill the engine with oil (see Chapter 1).

13 Fit the relay into its holder and connect the wiring connector **(see illustration 26.4a or b)**.

27 Starter relay – check and renewal

Check

1 If the starter circuit is faulty, first check the main fuse (see Section 5).

2 Remove the rider's seat, and on YZF1000R models the left-hand side cover (see Chapter 8). The starter relay is located behind the battery on YZF750R and SP models, and on the left-hand side of the battery box on YZF1000R models **(see illustrations)**. Lift the rubber terminal cover and unscrew the bolt securing the thick starter motor lead to the terminal marked 'M' **(see illustration)**; position the lead away from the relay terminal. With the ignition switch ON, the engine kill switch in the 'RUN' position, and the transmission in neutral, press the starter switch. The relay should be heard to click.

3 If the relay doesn't click, switch off the ignition and remove the relay as described below; test it as follows.

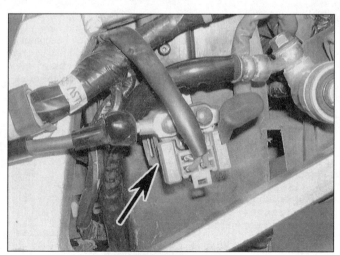

27.2b Starter relay (arrowed) – YZF1000R models

27.2c Starter motor (A) and battery (B) lead terminals

27.7 Disconnect the relay wiring connector

28.2 Pull back the rubber cover and unscrew the terminal nut (arrowed)

4 Set a multimeter to the ohms x 1 scale and connect it across the relay's starter motor and battery lead terminals (marked 'M' and 'B' respectively) **(see illustration 27.2c)**. Using a fully-charged 12 volt battery and two insulated jumper wires, connect the positive (+ve) terminal of the battery to the red/white wire terminal on the relay, and the negative (–ve) terminal to the blue (YZF1000R) or blue/white (YZF750R and SP) wire terminal on the relay. At this point the relay should be heard to click and the multimeter read 0 ohms (continuity). If this is the case the relay is proved good. If the relay does not click when battery voltage is applied and indicates no continuity (infinite resistance) across its terminals, it is faulty and must be replaced with a new one.

5 If the relay is good, check for battery voltage at the red/white wire terminal on the loom side of the relay wiring connector when the starter button is pressed. If voltage is present, check the other components in the starter circuit as described in the relevant sections of this Chapter. If no voltage was present, check the wiring between the various components (see *Wiring Diagrams* at the end of this Chapter).

Renewal

6 Remove the rider's seat, and on YZF1000R

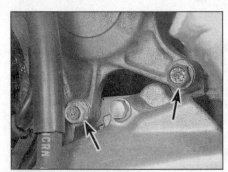

28.3a Unscrew the bolts (arrowed) . . .

models the left-hand side cover (see Chapter 8). The starter relay is located behind the battery on YZF750R and SP models, and on the left-hand side of the battery box on YZF1000R models **(see illustration 27.2a or b)**. Disconnect the battery negative (–ve) lead before removing the stater relay.
7 Disconnect the relay wiring connector **(see illustration)**. Unscrew the two bolts securing the starter motor and battery leads to the relay and detach the leads **(see illustration 27.2c)**. Remove the relay with its rubber sleeve from its mounting lug on the frame.
8 Installation is the reverse of removal. The starter motor lead connects to the terminal marked 'M', and the battery lead to the terminal marked 'B' **(see illustration 27.2c)**. Make sure the terminal nuts are securely tightened. Connect the negative (–ve) lead last when reconnecting the battery.

28 Starter motor – removal and installation

Removal

1 Remove the rider's seat and the left-hand fairing side panel (see Chapter 8), and the fuel tank (see Chapter 4). Disconnect the battery negative (–ve) lead. The starter motor is mounted on the crankcase, behind the cylinder block.
2 Peel back the rubber terminal cover and unscrew the nut securing the lead to the starter motor **(see illustration)**. Detach the lead.
3 Unscrew the two bolts securing the starter motor **(see illustration)**. Draw the starter motor out of the crankcase and remove it from the machine **(see illustration)**.
4 Remove the O-ring on the end of the starter motor and discard it as a new one must be used.

Installation

5 Fit a new O-ring onto the end of the starter motor, making sure it is seated in its groove, and smear it with grease.
6 Manoeuvre the motor into position and slide it into the crankcase **(see illustration 28.3b)**. Ensure that the starter motor teeth mesh correctly with those of the starter idle/reduction gear. Install the mounting bolts and tighten them to the torque setting specified at the beginning of the Chapter **(see illustration 28.3a)**.
7 Connect the lead to the starter motor and secure it with the nut **(see illustration 28.2)**. Make sure the rubber cover is correctly seated over the terminal.
8 Connect the battery negative (–ve) lead and install the seat (see Chapter 8).

29 Starter motor – disassembly, inspection and reassembly

Disassembly

1 Remove the starter motor (see Section 28) **(see illustration)**.
2 Note the alignment marks between the main housing and the front and rear covers, or

28.3b . . . and remove the starter motor

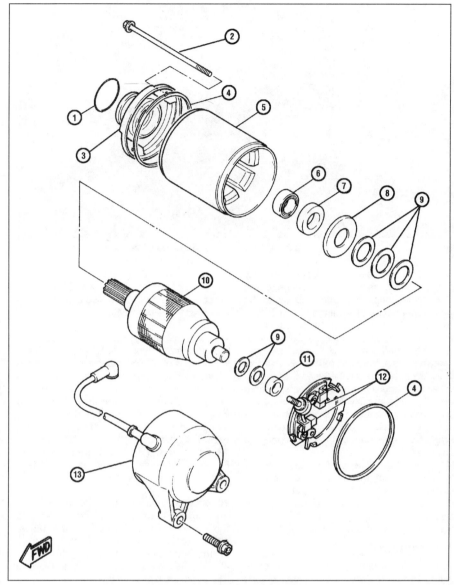

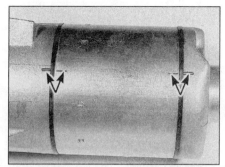

29.2 Note the alignment marks between the housing and end covers (arrowed)

29.1 Starter motor components

1 O-ring	6 Bearing	11 Bush
2 Long bolt	7 Oil seal	12 Brushes and
3 Front cover	8 Washer	brushplate
4 Housing O-ring	9 Shims	13 Rear cover
5 Main housing	10 Armature	

make your own if they aren't clear (see illustration).

3 Unscrew the two long bolts, noting how the washers locate, and withdraw them from the starter motor (see illustration).

4 Wrap some insulating tape around the teeth on the end of the starter motor shaft – this will protect the oil seal from damage as the front cover is removed. Remove the front cover from the motor. Remove the cover O-ring from the main housing and discard it as a new one must be used. Remove the washer and shims from the front end of the armature shaft or the inside of the front cover, noting their correct fitted locations.

5 Remove the rear cover and brushplate assembly from the motor (see illustration). Remove the cover O-ring from the main housing and discard it as a new one must be used. Remove the shims from the rear end of the armature shaft or from inside the rear cover after the brushplate assembly has been removed.

6 Withdraw the armature from the main housing.

7 Noting the correct fitted location of each component, unscrew the terminal nut and remove it along with its washer, the insulating washers and the O-ring. Withdraw the terminal bolt and brushplate assembly from the rear cover (see illustration).

8 Lift the brush springs and slide the brushes out from their holders.

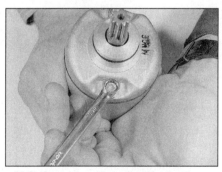

29.3 Unscrew and remove the two long bolts

29.5 Remove the rear cover

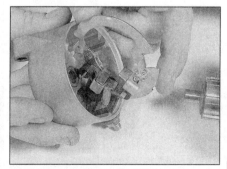

29.7 Remove the brushplate from the rear cover

9

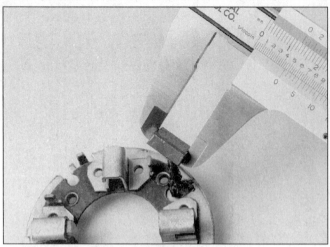

29.9 Measure the brush length

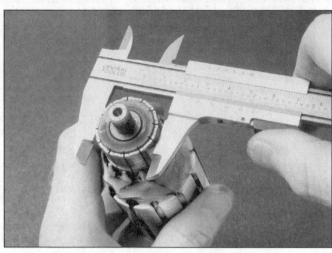

29.10 Measure the diameter of the commutator

Inspection

9 The parts of the starter motor that are most likely to require attention are the brushes. Measure the length of the brushes and compare the results to the length listed in this Chapter's Specifications **(see illustration)**. If any of the brushes are worn beyond the service limit, replace the brush assembly with a new one. If the brushes are not worn excessively, nor cracked, chipped, or otherwise damaged, they may be re-used.

10 Inspect the commutator bars on the armature for scoring, scratches and discoloration. The commutator can be cleaned and polished with crocus cloth, but do not use sandpaper or emery paper. After cleaning, wipe away any residue with a cloth soaked in electrical system cleaner or denatured alcohol. Measure the diameter of the commutator and compare it to the specifications **(see illustration)**. If it has worn below the wear limit, renew the starter motor. Measure the depth of the insulating Mica below the surface of the commutator bars. If the Mica is less than the depth specified, scrape it away until the specified depth is reached.

11 Using an ohmmeter or a continuity test light, check for continuity between the commutator bars **(see illustration)**. Continuity should exist between each bar and all of the others. Also, check for continuity between the commutator bars and the armature shaft **(see illustration)**. There should be no continuity (infinite resistance) between the commutator and the shaft. If the checks indicate otherwise, the armature is defective.

12 Check for continuity between the terminal bolt and the housing (when assembled). There should be no continuity (infinite resistance).

13 Check the front end of the armature shaft for worn, cracked, chipped and broken teeth. If the shaft is damaged or worn, renew the armature.

14 Inspect the end covers for signs of cracks or wear. Inspect the magnets in the main housing and the housing itself for cracks.

15 Inspect the insulating washers and front cover oil seal for signs of damage and replace them with new ones if necessary.

Reassembly

16 Slide the brushes back into position in their holders and place the brush spring ends onto the brushes.

17 Ensure that the inner rubber insulator is in place on the terminal bolt, then fit the O-ring over the terminal. Insert the bolt through the rear cover and fit the brushplate assembly in the rear cover, making sure its tab is correctly located in the slot in the cover **(see illustration 29.7)**. Fit the insulating washers over the terminal, then fit the standard washer and the nut.

18 Slide the shims onto the rear end of the armature shaft, then lubricate the shaft end with a drop of oil **(see illustration)**. Insert the armature into the rear cover, locating the brushes on the commutator bars as you do, taking care not to damage them. Check that each brush is securely pressed against the commutator by its spring and is free to move easily in its holder.

19 Fit a new O-ring onto the main housing. Fit the housing over the armature and onto the rear cover, aligning the marks made on removal.

20 Apply a smear of grease to the lips of the front cover oil seal and fit a new O-ring onto the front of the main housing. Fit the washer onto the cover. Slide the shims onto the front of the armature shaft. Install the cover, aligning the marks made on removal. Remove the protective tape from the shaft end.

21 Check the marks made on removal are correctly aligned, then install the long bolts and tighten them securely **(see illustrations 29.2 and 3)**.

22 Install the starter motor (see Section 28).

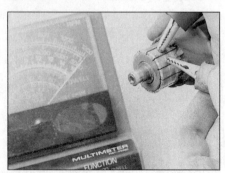

29.11a Continuity should exist between the commutator bars

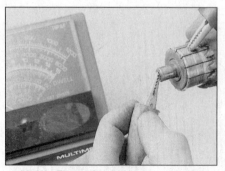

29.11b There should be no continuity between the commutator bars and the armature shaft

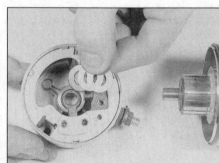

29.18 Fit the shims onto the shaft

30 Charging system testing – general information and precautions

1 If the performance of the charging system is suspect, the system as a whole should be checked first, followed by testing of the individual components. **Note:** *Before beginning the checks, make sure the battery is fully charged and that all system connections are clean and tight.*
2 Checking the output of the charging system and the performance of the various components within the charging system requires the use of a multimeter (with voltage, current and resistance checking facilities).
3 When making the checks, follow the procedures carefully to prevent incorrect connections or short circuits, as irreparable damage to electrical system components may result if short circuits occur.
4 If a multimeter is not available, the job of checking the charging system should be left to a Yamaha dealer or automotive electrician.

31 Charging system – leakage and output test

1 If the charging system of the machine is thought to be faulty, remove the seat (see Chapter 8) and perform the following checks.

Leakage test

Caution: Always connect an ammeter in series, never in parallel with the battery, otherwise it will be damaged. Do not turn the ignition ON or operate the starter motor when the ammeter is connected – a sudden surge in current will blow the meter's fuse.
2 Turn the ignition switch OFF and disconnect the lead from the battery negative (–ve) terminal.
3 Set the multimeter to the Amps function and connect its negative (–ve) probe to the battery negative (–ve) terminal, and positive (+ve) probe to the disconnected negative (–ve) lead **(see illustration)**. Always set the meter to a high amps range initially and then bring it down to the mA (milli Amps) range; if there is a high current flow in the circuit it may blow the meter's fuse.
4 No current flow should be indicated. If current leakage is indicated (generally greater than 0.1 mA), there is a short circuit in the wiring. Using the wiring diagrams at the end of this Chapter, systematically disconnect individual electrical components, checking the meter each time until the source is identified.
5 If no leakage is indicated, disconnect the meter and connect the negative (–ve) lead to the battery, tightening it securely.

Output test

6 Start the engine and warm it up to normal

operating temperature. Remove the seat (see Chapter 8).
7 To check the regulated voltage output, allow the engine to idle and connect a multimeter set to the 0 to 20 volts DC scale (voltmeter) across the terminals of the battery (positive (+ve) lead to battery positive (+ve) terminal, negative (–ve) lead to battery negative (–ve) terminal). Slowly increase the engine speed briefly to 5000 rpm and note the reading obtained. The regulated voltage should be as specified at the beginning of the Chapter. If the voltage is outside these limits, check the alternator/regulator/rectifier (see Section 32).

> **HAYNES HiNT** *Clues to a faulty regulator are constantly blowing bulbs, with brightness varying considerably with engine speed, and battery overheating.*

32 Alternator/regulator/rectifier – check, removal and installation

Check

⚠ *Warning: To prevent the risk of short circuits, remove the seat and disconnect the battery negative (–ve) lead before making any checks on the alternator.*
1 Remove the left-hand fairing side panel (see Chapter 8). Remove the three bolts securing the alternator end cover and remove the cover **(see illustration)**.

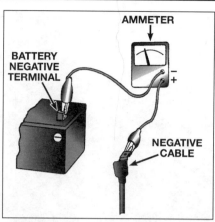

31.3 Checking the charging system leakage rate – connect the meter as shown

2 Remove the screws securing the brush holder, noting the lead secured by the bottom screw, and remove the holder, noting how it fits **(see illustration)**. Remove the cover from the holder **(see illustration)**. Inspect the holder for any signs of damage. Measure the brush lengths **(see illustration)**. Unfortunately, Yamaha provide no specifications for the standard and minimum brush lengths, but if the brushes are obviously worn short, replace the brush holder assembly with a new one. If the brushes are not worn excessively, nor cracked, chipped, or otherwise damaged, they may be re-used. Clean the slip rings (the rings on the shaft which contact the brushes) with a rag moistened with some solvent.

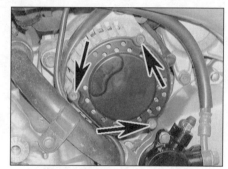

32.1 Unscrew the bolts (arrowed) and remove the cover

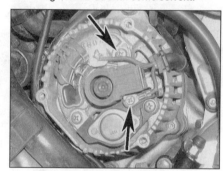

32.2a Undo the screws (arrowed) and remove the brushholder . . .

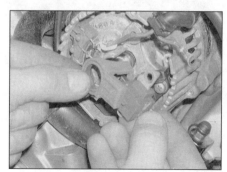

32.2b . . . then remove the cover . . .

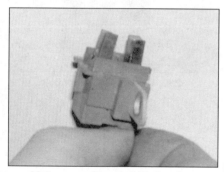

32.2c . . . and inspect the brushes

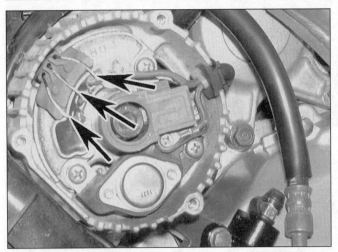

32.4 Check the stator coil resistance by testing between the three wires (arrowed) as described

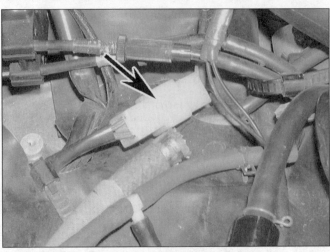

32.8a Alternator wiring connector (arrowed) – YZF750R and SP models

3 To check the rotor coil resistance, first remove the brushholder (see above), then set a multimeter to the ohms x 1 (ohmmeter) scale and measure the resistance between the slip rings (the rings on the shaft which contact the brushes) and compare the reading to the Specifications. If it is higher than specified, replace the rotor with a new one.

4 To check the stator coil resistance, set a multimeter to the ohms x 1 (ohmmeter) scale and measure the resistance between each of the white wires coming out of the left-hand side of the alternator, taking a total of three readings, then check for continuity between each terminal and earth (ground) **(see illustration)**. If the stator coil windings are in good condition the three readings should be within the range shown in the Specifications at the beginning of the Chapter, and there should be no continuity (infinite resistance) between any of the terminals and ground (earth). If not, the alternator stator coil

assembly is faulty and should be replaced with a new one.

5 Check for continuity between the slip rings and the armature housing. There should be no continuity (infinite resistance). If there is continuity, replace the rotor with a new one.

6 Yamaha do not provide any test Specifications for the regulator and rectifier. If none of the checks made here or in other Sections of the Chapter reveal any faults, then take the assembly to a Yamaha dealer for further tests. Individual components are available.

Removal

7 Remove the left-hand fairing side panel (see Chapter 8) and the fuel tank (see Chapter 4).

8 Trace the wiring from the alternator/regulator/rectifier and disconnect it at the connector **(see illustrations)**. Feed the wiring back to the alternator assembly.

9 Unscrew the three bolts securing the

32.8b Alternator wiring connector – YZF1000R models

alternator assembly to the crankcase and withdraw it **(see illustrations)**.

Installation

10 Installation is the reverse of removal. Tighten the bolts to the torque setting specified at the beginning of the Chapter.

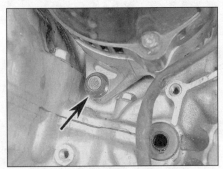

32.9a Unscrew the lower bolt (arrowed) . . .

32.9b . . . and the upper bolts (arrowed) . . .

32.9c . . . and remove the alternator

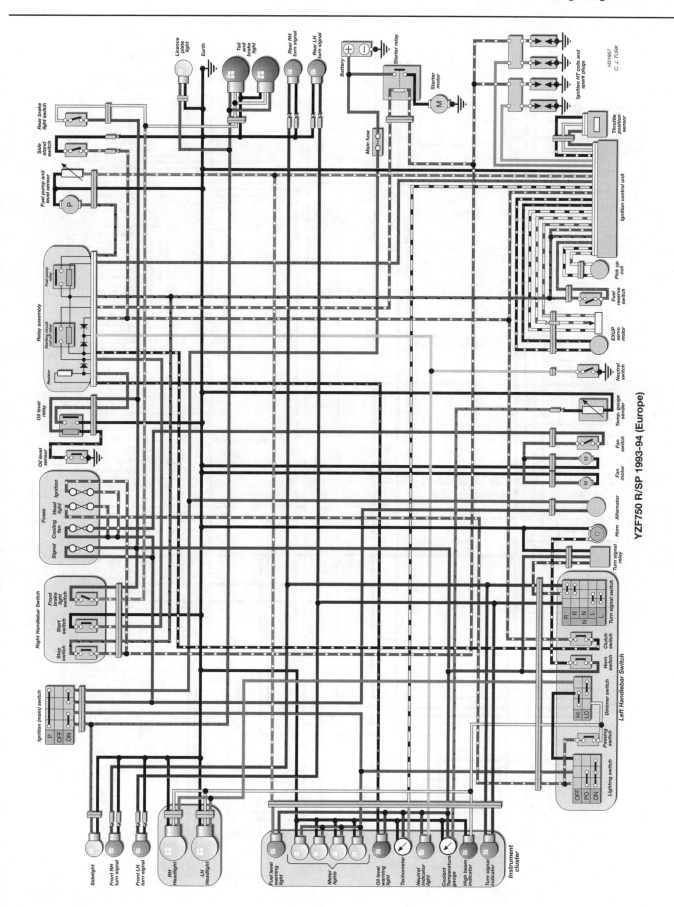

YZF750 R/SP 1993-94 (Europe)

H31667
C. J. TURK

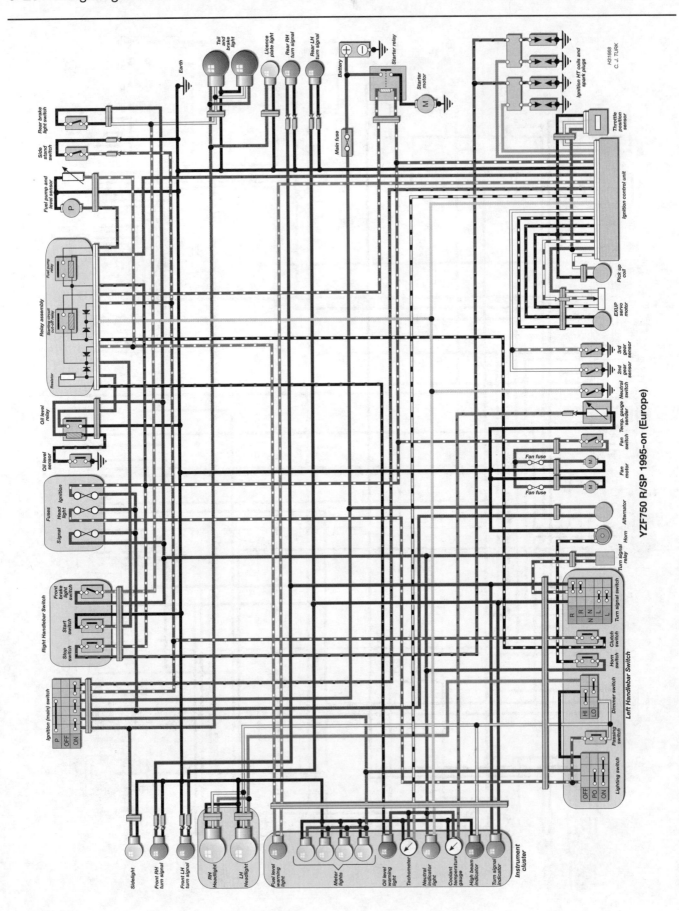

YZF750 R/SP 1995-on (Europe)

H31668
C. J. TURK

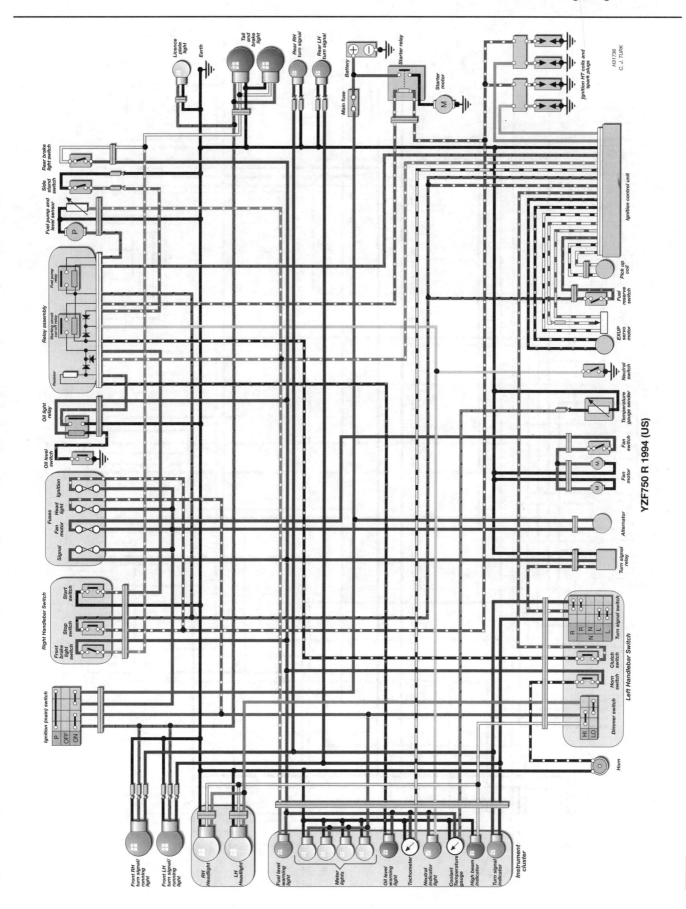

YZF750 R 1994 (US)

H31736
C. J. TURK

9

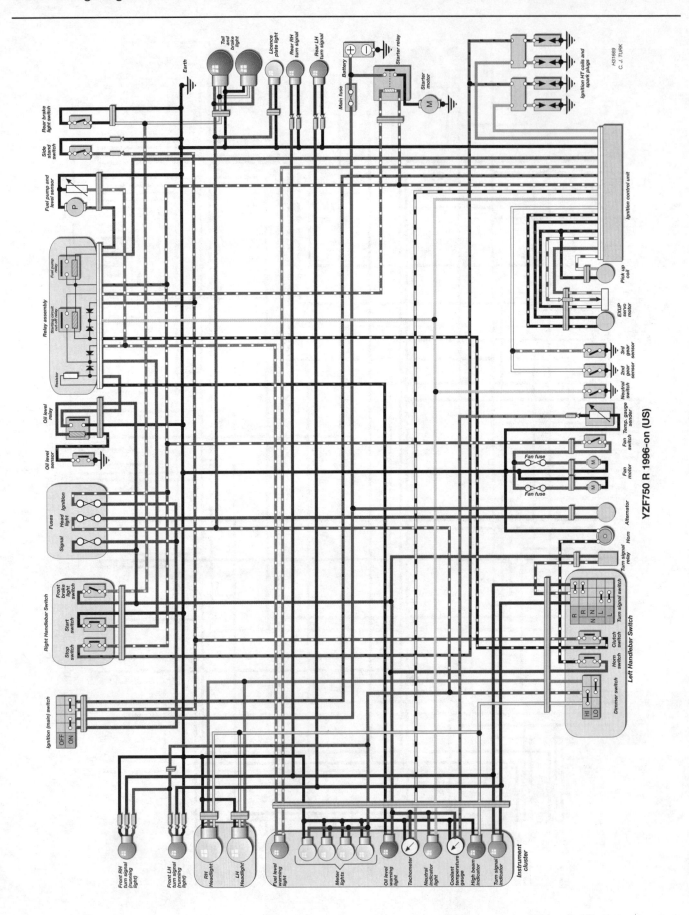

YZF750 R 1996-on (US)

H31669
C. J. TURK

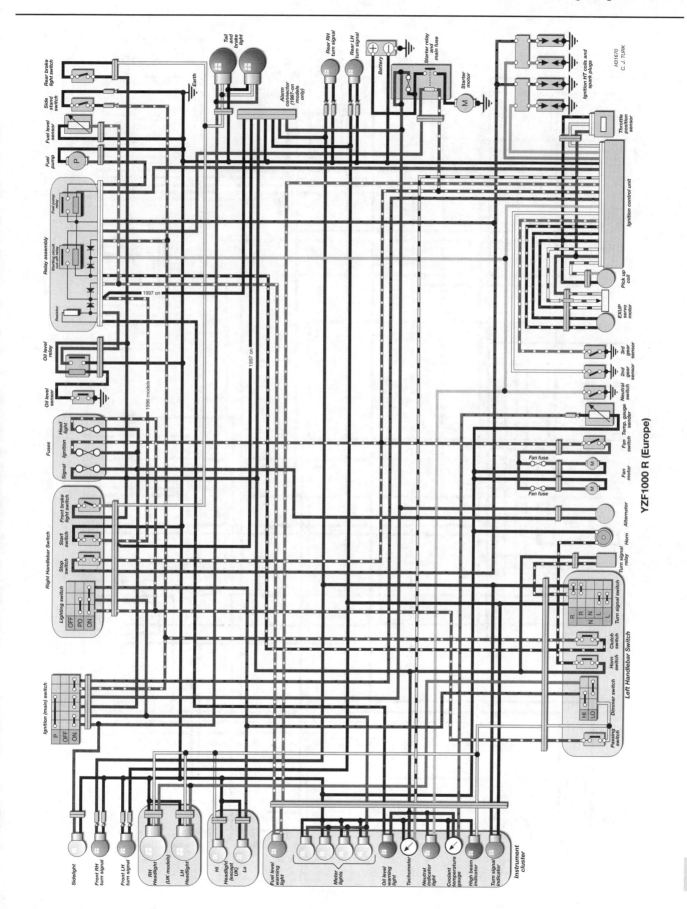

YZF1000 R (Europe)

H31670
C. J. TURK

Tail and brake light

Rear RH turn signal

Rear LH turn signal

Battery

Starter relay and main fuse

Starter motor

Ignition HT coils and spark plugs

Throttle position sensor

Ignition control unit

Pick up coil

EXUP servo motor

3rd gear sensor

2nd gear sensor

Neutral switch

Temp. gauge sender

Fan switch

Fan fuse

Fan motor

Fan fuse

Alternator

Horn

Turn signal relay

Turn signal switch

Clutch switch

Horn switch

Dimmer switch

Left Handlebar Switch

Passing switch

Alarm connector (1996 models only)

Rear brake light switch

Side stand switch

Fuel level sensor

Fuel pump

Relay assembly

Fuel pump relay

Starting circuit cut-off relay

Resistor

1997 on

1996 models

1997 on

Oil level relay

Oil level sensor

Fuses

Head light

Ignition

Signal

Right Handlebar Switch

Front brake light switch

Start switch

Stop switch

Lighting switch

OFF

PO

ON

Ignition (main) switch

P

OFF

ON

R R N N L L

HI LO

Sidelight

Front RH turn signal

Front LH turn signal

RH Headlight (UK models)

LH Headlight

Hi Headlight (except UK)

Lo

Fuel level warning light

Meter lights

Oil level warning light

Tachometer

Neutral indicator light

Coolant temperature gauge

High beam indicator

Turn signal indicator

Instrument cluster

9

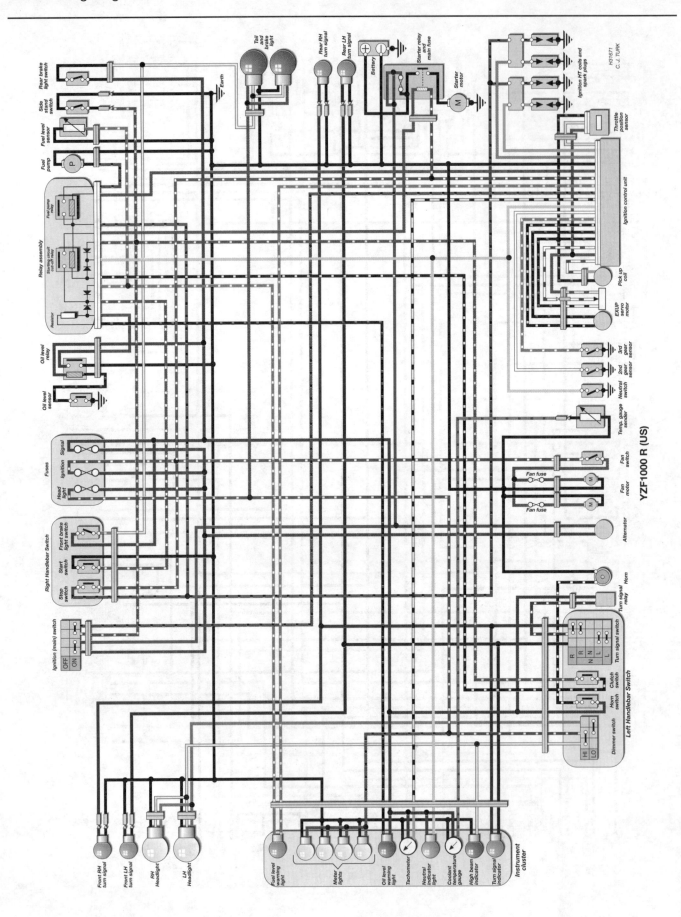

YZF1000 R (US)

H31671
C. J. TURK

Reference REF•1

Dimensions and weights

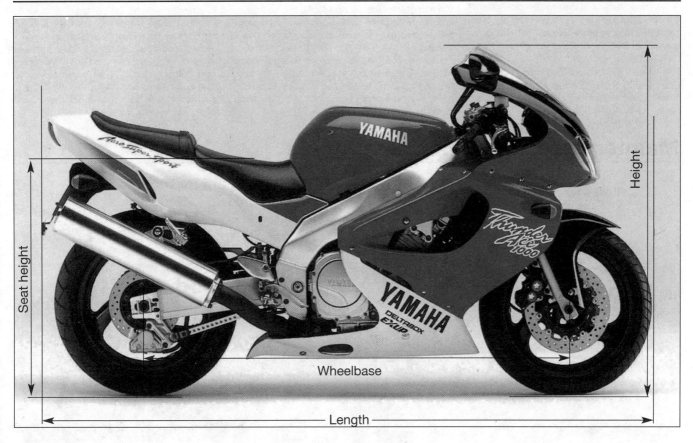

YZF750R

Overall length
  European models . . . . .2160 mm
  All US models . . . . .2070 mm
Overall width . . . . .730 mm
Overall height . . . . .1165 mm
Seat height . . . . .785 mm
Wheelbase . . . . .1420 mm
Ground clearance . . . . .140 mm
Weight (with fuel and oil)
  1993 and 1994 models . . . . .218 kg*
  1995-on models . . . . .221 kg*
*For California models add 1 kg

YZF750SP

Overall length . . . . .2160 mm
Overall widt . . . . .730 mm
Overall height . . . . .1145 mm
Seat height . . . . .785 mm
Wheelbase . . . . .1420 mm
Ground clearance . . . . .140 mm
Weight (with fuel and oil)
  1993 and 1994 models . . . . .215 kg
  1995-on models . . . . .218 kg

YZF1000R

Overall length . . . . .2085 mm
Overall width . . . . .740 mm
Overall height . . . . .1175 mm
Seat height
  1996 models . . . . .815 mm
  1997-on models . . . . .790 mm
Wheelbase . . . . .1430 mm
Ground clearance . . . . .140 mm
Weight (with fuel and oil) . . . . .224 kg*
*For California models add 1 kg

Buying tools

A toolkit is a fundamental requirement for servicing and repairing a motorcycle. Although there will be an initial expense in building up enough tools for servicing, this will soon be offset by the savings made by doing the job yourself. As experience and confidence grow, additional tools can be added to enable the repair and overhaul of the motorcycle. Many of the specialist tools are expensive and not often used so it may be preferable to hire them, or for a group of friends or motorcycle club to join in the purchase.

As a rule, it is better to buy more expensive, good quality tools. Cheaper tools are likely to wear out faster and need to be renewed more often, nullifying the original saving.

> ⚠️ **Warning: To avoid the risk of a poor quality tool breaking in use, causing injury or damage to the component being worked on, always aim to purchase tools which meet the relevant national safety standards.**

The following lists of tools do not represent the manufacturer's service tools, but serve as a guide to help the owner decide which tools are needed for this level of work. In addition, items such as an electric drill, hacksaw, files, soldering iron and a workbench equipped with a vice, may be needed. Although not classed as tools, a selection of bolts, screws, nuts, washers and pieces of tubing always come in useful.

For more information about tools, refer to the Haynes *Motorcycle Workshop Practice TechBook* (Bk. No. 3470).

Manufacturer's service tools

Inevitably certain tasks require the use of a service tool. Where possible an alternative tool or method of approach is recommended, but sometimes there is no option if personal injury or damage to the component is to be avoided. Where required, service tools are referred to in the relevant procedure.

Service tools can usually only be purchased from a motorcycle dealer and are identified by a part number. Some of the commonly-used tools, such as rotor pullers, are available in aftermarket form from mail-order motorcycle tool and accessory suppliers.

Maintenance and minor repair tools

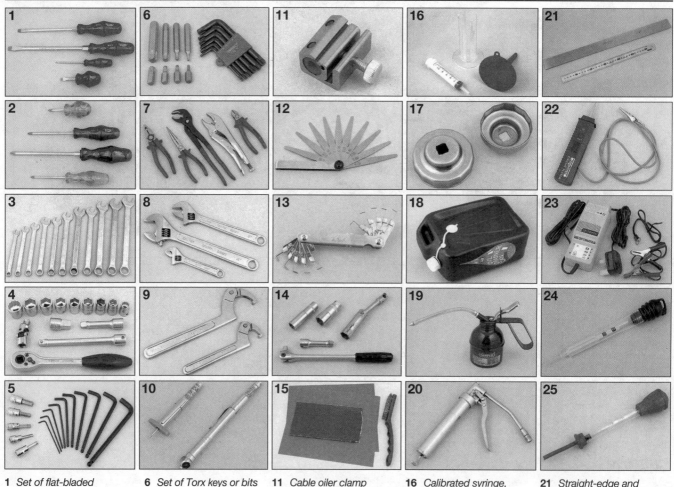

1 Set of flat-bladed screwdrivers
2 Set of Phillips head screwdrivers
3 Combination open-end and ring spanners
4 Socket set (3/8 inch or 1/2 inch drive)
5 Set of Allen keys or bits

6 Set of Torx keys or bits
7 Pliers, cutters and self-locking grips (Mole grips)
8 Adjustable spanners
9 C-spanners
10 Tread depth gauge and tyre pressure gauge

11 Cable oiler clamp
12 Feeler gauges
13 Spark plug gap measuring tool
14 Spark plug spanner or deep plug sockets
15 Wire brush and emery paper

16 Calibrated syringe, measuring vessel and funnel
17 Oil filter adapters
18 Oil drainer can or tray
19 Pump type oil can
20 Grease gun

21 Straight-edge and steel rule
22 Continuity tester
23 Battery charger
24 Hydrometer (for battery specific gravity check)
25 Anti-freeze tester (for liquid-cooled engines)

Repair and overhaul tools

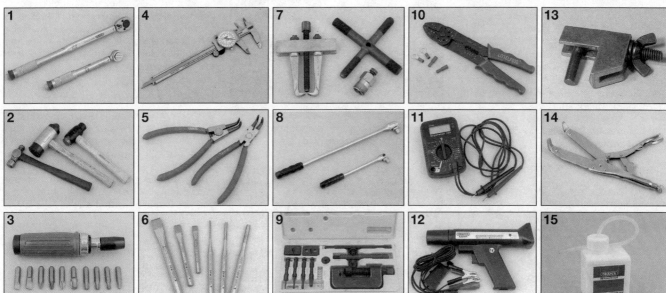

1 Torque wrench
   (small and mid-ranges)
2 Conventional, plastic or
   soft-faced hammers
3 Impact driver set
4 Vernier gauge
5 Circlip pliers (internal and
   external, or combination)
6 Set of cold chisels
   and punches
7 Selection of pullers
8 Breaker bars
9 Chain breaking/
   riveting tool set
10 Wire stripper and
    crimper tool
11 Multimeter (measures
    amps, volts and ohms)
12 Stroboscope (for
    dynamic timing checks)
13 Hose clamp
    (wingnut type shown)
14 Clutch holding tool
15 One-man brake/clutch
    bleeder kit

Specialist tools

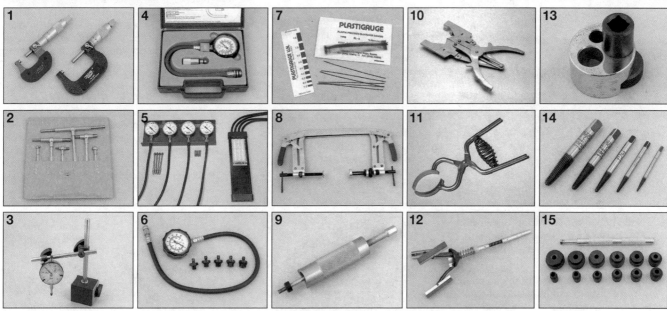

1 Micrometers
   (external type)
2 Telescoping gauges
3 Dial gauge
4 Cylinder
   compression gauge
5 Vacuum gauges (left) or
   manometer (right)
6 Oil pressure gauge
7 Plastigauge kit
8 Valve spring compressor
   (4-stroke engines)
9 Piston pin drawbolt tool
10 Piston ring removal and
    installation tool
11 Piston ring clamp
12 Cylinder bore hone
    (stone type shown)
13 Stud extractor
14 Screw extractor set
15 Bearing driver set

1 Workshop equipment and facilities

The workbench

● Work is made much easier by raising the bike up on a ramp - components are much more accessible if raised to waist level. The hydraulic or pneumatic types seen in the dealer's workshop are a sound investment if you undertake a lot of repairs or overhauls **(see illustration 1.1)**.

1.1 Hydraulic motorcycle ramp

● If raised off ground level, the bike must be supported on the ramp to avoid it falling. Most ramps incorporate a front wheel locating clamp which can be adjusted to suit different diameter wheels. When tightening the clamp, take care not to mark the wheel rim or damage the tyre - use wood blocks on each side to prevent this.
● Secure the bike to the ramp using tie-downs **(see illustration 1.2)**. If the bike has only a sidestand, and hence leans at a dangerous angle when raised, support the bike on an auxiliary stand.

1.2 Tie-downs are used around the passenger footrests to secure the bike

● Auxiliary (paddock) stands are widely available from mail order companies or motorcycle dealers and attach either to the wheel axle or swingarm pivot **(see illustration 1.3)**. If the motorcycle has a centrestand, you can support it under the crankcase to prevent it toppling whilst either wheel is removed **(see illustration 1.4)**.

1.3 This auxiliary stand attaches to the swingarm pivot

1.4 Always use a block of wood between the engine and jack head when supporting the engine in this way

Fumes and fire

● Refer to the Safety first! page at the beginning of the manual for full details. Make sure your workshop is equipped with a fire extinguisher suitable for fuel-related fires (Class B fire - flammable liquids) - it is not sufficient to have a water-filled extinguisher.
● Always ensure adequate ventilation is available. Unless an exhaust gas extraction system is available for use, ensure that the engine is run outside of the workshop.
● If working on the fuel system, make sure the workshop is ventilated to avoid a build-up of fumes. This applies equally to fume build-up when charging a battery. Do not smoke or allow anyone else to smoke in the workshop.

Fluids

● If you need to drain fuel from the tank, store it in an approved container marked as suitable for the storage of petrol (gasoline) **(see illustration 1.5)**. Do not store fuel in glass jars or bottles.

1.5 Use an approved can only for storing petrol (gasoline)

● Use proprietary engine degreasers or solvents which have a high flash-point, such as paraffin (kerosene), for cleaning off oil, grease and dirt - never use petrol (gasoline) for cleaning. Wear rubber gloves when handling solvent and engine degreaser. The fumes from certain solvents can be dangerous - always work in a well-ventilated area.

Dust, eye and hand protection

● Protect your lungs from inhalation of dust particles by wearing a filtering mask over the nose and mouth. Many frictional materials still contain asbestos which is dangerous to your health. Protect your eyes from spouts of liquid and sprung components by wearing a pair of protective goggles **(see illustration 1.6)**.

1.6 A fire extinguisher, goggles, mask and protective gloves should be at hand in the workshop

● Protect your hands from contact with solvents, fuel and oils by wearing rubber gloves. Alternatively apply a barrier cream to your hands before starting work. If handling hot components or fluids, wear suitable gloves to protect your hands from scalding and burns.

What to do with old fluids

● Old cleaning solvent, fuel, coolant and oils should not be poured down domestic drains or onto the ground. Package the fluid up in old oil containers, label it accordingly, and take it to a garage or disposal facility. Contact your local authority for location of such sites or ring the oil care hotline.

OIL CARE
OIL BANK LINE
0800 66 33 66

Note: It is antisocial and illegal to dump oil down the drain. To find the location of your local oil recycling bank, call this number free.

In the USA, note that any oil supplier must accept used oil for recycling.

2 Fasteners -
screws, bolts and nuts

Fastener types and applications

Bolts and screws

● Fastener head types are either of hexagonal, Torx or splined design, with internal and external versions of each type **(see illustrations 2.1 and 2.2)**; splined head fasteners are not in common use on motorcycles. The conventional slotted or Phillips head design is used for certain screws. Bolt or screw length is always measured from the underside of the head to the end of the item **(see illustration 2.11)**.

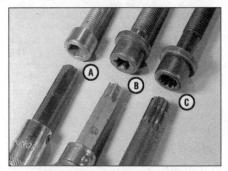

2.1 Internal hexagon/Allen (A), Torx (B) and splined (C) fasteners, with corresponding bits

2.2 External Torx (A), splined (B) and hexagon (C) fasteners, with corresponding sockets

● Certain fasteners on the motorcycle have a tensile marking on their heads, the higher the marking the stronger the fastener. High tensile fasteners generally carry a 10 or higher marking. Never replace a high tensile fastener with one of a lower tensile strength.

Washers (see illustration 2.3)

● Plain washers are used between a fastener head and a component to prevent damage to the component or to spread the load when torque is applied. Plain washers can also be used as spacers or shims in certain assemblies. Copper or aluminium plain washers are often used as sealing washers on drain plugs.

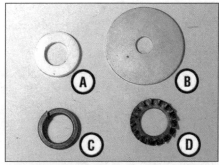

2.3 Plain washer (A), penny washer (B), spring washer (C) and serrated washer (D)

● The split-ring spring washer works by applying axial tension between the fastener head and component. If flattened, it is fatigued and must be renewed. If a plain (flat) washer is used on the fastener, position the spring washer between the fastener and the plain washer.

● Serrated star type washers dig into the fastener and component faces, preventing loosening. They are often used on electrical earth (ground) connections to the frame.

● Cone type washers (sometimes called Belleville) are conical and when tightened apply axial tension between the fastener head and component. They must be installed with the dished side against the component and often carry an OUTSIDE marking on their outer face. If flattened, they are fatigued and must be renewed.

● Tab washers are used to lock plain nuts or bolts on a shaft. A portion of the tab washer is bent up hard against one flat of the nut or bolt to prevent it loosening. Due to the tab washer being deformed in use, a new tab washer should be used every time it is disturbed.

● Wave washers are used to take up endfloat on a shaft. They provide light springing and prevent excessive side-to-side play of a component. Can be found on rocker arm shafts.

Nuts and split pins

● Conventional plain nuts are usually six-sided **(see illustration 2.4)**. They are sized by thread diameter and pitch. High tensile nuts carry a number on one end to denote their tensile strength.

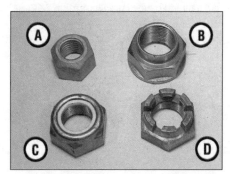

2.4 Plain nut (A), shouldered locknut (B), nylon insert nut (C) and castellated nut (D)

● Self-locking nuts either have a nylon insert, or two spring metal tabs, or a shoulder which is staked into a groove in the shaft - their advantage over conventional plain nuts is a resistance to loosening due to vibration. The nylon insert type can be used a number of times, but must be renewed when the friction of the nylon insert is reduced, ie when the nut spins freely on the shaft. The spring tab type can be reused unless the tabs are damaged. The shouldered type must be renewed every time it is disturbed.

● Split pins (cotter pins) are used to lock a castellated nut to a shaft or to prevent slackening of a plain nut. Common applications are wheel axles and brake torque arms. Because the split pin arms are deformed to lock around the nut a new split pin must always be used on installation - always fit the correct size split pin which will fit snugly in the shaft hole. Make sure the split pin arms are correctly located around the nut **(see illustrations 2.5 and 2.6)**.

2.5 Bend split pin (cotter pin) arms as shown (arrows) to secure a castellated nut

2.6 Bend split pin (cotter pin) arms as shown to secure a plain nut

Caution: If the castellated nut slots do not align with the shaft hole after tightening to the torque setting, tighten the nut until the next slot aligns with the hole - never slacken the nut to align its slot.

● R-pins (shaped like the letter R), or slip pins as they are sometimes called, are sprung and can be reused if they are otherwise in good condition. Always install R-pins with their closed end facing forwards **(see illustration 2.7)**.

**2.7 Correct fitting of R-pin.
Arrow indicates forward direction**

Circlips (see illustration 2.8)

● Circlips (sometimes called snap-rings) are used to retain components on a shaft or in a housing and have corresponding external or internal ears to permit removal. Parallel-sided (machined) circlips can be installed either way round in their groove, whereas stamped circlips (which have a chamfered edge on one face) must be installed with the chamfer facing away from the direction of thrust load **(see illustration 2.9)**.

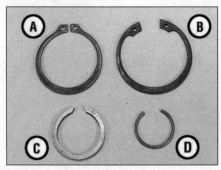

2.8 External stamped circlip (A), internal stamped circlip (B), machined circlip (C) and wire circlip (D)

● Always use circlip pliers to remove and install circlips; expand or compress them just enough to remove them. After installation, rotate the circlip in its groove to ensure it is securely seated. If installing a circlip on a splined shaft, always align its opening with a shaft channel to ensure the circlip ends are well supported and unlikely to catch **(see illustration 2.10)**.

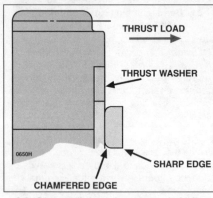

2.9 Correct fitting of a stamped circlip

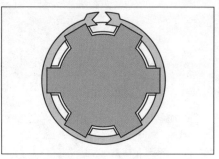

**2.10 Align circlip opening
with shaft channel**

● Circlips can wear due to the thrust of components and become loose in their grooves, with the subsequent danger of becoming dislodged in operation. For this reason, renewal is advised every time a circlip is disturbed.
● Wire circlips are commonly used as piston pin retaining clips. If a removal tang is provided, long-nosed pliers can be used to dislodge them, otherwise careful use of a small flat-bladed screwdriver is necessary. Wire circlips should be renewed every time they are disturbed.

Thread diameter and pitch

● Diameter of a male thread (screw, bolt or stud) is the outside diameter of the threaded portion **(see illustration 2.11)**. Most motorcycle manufacturers use the ISO (International Standards Organisation) metric system expressed in millimetres, eg M6 refers to a 6 mm diameter thread. Sizing is the same for nuts, except that the thread diameter is measured across the valleys of the nut.
● Pitch is the distance between the peaks of the thread **(see illustration 2.11)**. It is expressed in millimetres, thus a common bolt size may be expressed as 6.0 x 1.0 mm (6 mm thread diameter and 1 mm pitch). Generally pitch increases in proportion to thread diameter, although there are always exceptions.
● Thread diameter and pitch are related for conventional fastener applications and the accompanying table can be used as a guide. Additionally, the AF (Across Flats), spanner or socket size dimension of the bolt or nut **(see illustration 2.11)** is linked to thread and pitch specification. Thread pitch can be measured with a thread gauge **(see illustration 2.12)**.

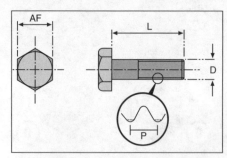

2.11 Fastener length (L), thread diameter (D), thread pitch (P) and head size (AF)

**2.12 Using a thread gauge
to measure pitch**

AF size	Thread diameter x pitch (mm)
8 mm	M5 x 0.8
8 mm	M6 x 1.0
10 mm	M6 x 1.0
12 mm	M8 x 1.25
14 mm	M10 x 1.25
17 mm	M12 x 1.25

● The threads of most fasteners are of the right-hand type, ie they are turned clockwise to tighten and anti-clockwise to loosen. The reverse situation applies to left-hand thread fasteners, which are turned anti-clockwise to tighten and clockwise to loosen. Left-hand threads are used where rotation of a component might loosen a conventional right-hand thread fastener.

Seized fasteners

● Corrosion of external fasteners due to water or reaction between two dissimilar metals can occur over a period of time. It will build up sooner in wet conditions or in countries where salt is used on the roads during the winter. If a fastener is severely corroded it is likely that normal methods of removal will fail and result in its head being ruined. When you attempt removal, the fastener thread should be heard to crack free and unscrew easily - if it doesn't, stop there before damaging something.
● A smart tap on the head of the fastener will often succeed in breaking free corrosion which has occurred in the threads **(see illustration 2.13)**.
● An aerosol penetrating fluid (such as WD-40) applied the night beforehand may work its way down into the thread and ease removal. Depending on the location, you may be able to make up a Plasticine well around the fastener head and fill it with penetrating fluid.

2.13 A sharp tap on the head of a fastener will often break free a corroded thread

• If you are working on an engine internal component, corrosion will most likely not be a problem due to the well lubricated environment. However, components can be very tight and an impact driver is a useful tool in freeing them **(see illustration 2.14)**.

2.14 Using an impact driver to free a fastener

• Where corrosion has occurred between dissimilar metals (eg steel and aluminium alloy), the application of heat to the fastener head will create a disproportionate expansion rate between the two metals and break the seizure caused by the corrosion. Whether heat can be applied depends on the location of the fastener - any surrounding components likely to be damaged must first be removed **(see illustration 2.15)**. Heat can be applied using a paint stripper heat gun or clothes iron, or by immersing the component in boiling water - wear protective gloves to prevent scalding or burns to the hands.

2.15 Using heat to free a seized fastener

• As a last resort, it is possible to use a hammer and cold chisel to work the fastener head unscrewed **(see illustration 2.16)**. This will damage the fastener, but more importantly extreme care must be taken not to damage the surrounding component.

Caution: Remember that the component being secured is generally of more value than the bolt, nut or screw - when the fastener is freed, do not unscrew it with force, instead work the fastener back and forth when resistance is felt to prevent thread damage.

2.16 Using a hammer and chisel to free a seized fastener

Broken fasteners and damaged heads

• If the shank of a broken bolt or screw is accessible you can grip it with self-locking grips. The knurled wheel type stud extractor tool or self-gripping stud puller tool is particularly useful for removing the long studs which screw into the cylinder mouth surface of the crankcase or bolts and screws from which the head has broken off **(see illustration 2.17)**. Studs can also be removed by locking two nuts together on the threaded end of the stud and using a spanner on the lower nut **(see illustration 2.18)**.

2.17 Using a stud extractor tool to remove a broken crankcase stud

2.18 Two nuts can be locked together to unscrew a stud from a component

• A bolt or screw which has broken off below or level with the casing must be extracted using a screw extractor set. Centre punch the fastener to centralise the drill bit, then drill a hole in the fastener **(see illustration 2.19)**. Select a drill bit which is approximately half to three-quarters the

2.19 When using a screw extractor, first drill a hole in the fastener . . .

diameter of the fastener and drill to a depth which will accommodate the extractor. Use the largest size extractor possible, but avoid leaving too small a wall thickness otherwise the extractor will merely force the fastener walls outwards wedging it in the casing thread.

• If a spiral type extractor is used, thread it anti-clockwise into the fastener. As it is screwed in, it will grip the fastener and unscrew it from the casing **(see illustration 2.20)**.

2.20 . . . then thread the extractor anti-clockwise into the fastener

• If a taper type extractor is used, tap it into the fastener so that it is firmly wedged in place. Unscrew the extractor (anti-clockwise) to draw the fastener out.

 Warning: Stud extractors are very hard and may break off in the fastener if care is not taken - ask an engineer about spark erosion if this happens.

• Alternatively, the broken bolt/screw can be drilled out and the hole retapped for an oversize bolt/screw or a diamond-section thread insert. It is essential that the drilling is carried out squarely and to the correct depth, otherwise the casing may be ruined - if in doubt, entrust the work to an engineer.

• Bolts and nuts with rounded corners cause the correct size spanner or socket to slip when force is applied. Of the types of spanner/socket available always use a six-point type rather than an eight or twelve-point type - better grip

2.21 Comparison of surface drive ring spanner (left) with 12-point type (right)

is obtained. Surface drive spanners grip the middle of the hex flats, rather than the corners, and are thus good in cases of damaged heads **(see illustration 2.21)**.

● Slotted-head or Phillips-head screws are often damaged by the use of the wrong size screwdriver. Allen-head and Torx-head screws are much less likely to sustain damage. If enough of the screw head is exposed you can use a hacksaw to cut a slot in its head and then use a conventional flat-bladed screwdriver to remove it. Alternatively use a hammer and cold chisel to tap the head of the fastener around to slacken it. Always replace damaged fasteners with new ones, preferably Torx or Allen-head type.

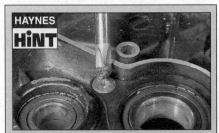

HAYNES HINT

A dab of valve grinding compound between the screw head and screw-driver tip will often give a good grip.

Thread repair

● Threads (particularly those in aluminium alloy components) can be damaged by overtightening, being assembled with dirt in the threads, or from a component working loose and vibrating. Eventually the thread will fail completely, and it will be impossible to tighten the fastener.

● If a thread is damaged or clogged with old locking compound it can be renovated with a thread repair tool (thread chaser) **(see illustrations 2.22 and 2.23)**; special thread

2.22 A thread repair tool being used to correct an internal thread

2.23 A thread repair tool being used to correct an external thread

chasers are available for spark plug hole threads. The tool will not cut a new thread, but clean and true the original thread. Make sure that you use the correct diameter and pitch tool. Similarly, external threads can be cleaned up with a die or a thread restorer file **(see illustration 2.24)**.

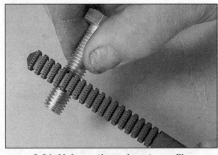

2.24 Using a thread restorer file

● It is possible to drill out the old thread and retap the component to the next thread size. This will work where there is enough surrounding material and a new bolt or screw can be obtained. Sometimes, however, this is not possible - such as where the bolt/screw passes through another component which must also be suitably modified, also in cases where a spark plug or oil drain plug cannot be obtained in a larger diameter thread size.

● The diamond-section thread insert (often known by its popular trade name of Heli-Coil) is a simple and effective method of renewing the thread and retaining the original size. A kit can be purchased which contains the tap, insert and installing tool **(see illustration 2.25)**. Drill out the damaged thread with the size drill specified **(see illustration 2.26)**. Carefully retap the thread **(see illustration 2.27)**. Install the

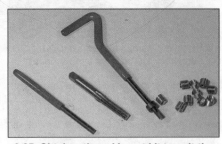

2.25 Obtain a thread insert kit to suit the thread diameter and pitch required

2.26 To install a thread insert, first drill out the original thread . . .

2.27 . . . tap a new thread . . .

2.28 . . . fit insert on the installing tool . . .

2.29 . . . and thread into the component . . .

2.30 . . . break off the tang when complete

insert on the installing tool and thread it slowly into place using a light downward pressure **(see illustrations 2.28 and 2.29)**. When positioned between a 1/4 and 1/2 turn below the surface withdraw the installing tool and use the break-off tool to press down on the tang, breaking it off **(see illustration 2.30)**.

● There are epoxy thread repair kits on the market which can rebuild stripped internal threads, although this repair should not be used on high load-bearing components.

Thread locking and sealing compounds

● Locking compounds are used in locations where the fastener is prone to loosening due to vibration or on important safety-related items which might cause loss of control of the motorcycle if they fail. It is also used where important fasteners cannot be secured by other means such as lockwashers or split pins.

● Before applying locking compound, make sure that the threads (internal and external) are clean and dry with all old compound removed. Select a compound to suit the component being secured - a non-permanent general locking and sealing type is suitable for most applications, but a high strength type is needed for permanent fixing of studs in castings. Apply a drop or two of the compound to the first few threads of the fastener, then thread it into place and tighten to the specified torque. Do not apply excessive thread locking compound otherwise the thread may be damaged on subsequent removal.

● Certain fasteners are impregnated with a dry film type coating of locking compound on their threads. Always renew this type of fastener if disturbed.

● Anti-seize compounds, such as copper-based greases, can be applied to protect threads from seizure due to extreme heat and corrosion. A common instance is spark plug threads and exhaust system fasteners.

3 Measuring tools and gauges

Feeler gauges

● Feeler gauges (or blades) are used for measuring small gaps and clearances (see illustration 3.1). They can also be used to measure endfloat (sideplay) of a component on a shaft where access is not possible with a dial gauge.

● Feeler gauge sets should be treated with care and not bent or damaged. They are etched with their size on one face. Keep them clean and very lightly oiled to prevent corrosion build-up.

3.1 Feeler gauges are used for measuring small gaps and clearances - thickness is marked on one face of gauge

● When measuring a clearance, select a gauge which is a light sliding fit between the two components. You may need to use two gauges together to measure the clearance accurately.

Micrometers

● A micrometer is a precision tool capable of measuring to 0.01 or 0.001 of a millimetre. It should always be stored in its case and not in the general toolbox. It must be kept clean and never dropped, otherwise its frame or measuring anvils could be distorted resulting in inaccurate readings.

● External micrometers are used for measuring outside diameters of components and have many more applications than internal micrometers. Micrometers are available in different size ranges, eg 0 to 25 mm, 25 to 50 mm, and upwards in 25 mm steps; some large micrometers have interchangeable anvils to allow a range of measurements to be taken. Generally the largest precision measurement you are likely to take on a motorcycle is the piston diameter.

● Internal micrometers (or bore micrometers) are used for measuring inside diameters, such as valve guides and cylinder bores. Telescoping gauges and small hole gauges are used in conjunction with an external micro-meter, whereas the more expensive internal micrometers have their own measuring device.

External micrometer

Note: *The conventional analogue type instrument is described. Although much easier to read, digital micrometers are considerably more expensive.*

● Always check the calibration of the micrometer before use. With the anvils closed (0 to 25 mm type) or set over a test gauge (for

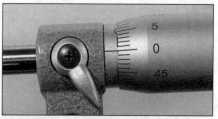

3.2 Check micrometer calibration before use

the larger types) the scale should read zero **(see illustration 3.2)**; make sure that the anvils (and test piece) are clean first. Any discrepancy can be adjusted by referring to the instructions supplied with the tool. Remember that the micrometer is a precision measuring tool - don't force the anvils closed, use the ratchet (4) on the end of the micrometer to close it. In this way, a measured force is always applied.

● To use, first make sure that the item being measured is clean. Place the anvil of the micrometer (1) against the item and use the thimble (2) to bring the spindle (3) lightly into contact with the other side of the item **(see illustration 3.3)**. Don't tighten the thimble down because this will damage the micrometer - instead use the ratchet (4) on the end of the micrometer. The ratchet mechanism applies a measured force preventing damage to the instrument.

● The micrometer is read by referring to the linear scale on the sleeve and the annular scale on the thimble. Read off the sleeve first to obtain the base measurement, then add the fine measurement from the thimble to obtain the overall reading. The linear scale on the sleeve represents the measuring range of the micrometer (eg 0 to 25 mm). The annular scale

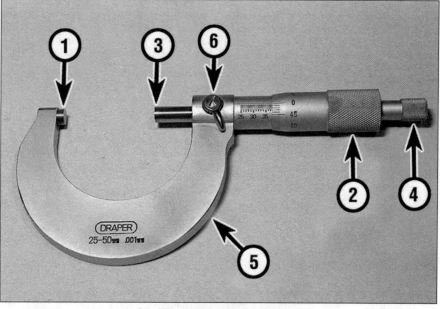

3.3 Micrometer component parts

1 Anvil	3 Spindle	5 Frame
2 Thimble	4 Ratchet	6 Locking lever

on the thimble will be in graduations of 0.01 mm (or as marked on the frame) - one full revolution of the thimble will move 0.5 mm on the linear scale. Take the reading where the datum line on the sleeve intersects the thimble's scale. Always position the eye directly above the scale otherwise an inaccurate reading will result.

In the example shown the item measures 2.95 mm **(see illustration 3.4)**:

Linear scale	2.00 mm
Linear scale	0.50 mm
Annular scale	0.45 mm
Total figure	**2.95 mm**

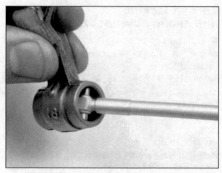

3.5 Micrometer reading of 46.99 mm on linear and annular scales . . .

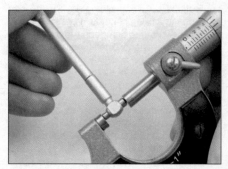

3.7 Expand the telescoping gauge in the bore, lock its position . . .

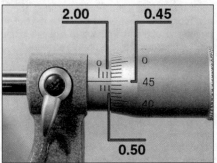

3.4 Micrometer reading of 2.95 mm

3.6 . . . and 0.004 mm on vernier scale

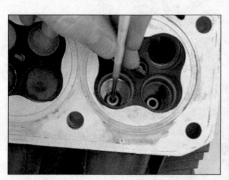

3.8 . . . then measure the gauge with a micrometer

Most micrometers have a locking lever (6) on the frame to hold the setting in place, allowing the item to be removed from the micrometer.
● Some micrometers have a vernier scale on their sleeve, providing an even finer measurement to be taken, in 0.001 increments of a millimetre. Take the sleeve and thimble measurement as described above, then check which graduation on the vernier scale aligns with that of the annular scale on the thimble **Note:** *The eye must be perpendicular to the scale when taking the vernier reading - if necessary rotate the body of the micrometer to ensure this.* Multiply the vernier scale figure by 0.001 and add it to the base and fine measurement figures.

In the example shown the item measures 46.994 mm **(see illustrations 3.5 and 3.6)**:

Linear scale (base)	46.000 mm
Linear scale (base)	00.500 mm
Annular scale (fine)	00.490 mm
Vernier scale	00.004 mm
Total figure	**46.994 mm**

Internal micrometer

● Internal micrometers are available for measuring bore diameters, but are expensive and unlikely to be available for home use. It is suggested that a set of telescoping gauges and small hole gauges, both of which must be used with an external micrometer, will suffice for taking internal measurements on a motorcycle.
● Telescoping gauges can be used to

measure internal diameters of components. Select a gauge with the correct size range, make sure its ends are clean and insert it into the bore. Expand the gauge, then lock its position and withdraw it from the bore **(see illustration 3.7)**. Measure across the gauge ends with a micrometer **(see illustration 3.8)**.
● Very small diameter bores (such as valve guides) are measured with a small hole gauge. Once adjusted to a slip-fit inside the component, its position is locked and the gauge withdrawn for measurement with a micrometer **(see illustrations 3.9 and 3.10)**.

Vernier caliper

Note: *The conventional linear and dial gauge type instruments are described. Digital types are easier to read, but are far more expensive.*
● The vernier caliper does not provide the precision of a micrometer, but is versatile in being able to measure internal and external diameters. Some types also incorporate a depth gauge. It is ideal for measuring clutch plate friction material and spring free lengths.
● To use the conventional linear scale vernier, slacken off the vernier clamp screws (1) and set its jaws over (2), or inside (3), the item to be measured **(see illustration 3.11)**. Slide the jaw into contact, using the thumb-wheel (4) for fine movement of the sliding scale (5) then tighten the clamp screws (1). Read off the main scale (6) where the zero on the sliding scale (5) intersects it, taking the whole number to the left of the zero; this provides the base measurement. View along the sliding scale and select the division which

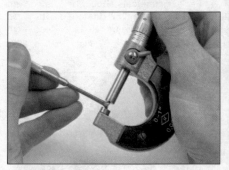

3.9 Expand the small hole gauge in the bore, lock its position . . .

3.10 . . . then measure the gauge with a micrometer

lines up exactly with any of the divisions on the main scale, noting that the divisions usually represents 0.02 of a millimetre. Add this fine measurement to the base measurement to obtain the total reading.

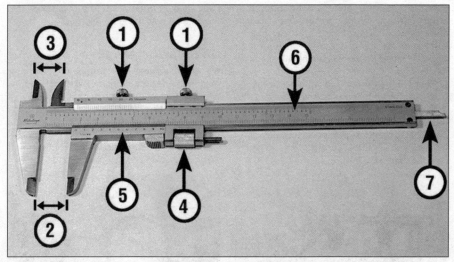

3.11 Vernier component parts (linear gauge)

1	Clamp screws	3	Internal jaws	5	Sliding scale	7	Depth gauge
2	External jaws	4	Thumbwheel	6	Main scale		

In the example shown the item measures 55.92 mm **(see illustration 3.12)**:

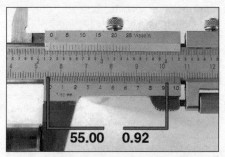

3.12 Vernier gauge reading of 55.92 mm

Base measurement	55.00 mm
Fine measurement	00.92 mm
Total figure	**55.92 mm**

● Some vernier calipers are equipped with a dial gauge for fine measurement. Before use, check that the jaws are clean, then close them fully and check that the dial gauge reads zero. If necessary adjust the gauge ring accordingly. Slacken the vernier clamp screw (1) and set its jaws over (2), or inside (3), the item to be measured **(see illustration 3.13)**. Slide the jaws into contact, using the thumbwheel (4) for fine movement. Read off the main scale (5) where the edge of the sliding scale (6) intersects it, taking the whole number to the left of the zero; this provides the base measurement. Read off the needle position on the dial gauge (7) scale to provide the fine measurement; each division represents 0.05 of a millimetre. Add this fine measurement to the base measurement to obtain the total reading.

In the example shown the item measures 55.95 mm **(see illustration 3.14)**:

Base measurement	55.00 mm
Fine measurement	00.95 mm
Total figure	**55.95 mm**

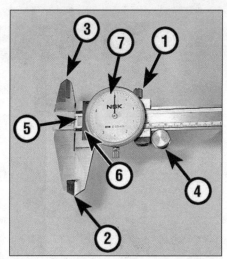

3.13 Vernier component parts (dial gauge)

1	Clamp screw	5	Main scale
2	External jaws	6	Sliding scale
3	Internal jaws	7	Dial gauge
4	Thumbwheel		

3.14 Vernier gauge reading of 55.95 mm

Plastigauge

● Plastigauge is a plastic material which can be compressed between two surfaces to measure the oil clearance between them. The width of the compressed Plastigauge is measured against a calibrated scale to determine the clearance.

● Common uses of Plastigauge are for measuring the clearance between crankshaft journal and main bearing inserts, between crankshaft journal and big-end bearing inserts, and between camshaft and bearing surfaces. The following example describes big-end oil clearance measurement.

● Handle the Plastigauge material carefully to prevent distortion. Using a sharp knife, cut a length which corresponds with the width of the bearing being measured and place it carefully across the journal so that it is parallel with the shaft **(see illustration 3.15)**. Carefully install both bearing shells and the connecting rod. Without rotating the rod on the journal tighten its bolts or nuts (as applicable) to the specified torque. The connecting rod and bearings are then disassembled and the crushed Plastigauge examined.

3.15 Plastigauge placed across shaft journal

● Using the scale provided in the Plastigauge kit, measure the width of the material to determine the oil clearance **(see illustration 3.16)**. Always remove all traces of Plastigauge after use using your fingernails.

Caution: Arriving at the correct clearance demands that the assembly is torqued correctly, according to the settings and sequence (where applicable) provided by the motorcycle manufacturer.

3.16 Measuring the width of the crushed Plastigauge

Dial gauge or DTI (Dial Test Indicator)

● A dial gauge can be used to accurately measure small amounts of movement. Typical uses are measuring shaft runout or shaft endfloat (sideplay) and setting piston position for ignition timing on two-strokes. A dial gauge set usually comes with a range of different probes and adapters and mounting equipment.

● The gauge needle must point to zero when at rest. Rotate the ring around its periphery to zero the gauge.

● Check that the gauge is capable of reading the extent of movement in the work. Most gauges have a small dial set in the face which records whole millimetres of movement as well as the fine scale around the face periphery which is calibrated in 0.01 mm divisions. Read off the small dial first to obtain the base measurement, then add the measurement from the fine scale to obtain the total reading.

In the example shown the gauge reads 1.48 mm (see illustration 3.17):

Base measurement	1.00 mm
Fine measurement	0.48 mm
Total figure	**1.48 mm**

3.17 Dial gauge reading of 1.48 mm

● If measuring shaft runout, the shaft must be supported in vee-blocks and the gauge mounted on a stand perpendicular to the shaft. Rest the tip of the gauge against the centre of the shaft and rotate the shaft slowly whilst watching the gauge reading (see illustration 3.18). Take several measurements along the length of the shaft and record the

3.18 Using a dial gauge to measure shaft runout

maximum gauge reading as the amount of runout in the shaft. **Note:** *The reading obtained will be total runout at that point - some manufacturers specify that the runout figure is halved to compare with their specified runout limit.*

● Endfloat (sideplay) measurement requires that the gauge is mounted securely to the surrounding component with its probe touching the end of the shaft. Using hand pressure, push and pull on the shaft noting the maximum endfloat recorded on the gauge (see illustration 3.19).

3.19 Using a dial gauge to measure shaft endfloat

● A dial gauge with suitable adapters can be used to determine piston position BTDC on two-stroke engines for the purposes of ignition timing. The gauge, adapter and suitable length probe are installed in the place of the spark plug and the gauge zeroed at TDC. If the piston position is specified as 1.14 mm BTDC, rotate the engine back to 2.00 mm BTDC, then slowly forwards to 1.14 mm BTDC.

Cylinder compression gauges

● A compression gauge is used for measuring cylinder compression. Either the rubber-cone type or the threaded adapter type can be used. The latter is preferred to ensure a perfect seal against the cylinder head. A 0 to 300 psi (0 to 20 Bar) type gauge (for petrol/gasoline engines) will be suitable for motorcycles.

● The spark plug is removed and the gauge either held hard against the cylinder head (cone type) or the gauge adapter screwed into the cylinder head (threaded type) (see illustration 3.20). Cylinder compression is measured with the engine turning over, but not running - carry out the compression test as described in

3.20 Using a rubber-cone type cylinder compression gauge

Fault Finding Equipment. The gauge will hold the reading until manually released.

Oil pressure gauge

● An oil pressure gauge is used for measuring engine oil pressure. Most gauges come with a set of adapters to fit the thread of the take-off point (see illustration 3.21). If the take-off point specified by the motorcycle manufacturer is an external oil pipe union, make sure that the specified replacement union is used to prevent oil starvation.

3.21 Oil pressure gauge and take-off point adapter (arrow)

● Oil pressure is measured with the engine running (at a specific rpm) and often the manufacturer will specify pressure limits for a cold and hot engine.

Straight-edge and surface plate

● If checking the gasket face of a component for warpage, place a steel rule or precision straight-edge across the gasket face and measure any gap between the straight-edge and component with feeler gauges (see illustration 3.22). Check diagonally across the component and between mounting holes (see illustration 3.23).

3.22 Use a straight-edge and feeler gauges to check for warpage

3.23 Check for warpage in these directions

● Checking individual components for warpage, such as clutch plain (metal) plates, requires a perfectly flat plate or piece or plate glass and feeler gauges.

4 Torque and leverage

What is torque?

● Torque describes the twisting force about a shaft. The amount of torque applied is determined by the distance from the centre of the shaft to the end of the lever and the amount of force being applied to the end of the lever; distance multiplied by force equals torque.

● The manufacturer applies a measured torque to a bolt or nut to ensure that it will not slacken in use and to hold two components securely together without movement in the joint. The actual torque setting depends on the thread size, bolt or nut material and the composition of the components being held.

● Too little torque may cause the fastener to loosen due to vibration, whereas too much torque will distort the joint faces of the component or cause the fastener to shear off. Always stick to the specified torque setting.

Using a torque wrench

● Check the calibration of the torque wrench and make sure it has a suitable range for the job. Torque wrenches are available in Nm (Newton-metres), kgf m (kilograms-force metre), lbf ft (pounds-feet), lbf in (inch-pounds). Do not confuse lbf ft with lbf in.

● Adjust the tool to the desired torque on the scale (see illustration 4.1). If your torque wrench is not calibrated in the units specified, carefully convert the figure (see Conversion Factors). A manufacturer sometimes gives a torque setting as a range (8 to 10 Nm) rather than a single figure - in this case set the tool midway between the two settings. The same torque may be expressed as 9 Nm ± 1 Nm. Some torque wrenches have a method of locking the setting so that it isn't inadvertently altered during use.

4.1 Set the torque wrench index mark to the setting required, in this case 12 Nm

● Install the bolts/nuts in their correct location and secure them lightly. Their threads must be clean and free of any old locking compound. Unless specified the threads and flange should be dry - oiled threads are necessary in certain circumstances and the manufacturer will take this into account in the specified torque figure. Similarly, the manufacturer may also specify the application of thread-locking compound.

● Tighten the fasteners in the specified sequence until the torque wrench clicks, indicating that the torque setting has been reached. Apply the torque again to double-check the setting. Where different thread diameter fasteners secure the component, as a rule tighten the larger diameter ones first.

● When the torque wrench has been finished with, release the lock (where applicable) and fully back off its setting to zero - do not leave the torque wrench tensioned. Also, do not use a torque wrench for slackening a fastener.

Angle-tightening

● Manufacturers often specify a figure in degrees for final tightening of a fastener. This usually follows tightening to a specific torque setting.

● A degree disc can be set and attached to the socket (see illustration 4.2) or a protractor can be used to mark the angle of movement on the bolt/nut head and the surrounding casting (see illustration 4.3).

4.2 Angle tightening can be accomplished with a torque-angle gauge . . .

4.3 . . . or by marking the angle on the surrounding component

Loosening sequences

● Where more than one bolt/nut secures a component, loosen each fastener evenly a little at a time. In this way, not all the stress of the joint is held by one fastener and the components are not likely to distort.

● If a tightening sequence is provided, work in the REVERSE of this, but if not, work from the outside in, in a criss-cross sequence (see illustration 4.4).

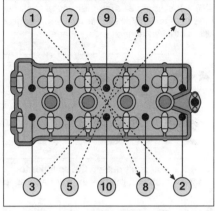

4.4 When slackening, work from the outside inwards

Tightening sequences

● If a component is held by more than one fastener it is important that the retaining bolts/nuts are tightened evenly to prevent uneven stress build-up and distortion of sealing faces. This is especially important on high-compression joints such as the cylinder head.

● A sequence is usually provided by the manufacturer, either in a diagram or actually marked in the casting. If not, always start in the centre and work outwards in a criss-cross pattern (see illustration 4.5). Start off by securing all bolts/nuts finger-tight, then set the torque wrench and tighten each fastener by a small amount in sequence until the final torque is reached. By following this practice,

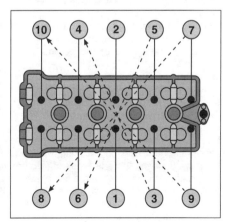

4.5 When tightening, work from the inside outwards

the joint will be held evenly and will not be distorted. Important joints, such as the cylinder head and big-end fasteners often have two- or three-stage torque settings.

Applying leverage

● Use tools at the correct angle. Position a socket wrench or spanner on the bolt/nut so that you pull it towards you when loosening. If this can't be done, push the spanner without curling your fingers around it **(see illustration 4.6)** - the spanner may slip or the fastener loosen suddenly, resulting in your fingers being crushed against a component.

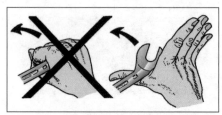

4.6 If you can't pull on the spanner to loosen a fastener, push with your hand open

● Additional leverage is gained by extending the length of the lever. The best way to do this is to use a breaker bar instead of the regular length tool, or to slip a length of tubing over the end of the spanner or socket wrench.
● If additional leverage will not work, the fastener head is either damaged or firmly corroded in place (see *Fasteners*).

5 Bearings

Bearing removal and installation

Drivers and sockets

● Before removing a bearing, always inspect the casing to see which way it must be driven out - some casings will have retaining plates or a cast step. Also check for any identifying markings on the bearing and if installed to a certain depth, measure this at this stage. Some roller bearings are sealed on one side - take note of the original fitted position.
● Bearings can be driven out of a casing using a bearing driver tool (with the correct size head) or a socket of the correct diameter. Select the driver head or socket so that it contacts the outer race of the bearing, not the balls/rollers or inner race. Always support the casing around the bearing housing with wood blocks, otherwise there is a risk of fracture. The bearing is driven out with a few blows on the driver or socket from a heavy mallet. Unless access is severely restricted (as with wheel bearings), a pin-punch is not recommended unless it is moved around the bearing to keep it square in its housing.

● The same equipment can be used to install bearings. Make sure the bearing housing is supported on wood blocks and line up the bearing in its housing. Fit the bearing as noted on removal - generally they are installed with their marked side facing outwards. Tap the bearing squarely into its housing using a driver or socket which bears only on the bearing's outer race - contact with the bearing balls/rollers or inner race will destroy it **(see illustrations 5.1 and 5.2)**.
● Check that the bearing inner race and balls/rollers rotate freely.

5.1 Using a bearing driver against the bearing's outer race

5.2 Using a large socket against the bearing's outer race

Pullers and slide-hammers

● Where a bearing is pressed on a shaft a puller will be required to extract it **(see illustration 5.3)**. Make sure that the puller clamp or legs fit securely behind the bearing and are unlikely to slip out. If pulling a bearing

5.3 This bearing puller clamps behind the bearing and pressure is applied to the shaft end to draw the bearing off

off a gear shaft for example, you may have to locate the puller behind a gear pinion if there is no access to the race and draw the gear pinion off the shaft as well **(see illustration 5.4)**.

> **Caution: Ensure that the puller's centre bolt locates securely against the end of the shaft and will not slip when pressure is applied. Also ensure that puller does not damage the shaft end.**

5.4 Where no access is available to the rear of the bearing, it is sometimes possible to draw off the adjacent component

● Operate the puller so that its centre bolt exerts pressure on the shaft end and draws the bearing off the shaft.
● When installing the bearing on the shaft, tap only on the bearing's inner race - contact with the balls/rollers or outer race with destroy the bearing. Use a socket or length of tubing as a drift which fits over the shaft end **(see illustration 5.5)**.

5.5 When installing a bearing on a shaft use a piece of tubing which bears only on the bearing's inner race

● Where a bearing locates in a blind hole in a casing, it cannot be driven or pulled out as described above. A slide-hammer with knife-edged bearing puller attachment will be required. The puller attachment passes through the bearing and when tightened expands to fit firmly behind the bearing **(see illustration 5.6)**. By operating the slide-hammer part of the tool the bearing is jarred out of its housing **(see illustration 5.7)**.
● It is possible, if the bearing is of reasonable weight, for it to drop out of its housing if the casing is heated as described opposite. If this

5.6 Expand the bearing puller so that it locks behind the bearing . . .

5.7 . . . attach the slide hammer to the bearing puller

method is attempted, first prepare a work surface which will enable the casing to be tapped face down to help dislodge the bearing - a wood surface is ideal since it will not damage the casing's gasket surface. Wearing protective gloves, tap the heated casing several times against the work surface to dislodge the bearing under its own weight (**see illustration 5.8**).

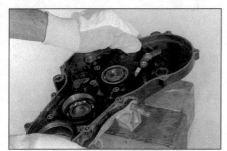

5.8 Tapping a casing face down on wood blocks can often dislodge a bearing

● Bearings can be installed in blind holes using the driver or socket method described above.

Drawbolts

● Where a bearing or bush is set in the eye of a component, such as a suspension linkage arm or connecting rod small-end, removal by drift may damage the component. Furthermore, a rubber bushing in a shock absorber eye cannot successfully be driven out of position. If access is available to a engineering press, the task is straightforward. If not, a drawbolt can be fabricated to extract the bearing or bush.

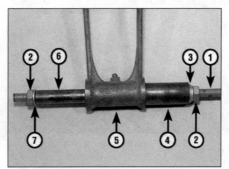

5.9 Drawbolt component parts assembled on a suspension arm

1 *Bolt or length of threaded bar*
2 *Nuts*
3 *Washer (external diameter greater than tubing internal diameter)*
4 *Tubing (internal diameter sufficient to accommodate bearing)*
5 *Suspension arm with bearing*
6 *Tubing (external diameter slightly smaller than bearing)*
7 *Washer (external diameter slightly smaller than bearing)*

5.10 Drawing the bearing out of the suspension arm

● To extract the bearing/bush you will need a long bolt with nut (or piece of threaded bar with two nuts), a piece of tubing which has an internal diameter larger than the bearing/bush, another piece of tubing which has an external diameter slightly smaller than the bearing/ bush, and a selection of washers (**see illustrations 5.9 and 5.10**). Note that the pieces of tubing must be of the same length, or longer, than the bearing/bush.
● The same kit (without the pieces of tubing) can be used to draw the new bearing/bush back into place (**see illustration 5.11**).

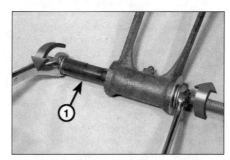

5.11 Installing a new bearing (1) in the suspension arm

Temperature change

● If the bearing's outer race is a tight fit in the casing, the aluminium casing can be heated to release its grip on the bearing. Aluminium will expand at a greater rate than the steel bearing outer race. There are several ways to do this, but avoid any localised extreme heat (such as a blow torch) - aluminium alloy has a low melting point.
● Approved methods of heating a casing are using a domestic oven (heated to 100°C) or immersing the casing in boiling water (**see illustration 5.12**). Low temperature range localised heat sources such as a paint stripper heat gun or clothes iron can also be used (**see illustration 5.13**). Alternatively, soak a rag in boiling water, wring it out and wrap it around the bearing housing.

> ⚠ *Warning: All of these methods require care in use to prevent scalding and burns to the hands. Wear protective gloves when handling hot components.*

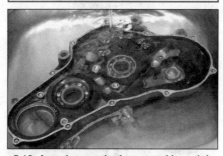

5.12 A casing can be immersed in a sink of boiling water to aid bearing removal

5.13 Using a localised heat source to aid bearing removal

● If heating the whole casing note that plastic components, such as the neutral switch, may suffer - remove them beforehand.
● After heating, remove the bearing as described above. You may find that the expansion is sufficient for the bearing to fall out of the casing under its own weight or with a light tap on the driver or socket.
● If necessary, the casing can be heated to aid bearing installation, and this is sometimes the recommended procedure if the motorcycle manufacturer has designed the housing and bearing fit with this intention.

● Installation of bearings can be eased by placing them in a freezer the night before installation. The steel bearing will contract slightly, allowing easy insertion in its housing. This is often useful when installing steering head outer races in the frame.

Bearing types and markings

● Plain shell bearings, ball bearings, needle roller bearings and tapered roller bearings will all be found on motorcycles (see illustrations 5.14 and 5.15). The ball and roller types are usually caged between an inner and outer race, but uncaged variations may be found.

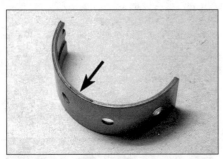

5.14 Shell bearings are either plain or grooved. They are usually identified by colour code (arrow)

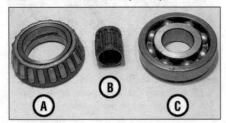

5.15 Tapered roller bearing (A), needle roller bearing (B) and ball journal bearing (C)

● Shell bearings (often called inserts) are usually found at the crankshaft main and connecting rod big-end where they are good at coping with high loads. They are made of a phosphor-bronze material and are impregnated with self-lubricating properties.
● Ball bearings and needle roller bearings consist of a steel inner and outer race with the balls or rollers between the races. They require constant lubrication by oil or grease and are good at coping with axial loads. Taper roller bearings consist of rollers set in a tapered cage set on the inner race; the outer race is separate. They are good at coping with axial loads and prevent movement along the shaft - a typical application is in the steering head.
● Bearing manufacturers produce bearings to ISO size standards and stamp one face of the bearing to indicate its internal and external diameter, load capacity and type (see illustration 5.16).
● Metal bushes are usually of phosphor-bronze material. Rubber bushes are used in suspension mounting eyes. Fibre bushes have also been used in suspension pivots.

5.16 Typical bearing marking

Bearing fault finding

● If a bearing outer race has spun in its housing, the housing material will be damaged. You can use a bearing locking compound to bond the outer race in place if damage is not too severe.
● Shell bearings will fail due to damage of their working surface, as a result of lack of lubrication, corrosion or abrasive particles in the oil (see illustration 5.17). Small particles of dirt in the oil may embed in the bearing material whereas larger particles will score the bearing and shaft journal. If a number of short journeys are made, insufficient heat will be generated to drive off condensation which has built up on the bearings.

5.17 Typical bearing failures

● Ball and roller bearings will fail due to lack of lubrication or damage to the balls or rollers. Tapered-roller bearings can be damaged by overloading them. Unless the bearing is sealed on both sides, wash it in paraffin (kerosene) to remove all old grease then allow it to dry. Make a visual inspection looking to dented balls or rollers, damaged cages and worn or pitted races (see illustration 5.18).
● A ball bearing can be checked for wear by listening to it when spun. Apply a film of light oil to the bearing and hold it close to the ear - hold the outer race with one hand and spin the inner

5.18 Example of ball journal bearing with damaged balls and cages

5.19 Hold outer race and listen to inner race when spun

race with the other hand (see illustration 5.19). The bearing should be almost silent when spun; if it grates or rattles it is worn.

6 Oil seals

Oil seal removal and installation

● Oil seals should be renewed every time a component is dismantled. This is because the seal lips will become set to the sealing surface and will not necessarily reseal.
● Oil seals can be prised out of position using a large flat-bladed screwdriver (see illustration 6.1). In the case of crankcase seals, check first that the seal is not lipped on the inside, preventing its removal with the crankcases joined.

6.1 Prise out oil seals with a large flat-bladed screwdriver

● New seals are usually installed with their marked face (containing the seal reference code) outwards and the spring side towards the fluid being retained. In certain cases, such as a two-stroke engine crankshaft seal, a double lipped seal may be used due to there being fluid or gas on each side of the joint.

● Use a bearing driver or socket which bears only on the outer hard edge of the seal to install it in the casing - tapping on the inner edge will damage the sealing lip.

Oil seal types and markings

● Oil seals are usually of the single-lipped type. Double-lipped seals are found where a liquid or gas is on both sides of the joint.
● Oil seals can harden and lose their sealing ability if the motorcycle has been in storage for a long period - renewal is the only solution.
● Oil seal manufacturers also conform to the ISO markings for seal size - these are moulded into the outer face of the seal (see illustration 6.2).

6.2 These oil seal markings indicate inside diameter, outside diameter and seal thickness

7 Gaskets and sealants

Types of gasket and sealant

● Gaskets are used to seal the mating surfaces between components and keep lubricants, fluids, vacuum or pressure contained within the assembly. Aluminium gaskets are sometimes found at the cylinder joints, but most gaskets are paper-based. If the mating surfaces of the components being joined are undamaged the gasket can be installed dry, although a dab of sealant or grease will be useful to hold it in place during assembly.
● RTV (Room Temperature Vulcanising) silicone rubber sealants cure when exposed to moisture in the atmosphere. These sealants are good at filling pits or irregular gasket faces, but will tend to be forced out of the joint under very high torque. They can be used to replace a paper gasket, but first make sure that the width of the paper gasket is not essential to the shimming of internal components. RTV sealants should not be used on components containing petrol (gasoline).
● Non-hardening, semi-hardening and hard setting liquid gasket compounds can be used with a gasket or between a metal-to-metal joint. Select the sealant to suit the application: universal non-hardening sealant can be used on virtually all joints; semi-hardening on joint faces which are rough or damaged; hard setting sealant on joints which require a permanent bond and are subjected to high temperature and pressure. **Note:** *Check first if the paper gasket has a bead of sealant*

impregnated in its surface before applying additional sealant.
● When choosing a sealant, make sure it is suitable for the application, particularly if being applied in a high-temperature area or in the vicinity of fuel. Certain manufacturers produce sealants in either clear, silver or black colours to match the finish of the engine. This has a particular application on motorcycles where much of the engine is exposed.
● Do not over-apply sealant. That which is squeezed out on the outside of the joint can be wiped off, whereas an excess of sealant on the inside can break off and clog oilways.

Breaking a sealed joint

● Age, heat, pressure and the use of hard setting sealant can cause two components to stick together so tightly that they are difficult to separate using finger pressure alone. Do not resort to using levers unless there is a pry point provided for this purpose (see illustration 7.1) or else the gasket surfaces will be damaged.
● Use a soft-faced hammer (see illustration 7.2) or a wood block and conventional hammer to strike the component near the mating surface. Avoid hammering against cast extremities since they may break off. If this method fails, try using a wood wedge between the two components.

Caution: If the joint will not separate, double-check that you have removed all the fasteners.

7.1 If a pry point is provided, apply gently pressure with a flat-bladed screwdriver

7.2 Tap around the joint with a soft-faced mallet if necessary - don't strike cooling fins

Removal of old gasket and sealant

● Paper gaskets will most likely come away complete, leaving only a few traces stuck on

HAYNES HiNT

Most components have one or two hollow locating dowels between the two gasket faces. If a dowel cannot be removed, do not resort to gripping it with pliers - it will almost certainly be distorted. Install a close-fitting socket or Phillips screwdriver into the dowel and then grip the outer edge of the dowel to free it.

the sealing faces of the components. It is imperative that all traces are removed to ensure correct sealing of the new gasket.
● Very carefully scrape all traces of gasket away making sure that the sealing surfaces are not gouged or scored by the scraper (see illustrations 7.3, 7.4 and 7.5). Stubborn deposits can be removed by spraying with an aerosol gasket remover. Final preparation of

7.3 Paper gaskets can be scraped off with a gasket scraper tool . . .

7.4 . . . a knife blade . . .

7.5 . . . or a household scraper

7.6 Fine abrasive paper is wrapped around a flat file to clean up the gasket face

7.7 A kitchen scourer can be used on stubborn deposits

the gasket surface can be made with very fine abrasive paper or a plastic kitchen scourer **(see illustrations 7.6 and 7.7).**

● Old sealant can be scraped or peeled off components, depending on the type originally used. Note that gasket removal compounds are available to avoid scraping the components clean; make sure the gasket remover suits the type of sealant used.

8 Chains

Breaking and joining final drive chains

● Drive chains for all but small bikes are continuous and do not have a clip-type connecting link. The chain must be broken using a chain breaker tool and the new chain securely riveted together using a new soft rivet-type link. Never use a clip-type connecting link instead of a rivet-type link, except in an emergency. Various chain breaking and riveting tools are available, either as separate tools or combined as illustrated in the accompanying photographs - read the instructions supplied with the tool carefully.

⚠️ *Warning: The need to rivet the new link pins correctly cannot be overstressed - loss of control of the motorcycle is very likely to result if the chain breaks in use.*

● Rotate the chain and look for the soft link. The soft link pins look like they have been

8.1 Tighten the chain breaker to push the pin out of the link . . .

8.2 . . . withdraw the pin, remove the tool . . .

8.3 . . . and separate the chain link

deeply centre-punched instead of peened over like all the other pins **(see illustration 8.9)** and its sideplate may be a different colour. Position the soft link midway between the sprockets and assemble the chain breaker tool over one of the soft link pins **(see illustration 8.1).** Operate the tool to push the pin out through the chain **(see illustration 8.2).** On an O-ring chain, remove the O-rings **(see illustration 8.3).** Carry out the same procedure on the other soft link pin.

> *Caution: Certain soft link pins (particularly on the larger chains) may require their ends to be filed or ground off before they can be pressed out using the tool.*

● Check that you have the correct size and strength (standard or heavy duty) new soft link - do not reuse the old link. Look for the size marking on the chain sideplates **(see illustration 8.10).**

● Position the chain ends so that they are engaged over the rear sprocket. On an O-ring

8.4 Insert the new soft link, with O-rings, through the chain ends . . .

8.5 . . . install the O-rings over the pin ends . . .

8.6 . . . followed by the sideplate

chain, install a new O-ring over each pin of the link and insert the link through the two chain ends **(see illustration 8.4).** Install a new O-ring over the end of each pin, followed by the sideplate (with the chain manufacturer's marking facing outwards) **(see illustrations 8.5 and 8.6).** On an unsealed chain, insert the link through the two chain ends, then install the sideplate with the chain manufacturer's marking facing outwards.

● Note that it may not be possible to install the sideplate using finger pressure alone. If using a joining tool, assemble it so that the plates of the tool clamp the link and press the sideplate over the pins **(see illustration 8.7).** Otherwise, use two small sockets placed over

8.7 Push the sideplate into position using a clamp

8.8 Assemble the chain riveting tool over one pin at a time and tighten it fully

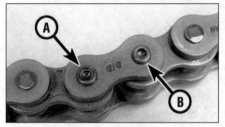

8.9 Pin end correctly riveted (A), pin end unriveted (B)

the rivet ends and two pieces of the wood between a G-clamp. Operate the clamp to press the sideplate over the pins.

● Assemble the joining tool over one pin (following the maker's instructions) and tighten the tool down to spread the pin end securely **(see illustrations 8.8 and 8.9)**. Do the same on the other pin.

> **Warning: Check that the pin ends are secure and that there is no danger of the sideplate coming loose. If the pin ends are cracked the soft link must be renewed.**

Final drive chain sizing

● Chains are sized using a three digit number, followed by a suffix to denote the chain type **(see illustration 8.10)**. Chain type is either standard or heavy duty (thicker sideplates), and also unsealed or O-ring/X-ring type.

● The first digit of the number relates to the pitch of the chain, ie the distance from the centre of one pin to the centre of the next pin **(see illustration 8.11)**. Pitch is expressed in eighths of an inch, as follows:

8.10 Typical chain size and type marking

8.11 Chain dimensions

Sizes commencing with a 4 (eg 428) have a pitch of 1/2 inch (12.7 mm)
Sizes commencing with a 5 (eg 520) have a pitch of 5/8 inch (15.9 mm)
Sizes commencing with a 6 (eg 630) have a pitch of 3/4 inch (19.1 mm)

● The second and third digits of the chain size relate to the width of the rollers, again in imperial units, eg the 525 shown has 5/16 inch (7.94 mm) rollers **(see illustration 8.11)**.

9 Hoses

Clamping to prevent flow

● Small-bore flexible hoses can be clamped to prevent fluid flow whilst a component is worked on. Whichever method is used, ensure that the hose material is not permanently distorted or damaged by the clamp.

a) A brake hose clamp available from auto accessory shops **(see illustration 9.1)**.
b) A wingnut type hose clamp **(see illustration 9.2)**.

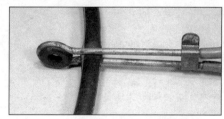

9.1 Hoses can be clamped with an automotive brake hose clamp . . .

9.2 . . . a wingnut type hose clamp . . .

c) Two sockets placed each side of the hose and held with straight-jawed self-locking grips **(see illustration 9.3)**.
d) Thick card each side of the hose held between straight-jawed self-locking grips **(see illustration 9.4)**.

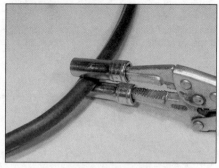

9.3 . . . two sockets and a pair of self-locking grips . . .

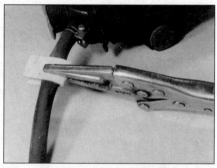

9.4 . . . or thick card and self-locking grips

Freeing and fitting hoses

● Always make sure the hose clamp is moved well clear of the hose end. Grip the hose with your hand and rotate it whilst pulling it off the union. If the hose has hardened due to age and will not move, slit it with a sharp knife and peel its ends off the union **(see illustration 9.5)**.

● Resist the temptation to use grease or soap on the unions to aid installation; although it helps the hose slip over the union it will equally aid the escape of fluid from the joint. It is preferable to soften the hose ends in hot water and wet the inside surface of the hose with water or a fluid which will evaporate.

9.5 Cutting a coolant hose free with a sharp knife

Length (distance)

Inches (in)	x 25.4	= Millimetres (mm)	x 0.0394	= Inches (in)
Feet (ft)	x 0.305	= Metres (m)	x 3.281	= Feet (ft)
Miles	x 1.609	= Kilometres (km)	x 0.621	= Miles

Volume (capacity)

Cubic inches (cu in; in³)	x 16.387	= Cubic centimetres (cc; cm³)	x 0.061	= Cubic inches (cu in; in³)
Imperial pints (Imp pt)	x 0.568	= Litres (l)	x 1.76	= Imperial pints (Imp pt)
Imperial quarts (Imp qt)	x 1.137	= Litres (l)	x 0.88	= Imperial quarts (Imp qt)
Imperial quarts (Imp qt)	x 1.201	= US quarts (US qt)	x 0.833	= Imperial quarts (Imp qt)
US quarts (US qt)	x 0.946	= Litres (l)	x 1.057	= US quarts (US qt)
Imperial gallons (Imp gal)	x 4.546	= Litres (l)	x 0.22	= Imperial gallons (Imp gal)
Imperial gallons (Imp gal)	x 1.201	= US gallons (US gal)	x 0.833	= Imperial gallons (Imp gal)
US gallons (US gal)	x 3.785	= Litres (l)	x 0.264	= US gallons (US gal)

Mass (weight)

Ounces (oz)	x 28.35	= Grams (g)	x 0.035	= Ounces (oz)
Pounds (lb)	x 0.454	= Kilograms (kg)	x 2.205	= Pounds (lb)

Force

Ounces-force (ozf; oz)	x 0.278	= Newtons (N)	x 3.6	= Ounces-force (ozf; oz)
Pounds-force (lbf; lb)	x 4.448	= Newtons (N)	x 0.225	= Pounds-force (lbf; lb)
Newtons (N)	x 0.1	= Kilograms-force (kgf; kg)	x 9.81	= Newtons (N)

Pressure

Pounds-force per square inch (psi; lbf/in²; lb/in²)	x 0.070	= Kilograms-force per square centimetre (kgf/cm²; kg/cm²)	x 14.223	= Pounds-force per square inch (psi; lbf/in²; lb/in²)
Pounds-force per square inch (psi; lbf/in²; lb/in²)	x 0.068	= Atmospheres (atm)	x 14.696	= Pounds-force per square inch (psi; lbf/in²; lb/in²)
Pounds-force per square inch (psi; lbf/in²; lb/in²)	x 0.069	= Bars	x 14.5	= Pounds-force per square inch (psi; lbf/in²; lb/in²)
Pounds-force per square inch (psi; lbf/in²; lb/in²)	x 6.895	= Kilopascals (kPa)	x 0.145	= Pounds-force per square inch (psi; lbf/in²; lb/in²)
Kilopascals (kPa)	x 0.01	= Kilograms-force per square centimetre (kgf/cm²; kg/cm²)	x 98.1	= Kilopascals (kPa)
Millibar (mbar)	x 100	= Pascals (Pa)	x 0.01	= Millibar (mbar)
Millibar (mbar)	x 0.0145	= Pounds-force per square inch (psi; lbf/in²; lb/in²)	x 68.947	= Millibar (mbar)
Millibar (mbar)	x 0.75	= Millimetres of mercury (mmHg)	x 1.333	= Millibar (mbar)
Millibar (mbar)	x 0.401	= Inches of water (inH₂O)	x 2.491	= Millibar (mbar)
Millimetres of mercury (mmHg)	x 0.535	= Inches of water (inH₂O)	x 1.868	= Millimetres of mercury (mmHg)
Inches of water (inH₂O)	x 0.036	= Pounds-force per square inch (psi; lbf/in²; lb/in²)	x 27.68	= Inches of water (inH₂O)

Torque (moment of force)

Pounds-force inches (lbf in; lb in)	x 1.152	= Kilograms-force centimetre (kgf cm; kg cm)	x 0.868	= Pounds-force inches (lbf in; lb in)
Pounds-force inches (lbf in; lb in)	x 0.113	= Newton metres (Nm)	x 8.85	= Pounds-force inches (lbf in; lb in)
Pounds-force inches (lbf in; lb in)	x 0.083	= Pounds-force feet (lbf ft; lb ft)	x 12	= Pounds-force inches (lbf in; lb in)
Pounds-force feet (lbf ft; lb ft)	x 0.138	= Kilograms-force metres (kgf m; kg m)	x 7.233	= Pounds-force feet (lbf ft; lb ft)
Pounds-force feet (lbf ft; lb ft)	x 1.356	= Newton metres (Nm)	x 0.738	= Pounds-force feet (lbf ft; lb ft)
Newton metres (Nm)	x 0.102	= Kilograms-force metres (kgf m; kg m)	x 9.804	= Newton metres (Nm)

Power

Horsepower (hp)	x 745.7	= Watts (W)	x 0.0013	= Horsepower (hp)

Velocity (speed)

Miles per hour (miles/hr; mph)	x 1.609	= Kilometres per hour (km/hr; kph)	x 0.621	= Miles per hour (miles/hr; mph)

Fuel consumption*

Miles per gallon (mpg)	x 0.354	= Kilometres per litre (km/l)	x 2.825	= Miles per gallon (mpg)

Temperature

Degrees Fahrenheit = (°C x 1.8) + 32   Degrees Celsius (Degrees Centigrade; °C) = (°F - 32) x 0.56

It is common practice to convert from miles per gallon (mpg) to litres/100 kilometres (l/100km), where mpg x l/100 km = 282

A number of chemicals and lubricants are available for use in motorcycle maintenance and repair. They include a wide variety of products ranging from cleaning solvents and degreasers to lubricants and protective sprays for rubber, plastic and vinyl.

● **Contact point/spark plug cleaner** is a solvent used to clean oily film and dirt from points, grime from electrical connectors and oil deposits from spark plugs. It is oil free and leaves no residue. It can also be used to remove gum and varnish from carburettor jets and other orifices.

● **Carburettor cleaner** is similar to contact point/spark plug cleaner but it usually has a stronger solvent and may leave a slight oily reside. It is not recommended for cleaning electrical components or connections.

● **Brake system cleaner** is used to remove grease or brake fluid from brake system components (where clean surfaces are absolutely necessary and petroleum-based solvents cannot be used); it also leaves no residue.

● **Silicone-based lubricants** are used to protect rubber parts such as hoses and grommets, and are used as lubricants for hinges and locks.

● **Multi-purpose grease** is an all purpose lubricant used wherever grease is more practical than a liquid lubricant such as oil. Some multi-purpose grease is coloured white and specially formulated to be more resistant to water than ordinary grease.

● **Gear oil** (sometimes called gear lube) is a specially designed oil used in transmissions and final drive units, as well as other areas where high friction, high temperature lubrication is required. It is available in a number of viscosities (weights) for various applications.

● **Motor oil**, of course, is the lubricant specially formulated for use in the engine. It normally contains a wide variety of additives to prevent corrosion and reduce foaming and wear. Motor oil comes in various weights (viscosity ratings) of from 5 to 80. The recommended weight of the oil depends on the seasonal temperature and the demands on the engine. Light oil is used in cold climates and under light load conditions; heavy oil is used in hot climates and where high loads are encountered. Multi-viscosity oils are designed to have characteristics of both light and heavy oils and are available in a number of weights from 5W-20 to 20W-50.

● **Petrol additives** perform several functions, depending on their chemical makeup. They usually contain solvents that help dissolve gum and varnish that build up on carburettor and inlet parts. They also serve to break down carbon deposits that form on the inside surfaces of the combustion chambers. Some additives contain upper cylinder lubricants for valves and piston rings.

● **Brake and clutch fluid** is a specially formulated hydraulic fluid that can withstand the heat and pressure encountered in brake/clutch systems. Care must be taken that this fluid does not come in contact with painted surfaces or plastics. An opened container should always be resealed to prevent contamination by water or dirt.

● **Chain lubricants** are formulated especially for use on motorcycle final drive chains. A good chain lube should adhere well and have good penetrating qualities to be effective as a lubricant inside the chain and on the side plates, pins and rollers. Most chain lubes are either the foaming type or quick drying type and are usually marketed as sprays. Take care to use a lubricant marked as being suitable for O-ring chains.

● **Degreasers** are heavy duty solvents used to remove grease and grime that may accumulate on engine and frame components. They can be sprayed or brushed on and, depending on the type, are rinsed with either water or solvent.

● **Solvents** are used alone or in combination with degreasers to clean parts and assemblies during repair and overhaul. The home mechanic should use only solvents that are non-flammable and that do not produce irritating fumes.

● **Gasket sealing compounds** may be used in conjunction with gaskets, to improve their sealing capabilities, or alone, to seal metal-to-metal joints. Many gasket sealers can withstand extreme heat, some are impervious to petrol and lubricants, while others are capable of filling and sealing large cavities. Depending on the intended use, gasket sealers either dry hard or stay relatively soft and pliable. They are usually applied by hand, with a brush, or are sprayed on the gasket sealing surfaces.

● **Thread locking compound** is an adhesive locking compound that prevents threaded fasteners from loosening because of vibration. It is available in a variety of types for different applications.

● **Moisture dispersants** are usually sprays that can be used to dry out electrical components such as the fuse block and wiring connectors. Some types can also be used as treatment for rubber and as a lubricant for hinges, cables and locks.

● **Waxes and polishes** are used to help protect painted and plated surfaces from the weather. Different types of paint may require the use of different types of wax polish. Some polishes utilise a chemical or abrasive cleaner to help remove the top layer of oxidised (dull) paint on older vehicles. In recent years, many non-wax polishes (that contain a wide variety of chemicals such as polymers and silicones) have been introduced. These non-wax polishes are usually easier to apply and last longer than conventional waxes and polishes.

About the MOT Test

In the UK, all vehicles more than three years old are subject to an annual test to ensure that they meet minimum safety requirements. A current test certificate must be issued before a machine can be used on public roads, and is required before a road fund licence can be issued. Riding without a current test certificate will also invalidate your insurance.

For most owners, the MOT test is an annual cause for anxiety, and this is largely due to owners not being sure what needs to be checked prior to submitting the motorcycle for testing. The simple answer is that a fully roadworthy motorcycle will have no difficulty in passing the test.

This is a guide to getting your motorcycle through the MOT test. Obviously it will not be possible to examine the motorcycle to the same standard as the professional MOT tester, particularly in view of the equipment required for some of the checks. However, working through the following procedures will enable you to identify any problem areas before submitting the motorcycle for the test.

It has only been possible to summarise the test requirements here, based on the regulations in force at the time of printing. Test standards are becoming increasingly stringent, although there are some exemptions for older vehicles. More information about the MOT test can be obtained from the TSO publications, *How Safe is your Motorcycle* and *The MOT Inspection Manual for Motorcycle Testing*.

Many of the checks require that one of the wheels is raised off the ground. If the motorcycle doesn't have a centre stand, note that an auxiliary stand will be required. Additionally, the help of an assistant may prove useful.

Certain exceptions apply to machines under 50 cc, machines without a lighting system, and Classic bikes - if in doubt about any of the requirements listed below seek confirmation from an MOT tester prior to submitting the motorcycle for the test.

Check that the frame number is clearly visible.

> **HAYNES HiNT**
> *If a component is in borderline condition, the tester has discretion in deciding whether to pass or fail it. If the motorcycle presented is clean and evidently well cared for, the tester may be more inclined to pass a borderline component than if the motorcycle is scruffy and apparently neglected.*

Electrical System

Lights, turn signals, horn and reflector

✔ With the ignition on, check the operation of the following electrical components. **Note:** *The electrical components on certain small-capacity machines are powered by the generator, requiring that the engine is run for this check.*

  a) *Headlight and tail light. Check that both illuminate in the low and high beam switch positions.*
  b) *Position lights. Check that the front position (or sidelight) and tail light illuminate in this switch position.*
  c) *Turn signals. Check that all flash at the correct rate, and that the warning light(s) function correctly. Check that the turn signal switch works correctly.*
  d) *Hazard warning system (where fitted). Check that all four turn signals flash in this switch position.*
  e) *Brake stop light. Check that the light comes on when the front and rear brakes are independently applied. Models first used on or after 1st April 1986 must have a brake light switch on each brake.*
  f) *Horn. Check that the sound is continuous and of reasonable volume.*

✔ Check that there is a red reflector on the rear of the machine, either mounted separately or as part of the tail light lens.
✔ Check the condition of the headlight, tail light and turn signal lenses.

Headlight beam height

✔ The MOT tester will perform a headlight beam height check using specialised beam setting equipment **(see illustration 1)**. This equipment will not be available to the home mechanic, but if you suspect that the headlight is incorrectly set or may have been maladjusted in the past, you can perform a rough test as follows.
✔ Position the bike in a straight line facing a brick wall. The bike must be off its stand, upright and with a rider seated. Measure the height from the ground to the centre of the headlight and mark a horizontal line on the wall at this height. Position the motorcycle 3.8 metres from the wall and draw a vertical

Headlight beam height checking equipment

line up the wall central to the centreline of the motorcycle. Switch to dipped beam and check that the beam pattern falls slightly lower than the horizontal line and to the left of the vertical line **(see illustration 2)**.

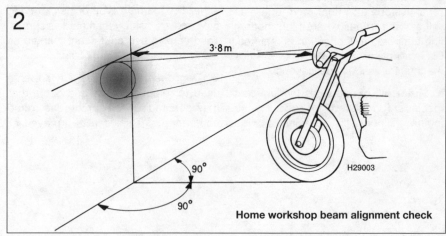

3·8 m

90°

90°

H29003

Home workshop beam alignment check

Exhaust System and Final Drive

Exhaust

✔ Check that the exhaust mountings are secure and that the system does not foul any of the rear suspension components.

✔ Start the motorcycle. When the revs are increased, check that the exhaust is neither holed nor leaking from any of its joints. On a linked system, check that the collector box is not leaking due to corrosion.

✔ Note that the exhaust decibel level ("loudness" of the exhaust) is assessed at the discretion of the tester. If the motorcycle was first used on or after 1st January 1985 the silencer must carry the BSAU 193 stamp, or a marking relating to its make and model, or be of OE (original equipment) manufacture. If the silencer is marked NOT FOR ROAD USE, RACING USE ONLY or similar, it will fail the MOT.

Final drive

✔ On chain or belt drive machines, check that the chain/belt is in good condition and does not have excessive slack. Also check that the sprocket is securely mounted on the rear wheel hub. Check that the chain/belt guard is in place.

✔ On shaft drive bikes, check for oil leaking from the drive unit and fouling the rear tyre.

Steering and Suspension

Steering

✔ With the front wheel raised off the ground, rotate the steering from lock to lock. The handlebar or switches must not contact the fuel tank or be close enough to trap the rider's hand. Problems can be caused by damaged lock stops on the lower yoke and frame, or by the fitting of non-standard handlebars.

✔ When performing the lock to lock check, also ensure that the steering moves freely without drag or notchiness. Steering movement can be impaired by poorly routed cables, or by overtight head bearings or worn bearings. The tester will perform a check of the steering head bearing lower race by mounting the front wheel on a surface plate, then performing a lock to lock check with the weight of the machine on the lower bearing (see illustration 3).

✔ Grasp the fork sliders (lower legs) and attempt to push and pull on the forks (see

Front wheel mounted on a surface plate for steering head bearing lower race check

illustration 4). Any play in the steering head bearings will be felt. Note that in extreme cases, wear of the front fork bushes can be misinterpreted for head bearing play.

✔ Check that the handlebars are securely mounted.

✔ Check that the handlebar grip rubbers are secure. They should by bonded to the bar left end and to the throttle cable pulley on the right end.

Front suspension

✔ With the motorcycle off the stand, hold the front brake on and pump the front forks up and down (see illustration 5). Check that they are adequately damped.

Checking the steering head bearings for freeplay

Hold the front brake on and pump the front forks up and down to check operation

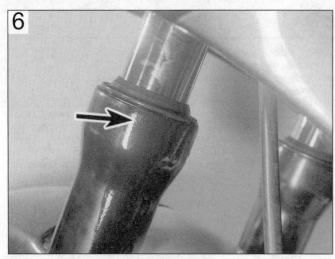

Inspect the area around the fork dust seal for oil leakage (arrow)

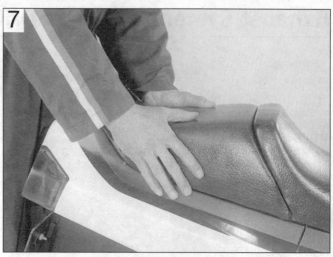

Bounce the rear of the motorcycle to check rear suspension operation

Checking for rear suspension linkage play

✔ Inspect the area above and around the front fork oil seals **(see illustration 6)**. There should be no sign of oil on the fork tube (stanchion) nor leaking down the slider (lower leg). On models so equipped, check that there is no oil leaking from the anti-dive units.

✔ On models with swingarm front suspension, check that there is no freeplay in the linkage when moved from side to side.

Rear suspension

✔ With the motorcycle off the stand and an assistant supporting the motorcycle by its handlebars, bounce the rear suspension **(see illustration 7)**. Check that the suspension components do not foul on any of the cycle parts and check that the shock absorber(s) provide adequate damping.

✔ Visually inspect the shock absorber(s) and check that there is no sign of oil leakage from its damper. This is somewhat restricted on certain single shock models due to the location of the shock absorber.

✔ With the rear wheel raised off the ground, grasp the wheel at the highest point and attempt to pull it up **(see illustration 8)**. Any play in the swingarm pivot or suspension linkage bearings will be felt as movement. **Note:** *Do not confuse play with actual suspension movement.* Failure to lubricate suspension linkage bearings can lead to bearing failure **(see illustration 9)**.

✔ With the rear wheel raised off the ground, grasp the swingarm ends and attempt to move the swingarm from side to side and forwards and backwards - any play indicates wear of the swingarm pivot bearings **(see illustration 10)**.

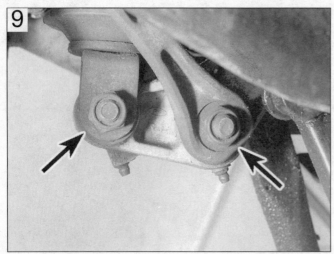

Worn suspension linkage pivots (arrows) are usually the cause of play in the rear suspension

Grasp the swingarm at the ends to check for play in its pivot bearings

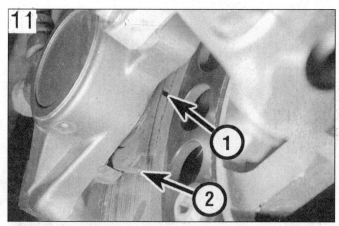

11

Brake pad wear can usually be viewed without removing the caliper. Most pads have wear indicator grooves (1) and some also have indicator tangs (2)

12

On drum brakes, check the angle of the operating lever with the brake fully applied. Most drum brakes have a wear indicator pointer and scale.

Brakes, Wheels and Tyres

Brakes

✔ With the wheel raised off the ground, apply the brake then free it off, and check that the wheel is about to revolve freely without brake drag.

✔ On disc brakes, examine the disc itself. Check that it is securely mounted and not cracked.

✔ On disc brakes, view the pad material through the caliper mouth and check that the pads are not worn down beyond the limit (see illustration 11).

✔ On drum brakes, check that when the brake is applied the angle between the operating lever and cable or rod is not too great (see illustration 12). Check also that the operating lever doesn't foul any other components.

✔ On disc brakes, examine the flexible hoses from top to bottom. Have an assistant hold the brake on so that the fluid in the hose is under pressure, and check that there is no sign of fluid leakage, bulges or cracking If there are any metal brake pipes or unions, check that these are free from corrosion and damage. Where a brake-linked anti-dive system is fitted, check the hoses to the anti-dive in a similar manner.

✔ Check that the rear brake torque arm is secure and that its fasteners are secured by self-locking nuts or castellated nuts with split-pins or R-pins (see illustration 13).

✔ On models with ABS, check that the self-check warning light in the instrument panel works.

✔ The MOT tester will perform a test of the motorcycle's braking efficiency based on a calculation of rider and motorcycle weight. Although this cannot be carried out at home, you can at least ensure that the braking systems are properly maintained. For hydraulic disc brakes, check the fluid level, lever/pedal feel (bleed of air if its spongy) and pad material. For drum brakes, check adjustment, cable or rod operation and shoe lining thickness.

Wheels and tyres

✔ Check the wheel condition. Cast wheels should be free from cracks and if of the built-up design, all fasteners should be secure. Spoked wheels should be checked for broken, corroded, loose or bent spokes.

✔ With the wheel raised off the ground, spin the wheel and visually check that the tyre and wheel run true. Check that the tyre does not foul the suspension or mudguards.

✔ With the wheel raised off the ground, grasp the wheel and attempt to move it about the axle (spindle) (see illustration 14). Any play felt here indicates wheel bearing failure.

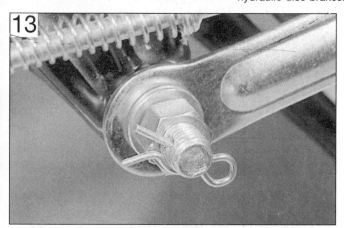

13

Brake torque arm must be properly secured at both ends

14

Check for wheel bearing play by trying to move the wheel about the axle (spindle)

Checking the tyre tread depth

Tyre direction of rotation arrow can be found on tyre sidewall

Castellated type wheel axle (spindle) nut must be secured by a split pin or R-pin

Two straightedges are used to check wheel alignment

✔ Check the tyre tread depth, tread condition and sidewall condition (see illustration 15).
✔ Check the tyre type. Front and rear tyre types must be compatible and be suitable for road use. Tyres marked NOT FOR ROAD USE, COMPETITION USE ONLY or similar, will fail the MOT.

✔ If the tyre sidewall carries a direction of rotation arrow, this must be pointing in the direction of normal wheel rotation (see illustration 16).
✔ Check that the wheel axle (spindle) nuts (where applicable) are properly secured. A self-locking nut or castellated nut with a split-pin or R-pin can be used (see illustration 17).
✔ Wheel alignment is checked with the motorcycle off the stand and a rider seated. With the front wheel pointing straight ahead, two perfectly straight lengths of metal or wood and placed against the sidewalls of both tyres (see illustration 18). The gap each side of the front tyre must be equidistant on both sides. Incorrect wheel alignment may be due to a cocked rear wheel (often as the result of poor chain adjustment) or in extreme cases, a bent frame.

General checks and condition

✔ Check the security of all major fasteners, bodypanels, seat, fairings (where fitted) and mudguards.

✔ Check that the rider and pillion footrests, handlebar levers and brake pedal are securely mounted.

✔ Check for corrosion on the frame or any load-bearing components. If severe, this may affect the structure, particularly under stress.

Sidecars

A motorcycle fitted with a sidecar requires additional checks relating to the stability of the machine and security of attachment and swivel joints, plus specific wheel alignment (toe-in) requirements. Additionally, tyre and lighting requirements differ from conventional motorcycle use. Owners are advised to check MOT test requirements with an official test centre.

Preparing for storage

Before you start

If repairs or an overhaul is needed, see that this is carried out now rather than left until you want to ride the bike again.

Give the bike a good wash and scrub all dirt from its underside. Make sure the bike dries completely before preparing for storage.

Engine

● Remove the spark plug(s) and lubricate the cylinder bores with approximately a teaspoon of motor oil using a spout-type oil can **(see illustration 1)**. Reinstall the spark plug(s). Crank the engine over a couple of times to coat the piston rings and bores with oil. If the bike has a kickstart, use this to turn the engine over. If not, flick the kill switch to the OFF position and crank the engine over on the starter **(see illustration 2)**. If the nature on the ignition system prevents the starter operating with the kill switch in the OFF position, remove the spark plugs and fit them back in their caps; ensure that the plugs are earthed (grounded) against the cylinder head when the starter is operated **(see illustration 3)**.

⚠️ **Warning: It is important that the plugs are earthed (grounded) away from the spark plug holes otherwise there is a risk of atomised fuel from the cylinders igniting.**

HAYNES HiNT *On a single cylinder four-stroke engine, you can seal the combustion chamber completely by positioning the piston at TDC on the compression stroke.*

● Drain the carburettor(s) otherwise there is a risk of jets becoming blocked by gum deposits from the fuel **(see illustration 4)**.

● If the bike is going into long-term storage, consider adding a fuel stabiliser to the fuel in the tank. If the tank is drained completely, corrosion of its internal surfaces may occur if left unprotected for a long period. The tank can be treated with a rust preventative especially for this purpose. Alternatively, remove the tank and pour half a litre of motor oil into it, install the filler cap and shake the tank to coat its internals with oil before draining off the excess. The same effect can also be achieved by spraying WD40 or a similar water-dispersant around the inside of the tank via its flexible nozzle.

● Make sure the cooling system contains the correct mix of antifreeze. Antifreeze also contains important corrosion inhibitors.

● The air intakes and exhaust can be sealed off by covering or plugging the openings. Ensure that you do not seal in any condensation; run the engine until it is hot,

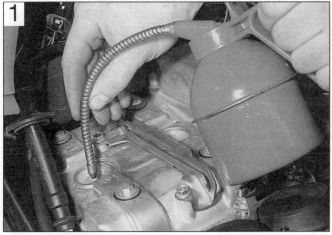

Squirt a drop of motor oil into each cylinder

Flick the kill switch to OFF . . .

. . . and ensure that the metal bodies of the plugs (arrows) are earthed against the cylinder head

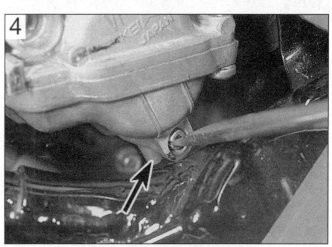

Connect a hose to the carburettor float chamber drain stub (arrow) and unscrew the drain screw

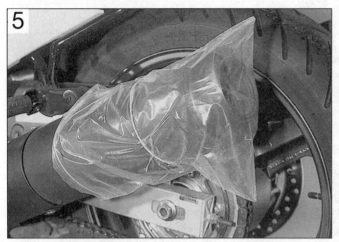

Exhausts can be sealed off with a plastic bag

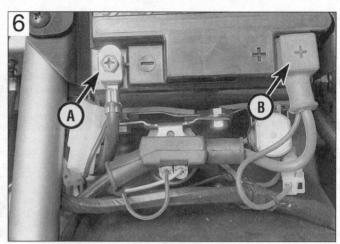

Disconnect the negative lead (A) first, followed by the positive lead (B)

Use a suitable battery charger - this kit also assess battery condition

then switch off and allow to cool. Tape a piece of thick plastic over the silencer end(s) (see illustration 5). Note that some advocate pouring a tablespoon of motor oil into the silencer(s) before sealing them off.

Battery

● Remove it from the bike - in extreme cases of cold the battery may freeze and crack its case (see illustration 6).

● Check the electrolyte level and top up if necessary (conventional refillable batteries). Clean the terminals.
● Store the battery off the motorcycle and away from any sources of fire. Position a wooden block under the battery if it is to sit on the ground.
● Give the battery a trickle charge for a few hours every month (see illustration 7).

Tyres

● Place the bike on its centrestand or an auxiliary stand which will support the motorcycle in an upright position. Position wood blocks under the tyres to keep them off the ground and to provide insulation from damp. If the bike is being put into long-term storage, ideally both tyres should be off the ground; not only will this protect the tyres, but will also ensure that no load is placed on the steering head or wheel bearings.
● Deflate each tyre by 5 to 10 psi, no more or the beads may unseat from the rim, making subsequent inflation difficult on tubeless tyres.

Pivots and controls

● Lubricate all lever, pedal, stand and

footrest pivot points. If grease nipples are fitted to the rear suspension components, apply lubricant to the pivots.
● Lubricate all control cables.

Cycle components

● Apply a wax protectant to all painted and plastic components. Wipe off any excess, but don't polish to a shine. Where fitted, clean the screen with soap and water.
● Coat metal parts with Vaseline (petroleum jelly). When applying this to the fork tubes, do not compress the forks otherwise the seals will rot from contact with the Vaseline.
● Apply a vinyl cleaner to the seat.

Storage conditions

● Aim to store the bike in a shed or garage which does not leak and is free from damp.
● Drape an old blanket or bedspread over the bike to protect it from dust and direct contact with sunlight (which will fade paint). This also hides the bike from prying eyes. Beware of tight-fitting plastic covers which may allow condensation to form and settle on the bike.

Getting back on the road

Engine and transmission

● Change the oil and replace the oil filter. If this was done prior to storage, check that the oil hasn't emulsified - a thick whitish substance which occurs through condensation.
● Remove the spark plugs. Using a spout-type oil can, squirt a few drops of oil into the cylinder(s). This will provide initial lubrication as the piston rings and bores comes back into contact. Service the spark plugs, or fit new ones, and install them in the engine.

● Check that the clutch isn't stuck on. The plates can stick together if left standing for some time, preventing clutch operation. Engage a gear and try rocking the bike back and forth with the clutch lever held against the handlebar. If this doesn't work on cable-operated clutches, hold the clutch lever back against the handlebar with a strong elastic band or cable tie for a couple of hours (see illustration 8).
● If the air intakes or silencer end(s) were blocked off, remove the bung or cover used.
● If the fuel tank was coated with a rust

Hold clutch lever back against the handlebar with elastic bands or a cable tie

preventative, oil or a stabiliser added to the fuel, drain and flush the tank and dispose of the fuel sensibly. If no action was taken with the fuel tank prior to storage, it is advised that the old fuel is disposed of since it will go off over a period of time. Refill the fuel tank with fresh fuel.

Frame and running gear

● Oil all pivot points and cables.
● Check the tyre pressures. They will definitely need inflating if pressures were reduced for storage.
● Lubricate the final drive chain (where applicable).
● Remove any protective coating applied to the fork tubes (stanchions) since this may well destroy the fork seals. If the fork tubes weren't protected and have picked up rust spots, remove them with very fine abrasive paper and refinish with metal polish.
● Check that both brakes operate correctly. Apply each brake hard and check that it's not possible to move the motorcycle forwards, then check that the brake frees off again once released. Brake caliper pistons can stick due to corrosion around the piston head, or on the sliding caliper types, due to corrosion of the slider pins. If the brake doesn't free after repeated operation, take the caliper off for examination. Similarly drum brakes can stick

due to a seized operating cam, cable or rod linkage.
● If the motorcycle has been in long-term storage, renew the brake fluid and clutch fluid (where applicable).
● Depending on where the bike has been stored, the wiring, cables and hoses may have been nibbled by rodents. Make a visual check and investigate disturbed wiring loom tape.

Battery

● If the battery has been previously removal and given top up charges it can simply be reconnected. Remember to connect the positive cable first and the negative cable last.
● On conventional refillable batteries, if the battery has not received any attention, remove it from the motorcycle and check its electrolyte level. Top up if necessary then charge the battery. If the battery fails to hold a charge and a visual checks show heavy white sulphation of the plates, the battery is probably defective and must be renewed. This is particularly likely if the battery is old. Confirm battery condition with a specific gravity check.
● On sealed (MF) batteries, if the battery has not received any attention, remove it from the motorcycle and charge it according to the information on the battery case - if the battery fails to hold a charge it must be renewed.

Starting procedure

● If a kickstart is fitted, turn the engine over a couple of times with the ignition OFF to distribute oil around the engine. If no kickstart is fitted, flick the engine kill switch OFF and the ignition ON and crank the engine over a couple of times to work oil around the upper cylinder components. If the nature of the ignition system is such that the starter won't work with the kill switch OFF, remove the spark plugs, fit them back into their caps and earth (ground) their bodies on the cylinder head. Reinstall the spark plugs afterwards.
● Switch the kill switch to RUN, operate the choke and start the engine. If the engine won't start don't continue cranking the engine - not only will this flatten the battery, but the starter motor will overheat. Switch the ignition off and try again later. If the engine refuses to start, go through the fault finding procedures in this manual. **Note:** *If the bike has been in storage for a long time, old fuel or a carburettor blockage may be the problem. Gum deposits in carburettors can block jets - if a carburettor cleaner doesn't prove successful the carburettors must be dismantled for cleaning.*
● Once the engine has started, check that the lights, turn signals and horn work properly.
● Treat the bike gently for the first ride and check all fluid levels on completion. Settle the bike back into the maintenance schedule.

This Section provides an easy reference-guide to the more common faults that are likely to afflict your machine. Obviously, the opportunities are almost limitless for faults to occur as a result of obscure failures, and to try and cover all eventualities would require a book. Indeed, a number have been written on the subject.

Successful troubleshooting is not a mysterious 'black art' but the application of a bit of knowledge combined with a systematic and logical approach to the problem. Approach any troubleshooting by first accurately identifying the symptom and then checking through the list of possible causes, starting with the simplest or most obvious and progressing in stages to the most complex.

Take nothing for granted, but above all apply liberal quantities of common sense.

The main symptom of a fault is given in the text as a major heading below which are listed the various systems or areas which may contain the fault. Details of each possible cause for a fault and the remedial action to be taken are given, in brief, in the paragraphs below each heading. Further information should be sought in the relevant Chapter.

1 Engine doesn't start or is difficult to start

☐ Starter motor doesn't rotate
☐ Starter motor rotates but engine does not turn over
☐ Starter works but engine won't turn over (seized)
☐ No fuel flow
☐ Engine flooded
☐ No spark or weak spark
☐ Compression low
☐ Stalls after starting
☐ Rough idle

2 Poor running at low speed

☐ Spark weak
☐ Fuel/air mixture incorrect
☐ Compression low
☐ Poor acceleration

3 Poor running or no power at high speed

☐ Firing incorrect
☐ Fuel/air mixture incorrect
☐ Compression low
☐ Knocking or pinking
☐ Miscellaneous causes

4 Overheating

☐ Engine overheats
☐ Firing incorrect
☐ Fuel/air mixture incorrect
☐ Compression too high
☐ Engine load excessive
☐ Lubrication inadequate
☐ Miscellaneous causes

5 Clutch problems

☐ Clutch slipping
☐ Clutch not disengaging completely

6 Gearchanging problems

☐ Doesn't go into gear, or lever doesn't return
☐ Jumps out of gear
☐ Overselects

7 Abnormal engine noise

☐ Knocking or pinking
☐ Piston slap or rattling
☐ Valve noise
☐ Other noise

8 Abnormal driveline noise

☐ Clutch noise
☐ Transmission noise
☐ Final drive noise

9 Abnormal frame and suspension noise

☐ Front end noise
☐ Shock absorber noise
☐ Brake noise

10 Oil pressure low

☐ Engine lubrication system

11 Excessive exhaust smoke

☐ White smoke
☐ Black smoke
☐ Brown smoke

12 Poor handling or stability

☐ Handlebars hard to turn
☐ Handlebars shake or vibrate excessively
☐ Handlebars pull to one side
☐ Poor shock absorbing qualities

13 Braking problems

☐ Brakes are spongy, don't hold
☐ Brake lever or pedal pulsates
☐ Brakes drag

14 Electrical problems

☐ Battery dead or weak
☐ Battery overcharged

1 Engine doesn't start or is difficult to start

Starter motor doesn't rotate

☐ Engine kill switch OFF.
☐ Fuse blown. Check main fuse (Chapter 9).
☐ Battery voltage low. Check and recharge battery (Chapter 9).
☐ Starter motor defective. Make sure the wiring to the starter is secure. Make sure the starter relay clicks when the start button is pushed. If the relay clicks, then the fault is in the wiring or motor.
☐ Starter relay faulty. Check it according to the procedure in Chapter 9.
☐ Starter switch not contacting. The contacts could be wet, corroded or dirty. Disassemble and clean the switch (Chapter 9).
☐ Wiring open or shorted. Check all wiring connections and harnesses to make sure that they are dry, tight and not corroded. Also check for broken or frayed wires that can cause a short to earth (ground) (see wiring diagram, Chapter 9).
☐ Ignition (main) switch defective. Check the switch according to the procedure in Chapter 9. Replace the switch with a new one if it is defective.
☐ Engine kill switch defective. Check for wet, dirty or corroded contacts. Clean or replace the switch as necessary (Chapter 9).
☐ Faulty starter cut-off relay, diodes, neutral, side stand or clutch switch. Check the wiring to each switch and the switch itself according to the procedures in Chapter 9.

Starter motor rotates but engine does not turn over

☐ Starter motor clutch defective. Inspect and repair or renew (Chapter 2).
☐ Damaged idler or starter gears. Inspect and renew the damaged parts (Chapter 2).

Starter works but engine won't turn over (seized)

☐ Seized engine caused by one or more internally damaged components. Failure due to wear, abuse or lack of lubrication. Damage can include seized valves, followers, camshafts, pistons, crankshaft, connecting rod bearings, or transmission gears or bearings. Refer to Chapter 2 for engine disassembly.

No fuel flow

☐ No fuel in tank.
☐ Fuel tank breather hose obstructed.
☐ Fuel filter clogged. Clean or renew filter (Chapter 4).
☐ Fuel tap vacuum hose split or detached (750 models). Check the hose.
☐ Fuel tap diaphragm split (750 models). Remove the tap and check the diaphragm (Chapter 4).
☐ Fuel line clogged. Pull the fuel line loose and carefully blow through it.
☐ Float needle valve clogged. For all of the valves to be clogged, either a very bad batch of fuel with an unusual additive has been used, or some other foreign material has entered the tank. Many times after a machine has been stored for many months without running, the fuel turns to a varnish-like liquid and forms deposits on the inlet needle valves and jets. The carburettors should be removed and overhauled if draining the float chambers doesn't solve the problem.
☐ Fuel pump faulty. Test as described in Chapter 4.

Engine flooded

☐ Float height too high. Check as described in Chapter 4.
☐ Float needle valve worn or stuck open. A piece of dirt, rust or other debris can cause the valve to seat improperly, causing excess fuel to be admitted to the float chamber. In this case, the float chamber should be cleaned and the needle valve and seat inspected. If the needle and seat are worn, then the leaking will persist and the parts should be replaced with new ones (Chapter 4).
☐ Starting technique incorrect. Under normal circumstances (ie, if all the carburettor functions are sound) the machine should start with little or no throttle. When the engine is cold, the choke should be operated and the engine started without opening the throttle. When the engine is at operating temperature, only a very slight amount of throttle should be necessary. If the engine is flooded, turn the fuel tap OFF or disconnect the vacuum hose (according to model – see Chapter 4) and hold the throttle open while cranking the engine. This will allow additional air to reach the cylinders. Remember to turn the fuel tap back ON or attach the vacuum hose.

No spark or weak spark

☐ Ignition switch OFF.
☐ Ignition circuit fuse blown.
☐ Engine kill switch turned to the OFF position.
☐ Battery voltage low. Check and recharge the battery as necessary (Chapter 9).
☐ Spark plugs dirty, defective or worn out. Locate reason for fouled plugs using spark plug condition chart and follow the plug maintenance procedures (Chapter 1).
☐ Spark plug caps or secondary (HT) wiring faulty. Check condition. Renew either or both components if cracks or deterioration are evident (Chapter 5).
☐ Spark plug caps not making good contact. Make sure that the plug caps fit snugly over the plug ends.
☐ Ignition control unit defective. Check the unit (Chapter 5).
☐ Pick-up coil defective. Check the unit (Chapter 5).
☐ Ignition HT coils defective. Check the coils (Chapter 5).
☐ Ignition or kill switch shorted. This is usually caused by water, corrosion, damage or excessive wear. The switches can be disassembled and cleaned with electrical contact cleaner. If cleaning does not help, renew the switches (Chapter 9).
☐ Wiring shorted or broken between:
  a) Ignition (main) switch and engine kill switch (or blown ignition fuse)
  b) Ignition control unit and engine kill switch
  c) Ignition control unit and ignition HT coils
  d) Ignition HT coils and spark plugs
  e) Ignition control unit and pick-up coil
☐ Make sure that all wiring connections are clean, dry and tight. Look for chafed and broken wires (Chapters 5 and 9).

1 Engine doesn't start or is difficult to start (continued)

Compression low

☐ Spark plugs loose. Remove the plugs and inspect their threads. Reinstall and tighten to the specified torque (Chapter 1).
☐ Cylinder head not sufficiently tightened down. If the cylinder head is suspected of being loose, then there's a chance that the gasket or head is damaged if the problem has persisted for any length of time. The head nuts should be tightened to the proper torque in the correct sequence (Chapter 2).
☐ Improper valve clearance. This means that the valve is not closing completely and compression pressure is leaking past the valve. Check and adjust the valve clearances (Chapter 1).
☐ Cylinder and/or piston worn. Excessive wear will cause compression pressure to leak past the rings. This is usually accompanied by worn rings as well. A top-end overhaul is necessary (Chapter 2).
☐ Piston rings worn, weak, broken, or sticking. Broken or sticking piston rings usually indicate a lubrication or carburation problem that causes excess carbon deposits or seizures to form on the pistons and rings. Top-end overhaul is necessary (Chapter 2).
☐ Piston ring-to-groove clearance excessive. This is caused by excessive wear of the piston ring lands. Piston replacement is necessary (Chapter 2).
☐ Cylinder head gasket damaged. If the head is allowed to become loose, or if excessive carbon build-up on the piston crown and combustion chamber causes extremely high compression, the head gasket may leak. Retorquing the head is not always sufficient to restore the seal, so gasket renewal is necessary (Chapter 2).
☐ Cylinder head warped. This is caused by overheating or improperly tightened head nuts. Machine shop resurfacing or head renewal is necessary (Chapter 2).
☐ Valve spring broken or weak. Caused by component failure or wear; the springs must be renewed (Chapter 2).
☐ Valve not seating properly. This is caused by a bent valve (from over-revving or improper valve adjustment), burned valve or seat

(improper carburation) or an accumulation of carbon deposits on the seat (from carburation or lubrication problems). The valves must be cleaned and/or renewed and the seats serviced if possible (Chapter 2).

Stalls after starting

☐ Improper choke action. Make sure the choke linkage shaft is getting a full stroke and staying in the out position (Chapter 4).
☐ Ignition malfunction (Chapter 5).
☐ Carburettor malfunction (Chapter 4).
☐ Fuel contaminated. The fuel can be contaminated with either dirt or water, or can change chemically if the machine is allowed to sit for several months or more. Drain the tank and float chambers (Chapter 4).
☐ Intake air leak. Check for loose carburettor-to-intake manifold connections, loose or missing vacuum gauge adapter screws or hose plugs, or loose carburettor tops (Chapter 4).
☐ Engine idle speed incorrect. Turn idle adjusting screw until the engine idles at the specified rpm (Chapter 1).

Rough idle

☐ Ignition malfunction (Chapter 5).
☐ Idle speed incorrect (Chapter 1).
☐ Incorrect air/fuel mixture setting (Chapter 4).
☐ Carburettors not synchronised. Adjust carburettors with vacuum gauge or manometer set as described in Chapter 1.
☐ Carburettor malfunction (Chapter 4).
☐ Fuel contaminated. The fuel can be contaminated with either dirt or water, or can change chemically if the machine is allowed to sit for several months or more. Drain the tank and float chambers (Chapter 4).
☐ Intake air leak. Check for loose carburettor-to-intake manifold connections, loose or missing vacuum gauge adapter screws or hose plugs, or loose carburettor tops (Chapter 4).
☐ Air filter clogged. Renew the air filter element (Chapter 1).

2 Poor running at low speeds

Spark weak

- ☐ Battery voltage low. Check and recharge battery (Chapter 9).
- ☐ Spark plugs fouled, defective or worn out. Refer to Chapter 1 for spark plug maintenance.
- ☐ Spark plug cap or HT wiring defective. Refer to Chapters 1 and 5 for details on the ignition system.
- ☐ Spark plug caps not making contact. Make sure they are securely pushed on to the plugs.
- ☐ Incorrect spark plugs. Wrong type, heat range or cap configuration. Check and install correct plugs listed in Chapter 1.
- ☐ Ignition control unit defective (Chapter 5).
- ☐ Pick-up coil defective (Chapter 5).
- ☐ Ignition HT coils defective (Chapter 5).

Fuel/air mixture incorrect

- ☐ Pilot screws out of adjustment (Chapter 4).
- ☐ Pilot jet or air passage clogged. Remove and overhaul the carburettors (Chapter 4).
- ☐ Air bleed holes clogged. Remove carburettor and blow out all passages (Chapter 4).
- ☐ Air filter clogged, poorly sealed or missing (Chapter 1).
- ☐ Air filter housing poorly sealed. Look for cracks, holes or loose clamps and renew or repair defective parts.
- ☐ Fuel level too high or too low. Check the level (Chapter 4).
- ☐ Fuel tank breather hose obstructed.
- ☐ Carburettor intake manifolds loose. Check for cracks, breaks, tears or loose clamps. Replace the rubber intake manifold joints if split or perished.

Compression low

- ☐ Spark plugs loose. Remove the plugs and inspect their threads. Reinstall and tighten to the specified torque (Chapter 1).
- ☐ Cylinder head not sufficiently tightened down. If the cylinder head is suspected of being loose, then there's a chance that the gasket and head are damaged if the problem has persisted for any length of time. The head nuts should be tightened to the proper torque in the correct sequence (Chapter 2).
- ☐ Improper valve clearance. This means that the valve is not closing completely and compression pressure is leaking past the valve. Check and adjust the valve clearances (Chapter 1).
- ☐ Cylinder and/or piston worn. Excessive wear will cause compression pressure to leak past the rings. This is usually accompanied by worn rings as well. A top-end overhaul is necessary (Chapter 2).
- ☐ Piston rings worn, weak, broken, or sticking. Broken or sticking piston rings usually indicate a lubrication or carburation problem that causes excess carbon deposits or seizures to form on the pistons and rings. Top-end overhaul is necessary (Chapter 2).
- ☐ Piston ring-to-groove clearance excessive. This is caused by excessive wear of the piston ring lands. Piston renewal is necessary (Chapter 2).
- ☐ Cylinder head gasket damaged. If the head is allowed to become loose, or if excessive carbon build-up on the piston crown and combustion chamber causes extremely high compression, the head gasket may leak. Retorquing the head is not always sufficient to restore the seal, so gasket renewal is necessary (Chapter 2).
- ☐ Cylinder head warped. This is caused by overheating or improperly tightened head nuts. Machine shop resurfacing or head renewal is necessary (Chapter 2).
- ☐ Valve spring broken or weak. Caused by component failure or wear; the springs must be renewed (Chapter 2).
- ☐ Valve not seating properly. This is caused by a bent valve (from over-revving or improper valve adjustment), burned valve or seat (improper carburation) or an accumulation of carbon deposits on the seat (from carburation, lubrication problems). The valves must be cleaned and/or renewed and the seats serviced if possible (Chapter 2).

Poor acceleration

- ☐ Carburettors leaking or dirty. Overhaul the carburettors (Chapter 4).
- ☐ Timing not advancing. The pick-up coil or the ignition control module may be defective. If so, they must be replaced with new ones, as they can't be repaired.
- ☐ Carburettors not synchronised. Adjust them with a vacuum gauge set or manometer (Chapter 1).
- ☐ Engine oil viscosity too high. Using a heavier oil than that recommended in Chapter 1 can damage the oil pump or lubrication system and cause drag on the engine.
- ☐ Brakes dragging. Usually caused by debris which has entered the brake piston seals, or from a warped disc or bent axle. Repair as necessary (Chapter 7).
- ☐ Fuel pump flow rate insufficient. Check the pump (Chapter 4).

3 Poor running or no power at high speed

Firing incorrect

☐ Air filter restricted. Clean or replace filter (Chapter 1).
☐ Spark plugs fouled, defective or worn out. See Chapter 1 for spark plug maintenance.
☐ Spark plug caps or HT wiring defective. See Chapters 1 and 5 for details of the ignition system.
☐ Spark plug caps not in good contact (Chapter 5).
☐ Incorrect spark plugs. Wrong type, heat range or cap configuration. Check and install correct plugs listed in Chapter 1.
☐ Ignition control unit defective (Chapter 5).
☐ Ignition coils defective (Chapter 5).

Fuel/air mixture incorrect

☐ Main jet clogged. Dirt, water or other contaminants can clog the main jets. Clean the fuel tap filter, the in-line filter, the float chamber area, and the jets and carburettor orifices (Chapter 4).
☐ Main jet wrong size. The standard jetting is for sea level atmospheric pressure and oxygen content.
☐ Throttle shaft-to-carburettor body clearance excessive. Refer to Chapter 4 for inspection and part replacement procedures.
☐ Air bleed holes clogged. Remove and overhaul carburettors (Chapter 4).
☐ Air filter clogged, poorly sealed, or missing (Chapter 1).
☐ Air filter housing poorly sealed. Look for cracks, holes or loose clamps, and replace or repair defective parts.
☐ Fuel level too high or too low. Check the level (Chapter 4).
☐ Fuel tank breather hose obstructed.
☐ Carburettor intake manifolds loose. Check for cracks, breaks, tears or loose clamps. Replace the rubber intake manifolds if they are split or perished (Chapter 4).

Compression low

☐ Spark plugs loose. Remove the plugs and inspect their threads. Reinstall and tighten to the specified torque (Chapter 1).
☐ Cylinder head not sufficiently tightened down. If the cylinder head is suspected of being loose, then there's a chance that the gasket and head are damaged if the problem has persisted for any length of time. The head nuts should be tightened to the proper torque in the correct sequence (Chapter 2).
☐ Improper valve clearance. This means that the valve is not closing completely and compression pressure is leaking past the valve. Check and adjust the valve clearances (Chapter 1).
☐ Cylinder and/or piston worn. Excessive wear will cause compression pressure to leak past the rings. This is usually accompanied by worn rings as well. A top-end overhaul is necessary (Chapter 2).
☐ Piston rings worn, weak, broken, or sticking. Broken or sticking piston rings usually indicate a lubrication or carburation problem that causes excess carbon deposits or seizures to form on the pistons and rings. Top-end overhaul is necessary (Chapter 2).
☐ Piston ring-to-groove clearance excessive. This is caused by excessive wear of the piston ring lands. Piston renewal is necessary (Chapter 2).
☐ Cylinder head gasket damaged. If the head is allowed to become loose, or if excessive carbon build-up on the piston crown and combustion chamber causes extremely high compression, the head gasket may leak. Retorquing the head is not always sufficient to restore the seal, so gasket renewal is necessary (Chapter 2).
☐ Cylinder head warped. This is caused by overheating or improperly tightened head nuts. Machine shop resurfacing or head renewal is necessary (Chapter 2).
☐ Valve spring broken or weak. Caused by component failure or wear; the springs must be renewed (Chapter 2).
☐ Valve not seating properly. This is caused by a bent valve (from over-revving or improper valve adjustment), burned valve or seat (improper carburation) or an accumulation of carbon deposits on the seat (from carburation or lubrication problems). The valves must be cleaned and/or renewed and the seats serviced if possible (Chapter 2).

Knocking or pinking

☐ Carbon build-up in combustion chamber. Use of a fuel additive that will dissolve the adhesive bonding the carbon particles to the crown and chamber is the easiest way to remove the build-up. Otherwise, the cylinder head will have to be removed and decarbonised (Chapter 2).
☐ Incorrect or poor quality fuel. Old or improper grades of fuel can cause detonation. This causes the piston to rattle, thus the knocking or pinking sound. Drain old fuel and always use the recommended fuel grade.
☐ Spark plug heat range incorrect. Uncontrolled detonation indicates the plug heat range is too hot. The plug in effect becomes a glow plug, raising cylinder temperatures. Install the proper heat range plug (Chapter 1).
☐ Improper air/fuel mixture. This will cause the cylinders to run hot, which leads to detonation. Clogged jets or an air leak can cause this imbalance. See Chapter 4.

Miscellaneous causes

☐ Throttle valve doesn't open fully. Adjust the throttle grip freeplay (Chapter 1).
☐ Clutch slipping. May be caused by loose or worn clutch components. Refer to Chapter 2 for clutch overhaul procedures.
☐ Timing not advancing.
☐ Engine oil viscosity too high. Using a heavier oil than the one recommended in Chapter 1 can damage the oil pump or lubrication system and cause drag on the engine.
☐ Brakes dragging. Usually caused by debris which has entered the brake piston seals, or from a warped disc or bent axle. Repair as necessary.
☐ Fuel pump flow rate insufficient. Check the pump (Chapter 4).

4 Overheating

Engine overheats

☐ Coolant level low. Check and add coolant (Chapter 1).
☐ Leak in cooling system. Check cooling system hoses and radiator for leaks and other damage. Repair or renew parts as necessary (Chapter 3).
☐ Thermostat sticking open or closed. Check and renew as described in Chapter 3.
☐ Faulty radiator cap. Remove the cap and have it pressure tested.
☐ Coolant passages clogged. Have the entire system drained and flushed, then refill with fresh coolant.
☐ Water pump defective. Remove the pump and check the components (Chapter 3).
☐ Clogged radiator fins. Clean them by blowing compressed air through the fins from the rear of the radiator.
☐ Cooling fan or fan switch fault (Chapter 3).

Firing incorrect

☐ Spark plugs fouled, defective or worn out. See Chapter 1 for spark plug maintenance.
☐ Incorrect spark plugs.
☐ Ignition control unit defective (Chapter 5).
☐ Faulty ignition HT coils (Chapter 5).

Fuel/air mixture incorrect

☐ Main jet clogged. Dirt, water and other contaminants can clog the main jets. Clean the fuel filters, the float chamber area and the jets and carburettor orifices (Chapter 4).
☐ Main jet wrong size. The standard jetting is for sea level atmospheric pressure and oxygen content.
☐ Air filter clogged, poorly sealed or missing (Chapter 1).
☐ Air filter housing poorly sealed. Look for cracks, holes or loose clamps and replace or repair.
☐ Fuel level too low. Check the level (Chapter 4).
☐ Fuel tank breather hose obstructed.
☐ Carburettor intake manifolds loose. Check for cracks, breaks, tears or loose clamps. Renew the rubber intake manifold joints if split or perished.
☐ Incorrect pilot screw setting (see Chapter 4).

Compression too high

☐ Carbon build-up in combustion chamber. Use of a fuel additive that will dissolve the adhesive bonding the carbon particles to the piston crown and chamber is the easiest way to remove the build-up. Otherwise, the cylinder head will have to be removed and decarbonised (Chapter 2).
☐ Improperly machined head surface or installation of incorrect gasket during engine assembly.

Engine load excessive

☐ Clutch slipping. Can be caused by damaged, loose or worn clutch components. Refer to Chapter 2 for overhaul procedures.
☐ Engine oil level too high. The addition of too much oil will cause pressurisation of the crankcase and inefficient engine operation. Check Specifications and drain to proper level (see Daily (pre-ride) checks).
☐ Engine oil viscosity too high. Using a heavier oil than the one recommended in Chapter 1 can damage the oil pump or lubrication system as well as cause drag on the engine.
☐ Brakes dragging. Usually caused by debris which has entered the brake piston seals, or from a warped disc or bent axle. Repair as necessary.

Lubrication inadequate

☐ Engine oil level too low. Friction caused by intermittent lack of lubrication or from oil that is overworked can cause overheating. The oil provides a definite cooling function in the engine. Check the oil level (Chapter 1).
☐ Poor quality engine oil or incorrect viscosity or type. Oil is rated not only according to viscosity but also according to type. Some oils are not rated high enough for use in this engine (see Daily (pre-ride) checks).

Miscellaneous causes

☐ Modification to exhaust system. Most aftermarket exhaust systems cause the engine to run leaner, which make them run hotter. When installing an accessory exhaust system, always seek advice on rejetting the carburettors.

5 Clutch problems

Clutch slipping

- [ ] Friction plates worn or warped. Overhaul the clutch assembly (Chapter 2).
- [ ] Plain plates warped (Chapter 2).
- [ ] Clutch springs broken or weak. Old or heat-damaged (from slipping clutch) springs should be replaced with new ones (Chapter 2).
- [ ] Clutch centre or housing unevenly worn. This causes improper engagement of the plates. Renew the damaged or worn parts (Chapter 2).

Clutch not disengaging completely

- [ ] Air in hydraulic release system. Bleed the system (see Chapter 2).
- [ ] Clutch plates warped or damaged. This will cause clutch drag, which in turn will cause the machine to creep. Overhaul the clutch assembly (Chapter 2).
- [ ] Clutch spring tension uneven. Usually caused by a sagged or broken spring. Check and renew the springs as a set (Chapter 2).
- [ ] Engine oil deteriorated. Old, thin, worn out oil will not provide proper lubrication for the plates, causing the clutch to drag. Change the oil and filter (Chapter 1).
- [ ] Engine oil viscosity too high. Using a heavier oil than recommended in Chapter 1 can cause the plates to stick together, putting a drag on the engine. Change to the correct weight oil (see Daily (pre-ride) checks).
- [ ] Clutch housing sleeve seized on input shaft. Lack of lubrication, severe wear or damage can cause the sleeve to seize on the shaft. Overhaul of the clutch, and perhaps transmission, may be necessary to repair the damage (Chapter 2).
- [ ] Clutch release mechanism defective. Overhaul the master and release cylinders (Chapter 2).
- [ ] Loose clutch centre nut. Causes housing and centre misalignment putting a drag on the engine. Engagement adjustment continually varies. Overhaul the clutch assembly (Chapter 2).

6 Gearchanging problems

Doesn't go into gear or lever doesn't return

- [ ] Clutch not disengaging. See above.
- [ ] Selector fork(s) bent or seized. Often caused by dropping the machine or from lack of lubrication. Overhaul the transmission (Chapter 2).
- [ ] Gear(s) stuck on shaft. Most often caused by a lack of lubrication or excessive wear in transmission bearings and bushings. Overhaul the transmission (Chapter 2).
- [ ] Selector drum binding. Caused by lubrication failure or excessive wear. Renew the drum and bearing (Chapter 2).
- [ ] Gearchange lever return spring weak or broken (Chapter 2).
- [ ] Gearchange lever broken. Splines stripped out of lever or shaft, caused by allowing the lever to get loose or from dropping the machine. Renew necessary parts (Chapter 2).
- [ ] Gearchange mechanism stopper arm broken or worn. Full engagement and rotary movement of selector drum results. Renew the arm (Chapter 2).
- [ ] Stopper arm spring broken. Allows arm to float, causing sporadic shift operation. Renew spring (Chapter 2).

Jumps out of gear

- [ ] Selector fork(s) worn. Overhaul the transmission (Chapter 2).
- [ ] Gear groove(s) worn. Overhaul the transmission (Chapter 2).
- [ ] Gear dogs or dog slots worn or damaged. The gears should be inspected and renewed. No attempt should be made to service the worn parts.

Overselects

- [ ] Stopper arm spring weak or broken (Chapter 2).
- [ ] Gearchange shaft return spring post broken or distorted (Chapter 2).

7 Abnormal engine noise

Knocking or pinking

☐ Carbon build-up in combustion chamber. Use of a fuel additive that will dissolve the adhesive bonding the carbon particles to the piston crown and chamber is the easiest way to remove the build-up. Otherwise, the cylinder head will have to be removed and decarbonised (Chapter 2).

☐ Incorrect or poor quality fuel. Old or improper fuel can cause detonation. This causes the pistons to rattle, thus the knocking or pinking sound. Drain the old fuel and always use the recommended grade fuel (Chapter 4).

☐ Spark plug heat range incorrect. Uncontrolled detonation indicates that the plug heat range is too hot. The plug in effect becomes a glow plug, raising cylinder temperatures. Install the proper heat range plug (Chapter 1).

☐ Improper air/fuel mixture. This will cause the cylinders to run hot and lead to detonation. Clogged jets or an air leak can cause this imbalance. See Chapter 4.

Piston slap or rattling

☐ Cylinder-to-piston clearance excessive. Caused by improper assembly. Inspect and overhaul top-end parts (Chapter 2).

☐ Connecting rod bent. Caused by over-revving, trying to start a badly flooded engine or from ingesting a foreign object into the combustion chamber. Renew the damaged parts (Chapter 2).

☐ Piston pin or piston pin bore worn or seized from wear or lack of lubrication. Renew damaged parts (Chapter 2).

☐ Piston ring(s) worn, broken or sticking. Overhaul the top-end (Chapter 2).

☐ Piston seizure damage. Usually from lack of lubrication or overheating. Rebore the cylinder block and fit new pistons (Chapter 2).

☐ Connecting rod upper or lower end clearance excessive. Caused by excessive wear or lack of lubrication. Replace worn parts with new ones.

Valve noise

☐ Incorrect valve clearances. Adjust the clearances by referring to Chapter 1.

☐ Valve spring broken or weak. Check and renew valve springs as a set (Chapter 2).

☐ Camshaft or cylinder head worn or damaged. Lack of lubrication at high rpm is usually the cause of damage. Insufficient oil or failure to change the oil at the recommended intervals are the chief causes. Since there are no replaceable bearings in the head, the camshaft case will have to be renewed if there is excessive wear or damage (Chapter 2).

Other noise

☐ Cylinder head gasket leaking.

☐ Exhaust pipe leaking at cylinder head connection. Caused by improper fit of pipe(s) or loose exhaust flange. All exhaust fasteners should be tightened evenly and carefully. Failure to do this will lead to a leak.

☐ Crankshaft runout excessive. Caused by a bent crankshaft (from over-revving) or damage from an upper cylinder component failure. Can also be attributed to dropping the machine on either of the crankshaft ends.

☐ Engine mounting bolts loose. Tighten all engine mount bolts (Chapter 2).

☐ Crankshaft bearings worn (Chapter 2).

☐ Cam chain or tensioner assembly defective. Renew according to the procedure in Chapter 2.

8 Abnormal driveline noise

Clutch noise

☐ Clutch housing/friction plate clearance excessive (Chapter 2).

☐ Loose or damaged clutch pressure plate and/or bolts (Chapter 2).

Transmission noise

☐ Bearings worn. Also includes the possibility that the shafts are worn. Overhaul the transmission (Chapter 2).

☐ Gears worn or chipped (Chapter 2).

☐ Metal chips jammed in gear teeth. Probably pieces from a broken clutch, gear or selector mechanism that were picked up by the gears. This will cause early bearing failure (Chapter 2).

☐ Engine oil level too low. Causes a howl from transmission. Also affects engine power and clutch operation (Chapter 1).

Final drive noise

☐ Chain not adjusted properly (Chapter 1).

☐ Front or rear sprocket loose. Tighten fasteners (Chapter 6).

☐ Sprockets and chain worn. Renew as a set (Chapter 6).

☐ Rear sprocket warped. Renew sprockets and chain as a set (Chapter 6).

☐ Loose or worn rear wheel or sprocket coupling bearings. Check and renew as needed (Chapter 7).

9 Abnormal frame and suspension noise

Front end noise

- [ ] Low fluid level or improper viscosity oil in forks. This can sound like spurting and is usually accompanied by irregular fork action (Chapter 6).
- [ ] Spring weak or broken. Makes a clicking or scraping sound. Fork oil, when drained, will have a lot of metal particles in it (Chapter 6).
- [ ] Steering head bearings loose or damaged. Clicks when braking. Check and adjust or renew as necessary (Chapters 1 and 6).
- [ ] Fork yokes loose. Make sure all clamp pinch bolts are tightened to the specified torque (Chapter 6).
- [ ] Fork tube bent. Good possibility if machine has been dropped. Replace tube with a new one (Chapter 6).
- [ ] Front axle bolt or axle clamp bolt loose. Tighten them to the specified torque (Chapter 7).
- [ ] Loose or worn wheel bearings. Check and renew as needed (Chapter 7).

Shock absorber noise

- [ ] Fluid level incorrect. Indicates a leak caused by defective seal. Shock will be covered with oil. Renew shock or seek advice on repair from a Yamaha dealer (Chapter 6).
- [ ] Defective shock absorber with internal damage. This is in the body of the shock and can't be remedied. The shock must be replaced with a new one (Chapter 6).

- [ ] Bent or damaged shock body. Replace the shock with a new one (Chapter 6).
- [ ] Loose or worn suspension linkage components. Check and renew as necessary (Chapter 6).

Brake noise

- [ ] Squeal caused by pad shim not installed or positioned correctly (where fitted) (Chapter 7).
- [ ] Squeal caused by dust on brake pads. Usually found in combination with glazed pads. Clean using brake cleaning solvent (Chapter 7).
- [ ] Contamination of brake pads. Oil, brake fluid or dirt causing brake to chatter or squeal. Clean or renew pads (Chapter 7).
- [ ] Pads glazed. Caused by excessive heat from prolonged use or from contamination. Do not use sandpaper, emery cloth, carborundum cloth or any other abrasive to roughen the pad surfaces as abrasives will stay in the pad material and damage the disc. A very fine flat file can be used, but pad renewal is suggested as a cure (Chapter 7).
- [ ] Disc warped. Can cause a chattering, clicking or intermittent squeal. Usually accompanied by a pulsating lever and uneven braking. Renew the disc(s) (Chapter 7).
- [ ] Loose or worn wheel bearings. Check and renew as needed (Chapter 7).

10 Oil pressure low

Engine lubrication system

☐ Engine oil level low. Inspect for leak or other problem causing low oil level and add recommended oil (Chapter 1).

☐ Engine oil viscosity too low. Very old, thin oil or an improper weight of oil used in the engine. Change to correct oil (Chapter 1).

☐ Engine oil pump defective, blocked oil strainer gauze or failed relief valve. Carry out oil pressure check (Chapter 1).

☐ Camshaft or journals worn. Excessive wear causing drop in oil pressure. Replace cam and/or camshaft case. Abnormal wear could be caused by oil starvation at high rpm from low oil level or improper weight or type of oil (Chapter 1).

☐ Crankshaft and/or bearings worn. Same problems as above. Check and renew crankshaft and/or bearings (Chapter 2).

11 Excessive exhaust smoke

White smoke

☐ Piston oil ring worn. The ring may be broken or damaged, causing oil from the crankcase to be pulled past the piston into the combustion chamber. Replace the rings with new ones (Chapter 2).

☐ Cylinders worn, cracked, or scored. Caused by overheating or oil starvation. Check the cylinder block, lubrication system and cooling system (see Chapters 2 and 3).

☐ Valve oil seal damaged or worn. Replace oil seals with new ones (Chapter 2).

☐ Valve guide worn. Perform a complete valve job (Chapter 2).

☐ Engine oil level too high, which causes the oil to be forced past the rings. Drain oil to the proper level (Chapter 1).

☐ Head gasket broken between oil return and cylinder. Causes oil to be pulled into the combustion chamber. Renew the head gasket and check the head for warpage (Chapter 2).

☐ Abnormal crankcase pressurisation, which forces oil past the rings. Clogged breather is usually the cause.

Black smoke

☐ Air filter clogged. Clean or renew the element (Chapter 1).

☐ Main jet too large or loose. Compare the jet size to the Specifications (Chapter 4).

☐ Choke cable or linkage shaft stuck, causing fuel to be pulled through choke circuit (Chapter 4).

☐ Fuel level too high. Check and adjust the float height(s) as necessary (Chapter 4).

☐ Float needle valve held off needle seat. Clean the float chambers and fuel line and renew the needles and seats if necessary (Chapter 4).

Brown smoke

☐ Main jet too small or clogged. Lean condition caused by wrong size main jet or by a restricted orifice. Clean float chambers and jets and compare jet size to Specifications (Chapter 4).

☐ Fuel flow insufficient – float needle valve stuck closed due to chemical reaction with old fuel; fuel level incorrect; restricted fuel line; faulty fuel pump (Chapter 4).

☐ Carburettor intake manifold clamps loose (Chapter 4).

☐ Air filter poorly sealed or not installed (Chapter 1).

12 Poor handling or stability

Handlebars hard to turn

- [ ] Steering head bearing adjuster nut too tight. Check adjustment as described in Chapter 1.
- [ ] Bearings damaged. Roughness can be felt as the bars are turned from side-to-side. Replace bearings and races (Chapter 6).
- [ ] Races dented or worn. Denting results from wear in only one position (eg, straight ahead), from a collision or hitting a pothole or from dropping the machine. Replace races and bearings (Chapter 6
- [ ] Steering stem lubrication inadequate. Causes are grease getting hard from age or being washed out by high pressure car washes. Disassemble steering head and repack bearings (Chapter 6).
- [ ] Steering stem bent. Caused by a collision, hitting a pothole or by dropping the machine. Renew damaged parts. Don't try to straighten the steering stem (Chapter 6).
- [ ] Front tyre air pressure too low (Chapter 1).

Handlebars shake or vibrate excessively

- [ ] Tyres worn or out of balance (Chapter 7).
- [ ] Swingarm bearings worn. Replace worn bearings (Chapter 6).
- [ ] Wheel rim(s) warped or damaged. Inspect wheels for runout (Chapter 7).
- [ ] Wheel bearings worn. Worn front or rear wheel bearings can cause poor tracking. Worn front bearings will cause wobble (Chapter 7).
- [ ] Handlebar clamp bolts loose (Chapter 6).
- [ ] Fork yoke bolts loose Tighten them to the specified torque (Chapter 6).
- [ ] Engine mounting bolts loose. Will cause excessive vibration with increased engine rpm (Chapter 2).

Handlebars pull to one side

- [ ] Frame bent. Definitely suspect this if the machine has been dropped. May or may not be accompanied by cracking near the bend. Renew the frame (Chapter 6).
- [ ] Wheels out of alignment. Caused by improper location of axle spacers or from bent steering stem or frame (Chapter 6).
- [ ] Swingarm bent or twisted. Caused by age (metal fatigue) or impact damage. Renew the arm (Chapter 6).
- [ ] Steering stem bent. Caused by impact damage or by dropping the motorcycle. Renew the steering stem (Chapter 6).
- [ ] Fork tube bent. Disassemble the forks and renew the damaged parts (Chapter 6).
- [ ] Fork oil level uneven. Check and add or drain as necessary (Chapter 6).

Poor shock absorbing qualities

- [ ] Too hard:
  - a) Fork oil level excessive (Chapter 6).
  - b) Fork oil viscosity too high. Use a lighter oil (see the Specifications in Chapter 6).
  - c) Fork tube bent. Causes a harsh, sticking feeling (Chapter 6).
  - d) Fork internal damage (Chapter 6).
  - e) Shock shaft or body bent or damaged (Chapter 6).
  - f) Shock internal damage.
  - g) Tyre pressure too high (Chapter 1).
- [ ] Too soft:
  - a) Fork or shock oil insufficient and/or leaking (Chapter 6).
  - b) Fork oil level too low (Chapter 6).
  - c) Fork oil viscosity too light (Chapter 6).
  - d) Fork springs weak or broken (Chapter 6).
  - e) Shock internal damage or leakage (Chapter 6).

13 Braking problems

Brakes are spongy, don't hold

☐ Air in brake line. Caused by inattention to master cylinder fluid level or by leakage. Locate problem and bleed brakes (Chapter 7).
☐ Pad or disc worn (Chapters 1 and 7).
☐ Brake fluid leak. See paragraph 1.
☐ Contaminated pads. Caused by contamination with oil, grease, brake fluid, etc. Clean or renew pads. Clean disc thoroughly with brake cleaner (Chapter 7).
☐ Brake fluid deteriorated. Fluid is old or contaminated. Drain system, replenish with new fluid and bleed the system (Chapter 7).
☐ Master cylinder internal parts worn or damaged causing fluid to bypass (Chapter 7).
☐ Master cylinder bore scratched by foreign material or broken spring. Repair or renew master cylinder (Chapter 7).
☐ Disc warped. Renew disc (Chapter 7).

Brake lever or pedal pulsates

☐ Disc warped. Renew disc (Chapter 7).
☐ Axle bent. Renew axle (Chapter 7).
☐ Brake caliper bolts loose (Chapter 7).
☐ Wheel warped or otherwise damaged (Chapter 7).
☐ Wheel bearings damaged or worn (Chapter 7).

Brakes drag

☐ Master cylinder piston seized. Caused by wear or damage to piston or cylinder bore (Chapter 7).
☐ Lever balky or stuck. Check pivot and lubricate (Chapter 7).
☐ Brake caliper piston seized in bore. Caused by wear or ingestion of dirt past deteriorated seal (Chapter 7).
☐ Brake pad damaged. Pad material separated from backing plate. Usually caused by faulty manufacturing process or from contact with chemicals. Renew pads (Chapter 7).
☐ Pads improperly installed (Chapter 7).

14 Electrical problems

Battery dead or weak

☐ Battery faulty. Caused by sulphated plates which are shorted through sedimentation. Also, broken battery terminal making only occasional contact (Chapter 9).
☐ Battery cables making poor contact (Chapter 9).
☐ Load excessive. Caused by addition of high wattage lights or other electrical accessories.
☐ Ignition (main) switch defective. Switch either earths (grounds) internally or fails to shut off system. Renew the switch (Chapter 9).
☐ Regulator/rectifier defective (Chapter 9).
☐ Alternator stator coil open or shorted (Chapter 9).
☐ Wiring faulty. Wiring earthed (grounded) or connections loose in ignition, charging or lighting circuits (Chapter 9).

Battery overcharged

☐ Regulator/rectifier defective. Overcharging is noticed when battery gets excessively warm (Chapter 9).
☐ Battery defective. Replace battery with a new one (Chapter 9).
☐ Battery amperage too low, wrong type or size. Install manufacturer's specified amp-hour battery to handle charging load (Chapter 9).

Checking engine compression

● Low compression will result in exhaust smoke, heavy oil consumption, poor starting and poor performance. A compression test will provide useful information about an engine's condition and if performed regularly, can give warning of trouble before any other symptoms become apparent.

● A compression gauge will be required, along with an adapter to suit the spark plug hole thread size. Note that the screw-in type gauge/adapter set up is preferable to the rubber cone type.

● Before carrying out the test, first check the valve clearances as described in Chapter 1.

1 Run the engine until it reaches normal operating temperature, then stop it and remove the spark plug(s), taking care not to scald your hands on the hot components.

2 Install the gauge adapter and compression gauge in No. 1 cylinder spark plug hole (see illustration 1).

Screw the compression gauge adapter into the spark plug hole, then screw the gauge into the adapter

3 On kickstart-equipped motorcycles, make sure the ignition switch is OFF, then open the throttle fully and kick the engine over a couple of times until the gauge reading stabilises.

4 On motorcycles with electric start only, the procedure will differ depending on the nature of the ignition system. Flick the engine kill switch (engine stop switch) to OFF and turn the ignition switch ON; open the throttle fully and crank the engine over on the starter motor for a couple of revolutions until the gauge reading stabilises. If the starter will not operate with the kill switch OFF, turn the ignition switch OFF and refer to the next paragraph.

5 Install the spark plugs back into their suppressor caps and arrange the plug electrodes so that their metal bodies are earthed (grounded) against the cylinder head; this is essential to prevent damage to the ignition system as the engine is spun over (see illustration 2). Position the plugs well

All spark plugs must be earthed (grounded) against the cylinder head

away from the plug holes otherwise there is a risk of atomised fuel escaping from the combustion chambers and igniting. As a safety precaution, cover the top of the valve cover with rag. Now turn the ignition switch ON and kill switch ON, open the throttle fully and crank the engine over on the starter motor for a couple of revolutions until the gauge reading stabilises.

6 After one or two revolutions the pressure should build up to a maximum figure and then stabilise. Take a note of this reading and on multi-cylinder engines repeat the test on the remaining cylinders.

7 The correct pressures are given in Chapter 2 Specifications. If the results fall within the specified range and on multi-cylinder engines all are relatively equal, the engine is in good condition. If there is a marked difference between the readings, or if the readings are lower than specified, inspection of the top-end components will be required.

8 Low compression pressure may be due to worn cylinder bores, pistons or rings, failure of the cylinder head gasket, worn valve seals, or poor valve seating.

9 To distinguish between cylinder/piston wear and valve leakage, pour a small quantity of oil into the bore to temporarily seal the piston rings, then repeat the compression tests (see illustration 3). If the readings show

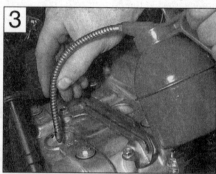

Bores can be temporarily sealed with a squirt of motor oil

a noticeable increase in pressure this confirms that the cylinder bore, piston, or rings are worn. If, however, no change is indicated, the cylinder head gasket or valves should be examined.

10 High compression pressure indicates excessive carbon build-up in the combustion chamber and on the piston crown. If this is the case the cylinder head should be removed and the deposits removed. Note that excessive carbon build-up is less likely with the used on modern fuels.

Checking battery open-circuit voltage

 Warning: The gases produced by the battery are explosive - never smoke or create any sparks in the vicinity of the battery. Never allow the electrolyte to contact your skin or clothing - if it does, wash it off and seek immediate medical attention.

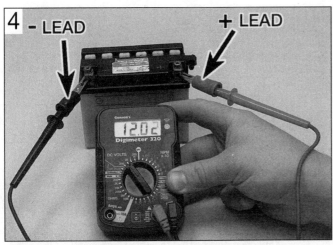

4 **- LEAD**   **+ LEAD**

Measuring open-circuit battery voltage

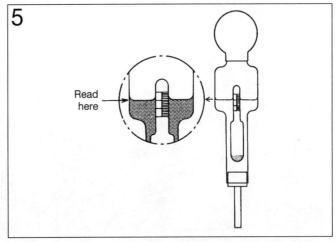

5

Read here

Float-type hydrometer for measuring battery specific gravity

● Before any electrical fault is investigated the battery should be checked.

● You'll need a dc voltmeter or multimeter to check battery voltage. Check that the leads are inserted in the correct terminals on the meter, red lead to positive (+ve), black lead to negative (-ve). Incorrect connections can damage the meter.

● A sound fully-charged 12 volt battery should produce between 12.3 and 12.6 volts across its terminals (12.8 volts for a maintenance-free battery). On machines with a 6 volt battery, voltage should be between 6.1 and 6.3 volts.

1 Set a multimeter to the 0 to 20 volts dc range and connect its probes across the battery terminals. Connect the meter's positive (+ve) probe, usually red, to the battery positive (+ve) terminal, followed by the meter's negative (-ve) probe, usually black, to the battery negative terminal (-ve) **(see illustration 4)**.

2 If battery voltage is low (below 10 volts on a 12 volt battery or below 4 volts on a six volt battery), charge the battery and test the voltage again. If the battery repeatedly goes flat, investigate the motorcycle's charging system.

Checking battery specific gravity (SG)

Warning: The gases produced by the battery are explosive - never smoke or create any sparks in the vicinity of the battery. Never allow the electrolyte to contact your skin or clothing - if it does, wash it off and seek immediate medical attention.

● The specific gravity check gives an indication of a battery's state of charge.

● A hydrometer is used for measuring specific gravity. Make sure you purchase one

which has a small enough hose to insert in the aperture of a motorcycle battery.

● Specific gravity is simply a measure of the electrolyte's density compared with that of water. Water has an SG of 1.000 and fully-charged battery electrolyte is about 26% heavier, at 1.260.

● Specific gravity checks are not possible on maintenance-free batteries. Testing the open-circuit voltage is the only means of determining their state of charge.

1 To measure SG, remove the battery from the motorcycle and remove the first cell cap. Draw

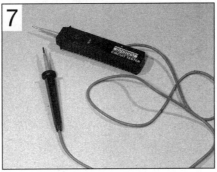

6

Digital multimeter can be used for all electrical tests

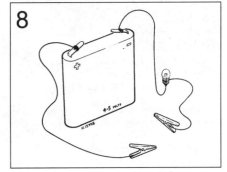

7

Battery-powered continuity tester

some electrolyte into the hydrometer and note the reading **(see illustration 5)**. Return the electrolyte to the cell and install the cap.

2 The reading should be in the region of 1.260 to 1.280. If SG is below 1.200 the battery needs charging. Note that SG will vary with temperature; it should be measured at 20°C (68°F). Add 0.007 to the reading for every 10°C above 20°C, and subtract 0.007 from the reading for every 10°C below 20°C. Add 0.004 to the reading for every 10°F above 68°F, and subtract 0.004 from the reading for every 10°F below 68°F.

3 When the check is complete, rinse the hydrometer thoroughly with clean water.

Checking for continuity

● The term continuity describes the uninterrupted flow of electricity through an electrical circuit. A continuity check will determine whether an **open-circuit** situation exists.

● Continuity can be checked with an ohmmeter, multimeter, continuity tester or battery and bulb test circuit **(see illustrations 6, 7 and 8)**.

8

Battery and bulb test circuit

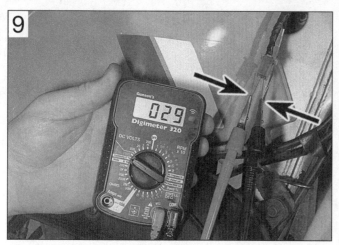

Continuity check of front brake light switch using a meter - note split pins used to access connector terminals

Continuity check of rear brake light switch using a continuity tester

● All of these instruments are self-powered by a battery, therefore the checks are made with the ignition OFF.

● As a safety precaution, always disconnect the battery negative (-ve) lead before making checks, particularly if ignition switch checks are being made.

● If using a meter, select the appropriate ohms scale and check that the meter reads infinity (∞). Touch the meter probes together and check that meter reads zero; where necessary adjust the meter so that it reads zero.

● After using a meter, always switch it OFF to conserve its battery.

Switch checks

1 If a switch is at fault, trace its wiring up to the wiring connectors. Separate the wire connectors and inspect them for security and condition. A build-up of dirt or corrosion here will most likely be the cause of the problem - clean up and apply a water dispersant such as WD40.

2 If using a test meter, set the meter to the ohms x 10 scale and connect its probes across the wires from the switch **(see illustration 9)**. Simple ON/OFF type switches, such as brake light switches, only have two wires whereas combination switches, like the ignition switch, have many internal links. Study the wiring diagram to ensure that you are connecting across the correct pair of wires. Continuity (low or no measurable resistance - 0 ohms) should be indicated with the switch ON and no continuity (high resistance) with it OFF.

3 Note that the polarity of the test probes doesn't matter for continuity checks, although care should be taken to follow specific test procedures if a diode or solid-state component is being checked.

4 A continuity tester or battery and bulb circuit can be used in the same way. Connect its probes as described above **(see illustration 10)**. The light should come on to indicate continuity in the ON switch position, but should extinguish in the OFF position.

Wiring checks

● Many electrical faults are caused by damaged wiring, often due to incorrect routing or chaffing on frame components.

● Loose, wet or corroded wire connectors can also be the cause of electrical problems, especially in exposed locations.

1 A continuity check can be made on a single length of wire by disconnecting it at each end and connecting a meter or continuity tester across both ends of the wire **(see illustration 11)**.

2 Continuity (low or no resistance - 0 ohms) should be indicated if the wire is good. If no continuity (high resistance) is shown, suspect a broken wire.

Checking for voltage

● A voltage check can determine whether current is reaching a component.

● Voltage can be checked with a dc voltmeter, multimeter set on the dc volts scale, test light or buzzer **(see illustrations 12 and 13)**. A meter has the advantage of being able to measure actual voltage.

● When using a meter, check that its leads are inserted in the correct terminals on the meter, red to positive (+ve), black to negative (-ve). Incorrect connections can damage the meter.

● A voltmeter (or multimeter set to the dc volts scale) should always be connected in parallel (across the load). Connecting it in series will destroy the meter.

● Voltage checks are made with the ignition ON.

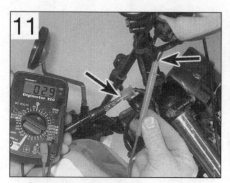

Continuity check of front brake light switch sub-harness

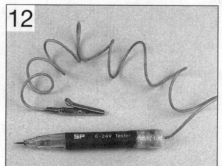

A simple test light can be used for voltage checks

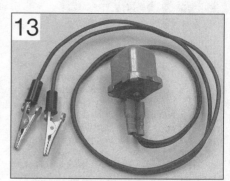

A buzzer is useful for voltage checks

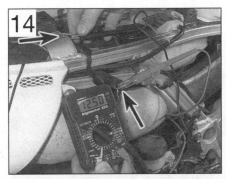

Checking for voltage at the rear brake light power supply wire using a meter . . .

1 First identify the relevant wiring circuit by referring to the wiring diagram at the end of this manual. If other electrical components share the same power supply (ie are fed from the same fuse), take note whether they are working correctly - this is useful information in deciding where to start checking the circuit.

2 If using a meter, check first that the meter leads are plugged into the correct terminals on the meter (see above). Set the meter to the dc volts function, at a range suitable for the battery voltage. Connect the meter red probe (+ve) to the power supply wire and the black probe to a good metal earth (ground) on the motorcycle's frame or directly to the battery negative (-ve) terminal **(see illustration 14)**. Battery voltage should be shown on the meter

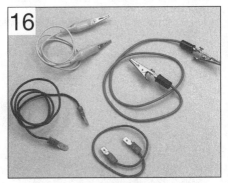

A selection of jumper wires for making earth (ground) checks

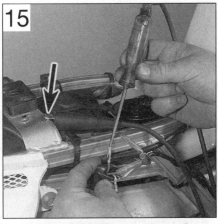

. . . or a test light - note the earth connection to the frame (arrow)

with the ignition switched ON.

3 If using a test light or buzzer, connect its positive (+ve) probe to the power supply terminal and its negative (-ve) probe to a good earth (ground) on the motorcycle's frame or directly to the battery negative (-ve) terminal **(see illustration 15)**. With the ignition ON, the test light should illuminate or the buzzer sound.

4 If no voltage is indicated, work back towards the fuse continuing to check for voltage. When you reach a point where there is voltage, you know the problem lies between that point and your last check point.

Checking the earth (ground)

● Earth connections are made either directly to the engine or frame (such as sensors, neutral switch etc. which only have a positive feed) or by a separate wire into the earth circuit of the wiring harness. Alternatively a short earth wire is sometimes run directly from the component to the motorcycle's frame.

● Corrosion is often the cause of a poor earth connection.

● If total failure is experienced, check the security of the main earth lead from the negative (-ve) terminal of the battery and also the main earth (ground) point on the wiring harness. If corroded, dismantle the connection and clean all surfaces back to bare metal.

1 To check the earth on a component, use an insulated jumper wire to temporarily bypass its earth connection **(see illustration 16)**. Connect one end of the jumper wire between the earth terminal or metal body of the component and the other end to the motorcycle's frame.

2 If the circuit works with the jumper wire installed, the original earth circuit is faulty. Check the wiring for open-circuits or poor connections. Clean up direct earth connections, removing all traces of corrosion and remake the joint. Apply petroleum jelly to the joint to prevent future corrosion.

Tracing a short-circuit

● A short-circuit occurs where current shorts to earth (ground) bypassing the circuit components. This usually results in a blown fuse.

● A short-circuit is most likely to occur where the insulation has worn through due to wiring chafing on a component, allowing a direct path to earth (ground) on the frame.

1 Remove any bodypanels necessary to access the circuit wiring.

2 Check that all electrical switches in the circuit are OFF, then remove the circuit fuse and connect a test light, buzzer or voltmeter (set to the dc scale) across the fuse terminals. No voltage should be shown.

3 Move the wiring from side to side whilst observing the test light or meter. When the test light comes on, buzzer sounds or meter shows voltage, you have found the cause of the short. It will usually shown up as damaged or burned insulation.

4 Note that the same test can be performed on each component in the circuit, even the switch.

A

ABS (Anti-lock braking system) A system, usually electronically controlled, that senses incipient wheel lockup during braking and relieves hydraulic pressure at wheel which is about to skid.

Aftermarket Components suitable for the motorcycle, but not produced by the motorcycle manufacturer.

Allen key A hexagonal wrench which fits into a recessed hexagonal hole.

Alternating current (ac) Current produced by an alternator. Requires converting to direct current by a rectifier for charging purposes.

Alternator Converts mechanical energy from the engine into electrical energy to charge the battery and power the electrical system.

Ampere (amp) A unit of measurement for the flow of electrical current. Current = Volts ÷ Ohms.

Ampere-hour (Ah) Measure of battery capacity.

Angle-tightening A torque expressed in degrees. Often follows a conventional tightening torque for cylinder head or main bearing fasteners **(see illustration)**.

Angle-tightening cylinder head bolts

Antifreeze A substance (usually ethylene glycol) mixed with water, and added to the cooling system, to prevent freezing of the coolant in winter. Antifreeze also contains chemicals to inhibit corrosion and the formation of rust and other deposits that would tend to clog the radiator and coolant passages and reduce cooling efficiency.

Anti-dive System attached to the fork lower leg (slider) to prevent fork dive when braking hard.

Anti-seize compound A coating that reduces the risk of seizing on fasteners that are subjected to high temperatures, such as exhaust clamp bolts and nuts.

API American Petroleum Institute. A quality standard for 4-stroke motor oils.

Asbestos A natural fibrous mineral with great heat resistance, commonly used in the composition of brake friction materials. Asbestos is a health hazard and the dust created by brake systems should never be inhaled or ingested.

ATF Automatic Transmission Fluid. Often used in front forks.

ATU Automatic Timing Unit. Mechanical device for advancing the ignition timing on early engines.

ATV All Terrain Vehicle. Often called a Quad.

Axial play Side-to-side movement.

Axle A shaft on which a wheel revolves. Also known as a spindle.

B

Backlash The amount of movement between meshed components when one component is held still. Usually applies to gear teeth.

Ball bearing A bearing consisting of a hardened inner and outer race with hardened steel balls between the two races.

Bearings Used between two working surfaces to prevent wear of the components and a build-up of heat. Four types of bearing are commonly used on motorcycles: plain shell bearings, ball bearings, tapered roller bearings and needle roller bearings.

Bevel gears Used to turn the drive through 90°. Typical applications are shaft final drive and camshaft drive **(see illustration)**.

Bevel gears are used to turn the drive through 90°

BHP Brake Horsepower. The British measurement for engine power output. Power output is now usually expressed in kilowatts (kW).

Bias-belted tyre Similar construction to radial tyre, but with outer belt running at an angle to the wheel rim.

Big-end bearing The bearing in the end of the connecting rod that's attached to the crankshaft.

Bleeding The process of removing air from an hydraulic system via a bleed nipple or bleed screw.

Bottom-end A description of an engine's crankcase components and all components contained there-in.

BTDC Before Top Dead Centre in terms of piston position. Ignition timing is often expressed in terms of degrees or millimetres BTDC.

Bush A cylindrical metal or rubber component used between two moving parts.

Burr Rough edge left on a component after machining or as a result of excessive wear.

C

Cam chain The chain which takes drive from the crankshaft to the camshaft(s).

Canister The main component in an evaporative emission control system (California market only); contains activated charcoal granules to trap vapours from the fuel system rather than allowing them to vent to the atmosphere.

Castellated Resembling the parapets along the top of a castle wall. For example, a castellated wheel axle or spindle nut.

Catalytic converter A device in the exhaust system of some machines which converts certain pollutants in the exhaust gases into less harmful substances.

Charging system Description of the components which charge the battery, ie the alternator, rectifer and regulator.

Circlip A ring-shaped clip used to prevent endwise movement of cylindrical parts and shafts. An internal circlip is installed in a groove in a housing; an external circlip fits into a groove on the outside of a cylindrical piece such as a shaft. Also known as a snap-ring.

Clearance The amount of space between two parts. For example, between a piston and a cylinder, between a bearing and a journal, etc.

Coil spring A spiral of elastic steel found in various sizes throughout a vehicle, for example as a springing medium in the suspension and in the valve train.

Compression Reduction in volume, and increase in pressure and temperature, of a gas, caused by squeezing it into a smaller space.

Compression damping Controls the speed the suspension compresses when hitting a bump.

Compression ratio The relationship between cylinder volume when the piston is at top dead centre and cylinder volume when the piston is at bottom dead centre.

Continuity The uninterrupted path in the flow of electricity. Little or no measurable resistance.

Continuity tester Self-powered bleeper or test light which indicates continuity.

Cp Candlepower. Bulb rating commonly found on US motorcycles.

Crossply tyre Tyre plies arranged in a criss-cross pattern. Usually four or six plies used, hence 4PR or 6PR in tyre size codes.

Cush drive Rubber damper segments fitted between the rear wheel and final drive sprocket to absorb transmission shocks **(see illustration)**.

Cush drive rubbers dampen out transmission shocks

D

Degree disc Calibrated disc for measuring piston position. Expressed in degrees.

Dial gauge Clock-type gauge with adapters for measuring runout and piston position. Expressed in mm or inches.

Diaphragm The rubber membrane in a master cylinder or carburettor which seals the upper chamber.

Diaphragm spring A single sprung plate often used in clutches.

Direct current (dc) Current produced by a dc generator.

Decarbonisation The process of removing carbon deposits - typically from the combustion chamber, valves and exhaust port/system.

Detonation Destructive and damaging explosion of fuel/air mixture in combustion chamber instead of controlled burning.

Diode An electrical valve which only allows current to flow in one direction. Commonly used in rectifiers and starter interlock systems.

Disc valve (or rotary valve) A induction system used on some two-stroke engines.

Double-overhead camshaft (DOHC) An engine that uses two overhead camshafts, one for the intake valves and one for the exhaust valves.

Drivebelt A toothed belt used to transmit drive to the rear wheel on some motorcycles. A drivebelt has also been used to drive the camshafts. Drivebelts are usually made of Kevlar.

Driveshaft Any shaft used to transmit motion. Commonly used when referring to the final driveshaft on shaft drive motorcycles.

E

Earth return The return path of an electrical circuit, utilising the motorcycle's frame.

ECU (Electronic Control Unit) A computer which controls (for instance) an ignition system, or an anti-lock braking system.

EGO Exhaust Gas Oxygen sensor. Sometimes called a Lambda sensor.

Electrolyte The fluid in a lead-acid battery.

EMS (Engine Management System) A computer controlled system which manages the fuel injection and the ignition systems in an integrated fashion.

Endfloat The amount of lengthways movement between two parts. As applied to a crankshaft, the distance that the crankshaft can move side-to-side in the crankcase.

Endless chain A chain having no joining link. Common use for cam chains and final drive chains.

EP (Extreme Pressure) Oil type used in locations where high loads are applied, such as between gear teeth.

Evaporative emission control system Describes a charcoal filled canister which stores fuel vapours from the tank rather than allowing them to vent to the atmosphere. Usually only fitted to California models and referred to as an EVAP system.

Expansion chamber Section of two-stroke engine exhaust system so designed to improve engine efficiency and boost power.

F

Feeler blade or gauge A thin strip or blade of hardened steel, ground to an exact thickness, used to check or measure clearances between parts.

Final drive Description of the drive from the transmission to the rear wheel. Usually by chain or shaft, but sometimes by belt.

Firing order The order in which the engine cylinders fire, or deliver their power strokes, beginning with the number one cylinder.

Flooding Term used to describe a high fuel level in the carburettor float chambers, leading to fuel overflow. Also refers to excess fuel in the combustion chamber due to incorrect starting technique.

Free length The no-load state of a component when measured. Clutch, valve and fork spring lengths are measured at rest, without any preload.

Freeplay The amount of travel before any action takes place. The looseness in a linkage, or an assembly of parts, between the initial application of force and actual movement. For example, the distance the rear brake pedal moves before the rear brake is actuated.

Fuel injection The fuel/air mixture is metered electronically and directed into the engine intake ports (indirect injection) or into the cylinders (direct injection). Sensors supply information on engine speed and conditions.

Fuel/air mixture The charge of fuel and air going into the engine. See **Stoichiometric ratio**.

Fuse An electrical device which protects a circuit against accidental overload. The typical fuse contains a soft piece of metal which is calibrated to melt at a predetermined current flow (expressed as amps) and break the circuit.

G

Gap The distance the spark must travel in jumping from the centre electrode to the side electrode in a spark plug. Also refers to the distance between the ignition rotor and the pickup coil in an electronic ignition system.

Gasket Any thin, soft material - usually cork, cardboard, asbestos or soft metal - installed between two metal surfaces to ensure a good seal. For instance, the cylinder head gasket seals the joint between the block and the cylinder head.

Gauge An instrument panel display used to monitor engine conditions. A gauge with a movable pointer on a dial or a fixed scale is an analogue gauge. A gauge with a numerical readout is called a digital gauge.

Gear ratios The drive ratio of a pair of gears in a gearbox, calculated on their number of teeth.

Glaze-busting see **Honing**

Grinding Process for renovating the valve face and valve seat contact area in the cylinder head.

Gudgeon pin The shaft which connects the connecting rod small-end with the piston. Often called a piston pin or wrist pin.

H

Helical gears Gear teeth are slightly curved and produce less gear noise that straight-cut gears. Often used for primary drives.

Installing a Helicoil thread insert in a cylinder head

Helicoil A thread insert repair system. Commonly used as a repair for stripped spark plug threads **(see illustration)**.

Honing A process used to break down the glaze on a cylinder bore (also called glaze-busting). Can also be carried out to roughen a rebored cylinder to aid ring bedding-in.

HT (High Tension) Description of the electrical circuit from the secondary winding of the ignition coil to the spark plug.

Hydraulic A liquid filled system used to transmit pressure from one component to another. Common uses on motorcycles are brakes and clutches.

Hydrometer An instrument for measuring the specific gravity of a lead-acid battery.

Hygroscopic Water absorbing. In motorcycle applications, braking efficiency will be reduced if DOT 3 or 4 hydraulic fluid absorbs water from the air - care must be taken to keep new brake fluid in tightly sealed containers.

I

lbf ft Pounds-force feet. An imperial unit of torque. Sometimes written as ft-lbs.

lbf in Pound-force inch. An imperial unit of torque, applied to components where a very low torque is required. Sometimes written as in-lbs.

IC Abbreviation for Integrated Circuit.

Ignition advance Means of increasing the timing of the spark at higher engine speeds. Done by mechanical means (ATU) on early engines or electronically by the ignition control unit on later engines.

Ignition timing The moment at which the spark plug fires, expressed in the number of crankshaft degrees before the piston reaches the top of its stroke, or in the number of millimetres before the piston reaches the top of its stroke.

Infinity (∞) Description of an open-circuit electrical state, where no continuity exists.

Inverted forks (upside down forks) The sliders or lower legs are held in the yokes and the fork tubes or stanchions are connected to the wheel axle (spindle). Less unsprung weight and stiffer construction than conventional forks.

J

JASO Quality standard for 2-stroke oils.

Joule The unit of electrical energy.

Journal The bearing surface of a shaft.

K

Kickstart Mechanical means of turning the engine over for starting purposes. Only usually fitted to mopeds, small capacity motorcycles and off-road motorcycles.

Kill switch Handebar-mounted switch for emergency ignition cut-out. Cuts the ignition circuit on all models, and additionally prevent starter motor operation on others.

km Symbol for kilometre.

kmh Abbreviation for kilometres per hour.

L

Lambda (λ) sensor A sensor fitted in the exhaust system to measure the exhaust gas oxygen content (excess air factor).

Lapping see **Grinding**.
LCD Abbreviation for Liquid Crystal Display.
LED Abbreviation for Light Emitting Diode.
Liner A steel cylinder liner inserted in a aluminium alloy cylinder block.
Locknut A nut used to lock an adjustment nut, or other threaded component, in place.
Lockstops The lugs on the lower triple clamp (yoke) which abut those on the frame, preventing handlebar-to-fuel tank contact.
Lockwasher A form of washer designed to prevent an attaching nut from working loose.
LT Low Tension Description of the electrical circuit from the power supply to the primary winding of the ignition coil.

M

Main bearings The bearings between the crankshaft and crankcase.
Maintenance-free (MF) battery A sealed battery which cannot be topped up.
Manometer Mercury-filled calibrated tubes used to measure intake tract vacuum. Used to synchronise carburettors on multi-cylinder engines.
Micrometer A precision measuring instrument that measures component outside diameters **(see illustration)**.

Tappet shims are measured with a micrometer

MON (Motor Octane Number) A measure of a fuel's resistance to knock.
Monograde oil An oil with a single viscosity, eg SAE80W.
Monoshock A single suspension unit linking the swingarm or suspension linkage to the frame.
mph Abbreviation for miles per hour.
Multigrade oil Having a wide viscosity range (eg 10W40). The W stands for Winter, thus the viscosity ranges from SAE10 when cold to SAE40 when hot.
Multimeter An electrical test instrument with the capability to measure voltage, current and resistance. Some meters also incorporate a continuity tester and buzzer.

N

Needle roller bearing Inner race of caged needle rollers and hardened outer race. Examples of uncaged needle rollers can be found on some engines. Commonly used in rear suspension applications and in two-stroke engines.
Nm Newton metres.
NOx Oxides of Nitrogen. A common toxic pollutant emitted by petrol engines at higher temperatures.

O

Octane The measure of a fuel's resistance to knock.
OE (Original Equipment) Relates to components fitted to a motorcycle as standard or replacement parts supplied by the motorcycle manufacturer.
Ohm The unit of electrical resistance. Ohms = Volts ÷ Current.
Ohmmeter An instrument for measuring electrical resistance.
Oil cooler System for diverting engine oil outside of the engine to a radiator for cooling purposes.
Oil injection A system of two-stroke engine lubrication where oil is pump-fed to the engine in accordance with throttle position.
Open-circuit An electrical condition where there is a break in the flow of electricity - no continuity (high resistance).
O-ring A type of sealing ring made of a special rubber-like material; in use, the O-ring is compressed into a groove to provide the sealing action.
Oversize (OS) Term used for piston and ring size options fitted to a rebored cylinder.
Overhead cam (sohc) engine An engine with single camshaft located on top of the cylinder head.
Overhead valve (ohv) engine An engine with the valves located in the cylinder head, but with the camshaft located in the engine block or crankcase.
Oxygen sensor A device installed in the exhaust system which senses the oxygen content in the exhaust and converts this information into an electric current. Also called a Lambda sensor.

P

Plastigauge A thin strip of plastic thread, available in different sizes, used for measuring clearances. For example, a strip of Plastigauge is laid across a bearing journal. The parts are assembled and dismantled; the width of the crushed strip indicates the clearance between journal and bearing.
Polarity Either negative or positive earth (ground), determined by which battery lead is connected to the frame (earth return). Modern motorcycles are usually negative earth.
Pre-ignition A situation where the fuel/air mixture ignites before the spark plug fires. Often due to a hot spot in the combustion chamber caused by carbon build-up. Engine has a tendency to 'run-on'.
Pre-load (suspension) The amount a spring is compressed when in the unloaded state. Preload can be applied by gas, spacer or mechanical adjuster.
Premix The method of engine lubrication on older two-stroke engines. Engine oil is mixed with the petrol in the fuel tank in a specific ratio. The fuel/oil mix is sometimes referred to as "petroil".
Primary drive Description of the drive from the crankshaft to the clutch. Usually by gear or chain.
PS Pfedestärke - a German interpretation of BHP.
PSI Pounds-force per square inch. Imperial measurement of tyre pressure and cylinder pressure measurement.
PTFE Polytetrafluroethylene. A low friction substance.

Pulse secondary air injection system A process of promoting the burning of excess fuel present in the exhaust gases by routing fresh air into the exhaust ports.

Q

Quartz halogen bulb Tungsten filament surrounded by a halogen gas. Typically used for the headlight **(see illustration)**.

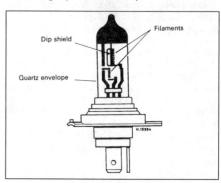

Quartz halogen headlight bulb construction

R

Rack-and-pinion A pinion gear on the end of a shaft that mates with a rack (think of a geared wheel opened up and laid flat). Sometimes used in clutch operating systems.
Radial play Up and down movement about a shaft.
Radial ply tyres Tyre plies run across the tyre (from bead to bead) and around the circumference of the tyre. Less resistant to tread distortion than other tyre types.
Radiator A liquid-to-air heat transfer device designed to reduce the temperature of the coolant in a liquid cooled engine.
Rake A feature of steering geometry - the angle of the steering head in relation to the vertical **(see illustration)**.

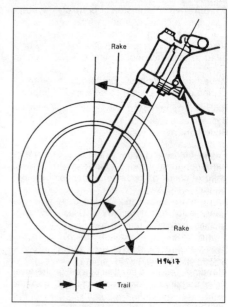

Steering geometry

Rebore Providing a new working surface to the cylinder bore by boring out the old surface. Necessitates the use of oversize piston and rings.

Rebound damping A means of controlling the oscillation of a suspension unit spring after it has been compressed. Resists the spring's natural tendency to bounce back after being compressed.

Rectifier Device for converting the ac output of an alternator into dc for battery charging.

Reed valve An induction system commonly used on two-stroke engines.

Regulator Device for maintaining the charging voltage from the generator or alternator within a specified range.

Relay A electrical device used to switch heavy current on and off by using a low current auxiliary circuit.

Resistance Measured in ohms. An electrical component's ability to pass electrical current.

RON (Research Octane Number) A measure of a fuel's resistance to knock.

rpm revolutions per minute.

Runout The amount of wobble (in-and-out movement) of a wheel or shaft as it's rotated. The amount a shaft rotates 'out-of-true'. The out-of-round condition of a rotating part.

S

SAE (Society of Automotive Engineers) A standard for the viscosity of a fluid.

Sealant A liquid or paste used to prevent leakage at a joint. Sometimes used in conjunction with a gasket.

Service limit Term for the point where a component is no longer useable and must be renewed.

Shaft drive A method of transmitting drive from the transmission to the rear wheel.

Shell bearings Plain bearings consisting of two shell halves. Most often used as big-end and main bearings in a four-stroke engine. Often called bearing inserts.

Shim Thin spacer, commonly used to adjust the clearance or relative positions between two parts. For example, shims inserted into or under tappets or followers to control valve clearances. Clearance is adjusted by changing the thickness of the shim.

Short-circuit An electrical condition where current shorts to earth (ground) bypassing the circuit components.

Skimming Process to correct warpage or repair a damaged surface, eg on brake discs or drums.

Slide-hammer A special puller that screws into or hooks onto a component such as a shaft or bearing; a heavy sliding handle on the shaft bottoms against the end of the shaft to knock the component free.

Small-end bearing The bearing in the upper end of the connecting rod at its joint with the gudgeon pin.

Spalling Damage to camshaft lobes or bearing journals shown as pitting of the working surface.

Specific gravity (SG) The state of charge of the electrolyte in a lead-acid battery. A measure of the electrolyte's density compared with water.

Straight-cut gears Common type gear used on gearbox shafts and for oil pump and water pump drives.

Stanchion The inner sliding part of the front forks, held by the yokes. Often called a fork tube.

Stoichiometric ratio The optimum chemical air/fuel ratio for a petrol engine, said to be 14.7 parts of air to 1 part of fuel.

Sulphuric acid The liquid (electrolyte) used in a lead-acid battery. Poisonous and extremely corrosive.

Surface grinding (lapping) Process to correct a warped gasket face, commonly used on cylinder heads.

T

Tapered-roller bearing Tapered inner race of caged needle rollers and separate tapered outer race. Examples of taper roller bearings can be found on steering heads.

Tappet A cylindrical component which transmits motion from the cam to the valve stem, either directly or via a pushrod and rocker arm. Also called a cam follower.

TCS Traction Control System. An electronically-controlled system which senses wheel spin and reduces engine speed accordingly.

TDC Top Dead Centre denotes that the piston is at its highest point in the cylinder.

Thread-locking compound Solution applied to fastener threads to prevent slackening. Select type to suit application.

Thrust washer A washer positioned between two moving components on a shaft. For example, between gear pinions on gearshaft.

Timing chain See Cam Chain.

Timing light Stroboscopic lamp for carrying out ignition timing checks with the engine running.

Top-end A description of an engine's cylinder block, head and valve gear components.

Torque Turning or twisting force about a shaft.

Torque setting A prescribed tightness specified by the motorcycle manufacturer to ensure that the bolt or nut is secured correctly. Undertightening can result in the bolt or nut coming loose or a surface not being sealed. Overtightening can result in stripped threads, distortion or damage to the component being retained.

Torx key A six-point wrench.

Tracer A stripe of a second colour applied to a wire insulator to distinguish that wire from another one with the same colour insulator. For example, Br/W is often used to denote a brown insulator with a white tracer.

Trail A feature of steering geometry. Distance from the steering head axis to the tyre's central contact point.

Triple clamps The cast components which extend from the steering head and support the fork stanchions or tubes. Often called fork yokes.

Turbocharger A centrifugal device, driven by exhaust gases, that pressurises the intake air. Normally used to increase the power output from a given engine displacement.

TWI Abbreviation for Tyre Wear Indicator. Indicates the location of the tread depth indicator bars on tyres.

U

Universal joint or U-joint (UJ) A double-pivoted connection for transmitting power from a driving to a driven shaft through an angle. Typically found in shaft drive assemblies.

Unsprung weight Anything not supported by the bike's suspension (ie the wheel, tyres, brakes, final drive and bottom (moving) part of the suspension).

V

Vacuum gauges Clock-type gauges for measuring intake tract vacuum. Used for carburettor synchronisation on multi-cylinder engines.

Valve A device through which the flow of liquid, gas or vacuum may be stopped, started or regulated by a moveable part that opens, shuts or partially obstructs one or more ports or passageways. The intake and exhaust valves in the cylinder head are of the poppet type.

Valve clearance The clearance between the valve tip (the end of the valve stem) and the rocker arm or tappet/follower. The valve clearance is measured when the valve is closed. The correct clearance is important - if too small the valve won't close fully and will burn out, whereas if too large noisy operation will result.

Valve lift The amount a valve is lifted off its seat by the camshaft lobe.

Valve timing The exact setting for the opening and closing of the valves in relation to piston position.

Vernier caliper A precision measuring instrument that measures inside and outside dimensions. Not quite as accurate as a micrometer, but more convenient.

VIN Vehicle Identification Number. Term for the bike's engine and frame numbers.

Viscosity The thickness of a liquid or its resistance to flow.

Volt A unit for expressing electrical "pressure" in a circuit. Volts = current x ohms.

W

Water pump A mechanically-driven device for moving coolant around the engine.

Watt A unit for expressing electrical power. Watts = volts x current.

Wear limit see Service limit

Wet liner A liquid-cooled engine design where the pistons run in liners which are directly surrounded by coolant **(see illustration)**.

Wet liner arrangement

Wheelbase Distance from the centre of the front wheel to the centre of the rear wheel.

Wiring harness or loom Describes the electrical wires running the length of the motorcycle and enclosed in tape or plastic sheathing. Wiring coming off the main harness is usually referred to as a sub harness.

Woodruff key A key of semi-circular or square section used to locate a gear to a shaft. Often used to locate the alternator rotor on the crankshaft.

Wrist pin Another name for gudgeon or piston pin.

Note: *References throughout this index are in the form - "Chapter number" • "Page number"*

Haynes Motorcycle Manuals – The Complete List

Title	Book No
APRILIA RSV1000 Mille (98 - 03)	4255
BMW 2-valve Twins (70 - 96)	◆ 0249
BMW K100 & 75 2-valve Models (83 - 96)	◆ 1373
BMW R850, 1100 & 1150 4-valve Twins (93 - 04)	◆ 3466
BSA Bantam (48 - 71)	0117
BSA Unit Singles (58 - 72)	0127
BSA Pre-unit Singles (54 - 61)	0326
BSA A7 & A10 Twins (47 - 62)	0121
BSA A50 & A65 Twins (62 - 73)	0155
DUCATI 600, 750 & 900 2-valve V-Twins (91 - 96)	◆ 3290
Ducati MK III & Desmo Singles (69 - 76)	◇ 0445
Ducati 748, 916 & 996 4-valve V-Twins (94 - 01)	◆ 3756
GILERA Runner, DNA, Stalker & Ice (97 - 04)	4163
HARLEY-DAVIDSON Sportsters (70 - 03)	◆ 2534
Harley-Davidson Shovelhead and Evolution Big Twins (70 - 99)	2536
Harley-Davidson Twin Cam 88 (99 - 03)	◆ 2478
HONDA NB, ND, NP & NS50 Melody (81 - 85)	◇ 0622
Honda NE/NB50 Vision & SA50 Vision Met-in (85 - 95)	◇ 1278
Honda MB, MBX, MT & MTX50 (80 - 93)	0731
Honda C50, C70 & C90 (67 - 99)	0324
Honda XR80R & XR100R (85 - 04)	2218
Honda XL/XR 80, 100, 125, 185 & 200 2-valve Models (78 - 87)	0566
Honda H100 & H100S Singles (80 - 92)	◇ 0734
Honda CB/CD125T & CM125C Twins (77 - 88)	◇ 0571
Honda CG125 (76 - 00)	◇ 0433
Honda NS125 (86 - 93)	◇ 3056
Honda MBX/MTX125 & MTX200 (83 - 93)	◇ 1132
Honda CD/CM185 200T & CM250C 2-valve Twins (77 - 85)	0572
Honda XL/XR 250 & 500 (78 - 84)	0567
Honda XR250L, XR250R & XR400R (86 - 03)	2219
Honda CB250 & CB400N Super Dreams (78 - 84)	◇ 0540
Honda CR Motocross Bikes (86 - 01)	2222
Honda CBR400RR Fours (88 - 99)	◇ ◆ 3552
Honda VFR400 (NC30) & RVF400 (NC35) V-Fours (89 - 98)	◇ ◆ 3496
Honda CB500 (93 - 01)	◇ ◆ 3753
Honda CB400 & CB550 Fours (73 - 77)	0262
Honda CX/GL500 & 650 V-Twins (78 - 86)	0442
Honda CBX550 Four (82 - 86)	◇ 0940
Honda XL600R & XR600R (83 - 00)	2183
Honda XL600/650V Transalp & XRV750 Africa Twin (87 - 02)	◇ ◆ 3919
Honda CBR600F1 & 1000F Fours (87 - 96)	◆ 1730
Honda CBR600F2 & F3 Fours (91 - 98)	◆ 2070
Honda CBR600F4 (99 - 02)	◆ 3911
Honda CB600F Hornet (98 - 02)	◇ ◆ 3915
Honda CB650 sohc Fours (78 - 84)	0665
Honda NTV600 Revere, NTV650 & NT650V Deauville (88 - 01)	◇ ◆ 3243
Honda Shadow VT600 & 750 (USA) (88 - 03)	2312
Honda CB750 sohc Four (69 - 79)	0131
Honda V45/65 Sabre & Magna (82 - 88)	0820
Honda VFR750 & 700 V-Fours (86 - 97)	◆ 2101
Honda VFR800 V-Fours (97 - 01)	◆ 3703
Honda VFR800 V-Tec V-Fours (02 - 05)	◆ 4196
Honda CB750 & CB900 dohc Fours (78 - 84)	0535
Honda VTR1000 (FireStorm, Super Hawk) & XL1000V (Varadero) (97 - 00)	◆ 3744
Honda CBR900RR FireBlade (92 - 99)	◆ 2161
Honda CBR900RR FireBlade (00 - 03)	◆ 4060
Honda CBR1100XX Super Blackbird (97 - 02)	◆ 3901
Honda ST1100 Pan European V-Fours (90 - 01)	◆ 3384
Honda Shadow VT1100 (USA) (85 - 98)	2313

Title	Book No
Honda GL1000 Gold Wing (75 - 79)	0309
Honda GL1100 Gold Wing (79 - 81)	0669
Honda Gold Wing 1200 (USA) (84 - 87)	2199
Honda Gold Wing 1500 (USA) (88 - 00)	2225
KAWASAKI AE/AR 50 & 80 (81 - 95)	1007
Kawasaki KC, KE & KH100 (75 - 99)	1371
Kawasaki KMX125 & 200 (86 - 02)	◇ 3046
Kawasaki 250, 350 & 400 Triples (72 - 79)	0134
Kawasaki 400 & 440 Twins (74 - 81)	0281
Kawasaki 400, 500 & 550 Fours (79 - 91)	0910
Kawasaki EN450 & 500 Twins (Ltd/Vulcan) (85 - 04)	2053
Kawasaki EX & ER500 (GPZ500S & ER-5) Twins (87 - 99)	◆ 2052
Kawasaki ZX600 (Ninja ZX-6, ZZ-R600) Fours (90 - 00)	◆ 2146
Kawasaki ZX-6R Ninja Fours (95 - 02)	◆ 3541
Kawasaki ZX600 (GPZ600R, GPX600R, Ninja 600R & RX) & ZX750 (GPX750R, Ninja 750R) Fours (85 - 97)	◆ 1780
Kawasaki 650 Four (76 - 78)	0373
Kawasaki Vulcan 700/750 & 800 (85 - 04)	◆ 2457
Kawasaki 750 Air-cooled Fours (80 - 91)	0574
Kawasaki ZR550 & 750 Zephyr Fours (90 - 97)	◆ 3382
Kawasaki ZX750 (Ninja ZX-7 & ZXR750) Fours (89 - 96)	◆ 2054
Kawasaki Ninja ZX-7R & ZX-9R (94 - 04)	◆ 3721
Kawasaki 900 & 1000 Fours (73 - 77)	0222
Kawasaki ZX900, 1000 & 1100 Liquid-cooled Fours (83 - 97)	◆ 1681
MOTO GUZZI 750, 850 & 1000 V-Twins (74 - 78)	0339
MZ ETZ Models (81 - 95)	◇ 1680
NORTON 500, 600, 650 & 750 Twins (57 - 70)	0187
Norton Commando (68 - 77)	0125
PEUGEOT Speedfight, Trekker & Vivacity (96 - 02)	◇ 3920
PIAGGIO (Vespa) Scooters (91 - 03)	◇ 3492
SUZUKI GT, ZR & TS50 (77 - 90)	◇ 0799
Suzuki TS50X (84 - 00)	◇ 1599
Suzuki 100, 125, 185 & 250 Air-cooled Trail bikes (79 - 89)	0797
Suzuki GP100 & 125 Singles (78 - 93)	◇ 0576
Suzuki GS, GN, GZ & DR125 Singles (82 - 99)	◇ 0888
Suzuki 250 & 350 Twins (68 - 78)	0120
Suzuki GT250X7, GT200X5 & SB200 Twins (78 - 83)	◇ 0469
Suzuki GS/GSX250, 400 & 450 Twins (79 - 85)	0736
Suzuki GS500 Twin (89 - 02)	◆ 3238
Suzuki GS550 (77 - 82) & GS750 Fours (76 - 79)	0363
Suzuki GS/GSX550 4-valve Fours (83 - 88)	1133
Suzuki SV650 (99 - 02)	◆ 3912
Suzuki GSX-R600 & 750 (96 - 00)	◆ 3553
Suzuki GSX-R600 (01 - 02), GSX-R750 (00 - 02) & GSX-R1000 (01 - 02)	◆ 3986
Suzuki GSF600 & 1200 Bandit Fours (95 - 04)	◆ 3367
Suzuki GS850 Fours (78 - 88)	0536
Suzuki GS1000 Four (77 - 79)	0484
Suzuki GSX-R750, GSX-R1100 (85 - 92), GSX600F, GSX750F, GSX1100F (Katana) Fours (88 - 96)	◆ 2055
Suzuki GSX600/750F & GSX750 (98 - 02)	◆ 3987
Suzuki GS/GSX1000, 1100 & 1150 4-valve Fours (79 - 88)	0737
Suzuki TL1000S/R & DL1000 V-Strom (97 - 04)	◆ 4083
Suzuki GSX1300R Hayabusa (99 - 04)	◆ 4184
TRIUMPH Tiger Cub & Terrier (52 - 68)	0414
Triumph 350 & 500 Unit Twins (58 - 73)	0137
Triumph Pre-Unit Twins (47 - 62)	0251
Triumph 650 & 750 2-valve Unit Twins (63 - 83)	0122
Triumph Trident & BSA Rocket 3 (69 - 75)	0136
Triumph Fuel Injected Triples (97 - 00)	◆ 3755
Triumph Triples & Fours (carburettor engines) (91 - 99)	◆ 2162
VESPA P/PX125, 150 & 200 Scooters (78 - 03)	0707
Vespa Scooters (59 - 78)	0126
YAMAHA DT50 & 80 Trail Bikes (78 - 95)	◇ 0800

Title	Book No
Yamaha T50 & 80 Townmate (83 - 95)	◇ 1247
Yamaha YB100 Singles (73 - 91)	◇ 0474
Yamaha RS/RXS100 & 125 Singles (74 - 95)	0331
Yamaha RD & DT125LC (82 - 87)	◇ 0887
Yamaha TZR125 (87 - 93) & DT125R (88 - 02)	◇ 1655
Yamaha TY50, 80, 125 & 175 (74 - 84)	◇ 0464
Yamaha XT & SR125 (82 - 02)	◇ 1021
Yamaha Trail Bikes (81 - 00)	2350
Yamaha 250 & 350 Twins (70 - 79)	0040
Yamaha XS250, 360 & 400 sohc Twins (75 - 84)	0378
Yamaha RD250 & 350LC Twins (80 - 82)	0803
Yamaha RD350 YPVS Twins (83 - 95)	1158
Yamaha RD400 Twin (75 - 79)	0333
Yamaha XT, TT & SR500 Singles (75 - 83)	0342
Yamaha XZ550 Vision V-Twins (82 - 85)	0821
Yamaha FJ, FZ, XJ & YX600 Radian (84 - 92)	2100
Yamaha XJ600S (Diversion, Seca II) & XJ600N Fours (92 - 03)	◆ 2145
Yamaha YZF600R Thundercat & FZS600 Fazer (96 - 03)	◆ 3702
Yamaha YZF-R6 (98 - 02)	◆ 3900
Yamaha 650 Twins (70 - 83)	0341
Yamaha XJ650 & 750 Fours (80 - 84)	0738
Yamaha XS750 & 850 Triples (76 - 85)	0340
Yamaha TDM850, TRX850 & XTZ750 (89 - 99)	◇ ◆ 3540
Yamaha YZF750R & YZF1000R Thunderace (93 - 00)	◆ 3720
Yamaha FZR600, 750 & 1000 Fours (87 - 96)	◆ 2056
Yamaha XV (Virago) V-Twins (81 - 03)	◆ 0802
Yamaha XVS650 & 1100 Dragstar/V-Star (97 - 05)	◆ 4195
Yamaha XJ900F Fours (83 - 94)	◆ 3239
Yamaha XJ900S Diversion (94 - 01)	◆ 3739
Yamaha YZF-R1 (98 - 03)	◆ 3754
Yamaha FJ1100 & 1200 Fours (84 - 96)	◆ 2057
Yamaha XJR1200 & 1300 (95 - 03)	◆ 3981
Yamaha V-Max (85 - 03)	◆ 4072
ATVs	
Honda ATC70, 90, 110, 185 & 200 (71 - 85)	0565
Honda TRX300 Shaft Drive ATVs (88 - 00)	2125
Honda TRX300EX & TRX400EX ATVs (93 - 04)	2318
Honda Foreman 400 and 450 ATVs (95 - 02)	2465
Kawasaki Bayou 220/250/300 & Prairie 300 ATVs (86 - 03)	2351
Polaris ATVs (85 - 97)	2302
Polaris ATVs (98 - 03)	2508
Yamaha YFS200 Blaster ATV (88 - 02)	2317
Yamaha YFB250 Timberwolf ATVs (92 - 00)	2217
Yamaha YFM350 & YFM400 (ER and Big Bear) ATVs (87 - 03)	2126
Yamaha Banshee and Warrior ATVs (87 - 03)	2314
ATV Basics	10450
TECHBOOK SERIES	
Motorcycle Basics TechBook (2nd Edition)	3515
Motorcycle Electrical TechBook (3rd Edition)	3471
Motorcycle Fuel Systems TechBook	3514
Motorcycle Maintenance TechBook	4071
Motorcycle Workshop Practice TechBook (2nd Edition)	3470
GENERAL MANUALS	
Twist and Go (automatic transmission) Scooters Service and Repair Manual	4082

◇ = not available in the USA   ◆ = Superbike

The manuals on this page are available through good motorcycle dealers and accessory shops. In case of difficulty, contact: **Haynes Publishing**
(UK) +44 1963 442030   (USA) +1 805 498 6703
(FR) +33 1 47 17 66 29   (SV) +46 18 124016
(Australia/New Zealand) +61 3 9763 8100

MCL18.04/05

Preserving Our Motoring Heritage

< *The Model J Duesenberg Derham Tourster. Only eight of these magnificent cars were ever built – this is the only example to be found outside the United States of America*

Almost every car you've ever loved, loathed or desired is gathered under one roof at the Haynes Motor Museum. Over 300 immaculately presented cars and motorbikes represent every aspect of our motoring heritage, from elegant reminders of bygone days, such as the superb Model J Duesenberg to curiosities like the bug-eyed BMW Isetta. There are also many old friends and flames. Perhaps you remember the 1959 Ford Popular that you did your courting in? The magnificent 'Red Collection' is a spectacle of classic sports cars including AC, Alfa Romeo, Austin Healey, Ferrari, Lamborghini, Maserati, MG, Riley, Porsche and Triumph.

A Perfect Day Out

Each and every vehicle at the Haynes Motor Museum has played its part in the history and culture of Motoring. Today, they make a wonderful spectacle and a great day out for all the family. Bring the kids, bring Mum and Dad, but above all bring your camera to capture those golden memories for ever. You will also find an impressive array of motoring memorabilia, a comfortable 70 seat video cinema and one of the most extensive transport book shops in Britain. The Pit Stop Cafe serves everything from a cup of tea to wholesome, home-made meals or, if you prefer, you can enjoy the large picnic area nestled in the beautiful rural surroundings of Somerset.

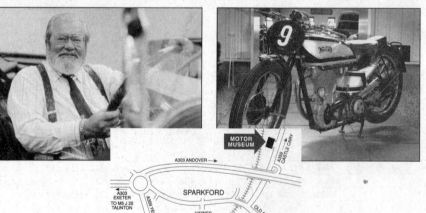

John Haynes O.B.E., Founder and Chairman of the museum at the wheel of a Haynes Light 12. >

< *The 1936 490cc sohc-engined International Norton – well known for its racing success*

The Museum is situated on the A359 Yeovil to Frome road at Sparkford, just off the A303 in Somerset. It is about 40 miles south of Bristol, and 25 minutes drive from the M5 intersection at Taunton.

Open 9.30am - 5.30pm (10.00am - 4.00pm Winter) 7 days a week, *except Christmas Day, Boxing Day and New Years Day*

Special rates available for schools, coach parties and outings Charitable Trust No. 292048